SAMUEL PEPYS

Born in 1633, the son of a London tailor. In
1659 entered the Civil Service, and distinguished
himself as Secretary of the Admiralty. Committed to the Tower of London, 1679; released,
1680; reinstated in the Admiralty, 1683; dismissed after the Revolution and lived in retire-
ment, chiefly at Clapham. Died in 1703.

The Diary of
Samuel Pepys

IN THREE VOLUMES · VOLUME THREE

EDITED WITH AN INTRODUCTION BY
JOHN WARRINGTON

DENT: LONDON
EVERYMAN'S LIBRARY
DUTTON: NEW YORK

All rights reserved
Made in Great Britain
at the
Aldine Press · Letchworth · Herts
for
J. M. DENT & SONS LTD
Aldine House · Bedford Street · London
First included in Everyman's Library 1953
Last reprinted 1973

No. 55   ISBN (if a hardback) 0 460 00055 1
No. 1055   ISBN (if a paperback) 0 460 01055 7

DIARY OF SAMUEL PEPYS

1667 (*continued*)

July 1st. We took coach, and, being very sleepy, drowsed most part of the way to Gravesend, and there 'light, and down to the new batteries, which are like to be very fine; and there did hear a plain fellow cry out upon the folly of the King's officers above, to spend so much money in works at Woolwich and Deptford, and sinking of good ships loaden with goods, when, if half the charge had been laid out here, it would have secured all that, and this place, too, before now. And I think it is not only true, but that the best of the actions of us all are so silly, that the meanest people do begin to see through them, and contemn them. Besides, says he, they spoil the River by it. We got home by noon, where all well. Then to the office, where I am sorry to hear that Sir J. Minnes is likely to die this night.

2d. To the office, where W. Pen and myself and Sir T. Harvey met, the first time we have had a meeting since the coming of the Dutch upon this coast. Busy till night, and then comes Mrs. Turner and tells me how she hears at the other end of the town how bad our Office is spoken of by the King and Prince and Duke of Albemarle; and that there is not a good word said of any of us but of me, and me they all do speak mightily of. So, she gone, comes my wife, and to walk in the garden, Sir J. Minnes being still ill and so keeping us from singing. And by and by Sir W. Pen came and walked with us and gave us a bottle of cider, and so we home to supper.

3d. Sir Richard Ford tells us how he hath been at the Sessions-house, and there it is plain that there is a combination of rogues in the town, that do make it their business to set houses on fire, and that one house they did set on fire in Aldersgate Street last Easter; and that this is proved by two young men, whom one of them debauched by degrees to steal their fathers' plate and clothes, and at last to be of their company; and they had their places to take up what goods were flung into the streets out of the windows, when the houses were on fire; and this is like to be proved to a great number of rogues, whereof five are already found, and some found guilty this day. One of these boys is a son of a Montagu,[1] of my Lord Manchester's family; but whose son he could not tell me. To the Council-chamber, to deliver a letter to their Lordships about the state of the six merchantmen which we have been so long fitting out. When I came the King and the whole table full of Lords were hearing of a pitiful cause of a complaint of an old man, with a great grey beard, against his son, for not allowing him something to live on; and at last came to the ordering the son to allow his father £10 a year. This cause lasted them near two hours: which, methinks, at this time to be the work of the Council-board of England, is a scandalous thing. Here I find all the news is the enemy's landing 3000 men near Harwich, and attacking Landguard Fort, and being beat off thence with our great guns, killing some of their men, and they leaving their ladders behind them; but we had no Horse in the way on Suffolk side, otherwise we might have galled their Foot. The Duke of York is gone down thither this day, while the General [2] sat sleeping this afternoon at the Council-table.

4th. To the Sessions-house, where I have a mind to hear Basil Feilding's case tried; and so got up to the Bench, my Lord Chief Justice Keeling [3] being Judge. Here I stood bare, not challenging, though I might well enough, to be covered. But here were several fine trials: among others, several brought in for making it their trade to set houses on fire merely to get plunder; and all proved by the two little boys spoken of yesterday by Sir R. Ford, who did give so good account of particulars that I never heard children in my life. And I confess, though I was unsatisfied with the force given to such little boys to take away men's lives, yet, when I was told that my Lord Chief Justice did declare that there was no law against taking the oath of children above twelve years old, and then heard from Sir R. Ford the good account which the boys had given of their understanding the nature and consequence of an oath, and now my own observation of the sobriety and readiness of their answers, further than of any man of any rank that came to give witness this day, though some men of years and learning, I was a little amazed, and fully satisfied that they ought to have as

[1] A son of James Montagu, third son of the first Earl of Manchester, by his wife Mary, daughter of Sir R. Baynard, of Lackham, Wiltshire.

[2] The Duke of Albemarle.

[3] Sir John Keeling, King's Serjeant 1661, Chief Justice of the King's Bench 1665.

much credit as the rest.   They proved against several their consulting several times at a brothel in Moorfields, called the Russia
House, among many other rogueries, of setting houses on fire,
that they might gather the goods that were flung into the streets;
and it is worth considering how unsafe it is to have children play
up and down this lewd town.   For these two boys (one my Lady
Montagu's, I know not what Lady Montagu's, son, and the other of
good condition) were playing in Moorfields, and one rogue,
Gabriel Holmes, did come to them and teach them to drink, and
then to bring him plate and clothes from their fathers' houses, and
carry him into their houses, and leaving open the doors for him,
and at last were made of their conspiracy, and were at the very
burning of this house in Aldersgate Street on Easter Sunday night
last, and did gather up goods, as they had resolved before: and this
Gabriel Holmes did advise to have had two houses set on fire, one
after another, that, while they were quenching of one, they might
be burning another.   And it is pretty that G. Holmes did tell his
fellows, and these boys swore it, that he did set fire to a box of
linen in the Sheriff, Sir Joseph Sheldon's, house, while he was
attending the fire in Aldersgate Street, and the Sheriff himself said
that there was a fire in his house, in a box of linen, at the same time,
but cannot conceive how this fellow should do it.   The boys did
swear against one of them, that he had made it his part to pull the
plug out of the engine while it was a-playing; and it really was so.
And goods they did carry away, and the manner of the setting the
house on fire was, that Holmes did get to a cockpit, where, it
seems, there was a public cockpit, and set fire to the straw in it,
and hath a fire-ball at the end of the straw, which did take fire, and
so it prevailed, and burned the house; and, among other things
they carried away, he took six of the cocks that were at the cockpit;
and afterwards the boys told us how they had one dressed, by the
same token it was so hard they could not eat it.   But that which
was most remarkable was the impudence of this Holmes, who hath
been arraigned often, and still got away; and on this business was
taken, and broke loose just at Newgate Gate; and was last night
luckily taken about Bow, where he got loose, and run into the
river, and hid himself in the rushes; and they pursued him with a
dog, and the dog got him, and held him till he was taken.   But the
impudence of the fellow was such, that he denied he ever saw the
boys before, or ever knew the Russia House, or that the people
knew him; and by and by the mistress of the Russia House was

3

called in, being indicted, at the same time, about another thing; and she denied that the fellow was of her acquaintance, when it was pretty to see how the little boys did presently fall upon her, and ask her how she durst say so, when she was always with them when they met at her house, and particularly when she came in her smock before a dozen of them, at which the Court laughed, and put the woman away. Well, this fellow Holmes[1] was found guilty of the act of burning the house, and other things that he stood indicted for. And then there were other good cases, as of a woman that came to serve a gentlewoman, and in three days run away, betimes in the morning, with a good deal of plate and rings, and other good things. It was time very well spent to be here. Here I saw how favourable the judge was to a young gentleman that struck one of the officers for not making him room: told him he had endangered the loss of his hand, but that he hoped he had not struck him, and would suppose that he had not struck him. The Court then rose, and I to dinner with my Lord Mayor and Sheriffs;where a good dinner and good discourse, the Judge being there. There was also tried this morning Feilding, which I thought had been Basil (but it proved the other, and Basil was killed), that killed his brother; who was found guilty of murder, and nobody pitied him. The Judge seems to be a worthy man, and able: and do intend, for these rogues that burned this house, to be hung in some conspicuous place in the town, for an example.

5th. Sir G. Carteret did come to us. He told us that the great seal is passed to my Lord Anglesey for Treasurer of the Navy: so that now he do no more belong to us, and I confess, for his sake, I am glad of it. At noon home to dinner with my wife, and after dinner to sing, and then to the office a little and Sir W. Batten's, where I am vexed to hear that Nan Wright, now Mrs. Markham, Sir W. Pen's maid and mistress, is come to sit in our pew at church, and did so while my Lady Batten was there. I confess I am very much vexed at it and ashamed. No news, but that the Dutch are gone clear from Harwich northward, and have given out that they are going to Yarmouth.

6th. Mr. Williamson told me that Mr. Coventry is coming over with a project of a peace; which, if the States agree to, and our King, when their Ministers on both sides have showed it them, we shall agree, and that is all: but the King, I hear, do give it out plain

---

[1] According to Smith's *Obituary* Gabriel Holmes was hanged on 11th July 1667, and buried in the new churchyard in the fields in Cripplegate parish.

that the peace is concluded. This afternoon I met with Mr. Rolt, who tells me that he is going cornet under Colonel Ingoldsby; but it was an ominous thing, methought, just as he was bidding me his last adieu his nose fell a-bleeding, which ran in my mind a pretty while after. This day, with great satisfaction, I hear that my Lady Jemimah is brought to bed, at Hinchingbroke, of a boy.[1]

7th. (Lord's day.) Mr. Moore tells me that the discontented Parliament-men are fearful that, the next sitting, the King will try for a general excise, by which to raise him money, and then to fling off the Parliament, and raise a land-army and keep them all down like slaves. And it is gotten among them that Bab. May, the Privy Purse, had been heard to say that £300 a year is enough for any country gentleman; which makes them mad, and they do talk of 6 or £800,000 gone into the Privy Purse this war, when in King James's time it arose but to £5,000, and in King Charles's time but £10,000 in a year. He tells me that a goldsmith in town told him that, being with some plate with my Lady Castlemaine lately, she directed her woman (the great beauty), 'Wilson,' says she, 'make a note for this, and for that, to the Privy Purse for money.' He tells me a little more of the baseness of the courses taken at Court in the case of Mr. Moyer, who is at liberty, and is to give £500 for his liberty; but now the great ones are divided, who shall have the money, the Duke of Albemarle on one hand, and another Lord on the other; and that it is fain to be decided by having the person's name put into the King's warrant for his liberty, at whose intercession the King shall own that he is set at liberty; which is a most lamentable thing, that we do professedly own that we do these things, not for right and justice sake, but only to gratify this or that person about the King. God forgive us all! Busy till the evening, and then with my wife and Jane over to Half-way house,[2] a very good walk; and there drank, and in the cool of the evening back again, and sang with pleasure upon the water, and were mightily pleased in hearing a boatful of Spaniards sing. Jane of late mighty fine, by reason of a laced whisk her mistress hath given her, which makes her a very graceful servant. But, above all, my wife and I were the most surprised in the beauty of a plain girl which we met in the little lane going from Redriffe stairs into the

---

[1] George Carteret, in 1681 created Baron Carteret of Hawnes, county Bedfordshire, in consideration of the eminent services rendered by his father and grandfather to Charles II.

[2] Probably the Jamaica House.

fields, one of the prettiest faces that we think we ever saw in our lives.

8th. Mr. Coventry is come from Breda, as was expected; but contrary to expectation, brings with him two or three articles which do not please the King: as, to retrench the Act of Navigation, and then to ascertain what are contraband goods; and then that those exiled persons, who are or shall take refuge in their country, may be secure from any further prosecution. Whether these will be enough to break the peace upon, or no, he cannot tell; but I perceive the certainty of peace is blown over. To Charing Cross, there to see the great boy and girl that are lately come out of Ireland, the latter eight, the former but four years old, of most prodigious bigness for their age. I tried to weigh them in my arms, and find them twice as heavy as people almost twice their age; and yet I am apt to believe they are very young. Their father a little sorry fellow, and their mother an old Irish woman. They have had four children of this bigness, and four of ordinary growth, whereof two of each are dead. If, as my Lord Ormond certifies, it be true that they are no older, it is very monstrous.

9th. This day my Lord Anglesey, our new Treasurer, came the first time to the Board; and I do perceive he is a very notable man, and understanding, and will do things regular, and understand them himself, not trust Fenn, as Sir G. Carteret did, and will solicit soundly for money, which I do fear was Sir G. Carteret's fault, that he did not do that enough, considering the age we live in. This evening news comes for certain that the Dutch are with their fleet before Dover, and that it is expected they will attempt something there. The business of the peace is quite dashed again.

10th. This day our girl Mary did go away, declaring that she must be where she might earn something one day and spend it and play away the next. But a good civil wench, and one neither wife nor I did ever give angry word to, but she has a silly vanity that she must play.

11th. Sir T. Harvey tells me that the Council last night did sit close to determine of the King's answer about the peace, and that, though he do not certainly know, yet by all discourse yesterday he do believe it is peace, and that the King had said it should be peace, and had been with Alderman Backwell to declare it upon the 'Change.

12th. Up betimes, and by and by comes Greeting, and begun a new month with him and now to learn to set anything from the notes upon the flageolet. But Lord! to see how like a fool he goes about to give me direction would make a man mad. Met at White Hall with Sir H. Cholmley, he telling me that undoubtedly the peace is concluded; for he did stand yesterday where he did hear part of the discourse at the Council-table, and there did hear the King argue for it. Among other things, that the spirits of the seamen were down, and the forces of our enemies were grown too great and many for us, and he would not have his subjects overpressed; for he knows an Englishman would do as much as any man upon hopeful terms; but where he sees he is overpressed, he despairs as soon as any other; and, besides that, they have already such a load of dejection upon them, that they will not be in temper a good while again. He heard my Lord Chancellor say to the King, 'Sir,' says he, 'the whole world do complain publilcy of treachery, that things have been managed falsely by some of your great Ministers. Sir,' says he, 'I am for Your Majesty's falling into a speedy inquiry into the truth of it, and, where you meet with it, punish it. But, at the same time, consider what you have to do, and make use of your time for having a peace; for more money will not be given without much trouble, nor is it, I fear, to be had of the people, nor will a little do it to put us into condition of doing our business.' But the other day, Sir H. Cholmley tells me, he [the Chancellor] did say at his table, 'Treachery!' says he; 'I could wish we could prove there was anything of that sort in it, for that would imply some wit and thoughtfulness; but we are ruined merely by folly and neglect.' And so they did all argue for peace, and so he do believe that the King hath agreed to the three points Mr. Coventry brought over, which I have mentioned before, and is gone with them back. He tells me further that the Duke of Buckingham was before the Council the other day, and there did carry it very submissively and pleasingly to the King; but to my Lord Arlington, who did prosecute the business, he was most bitter and sharp, and very slighting. As to the letter about his employing a man to cast the King's nativity, says he to the King, 'Sir, this is none of my hand, and I refer it to your Majesty whether you do not know this hand.' The King answered that it was indeed none of his, and that he knew whose it was, but could not recall it presently. 'Why,' says he, 'it is my sister of Richmond's, some frolic or other of hers about some certain person; and there is nothing of the King's name in it, but it is only said to be his by supposition, as is said.' The King, it seems, was not very much displeased with what the Duke had said; but, however, he is still in the Tower, and no discourse of his being out in haste, though my Lady Castlemaine hath so far solicited for him, that the King and she are quite fallen out: he comes not to her, nor hath for some three or four days; and parted with very foul words, the King calling her a jade that meddled with things she had nothing to do with at all, and she calling him fool; and told him if he was not a fool, he would not suffer his businesses to be carried on by fools that did not understand them, and cause his best subjects, and those best able to serve him, to be imprisoned; meaning the Duke of Buckingham. And it seems she was not only for his liberty, but to be restored to all his places; which, it is thought, he will never be. It was computed that the Parliament had given the King for this war only, besides all prizes, and besides the £200,000 which he was to spend of his own revenue, to guard the sea above £5,000,000 and odd £100,000; which is a most prodigious sum. Sir H. Cholmley, as a true English gentleman, do decry the King's expenses of his Privy Purse, which in King James's time did not rise to above £5000 a year, and in King Charles's to £10,000, do now cost us above £100,000, besides the great charge of the monarchy, as the Duke of York £100,000 of it, and other limbs of the Royal family, and the Guards, which, for his part, says he, 'I would have all disbanded, for the King is not the better by them, and would be as safe without them; for we have had no rebellions to make him fear anything.' But, contrarily, he is now raising of a land-army, which this Parliament and kingdom will never bear; besides, the commanders they put over them are such as will never be able to raise or command them. But the design is, and the Duke of York, he says, is hot for it, to have a land-army, and so to make the government like that of France. But our princes have not brains, or at least care and forecast, enough to do that. It is strange how everybody do nowadays reflect upon Oliver, and commend him, what brave things he did, and made all the neighbour princes fear him; while here a prince, come in with all the love and prayers and good liking of his people, who have given greater signs of loyalty and willingness to serve him with their estates than ever was done by any people, hath lost all so soon, that it is a miracle what way a man could devise to lose so much in so little time. Sir Thomas Crewe tells me how I am mightily in esteem with the Parliament, there being harangues made in the House to the Speaker, of Mr. Pepys's readiness and civility to show

8

them everything. Home, and there find my wife in a dogged humour for my not dining at home, and I did give her a pull by the nose and some ill words, which she provoked me to by something she spoke, that we fell extraordinarily out, insomuch that, I going to the office to avoid further anger, she followed me in a devilish manner thither; and with much ado I got her into the garden out of hearing, to prevent shame, and by degrees I found it necessary to calm her, and did, and then to the office, where pretty late, and then to walk with her in the garden, and pretty good friends, and so to bed with my mind very quiet.

13th. Mighty hot weather, I lying this night, which I have not done, I believe, since a boy, with only a rug and a sheet upon me. Mr. Pierce tells us what troubles me, that my Lord Buckkurst hath got Nell away from the King's House, and gives her £100 a year, so as she hath sent her parts to the house, and will act no more. And yesterday Sir Thomas Crewe told me that Lacy lies a-dying, nor will receive any ghostly advice from a Bishop, an old acquaintance of his, that went to see him. My wife and I to the New Exchange, to pretty maid Mrs. Smith's shop, where I left my wife; and I mightily pleased with this Mrs. Smith, being a very pleasant woman. It is an odd and sad thing to say, that though this be a peace worse than we had before, yet everybody's fear, almost, is that the Dutch will not stand by their promise, now the King hath consented to all they would have. And yet no wise man that I meet with, when he comes to think if it, but wishes, with all his heart, a war; but that the King is not a man to be trusted with the management of it. It was pleasantly said by a man in this City, a stranger, to one that told him the peace was concluded, 'Well,' says he, 'and have you a peace?'—'Yes,' says the other.—'Why, then,' says he, 'hold your peace!' partly reproaching us for the disgracefulness of it, that it is not fit to be mentioned, and next, that we are not able to make the Dutch keep it, when they have a mind to break it. Sir Thomas Crewe yesterday, speaking of the King of France, how great a man he is, 'Why,' says he, 'all the world thought that when the last Pope died [1] there would have been such bandying between the Crowns of France and Spain, whereas, when he was asked what he would have his ministers at Rome do, "Why," says he, "let them choose who they will; if the Pope will do what is fit, the Pope and I will be friends. If he will not, I will take a course with him: therefore, I will not trouble myself"; and

[1] Alexander VII. He died 22nd May 1667, N.S.

thereupon the election [1] was despatched in a little time—I think in a day—and all ended.'

14th. (Lord's day.) Up, and my wife, a little before four, and to make us ready; and by and by Mrs. Turner came to us, by agreement, and she and I stayed talking below while my wife dressed herself, which vexed me that she was so long about it, keeping us till past five o'clock before she was ready. She ready; and, taking some bottles of wine and beer and some cold fowl with us into the coach, we took coach and four horses, which I had provided last night, and so away. A very fine day, and so towards Epsom, talking all the way pleasantly, and particularly of the pride and ignorance of Mrs. Lowther, in having of her train carried up. The country very fine, only the way very dusty. To Epsom, by eight o'clock, to the well; where much company, and I drank the water: they did not, but I did drink four pints. And to the town, to the King's Head, and hear that my Lord Buckhurst and Nelly are lodged at the next house, and Sir Charles Sedley with them: and keep a merry house. Poor girl! I pity her; but more the loss of her at the King's House. W. Hewer rode with us, and I left him and the women, and myself walked to church, where few people to what I expected, and none I knew, but all the Houblons, brothers, and them after sermon I did salute and walk with towards my inn. James did tell me that I was the only happy man of the Navy, of whom, he says, during all this freedom the people have taken to speaking treason, he hath not heard one bad word of me; which is a great joy to me, for I hear the same of others, but do know that I have deserved as well as most. We parted to meet anon, and I to my women into a better room, which the people of the house borrowed for us: and there to a good dinner, and were merry; and Pembleton came to us, who happened to be in the house, and there talked and were merry. After dinner, he gone, we all lay down, the day being wonderful hot, to sleep, and each of us took a good nap, and then rose; and here Tom Wilson come to see me, and sat and talked an hour; and I perceive he hath been much acquainted with Dr. Fuller (Tom) and Dr. Pierson, and several of the great cavalier parsons during the late troubles; and I was glad to hear him talk of them, which he did very ingenuously, and very much of Dr. Fuller's art of memory, which he did tell me several instances of. By and by he parted, and we took coach, and to take the air, there being a fine breeze abroad; and I carried

[1] Of Clement IX, Giulio Rospigliosi, elected 20th June 1667, N.S.

them to the well, and there filled some bottles of water to carry home with me; and there I talked with the two women that farm the well, at £12 per annum, of the lord of the manor.   Mr. Evelyn [1] with his lady, and also my Lord George Berkeley's lady,[2] and their fine daughter, that the King of France liked so well, and did dance so rich in jewels before the King at the ball I was at, at our Court, last winter, and also their son,[3] a Knight of the Bath, were at church this morning.   Here W. Hewer's horse broke loose, and we had the sport to see him taken again.   Then I carried them to see my cousin Pepys's house, and 'light, and walked round about it, and they like it, as indeed it deserves, very well, and is a pretty place; and then I walked them to the wood hard by, and there got them in the thickets till they had lost themselves, and I could not find the way into any of the walks in the wood, which indeed are very pleasant, if I could have found them.   At last got out of the wood again; and I, by leaping down the little bank, coming out of the wood, did sprain my right foot, which brought me great present pain, but presently, with walking, it went away for the present, and so the women and W. Hewer and I walked upon the Downs, where a flock of sheep was; and the most pleasant and innocent sight that ever I saw in my life.   We found a shepherd and his little boy reading, far from any houses or sight of people, the Bible to him; so I made the boy read to me, which he did, with the forced tone that children do usually read, that was mighty pretty, and then I did give him something, and went to the father, and talked with him; and I find he had been a servant in my cousin Pepys's house, and told me what was become of their old servants.   He did content himself mightily in my liking his boy's reading, and did bless God for him, the most like one of the old patriarchs that ever I saw in my life, and it brought those thoughts of the old age of the world in my mind for two or three days after.   We took notice of his woollen knit stockings of two colours mixed, and of his shoes shod with iron, both at the toe and heels, and with great nails in the soles of his feet, which was mighty pretty: and, taking notice of them, 'Why,' says the poor man, 'the downs, you see, are full of stones, and we are fain to shoe

[1] This was probably Richard Evelyn, of Woodcote Park, near Epsom, and his wife Elizabeth, daughter and heir of George Mynne, Esq., of Horton in Epsom, both of which places belonged to her.

[2] Elizabeth, daughter and co-heir of John Massingberd.

[3] Charles, eldest son, summoned to Parliament as Baron Berkeley, *vitâ patris*, 1680: *ob.* 1710, having succeeded his father in the earldom 1698.

ourselves thus; and these,' says he, 'will make the stones fly till they ring before me.' I did give the poor man something, for which he was mighty thankful, and I tried to cast stones with his horn crook. He values his dog mightily, that would turn a sheep any way which he would have him, when he goes to fold them: told me there was about eighteen score sheep in his flock, and that he hath four shillings a week the year round for keeping of them. And Mrs. Turner, in the common fields here, did gather one of the prettiest nosegays that ever I saw in my life. So to our coach, and through Mrs. Minnes's wood, and looked upon Mr. Evelyn's house; and so over the common, and through Epsom town to our inn, in the way stopping a poor woman with her milk-pail, and in one of my gilt tumblers, did drink our bellyfuls of milk, better than any cream; and so to our inn, and there had a dish of cream, but it was sour, and so had no pleasure in it; and so paid our reckoning, and took coach, it being about seven at night, and passed and saw the people walking with their wives and children to take the air, and we set out for home, the sun by and by going down, and we in the cool of the evening all the way with much pleasure home, talking and pleasing ourselves with the pleasures of this day's work. Mrs. Turner mightily pleased with my resolution, which, I tell her, is never to keep a country house, but to keep a coach, and with my wife on the Saturday to go sometimes for a day to this place, and then quit to another place: and there is more variety and as little charge, and no trouble, as there is in a country house. Anon it grew dark, and we had the pleasure to see several glow-worms, which was mighty pretty, but my foot begins more and more to pain me, which Mrs. Turner, by keeping her warm hand upon it, did much ease; but so that when we come home, which was just at eleven at night, I was not able to walk from the lane's end to my house without being helped. So to bed, and there had a cerecloth laid to my foot, but in great pain all night long.

15th. I was not able to go today to wait on the Duke of York with my fellows, but was forced in bed to write out particulars for their discourse there. Anon comes Mrs. Turner, and new-dressed my foot, and did it so that I was at much ease presently. Our poor Jane very sad for the death of her poor brother, who hath left a wife and two small children. I did give her 20s. in money, and what wine she needed, for the burying him.

16th. To the office without much pain, and there sat all the morning.

17th. Home, where I am saluted with the news of Hogg's bringing a rich Canary prize to Hull: and Sir W. Batten do offer me £1000 down for my particular share, beside Sir Richard Ford's part, which do tempt me; but yet I would not take it, but will stand and fall with the company. He and two more, the Panther and Fanfan, did enter into consortship; and so they have all brought in each a prize, though ours worth as much as both theirs, and more. However, it will be well worth having, God be thanked for it! This news makes us all very glad. I at Sir W. Batten's did hear the particulars of it; and there for joy he did give the company that were there a bottle or two of his own last year's wine, growing at Walthamstow, than which the whole company said they never drank better foreign wine in their lives. The Duke of Buckingham is, it seems, set at liberty, without any further charge against him or other clearing of him, but let to go out; which is one of the strangest instances of the fool's play with which all public things are done in this age, that is to be apprehended. And it is said that when he was charged with making himself popular—as indeed he is, for many of the discontented Parliament, Sir Robert Howard, and Sir Thomas Meres, and others, did attend at the Council-chamber when he was examined—he should answer, that whoever was committed to prison by my Lord Chancellor or my Lord Arlington could not want being popular. But it is worth considering the ill state a Minister of State is in, under such a Prince as ours is; for, undoubtedly, neither of those two great men would have been so fierce against the Duke of Buckingham at the Council-table the other day, had they not been assured of the King's good liking and supporting them therein: whereas, perhaps at the desire of my Lady Castlemaine, who, I suppose, hath at last overcome the King, the Duke of Buckingham is well received again, and now these men delivered up to the interest he can make for his revenge. He told me over the story of Mrs. Stuart, much after the manner which I was told it by Mr. Evelyn; only he says it is verily believed that the King did never intend to marry her to any but himself, and that the Duke of York and Lord Chancellor were jealous of it; and that Mrs. Stuart might be got with child by the King, or somebody else, and the King own a marriage before his contract, for it is but a contract, as he tells me, to this day, with the Queen, and so wipe their noses of the Crown; and that, therefore, the Duke of York and Chancellor did do all they could to forward the match with my Lord Duke of Richmond, that she might be married out of the way: but, above all, it is a worthy part that this good lady hath acted. My sister Michell[1] came from Leigh[2] to see us, but do tattle so much of the late business of the Dutch coming thither, that I am weary of it. Yet it is worth remembering what she says: that she hath heard both seamen and soldiers swear they would rather serve the Dutch than the King, for they should be better used. She saw the Royal Charles brought into the River by them; and how they shot off their great guns for joy, when they got her out of Chatham river.

18th. Very well employed at the office till evening; and then, being weary, took out my wife and Will Batelier by coach to Islington, but no pleasure in our going, the way being so dusty that one durst not breathe. Drank at the old house, and so home.

19th. Comes the flageolet master and brings me two new great ivory pipes which cost me 32s., and so to play; and he being done, I to Westminster. So home, and in my way by coach down Mark Lane, mightily pleased and smitten to see, as I thought, in passing, the pretty woman, the linen-maker's wife that lived in Fenchurch Street; and I had a great mind to have gone back to have seen, but yet would correct my nature and would not. One tells me that, by letter from Holland, the people there are made to believe that our condition in England is such as they may have whatever they will ask; and that so they are mighty high, and despise us, or a peace with us: and there is too much reason for them to do so. The Dutch fleet are in great squadrons everywhere still about Harwich, and were lately at Portsmouth; and the last letters say at Plymouth, and now gone to Dartmouth to destroy our Straits fleet lately got in thither: but God knows whether they can do it any hurt, or no.

20th. Towards the 'Change at noon, in my way observing my mistake yesterday in Mark Lane, that the woman I saw was not the pretty woman I meant, the linen-maker's wife, but a new-married woman, very pretty, a strong-water seller. And in going by, to my content, I find that the very pretty daughter at the Ship tavern, at the end of Billiter Lane, is there still, and in the bar: and, I believe, is married to him that is new come, and hath new trimmed the house. Home to dinner, and then to the office, we having dispatched away Mr. Oviatt to Hull, about our prizes there; and

[1] The wife of Balthazar St. Michel, Mrs. Pepys's brother.
[2] Opposite to Sheerness.

I have wrote a letter of thanks by him to Lord Bellassis, who had writ to me to offer all his service for my interest there, but I dare not trust him.

21st. (Lord's day.) I and my wife and Mercer up by water to Barn Elms, where we walked by moonshine, and called at Lambeth, and drank and had cold meat in the boat, and did eat and sang, and down home, by almost twelve at night, very fine and pleasant, only could not sing ordinary songs with the freedom that otherwise I would.   Here Mercer tells me that the pretty maid of the Ship tavern is married there, which I am glad of.   So having spent this night, with much serious pleasure to consider that I am in condition to fling away an angel [1] in such a refreshment to myself and family, we home and to bed, leaving Mercer, by the way, at her own door.

22d.   Up to my Lord Chancellor's, where was a Committee of Tangier in my Lord's room, where he sits to hear causes, and where all the Judges' pictures hung up, very fine.   But to see how Sir W. Coventry did oppose both my Lord Chancellor and the Duke of York himself, about the Order of the Commissioners of the Treasury to me for not paying of pensions, and with so much reason, and eloquence so natural, was admirable.   And another thing, about his pressing for the reduction of the charge of Tangier, which they would have put off to another time; 'But,' says he, 'the King suffers so much by the putting off of the consideration of reductions of charge, that he is undone: and therefore I do pray you, sir,' to his Royal Highness, 'that when anything offers of the kind, you will not let it escape you.'   Here was a great bundle of letters brought hither, sent up from sea, from a vessel of ours that hath taken them after they had been flung over by a Dutchman; wherein, among others, the Duke of York did read the superscription of one to De Witt, thus—'To the most wise, foreseeing, and discreet, These, &c.'; which, I thought with myself, I could have been glad might have been duly directed to any one of them at the table, though the greatest men in this kingdom.   The Duke of York, the Lord Chancellor, my Lord Duke of Albemarle, Arlington, Ashley, Peterborough, and Coventry, the best of them all for parts, I perceive they do all profess their expectation of a peace, and that suddenly.   Sir W. Coventry did declare his opinion that if Tangier were offered us now, as the King's condition is, he would advise against the taking it; saying that the King's charge is too

[1] The ancient English gold coin, of the value of ten shillings.

great, and must be brought down, it being, like the fire of this City, never to be mastered till you have brought it under you; and that these places abroad are but so much charge to the King, and we do rather herein strive to greaten them than lessen them; and then the King is forced to part with them, 'as,' says he, 'he did with Dunkirk, by my Lord Teviot's making it so chargeable to the King as he did that, and would have done Tangier, if he had lived.' I perceive he is the only man that do seek the King's profit, and is bold to deliver what he thinks on every occasion. With much pleasure reflecting upon our discourse today at the Tangier meeting, and crying up the worth of Sir W. Coventry. Creed tells me of the fray between the Duke of Buckingham at the Duke's playhouse the last Saturday (and it is the first day I have heard that they have acted at either the King's or Duke's Houses this month or six weeks), and Henry Killigrew, whom the Duke of Buckingham did soundly beat and take away his sword, and make a fool of, till the fellow prayed him to spare his life: and I am glad of it, for it seems in this business the Duke of Buckingham did carry himself very innocently and well, and I wish he had paid this fellow's coat well. I heard something of this at the 'Change today: and it is pretty to hear how people do speak kindly of the Duke of Buckingham, as one that will enquire into faults; and therefore they do mightily favour him. And it puts me in mind that, this afternoon, Billing, the Quaker, meeting me in the Hall, came to me, and after a little discourse did say, 'Well,' says he, 'now you will be all called to an account'; meaning the Parliament is drawing near.

23d. Comes sudden news to me by letter from the Clerk of the Cheque at Gravesend, that there were thirty sail of Dutch men-of-war coming up into the Hope this last tide: which I told Sir W. Pen of; but he would not believe it, but laughed, and said it was a fleet of billanders [coasters], and that the guns that were heard was the salutation of the Swede's Ambassador that comes over with them. But within half an hour comes another letter from Captain Proud, that eight of them were come into the Hope, and thirty more following them, at ten this morning. By and by comes an order from White Hall to send down one of our number to Chatham, fearing that, as they did before, they may make a show first up hither, but then go to Chatham. So my Lord Brouncker do go, and we here are ordered to give notice to the merchantmen-of-war, gone below the barricado at Woolwich, to come up again.

24th. Betimes this morning comes a letter from the Clerk of the Cheque at Gravesend to me, to tell me that the Dutch fleet did come all into the Hope yesterday noon, and held a fight with our ships from thence till seven at night; that they had burned twelve fire-ships, and we took one of theirs, and burned five of our fire-ships. But then rising and going to Sir W. Batten, he tells me that we have burned one of their men-of-war, and another of theirs is blown up: but how true this is, I know not. But these fellows are mighty bold, and have had the fortune of the wind easterly this time to bring them up, and prevent our troubling them with our fire-ships; and, indeed, have had the winds at their command from the beginning, and now do take the beginning of the spring, as if they had some great design to do. At noon home to dinner, where my wife mighty musty, but I took no notice of it. About five o'clock down to Gravesend, all the way with extraordinary content reading of Boyle's Hydrostatics, which the more I read and understand, the more I admire, as a most excellent piece of philosophy. And as we come nearer Gravesend, we hear the Dutch fleet and ours a-firing their guns most distinctly and loud. So I landed, and discoursed with the landlord of the Ship, who undeceives me in what I heard this morning about the Dutch having lost two men-of-war, for it is not so, but several of their fire-ships. He do say that this afternoon they did force our ships to retreat, but that now they are gone down as far as Shell-haven:[1] but what the event hath been of this evening's guns they know not, but suppose not much, for they have all this while shot at good distance one from another. They seem confident of the security of this town and the River above it, if the enemy should come up so high, their fortifications being so good, and guns many. But he do say that people do complain of Sir Edward Spragg, that he hath not done extraordinary; and more of Sir W. Jennings, that he came up with his tamkins[2] in his guns. Having eat a bit of cold venison and drank, I away, took boat, and homeward again, with great pleasure, the moon shining, and it being a fine pleasant cool evening, and got home by half-past twelve at night, and so to bed.

25th. At night Sir W. Batten, W. Pen, and myself and Sir R. Ford did meet in the garden to discourse about our prizes at Hull. It appears that Hogg is the veriest rogue, the most observable

---

[1] Shellhaven, on the Essex coast, opposite to Cliffe on the Kentish side.
[2] Tamkin, or tompion, the stopple of a great gun.

embezzler, that ever was known.   This vexes us, and made us
very free and plain with Sir W. Pen, who hath been his great
patron, and as very a rogue as he.   But he do now seem to own
that his opinion is changed of him, and that he will join with us in
our strictest inquiries, and did sign to the letters we had drawn,
which he had refused before, and so seemingly parted good friends.
I demanded of Sir R. Ford and the rest what passed today at the
meeting of Parliament: who told me that, contrary to all expectation by the King that there would be but a thin meeting, there met
above 300 this first day, and all the discontented party; and,
indeed, the whole House seems to be no other almost.   The
Speaker told them, as soon as they were sat, that he was ordered
by the King to let them know he was hindered by some important
business to come to them and speak to them, as he intended; and,
therefore, ordered him to move that they would adjourn themselves
till Monday next, it being very plain to all the House that he expects
to hear by that time of the sealing of the peace, which by letters, it
seems, from my Lord Hollis, was to be sealed the last Sunday.[1]
But before they would come to the question whether they
would adjourn, Sir Thomas Tomkins steps up and tells them that
all the country is grieved at this new-raised standing army; and
that they thought themselves safe enough in their train-bands; and
that, therefore, he desired the King might be moved to disband
them.   Then rises Garraway and seconds him, only with this
explanation, which he said he believed the other meant, that, as
soon as peace should be concluded, they might be disbanded.
Then rose Sir W. Coventry and told them that he did approve of
what the last gentleman said; but also, that at the same time he did
no more than what, he durst be bold to say, he knew to be the
King's mind, that as soon as peace was concluded he would do it
of himself.   Then rose Sir Thomas Littleton and did give several
reasons from the uncertainty of their meeting again but to adjourn,
in case news comes of the peace being ended before Monday next,
and the possibility of the King's having some about him that may
endeavour to alter his own and the good part of his Council's
advice, for the keeping up of the land-army; and, therefore, it was
fit that they did present it to the King as their desire that, as soon
as peace was concluded, the land-army might be laid down, and
that this their request might be carried to the King by them of their
House that were Privy Councillors; which was put to the vote and

[1] The peace was signed on the 31st.

carried *nemine contradicente.* So after this vote passed, they adjourned: but it is plain what the effects of this Parliament will be, if they be suffered to sit, that they will fall foul upon the faults of the Government; and I pray God they may be permitted to do it, for nothing else, I fear, will save the King and kingdom than the doing it betimes.

26th. No news all this day what we have done to the enemy, but that the enemy is fallen down, and we after them, but to little purpose.

27th. To the office, where I hear that Sir John Coventry [1] is come over from Breda, a nephew, I think, of Sir W. Coventry's: but what message he brings, I know not. This morning news is come that Sir Jos. Jordan is come from Harwich with sixteen fire-ships and four other little ships of war, and did attempt to do some execution upon the enemy, but did it without discretion, as most do say, so as they have been able to do no good, but have lost four of their fire-ships. They attempted this, it seems, when the wind was too strong, that our grapplings could not hold: others say we came to leeward of them, but all condemn it as a foolish management. They are come to Sir Edward Spragg about Leigh, and the Dutch are below at the Nore. At the office all the morning, and at noon to the 'Change, where I met Fenn; and he tells me that Sir John Coventry do bring the confirmation of the peace: but I do not find the 'Change at all glad of it, but rather the worse, they looking upon it as a peace made only to preserve the King for a time in his lusts and ease, and to sacrifice trade and his kingdoms only to his own pleasures; so that the hearts of merchants are quite down. He tells me that the King and my Lady Castlemaine are quite broke off, and she is gone away, and is with child, and swears the King shall own it,[2] and she will have it christened in the Chapel at White Hall so, and owned for the King's, as other Kings have done; or she will bring it into White Hall Gallery, and

---

[1] Created K.B. at Charles II's coronation and M.P. for Weymouth in several Parliaments. He was the son of John Coventry, the eldest brother of Sir W. Coventry; and the outrage committed on his person, on 21st December 1670, by Sir Thomas Sandys, O'Bryan, and others, who cut his nose to the bone, gave rise to the passing the Bill still known by the name of The Coventry Act, under which persons so offending were to suffer death.

[2] Charles owned only four children by Lady Castlemaine—Anne, Countess of Sussex, and the Dukes of Southampton, Grafton, and Northumberland. The last of these was born in 1665. The paternity of all her other children was certainly doubtful.

dash the brains of it out before the King's face. He tells me that the King and Court were never in the world so bad as they are now for gaming, swearing, women, and drinking, and the most abominable vices that ever were in the world; so that all must come to naught. He told me that Sir G. Carteret was at this end of the town; so I went to visit him in Broad Street, and there he and I together: and he is mightily pleased with my Lady Jem's having a son, and a mighty glad man he is. He [Sir George Carteret] tells me, as to news, that the peace is now confirmed, and all that over. He says it was a very unhappy motion in the House the other day about the land-army; for, whether the King hath a mind of his own to do the thing desired or no, his doing it will be looked upon as a thing done only in fear of the Parliament. He says that the Duke of York is suspected to be the great man that is for raising of this army, and bringing things to be commanded by an army; but that he do know that he is wronged therein. He do say that the Court is in a way to ruin all for their pleasures; and says that he himself hath once taken the liberty to tell the King the necessity of having at least a show of religion in the Government, and sobriety; and that it was that that did set up and keep up Oliver though he was the greatest rogue in the world. He tells me the King adheres to no man, but this day delivers himself up to this, and the next to that, to the ruin of himself and business; that he is at the command of any woman like a slave, though he be the best man to the Queen in the world, with so much respect, and never lies a night from her: but yet cannot command himself in the presence of a woman he likes. It raining this day all day to our great joy, it having not rained, I think, this month before, so as the ground was everywhere so burned and dry as could be; and no travelling in the road or streets in London, for dust.

28th. All the morning close, to draw up a letter to Sir W. Coventry upon the tidings of peace, taking occasion, before I am forced to it, to resign up to his Royal Highness my place of the Victualling, and to recommend myself to him by promise of doing my utmost to improve this peace in the best manner we may, to save the kingdom from ruin.

29th. Up, and with Sir W. Batten to St. James's, to Sir W. Coventry's chamber; where, among other things, he came to me, and told me that he had received my yesterday's letters, and that we concurred very well in our notions; and that, as to my place which I had offered to resign of the Victualling, he had drawn up a letter at the same time for the Duke of York's signing for the like places in general raised during this war; and that he had done me right to the Duke of York, to let him know that I had, of my own accord, offered to resign mine. The letter do bid us to do all things, particularizing several, for the laying up of the ships and easing the King of charge; so that the war is now professedly over. By and by up to the Duke of York's chamber; and there all the talk was about Jordan's coming with so much indiscretion, with his four little frigates and sixteen fire-ships from Harwich, to annoy the enemy. His failures were of several sorts, I know not which the truest: that he came with so strong a gale of wind, that his grapplings would not hold; that he did come by their lee, whereas if he had come athwart their hawse, they would have held; that they did not stop a tide, and come up with a windward tide, and then they would not have come so fast. Now, there happened to be Captain Jenifer by, who commanded the Lily in this business, and thus says: that, finding the Dutch not so many as they expected, they did not know that there were more of them above, and so were not so earnest to the setting upon these; that they did do what they could to make the fire-ships fall in among the enemy; and, for their lives, neither Sir J. Jordan nor others could, by shooting several times at them, make them go in. And it seems they were commanded by some idle fellows, such as they could of a sudden gather up at Harwich; which is a sad consideration that, at such a time as this, where the saving the reputation of the whole nation lay at stake, and after so long a war, the King had not credit to gather a few able men to command these vessels. He says that if they had come up slower, the enemy would (with their boats and their great sloops, which they have to row with a great many men, and did) come and cut up several of our fire-ships, and would certainly have taken most of them; for they do come with a great provision of these boats on purpose, and to save their men, which is bravely done of them, though they did, on this very occasion, show great fear, as they say, by some men leaping overboard out of a great ship, as these were all of them of sixty and seventy guns apiece, which one of our fire-ships laid on board, though the fire did not take. But yet it is brave to see what care they do take to encourage their men to provide great stores of boats to save them, while we have not credit to find one boat for a ship. And, further, he told us that this new way used by Deane (and this Sir W. Coventry observed several times) of preparing of fire-ships, do not

do the work; for the fire, not being strong and quick enough to
flame up, so as to take the rigging and sails, lies smothering a great
while, half an hour before it flames, in which time they can get
the fire-ship off safely, though, which is uncertain and did fail
in one or two this bout, it do serve to burn our own ships.   But
what a shame it is to consider how two of our ships' companies
did desert their ships for fear of being taken by their boats, our
little frigates being forced to leave them, being chased by their
greater!   And one more company did set their ship on fire, and
leave her; which afterwards a Faversham fisherman came up to,
and put out the fire, and carried safe into Faversham, where she
now is: which was observed by the Duke of York and all the
company with him, that it was only want of courage, and a general
dismay and abjectness of spirit upon all our men.   And others did
observe our ill management and God Almighty's curse upon all
that we have in hand, for never such an opportunity was of de-
stroying so many good ships of theirs as we now had.   But to see
how negligent we were in this business, that our fleet of Jordan's
should not have any notice where Spragg was, nor Spragg of
Jordan's, so as to be able to meet and join in the business, and help
one another; but Jordan, when he saw Spragg's fleet above, did
think them to be another part of the enemy's fleet!   While, on
the other side, notwithstanding our people at Court made such a
secret of Jordan's design that nobody must know it, and even this
Office itself must not know it; nor for my part I did not, though
Sir W. Batten says by others' discourse to him he had heard something of it; yet De Ruyter, or he that commanded this fleet, had
notice of it, and told it to a fisherman of ours that he took and
released on Thursday last, which was the day before our fleet came
to him.   But then, that that seems most to our disgrace, and which
the Duke of York did take special and vehement notice of, is
that when the Dutch saw so many fire-ships provided for them,
themselves lying, I think, about the Nore, they did with all their
great ships (with a North-east wind, as I take it they said, but whatever it was, it was a wind that we should not have done it with)
turn down to the Middleground; which, the Duke of York observed, never was nor would have been undertaken by ourselves.
And whereas some of the company answered it was their great fear,
not their choice, that made them do it, the Duke of York answered
that it was, it may be, their fear and wisdom that made them do it.
But yet their fear did not make them mistake, as we should have

done, when we have had no fear upon us and have run our ships on ground. And this brought it into my mind that they managed their retreat down this difficult passage, with all their fear, better than we could do ourselves in the main sea, when the Duke of Albemarle ran away from the Dutch, when the Prince was lost, and the Royal Charles and the other great ships came on ground upon the Galloper. Thus, in all things, in wisdom, courage, force, knowledge of our own streams, and success, the Dutch have the best of us, and do end the war with victory on their side. The Duke of York being ready, we into his closet, but, being in haste to go to the Parliament House, he could not stay. So we parted, and to Westminster Hall, where the Hall full of people to see the issue of the day, the King being to come to speak to the House today. One thing extraordinary was this day, a man, a Quaker, came naked through the Hall, only very civilly tied about the loins to avoid scandal, and with a chafing-dish of fire and brimstone burning upon his head, did pass through the Hall, crying, 'Repent! repent!' Presently comes down the House of Commons, the King having made them a very short and no pleasing speech to them at all, not at all giving them thanks for their readiness to come up to town at this busy time; but told them that he did think he should have had occasion for them, but had none, and therefore did dismiss them to look after their own occasions till October; and that he did wonder any should offer to bring in a suspicion that he intended to rule by an army, or otherwise than by the laws of the land, which he promised them he would do; and so bade them go home and settle the minds of the country in that particular; and only added that he had made a peace which he did believe they would find reasonable, and a good peace, but did give them none of the particulars thereof. Thus they are dismissed again, to their general great distaste: I believe the greatest that ever Parliament was, to see themselves so fooled, and the nation in certain condition of ruin, while the King, they see, is only governed by his lust, and women and rogues about him. The Speaker, they found, was kept from coming in the morning to the House on purpose, till after the King was come to the House of Lords, for fear they should be doing anything in the House of Commons to the further dissatisfaction of the King and his courtiers. They do all give up the kingdom for lost, that I speak to; and do hear what the King says, how he and the Duke of York do do what they can to get up an army, that they may need no more Parliaments; and how my Lady Castlemaine hath, before the late breach between her and the King, said to the King that he must rule by an army, or all would be lost; and that Bab. May hath given the like advice to the King, to crush the English gentlemen, saying that £300 a year was enough for any man but them that lived at Court.   I am told that many petitions were provided for the Parliament, complaining of the wrongs they have received from the Court and courtiers, in city and country, if the Parliament had but sat.   And I do perceive they all do resolve to have a good account of the money spent before ever they give a farthing more; and the whole kingdom is everywhere sensible of their being abused, insomuch that they forced their Parliament-men to come up to sit.   And my cousin Roger told me that, but that was in mirth, he believed, if he had not come up, he should have had his house burned.   The kingdom never in so troubled a condition in this world as now: nobody pleased with the peace, and yet nobody daring to wish for the continuance of the war, it being plain that nothing do nor can thrive under us.   Here I saw old good Mr. Vaughan,[1] and several of the great men of the Commons, and some of them old men, that are come 200 miles and more, to attend this session of Parliament; and have been at great charge and disappointments in their other private business; and now all to no purpose, neither to serve their country, content themselves, nor receive any thanks from the King. It is verily expected by many of them that the King will continue the prorogation in October, so as, if it be possible, never to have this Parliament more.   My Lord Bristol took his place in the House of Lords this day, but not in his robes; and when the King came in he withdrew: but my Lord of Buckingham was there as brisk as ever, and sat in his robes; which is a monstrous thing, that a man should be proclaimed against, and put in the Tower, and released without any trial, and yet not restored to his places. But, above all, I saw my Lord Mordaunt as merry as the best, that it seems hath done such further indignities to Mr. Taylor since the last sitting of Parliament as would hang him, if there were nothing else, would the King do what were fit for him; but nothing of that is now likely to be.   After having spent an hour or two in the hall, my cousin Roger and I and Creed to the Old Exchange, where I find all the merchants sad at this peace and breaking up of the Parliament, as men despairing of any good to the nation, which is a grievous consideration.   And so home.   Cousin Roger and Creed

---

[1] John Vaughan, M.P. for Cardiganshire.

to dinner with me, and very merry; but among other things they told me of the strange, bold sermon of Dr. Creeton yesterday, before the King: how he preached against the sins of the Court, and particularly against adultery, over and over instancing how for that single sin in David the whole nation was undone; and of our negligence in having our castles without ammunition and powder when the Dutch came upon us; and how we have no courage nowadays, but let our ships be taken out of our harbour. Here Creed did tell us the story of the duel last night, in Covent Garden, between Sir H. Bellassis and Tom Porter. It is worth remembering the silliness of the quarrel, and is a kind of emblem of the general complexion of this whole kingdom at present. They two dined yesterday at Sir Robert Carr's,[1] where it seems people do drink high, all that come. It happened that these two, the greatest friends in the world, were talking together: and Sir H. Bellassis talked a little louder than ordinary to Tom Porter, giving of him some advice. Some of the company standing by said, 'What! are they quarrelling, that they talk so high?' Sir H. Bellassis, hearing it, said, 'No!' says he: 'I would have you know I never quarrel, but I strike; and take that as a rule of mine!' 'How?' says Tom Porter, 'strike! I would I could see the man in England that durst give me a blow!' with that Sir H. Bellassis did give him a box of the ear; and so they were going to fight there, but were hindered. And by and by Tom Porter went out, and, meeting Dryden the poet, told him of the business, and that he was resolved to fight Sir H. Bellassis presently; for he knew, if he did not, they should be friends tomorrow, and then the blow would rest upon him; which he would prevent, and desired Dryden to let him have his boy to bring him notice which way Sir H. Bellassis goes. By and by he is informed that Sir H. Bellassis's coach was coming: so Tom Porter went down out of the coffee-house where he stayed for the tidings, and stopped the coach, and bade Sir H. Bellassis come out. 'Why,' says H. Bellassis, 'you will not hurt me coming out, will you?'—'No,' says Tom Porter. So out he went, and both drew: and H. Bellassis having drawn and flung away his scabbard, Tom Porter asked him whether he was ready. The other answering him he was, they fell to fight, some of their acquaintance by. They wounded one another, and H. Bellassis so much that it is feared he will die: and finding himself severely

---

[1] Baronet of Sleaford, Lincolnshire, and one of the proposed Knights of the Royal Oak for that county.

wounded, he called to Tom Porter, and kissed him, and bade him shift for himself; 'for,' says he, 'Tom, thou hast hurt me; but I will make shift to stand upon my legs till thou mayest withdraw, and the world not take notice of you, for I would not have thee troubled for what thou hast done.' And so whether he did fly or no I cannot tell; but Tom Porter showed H. Bellassis that he was wounded too: and they are both ill, but H. Bellassis to fear of life. And this is a fine example; and H. Bellassis a Parliament man,[1] too, and both of them extraordinary friends! Among other discourse, my cousin Roger told us a thing certain, that the Archbishop of Canterbury[2] that now is do keep a wench, and that he is as very a wencher as can be; and tells us it is a thing publicly known that Sir Charles Sedley had got away one of the Archbishop's wenches from him, and the Archbishop sent to him to let him know that she was his kinswoman, and did wonder that he would offer any dishonour to one related to him. To which Sir Charles Sedley is said to answer, 'Pray, tell his Grace that I believe he finds himself too old, and is afraid that I should outdo him among his girls, and spoil his trade.' But he makes no more of doubt to say that the Archbishop is a wencher, and known to be so, which is one of the most astonishing things that I have heard of, unless it be, what for certain he says is true, that my Lady Castlemaine hath made a Bishop lately, namely, her uncle, Dr. Glenham,[3] who, I think they say, is Bishop of Carlisle: a drunken, swearing rascal, and a scandal to the Church; and do now pretend to be Bishop of Lincoln[4] in competition with Dr. Rainbow,[5] who is reckoned as worthy a man as most in the Church for piety and learning: which are things so scandalous to consider, that no man can doubt but we must be undone that hears of them. Cousin Roger did acquaint me in private with an offer made of his marrying of Mrs. Elizabeth Wiles, whom I know; a kinswoman of Mr. Honiwood's, an ugly old maid, but good housewife, and is said to have £2500 to her portion. But if I can find that she hath but £2000, which he prays me to examine, he says he will have her, she being

[1] He was serving for Grimsby.

[2] Gilbert Sheldon.

[3] Henry Glenham, D.D., was Dean of Bristol 1661; but never raised to the Bench.

[4] Lincoln was vacant by the translation of Benjamin Laney to Ely, on 24th May previously. William Fuller, Bishop of Limerick, was made Bishop of Lincoln on 17th September following.

[5] Dr. Rainbow was Bishop of Carlisle from 1664 to 1684.

one he hath long known intimately, and a good housewife, and discreet woman; though I am against it in my heart, she being not handsome at all. And it hath been the very bad fortune of the Pepyses that ever I knew, never to marry an handsome woman, excepting Ned Pepys.[1] To White Hall; and, looking out of the window into the garden, I saw the King (whom I have not had any desire to see since the Dutch came upon the coast first to Sheerness, for shame that I should see him, or he me, methinks, after such a dishonour) come upon the garden: with him two or three idle Lords; and instantly after him, in another walk, my Lady Castlemaine led by Bab. May: at which I was surprised, having but newly heard the stories of the King and her being parted for ever. So I took Mr. Povy, who was there, aside, and he told me all— how imperious this woman is, and hectors the King to whatever she will. It seems she is with child, and the King says he did not get it: with that she made a slighting puh with her mouth, and went out of the house, and never came in again till the King went to Sir Daniel Harvey's to pray her; and so she is come today, when one would think his mind should be full of some other cares, having but this morning broken up such a Parliament, with so much discontent and so many wants upon him, and but yesterday heard such a sermon against adultery. But it seems she hath told the King that, whoever did get it, he should own it; and the bottom of the quarrel is this: She is fallen in love with young Jermyn,[2] who hath of late been with her oftener than the King and is now going to marry my Lady Falmouth.[3] The King is mad at her entertaining Jermyn, and she is mad at Jermyn's going to marry from her: so they are all mad, and thus the kingdom is governed! But he tells me for certain that nothing is more sure than that the King and Duke of York and the Chancellor are desirous and labouring all they can to get an army, whatever the King say to the Parliament; and he believes that they are at last resolved to stand and fall all three together, so that he says in terms that the match of the Duke of York with the Chancellor's daughter hath undone the nation. He tells me also that the King hath not greater enemies in the world than those of his own family; for there is not an officer in the house almost but curses him for letting them starve,

[1] Edward Pepys, of Broomthorpe, who married Elizabeth Walpole.
[2] Henry Jermyn, afterwards Earl of Dover.
[3] Lady Falmouth, remarried Charles Lord Buckhurst, afterwards the sixth Earl of Dorset.

and there is not a farthing of money to be raised for the buying them bread. To walk in the garden with my wife, telling her of my losing £300 a year by my place that I am to part with, which do a little trouble me, but we must live with somewhat more thrift. Many guns were heard this afternoon, it seems, at White Hall and in the Temple garden very plain; but what it should be nobody knows, unless the Dutch be driving our ships up the river. To-morrow we shall know.

30th. To the Treasury-chamber, where I did speak with the Lords. Here I do hear that there are three Lords more to be added to them: my Lord Bridgewater, my Lord Anglesey, and my Lord Chamberlain.[1] Thence with Creed to White Hall, in our way meeting with Mr. Cooling, my Lord Chamberlain's secretary, on horseback, who stopped to speak with us; and he proved very drunk, and did talk, and would have talked all night with us, I not being able to break loose from him, he holding me so by the hand. But, Lord! to see his present humour, how he swears at every word, and talks of the King and my Lady Castlemaine in the plainest words in the world. And from him I gather that the story I learned yesterday is true—that the King hath declared that he did not get the child of which she is conceived at this time. But she told him, 'God damn me, but you shall own it!' It seems he is jealous of Jermyn, and she loves him so, that the thoughts of his marrying of my Lady Falmouth puts her into fits of the mother;[2] and he, it seems, hath been in her good graces from time to time, continually, for a good while; and once, as this Cooling says, the King had like to have taken him abed with her, but that he was fain to creep under the bed into her closet. Mr. Cooling told us how the King, once speaking of the Duke of York's being mastered by his wife, said to some of the company by that he would go no more abroad with this Tom Otter,[3] meaning the Duke of York, and his wife. Tom Killigrew, being by, said, 'Sir, pray which is the best for a man, to be a Tom Otter to his wife or to his mistress?' meaning the King's being so to my Lady Castlemaine. Thus he went on; and speaking then of my Lord Sandwich, whom he professed to love exceedingly, says

___

[1] Earl of Manchester.   [2] Hysteria.

[3] In the play of *Epicene, or the Silent Woman*, Mrs. Otter thus addresses her henpecked husband, Thomas Otter: 'Is this according to the instrument when I married you, that I would be princess and reign in my own house, and you would be my subject, and obey me?'—Act III, scene i.

Creed, 'I know not what, but he is a man, methinks, that I could love for himself, without other regards.' He talked very lewdly; and then took notice of my kindness to him on shipboard seven years ago, when the King was coming over, and how much he was obliged to me; but says, 'Pray look upon this acknowledgment of a kindness in me to be a miracle; for,' says he, 'it is against the law at Court for a man that borrows money of me, even to buy his place with, to own it the next Sunday'; and then told us his horse was a bribe, and his boots a bribe; and told us he was made up of bribes, as an Oxford scholar is set out with other men's goods when he goes out of town, and that he makes every sort of tradesman to bribe him; and invited me home to his house, to taste of his bribe wine. I never heard so much vanity from a man in my life: so, being now weary of him, we parted, and I took coach, and carried Creed to the Temple. There set him down, and to my office till my eyes begun to ache, and then home to supper: a pullet, with good sauce, to my liking, and then to play on the flageolet with my wife, which she now does very prettily, and so to bed.

31st. Among other things, did examine a fellow of our private man-of-war, who we have found come up from Hull, with near £500 worth of pieces of eight, though he will confess but 100 pieces. But it appears that there have been fine doings there. Major Halsey, speaking much of my doing business and understanding business, told me how my Lord General do say that I am worth them all. To Marrowbone,[1] where my Lord Mayor and Aldermen, it seems, dined today: and were just now going away, methought, in a disconsolate condition, compared with their splendour they formerly had, when the City was standing.

August 1st. Dined at Sir W. Pen's, only with Mrs. Turner and her husband, on a venison pasty that stunk like a devil. However, I did not know it till dinner was done. We had nothing but only this, and a leg of mutton, and a pullet or two. Mrs. Markham was here, with her great belly. I was very merry, and after dinner, upon a motion of the women, I was got to go to the play with them —the first I have seen since before the Dutch's coming upon our coast: and so to the King's House, to see 'The Custom of the Country.' The house mighty empty—more than ever I saw it— and an ill play. After the play we went into the house, and spoke with Knipp, who went abroad with us by coach to the Neat

[1] To the Lord Mayor's Banqueting House, on the site of what was Stratford Place, Oxford Street.

Houses,[1] in the way to Chelsea.   And there, in a box in a tree,[2] we sat and sang, and talked and eat : my wife out of humour, as she always is, when this woman is by.   So, after it was dark, we home. Set Knipp down at home, who told us the story how Nell is gone from the King's House, and is kept by my Lord Buckhurst.   Home, the gates of the City shut, it being so late : and at Newgate we find them in trouble, some thieves having this night broke open prison. So we through, and home ; and our coachman was fain to drive hard from two or three fellows, which he said were rogues, that he met at the end of Blowbladder Street, next Cheapside.   So set Mrs. Turner home, and then we home, and I to the Office a little ; and so home and to bed, my wife in an ill humour still.

2d. To the office, where Mr. Gauden came to me ; and he and I home to my chamber, and there reckoned, and I received my profits for Tangier of him, and £250 on my victualling score.   He is a most noble-minded man as ever I met with, and seems to own himself much obliged to me, which I will labour to make him ; for he is a good man also.   And, in fine, I had much matter of joy by this morning's work, receiving above £400 of him, on one account or other, and a promise that, though I lay down my victualling place, yet, as long as he continues Victualler, I shall be the better by him.

3d. To the office, there to enable myself, by finishing our great account, to give it to the Lords Commissioners of the Treasury ; which I did, and there was called in to them, to tell them only the total of our debt of the Navy on the 25th of May last, which is above £950,000.   Here I find them mighty hot in their answers to the Council-board about our Treasurer's threepences of the Victualling, and also against the present farm of the Customs, which they do most highly inveigh against.

4th. (Lord's day.) Busy at my office from morning till night, in writing with my own hand, fair, our large general account of the expense and debt of the Navy, which lasted me till midnight to do, that I was almost blind.

5th. To St. James's, where we did our ordinary business with the Duke of York, where I perceive they have taken the highest

[1] Situated on the site of St. George's Row, Sutherland Street, Pimlico.
[2] Within the hollow of the trunk of Sir Philip Sidney's oak at Penshurst, celebrated by several of our poets, was a seat which contained five or six persons with ease and convenience.   Pepys probably means a summer-house erected in the branches.

resolution in the world to become good husbands, and to retrench all charge. And to that end we are commanded to give him an account of the establishment in the seventh year of the late King's reign, and how offices and salaries had been increased since. And I hope it will end in the taking away some of our Commissioners. After done with the Duke of York, and coming out through his dressing-room, I there spied Signor Francisco tuning his guitar, and Monsieur de Puy with him, who did make him play to me, which he did most admirably—so well that I was mightily troubled that all that pains should have been taken upon so bad an instrument. I hear the ill news of our loss lately of four rich ships, two from Guinea, one from Gallipoli, all with rich oils; and the other from Barbadoes, worth, as is guessed, £80,000. But here is strong talk, as if Harman had taken some of the Dutch East India ships (but I dare not yet believe it) and brought them into Lisbon. To the Duke of York's House, and there saw 'Love's Tricks, or the School of Compliments';[1] a silly play, only Miss Davis's dancing in a shepherd's clothes did please us mightily.

6th. A full Board. Here, talking of news, my Lord Anglesey did tell us that the Dutch do make a further boggle with us about two or three things, which they will be satisfied in, he says, by us easily; but only in one, it seems, they do demand that we shall not interrupt their East Indiamen coming home, and of which they are in some fear; and we are full of hopes that we have light upon some of them, and carried them into Lisbon, by Harman; which God send! But they, which do show the low esteem they have of us, have the confidence to demand that we shall have a cessation on our parts, and yet they at liberty to take what they will; which is such an affront, as another cannot be devised greater. At noon home to dinner, where I find Mrs. Wood, Bab. Shelden, and our Mercer, who is dressed today in a pagan dress, that looks mighty pretty. We dined and sang and laughed mighty merry; and then I to the office, only met at the door with Mrs. Martin and Mrs. Burroughs, who I took in and drank with, but was afeard my wife should see them, they being, especially the first, tattling gossips. And so, after drinking with them, parted, and I to the office, busy as long as my poor eyes would endure, which troubles me mightily. My wife, as she said last night, hath put away Nell today, for her gossiping abroad and telling of stories.

[1] A comedy by James Shirley.

7th. My wife abroad with her maid Jane and Tom all the afternoon, being gone forth to eat some pasties at the Bottle of Hay, in John's Street, as you go to Islington, of which she is mighty fond; and I dined at home alone. Mr. Pierce, the surgeon, tells me that though the King and my Lady Castlemaine are friends again, she is not at White Hall, but at Sir D. Harvey's, whither the King goes to her; and he says she made him ask her forgiveness upon his knees, and promise to offend her no more so; and that, indeed, she did threaten to bring all his bastards to his closet door, and hath nearly hectored him out of his wits.

8th. Sir Henry Bellassis is dead of the duel he fought about ten days ago with Tom Porter; and it is pretty to see how the world do talk of them as a couple of fools, that killed one another out of love. I to my booksellers', where by and by I met Mr. Evelyn, and talked of several things, but particularly of the times: and he tells me that wise men do prepare to remove abroad what they have, for that we must be ruined, our case being past relief, the kingdom so much in debt, and the King minding nothing but his lust, going two days a week to see my Lady Castlemaine at Sir D. Harvey's. I met with Mr. Moore, who tells me that my Lord Hinchingbroke is now with his mistress, but that he is not married, as W. Howe came and told us the other day. To White Hall, and so took up my wife: and as far as Bow, where we stayed and drank. And there, passing by Mr. Lowther and his lady, they stopped; and we talked a little with them, they being in their gilt coach. Presently came to us Mr. Andrews, whom I had not seen a good while, who, as other merchants do, do all give over any hopes of things doing well, and so he spends his time here most, playing at bowls. After dining together at the coach-side, we with great pleasure home.

9th. To Westminster, to Mr. Burges, and he and I talked: and he do really declare that he expects that of necessity this kingdom will fall back again to a commonwealth, and other wise men are of the same mind, this family doing all that silly men can do to make themselves unable to support their kingdom, minding their lust and their pleasure, and making their government so chargeable, that people do well remember better things were done, and better managed, and with much less charge, under a commonwealth than they have been by this King. Home, and find Mr. Goodgroome, my wife's singing-master. There I did soundly rattle him for neglecting her so much as he has done—she not having learned three songs these three months and more. To St. James's, and there met Sir W. Coventry; and he and I walked in the Park an hour. And then to his chamber, where he read to me the heads of the late dispute between him and the rest of the Commissioners of the Treasury, and our new Treasurer of the Navy: where they have overthrown him the last Wednesday, in the great dispute touching his having the payment of the Victualler, which is now settled by Council that he is not to have it. And, indeed, they have been most just, as well as most severe and bold, in the doing this against a man of his quality: but I perceive Sir W. Coventry does really make no difference between any man. He tells me this day it is supposed the peace is ratified at Breda,[1] and all that matter over. We did talk of many retrenchments of charge of the Navy, which he will put in practice, and everywhere else; though, he tells me, he despairs of being able to do what ought to be done for the saving of the kingdom, which I tell him, indeed, all the world is almost in hopes of, upon the proceeding of these gentlemen for the regulating of the Treasury, it being so late, and our poverty grown so great, that they want where to set their feet, to begin to do anything. He tells me how weary he hath for this year and a half been of the war; and how, in the Duke of York's bedchamber at Christ Church at Oxford, when the Court was there, he did labour to persuade the Duke to fling off the care of the Navy, and get it committed to other hands; which, if he had done, would have been much to his honour, being just come home with so much honour from sea as he was. I took notice of the sharp letter he wrote, which he sent us to read, to Sir Edward Spragg, where he is very plain about his leaving his charge of the ships at Gravesend, when the enemy came last up, and several other things: a copy whereof I have kept. But it is done like a most worthy man; and he says it is good, now and then, to tell these gentlemen their duties, for they need it. And it seems, as he tells me, all our Knights are fallen out one with another, he and Jennings and Hollis; and, his words were, they are disputing which is the coward among them, and yet men that take the greatest liberty of censuring others! Here with him very late, till I could hardly get a coach or link

[1] The peace was signed at Breda, on 31st July. There were three separate acts or instruments—the first between France and England, by which D'Estrades and Courtin agreed that all conquests made during the war should be mutually restored; the second between England and Denmark; the third between England and Holland. In this last it is to be observed that England retained the right of the flag.

willing to go through the ruins; but I do, but I will not do it again, being, indeed, very dangerous.

10th. To the office, and at noon to dinner, where I sang and piped with my wife with great pleasure. To the New Exchange, to the bookseller's [1] there, where I hear of several new books coming out—Mr. Sprat's History of the Royal Society,[2] and Mrs. Philips's [3] poems. Sir John Denham's poems are going to be all printed together; and, among others, some new things; and among them he showed me a copy of verses of his upon Sir John Minnes's going heretofore to Boulogne to eat a pig.[4] Cowley, he tells me, is dead; who, it seems, was a mighty civil, serious man; which I did not know before.[5] Several good plays are also likely to be abroad soon, as 'Mustapha' and 'Henry the 5th.'

11th. (Lord's day.) Up by four o'clock, and ready, with Mrs. Turner, to take coach before five; and set on our journey, and got to the Wells at Barnet by seven o'clock, and there found many people a-drinking: but the morning is a very cold morning, so as we were very cold all the way in the coach. Here we met Joseph Batelier and W. Hewer also, and his uncle Steventon. So, after drinking three glasses and the women nothing, we back by coach to Barnet, where to the Red Lion, where we 'light, and went up into the great Room, and there drank, and eat some of the best cheese-cakes that ever I eat in my life. And so took coach again, and W. Hewer on horseback with us, and so to Hatfield, to the inn, next my Lord Salisbury's house, and there rested ourselves,

[1] To Herringman's, at the Blue Anchor, in the Lower Walk of the New Exchange. He died rich, and is buried under a handsome monument, at Chislehurst, in Kent.

[2] By Thomas Sprat.

[3] Katherine Fowler, wife of James Philips, of Cardigan, and once celebrated as a distinguished poetess; best known as the 'matchless Orinda.' She died at the early age of thirty-three in 1664 but the praise of her contemporaries has not been sufficient to preserve her works from oblivion.

[4] This was before the Restoration, when Sir John Minnes was at Calais.

[5] We have here a striking instance of the slow communication of intelligence. Cowley died on 28th July at Chertsey; and Pepys, though in London, and at all times a great newsmonger, did not learn till 10th August that so eminent a man was dead. Evelyn says that he attended Cowley's funeral on 3rd August, which shows that he did not keep his *Diary* entered up as regularly as our journalist, for the interment is thus recorded in the register of Westminster Abbey: 'On the 17th of August, Mr. Cowley, a famous poet, was buried at the foot of the steps to Henry VII's Chapel.' Cowley's corpse lay in state at Wallingford House, then the residence of the Duke of Buckingham.

and drank, and bespoke dinner; and so to church, it being just church-time. Did hear a most excellent good sermon, which pleased me mightily, and very devout; it being upon the designs of saving grace, where it is in a man, and one sign, which held him all this day, was, that where that grace was, there is also the grace of prayer, which he did handle very finely. In this church lies the former Lord of Salisbury, Cecil,[1] buried in a noble tomb. Then we to our inn, and there dined very well, and mighty merry; and walked out into the Park through the fine walk of trees, and to the vineyard, and there showed them that, which is in good order, and indeed a place of great delight; which, together with our fine walk through the Park, was of as much pleasure as could be desired in the world for country pleasure and good air. Being come back, and weary with the walk, the women had pleasure in putting on some straw hats, which are much worn in this country, and did become them mightily, but especially my wife. So, after resting awhile, we took coach again, and back to Barnet, where W. Hewer took us into his lodging, which is very handsome, and there did treat us very highly with cheese-cakes, cream, tarts, and other good things; and then walked into the garden, which was pretty, and there filled my pockets full of filberts, and so with much pleasure. Among other things, I met in this house with a printed book of the Life of O. Cromwell,[2] to his honour as a soldier and politician, though as a rebel, the first of that kind that ever I saw, and it is well done. Took coach again, and got home with great content.

12th. To St. James's, where we find the Duke gone a-hunting with the King. To my bookseller's, and did buy Scott's Discourse of Witches; and do hear Mr. Cowley mightily lamented his death, by Dr. Ward, the Bishop of Winchester,[3] and Dr. Bates, who were standing there, as the best poet of our nation, and as good a man. Thence I to the print-seller's, over against the Exchange towards Covent Garden, and there bought a few more prints of cities. So home, and my wife and maids being gone over the water to the

---

[1] Robert Cecil, the first earl, son of the great Lord Burghley. He died in 1612.

[2] 'The History of the Life and Death of Oliver Cromwell, the late Usurper and pretended Protector of England, &c., truly collected and published for a warning to all tyrants and usurpers, by I. H. Gent, London, printed for F. Coles, at the Lamb, in the Old Bailey, 1663.' 4to, pp. 22; reprinted in *Harl. Miscel.*, i, p. 279.

[3] Dr. George Morley.

whitster's [1] with their clothes, this being the first time of her trying this way of washing her linen. After dinner, all alone to the King's playhouse, and there did happen to sit just before Mrs. Pierce, and Mrs. Knipp, who pulled me by the hair; and I so addressed myself to them, and talked to them all the intervals of the play, and did give them fruit. The play is 'Brenoralt,' which I do find but little in, for my part. Here was many fine ladies—among others, the German Baron, with his lady, who is envoy from the Emperor, and their fine daughter, which hath travelled all Europe over with them, it seems; and is accordingly accomplished, and, indeed, is a wonderful pretty woman. Here Sir Philip Frowde,[2] who sat next to me, did tell me how Sir H. Bellassis is dead, and that the quarrel between him and Tom Porter, who is fled, did rise in the ridiculous fashion that I was first told it, which is a strange thing between two so good friends. The play being done, I took the women and Mrs. Corbett, who was with them, by coach, it raining, to Mrs. Manuel's, the Jew's widow, formerly a player, whom we heard sing with one of the Italians that was there; and, indeed, she sings mightily well, and just after the Italian manner, but yet do not please me like one of Mrs. Knipp's songs, to a good English tune, the manner of their air not pleasing me so well as the fashion of our own, nor so natural. Then home, and my wife come; and so, saying nothing where I had been, we to supper and pipe, and so to bed.

13th. Attended the Duke of York, with our usual business; who, upon occasion, told us that he did expect this night or to-morrow to hear from Breda of the consummation of the peace. Thence Sir W. Pen and I to the King's House, and there saw 'The Committee,' which I went to with some prejudice, not liking it before; but I do now find it a very good play, and a great deal of good invention in it: but Lacy's part is so well performed that it would set off anything. Home to my chamber to sing and pipe till my wife comes home from her washing, which was nine at night, and a dark rainy night, that I was troubled at her staying out so long.

14th. To dinner to Sir W. Batten's. By and by to talk of our prize at Hull, and Sir W. Batten offering, again and again, seriously how he would sell his part for £1000, and I considering the knavery of Hogg and his company, and the trouble we may have with the

[1] Whitester: a bleacher of linen.
[2] *Ob.* 6th August 1674. There is a monument to Sir Philip Frowde in Bath Abbey Church.

Prince Rupert about the consort ship, and how we are linked with Sir R. Ford, and then the danger of the sea, I did offer my part to him for £700. With a little beating the bargain, we came to a perfect agreement for £666 13s. 4d., which is two-thirds of £1000, which is my proportion of the prize. I went to my office full of doubts and joy concerning what I had done; but, however, did put into writing the heads of our agreement, and we both signed them; and Sir R. Ford, being come thither since, witnessed them. I away, satisfied, and to the King's playhouse, and there saw 'The Country Captain,' which is a very ordinary play.

15th. Sir W. Pen and I to the Duke's House; where a new play. The King and Court there: the house full, and an act begun. And so we went to the King's, and there saw 'The Merry Wives of Windsor,' which did not please me at all, in no part of it.

16th. My wife and I to the Duke's playhouse, where we saw the new play acted yesterday, 'The Feigned Innocence, or Sir Martin Mar-all'; a play made by my Lord Duke of Newcastle, but, as everybody says, corrected by Dryden.[1] It is the most entire piece of mirth, a complete farce from one end to the other, that certainly was ever writ. I never laughed so in all my life, and at very good wit therein, not fooling. The house full, and in all things of mighty content to me. To the New Exchange, where, at my bookseller's, I saw 'The History of the Royal Society,'[2] which, I believe, is a fine book, and have bespoke one in quires. To my chamber, and read the history of 88[3] in Speed, in order to my seeing the play thereof acted tomorrow at the King's House. Everybody wonders that we have no news from Breda of the ratification of the peace; and do suspect that there is some stop in it.

17th. My wife and I and Sir W. Pen to the King's playhouse, where the house extraordinary full; and there the King and Duke of York to see the new play, 'Queen Elizabeth's Troubles, and the History of Eighty Eight.'[4] I confess I have sucked in so much

[1] Downes says that the duke gave this comedy to Dryden, who adapted it to the stage; but it is entered on the books of the Stationers' Company as the production of His Grace.

[2] Sprat's.   [3] 1588.

[4] Pepys here, as elsewhere, took the second title of the piece, as, perhaps, it appeared in the bills of the day. He alludes to the revival of a play by Thomas Heywood, originally printed in 1605, under the title of *If you know not me, you know nobody, or the Troubles of Queen Elizabeth*, which especially relates to the defeat of the Armada in 1588. It was so popular that it went through eight or nine early editions. In 1667 it was no doubt brought out with some alterations, but probably not printed.

of the sad story of Queen Elizabeth from my cradle, that I was
ready to weep for her sometimes; but the play is the most ridiculous
that sure ever came upon the stage, and, indeed, is merely a show,
only shows the true garb of the Queen in those days, just as we see
Queen Mary and Queen Elizabeth painted: but the play is merely
a puppet play, acted by living puppets. Neither the design nor
language better; and one stands by and tells us the meaning of
things. Only I was pleased to see Knipp dance among the milk-
maids, and to hear her sing a song to Queen Elizabeth; and to see
her come out in her night-gown with no locks on, but her bare
face and hair only tied up in a knot behind; which is the comeliest
dress that ever I saw her in to her advantage. Went as far as
Mile End with Sir W. Pen, whose coach took him up there for his
country house; and, after having drunk there, at the Rose and
Crown, a good house for Alderman Bide's [1] ale, we parted.

18th. To Cree Church, to see it how it is: but I find no alteration
there, as they say there was, for my Lord Mayor and Aldermen to
come to sermon, as they do every Sunday, as they did formerly to
Paul's.[2] There dined with me Mr. Turner and his daughter Betty.
Betty is grown a fine young lady as to carriage and discourse. We
had a good haunch of venison, powdered and boiled, and a good
dinner. I walked towards White Hall, but, being wearied, turned
into St. Dunstan's Church, where I heard an able sermon of the
minister [3] of the place, and stood by a pretty, modest maid, whom
I did labour to take by the hand, but she would not, but got
further and further from me; and, at last, I could perceive her to
take pins out of her pocket to prick me if I should touch her again
—which, seeing, I did forbear, and was glad I did spy her design.
And then I fell to gaze upon another pretty maid, in a pew close
to me, and she on me; and I did go about to take her by the hand,
which she suffered a little, and then withdrew. So the sermon
ended, and the church broke up, and my amours ended also.
Took coach and home, and there took up my wife, and to Islington. Between that and Kingsland there happened an odd
adventure: one of our coach-horses fell sick of the staggers, so as
he was ready to fall down. The coachman was fain to 'light, and
hold him up, and cut his tongue to make him bleed, and his tail.

[1] John Bide, brewer, sheriff of London in 1647.
[2] The church of St. Catherine Cree, having escaped the fire, was resorted
to by the corporation after the destruction of St. Paul's.
[3] John Thompson, vicar of St. Dunstan's in the West.

The horse continued shaking every part of him, as if he had been in an ague, a good while, and the coachman thought and believed he would presently drop down dead; then he blew some tobacco in his nose, upon which the horse sneezed, and, by and by, grew well, and drew us all the rest of our way, as well as ever he did; which was one of the strangest things of a horse I ever observed.

19th. To the Duke of York's House all alone, and there saw 'Sir Martin Mar-all' again, though I saw him but two days since, and do find it the most comical play that ever I saw in my life. Mr. Moore do agree with most people that I meet with, that we shall fall into a commonwealth in a few years, whether we will or no; for the charge of a monarchy is such as the kingdom cannot be brought to bear willingly, nor are things managed so well nowadays under it, as heretofore.

20th. Sir W. Coventry fell to discourse of retrenchments; and therein he tells how he would have but only one Clerk of the Acts. He do tell me he hath propounded how the charge of the Navy in peace shall come within £200,000, by keeping out twenty-four ships in summer, and ten in the winter. And several other particulars we went over of retrenchment: and I find I must provide some things to offer, that I may be found studious to lessen the King's charge. We up to the Duke of York, but no money to be heard of—nay, not £100 upon the most pressing service that can be imagined of bringing in the King's timber from Whittlewood,[1] while we have the utmost want of it. Sir W. Coventry did single out Sir W. Pen and me, and desired us to lend the King some money, out of the prizes we have taken by Hogg. He did not much press it, and we made but a merry answer thereto: but I perceive he did ask it seriously, and did tell us that there never was so much need of it in the world as now, we being brought to the lowest straits that can be in the world. My wife mighty pressing for a new pair of cuffs, which I am against the laying out of money upon yet, which makes her angry.

21st. I sent my cousin Roger a tierce of claret, which I give him. This morning come two of Captain Cocke's boys, whose voices are broke, and are gone from the Chapel, but have extraordinary skill; and they and my boy, with his broken voice, did sing three parts; their names were Blaew and Loggings. But, notwithstanding their skill, yet to hear them sing with their broken

---
[1] Whittlebury Forest.

voices, which they could not command to keep in tune, would make a man mad—so bad it was.

22d. Up, and to the office; whence Lord Brouncker, J. Minnes, W. Pen, and I went to examine some men that are put in there, for rescuing of men that were pressed into the service: and we do plainly see that the desperate condition that we put men into for want of their pay makes them mad, they being as good men as ever were in the world, and would as readily serve the King again, were they but paid. Two men leaped overboard, among others, into the Thames, out of the vessel into which they were pressed, and were shot by the soldiers placed there to keep them, two days since; so much people do avoid the King's service! And then these men are pressed without money, and so we cannot punish them for anything, so that we are forced only to make a show of severity by keeping them in prison, but are unable to punish them. Returning to the office, I did ask whether we might visit Commissioner Pett, to which, I confess, I have no great mind; and it was answered that he was close prisoner, and we could not; but the Lieutenant of the Tower would send for him to his lodgings, if we would: so we put it off to another time. To Captain Cocke's to dinner; where Lord Brouncker and his lady, Matt. Wren, and Bulteel, and Sir Allan Apsley; the last of whom did make good sport, he being already fallen under the retrenchments of the new Committee, as he is Master Falconer, which makes him mad, and swears that we are doing what the Parliament would have done— that is, that we are now endeavouring to destroy one another. But it was well observed by some at the table that they do not think this retrenchment of the King's charge will be so acceptable to the Parliament, they having given the King a revenue of so many £100,000 a year more than his predecessors had, that he might live in pomp, like a king. With my Lord Brouncker and his mistress to the King's playhouse, and there saw 'The Indian Emperor': where I find Nell come again, which I am glad of; but was most infinitely displeased with her being put to act the Emperor's daughter, which is a great and serious part, which she does most basely. The rest of the play, though pretty good, was not well acted by most of them, methought; so that I took no great content in it. But that that troubled me most was that Knipp sent by Moll [1] to desire to speak to me after the play: and she beckoned to me at the end of the play, and I promised to come; but it was so

[1] Orange Moll, mentioned before.

late, and I forced to step to Mrs. Williams's lodgings with my Lord Brouncker and her, where I did not stay, however, for fear of her showing me her closet and thereby forcing me to give her something; and it was so late, that, for fear of my wife's coming home before me, I was forced to go straight home, which troubled me. Anon, late, comes home my wife with Mr. Turner and Mrs. Turner, with whom she supped, having been with Mrs. Turner today at her daughter's school, to see her daughters dancing, and the rest, which she says is fine. My wife very fine today, in her new suit of laced cuffs and perquisites. This evening Mr. Pelling comes to me, and tells me that this night the Dutch letters are come, and that the peace was proclaimed there the 19th inst., and that all is finished; which, for my life, I know not whether to be glad or sorry for, a peace being so necessary, and yet so bad in its terms.

23d. Abroad to White Hall in a hackney coach with Sir W. Pen; and in our way, in the narrow street near Paul's (going the back way by Tower Street, and the coach being forced to put back), he was turning himself into a cellar,[1] which made people cry out to us, and so we were forced to leap out—he out of one, and I out of the other door. *Query*, whether a glass coach would have permitted us to have made the escape, neither of us getting any hurt; nor could the coach have got much hurt had we been in it; but, however, there was cause enough for us to do what we could to save ourselves. So, being all dusty, we put into the Castle tavern, by the Savoy, and there brushed ourselves. To White Hall, to attend the Council. The King there: and it was about considering how the fleet might be discharged at their coming in shortly, the peace being now ratified, and it takes place on Monday next. I to Westminster to the Exchequer, to see what sums of money other people lend upon the Act; and find of all sizes from £1000 to £100—nay, to £50, and to £20, and to £5: for I find that one Dr. Reade, Doctor of Law, gives no more, and others of them £20; which is a poor thing, methinks, that we should stoop so low as to borrow such sums. Upon the whole, I do think to lend, since I must lend, £300, though, God knows! it is much against my will to lend any unless things were in better condition, and likely to continue so. To the Treasury-chamber, where I waited, talking with Sir G. Downing, till the Lords met. He tells me how he will make all the Exchequer officers, of one side and

_____
[1] So much of London was yet in ruins.

the other, to lend the King money upon the Act; and that the least clerk shall lend money, and he believes the least will £100: but this I do not believe. He made me almost ashamed that we of the Navy had not in all this time lent any; so that I find it necessary I should, and so will speedily do it, before any of my fellows begin, and lead me to a bigger sum. By and by the Lords come; and I perceive Sir W. Coventry is the man, and nothing done till he comes. Among other things, I heard him observe, looking over a paper, that Sir John Shaw is a miracle of a man, for he thinks he executes more places than any man in England; for there he finds him a Surveyor of some of the King's woods, and so reckoned up many other places, the most inconsistent in the world. Their business with me was to consider how to assign such of our commanders as will take assignments upon the Act for their wages; and the consideration thereof was referred to me to give them an answer the next sitting: which is a horrid poor thing, but they scruple at nothing of honour in the case. So away, and called my wife, and to the King's House, and saw 'The Maiden Queen,' which pleased us mightily; and then away, and took up Mrs. Turner at her door, and so to Mile End, and there drank, and so back to her house, it being a fine evening, and there supped. The first time I ever was there since they lived there; and she hath all things so neat and well done, that I am mightily pleased with her and all she do. So here very merry, and then home and to bed. I find most people pleased with their being at ease, and safe of a peace, that they may know no more charge or hazard of an ill-managed war: but nobody speaking of the peace with any content or pleasure, but are silent in it, as of a thing they are ashamed of; no, not at Court, much less in the City.

24th. (St. Bartholomew's day.) This morning was proclaimed the peace between us and the States of the United Provinces, and also of the King of France and Denmark; and in the afternoon the Proclamations were printed and came out; and at night the bells rung, but no bonfires that I hear of anywhere, partly from the dearness of firing, but principally from the little content most people have in the peace. After dinner to a play, and there saw 'The Cardinal' at the King's House, wherewith I am mightily pleased: but, above all, with Beck Marshall. But it is pretty to see how I look up and down for, and did spy Knipp; but durst not own it to my wife, for fear of angering her, and so I was forced not to take notice of her, and so homeward: and my belly now full with plays, that I do intend to bind myself to see no more till Michael-mas. Most of our discourse is about our keeping a coach the next year, which pleases my wife mightily; and, if I continue as able as now, it will save us money. This day comes a letter from the Duke of York to the Board to invite us, which is as much as to fright us, into the lending the King money; which is a poor thing, and most dishonourable, and shows in what a case we are at the end of the war to our neighbours. And the King do now declare publicly to give 10 per cent to all lenders; which makes some think that the Dutch themselves will send over money, and lend it upon our public faith, the Act of Parliament.

25th. (Lord's day.) Up and to church, and thence home; and Pelling comes by invitation to dine with me, and much pleasant discourse with him. After dinner, away by water to White Hall, where I landed Pelling, who is going to his wife, where she is in the country, at Parson's Green; and myself to Westminster, and to the parish church, thinking to see Betty Michell; and did stay an hour in the crowd, thinking, by the end of a nose that I saw, that it had been her; but at last the head turned towards me, and it was her mother, which vexed me. So I back to my boat, which had broke one of her oars in rowing, and had now fastened it again; and so I up to Putney, and there stepped into the church, to look upon the fine people there, whereof there is great store, and the young ladies; and so walked to Barn Elms, whither I sent Russel,[1] reading of Boyle's Hydrostatics, which are of infinite delight. I walked in the Elms a good while, and then to my boat, and leisurely home, with great pleasure to myself; and there supped, and W. Hewer with us, with whom a great deal of good talk touching the Office, and so to bed.

26th. To the office, where we sat upon a particular business all the morning, and my Lord Anglesey with us: who, and my Lord Brouncker, do bring us news how my Lord Chancellor's Seal is to be taken away from him today. The thing is so great and sudden to me, that it put me into a very great admiration what should be the meaning of it; and they do not own that they know what it should be: but this is certain, that the King did resolve it on Saturday, and did yesterday send the Duke of Albemarle, the only man fit for those works, to him for his purse. To which the Chancellor answered that he received it from the King, and would deliver it to the King's own hand, and so civilly returned the Duke

---

[1] His waterman.

of Albemarle without it; and this morning my Lord Chancellor
is to be with the King, to come to an end in the business.   Dined
at Sir W. Batten's, where Mr. Boreman was, who came from White
Hall, who tells us that he saw my Lord Chancellor come in his
coach with some of his men, without his Seal, to White Hall to his
chamber; and thither the King and Duke of York came and stayed
together alone, an hour or more; and it is said that the King do say
that he will have the Parliament meet, and that it will prevent much
trouble by having of him out of their enmity, by his place being
taken away, for that all their enmity will be at him.   It is said, also,
that my Lord Chancellor answers that he desires he may be
brought to his trial, if he have done anything to lose his office; and
that he will be willing, and is most desirous, to lose that and
his head both together.   Upon what terms they parted nobody
knows: but the Chancellor looked sad, he says.   Then in comes
Sir Richard Ford, and says he hears that there is nobody more
presses to reconcile the King and Chancellor than the Duke of
Albemarle and Duke of Buckingham: the latter of which is very
strange, not only that he who was so lately his enemy should do it,
but that this man that but the other day was in danger of losing his
own head, should so soon come to be a mediator for others: it
shows a wise Government.   They all say that he [Clarendon] is
but a poor man, not worth above £3000 a year in land; but this I
cannot believe: and all do blame him for having built so great a
house till he had got a better estate.   So I walked to the King's
playhouse, and saw 'The Surprisal,'[1] a very mean play, I thought
(or else it was because I was out of humour), and but very little
company in the house.   Sir W. Pen and I had a great deal of discourse with Moll, who tells us that Nell is already left by my Lord
Buckhurst, and that he makes sport of her, and swears she hath
had all she could get of him; and Hart,[2] her great admirer, now
hates her; and that she is very poor, and hath lost my Lady Castlemaine, who was her great friend also: but she is come to the House,
but is neglected by them all.[3]

27th.   To White Hall, and there hear how it is like to go well
enough with my Lord Chancellor; that he is like to keep his Seal,

[1] A comedy by Sir Robert Howard.
[2] The celebrated actor.
[3] The king afterwards took her into keeping. His son by her was born
8th May 1670, and was subsequently made Duke of St. Albans. It may be
well doubted if Charles were indeed the father.

desiring that he may stand his trial in Parliament, if they will accuse him of anything. Here Sir J. Minnes and I looking upon the pictures; and Mr. Chiffinch,[1] being by, did take us, of his own accord, into the King's closet, to show us some pictures, which, indeed, is a very noble place, and exceeding great variety of brave pictures, and the best hands. I could have spent three or four hours there well, and we had great liberty to look; and Cheffins seemed to take pleasure to show us, and commend the pictures. I to visit Colonel Fitzgerald,[2] who hath been sick at Woolwich, where most of the officers and soldiers quartered there, since the Dutch being in the river, have died or been sick, and he among the rest; and, by the growth of his beard and grey hairs, I did not know him. This day Mr. Pierce, the surgeon, was with me; and tells me how this business of my Lord Chancellor's was certainly designed in my Lady Castlemaine's chamber; and that when he went from the King on Monday morning she was in bed, though about twelve o'clock, and ran out in her smock into her aviary looking into White Hall; and thither her woman brought her her night-gown; and stood joying herself at the old man's going away: and several of the gallants of White Hall, of which there were many staying to see the Chancellor return, did talk to her in her bird-cage; among others, Blanquefort, telling her she was the bird of paradise.[3]

28th. Up; and stayed undressed till my tailor's boy did mend my vest, in order to my going to the christening anon. To White Hall: till past twelve in a crowd of people in the lobby, expecting the hearing of the great cause of Alderman Barker [4] against my Lord Deputy of Ireland, for his ill usage in his business of land there; but the King and Council sat so long, as they neither heard them, nor me. So when they rose, I into the House, and saw the King and Queen at dinner, and heard a little of their violins' music, and so home. In the afternoon with my Lady Batten, Pen and her daughter, and my wife, to Mrs. Poole's, where I mighty merry among the women, and christened the child, a girl, Elizabeth, which, though a girl, yet my Lady Batten would have me to give the name. After christening comes Sir W. Batten, W. Pen, and

---

[1] William Chiffinch.

[2] Deputy governor of Tangier.

[3] See Clarendon's account of this scene, *Life*, vol. iii, p. 832. 8vo. 1761.

[4] William Barker, who married Martha, daughter of William Turner, and widow of Daniel Williams. His son William was created a baronet in 1676.

Mr. Lowther, and mighty merry there; and I forfeited for not kissing the two godmothers presently after the christening, before I kissed the mother, which made good mirth.   Went twice round Bartholomew fair, which I was glad to see again after two years missing it by the plague.

29th.   Mr. Moore tells me that my Lord Crewe and his friends take it very ill of me that my Lord Sandwich's sea-fee should be retrenched, and so reported from this Office, and I give them no notice of it.   The thing, though I know it to be false—at least, that nothing went from our Office towards it—yet it troubled me; and therefore I went and dined with my Lord Crewe, and I did enter into that discourse, and laboured to satisfy him, but found, though he said little, yet that he was not yet satisfied; but after dinner did pray me to go and see how it was, whether true or no. Did tell me that if I was not their friend, they could trust to nobody, and that he did not forget my service and love to my Lord, and adventures for him in dangerous times, and therefore would not willingly doubt me now; but yet asked my pardon if, upon this news, he did begin to fear it.   This did mightily trouble me: so I away thence to White Hall, but could do nothing.   In the evening to White Hall again, and there met Sir Richard Browne, Clerk to the Committee for retrenchments, who assures me no one word was ever yet mentioned about my Lord's salary; and the mistake ended very merrily, and to all our contents.   I find at Sir G. Carteret's that they do mightily joy themselves in the hopes of my Lord Chancellor's getting over this trouble; and I make them believe, and so, indeed, I do believe he will, that my Lord Chancellor is become popular by it.   I find by all hands that the Court is at this day all to pieces, every man of a faction of one sort or other, so as it is to be feared what it will come to.   But that that pleases me is, I hear tonight that Mr. Brouncker is turned away yesterday by the Duke of York, for some bold words he was heard by Colonel Werden [1] to say in the garden, the day the Chancellor was with the King—that he believed the King would be hectored out of everything.   For this the Duke of York, who all say hath been very strong for his father-in-law at this trial, hath turned him away: and everybody, I think, is glad of it; for he was a pestilent rogue, an atheist, that would have sold his King and country for *6d.* almost, so covetous and wicked a rogue he is, by all men's

---

[1] His eldest son, John, was created a baronet in 1672.

report.   But one observed to me that there never was the occasion of men's holding their tongues at Court and everywhere else as there is at this day, for nobody knows which side will be uppermost.

30th.   At White Hall I met with Sir G. Downing, who tells me of Sir W. Pen's offering to lend £500; and I tell him of my £300 which he would have me to lend upon the credit of the latter part of the Act, saying that by that means my 10 per cent will continue to me the longer.   But I understand better, and will do it upon the £380,000 which will come to be paid the sooner; there being no delight in lending money now, to be paid by the King two years hence.   But here he and Sir William Doyly were attending the Council as Commissioners for sick and wounded and prisoners: and they told me their business, which was to know how we shall do to release our prisoners; for it seems the Dutch have got us to agree in the treaty, as they fool us in anything, that the diet of the prisoners on both sides shall be paid for before they be released; which they have done, knowing ours to run high, they having more prisoners of ours than we have of theirs; so that they are able and most ready to discharge the debt of theirs, but we are neither able nor willing to do that for ours, the debt of those in Zealand only amounting to above £5000 for men taken in the King's own ships, besides others taken in merchantmen, who expect, as is usual, that the King should redeem them; but I think he will not, by what Sir G. Downing says.   This our prisoners complain of there; and say in their letters, which Sir G. Downing showed me, that they have made a good feat that they should be taken in the service of the King, and the King not pay for their victuals while prisoners for him.   But so far they are from doing thus with their men, as we do to discourage ours, that I find in the letters of some of our prisoners there, which he showed me, that they have with money got our men, that they took, to work and carry their ships home for them; and they have been well rewarded, and released when they came into Holland: which is done like a noble, brave, and wise people.   To Walthamstow, to Sir W. Pen's by invitation: a very bad dinner, and everything suitable, that I never knew people in my life that make their flutter, that do things so meanly.   I was sick to see it, but was merry at some ridiculous humours of my Lady Batten, who, as being an ill-bred woman, would take exceptions at anything anybody said, and I made good sport at it.   Into the garden and wilderness, which is like the rest of the house, nothing in order, nor looked after.   By and by comes news that my Lady Viner was come to see Mrs. Lowther; and all the pleasure I had here was to see her, which I did, and saluted her, and find she is pretty, though not so eminently so as people talked of her, and of very pretty carriage and discourse.   Leaving my wife to come home with them, I to Bartholomew fair, to walk up and down; and there among other things find my Lady Castle-maine at a puppet-play, 'Patient Grizell,'[1] and the street full of people expecting her coming out.   I confess I did wonder at her courage to come abroad, thinking the people would abuse her: but they, silly people! do not know the work she makes, and there-fore suffered her with great respect to take coach, and she away, without any trouble at all.   I, among others, saw Tom Pepys, the turner, who has a shop, and I think lives in the Fair, when the fair is not.   Captain Cocke tells me that there is yet expectation that the Chancellor will lose the Seal; and assures me that there have been high words between the Duke of York and Sir W. Coventry, for his being so high against the Chancellor, so as the Duke of York would not sign some papers that he brought, saying that he could not endure the sight of him; and that Sir W. Coventry answered, that what he did was in obedience to the King's commands, and that he did not think any man fit to serve a prince, that did not know how to retire and live a country life.

31st.   At the office all the morning, where by Sir W. Pen I do hear that the Seal was fetched away to the King yesterday from the Lord Chancellor by Secretary Morrice; which puts me into a great horror.   My Lord Brouncker tells me that he hath of late discoursed about this business with Sir W. Coventry, who he finds is the great man in the doing this business of the Chancellor's, and that he do persevere in it, though against the Duke of York's opinion; to which he says that the Duke of York was once of the same mind, and if he had thought fit since, for any reason, to alter his mind, he hath not found any to alter his own, and so desires to be excused, for it is for the King's and kingdom's good.   And it seems that the Duke of York himself was the first man that did speak to the King of this, though he hath since altered his mind; and that W. Coventry did tell the Duke of York that he was not fit to serve a prince, that did not know how to retire and live a private life; and that he was ready for that, if it be his and the King's

---

[1] The well-known story, first told by Boccaccio, then by Petrarch, after-wards by Chaucer, and which has since become proverbial.

pleasure. In the evening Mr. Ball, of the Excise Office, tells me that the Seal is delivered to Sir Orlando Bridgeman, the man of the whole nation that is the best spoken of and will please most people; and therefore I am mighty glad of it. He was then at my Lord Arlington's, whither I went, expecting to see him come out; but stayed so long, and Sir W. Coventry coming there, whom I had not a mind should see me there idle upon a post-night, I went home without seeing him; but he is there with his Seal in his hand. This day, being dissatisfied with my wife's learning so few songs of Goodgroome, I did come to a new bargain with him to teach her songs at so much, viz., 10s. a song, which he accepts of, and will teach her.

September 1st. (Lord's day.) Up, and betimes by water from the Tower, and called at the Old Swan for a glass of strong water, and sent word to have little Michell and his wife come and dine with us today; and so, taking in a gentleman and his lady that wanted a boat, to Westminster. Our new Lord Keeper, Bridgeman, did this day, the first time, attend the King to chapel with his Seal. Sir H. Cholmley tells me there are hopes that the women also will have a rout, and particularly that my Lady Castlemaine is coming to a composition with the King to be gone; but how true this is, I know not. Blanquefort is made Privy Purse to the Duke of York; the Attorney-General is made Chief Justice, in the room of my Lord Bridgman; the Solicitor-General is made Attorney-General; and Sir Edward Turner made Solicitor-General.[1] It is pretty to see how strange everybody looks, nobody knowing whence this arises, whether from my Lady Castlemaine, Bab. May, and their faction, or from the Duke of York, notwithstanding his great appearance of defence of the Chancellor, or from Sir William Coventry and some few with him. But greater changes are yet expected. Spent all the afternoon, Pelling, Howe, and I and my boy, singing of Locke's response to the Ten Commandments, which he hath set very finely, and was a good while since sung before the King, and spoiled in the performance, which occasioned his printing them for his vindication, and are excellent good. In the evening my wife and I to walk in the garden, and there scolded a little, I being doubtful that she had received a couple of fine pinners (one of point de Gênes), which I feared she hath from someone or other of a

---

[1] This was a false report; Bridgeman continued to preside in the Common Pleas till 23rd May 1668, when he was succeeded by Lord Chief Justice Vaughan, and neither of the other changes took place.

present; but, on the contrary, I find she hath bought them for me
to pay for them, without my knowledge. This do displease me
much; but yet do so much please me better than if she had received
them the other way, that I was not much angry, but fell to other
discourse.

2d. This day is kept in the City as a public fast for the fire this
day twelve months: but I was not at church, being commanded,
with the rest, to attend the Duke of York; and, therefore, with Sir
J. Minnes to St. James's, where we had much business before the
Duke of York, and observed all things to be very kind between
the Duke of York and Sir W. Coventry; which did mightily joy
me. When we had done, Sir W. Coventry called me down with
him to his chamber, and there told me that he is leaving the Duke
of York's service, which I was amazed at. But he tells me that it
is not with the least unkindness on the Duke of York's side, though
he expects, and I told him he was in the right, it will be interpreted
otherwise, because done just at this time; 'but,' says he, 'I did desire
it a good while since, and the Duke of York did, with much
entreaty, grant it, desiring that I would say nothing of it, that he
might have time and liberty to choose his successor without being
importuned for others whom he should not like': and that he hath
chosen Mr. Wren, which I am glad of, he being a very ingenious
man; and so Sir W. Coventry says of him, though he knows him
little; but particularly commends him for the book he writ in
answer to Harrington's 'Oceana,' which, for that reason, I intend
to buy. He tells me the true reason is, that he, being a man not
willing to undertake more business than he can go through, and
being desirous to have his whole time to spend upon the business
of the Treasury, and a little for his own ease, he did desire this of
the Duke of York. He assures me that the kindness with which he
goes away from the Duke of York is one of the greatest joys that
ever he had in the world. I used some freedom with him, telling
him how the world hath discoursed of his having offended the
Duke of York about the late business of the Chancellor. He does
not deny it, but says that perhaps the Duke of York might have
some reason for it, he opposing him in a thing wherein he was so
earnest: but tells me that, notwithstanding all that, the Duke of
York does not now, nor can, blame him, for he was the man that
did propose the removal of the Chancellor; and that he did still
persist in it, and at this day publicly owns it and is glad of it; but
that the Duke of York knows that he did first speak of it to the

Duke of York, before he spoke to any mortal creature besides, which was fair dealing; and the Duke of York was then of the same mind with him, and did speak of it to the King; though since, for reasons best known to himself, he afterwards altered. I did then desire to know what was the great matter that grounded his desire of the Chancellor's removal? He told me many things not fit to be spoken, and yet not anything of his being unfaithful to the King; but, *instar omnium*, he told me that while he was so great at the Council-board, and in the administration of matters, there was no room for anybody to propose any remedy to what was amiss, or to compass anything, though never so good, for the kingdom, unless approved of by the Chancellor, he managing all things with that greatness which now will be removed, that the King may have the benefit of others' advice. I then told him that the world hath an opinion that he hath joined himself with my Lady Castlemaine's faction: but in this business, he told me, he cannot help it, but says they are in an error; for he will never, while he lives, truckle under anybody or any faction, but do just as his own reason and judgment directs; and, when he cannot use that freedom, he will have nothing to do in public affairs. But then he added that he never was the man that ever had any discourse with my Lady Castlemaine, or with others from her, about this or any public business, or ever made her a visit, or at least not this twelvemonth, or been in her lodgings but when called on any business to attend the King there, nor hath had anything to do in knowing her mind in this business. He ended all with telling me that he knows that he that serves a prince must expect, and be contented to stand, all fortunes, and be provided to retreat; and that he is most willing to do whatever the King shall please. And so we parted, he setting me down out of his coach at Charing Cross, and desired me to tell Sir W. Pen what he had told me of his leaving the Duke of York's service, that his friends might not be the last that know it. I took a coach and went homewards: but then turned again, and to White Hall, where I met with many people; and, among other things, do learn that there is some fear that Mr. Brouncker is got into the King's favour and will be cherished there, which will breed ill will between the King and Duke of York, he lodging at this time in White Hall since he was put away from the Duke of York; and he is great with Bab. May, my Lady Castlemaine, and that wicked crew. But I find this denied by Sir G. Carteret, who tells me that he is sure he hath no

kindness from the King; that the King at first, indeed, did endeavour to persuade the Duke of York from putting him away;
but when, besides this business of his ill words concerning His
Majesty in the business of the Chancellor, he told him that he hath
had, a long time, a mind to put him away for his ill offices, done
between him and his wife, the King held his peace and said no
more, but wished him to do what he pleased with him; which was
very noble.   I met with Fenn, and he tells me, as I do hear from
some others, that the business of the Chancellor's had proceeded
from something of a mistake, for the Duke of York did first tell
the King that the Chancellor had a desire to be eased of his great
trouble; and that the King, when the Chancellor came to him, did
wonder to hear him deny it, and the Duke of York was forced to
deny to the King that ever he did tell him so in those terms; but
the King did answer that he was sure that he did say some such
things to him: but, however, since it had gone so far, did desire
him to be contented with it, as a thing very convenient for him as
well as for himself, the King: and so matters proceeded, as we find.
Now it is likely the Chancellor might, some time or other, in a
compliment or vanity, say to the Duke of York that he was weary
of this burden, and I know not what; and this comes of it.   Some
people, and myself among them, are of good hope from this change
that things are reforming; but there are others that do think it is a
hit of chance, as all other our greatest matters are, and that there
is no general plot or contrivance in any number of people what to
do next, though, I believe, Sir W. Coventry may in himself have
further designs; and so that, though other changes may come, yet
they shall be accidental, and laid upon [no] good principles of
doing good.   Mr. May [1] showed me the King's new buildings, in
order to their having of some old sails for the closing of the
windows this winter.   I dined with Sir G. Carteret, with whom
dined Mr. Jack Ashburnham and Dr. Creeton, who I observe to
be a most good man and scholar.   In discourse at dinner concerning the change of men's humours and fashions touching meats,
Mr. Ashburnham told us that he remembers since the only fruit
in request, and eaten by the King and Queen at table as the best
fruit, was the Catharine pear,[2] though they knew at the time other
fruits of France and our own country.   After dinner comes in Mr.
Townsend: and there I was witness of a horrid rating which Mr.

---

[1] Hugh May.   [2] A small red fruit.

Ashburnham, as one of the Grooms of the King's Bed-chamber, did give him for want of linen for the King's person; which he swore was not to be endured, and that the King would not endure it, and that the King, his father, would have hanged his Wardrobe-man should he have been served so; the King having at this day no handkerchers, and but three bands to his neck, he swore. Mr. Townsend pleaded want of money and the owing of the linen-draper £5000; and that he hath of late got many rich things made —beds and sheets and saddles—without money, and that he can go no further: but still this old man, indeed, like an old loving servant, did cry out for the King's person to be neglected. But when he was gone Townsend told me that it is the grooms taking away the King's linen at the quarter's end, as their fee, which makes this great want: for, whether the King can get it or no, they will run away at the quarter's end with what he hath had, let the King get more as he can. All the company gone, Sir G. Carteret and I to talk: and it is pretty to observe how already he says that he did always look upon the Chancellor indeed as his friend, though he never did do him any service at all, nor ever got anything by him, nor was he a man apt (and that, I think, is true) to do any man any kindness of his own nature; though I do know that he was believed by all the world to be the greatest support of Sir G. Carteret with the King of any man in England: but so little is now made of it! He observes that my Lord Sandwich will lose a great friend in him; and I think so too, my Lord Hinchingbroke being about a match calculated purely out of respect to my Lord Chancellor's family. By and by Sir G. Carteret and Townsend and I to consider of an answer to the Commissioners of the Treasury about my Lord Sandwich's profits in the Wardrobe; which seems, as we make them, to be very small, not £1000 a year, but only the difference in measure at which he buys and delivers out to the King, and then 6d. in the pound from the tradesmen for what money he receives for him; but this, it is believed, these Commissioners will endeavour to take away. From him I went to see a great match at tennis, between Prince Rupert and one Captain Cooke, against Bab. May and the elder Chicheley; where the King was, and Court; and it seems they are the best players at tennis in the nation. But this puts me in mind of what I observed in the morning, that the King, playing at tennis, had a steel-yard carried to him; and I was told it was to weigh him after he had done playing: and at noon Mr. Ashburnham told me that it is only the

King's curiosity, which he usually hath of weighing himself before and after his play, to see how much he loses in weight by playing; and this day he lost 4½ lbs.   I to Sir W. Batten and Sir W. Pen, and there discoursed of Sir W. Coventry's leaving the Duke of York, and Mr. Wren's succeeding him.   They told me both seriously that they had long cut me out for Secretary to the Duke of York, if ever Sir W. Coventry left him; which, agreeing with what I have heard from other hands heretofore, do make me not only think that something of that kind hath been thought on, but do comfort me to see that the world hath such an esteem of my qualities as to think me fit for any such thing: though I am glad with all my heart that I am not so, for it would never please me to be forced to the attendance that that would require, and leave my wife and family to themselves, as I must do in such a case; thinking myself now in the best place that ever man was in to please his own mind in, and, therefore, I will take care to preserve it.

3d.   Attended the Duke of York about the list of ships that we propose to sell: and here there attended Mr. Wren the first time, who hath not yet, I think, received the Duke of York's seal and papers.   At our coming hither we found the Duke and Duchess all alone at dinner, methought melancholy; or else I thought so, from the late occasion of the Chancellor's fall, who, they say, however, takes it very contentedly.

4th.   By coach to White Hall, to the Council-chamber, and there met with Sir W. Coventry going in, who took me aside, and told me that he was just come from delivering up his seal and papers to Mr. Wren; and told me he must now take his leave of me as a naval man, but that he shall always bear respect to his friends there, and particularly to myself, with great kindness; which I returned to him with thanks, and so, with much kindness, parted; and he into the Council.   Sir Samuel Morland showed me two orders upon the Exchequer, one of £600, and another of £400, for money assigned to him, which he would have me lend him money upon, and he would allow 12 per cent.   I would not meddle with them, though they are very good, and I would, had I not so much money out already on public credit.   But I see by this his condition all trade will be bad.   Stayed and heard Alderman Barker's case of his being abused by the Council of Ireland, touching his lands there: all I observed there is the silliness of the King, playing with his dog all the while, and not minding the business; and what he said was mighty weak, but my Lord Keeper I observe to be a mighty able man. With my wife and W. Hewer to Bartholomew fair, and there Polichinelli, where we saw Mrs. Clerke and all her crew; and so to a private house, and sent for a side of pig, and eat it at an acquaintance of W. Hewer's, where there was some learned physic and chemical books, and, among others, a natural Herbal, very fine. To the Duke of York's playhouse, and there saw 'Mustapha'; which, the more I see, the more I like; and is a most admirable poem, and bravely acted; only both Betterton and Harris could not contain from laughing in the midst of a most serious part, from the ridiculous mistake of one of the men upon the stage; which I did not like.

5th. To the Duke of York's House, and there saw 'Heraclius,' which is a good play; but they did so spoil it with their laughing, and being all of them out, and with the noise they made within the theatre, that I was ashamed of it, and resolved not to come thither again a good while, believing that this negligence, which I never observed before, proceeds only from their want of company in the pit, that they have no care how they act. This morning I was told by Sir W. Batten that he do hear from Mr. Grey, who hath good intelligence, that our Queen is to go into a nunnery, there to spend her days; and that my Lady Castlemaine is going into France, and is to have a pension of £4000 a year. This latter I do more believe than the other, it being very wise in her to do it, and save all she hath, besides easing the King and kingdom of a burden and reproach.

6th. To Westminster, and then into the Hall, and there bought Guillim's 'Heraldry.' [1] To Bartholomew fair, and there, it being very dirty and now night, we saw a poor fellow, whose legs were tied behind his back, dance upon his hands with his breech above his head, and also dance upon his crutches, without any legs upon the ground to help him, which he did with that pain that I was sorry to see it, and did pity him and give him money after he had done. Then we to see a piece of clock-work, made by an Englishman—indeed, very good, wherein all the several states of man's age, to 100 years old, is shown very pretty and solemn; and several other things more cheerful. And so we ended, and took a link, the women resolving to be dirty, and walked up

---

[1] This book first appeared in 1610, and has often been reprinted with additions.

and down to get a coach; and my wife, being a little before me, had like to be taken up by one, whom we saw to be Sam Hartlib. My wife had her vizard on: yet we cannot say that he meant any hurt, for it was just as she was by a coach-side, which he had or had a mind to take up, and he asked her, 'Madam, do you go in this coach?' but as soon as he saw a man come to her, I know not whether he knows me, he departed away apace. By and by did get a coach, and so away home, and there to supper, and to bed.

7th. To the office. At noon home to dinner, where Good-groome was teaching my wife; and I did tell him of my intention to learn to trill, which he will not promise I shall obtain, but he will do what can be done, and I am resolved to learn. By coach with my wife, she to the 'Change and I to see the price of a copper cistern for the table, which is very pretty, and they demand £6 or £7 for one; but I will have one. Bought a night-gown for my wife; cost but 24s.

8th. To St. James's, but there I find Sir W. Coventry gone from his chamber, and Mr. Wren not yet come thither. With my Lord Brouncker, and he told me, in discourse, how that, though it is true that Sir W. Coventry did long since propose to the Duke of York the leaving his service (as being unable to fulfil it as he should do, now he hath so much public business, and that the Duke of York did bid him to say nothing of it, but that he would take time to please himself in another to come in his place), yet the Duke, doing it at this time, declaring that he hath found out another, and this one of the Chancellor's servants, he cannot but think was done with some displeasure, and that it could not well be otherwise, that the Duke of York should keep one in that place, that had so eminently opposed him in the defence of his father-in-law, nor could the Duchess ever endure the sight of him, to be sure. But he thinks that the Duke of York and he are parted upon clear terms of friendship. Lord Brouncker says he do believe that my Lady Castlemaine is compounding with the King for a pension and to leave the Court, but that her demands are mighty high. But he believes the King is resolved, and so do everybody else I speak with, to do all possible to please the Parliament. And he do declare that he will deliver everybody up to give an account of their actions; and that last Friday, it seems, there was an Act of Council passed, to put out all Papists in office, and to keep out any from coming in. I went to the King's Chapel to the closet, and there I heard Cresset [1] sing a tenor part along with the Church music very handsomely, but so loud that people did laugh at him, as a thing done for ostentation. Here I met Sir **G. Downing**, who would speak with me, and first to enquire what I paid for my kid's leather gloves I had on my hand, and showed me others on his, as handsome as this in all points, cost him but 12*d.* a pair, and mine me 2*s.* He told me he had been seven years finding out a man that could dress English sheepskin as it should be—and, indeed, it is now as good in all respects as kid, and he says will save £100,000 a year, that goes out to France for kid's skins. Thus he labours very worthily to advance our own trade, but do it with mighty vanity and talking. But then he told me of our base condition, in the treaty with Holland and France, about our prisoners: that whereas before we did clear one another's prisoners, man for man, and we, upon the publication of the peace, did release all ours, 300 at Leith and others in other places, for nothing, the Dutch do keep theirs, and will not discharge them without paying their debts according to the Treaty. That his instruments in Holland, writing to our Ambassadors about this to Breda, they answer them that they do not know of anything that they have done therein, but left it just as it was before. To which when they answer that by the treaty their Lordships had not bound our countrymen to pay their debts in prison, they answer they cannot help it, and we must get them off as cheap as we can. On this score they demand £1100 for Sir G. Ascue, and £5000 for the one province of Zealand, for the prisoners that we have therein. He says that this is a piece of shame that never any nation committed, and that our very Lords here of the Council, when he related this matter to them, did not remember that they had agreed to this article; and swears that all their articles are alike, as the giving away Polleron and Surinam and Nova Scotia, which hath a river 300 miles up the country, with copper mines more than Swedeland, and Newcastle coals, the only place in America that hath coals that we know of; and that Cromwell did value those places, and would for ever have made much of them; but we have given them away for nothing, besides a debt to the King of Denmark. But, which is most of all, they have discharged those very particular demands of merchants of the

[1] This was most likely Francis Cresset, a Shropshire gentleman, whose father and brother had fallen in the king's service during the Civil War, and he was on that account strongly recommended to Charles II at the Restoration (Kennett's *Register*).

Guinea company and others, which he, when he was there, had adjusted with the Dutch, and come to an agreement in writing, and they undertaken to satisfy, and that this was done in black and white under their hands; and yet we have forgiven all these, and not so much as sent to Sir G. Downing to know what he had done, or to confer with him about any one point of the treaty, but signed to what they would have, and we here signed to whatever in gross was brought over by Mr. Coventry. And Sir G. Downing tells me, just in these words, 'My Lord Chancellor had a mind to keep himself from being questioned by clapping up a peace upon any terms.' When I answered that there was other privy-councillors to be advised with besides him, and that, therefore, this whole peace could not be laid to his charge, he answered that nobody durst say anything at the Council-table but himself, and that the King was as much afraid of saying anything there as the meanest privy-councillor; and says more, that at this day the King, in familiar talk, do call the Chancellor 'the insolent man,' and says that he would not let him speak himself in Council: which is very high, and do show that the Chancellor is like to be in a bad state, unless he can defend himself better than people think. And yet Creed tells me that he do hear that my Lord Cornbury [1] do say that his father do long for the coming of the Parliament, in order to his own vindication, more than any one of his enemies. And here it comes into my head to set down what Mr. Rawlinson, whom I met in Fenchurch Street on Friday last, looking over his ruins there, told me, that he was told by one of my Lord Chancellor's gentlemen lately, that a grant coming to him to be sealed, wherein the King hath given my Lady Castlemaine, or somebody by her means, a place which he did not like well of, he did stop the grant, saying, that he thought this woman would sell everything shortly: which she hearing of, she sent to let him know that she had disposed of this place, and did not doubt, in a little time, to dispose of his. To White Hall, and saw the King and Queen at dinner; and observed, which I never did before, the formality (but it is but a formality) of putting a bit of bread wiped upon each dish into the mouth of every man that brings a dish; [2] but it should be in the sauce. Here were some Russes come to see the King at dinner: among others, the interpreter, a comely Englishman, in the Envoy's own clothes; which

---

[1] Henry Hyde, afterwards second Earl of Clarendon.
[2] A vestige of the old custom of tasting, or assay.

the Envoy, it seems, in vanity did send to show his fine clothes upon this man's back, he being one, it seems, of a comelier presence than himself: and yet it is said that none of their clothes are their own, but taken out of the King's own Wardrobe; and which they dare not bring back dirty or spotted, but clean, or are in danger of being beaten, as they say: insomuch that, Sir Charles Cotterell [1] says, when they are to have an audience they never venture to put on their clothes till he appears to come to fetch them; and, as soon as ever they come home, put them off again.   I to Sir G. Carteret's to dinner, where Mr. Cofferer Ashburnham, who told a good story of a prisoner's being condemned at Salisbury for a small matter.   While he was on the bench with his father-in-law, Judge Richardson,[2] and while they were considering to transport him to save his life, the fellow flung a great stone at the Judge, that missed him, but broke through the wainscot.   Upon this, he had his hand cut off, and was hanged presently.[3]   Here was a gentleman, one Sheres, one come lately from my Lord Sandwich with an express; but, Lord! I was almost ashamed to see him, lest he should know that I have not yet wrote one letter to my Lord since his going.

9th. After dinner, Creed and I and my wife to the bear garden, to see a prize fought there.   To White Hall, and here do hear by Tom Killigrew and Mr. Progers that for certain news is come of Harman's having spoiled nineteen of twenty-two French ships, somewhere about the Barbadoes, I think they said; but wherever it is, it is a good service, and very welcome.   I fell in talk with Tom Killigrew about music, and he tells me that he will bring me to the best music in England, of which, indeed, he is master, and that is two Italians and Mrs. Yates, who, he says, is come to sing the Italian manner as well as ever he heard any.   He says that Knipp won't take pains enough, but that she understands her part so well upon the stage, that no man nor woman in the House do the like.

[1] Master of the ceremonies from 1641 to 1686, when he resigned in favour of his son.

[2] Elizabeth, eldest daughter of Sir Thomas Beaumont, widow of Sir John Ashburnham, and mother of John Ashburnham and William Ashburnham, the Cofferer, remarried Sir Thomas Richardson, Chief Justice of the Common Pleas.   She was, in 1629, created Baroness Cramond, in Scotland, for her life only, *with remainder to the heirs male of her second husband by a former wife.*   No reason is assigned for this strange limitation of the patent.

[3] This anecdote is confirmed in Chief Justice Treby's *Notes to Dyer's Reports*, folio edition, p. 188, b.

To the bear garden, where now the yard was full of people, and
those most of them seamen, striving by force to get in, that I was
afraid to be seen among them, but got into the ale-house, and so
by a back way was put into the bull-house, where I stood a good
while all alone among the bulls, and was afeard I was among the
bears, too; but by and by the door opened, and I got into the
common pit; and there, with my cloak about my face, I stood and
saw the prize fought, till one of them, a shoemaker, was so cut in
both his wrists that he could not fight any longer, and then they
broke off: his enemy was a butcher. The sport very good, and
various humours to be seen among the rabble that is there. To
Sir W. Batten's, to invite them to dinner on Wednesday next,
having a whole buck come from Hampton Court, by the warrant
which Sir Stephen Fox did give me.

10th. At the office, where little to do but bemoan ourselves
under the want of money; and indeed little is, or can be, done, we
having not now received one penny for any service in many weeks,
and none in view, saving for paying of some seamen's wages. To
St. James's, where we all met, and did our usual weekly business
with the Duke of York. But, Lord! methinks both he and we are
mighty flat and dull to what we used to be when Sir W. Coventry
was among us. Met Mr. Povy, and he and I to walk an hour or
more in the Pall Mall, talking of the times. He tells me, among
other things, that this business of the Chancellor do breed a kind
of inward distance between the King and the Duke of York, and
that it cannot be avoided; for though the latter did at first move it
through his folly, yet he is made to see that he is wounded by it,
and is become much a less man than he was, and so will be: but he
tells me that they are, and have always been, great dissemblers one
towards another; and that their parting heretofore in France [1] is
never to be thoroughly reconciled between them. He tells me
that he believes there is no such thing likely to be, as a composition
with my Lady Castlemaine, and that she shall be got out of the
way before the Parliament comes; for he says she is as high as
ever she was, though he believes the King is as weary of her as is
possible, and would give anything to remove her, but he is so
weak in his passion that he dare not do it; that he do believe that
my Lord Chancellor will be doing some acts in the Parliament

[1] In 1652. See an account of it in Clarendon's *History of the Rebellion*,
book xiii, and of Sir John Berkeley's part in the matter, to which he is said
to have owed his peerage.

which shall render him popular; and that there are many people now do speak kindly of him that did not before; but that, if he do do this, it must provoke the King, and that party that removed him. He seems to doubt what the King of France will do, in case an accommodation shall be made between Spain and him for Flanders, for then he will have nothing more easy to do with his army than to subdue us.

11th. Up, and with Mr. Gauden to the Exchequer. By the way, he tells me this day he is to be answered whether he must hold Sheriff or no; for he would not hold unless he may keep it at his office, which is out of the City, and so my Lord Mayor must come with his sword down whenever he comes thither, which he do, because he cannot get a house fit for him in the City, or else he will fine for it. Among others that they have in nomination for Sheriff, one is little Chaplin,[1] who was his servant, and a very young man to undergo that place: but as the City is now, there is no great honour nor joy to be had in being a public officer. To the 'Change and there bought a case of knives for dinner, and a dish of fruit for 5s.; and then home, and here I find all things in good order, and a good dinner towards. Anon comes Sir W. Batten and his lady, and Mr. Griffith, their ward, and Sir W. Pen and his lady, and Mrs. Lowther, who is grown, either through pride or want of manners, a fool, having not a word to say; and, as a further mark of a beggarly, proud fool, hath a bracelet of diamonds and rubies about her wrist, and a sixpenny necklace about her neck, and not one good rag of clothes upon her back; and Sir John Chicheley in their company, and Mrs. Turner. Here I had an extraordinary good and handsome dinner for them, better than any of them deserve or understand, saving Sir John Chicheley and Mrs. Turner, and not much mirth, only what I by discourse made, and that against my genius. After dinner I took care to break up the party as soon as I could. To the Duke of York's playhouse, and there saw part of 'The Ungrateful Lovers';[2] and sat by Beck Marshall, who is very handsome near hand. Home, and here came Mr. Moore, and sat and discoursed with me of public matters: the sum of which is, that he do doubt that there is more at the bottom than the removal of the Chancellor; that is, he do verily believe

---

[1] Francis Chaplin, cloth-worker, son of Robert Chaplin, of Bury St. Edmund's: Sheriff of London in 1668, knighted and lord mayor in 1678.

[2] *The Ungrateful Lovers* is an odd title; nor has a play of that name been traced. Is it a mistake for Davenant's *Unfortunate Lovers?*

that the King do resolve to declare the Duke of Monmouth legitimate, and that we shall soon see it. This I do not think the Duke of York will endure without blows; but his poverty, and being lessened by having the Chancellor fallen and Sir W. Coventry gone from him, will disable him from being able to do anything almost, he being himself almost lost in the esteem of people; and will be more and more, unless my Lord Chancellor, who is already begun to be pitied by some people, and to be better thought of than was expected, do recover himself in Parliament. He do say that that is very true, that my Lord Chancellor did lately make some stop of some grants of £2000 a year to my Lord Grandison,[1] which was only in his name, for the use of my Lady Castlemaine's children; and that this did incense her, and she did speak very scornful words, and sent a scornful message to him about it.

12th. To the Exchequer for some tallies for Tangier; and that being done, to the Dog tavern, and there I spent half a piece upon the clerks. To the Duke's House, where 'Tu Quoque'[2] was the first time acted, with some alterations of Sir W. Davenant's; but the play is a very silly play, methinks; for I, and others that sat by me, Mr. Povy and Mr. Progers, were weary of it; but it will please the citizens.

13th. Called up by people come to deliver in ten chaldron of coals, brought in one of our prizes from Newcastle. The rest we intend to sell, we having above ten chaldron between us. They sell at about 28s. or 29s. per chaldron: but Sir W. Batten hath sworn that he was a cuckold that sells under 30s., and that makes us lay up all but what we have for our own spending, which is very pleasant; for I believe we shall be glad to sell them for less. With Sir W. Batten and my wife and Mrs. Turner to Walthamstow, to Mr. Shipman's to dinner, where Sir W. Pen and my Lady and Mrs. Lowther (the latter of which hath got a sore nose, which made me I could not look upon her with any pleasure).

14th. The King and Duke of York and the whole Court is mighty joyful at the Duchess of York's being brought to bed this

---

[1] George Villiers, fourth Viscount Grandison, and younger brother of Lady Castlemaine's father, who had died without issue male.

[2] This play, which was called *Greene's Tu Quoque*, on account of the celebrity of the actor Thomas Greene in the part of Bubble, was written by John Cooke, and first printed in 1614, having been published by the well-known dramatist Thomas Heywood. It was afterwards known as *The City Gallant*, the second title being made the first: it is reprinted in all the editions of Dodsley's *Old Plays*.

day, or yesterday, of a son;[1] which will settle men's minds mightily. And Pierce tells me that he do think that what the King do, of giving the Duke of Monmouth the command of his Guards, and giving my Lord Gerard £12,000 for it, merely to find an employment for him upon which he may live, and not out of any design to bring him into any title to the Crown; which Mr. Moore did the other day put me into great fear of. To the King's playhouse to see 'The Northern Castle,' which I think I never did see before. Knipp acted in it, and did her part very extraordinary well; but the play is but a mean, sorry play; but the house very full of gallants. It seems, it hath not been acted a good while. To bed mightily troubled in mind at the liberty I give myself of going to plays upon pretence of the weakness of my eyes.

15th. (Lord's day.) To church, where I stood in continual fear of Mrs. Markham's coming and offering to come into our pew, to prevent which, soon as ever I heard the great door open, I did step back and clap my breech to our pew-door, that she might be forced to shove me to come in; but, as God would have it, she did not come. Mr. Mills preached, and after sermon, by invitation, he and his wife came to dine with me, which is the first time they have been in my house, I think, these five years, I thinking it not amiss, because of their acquaintance in our country, to show them some respect. Mr. Turner and his wife, and their son the Captain, dined with me, and I had a very good dinner for them, and very merry; and after dinner, Mr. Mills was forced to go, though it rained, to Stepney, to preach. We also to church, and then home, and there comes Mr. Pelling with two men, by promise, one Wallington and Piggott, the former whereof, being a very little fellow, did sing a most excellent bass, and yet a poor fellow, a working goldsmith, that goes without gloves to his hands. Here we sung several good things, but I am more and more confirmed that singing with many voices is not singing, but a sort of instrumental music, the sense of the words being lost by not being heard. They supped with me, and so broke up.

16th. Sir H. Cholmley was with me a good while; who tells me that the Duke of York's child is christened, the Duke of Albemarle and the Marquis of Worcester [2] godfathers, and my Lady Suffolk

---

[1] Edgar, created Duke of Cambridge, the third of James's sons who had borne that title.

[2] Henry Somerset, third Marquis of Worcester, afterwards created Duke of Beaufort.

godmother; and they have named it Edgar, which is a brave name. But it seems they are more joyful in the Chancellor's family, at the birth of this Prince, than in wisdom they should, for fear it should give the King cause of jealousy. Sir H. Cholmley thinks there may possibly be some persons that would be glad to have the Queen removed to some monastery, or somewhere or other, to make room for a new wife; for they will all be unsafe under the Duke of York. He says the King and Parliament will agree: that is, that the King will do anything that they will have him. At the New Exchange I stayed reading Mrs. Philips's poems till my wife and Mercer called me to Mrs. Pierce's, by invitation, to dinner; where I find her painted, which makes me loathe her, and the nastiest poor dinner that made me sick. Here I met with 'A Fourth Advice to the Painter upon the coming in of the Dutch to the River and end of the war,' that made my heart ache to read, it being too sharp, and so true. Here I also saw a printed account of the examinations taken, touching the burning of the City of London, showing the plot of the Papists therein; which, it seems, hath been ordered to be burnt by the hands of the common hangman, in Westminster Palace. My wife and Mercer and I away to the King's playhouse, to see 'The Scornful Lady'; but it being now three o'clock, there was not one soul in the pit; whereupon, for shame, we could not go in, but, against our wills, went all to see 'Tu Quoque' again, where there was pretty store of company. Here we saw Madam Morland,[1] who is grown mighty fat, but is very comely. But one of the best parts of our sport was a mighty pretty lady that sat behind us, that did laugh so heartily and constantly, that it did me good to hear her. Thence to the King's House, upon a wager of mine with my wife, that there would be no acting there today, there being no company: so I went in and found a pretty good company there, and saw their dance at the end of the play.

17th. This evening Captain Cocke and Sir W. Batten did come to me, and sat, and drank a bottle of wine, and told me how Sir W. Pen hath got an order for the Flying Greyhound for himself, which is so false a thing, and the part of a knave, as nothing almost can be more. This vexed me; but I resolve to bring it before the Duke, and try a pull for it.

18th. I walked in the Exchange, which is now made pretty, by

[1] Sir Samuel Morland's first wife, Caroline Harsnet, buried in Westminster Abbey.

having windows and doors before all their shops, to keep out the cold.

19th. Comes my cousin, Kate Joyce, and an aunt of ours, Lettice, formerly Haynes, and now Howlett, come to town to see her friends, and also Sarah Kite, with her little boy in her arms. The child I like very well, and could wish it my own. My wife, being all unready, did not appear. I made as much of them as I could such ordinary company; and yet my heart was glad to see them, though their condition was a little below my present state, to be familiar with. She tells me how the Life-guard, which we thought a little while since was sent down into the country about some insurrection, was sent to Winchcombe,[1] to spoil the tobacco there, which, it seems, the people there do plant contrary to law, and have always done, and still been under force and danger of having it spoiled, as it hath been oftentimes, and yet they will continue to plant it. The place, she says, is a miserable poor place.

20th. I out to pay some debts; among others to the tavern at the end of Billiter Lane, where my design was to see the pretty mistress of the house, which I did, and indeed is, as I always thought, one of the modestest, prettiest, plain women that ever I saw. By coach to the King's playhouse, and there saw 'The Mad Couple,'[2] my wife having been at the same play with Jane, in the 18d. seat.

21st. The King, Duke of York, and the men of the Court have been these four or five days a-hunting at Bagshot.

22d. (Lord's day.) At noon comes Mr. Sheeres, whom I find a good, ingenious man, but do talk a little too much of his travels. He left my Lord Sandwich well, but in pain to be at home for want of money, which comes very hardly. I have indulged myself more in pleasure for these last two months than ever I did in my life before since I came to be a person concerned in business; and I doubt, when I come to make up my accounts, I shall find it so by the expense.

23d. To Westminster, and there, among other things, bought the examinations of the businesses about the Fire of London, which is a book that Mrs. Pierce tells me hath been commanded to be

[1] Winchcombe St. Peter, a market-town in Gloucestershire. Tobacco was first cultivated in this parish, after its introduction into England, in 1583, and it proved a considerable source of profit to the inhabitants, till the trade was placed under restrictions.

[2] *All Mistaken; or A Mad Couple*, a comedy, by the Honourable James Howard.

burnt.[1]   The examinations indeed are very plain.   At my Lord Ashley's, by invitation, to dine there: at table it is worth remembering that my Lord tells us that the House of Lords is the last appeal that a man can make upon a point of interpretation of the law, and that therein they are above the Judges; and that he did assert this in the Lords' House upon the late occasion of the quarrel between my Lord Bristol and the Chancellor, when the former did accuse the latter of treason, and the Judges did bring it in not to be treason.   My Lord Ashley did declare that the judgment of the Judges was nothing in the presence of their Lordships, but only as far as they were the properest men to bring precedents; but not to interpret the law to their Lordships, but only the inducements of their persuasions: and this the Lords did concur in.   Another pretty thing was my Lady Ashley's [2] speaking of the bad qualities of glass coaches; among others, the flying open of the doors upon any great shake: but another was, that my Lady Peterborough being in her glass coach, with the glass up, and seeing a lady pass by in a coach, whom she would salute, the glass was so clear, that she thought it had been open, and so ran her head through the glass!   We were put into my Lord's room before he could come to us, and there had opportunity to look over his state of his accounts of the prizes; and there saw how bountiful the King hath been to several people: and hardly any man almost, commander of the Navy of any note, but hath had some reward or other out of them; and many sums to the Privy Purse, but not so many, I see, as I thought there had been: but we could not look quite through it.   But several Bedchamber men and people about the Court had good sums; and, among others, Sir John Minnes and Lord Brouncker have £200 apiece for looking to the East India prizes, while I did their work for them.   By and by my Lord came, and we did look over Yeabsly's business a little; and I find how prettily this cunning Lord can be partial and dissemble it in this case, being privy to the bribe he is to receive.   With Sir H. Cholmley to Westminster; who by the way told me how merry the King and Duke of York and Court were the other day, when they were

[1] The tract alluded to was called 'A true and faithful account of the several informations exhibited to the Honourable Committee appointed by the Parliament to enquire into the late dreadful burning of the City of London,' 1667: reprinted in the *Antiquarian Repertory*, vol. i, p. 123.

[2] Margaret, daughter of William, Lord Spencer of Wormleighton, was third wife of Lord Ashley, according to Collins; but second according to Dugdale.

abroad a-hunting. They came to Sir G. Carteret's house at Cranborne, and there were entertained, and all made drunk; and all being drunk, Armorer [1] did come to the King, and swore to him, 'By God, Sir,' says he, 'you are not so kind to the Duke of York of late as you used to be.'—'Not I?' says the King. 'Why so?'—'Why,' says he, 'if you are, let us drink his health.'—'Why, let us,' says the King. Then he fell on his knees and drank it; and having done, the King began to drink it. 'Nay, Sir,' says Armorer, 'by God you must do it on your knees!' So he did, and then all the company: and having done it, all fell a-crying for joy, being all maudlin and kissing one another, the King the Duke of York, and the Duke of York the King, and in such a maudlin pickle as never people were: and so passed the day. But Sir H. Cholmley tells me that the King hath this good luck, that the next day he hates to have anybody mention what he had done the day before, nor will suffer anybody to gain upon him that way; which is a good quality. By and by comes Captain Cocke about business; who tells me that Mr. Brouncker is lost for ever, notwithstanding my Lord Brouncker hath advised with him, Cocke, how he might make a peace with the Duke of York and Chancellor, upon promise of serving him in the Parliament: but Cocke says that is base to offer, and will have no success neither. He says that Mr. Wren hath refused a present of Tom Wilson's for his place of Store-keeper at Chatham, and is resolved never to take anything; which is both wise in him, and good to the King's service.

24th. To the office, where all the morning very busy. Home, where there dined with me Anthony Joyce and his wife, and Will and his wife, and my aunt Lettice, that was here the other day, and Sarah Kite; and I had a good dinner for them, and were as merry as I could be in that company where W. Joyce is, who is still the same impertinent fellow that ever he was. After dinner to St. James's, where we had an audience of the Duke of York of many things of weight, about which we stayed till past candle-light, and so Sir W. Batten and W. Pen and I fain to go in a hackney coach all round by London Wall, for fear of cellars. We tired one coach upon Holborn-Conduit Hill, and got another, and made it a long journey home. At my business till twelve at night, writing in shorthand the draft of a report to make to the King and Council tomorrow, about the reason of not having the book of the Treasurer made up. My wife tells me that W. Batelier hath been here

[1] Sir William Armorer, equerry to the king.

today, and brought with him the pretty girl he speaks of, to come
to serve my wife as a woman, out of the school at Bow. My wife
says she is extraordinary handsome, and inclines to have her, and I
am glad of it—at least, that if we must have one, she should be
handsome. But I shall leave it wholly to my wife, to do what she
will therein.

25th. With Sir H. Cholmley, who came to me about his business, to White Hall: and thither came also my Lord Brouncker: and
we by and by called in, and our paper read; and much discourse
thereon by Sir G. Carteret, my Lord Anglesey, Sir W. Coventry,
and my Lord Ashley, and myself: but I could easily discern that
they none of them understood the business: and the King at last
ended it with saying lazily, 'Why,' says he, 'after all this discourse,
I now come to understand it; and that is, that there can nothing
be done in this more than is possible,' which was so silly as I never
heard: 'and therefore,' says he, 'I would have these gentlemen do
as much as possible to hasten the Treasurer's accounts; and that is
all.' And so we broke up: and I confess I went away ashamed,
to see how slightly things are advised upon there. Here I saw
the Duke of Buckingham sit in Council again, where he was re-
admitted, it seems, the last Council-day: and it is wonderful to see
how this man is come again to his places, all of them, after the
reproach and disgrace done him: so that things are done in a most
foolish manner quite through. The Duke of Buckingham did
second Sir W. Coventry in the advising the King that he would
not concern himself in the owning or not owning any man's
accounts, or anything else, wherein he had not the same satisfaction
that would satisfy the Parliament; saying that nothing would
displease the Parliament more than to find him defending anything
that is not right, nor justifiable to the utmost degree: but methought he spoke it but very poorly. After this I walked up and
down the Gallery till noon; and here I met with Bishop Fuller,
who, to my great joy, is made, which I did not hear before,
Bishop of Lincoln. At noon I took coach, and to Sir G. Carteret's,
in Lincoln's Inn Fields, to the house that is my Lord's, which my
Lord lets him have: and this is the first day of dining there. And
there dined with him and his lady my Lord Privy Seal, who is
indeed a very sober man; who, among other talk, did mightily
wonder at the reason of the growth of the credit of bankers, since
it is so ordinary a thing for citizens to break, out of knavery.
Upon this we had much discourse; and I observed therein, to the

honour of this City, that I have not heard of one citizen of London broke in all this war, this plague, or this fire, and this coming up of the enemy among us; which he owned to be very considerable. I to the King's playhouse, my eyes being so bad since last night's straining of them, that I am hardly able to see, besides the pain which I have in them. The play was a new play, and infinitely full: the King and all the Court almost there. It is 'The Storm,' a play of Fletcher's, which is but so-so, methinks; only there is a most admirable dance at the end, of the ladies, in a military manner, which indeed did please me mightily. So, it being a mighty wet day and night, I with much ado got a coach, and, with twenty stops which he made, I got him to carry me quite through, and paid dear for it, and so home; and then comes my wife home from the Duke of York's playhouse, where she hath been with my aunt and Kate Joyce.

26th. To my chamber, whither Jonas Moore comes, and tells me the mighty use of Napier's bones;[1] so that I will have a pair presently. With my wife abroad to the King's playhouse, to show her yesterday's new play, which I like as I did yesterday, the principal thing extraordinary being the dance, which is very good.

27th. While I was busy at the office my wife sends for me to come home, and what was it but to see the pretty girl which she is taking to wait upon her: and though she seems not altogether so great a beauty as she had before told me, yet indeed she is mighty pretty; and so pretty, that I find I shall be too much pleased with it, and therefore could be contented as to my judgment, though not to my passion, that she might not come, lest I may be found too much minding her, to the discontent of my wife. She is to come next week. She seems, by her discourse, to be grave beyond her bigness and age, and exceeding well bred as to her deportment, having been a scholar in a school at Bow these seven or eight years. Creed and Sheres came and dined with me; and we had a great deal of pretty discourse of the ceremoniousness of the Spaniards, whose ceremonies are so many and so known, that, Sheres tells me, upon all occasions of joy or sorrow in a Grandee's family, my Lord Ambassador is fain to send one with an *en hora buena*, if it be upon a marriage, or birth of a child, or a *pesa me*, if it be upon the death of a child, or so. And these ceremonies are so set, and the words

---

[1] Napier's bones, or rods, an instrument contrived by John Lord Napier, of Murcheston, for simplifying arithmetical operations, first described in his *Rabdologiæ seu Numerationes per virgulas, Libri duo.* Edition 1617.

of the compliment, that he hath been sent from my Lord, when he hath done no more than send in word to the Grandee that one was there from the Ambassador; and he knowing what was his errand, that hath been enough, and he hath never spoken with him: nay, several Grandees having been to marry a daughter, have wrote letters to my Lord to give him notice, and out of the greatness of his wisdom to desire his advice, though people he never saw; and then my Lord he answers by commending the greatness of his discretion in making so good an alliance, etc., and so ends. He says that it is so far from dishonour to a man to give private revenge for an affront, that the contrary is a disgrace, they holding that he that receives an affront is not fit to appear in the sight of the world till he hath revenged himself; and therefore, that a gentleman there that receives an affront oftentimes never appears again in the world till he hath, by some private way or other, revenged himself: and that, on this account, several have followed their enemies privately to the Indies, thence to Italy, thence to France and back again, watching for an opportunity to be revenged. He says my Lord was fain to keep a letter from the Duke of York to the Queen of Spain a great while in his hands, before he could think fit to deliver it, till he had learnt whether the Queen could receive it, it being directed to his cousin. He says that many ladies in Spain, after they are found to be with child, do never stir out of their beds or chambers till they are brought to bed: so ceremonious they are in that point also. He tells me of their wooing by serenades at the window, and that their friends do always make the match; but yet they have opportunities to meet at mass at church, and there they make love; that the Court there hath no dancing, nor visits at night to see the King or Queen, but is always just like a cloister, nobody stirring in it; that my Lord Sandwich wears a beard now, turned up in the Spanish manner. But that which pleased me most indeed is, that the peace which he hath made with Spain is now printed here, and is acknowledged by all the merchants to be the best peace that ever England had with them: and it appears that the King thinks it so, for this is printed before the ratification is gone over; whereas that with France and Holland was not in a good while after, till copies came over of it in English out of Holland and France, that it was a reproach not to have it printed here. This I am mighty glad of, and is the first and only piece of good news, or thing fit to be owned, that this nation hath done several years. Anon comes Pelling, and he and I to Gray's Inn

Fields, thinking to have heard Mrs. Knight [1] sing at her lodgings, by a friend's means of his; but we come too late, so must try another time.

28th. All the morning at the office, busy upon an Order of Council, wherein they are mightily at a loss what to advise about our discharging of seamen by ticket, there being no money to pay their wages before January. And this did move Mr. Wren at the table today to say that he did believe that if ever there be occasion more to raise money, it will become here, as it is in Poland, that there are two treasurers—one for the King, and the other for the kingdom. Mr. Pierce, the surgeon, dropped in, who I feared did come to bespeak me to be godfather to his son, which I am unwilling now to be, having ended my liking to his wife since I find she paints. After dinner comes Sir Fr. Hollis to me about business; and I with him by coach to the Temple, and there I 'light; all the way he telling me romantic lies of himself and his family, how they have been Parliament-men for Grimsby, he and his forefathers, this 140 years; and his father is now, and himself, at this day, stands for to be, with his father,[2] by the death of his fellow burgess; and that he believes it will cost him as much as it did his predecessor, which was £300 in ale, and £52 in buttered ale;[3] which I believe is one of his devilish lies. To the Duke of York's playhouse, and there saw a piece of 'Sir Martin Mar-all,' with great delight.

29th. (Lord's day.) Put off first my summer's silk suit, and put on a cloth one. Then to church. All the afternoon talking in my chamber with my wife about my keeping a coach the next year, and doing some things to my house, which will cost money—that is, furnish our best chamber with tapestry, and other rooms with pictures. In the evening read good books—my wife to me; and I did even my kitchen accounts.

30th. To the Duke of York to Council, where the officers of the Navy did attend. Speaking concerning the difficulty of pleasing of seamen and giving them assurance to their satisfaction that they should be paid their arrears of wages, my Lord Ashley did move that an assignment for money on the Act might be put into the hands of the East India Company or City of London, which

---

[1] Mrs. Knight, a celebrated singer, and favourite of Charles II.

[2] He succeeded Sir Henry Bellassis, who had been returned for Grimsby on the death of Sir Adrian Scrope, and who had been killed in a duel with Porter.

[3] Composed of sugar, cinnamon, butter, and beer brewed without hops.

he thought the seamen would believe.   But this my Lord Anglesey
did very handsomely oppose, and I think did carry it that it will
not be: and it is indeed a mean thing that the King should so far
own his own want of credit as to borrow theirs in this manner.
My Lord Anglesey told him that this was the way indeed to teach
the Parliament to trust the King no more for the time to come, but
to have a kingdom's Treasurer distinct from the King's.   To Mrs.
Martin's, to bespeak some linen, and drank, and away, having first
promised my god-daughter a new coat—her first coat.   So home,
and there find our pretty girl Willett come, brought by Mr. Batelier,
and she is very pretty, and so grave as I never saw a little thing in
my life.   I wish my wife may use her well.

October 1st.   To White Hall; and there in the Boarded Gallery
did hear the music with which the King is presented this night by
Monsieur Grabut,[1] the master of his music; both instrumental—
I think twenty-four violins—and vocal; an English song upon
Peace.   But, God forgive me! I never was so little pleased with a
concert of music in my life.   The manner of setting of words and
repeating them out of order, and that with a number of voices,
makes me sick, the whole design of vocal music being lost by it.
Here was a great press of people; but I did not see many pleased
with it, only the instrumental music he had brought by practice
to play very just.

2d.   This morning came to me Mr. Gauden about business, with
his gold chain about his neck, as being Sheriff of the City this year.
To the New Exchange, and there met my wife and girl, and took
them to the King's House to see 'The Traitor,' which still I like as
a very good play, and thence, round by the wall, home, having
drunk at the Cock ale-house, as I of late have used to do.

3d.   I understand that Sir W. Batten is gone to bed on a sudden
again this morning, being struck very ill.   To St. James's, where
Sir W. Coventry took me into the gallery, and walked with me an
hour, discoursing of Navy business, and with much kindness to,
and confidence in, me still; which I must endeavour to preserve,
and will do; and, good man! all his care how to get the Navy paid
off, and that all other things therein may go well.   He gone, I

---

[1] Louis Grabut, or Grabu, a French composer, and Master of the King's
Band, whom Charles had the bad taste to prefer to Purcell.   In 1685, Dryden's
opera of *Albion and Albanius* was set to music by Grabut; but the piece did
not succeed, and the favourers of the English school triumphed in its downfall
(Dryden's *Works*, vol. vii, p. 212).

thence to my Lady Peterborough, who sent for me; and with her an hour talking about her husband's pension, and how she hath got an order for its being paid again, though I believe, for all that order, it will hardly be; but of that I said nothing. But her design is to get it paid again, and how to raise money upon it, to clear it from the engagement which lies upon it to some citizens who lent her husband money, without her knowledge, upon it, to vast loss. She intends to force them to take their money again and release her husband of those hard terms. The woman is a very wise woman, and is very plain in telling me how her plate and jewels are at pawn for money, and how they are forced to live beyond their estate, and do get nothing by his being a courtier. The lady I pity, and her family. Took out my wife and Willett, thinking to have gone to a play, but both houses were begun, and so we to the 'Change, and thence to my tailor's, and there, the coachman desiring to go home to change his horses, we went with him to a nasty end of all St. Giles's, and there went into a nasty room, a chamber of his, where he hath a wife and child, and there stayed, it growing dark, too, and I angry thereat, till he shifted his horses, and then home apace.

4th. To White Hall; and in the Robe-Chamber the Duke of York came to us, the officers of the Navy, and there did meet together about business, where Sir W. Coventry did recommend his Royal Highness, now the prizes were disposing, to remember Sir John Harman to the King for some bounty, and also for my Lady Minnes, which was very nobly done of him. Thence all of us to attend the Council, where we were anon called on, and there was a long hearing of Commissioner Pett, who was there, and there were the two Masters Attendant of Chatham called in, who did deny their having any order from Commissioner Pett about bringing up the great ships, which gives the lie to what he says; but, in general, I find him to be but a weak, silly man, and that is guilty of horrid neglect in this business all along. Here broke off without coming to any issue, but that there should be another hearing on Monday next. I to my Lord Crewe's to dinner; but he having dined, I took a very short leave, confessing I had not dined; and so to an ordinary hard by the Temple gate, where I have heretofore been, and there dined—cost me 10*d*. And so to my Lord Ashley's; and thence to my Lord Crewe's, and there did stay with him an hour till almost night, discoursing about the ill state of my Lord Sandwich, that he can neither be got to be called home, nor money got to maintain him there;[1] which will ruin his family. And the truth is, he do almost deserve it: for, by all relation, he hath, in a little more than a year and a half, spent £20,000 of the King's money, and the best part of £10,000 of his own; which is a most prodigious expense, more than ever Ambassador spent there, and more than these Commissioners of the Treasury will or do allow. And they demand an account before they will give him any more money; which puts all his friends to a loss what to answer. But more money we must get him, or be called home. I offer to speak to Sir W. Coventry about it; but my Lord will not advise us to it, without consent of Sir G. Carteret. To see Sir W. Batten: he is asleep, and so I could not see him, but in an hour after word is brought to me that he is so ill, that it is believed he cannot live till tomorrow, which troubles me and my wife mightily, partly out of kindness—he being a good neighbour—and partly because of the money he owes me upon our bargain of the late prize.

5th. Up, and to the office; and there all the morning, none but my Lord Anglesey and myself. But much surprised with the news of the death of Sir W. Batten, who died this morning, having been but two days sick. Sir W. Pen and I did despatch a letter this morning to Sir W. Coventry, to recommend Colonel Middleton, who we think a most honest and understanding man, and fit for that place. Sir G. Carteret did also come this morning, and walked with me in the garden, and concluded not to concern himself or have any advice made to Sir W. Coventry in behalf of my Lord Sandwich's business: so I do rest satisfied, though I do think they are all mad, that they will judge Sir W. Coventry an enemy, when he is indeed no such man to anybody, but is severe and just, as he ought to be, where he sees things ill done. To my Lord Crewe, and there met my Lord Hinchingbroke and Lady Jemimah, and there dined with them and my Lord, where pretty merry. To my tailor's, and there took up my wife and Willett, and to the King's House: and there, going in, met with Knipp, and she took us up into the tiring-rooms and to the women's shift, where Nell was dressing herself, and was all unready, and is very pretty, prettier than I thought. And so walked all up and down the house above, and then below into the scene-room, and there sat down, and she gave us fruit: and here I read the questions to Knipp, while she answered me, through all her part of 'Flora's Figaries,' which was acted today. But, Lord! to see how they

[1] In Spain.

were both painted would make a man mad, and did make me loathe them; and what base company of men comes among them, and how lewdly they talk! and how poor the men are in clothes, and yet what a show they make on the stage by candle-light, is very observable. But to see how Nell cursed, for having so few people in the pit, was pretty; the other house carrying away all the people at the new play, and is said, nowadays, to have generally most company, as being better players. By and by into the pit, and there saw the play, which is pretty good.

6th. (Lord's day.) Up, and walked out with the boy to Smithfield to Cow Lane, to Lincoln's, and there spoke with him, and agreed upon the hour tomorrow, to set out towards Brampton; but vexed that he is not likely to go himself, but sends another for him. Here I took a hackney coach, and to White Hall, and there met Sir W. Coventry, and discoursed with him; and then with my Lord Brouncker and many others, to end my matters in order to my going into the country tomorrow for five or six days, which I have not been now for above three years. Walked with Creed into the park a little, and at last went into the Queen's side, and there saw the King and Queen, and saw the ladies, in order to my hearing any news stirring to carry into the country, but met with none. Pelling tells us how old Mr. Batelier is dead last night, going to bed well, which I am mightily troubled for, he being a good man.

7th. Up betimes, in order to my journey this day, and did leave my chief care, and the key of my closet, with Mr. Hater, with directions what papers to secure in case of fire or other accident; and so, about nine o'clock, I and my wife and Willett set out in a coach I have hired, with four horses; and W. Hewer and Murford rode by us on horseback: and so my wife and she in their morning gowns, very handsome and pretty, and to my great liking. We set out, and so out at Aldgate, and so to the Green Man, and so on to Enfield, in our way seeing Mr. Lowther and his lady in a coach, going to Walthamstow; and he told us that he would overtake us at night, he being to go that way. So we to Enfield, and there baited, it being but a foul, bad day, and there Lowther and Mr. Burford, an acquaintance of his, did overtake us, and there drank and eat together; and, by and by, we parted, we going before them, and very merry, my wife and girl and I, talking and telling tales and singing, and before night come to Bishop's Stortford, where Lowther and his friend did meet us again, and carried us to the Reindeer, where Mrs. Aynsworth,[1] who lived heretofore at Cambridge, and whom I knew better than they think for, do live.   It was the woman that, among other things, was great with my cousin Barnston, of Cottenham, and did use to sing to him, and did teach me 'Full forty times over,' a very lewd song: a woman they are very well acquainted with, and is here what she was at Cambridge, and all the good fellows of the country come hither.   Lowther and his friend stayed and drank, and then went further this night; but here we stayed, and supped, and lodged. But, as soon as they were gone, and my supper getting ready, I fell to write my letter to my Lord Sandwich, which I could not finish before my coming from London, and a good letter, telling him the present state of all matters, and did get a man to promise to carry it tomorrow morning, to be there, at my house, by noon, and I paid him well for it.   So, that being done, and my mind at ease, we to supper, and so to bed, my wife and I in one bed, and the girl in another, in the same room, and lay very well, but there was so much tearing company in the house, that we could not see the landlady; so I had no opportunity of renewing my old acquaintance with her.

8th.   Up pretty betimes, though not so soon as we intended, by reason of Murford's not rising, and then not knowing how to open our door, which, and some other pleasant simplicities of the fellow, did give occasion to us to call him Sir Martin Mar-all, and W. Hewer being his helper and counsellor, we did call him, all this journey, Mr. Warner, which did give us good occasion of mirth now and

---

[1] Elizabeth Aynsworth, here mentioned, is said to have been a noted procuress at Cambridge, banished from that town by the university authorities for her evil courses.   She subsequently kept the Reindeer Inn at Bishop's Stortford, at which the vice-chancellor, and some of the heads of colleges, had occasion to sleep, in their way to London, and were nobly entertained, their supper being served off plate.   The next morning their hostess refused to make any charge, saying, that she was still indebted to the vice-chancellor, who, by driving her out of Cambridge, had made her fortune.   No tradition of this woman has been preserved at Bishop's Stortford; but it appears, from the register of that parish, that she was buried there 26th March 1686.   It is recorded in the *History of Essex*, vol. iii, p. 130, 8vo, 1770, and in a pamphlet in the British Museum, entitled 'Boteler's Case,' that she was implicated in the murder of Captain Wood, a Hertfordshire gentleman, at Manuden, in Essex, and for which offence a person named Boteler was executed at Chelmsford, 10th September 1667, and that Mrs. Aynsworth, tried at the same time as an accessory before the fact, was acquitted for want of evidence, though in her way to the jail she endeavoured to throw herself into the river but was prevented.

then. At last, rose and up, and broke our fast, and then took coach, and away, and at Newport did call on Mr. Lowther, and he and his friend, and the master of the house, their friend, where they were, a gentleman, did presently get a-horseback, and went with us to Audley End, and did go along with us all over the house and garden: and mighty merry we were. The house indeed do appear very fine, but not so fine as it hath heretofore to me; particularly the ceilings are not so good as I always took them to be, being nothing so well wrought as my Lord Chancellor's are; and though the figure of the house without be very extraordinary good, yet the staircase is exceeding poor; and a great many pictures, and not one good one in the house but one of Harry the Eighth, done by Holbein; and not one good suit of hangings in all the house, but all most ancient things, such as I would not give the hanging-up of in my house; and the other furniture, beds and other things, accordingly. Only the gallery is good, and, above all things, the cellars, where we went down and drank of much good liquor; and indeed the cellars are fine: and here my wife and I did sing to my great content. And then to the garden, and there eat many grapes, and took some with us: and so away thence, exceeding well satisfied, though not to that degree that, by my old esteem of the house, I ought and did expect to have done, the situation of it not pleasing me. Here we parted with Lowther and his friends, and away to Cambridge, it being foul, rainy weather, and there did take up at the Rose, for the sake of Mrs. Dorothy Drawwater, the vintner's daughter, which is mentioned in the play of 'Sir Martin Mar-all.' Here we had a good chamber, and bespoke a good supper; and then I took my wife and W. Hewer and Willett, it holding up a little, and showed them Trinity College and St. John's library, and went to King's College Chapel, to see the outside of it only; and so to our inn, and with much pleasure did this, they walking in their pretty morning gowns, very handsome, and I proud to find myself in condition to do this; and so home to our lodging, and there, by and by, to supper, with much good sport, talking with the drawers concerning matters of the town, and persons whom I remember: and so, after supper, to cards and then to bed, lying, I in one bed, and my wife and girl in another, in the same room, and very merry talking together, and mightily pleased both of us with the girl. Saunders, the only violin in my time, is, I hear, dead of the plague in the late plague there.

9th. Up, and got ready and eat our breakfast, and then took

coach: and the poor, as they did yesterday, did stand at the coach to have something given them, as they do to all great persons, and I did give them something: and the town music did also come and play, but, Lord! what sad music they made! So through the town, and observed at our College of Magdalene the posts new painted, and understand that the Vice-Chancellor [1] is there this year. And so away for Huntingdon; and come to Brampton at about noon, and there find my father and sister and brother all well: and up and down to see the garden with my father, and the house, and do altogether find it very pretty, especially the little parlour and the summer-houses in the garden, only the wall do want greens upon it, and the house is too low-roofed; but that is only because of my coming from a house with higher ceilings. But altogether is very pretty, and I bless God that I am like to have such a pretty place to retire to. After dinner I walked up to Hinchingbroke, where my Lady expected me, and there spent all the afternoon with her: the same most excellent, good, discreet lady that ever she was, and, among other things, is mightily pleased with the lady that is like to be her son Hinchingbroke's wife. By and by my wife comes with Willett, my wife in her velvet vest, which is mighty fine, and becomes her exceedingly. I am pleased with my Lady Paulina and Anne,[2] who both are grown very proper ladies, and handsome enough. But a thousand questions my Lady asked me, till she could think of no more almost, but walked up and down the house with me. But I do find, by her, that they are reduced to great straits for money, having been forced to sell her plate, 8 or £900 worth; and she is now going to sell a suit of her best hangings, of which I could almost wish to buy a piece or two, if the pieces will be broke. But the house is most excellently furnished, and brave rooms and good pictures, so that it do please me infinitely beyond Audley End. Home, and there Mr. Shepley stayed with us and supped. Night being come, we took leave with all possible kindness, and so home. Supper done, we all to bed, only I a little troubled that my father tells me that he is troubled that my wife shows my sister no countenance, and him but very little, but is as a stranger in the house; and I do observe she do carry herself very high; but I perceive there was some great falling

---

[1] John Howarth, D.D., prebendary of Peterborough.
[2] She became the wife of Sir Richard Edgcumbe, and by him had a son Richard, created an English baron in 1742. She married, secondly, the Honourable Christopher Montagu, elder brother of Charles, Lord Halifax.

out when she was here last, but the reason I have no mind to enquire after, for vexing myself, being desirous to pass my time with as much mirth as I can while I am abroad. My wife and I in the high bed in our chamber, and Willett in the trundle bed, which she desired to lie in, by us.

10th. Up, to walk up and down in the garden with my father, to talk of all our concernments: about a husband for my sister, whereof there is at present no appearance; but we must endeavour to find her one now, for she grows old and ugly: then for my brother, and resolve he shall stay here this winter, and then I will either send him to Cambridge for a year, till I get him some church promotion, or send him to sea as a chaplain, where he may study, and earn his living. Then walked round about our Green, to see whether, in case I cannot buy out my uncle Thomas and his son's right in this house, that I can buy another place as good thereabouts to build on, and I do not see that I can. But this, with new building, may be made an excellent pretty thing, and I resolve to look after it as soon as I can, and Goody Gorum dies. By coach round the town of Brampton, to observe any other place as good as ours, and find none; and so back with great pleasure; and thence went all of us, my sister and brother and W. Hewer, to dinner to Hinchingbroke, where we had a good plain country dinner, but most kindly used; and here dined the Minister of Brampton and his wife, who is reported a very good, but poor man. Here I spent alone with my Lady, after dinner, the most of the afternoon, and anon the two twins [1] were sent for from school, at Mr. Taylor's, to come to see me, and I took them into the garden, and there, in one of the summer-houses, did examine them, and do find them so well advanced in their learning, that I am amazed at it: they repeating a whole ode without book out of Horace, and did give me a very good account of anything almost, and did make me very readily very good Latin, and did give me good account of their Greek grammar, beyond all possible expectation; and so grave and manly as I never saw, I confess, nor could have believed; so that they will be fit to go to Cambridge in two years at most. They are both little, but very like one another, and well-looked

----

[1] The twins were the third and fourth sons of Lord Sandwich: Oliver Montagu, afterwards M.P. for Huntingdon, and in 1685 solicitor-general to the queen; he died unmarried in 1693: and John Montagu, made Master of Trinity College, Cambridge, in 1683, and Dean of Durham, 1699, who also died a bachelor, in 1729.

children.   Took leave for a great while again, but with extraordinary kindness from my Lady, who looks upon me like one of
her own family and interest.   Thence I walked over the park
with Mr. Shepley, and through the grove, which is mighty pretty,
as is imaginable, and so over their drawbridge to Nun's Bridge,
and so to my father's, and there sat and drank, and talked a little,
and then parted.   And he being gone, and what company there
was, my father and I with a dark lantern, it being now night, into
the garden with my wife, and there went about our great work to
dig up my gold.   But, Lord! what a toss I was for some time in,
that they could not justly tell where it was, that I begun heartily
to sweat and be angry, that they should not agree better upon the
place, and at last to fear that it was gone: but by and by poking
with a spit, we found it, and then begun with a spud to lift up the
ground.   But, good God! to see how sillily they did it, not half a
foot underground, and in the sight of the world from a hundred
places, if anybody by accident were near hand, and within sight
of a neighbour's window: only my father says that he saw them all
gone to church before he began the work, when he laid the money.
But I was out of my wits almost, and the more from that, upon my
lifting up the earth with the spud, I did discern that I scattered
the pieces of gold round about the ground among the grass and
loose earth.   And taking up the iron head-pieces wherein they were
put, I perceived the earth was got among the gold, and wet, so that
the bags were all rotten, and all the notes, that I could not tell what
in the world to say to it, not knowing how to judge what was
wanting or what had been lost by Gibson in his coming down:
which, all put together, did make me mad; and at last I was forced
to take up the head-pieces, dirt and all, and as many of the scattered
pieces as I could with the dirt discern by candle-light, and carry
them up into my brother's chamber, and there lock them up till I
had eat a little supper.   And then, all people going to bed, W. Hewer
and I did all alone, with several pails of water and besoms, at last
wash the dirt off of the pieces, and parted the pieces and the dirt,
and then began to tell them, by a note which I had of the value of
the whole, in my pocket; and do find that there was short above a
hundred pieces, which did make me mad; and considering that
the neighbour's house was so near, that we could not suppose we
could speak one to another in the garden at that place where the
gold lay—especially my father being deaf—but they must know
what we had been doing, I feared that they might in the night come

and gather some pieces and prevent us the next morning; so W. Hewer and I out again about midnight, for it was now grown so late, and there by candle-light did make shift to gather forty-five pieces more.   And so in, and to cleanse them: and by this time it was past two in the morning; and so to bed, with my mind pretty quiet to think that I have recovered so many.   I lay in the trundle-bed, the girl being gone to bed to my wife, and there lay in some disquiet all night, telling of the clock till it was daylight.

11th. And then W. Hewer and I, with pails and a sieve, did lock ourselves into the garden, and there gather all the earth about the place into pails, and then sift those pails in one of the summer-houses, just as they do for diamonds in other parts of the world; and there, to our great content, did by nine o'clock make the last night's forty-five up to seventy-nine: so that we are come to about twenty or thirty of what I think the true number should be, and perhaps within less; and of them I may reasonably think that Mr. Gibson might lose some, so that I am pretty well satisfied that my loss is not great, and do bless God that it is so well.   So do leave my father to make a second examination of the dirt; and my mind at rest in it, being but an accident: and so gives me some kind of content to remember how painful it is sometimes to keep money, as well as to get it, and how doubtful I was to keep it all night, and how to secure it to London: so got all my gold put up in bags. And so, having the last night wrote to my Lady Sandwich to lend me John Bowles to go along with me my journey, not telling her the reason, that it was only to secure my gold, we to breakfast, and about ten o'clock took coach, my wife and I, and Willett and W. Hewer, and Murford and Bowles, and my brother John on horse-back; and with these four I thought myself pretty safe.   But, before we went out, the Huntingdon music came to me and played, and it was better than that of Cambridge.   Here I took leave of my father and did give my sister 20s.   She cried at my going; but whether it was at her unwillingness for my going, or any unkind-ness of my wife's, or no, I know not.   But, God forgive me! I take her to be so cunning and ill-natured, that I have no great love for her; but only [she] is my sister, and must be provided for.   My gold I put into a basket, and set under one of the seats; and so my work every quarter of an hour was to look to see whether all was well; and I did ride in great fear all the day.   Mr. Shepley saw me beyond St. Neots, and there parted, and we straight to Stevenage, through Bald Lanes, which are already very bad; and at Stevenage

we come well before night, and all sat, and there with great care I
got the gold up to my chamber, my wife carrying one bag, and the
girl another, and W. Hewer the rest in the basket, and set it all
under a bed in our chamber, and then sat down to talk, and were
very pleasant, satisfying myself, among other things, from John
Bowles, in some terms of hunting, and about deer, bucks, and
does.   Brecocke alive still, and the best host I know almost.

12th. Up, and eat our breakfast, and set out about nine o'clock,
and so to Barnet, where we baited.   By five o'clock got home,
where I find all well; and did bring my gold, to my heart's content,
very safe, having not this day carried it in a basket, but in our
hands.   The girl took care of one, and my wife another bag, and I
the rest, I being afraid of the bottom of the coach, lest it should
break.   At home we find that Sir W. Batten's body was today
carried from hence, with a hundred or two of coaches, to Walthamstow, and there buried.   The Parliament met on Thursday last, and
adjourned to Monday next.   The King did make them a very kind
speech, promising them to leave all to them to do, and call to
account what and whom they pleased; and declared by my Lord
Keeper how many, thirty-six, acts he had done since he saw them:
among others, disbanding the army, and putting all Papists out of
employment, and displacing persons that had managed their
business ill.   The Parliament is mightily pleased with the King's
speech, and voted giving him thanks for what he said and hath
done; and, among other things, would by name thank him for
displacing my Lord Chancellor, for which a great many did speak
in the House, but it was opposed by some, and particularly Harry
Coventry, who got that it should be put to a Committee to consider what particulars to mention in their thanks to the King, saying
that it was too soon to give thanks for the displacing of a man,
before they knew or had examined what was the cause of his displacing.   And so it rested: but this do show that they are and will
be very high; and Mr. Pierce do tell me that he fears, and do hear
that it hath been said among them, that they will move for the
calling my Lord Sandwich home, to bring him to account; which
do trouble me mightily, but I trust it will not be so.   Anon comes
home Sir W. Pen from the burial; and he says that Lady Batten and
her children-in-law are all broke in pieces, and that there is but
£800 found in the world, of money; and is in great doubt what we
shall do towards the doing ourselves right with them, about the
prize-money.   With Sir W. Pen to my Lady Batten, whom I had

not seen since she was a widow, which she took unkindly, but I did excuse it; and the house being full of company, and of several factions, she against the children, and they against one another and her, I away.

13th. (Lord's day.) To St. James's, and there to the Duke of York's chamber; and there he was dressing, and many Lords and Parliament-men came to kiss his hands, they being newly come to town. And there the Duke of York did of himself call me to him, and tell me that he had spoke to the King, and that the King had granted me the ship I asked for; and did, moreover, say that he was mightily satisfied with my service, and that he would be willing to do anything that was in his power for me: which he said with mighty kindness; which I did return him thanks for, and departed with mighty joy, more than I did expect. And so walked over the Park to White Hall, and then met Sir H. Cholmley, who walked with me, and told me most of the news I heard last night of the Parliament; and thinks they will do all things very well, only they will be revenged of my Lord Chancellor; and says, however, that he thinks there will be but two things proved on him: and that one is, that he may have said to the King, and to others, words to breed in the King an ill opinion of the Parliament—that they were factious, and that it was better to dissolve them; and this, he thinks, they will be able to prove; but what this will amount to, he knows not. And next, that he hath taken money for several bargains that have been made with the Crown, and did instance one that is already complained of: but there are so many more involved in it, that, should they unravel things of this sort, everybody almost will be more or less concerned. But these are the two great points which he thinks they will insist on, and prove against him. Walked with Sir W. Pen, and told him what the Duke of York told me today about the ship I begged; and he was knave enough, of his own accord, but, to be sure, in order to his own advantage, to offer me to send for the master of the vessel, the Maybolt galliot, and bid him to get her furnished as for a long voyage, and I to take no notice of it, that she might be the more worth to me: so that here he is a very knave to the King, and I doubt not his being the same to me on occasion. Evened with W. Hewer for my expenses upon the road this last journey, and do think that the whole journey will cost me little less than £18 or £20, one way or other; but I am well pleased with it.

14th. To Mr. Wren's; and he told me that my business was

done about my warrant on the Maybolt galliot, which I did see, and thought it was not so full in the reciting of my services as the other was in that of Sir W. Pen's; yet I was well pleased with it, and do intend to fetch it away anon.   With Sir Thomas Allen, in a little sorry coach that he hath set up of late, and Sir Jeremy Smith, to White Hall, and there hear that the House is this day again upon the business of giving the King the thanks of the House for his speech, and, among other things, for laying aside of my Lord Chancellor.   To visit Sir G. Carteret, and from him do understand that the King himself (but this he told me as a great secret) is satisfied that these thanks which he expects from the House, for the laying aside of my Lord Chancellor, are a thing irregular; but, since it is come into the House, he do think it necessary to carry it on, and will have it, and hath made his mind known to be so, to some of the House.   But Sir G. Carteret do say he knows nothing of what my Lord Brouncker told us today, that the King was angry with the Duke of York yesterday, and advised him not to hinder what he had a mind to have done touching this business; which is news very bad, if true.   Thence to my Lord Crewe.   He tells me also that the King will have the thanks of the House go on, and commends my Lord Keeper's speech for all but what he was forced to say, about the reason of the King's sending away the House so soon the last time, when they were met.   Walked with Mr. Scowen, who tells me that it is at last carried in the House that the thanks shall be given to the King—among other things particularly for the removal of my Lord Chancellor; but he tells me that it is a strange act, and that which he thinks would never have been, but that the King did insist upon it, that, since it come into the House, it might not be let fall.   To the Duke of York's House, and there went in for nothing into the pit, at the last act, to see 'Sir Martin Mar-all,' and met my wife, who was there, and my brother, and W. Hewer and Willett, and carried them home, and there do find that John Bowles is not yet come thither.   I suppose he is playing the good fellow in the town.

15th. My wife and I and Willett to the Duke of York's House, where, after long stay, the King and Duke of York came, and there saw 'The Coffee-house,' [1] the most ridiculous, insipid play that ever I saw in my life, and glad we were that Betterton had no part in it.   But here, before the play begun, my wife begun to

[1] *Tarugo's Wiles, or, The Coffee House.*   By Thomas St. Serfe; printed in 1668.   See the Earl of Dorset's lines on this play, printed in his *Works.*

complain to me of Willett's confidence in sitting cheek by jowl by us, which was a poor thing; but I perceive she is already jealous of my kindness to her, so that I begin to fear this girl is not likely to stay long with us.

16th. At home most of the morning with Sir H. Cholmley, about some accounts of his; and for news he tells me that the Commons and Lords have concurred, and delivered the King their thanks, among other things, for his removal of the Chancellor; who took their thanks very well, and, among other things, promised them, in these words, never, in any degree, to give the Chancellor any employment again. And he tells me that it is very true, he hath it from one that was by, that the King did give the Duke of York a sound reprimand; told him that he had lived with him with more kindness than ever any other King lived with a brother, and that he lived as much like a monarch as himself, but advised him not to cross him in his designs about the Chancellor; in which the Duke of York do very wisely acquiesce, and will be quiet as the King bade him, but presently commands all his friends to be silent in the business of the Chancellor, and they were so: but that the Chancellor hath done all that is possible to provoke the King, and to bring himself to lose his head by enraging of people. To White Hall, where the Duke of York is now newly come for this winter, and there did our usual business with him. To the Duke of York's House; and I was vexed to see Young, who is but a bad actor at best, act Macbeth in the room of Betterton, who, poor man! is sick: but, Lord! what a prejudice it wrought in me against the whole play, and everybody else agreed in disliking this fellow. Thence home, and there find my wife gone home; because of this fellow's acting of the part, she went out of the house again.

17th. Sent for by my Lady Batten. I to her, and there she found fault with my not seeing her since her being a widow,[1] which I excuse as well as I could, though it is a fault, but it is my nature not to be forward in visits. But here she told me her condition, which is good enough, being sole executrix, to the disappointment of all her husband's children, and prayed my friendship about the accounts of the prizes, which I promised her. And here do see what creatures widows are in weeping for their husbands, and then presently leaving off; but I cannot wonder at it, the cares of the world taking place of all other passions. Mr. John Andrews and his wife came and dined with me, and pretty merry we were, only

[1] He seems to have forgotten his visit on the 12th.

I out of humour the greatest part of the dinner, by reason that my people had forgot to get wine ready (I having none in the house, which I cannot say now these almost three years, I think, without having two or three sorts), by which we were fain to stay a great while, while some could be fetched. It was an odd, strange thing to observe of Mr. Andrews what a fancy he hath to raw meat, that he eats it with no pleasure unless the blood run about his chops, which it did now by a leg of mutton that was not above half boiled; but, it seems, at home all his meat is dressed so, and beef and all, and [he] eats it so at nights also. The Parliament run on mighty furiously, having yesterday been almost all the morning complaining against some high proceedings of my Lord Chief Justice Kelyng, that the gentlemen of the country did complain against him in the House, and run very high. It is the man that did fall out with my cousin Roger Pepys[1] once, at the Assizes there, and would have laid him by the heels; but, it seems, a very able lawyer.[2] This afternoon my Lord Anglesey tells us that the House of Commons have this morning run into the inquiry in many things: as, the sale of Dunkirk, the dividing of the fleet the last year, the business of the prizes with my Lord Sandwich, and many other things; so that now they begin to fall close upon it, and God knows what will be the end of it, but a Committee they have chosen to enquire into the miscarriages of the war.

18th. To White Hall, and there attended the Duke of York; but first we find him to spend above an hour in private in his closet with Sir W. Coventry; which I was glad to see, that there is so much confidence between them. By and by we were called in. The Duke of York considering what third-rate ship to keep abroad, the Rupert was thought on, but then it was said that Captain Hubbert was commander of her, and that the King had a mind for Spragg to command the Rupert, which would not be well, by turning out Hubbert, who is a good man; but one said the Duke of York did not know whether he did so well conform, as at this time to please the people and Parliament. Sir W. Coventry answered, and the Duke of York merrily agreed to it, that it was

---

[1] At the Cambridge Assizes held before Judge Kelyng, 9th March 1665, Roger Pepys, the Recorder, was bound over to his good behaviour for speaking slightingly of Lord Chief Justice Hyde at the Town Sessions, on an appeal by Dr. Eade against a poor-rate (Cooper's *Cambridge Annals*, vol. iii, p. 516).
[2] To Kelyng was entrusted the drawing up of the Act of Uniformity (Burnet, *Own Time*, vol. i, p. 316). No record of the 'high proceedings,' referred to by Pepys, is to be found in the parliamentary history.

very hard to know what it was that the Parliament would call conformity at this time. To several places to buy a hat and books and neckcloths; and several errands I did before I got home, and, among others, bought me two new pair of spectacles of Turlington, who, it seems, is famous for them; and his daughter, he being out of the way, do advise me two very young sights, and that that will help me most, and promises me great ease from them, and I will try them. I met Creed, and he tells me that Sir Robert Brookes is the man that did mention the business in Parliament yesterday about my Lord Sandwich, but that it was seconded by nobody, but that the matter will come before the Committee for miscarriages. To the King's House, and saw 'Brenoralt,' which is a good tragedy.

19th. Full of my desire of seeing my Lord Orrery's new play this afternoon at the King's House, 'The Black Prince,' the first time it is acted; where, though we came by two o'clock, yet there was no room in the pit, but were forced to go into one of the upper boxes, at 4s. apiece, which is the first time I ever sat in a box in my life. And in the same box came, by and by, behind me, my Lord Berkeley [of Stratton] and his lady,[1] but I did not turn my face to them to be known, so that I was excused from giving them my seat. And this pleasure I had, that from this place the scenes do appear very fine indeed, and much better than in the pit. The house infinite full, and the King and Duke of York there. By and by the play begun, and in it nothing particular but a very fine dance for variety of figures, but a little too long. But, as to the contrivance, and all that was witty (which, indeed, was much, and very witty), was almost the same that had been in his former plays of 'Henry the 5th' and 'Mustapha,' and the same points and turns of wit in both, and in this very same play often repeated, but in excellent language, and were so excellent that the whole house was mightily pleased all along till the reading of a letter,[2] which was so long and so unnecessary that they frequently began to laugh, and to hiss twenty times, that, had it not been for the King's being there, they had certainly hissed it off the stage. But I must confess that, as my Lord Berkeley said behind me, the having of that long letter was a thing so absurd, that he could not imagine how a man

[1] Lady Berkeley was Christian, daughter of Sir Andrew Rickard, and widow of Henry Rich, Lord Kensington.
[2] It occurs in the fifth act, and is certainly very long. It was read by Hart, but was afterwards omitted in the acting.

of his parts could possibly fall into it; or, if he did, if he had but let any friend read it, the friend would have told him of it; and, I must confess, it is one of the most remarkable instances of a wise man's not being wise at all times. After the play done, and nothing pleasing them from the time of the letter to the end of the play, people being put into a bad humour of disliking, which is another thing worth the noting, I home by coach, and could not forbear laughing almost all the way, and all the evening to my going to bed, at the ridiculousness of the letter, and the more because my wife was angry with me and the world for laughing, because the King was there.

20th. (Lord's day.) Up, and put on my new tunic of velvet, which is very plain, but good. This morning is brought to me an order for the presenting the Committee of Parliament tomorrow with a list of the commanders and ships' names of all the fleets set out since the war, and particularly of those ships which are divided from the fleet with Prince Rupert; which gives me occasion to see that they are busy after that business, and I am glad of it. This afternoon comes to me Captain O'Bryan, about a ship that the King hath given him; and he and I to talk of the Parliament; and he tells me that the business of the Duke of York's slackening sail in the first fight, at the beginning of the war, is brought into question, and Sir W. Pen and Captain Cox are to appear tomorrow about it; and it is thought will at last be laid upon Mr. Brouncker's giving orders from the Duke of York, which the Duke of York do not own, to Captain Cox to do it; but it seems they do resent this very highly, and are mad in going through all business, where they can lay any fault. I am glad to hear that in the world I am as kindly spoke of as anybody; for, for aught I see, there is bloody work like to be, Sir W. Coventry having been forced to produce a letter in Parliament wherein the Duke of Albemarle did from Sheerness write in what good posture all things were at Chatham, and that the chain was so well placed that he feared no attempt of the enemy: so that, among other things, I do see everybody is upon his own defence, and spares not to blame another to defend himself, and the same course I shall take. But God knows where it will end! Pelling tells me that my Lady Duchess Albemarle was at Mrs. Turner's this afternoon, she being ill, and did there publicly talk of business, and of our Office; and that she believed that I was safe, and had done well; and so, I thank God! I hear everybody speaks of me; and indeed, I think, without vanity, I may expect to be profited rather than injured by this inquiry, which the Parliament makes into business.

21st. To Westminster, and up to the lobby, where many commanders of the fleet were, and Captain Cox, and Mr. Pierce, the surgeon; the last of whom hath been in the House, and declared that he heard Brouncker advise and give arguments to Cox, for the safety of the Duke of York's person, to shorten sail, that they might not be in the middle of the enemy in the morning alone; and Cox denying to observe his advice, having received the Duke of York's commands over night to keep within gun-shot, as they then were, of the enemy, Brouncker did go to Harman, and used the same arguments, and told him that he was sure it would be well pleasing to the King that care should be taken of not endangering the Duke of York; and, after much persuasion, Harman was heard to say, 'Why, if it must be, then lower the topsail.' And so did shorten sail, to the loss, as the Parliament will have it, of the greatest victory that ever was, and which would have saved all the expense of blood, and money, and honour, that followed; and this they do resent, so as to put it to the question, whether Brouncker should not be carried to the Tower: who do confess that, out of kindness to the Duke of York's safety, he did advise that they should do so, but did not use the Duke of York's name therein; and so it was only his error in advising it, but the greatest theirs in taking it, contrary to order. At last it ended that it should be suspended till Harman comes home; and then the Parliament-men do all tell me that it will fall heavy, and, they think, be fatal to Brouncker or him. Sir W. Pen tells me he was gone to bed, having been all day labouring, and then not able to stand, of the gout, and did give order for the keeping the sails standing, as they then were, all night. But, which I wonder at, he tells me that he did not know the next day that they had shortened sail, nor ever did enquire into it till about ten days ago, that this began to be mentioned; and, indeed, it is charged privately as a fault on the Duke of York, that he did not presently examine the reason of the breach of his orders, and punish it. But Cox tells me that he did finally refuse it; and what prevailed with Harman he knows not, and do think that we might have done considerable service on the enemy the next day, if this had not been done. Thus this business ended today, having kept them [1] till almost two o'clock; and then I by coach with Sir W. Pen as far as St. Clement's, talking of this matter, and there set

[1] The House of Commons.

down; and I walked to Sir G. Carteret's, and there dined with him and several Parliament-men, who, I perceive, do all look upon it as a thing certain that the Parliament will enquire into everything, and will be very severe where they can find any fault.   Sir W. Coventry, I hear, did this day make a speech, in apology for his reading the letter of the Duke of Albemarle concerning the good condition which Chatham was in before the enemy came thither: declaring his simple intention therein, without prejudice to my Lord.   And I am told that he was also with the Duke of Albemarle yesterday to excuse it; but this day I do hear, by some of Sir W. Coventry's friends, that they think he hath done himself much injury by making this man, and his interest, so much his enemy. After dinner, I away to Westminster, and up to the Parliament-house, and there did wait with great patience, till seven at night, to be called in to the Committee, who sat all this afternoon examining the business of Chatham; and at last was called in, and told that the least they expected from us Mr. Wren had promised them, and only bade me to bring all my fellow officers thither tomorrow afternoon.   Sir Robert Brookes in the chair: methinks a sorry fellow to be there, because a young man; and yet he seems to speak very well.   I gone thence, my cousin Pepys comes out to me, and walks in the Hall with me, and bids me prepare to answer to every-thing; for they do seem to lay the business of Chatham upon the Commissioners of the Navy, and they are resolved to lay the fault heavy somewhere, and to punish it; and prays me to prepare to save myself, and gives me hints what to prepare against; which I am obliged to him for.   This day I did get a list of the fourteen particular miscarriages which are already before the Committee to be examined; wherein, besides two or three that will concern this Office much, there are those of the prizes, and that of Bergen, and not following the Dutch ships, against my Lord Sandwich; that, I fear, will ruin him, unless he hath very good luck, or they may be in better temper before he can come to be charged: but my heart is full of fear for him and his family.   I hear that they do prosecute the business against my Lord Chief Justice Kelyng with great severity.

22d.   Slept but ill all the last part of the night, for fear of this day's success in Parliament; therefore up, and all of us all the morning close, till almost two o'clock, collecting all we had to say and had done from the beginning, touching the safety of the River Medway and Chatham.   And, having done this, and put it into order, we away, I not having time to eat my dinner; and so all in my Lord Brouncker's coach, that is to say, Brouncker, W. Pen, T. Hater, and myself, talking of the other great matter with which they charge us, that is, of discharging men by ticket, in order to our defence in case that should be asked. We came to the Parliament-door, and there, after a little waiting till the Committee was sat, we were, the House being very full, called in. Sir W. Pen went in and sat as a Member; and my Lord Brouncker would not at first go in, expecting to have a chair set for him, and his brother had bid him not go in till he was called for; but, after a few words, I had occasion to mention him, and so he was called in, but without any more chair or respect paid him than myself. And so Brouncker and T. Harvey and I were there to answer, and I had a chair brought me to lean my books upon: and so did give them such an account, in a series of the whole business that had passed the Office touching the matter, and so answered all questions given me about it, that I did not perceive but they were fully satisfied with me and the business as to our office. And then Commissioner Pett (who was by at all my discourse, and this held till within an hour after candle-light, for I had candles brought in to read my papers by) was to answer for himself, we having lodged all matters with him for execution. But, Lord! what a tumultuous thing this Committee is, for all the reputation they have of a great Council, is a strange consideration; there being as impertinent questions, and as disorderly, proposed as any man could make. But Commissioner Pett, of all men living, did make the weakest defence for himself: nothing to the purpose, nor to satisfaction, nor certain; but sometimes one thing and sometimes another, sometimes for himself and sometimes against him; and his greatest failure was, that I observed, from his [not] considering whether the question propounded was his part to answer or no, and the thing to be done was his work to do: the want of which distinction will overthrow him; for he concerns himself in giving an account of the disposal of the boats, which he had no reason at all to do, or take any blame upon him for them. He charged the not carrying up of the Charles upon the Tuesday, to the Duke of Albemarle; but I see the House is mighty favourable to the Duke of Albemarle, and would give little weight to it. And something of want of arms he spoke, which Sir J. Duncomb answered with great imperiousness and earnestness; but, for all that, I do see the House is resolved to be better satisfied in the business of the unreadiness of Sheerness, and want of arms and ammunition there and everywhere: and all their officers [1] were here today attending, but only one called in, about arms for boats, to answer Commissioner Pett. None of my brethren said anything but myself: only two or three silly words my Lord Brouncker gave, in answer to one question about the number of men there were in the King's Yard at the time. At last, the House dismissed us, and shortly after did adjourn the debate till Friday next: and my cousin Pepys did come out and joy me in my acquitting myelf so well, and so did several others, and my fellow officers all very brisk to see themselves so well acquitted; which makes me a little proud, but not yet secure but we may yet meet with a back-blow which we see not.

23d. To White Hall, there to attend the Duke of York; but came a little too late, and so missed it: only spoke with him, and heard him correct my Lord Berkeley, who fell foul on Sir Edward Spragg, who, it seems, said yesterday to the House, that if the Officers of the Ordnance had done as much work at Sheerness in ten weeks as the Prince [Rupert] did in ten days, he could have defended the place against the Dutch. But the Duke of York told him that everybody must have liberty, at this time, to make their own defence, though it be to the charging of the fault upon any other, so it be true; so I perceive the whole world is at work in blaming one another. Thence Sir W. Pen and I back into London; and there saw the King, with his kettledrums and trumpets, going to the Exchange, to lay the first stone of the first pillar of the new building of the Exchange; which, the gates being shut, I could not get in to see. So, with Sir W. Pen, to Captain Cocke's, and then again towards Westminster; but in my way stopped at the Exchange and got in, the King being newly gone; and there find the bottom of the first pillar laid. And here was a shed set up, and hung with tapestry, and a canopy of state, and some good victuals and wine for the King, who, it seems, did it; [2] and so a great many people, as Tom Killigrew, and others of the Court, there. I do find Mr. Gauden in his gown as Sheriff, and understand that the King hath this morning knighted him upon the place, which I am mightily pleased with; and I think the other Sheriff, who is Davis,[3]

---

[1] Of the Ordnance.

[2] i.e. laid the stone.

[3] Thomas Davies, draper, son of John Davies, of London, knighted and lord mayor in 1677: *ob.* 1689. There is a monument to his memory in St. Sepulchre's Church, Snow Hill.

the little fellow, my schoolfellow, the bookseller, who was one of Audley's [1] Executors, and now become Sheriff; which is a strange turn, methinks.   To Westminster Hall, where I came just as the House rose; and there, in the Hall, met with Sir W. Coventry, who is in pain to defend himself in the business of tickets, it being said that the paying of the ships at Chatham by ticket was by his direction, and he hath wrote to me to find his letters, and show them him, but I find none; but did there argue the case with him, and I think no great blame can be laid on us for that matter, only I see he is fearful.   And he tells me his mistake in the House the other day, which occasions him much trouble, in showing of the House the Duke of Albemarle's letter about the good condition of Chatham; which he is sorry for, and owns as a mistake, the thing not being necessary to have been done, and confesses that nobody can escape from such error some times or other.   He says the House was well satisfied with my Report yesterday; and so several others told me in the Hall that my Report was very good and satisfactory, and that I have got advantage by it in the House: I pray God it may prove so!   To the King's playhouse, and saw 'The Black Prince,' which is now mightily bettered by that long letter being printed, and so delivered to everybody at their going in, and some short reference made to it in the play; but, when all is done, I think it the worst play of my Lord Orrery's.   But here, to my great satisfaction, I did see my Lord Hinchingbroke and his mistress, with her father and mother; and I am mightily pleased with the young lady, being handsome enough—and, indeed, to my great liking, as I would have her.   Home, and then to my chamber, to read the true story, in Speed, of the Black Prince.   This day it was moved in the House that a day might be appointed to bring in an impeachment against the Chancellor, but it was decried as being irregular; but that, if there was ground for complaint, it might be brought to the Committee for miscarriages, and, if they thought good, to present it to the House; and so it was carried. They did also vote this day thanks to be given to the Prince [2] and Duke of Albemarle for their care and conduct in the last year's war, which is a strange act; but, I know not how, the blockhead Albemarle hath strange luck to be loved, though he be, and every man must know it, the heaviest man in the world, but stout and honest to his country.   This evening, late, Mr. Moore come to me to prepare matters for my Lord Sandwich's defence; wherein I

---

[1] Audley, the usurer.   [2] Rupert.

can little assist, but will do all I can; and am in great fear of nothing but the damned business of the prizes, but I fear my Lord will receive a cursed deal of trouble by it.

24th. To write what letters I had to write, that I might go abroad with my wife, who was not well, only to jumble her, and so to the Duke of York's playhouse; and there, Betterton not being yet well, we would not stay, though since I hear that Smith do act his part in 'The Villain,' which was then acted, as well or better than he, which I do not believe: but to Charing Cross, there to see Polichinelli. But, it being begun, we in to see a Frenchman, at the house where my wife's father last lodged, one Monsieur Prin, play on the trump-marine, [1] which he do beyond belief; and, the truth is, it do so far outdo a trumpet as nothing more, and he do play anything very true, and it is most admirable and at first was a mystery to me that I should hear a whole concert of chords together, at the end of a pause; but he showed me that it was only when the last notes were 5ths or 3rds, one to another, and then their sounds like an echo did last so as they seemed to sound all together. The instrument is open at the end, I discovered, but he would not let me look into it. Here we also saw again the two fat children come out of Ireland, and a brother and sister of theirs now come, which are of little ordinary growth, like other people. But, Lord! how strange it is to observe the difference between the same children, come out of the same little woman's belly! Thence to Mile End Green, and there drank, and so home, bringing home night with us.

25th. Up, and to make our answer ready for the Parliament this afternoon, to show how Commissioner Pett was singly concerned in the execution of all orders from Chatham, and that we did properly lodge all orders with him. Thence with Sir W. Pen to the Parliament Committee, and there I had no more matters asked me. They were examining several about the business of Chatham again, and particularly my Lord Brouncker did meet with two or three blurs that he did not think of. One from Spragg, who says that 'The Unity' was ordered up, contrary to his order, by my Lord Brouncker and Commissioner Pett. Another by Crispin, the waterman, who said he was upon the Charles, and spoke to Lord Brouncker coming by in his boat, to know whether they should carry up the Charles, they being a great many naked men without arms; and he told him she was well as she was. Both

[1] See the note on Tromba marina in *Everyman's Dictionary af Music.*

these have little in them indeed, but yet both did stick close against him; and he is the weakest man in the world to make his defence, and so is like to have much fault laid on him, for a man that minds his pleasure and little else of his whole charge. The Commissioners of the Ordnance, being examined with all severity and hardly used, did go away with mighty blame; and I am told by everybody that is likely to stick mighty hard upon them: at which everybody is glad, because of Duncomb's pride, and their expecting to have the thanks of the House; whereas they have deserved, as the Parliament apprehends, as bad as bad can be. Here is great talk of an impeachment brought in against my Lord Mordaunt, and that another will be brought in against my Lord Chancellor in a few days. Here I understand for certain that they have ordered that my Lord Arlington's letters, and Secretary Morrice's letters of intelligence, be consulted, about the business of the Dutch fleet's coming abroad; and I do hear how Birch [1] is the man that do examine and trouble everybody with his questions.

26th. Mrs. Pierce tells me that the two Marshalls at the King's House was Stephen Marshall's,[2] the great Presbyterian's daughters: and that Nelly and Beck Marshall falling out the other day, the latter called the other my Lord Buckhurst's mistress. Nell answered her, 'I was but one man's mistress, though I was brought up in a brothel to fill strong waters to the gentlemen; and you are a mistress to three or four, though a Presbyter's praying daughter'; which was very pretty. Mrs. Pierce is still very pretty, but paints red on her face, which makes me hate her.

27th. (Lord's day.) After dinner, I down to Deptford, the first time that I went to look upon the Maybolt, which the King hath given me, and there she is; and I did meet with Mr. Unthwayte, who do tell me that there are new sails ordered to be delivered her,

[1] Colonel John Birch, M.P. for Penryn.
[2] There is an account of Stephen Marshall, the Presbyterian minister, in Neal's *History of the Puritans*. Sir Peter Leycester, who married a daughter of Lord Gerard, of Bromley, observes, in his *History of Cheshire*, that 'the two famous women-actors in London' were daughters of —— Marshall, chaplain to Lord Gerard, by Elizabeth, bastard daughter of John Dutton, of Dutton. Sir Peter, being connected by marriage with the Duttons, ought to have known the fact; but it is difficult to suppose that Mrs. Pierce and Nell Gwynn could have been ignorant of the actress's real history. Nor does it seem likely that Lord Gerard, who was a staunch Royalist, would have selected a Presbyterian minister for his chaplain. If Nell Gwynn's story was untrue, the remark would have lost all its point.

and a cable, which I did not speak of at all to him. So, thereupon, I told him I would not be my own hindrance so much as to take her into my custody before she had them, which was all I said to him, but desired him to take a strict inventory of her, that I might not be cheated by the master nor the company when they come to understand that the vessel is gone away, which he hath promised me. This evening came Sir J. Minnes to me, to let me know that a Parliament-man hath been with him, to tell him that the Parliament intend to examine him particularly about Sir W. Coventry's selling of places, and about my Lord Brouncker's discharging the ships at Chatham by ticket: for the former of which I am more particularly sorry, that that business of Sir W. Coventry should come up again; though this old man tells me, and I believe, that he can say nothing to it.

28th. To Sir W. Coventry's lodging, but he was gone out, and I find him at his house, which is fitting for him; and there I to him, and was with him above an hour alone, discoursing of the matters of the nation, and our Office, and himself. He owns that he is, at this day, the chief person aimed at by the Parliament—that is, by the friends of my Lord Chancellor, and also of the Duke of Albemarle—by reason of his unhappy showing of the Duke of Albemarle's letter, the other day, in the House; but that he thinks that he is not liable to any hurt they can fasten on him for anything. He says he is so well armed to justify himself in everything, unless in the old business of selling places, when, he says, everybody did; and he will now not be forward to tell his own story, as he hath been; but tells me he is grown wiser, and will put them to prove anything, and he will defend himself: besides that, he will dispute the statute, thinking that it will not be found to reach him. We did talk many things, which, as they come into my mind now, I shall set down without order: That he is weary of public employment, and neither ever designed, nor will ever, if his commission were brought to him wrapped in gold, accept of any single place in the State, as particularly Secretary of State; which, he says, the world discourses Morrice is willing to resign, and he thinks the King might have thought of him, but he would not, by any means, now take it, if given him, nor anything, but in commission with others, who may bear part of the blame; for now he observes well, that whoever did do anything singly are now in danger, however honest and painful they were, saying that he himself was the only man, he thinks, at the Council-board that spoke his mind clearly, as he thought, to the good of the King; and the rest, who sat silent, have nothing said to them, nor are taken notice of. That the first time the King did take him so closely into his confidence and ministry of affairs was upon the business of Chatham, when all the disturbances were there and in the kingdom; and then, while everybody was fancying for himself, the King did find him to persuade him to call for the Parliament, declaring that it was against his own proper interest, forasmuch as it was likely they would find faults with him as well as with others, but that he would prefer the service of the King before his own. And thereupon the King did take him into his special notice, and from that time to this hath received him so. And that then he did see the folly and mistakes of the Chancellor in the management of things, and that matters were never likely to be done well in that sort of conduct; and did persuade the King to think fit of the taking away the seals from the Chancellor, which, when it was done, he told me that he himself, in his own particular, was sorry for it, for, while he stood, there was he and my Lord Arlington to stand between him and harm, whereas now there is only my Lord Arlington, and he is now done, so that all their fury is placed upon him: but that he did tell the King, when he first moved it, that, if he thought the laying of him, W. Coventry, aside would at all facilitate the removing of the Chancellor, he would most willingly submit to it. Whereupon the King did command him to try the Duke of York about it, and persuade him to it; which he did, by the King's command, undertake and compass. And the Duke of York did own his consent to the King, but afterwards was brought to be of another mind for the Chancellor, and now is displeased with him, and [so is] the Duchess, so that she will not see him; but he tells me that the Duke of York seems pretty kind, and hath said that he do believe that W. Coventry did mean well, and do it only out of judgment. He tells me that he never was an intriguer in his life, nor will be, nor of any combination of persons to set up this, or fling down that, nor hath, in his own business, this Parliament, spoke to three members to say anything for him, but will stand upon his own defence, and will stay by it, and thinks that he is armed against all they can [say], but the old business of selling places, and in that thinks they cannot hurt him. However, I do find him mighty willing to have his name used as little as he can, and he was glad when I did deliver him up a letter of his to me, which did give countenance to the discharging of men by ticket at Chatham, which is now coming in question; and wherein, I confess, I am sorry to find him so tender of appearing, it being a thing not only good and fit, all that was done in it, but promoted and advised by him. But he thinks the House is set upon wresting anything to his prejudice that they can pick up. He tells me he did never, as a great many have, call the Chancellor rogue and knave, and I know not what; but all that he hath said, and will stand by, is, that his counsels were not good, nor his manner of managing things. I suppose he means suffering the King to run in debt; for by and by, the King walking in the park with a great crowd of his idle people about him, I took occasion to say that it was a sorry thing to be a poor King, and to have others to come to correct the faults of his own servants, and that this was it that brought us all into this condition. He answered that he would never be a poor King, and then the other would mend of itself. 'No,' says he, 'I would eat bread and drink water first, and this day discharge all the idle company about me, and walk only with two footmen; and this I have told the King, and this must do it at last.' I asked him how long the King would suffer this. He told me the King must suffer it yet longer; that he would not advise the King to do otherwise; for it would break out again worse, if he should break them up before the core be come up. After this we fell to other talk, of my waiting upon him hereafter, it may be to read a chapter in Seneca, in this new house which he hath bought and is making very fine, when he may be out of employment, which he seems to wish more than to fear, and I do believe him heartily. Thence home, and met news from Townsend of the Wardrobe, that old Young, the yeoman tailor, whose place my Lord Sandwich promised my father, is dead. Upon which, resolving presently that my father shall not be troubled with it, but I hope I shall be able to enable him to end his days where he is, in quiet. At the new Exchange, and there buying 'The Indian Emperor,' newly printed. After dinner my wife, and Mercer who grows fat, and Willett and I, to the King's House, and there saw 'The Committee.'

29th. To Westminster Hall, the House sitting all this day about the method of bringing in the charge against my Lord Chancellor; and at last resolved for a Committee to draw up the heads.

30th. To White Hall, where we did a little business with the Duke of York, only I perceive that he do leave all of us, as the King do those about him, to stand and fall by ourselves; and I think is not without some cares himself what the Parliament may do in matters wherein his honour is concerned. To the Parliament-house, where, after the Committee was sat, I was called in: and the first thing was upon the complaint of a dirty slut that was there, about a ticket which she had lost, and had applied herself to me for another. I did give them a short and satisfactory answer to that; and so they sent her away, and were ashamed of their foolery in giving occasion to 500 seamen and seamen's wives to come before them, as there were this afternoon. When I come home, I did find my wife and Betty Turner, the two Mercers, and Mrs. Parker, an ugly lass, but yet dances well, and speaks the best of them, and W. Batelier and Pembleton, dancing; and here I danced with them, and had a good supper, and as merry as I could be.

31st. After dinner in comes Mr. Turner, of Eynesbury,[1] lately come to town, and also after him Captain Hill of the Coventry, who lost her at Barbadoes, and hath come out of France, where he hath been long prisoner. I to Westminster; and there at the lobby do hear by Commissioner Pett, to my great amazement, that he is in worse condition than before, by the coming in of the Duke of Albemarle's and Prince Rupert's narratives[2] this day; wherein the former do most severely lay matters upon him, so as the House this day have, I think, ordered him to the Tower again, or something like it; so that the poor man is likely to be overthrown, I doubt, right or wrong, so infinite fond they are of anything the Duke of Albemarle says or writes to them! I did then go down, and there met with Colonel Reames and cousin Roger Pepys; and there they do tell me how the Duke of Albemarle and the Prince have laid blame on a great many, and particularly on our Office in general; and particularly for want of provision, wherein I shall come to be questioned again in that business myself; which do trouble me. But my cousin Pepys and I had much discourse alone: and he do bewail the constitution of this House, and says there is a direct cabal and faction, as much as is possible between

---

[1] John Turner, B.D., whose ancestors were of Hemel Hempstead, had been a Fellow of Magdalene College, Cambridge, and became rector of Eynesbury in 1649. He resigned the living, of which Lord Sandwich was the patron, to his son, Edward Turner, in 1689; and dying in 1705, *æt.* 84, had sepulture in the parish church, *M.I.*

[2] See these narratives, each dated 31st October 1667, in the Harleian MSS., 7170, entitled, 'Notes of Transactions in Parliament addressed to Pepys and Hewer.' They are printed at length in the journals of the day.

those for and against the Chancellor, and so in other factions, that there is nothing almost done honestly and with integrity; only some few, he says, there are, that do keep out of all plots and combinations, and when their time comes will speak and see right done, if possible; and that he himself is looked upon to be a man that will be of no faction, and so they do shun to make him; and I am glad of it. He tells me that he thanks God that he never knew what it was to be tempted to be a knave in his life, till he did come into the House of Commons, where there is nothing done but by passion and faction and private interest. Reames did tell me of a fellow last night, one Kelsy, a commander of a fire-ship, who complains for want of his money paid him, did say that he did see one of the Commissioners of the Navy bring in three waggon-loads of prize-goods into Greenwich one night; but that the House did take no notice of it, nor enquire; but this is me, and I must expect to be called to account, and answer what I did as well as I can. I espied Sir D. Gauden's coach, and so went out of mine into his; and there had opportunity to talk of the business of victuals, which the Duke of Albemarle and Prince did complain that they were in want of the last year: but we do conclude we shall be able to show quite the contrary of that; only it troubles me that we must come to contend with these great persons, which will overrun us. Mr. Yeabsly and I to even some accounts, wherein I shall be a gainer about £200, which is a seasonable profit; for I have got nothing a great while.

November 1st. To Sir W. Coventry's. The Duke of Albemarle's and Prince's narratives, given yesterday by the House, fall foul of him and Sir G. Carteret in something about the dividing of the fleet, and the Prince particularly charging the Commissioners of the Navy with negligence, whereof Sir W. Coventry is one. The Duke of Albemarle charges W. Coventry that he should tell him, when he came down to the fleet with Sir G. Carteret to consult about the dividing the fleet, that the Dutch would not be out in six weeks, which W. Coventry says is as false as is possible, and he can prove the contrary by the Duke of Albemarle's own letters. The Duke says that he did, upon sight of the Dutch, call a council of officers, and they did conclude they could not avoid fighting the Dutch; and yet we did go to the enemy, and found them at anchor, which is a pretty contradiction. And he tells me that Spragg did the other day say in the House that the Prince, upon his going from the Duke of Albemarle with his fleet, did tell him that if the Dutch should come on, the Duke was to follow him, the Prince, with his fleet, and not fight the Dutch.   But it is a sad consideration that all this picking of holes in one another's coats —nay, and the thanks of the House to the Prince and the Duke of Albemarle, and all this envy and design to ruin Sir W. Coventry —did arise from Sir W. Coventry's unfortunate mistake the other day in producing of a letter from the Duke of Albemarle touching the good condition of all things at Chatham just before the Dutch came up, and did us that fatal mischief; for upon this they are resolved to undo him, and I pray God they do not.   To chapel, it being All-Hallows day, and heard a fine anthem, made by Pelham,[1] who is come over.   I this morning before chapel visited Sir G. Carteret, who is vexed to see how things are likely to go, but cannot help it, and yet seems to think himself mighty safe.   I also visited my Lord Hinchingbroke at his chamber at White Hall; I am mightily pleased with his sobriety and few words.   There I found Mr. Turner, Moore, and Creed talking of my Lord Sandwich, whose case I doubt is but bad, and, I fear, will not escape being worse.   My wife and I to the King's playhouse, and there saw a silly play and an old one, 'The Taming of a Shrew.'

2d. To the King's playhouse, and there saw 'Henry the Fourth:' and, contrary to expectation, was pleased in nothing more than in Cartwright's [2] speaking of Falstaff's speech about 'What is Honour?'   The house full of Parliament-men, it being holiday with them: and it was observable how a gentleman of good habit, sitting just before us, eating of some fruit in the midst of the play, did drop down as dead, being choked; but with much ado Orange Moll did thrust her finger down his throat, and brought him to life again.

3d. To church, and thither comes Roger Pepys to our pew; and thence home to dinner, whither comes, by invitation, Mr. Turner, the Minister, and my cousin Roger brought with him Jeffreys, the apothecary at Westminster, who is our kinsman, and we had

---

[1] Pelham Humfrey, who had been educated under Captain Henry Cooke, was admitted a Gentleman of the Chapel Royal in 1667, and distinguished himself so much as to excite the envy of his instructor, who died of discontent at his pupil's excelling him.   Humfrey succeeded him as Master of the Children; but his career was very short; for he deceased at Windsor 14th July 1674, *æt.* 27.

[2] William Cartwright, one of Killigrew's Company at the original establishment of Drury Lane.   By his will, dated 1686, he left his books, pictures, and furniture to Dulwich College, where also his portrait still remains.

much discourse of Cottinghamshire.[1] Roger did tell me of a bargain which I may now have in Norfolk, that my she-cousin Nan Pepys is going to sell, the title whereof is very good, and the pennyworth is also good enough; but it is out of the way so of my life, that I shall never enjoy it, nor, it may be, see it, and so I shall have nothing to do with it. I find by discourse Mr. Turner to be a man mighty well read in the Roman history, which is very pleasant.

4th. To Westminster, and there, landing at the New Exchange stairs, I to Sir W. Coventry: and there he read over to me the Prince's and the Duke of Albemarle's narratives, wherein they are very severe against him and our Office. But Sir W. Coventry do contemn them; only that their persons and qualities are great, and so I do perceive he is afraid of them, though he will not confess it. But he do say that, if he can get out of these briars, he will never trouble himself with Princes nor Dukes again. He finds several things in their narratives, which are both inconsistent and foolish, as well as untrue. I confess I do see so much, that, were I but well possessed of what I should have in the world, I think I could willingly retreat, and trouble myself no more. Sir H. Cholmley owns Sir W. Coventry, in his opinion, to be one of the worthiest men in the nation, as I do really think he is. He tells me he do think really that they will cut off my Lord Chancellor's head, the Chancellor at this day having as much pride as is possible to those few that venture their fortunes by coming to see him; and that the Duke of York is troubled much, knowing that those that fling down the Chancellor cannot stop there, but will do something to him, to prevent his having it in his power hereafter to avenge himself and father-in-law upon them. And this Sir H. Cholmley fears may be by divorcing the Queen and getting another, or declaring the Duke of Monmouth legitimate: which God forbid! He tells me he do verily believe that there will come in an impeachment of High Treason against my Lord of Ormond: among other things, for ordering the quartering of soldiers in Ireland on free quarters; which, it seems, is high treason in that country, and was one of the things that lost the Lord Strafford his head, and the law is not yet repealed; which, he says, was a mighty oversight of him not to have it repealed, which he might with ease have done, or have justified himself by an Act. To Turlington, the great spectacle-maker, for advice, who dissuades me from using old spectacles, but rather young ones, and do tell me that nothing can

[1] Pepys's ancestors were seated at Cottenham, in Cambridgeshire.

wrong my eyes more than for me to use reading-glasses, which do magnify much.

6th. The House is just now upon taking away the charter from the Company of Woodmongers,[1] whose frauds, it seems, have been mightily laid before them. I to the House of Lords, and there first saw Dr. Fuller, as Bishop of Lincoln, to sit among the Lords. Here I spoke with the Duke of York and the Duke of Albemarle about Tangier; but methinks both of them do look very coldly upon one another, and their discourse mighty cold, and little to the purpose about our want of money. Thence called at Allestry's, the bookseller, who is bookseller to the Royal Society, and there did buy three or four books, and find great variety of French and foreign books. With my wife to a play, and the girl —'Macbeth,' which we still like mightily, though mighty short of the content we used to have when Betterton acted, who is still sick. This day, in the Painted Chamber, I met and walked with Mr. George Montagu, who thinks it may go hard with my Lord Sandwich; but he says the House is offended with Sir W. Coventry much, and that he do endeavour to gain them again in the most precarious manner in all things that is possible.

7th. At noon resolved with Sir W. Pen to go to see 'The Tempest,' an old play of Shakespeare's, acted, I hear, the first day; and so my wife and girl and W. Hewer by themselves, and Sir W. Pen and I afterwards by ourselves: and forced to sit in the side balcony over against the music-room at the Duke's house, close by my Lady Dorset [2] and a great many great ones. The house mighty full; the King and Court there; and the most innocent play that ever I saw; and a curious piece of music,[3] in an echo of half sentences, the echo repeating the former half while the man goes on to the latter, which is mighty pretty. The play has no great wit, but yet good, above ordinary plays.

8th. Called up betimes by Sir H. Cholmley, and he and I to good purpose most of the morning—I in my dressing-gown with him—on our Tangier accounts, and stated them well; and here he tells me that he believes it will go hard with my Lord Chancellor.

---

[1] The Woodmongers' Company of London were incorporated by James I on 29th August 1605; but, for their malpractices, they, in the year 1668, found it convenient, in order to avoid punishment, to surrender their charter.

[2] Frances, daughter of Lionel Cranfield, first Earl of Middlesex, wife of Richard Sackville, fifth Earl of Dorset.

[3] Evidently the song sung by Ferdinand, wherein Ariel echoes 'Go thy way,' from Davenant's and Dryden's adaptation. The music was by Banister.

Thence I to the office, where met on some special business; and here I hear that the Duke of York is very ill; and by and by word brought us that we shall not need to attend today on the Duke of York, for he is not well, which is bad news.   They being gone, I to my workmen, who this day came to alter my office by beating down the wall, and making me a fair window there, and increasing the window of my closet, which do give me some present trouble, but will be mighty pleasant.   So all the whole day among them till very late, and so home weary, to supper and to bed, troubled for the Duke of York his being sick.

9th.   The House very busy, and like to be so all day, about my Lord Chancellor's impeachment, whether treason or not.   I spoke with my cousin Roger, he desirous to get back into the House, he having his notes in his hands, the lawyers being now speaking to the point of whether treason or not treason, the article of advising the King to break up the Parliament and to govern by the sword. To the Hall, and there met Mr. King,[1] the Parliament man for Harwich, and there he did show, and let me take a copy of, all the articles against my Lord Chancellor, and what members they were that undertook to bring witnesses to make them good.   So away home, and there, by W. Pen, do hear that this article was over-voted in the House not to be a ground of impeachment of treason, at which I was glad, being willing to have no blood spilt, if I could help it.

10th. (Lord's day.) To church.   Here was my Lady Batten in her mourning.   To White Hall, to speak with Sir W. Coventry; and there, beyond all we looked for, do hear that the Duke of York hath got, and is full of, the small-pox.   And so we to his lodgings, and there find most of the family going to St. James's, and the gallery-doors locked up, that nobody might pass to nor fro: and a sad house, I am sure.   I am sad to consider the effects of his death, if he should miscarry; but Dr. Frazier tells me that he is in as good condition as a man can be in his case.   The eruption appeared last night: it seems he was let blood on Friday.   W. Coventry told us that the counsel he hath too late learned is, to spring nothing in the House, nor offer anything, but just what is drawn out of a man: that this is the best way of dealing with a Parliament, and that he hath paid dear, and knows not how much more he may pay, for not knowing it sooner, when he did unnecessarily produce the Duke of Albemarle's letter about Chatham.

[1] Thomas King.

11th. Sir G. Carteret and I towards the Temple in coach together; and there he did tell me how the King do all he can in the world to overthrow my Lord Chancellor, and that notice is taken of every man about the King that is not seen to promote the ruin of the Chancellor; and that this being another great day in his business, he dares not but be there.   He tells me that as soon as Secretary Morrice brought the Great Seal from my Lord Chancellor, Bab. May fell upon his knees, and catched the King about the legs, and joyed him, and said that this was the first time that ever he could call him King of England, being freed from this great man: which was a most ridiculous saying.   And he told me that when first my Lord Gerard, a great while ago, came to the King and told him that the Chancellor did say openly that the King was a lazy person and not fit to govern (which is now made one of the things in people's mouths against the Chancellor), 'Why,' says the King, 'that is no news, for he hath told me so twenty times, and but the other day he told me so'; and made matter of mirth at it: but yet this light discourse is likely to prove bad to him.   After dinner my wife and I and Willett to the King's playhouse, and there saw 'The Indian Emperor,' a good play, but not so good as people cry it up, I think, though above all things Nell's ill speaking of a great part made me mad.   Thence with great trouble and charge getting a coach.   This day I had a whole doe sent me by Mr. Hozier, which is a fine present, and I had the umbles of it for dinner.   I hear Kirton, my bookseller, poor man, is dead, I believe of grief for his losses by the fire.

12th. Up, and to the office, where sat all the morning; and there hear that the Duke of York do yet do very well with his small-pox: pray God he may continue to do so!   This morning also, to my astonishment, I hear that yesterday my Lord Chancellor, to another of his Articles, that of betraying the King's counsels to his enemies, is voted to have matter against him for an impeachment of high treason, and that this day the impeachment is to be carried up to the House of Lords: which is very high, and I am troubled at it; for God knows what will follow, since they that do this must do more to secure themselves against any that will revenge this, if it ever come in their power!

13th. To Westminster, where I find the House sitting, and in a mighty heat about Commissioner Pett, that they would have him impeached, though the Committee have yet brought in but part of their Report.   And this heat of the House is much heightened by

Sir Thomas Clifford telling them that he was the man that did, out of his own purse, employ people at the outports to prevent the King of Scots to escape after the battle of Worcester. The House was in a great heat all this day about it; and at last it was carried, however, that it should be referred back to the Committee to make further inquiry. By and by I met with Mr. Wren, who tells me that the Duke of York is in as good condition as is possible for a man in his condition of the small-pox. He, I perceive, is mightily concerned in the business of my Lord Chancellor, the impeachment against whom is gone up to the House of Lords; and great differences there are in the Lords' House about it, and the Lords are very high one against another. To the Duke of York's House, and there saw 'The Tempest' again, which is very pleasant, and full of so good variety, that I cannot be more pleased almost in a comedy, only the seaman's part a little too tedious. To my chamber, and do begin anew to bind myself to keep my old vows, and, among the rest, not to see a play till Christmas but once in every other week, and have laid aside £10, which is to be lost to the poor if I do. This day Mr. Chicheley told me, with a seeming trouble, that the House have stopped his son Jack [Sir John] his going to France, that he may be a witness against my Lord Sandwich: which do trouble me, though he can, I think, say little.

14th. At noon, all my clerks with me to dinner, to a venison pasty; and there comes Creed, and dined with me, and he tells me how high the Lords were in the Lords' House about the business of the Chancellor, and that they were not yet agreed to impeach him. After dinner he and I and my wife and girl, the latter two to their tailor's, and he and I to the Committee of the Treasury, where I had a hearing, but can get but £6,000 for the pay of the garrison, in lieu of above £16,000; and this Alderman Backwell gets remitted there, and I am glad of it. Thence by coach took up my wife and girl, and so home, and set down Creed at Arundel House, going to the Royal Society, whither I would be glad to go, but cannot. Thence home, and to the office, where about my letters, and so home to supper, and to bed, my eyes being bad again; and by this means, the nights, nowadays, do become very long to me, longer than I can sleep out.

15th. To Westminster, and do hear that there is to be a conference between the two Houses today. So I stayed: and it was only to tell the Commons that the Lords cannot agree to the confining or sequestering of the Earl of Clarendon from the Parliament, forasmuch as they do not specify any particular crime which they lay upon him and call treason. This the House did receive, and so parted: at which, I hear, the Commons are like to grow very high, and will insist upon their privileges, and the Lords will own theirs, though the Duke of Buckingham, Bristol, and others, have been very high in the House of Lords to have had him committed. This is likely to breed ill blood. Home, and there find, as I expected, Mr. Cæsar and little Pelham Humphreys, lately returned from France, and is an absolute Monsieur, as full of form and confidence and vanity, and disparages everything and everybody's skill but his own. But to hear how he laughs at all the King's music here, as Blagrave [1] and others, that they cannot keep time nor tune, nor understand anything; and that Grabut, the Frenchman, the King's master of the music, how he understands nothing, nor can play on any instrument, and so cannot compose; and that he will give him a lift out of his place; and that he and the King are mighty great! I had a good dinner for them, as a venison pasty and some fowl; and after dinner we did play, he on the theorbo, Mr. Cæsar on his French lute, and I on the viol. And I see that this Frenchman do so much wonders on the theorbo, that without question he is a good musician, but his vanity do offend me. Mr. Moore tells me that the King hath, as he says Sir Thomas Crewe told him, been heard to say that the quarrel is not between my Lord Chancellor and him, but his brother and him; which will make sad work among us if that be once promoted, as to be sure it will, Buckingham and Bristol being now the only counsel the King follows, so as Arlington and Coventry are come to signify little. He tells me they are likely to fall upon my Lord Sandwich; but, for my part, sometimes I am apt to think they cannot do him much harm, he telling me that there is no great fear of the business of Resumption.[2] This day, Poundy the waterman, was with me, to let me know that he was summoned to bear witness against me to Prince Rupert's people, who have a commission to look after the business of prize-goods, about the business of the prize-goods

---

[1] Thomas Blagrave, a Gentleman of the Chapel of Charles II, and a performer on the cornett there; he was of the Berkshire family of that name. A few of his songs are printed in *Select Ayres and Dialogues*, folio 1669.

[2] Resumption, in a legal sense, signifies the taking again into the king's hands such lands or tenements as before, upon false suggestions, or other error, he had delivered to the heir, or granted by letters patent to any man. The Bill for effecting these objects was brought into the House of Commons, but never passed.

I was concerned in: but I did desire him to speak all he knew and not to spare me, nor did promise nor give him anything, but sent him away with good words.

16th. To White Hall, where there is to be a performance of music of Pelham's before the King. The company not come; but I did go into the music-room, where Captain Cocke and many others; and here I did hear the best and the smallest organ go that ever I saw in my life, and such a one as, by the grace of God, I will have the next year, if I continue in this condition, whatever it cost me. Met Mr. Gregory, my old acquaintance, an understanding gentleman; and he and I walked an hour together, talking of the bad prospect of the times. And the sum of what I learn from him is this: That the King is the most concerned in the world against the Chancellor and all people that do not appear against him, and therefore is angry with the Bishops, having said that he had one Bishop on his side, Crofts, and but one: that Buckingham and Bristol are now his only Cabinet Council; and that, before the Duke of York fell sick, Buckingham was admitted to the King of his Cabinet, and there stayed with him several hours, and the Duke of York shut out. That it is plain that there is dislike between the King and Duke of York, and that it is to be feared that the House will go so far against the Chancellor, that they must do something to undo the Duke of York, or will not think themselves safe. That this Lord Vaughan,[1] that is so great against the Chancellor, is one of the lewdest fellows of the age, worse than Sir Charles Sedley; and that he was heard to swear he would do my Lord Clarendon's business. That he do find that my Lord Clarendon hath more friends in both Houses than he believes he would have, by reason that they do see what are the hands that pull him down; which they do not like. That Harry Coventry was scolded at by the King severely the other day; and that his answer was that, if he must not speak what he thought in this business in Parliament, he must not come thither. And he says that by this very business Harry Coventry hath got more fame and common esteem than any gentleman in England hath at this day, and is an excellent and able person. That the King, who not long ago did say of Bristol that he was a man able in three years to get himself a fortune in

[1] John Vaughan, Lord Vaughan, eldest surviving son to Richard Earl of Carbery, whom he succeeded. He was well versed in literature, and President of the Royal Society from 1686 to 1689, and had been Governor of Jamaica. He was amongst Dryden's earliest patrons. *Ob.* 1713.

any kingdom in the world and lose all again in three months, do now hug him, and commend his parts everywhere, above all the world. How fickle is this man [the King], and how unhappy we like to be! That he fears some furious courses will be taken against the Duke of York; and that he hath heard that it was designed, if they cannot carry matters against the Chancellor, to impeach the Duke of York himself: which God forbid! That Sir Edward Nicholas, whom he served while Secretary, is one of the best men in the world, but hated by the Queen-mother for a service he did the old King against her mind and her favourites; and that she and my Lady Castlemaine did make the King to lay him aside: but this man [1] says that he is one of the most heavenly and charitable men in the whole world. That the House of Commons resolve to stand by their proceedings, and have chosen a Committee to draw up the reasons thereof to carry to the Lords; which is likely to breed great heat between them. That the Parliament, after all this, is likely to give the King no money; and, therefore, that it is to be wondered what makes the King give way to so great extravagancies, which do all tend to the making him less than he is, and so will, every day more and more: and by this means every creature is divided against the other, that there never was so great an uncertainty in England of what would be the event of things as at this day, nobody being at ease or safe. To White Hall, and there got into the theatre-room; and there heard both the vocal and instrumental music, where the little fellow [2] stood keeping time: but for my part, I see no great matter, but quite the contrary in both sorts of music. Here was the King and Queen, and some of the ladies; among whom none more jolly than my Lady Buckingham,[3] her Lord being once more a great man.

17th. (Lord's day.) Comes Captain Cocke, who sat with me all the evening. He tells me that he hears that Sir W. Coventry was, a little before the Duke of York fell sick, with the Duke of York in his closet, and fell on his knees, and begged his pardon for what he hath done to my Lord Chancellor; but this I dare not soon believe. But he tells me another thing, which he says he had from the person himself who spoke with the Duke of Buckingham; who, he says, is a very sober and worthy man, that he did lately speak with the Duke of Buckingham about his greatness now with the King, and told him—'But, sir, these things that the

[1] Gregory. [2] Pelham Humfrey. [3] The daughter of Fairfax.

King do now, in suffering the Parliament to do all this, you know
are not fit for the King to suffer; and you know how often you
have said to me that the King was a weak man, and unable to
govern, but to be governed, and that you could command him as
you listed.   Why do you suffer him to go on in these things?'—
'Why,' says the Duke of Buckingham, 'I do suffer him to do this,
that I may hereafter the better command him.'   He told me of one
odd passage by the Duke of Albemarle, speaking how hasty a
man he is, and how for certain he would have killed Sir W.
Coventry, had he met him in a little time after his showing his
letter in the House.   He told me that a certain lady whom he
knows did tell him that, she being certainly informed that some of
the Duke of Albemarle's family did say that the Earl of Torrington [1] was a bastard, [she] did think herself concerned to tell the
Duke of Albemarle of it, and did first tell the Duchess, and was
going to tell the old man, when the Duchess pulled her back by
the sleeve and hindered her, swearing to her that if he should hear
it he would certainly kill the servant that should be found to have
said it, and therefore prayed her to hold her peace.

18th.   To White Hall, to the Commissioners of the Treasury,
and so home, leaving multitudes of solicitors at their door, of one
sort or other, complaining for want of such dispatch as they had
in my Lord Treasurer's time.   Among others, there was Gresham

---

[1] In 1652 General Monk was married at the church of St. George, Southwark, to Anne, daughter of his regimental farrier, John Clarges, and in the
following year had by her a son, Christopher, the 'Earl of Torrington' here
mentioned.   The child was suckled by Honour Mills, a vendor of apples and
oysters, and succeeded his father as Duke of Albemarle in 1670; but, dying in
1688, *s. p.*, all the honours and titles of the family became extinct.   It came
out, on a trial of trespass between William Sherwen, plaintiff, and Sir Walter
Clarges, Bart., and others, defendants, at the bar of the King's Bench, 15th
November 1702, that Anne Clarges had married for her fi·st husband Thomas
Ratford, in 1632, and was separated from him in 1649; but no certificate of
his death had ever appeared.   This fact would invalidate the legitimacy of
the Earl of Torrington: and the suspicion is strengthened by the low origin
and vulgar habits of the duchess, and the threats which she resorted to, to
prevent the story being made public.   One Pride, who, as the son of a daughter
of an elder brother of George, Duke of Albemarle, claimed to be heir to Duke
George, brought an ejectment against the Earl of Bath (who claimed under a
deed from Duke Christopher), in the King's Bench in Hilary Term, 6 Wm.
III, attempting to bastardize Duke Christopher, on the ground mentioned in
the note.   After a long trial, the jury, not being satisfied with the evidence,
found for the Earl of Bath.   This case, which is a different one from that
given above, is reported in 1 Salkeld, 120; 3 Leving, 410; and Holt, 286.
Leving was one of the counsel for the Earl of Bath.

College come, about getting a grant of Chelsea College[1] for their Society, which the King, it seems, hath given them his right in; but they met with some other pretences, I think, to it, besides the King's.

19th. To the Parliament House. Here Sir R. Brookes did take me alone, and pray me to prevent their trouble by discovering the order he would have. I told him I would suppress none, nor could, but this would not satisfy him. Here I did stand by unseen, and did hear their impertinent yet malicious examinations of some rogues about the business of Bergen, wherein they would wind in something against my Lord Sandwich, which was plain by their manner of examining, as Sir Thomas Crewe did afterwards observe to me. But Sir Thomas Crewe and W. Hewer did tell me that they did hear Captain Downing give a cruel testimony against my Lord Brouncker, for his neglect, and doing nothing, in the time of straits at Chatham, when he was spoke to, and did tell the Committee that he, Downing, did presently after, in Lord Brouncker's hearing, tell the Duke of Albemarle that, if he might advise the King, he should hang both my Lord Brouncker and Pett. This is very hard. This night I wrote to my father, in answer to a new match which is proposed, the executor of Ensum, my sister's former servant, for my sister, that I will continue my mind of giving her £500, if he likes of the match. My father did also this week, by Shepley, return me up a guinea, which, it seems, upon searching the ground, they have found since I was there. I was told this day that Lory Hyde,[2] second son of my Lord Chancellor, did some time since in the House say that if he thought his father was guilty but of one of the things then said against him, he would be the first that should call for judgment against him: which Mr. Waller, the poet, did say was spoke like the old Roman, Brutus, for its greatness and worthiness.

20th. This afternoon Mr. Mills told me how fully satisfactory my first Report was to the House in the business of Chatham: which I am glad to hear, and the more, for that I know that he is a great creature of Sir R. Brookes's.

21st. My wife not very well, but is to go to Mr. Mills's child's

---

[1] In 1669 Charles gave the ground and buildings of St. James's College, Chelsea to the Royal Society, who sold them again to Sir Stephen Fox, for the Crown, in January 1682 for £1,300.

[2] Laurence Hyde, Master of the Robes in 1682, created Earl of Rochester: *ob.* 1711.

christening, where she is godmother.   Among other things of
news, I do hear that, upon the reading of the House of Commons'
Reasons of the manner of their proceedings in the business of my
Lord Chancellor, the Reasons were so bad, that my Lord Bristol
himself did declare that he would not stand to what he had, and
did still, advise the Lords to concur to, upon any of the Reasons
of the House of Commons; but if it was put to the question whether
it should be done on their Reasons, he would be against them.   And
indeed it seems the Reasons—however they come to escape the
House of Commons, which shows how slightly the greatest matters
are done in this world, and even in Parliaments—were none of
them of strength, but the principle of them untrue; they saying
that where any man is brought before a Judge, accused of treason
in general, without specifying the particular, the Judge is obliged
to commit him.   The question being put by the Lords to my Lord
Keeper, he said that quite the contrary was true: and then, in the
Sixth Article (I will get a copy of them if I can) there are two or
three things strangely asserted to the diminishing of the King's
power, as is said at least; things that heretofore would not have
been heard of.   But then the question being put among the Lords,
as my Lord Bristol advised, whether, upon the whole matter and
Reasons that had been laid before them, they would commit my
Lord Clarendon, it was carried five to one against it; there being
but three Bishops against him, of whom Cosin [1] and Dr. Reynolds
were two, and I know not the third.[2]   This made the opposite
Lords, as Bristol and Buckingham, so mad, that they declared and
protested against it, speaking very broad that there was mutiny
and rebellion in the hearts of the Lords, and that they desired they
might enter their dissents: which they did do, in great fury.   So
that upon the Lords' sending to the Commons, as I am told, to
have a conference for them to give their answer to the Commons'
Reasons, the Commons did desire a free conference: but the Lords
do deny it; and the reason is, that they hold not the Commons any
Court, but that themselves only are a Court, and the Chief Court
of Judicature, and therefore are not to dispute the laws and method
of their own Court with them that are none, and so will not submit
so much as to have their power disputed.   And it is conceived that

[1] John Cosin, Master of Peterhouse and Dean of Peterborough in the
time of Charles I; afterwards Bishop of Durham: *ob.* 1672, aged seventy-
eight.
[2] Probably Crofts.

much of this eagerness among the Lords do arise from the fear some of them have, that they may be dealt with in the same manner themselves, and therefore do stand upon it now. It seems my Lord Clarendon hath, it is said and believed, had his horses several times in his coach, ready to carry him to the Tower, expecting a message to that purpose; but by this means his case is like to be laid by. From this to other discourse, and very good: among the rest, of a man that is a little frantic, that hath been a kind of minister (Dr. Wilkins saying that he hath read for him in his church), that is poor and a debauched man, that the College [1] have hired for 20*s.* to have some of the blood of a sheep let into his body; [2] and it is to be done on Saturday next. They purpose to let in about twelve ounces; which, they compute, is what will be let in in a minute's time by a watch. They differ in the opinion they have of the effects of it: some think it may have a good effect upon him as a frantic man by cooling his blood, others that it will not have any effect at all. But the man is a healthy man, and will be able to give an account what alteration, if any, he do find in himself, and so may be useful. On this occasion Dr. Whistler told a pretty story related by Muffet, [3] a good author, of Dr. Caius, that built Caius College: that, being very old, and living only at that time upon woman's milk, he, while he fed upon the milk of an angry, fretful woman, was so himself; and then, being advised to take it of a good-natured, patient woman, he did become so, beyond the common temper of his age. Their discourse was very fine; and if I should be put out of my office, I do take great content in the liberty I shall be at, of frequenting these gentlemen's company. Home, and there my wife tells me great stories of the gossiping women of the parish—what this, and what that woman was; and, among the rest, how Mrs. Hollworthy is the veriest confident bragging gossip of them all, which I should not have believed; but that Sir R. Brookes, her partner, [4] was mighty civil to her, and taken with her, and what not. Inventing a cypher to put on a piece of

---

[1] The Royal Society, meeting at Gresham College.

[2] See an account of the experiment of transfusion performed at Arundel House, 23rd November 1667, upon the person of Arthur Coga.—*Philosophical Transactions*, No. 30, p. 557.

[3] The work alluded to is *Health's Improvement, or Rules for preparing all sorts of Food*, London, 1655, 4to, enlarged by Christopher Bennett, from a treatise written by Thomas Moufet, or Muffet, an English physician and naturalist.

[4] As sponsor, at the christening.

plate, which I must give, better than ordinary, to the Parson's child.

22d. Met with Cooling, my Lord Chamberlain's Secretary, and from him to learn the truth of all I heard last night; and understand further, that this stiffness of the Lords is in no manner of kindness to my Lord Chancellor, for he neither hath, nor do, nor for the future can oblige any of them, but rather the contrary: but that they do fear what the consequence may be to themselves, should they yield in his case, as many of them have reason. And more, he showed me how this is rather to the wrong and prejudice of my Lord Chancellor; for that it is better for him to come to be tried before the Lords, where he can have right and make interest, than, when the Parliament is up, be committed by the King, and tried by a Court on purpose made by the King, of what Lords the King pleases, who have a mind to have his head. So that my Lord Cornbury himself his son, he tells me, hath moved, that if they have treason against my Lord of Clarendon, that they would specify it and send it up to the Lords, that he might come to his trial; so full of intrigues this business is! Walked a good while in the Temple church, observing the plainness of Selden's tomb, and how much better one of his executors hath, who is buried by him.[1]

23d. Busy till late preparing things to fortify myself and fellows against the Parliament; and particularly myself against what I fear is thought, that I have suppressed the Order of the Board by which the discharging the great ships at Chatham by tickets was directed; whereas, indeed, there was no such Order.

24th. (Lord's day.) For want of other of my clerks, sent to Mr. Gibbs, whom I never used till now, for the writing over of my little pocket Contract-book; and there I laboured till nine at night with him, in drawing up the history of all that hath passed concerning tickets, in order to the laying the whole, and clearing myself and Office, before Sir R. Brookes. And in this I took great pains, and then sent him away, and proceeded, and had W. Hewer come to me; and he and I till past twelve at night in the office. And he, which was a good service, did so inform me in the consequence of writing this report, and that what I said would not hold water, in denying this Board to have ever ordered the discharging out of the service whole ships by ticket, that I did alter my whole counsel,

[1] Selden's executors were Matthew Hale, John Vaughan, and Rowland Jewks, here alluded to, who was buried in the Temple Church in 1665. Vaughan survived till 1674, and had also sepulture there.

and fall to arm myself with good reasons to justify the Office in so doing, which hath been but rare. Having done this, I went, with great quiet in my mind, home, though vexed that so honest a business should bring me so much trouble; but mightily was pleased to find myself put out of my forner design; and so, after supper, to bed.

25th. This morning Sir W. Pen tells me that the House was very hot on Saturday last upon the business of liberty of speech in the House, and damned the vote in the beginning of the Long Parliament against it; so that he fears that there may be some bad thing which they have a mind to broach, which they dare not do without more security than they now have. God keep us, for things look mighty ill!

26th. By coach as far as the Temple, and there saw a new book [1] in folio, of all that suffered for the King in the late times, which I will buy. At my goldsmith's, bought a basin for my wife to give the Parson's child, to which the other day she was godmother. It cost me £10 14s. besides graving, which I do with the cypher of the name, Daniel Mills. After dinner came to me Mr. Warren, and there did tell me that he came to pay his debt to me for the kindness I did him in getting his last ship out, which I must also remember was a service to the King, though I did not tell him so. He would present me with sixty pieces of gold. I told him I would demand nothing of his promises, though they were much greater, nor would have thus much; but if he could afford to give me but fifty pieces, it should suffice me. So now he brought something in a paper, which since proves to be fifty pieces. This evening comes to me to my closet at the Office Sir John Chicheley, of his own accord, to tell me what he shall answer to the Committee, when, as he expects, he shall be examined about my Lord Sandwich; which is so little as will not hurt my Lord at all, I know.

27th. Mr. Pierce comes to me, and there, in general, tells me how the King is now fallen in and become a slave to the Duke of Buckingham, led by none but him, whom he, Mr. Pierce, swears he knows do hate the very person of the King, and would, as well as will, certainly ruin him. He do say, and I think is right, that the King do in this do the most ungrateful part of a master to a servant that ever was done, in this carriage of his, to my Lord Chancellor: that, it may be, the Chancellor may have faults, but none such as these they speak of: that he do now really fear that

---

[1] David Lloyd's *Memoirs of the Loyalists of Charles the First's time.*

all is going to ruin, for he says he hears that Sir W. Coventry hath been, just before his sickness, with the Duke of York, to ask his forgiveness and peace for what he had done; for that he never could foresee that what he meant so well, in the counselling to lay by the Chancellor, should come to this.

28th. To the King's playhouse, and there sat by my wife, and saw 'The Mistaken Beauty,' [1] which I never, I think, saw before, though an old play; and there is much in it that I like, though the name is but improper to it—at least, that name, it being also called 'The Liar,' which is proper enough.

29th. Waked about seven o'clock this morning with a noise I supposed I heard, near our chamber, of knocking, which, by and by, increased: and I, more awake, could disinguish it better. I then waked my wife, and both of us wondered at it and so lay a great while, while that increased, and at last heard it plainer, knocking, as if it were breaking down a window for people to get out; and then removing of stools and chairs; and plainly, by and by, going up and down our stairs. We lay, both of us, afraid; yet I would have rose, but my wife would not let me. Besides, I could not do it without making noise; and we did both conclude that thieves were in the house, but wondered what our people did, whom we thought either killed, or afraid, as we were. Thus we lay till the clock struck eight, and high day. At last, I removed my gown and slippers safely to the other side of the bed over my wife; and there safely rose, and put on my gown and breeches, and then, with a firebrand in my hand, safely opened the door, and saw nor heard anything. Then, with fear, I confess, went to the maid's chamber-door, and all quiet and safe. Called Jane up, and went down safely, and opened my chamber-door, where all well. Then more freely about, and to the kitchen, where the cook-maid up, and all safe. So up again, and when Jane came, and we demanded whether she heard no noise, she said, 'yes, but was afraid,' but rose with the other maid, and found nothing; but heard a noise in the great stack of chimneys that goes from Sir J. Minnes through our house. And so we sent, and their chimneys have been swept this morning, and the noise was that, and nothing else. It is one of the most extraordinary accidents in my life, and gives ground to think of Don Quixote's adventures, how people may be surprised;

---

[1] *The Mistaken Beauty, or, The Liar*, a comedy, taken from the *Menteur* of Corneille, printed, in 1661, by its second title only, and without any author's name.

and the more from an accident last night, that our young gib-cat did leap down our stairs from top to bottom, at two leaps, and frighted us, that we could not tell well whether it was the cat or a spirit, and do sometimes think this morning that the house might be haunted.

30th. To Arundel House, to the election of Officers [1] for the next year; where I was near being chosen of the Council, but am glad I was not, for I could not have attended, though, above all things, I could wish it, and do take it as a mighty respect to have been named there. Then to Cary House, a house now of entertainment, next my Lord Ashley's; where I have heretofore heard Common Prayer in the time of Dr. Mossum. Here was good company: among others, Dr. Wilkins, talking of the universal speech, of which he has a book coming out, did first inform me how man was certainly made for society, he being of all creatures the least armed for defence, and of all creatures in the world the young ones are not able to help themselves; and, he says, were it not for speech, man would be a very mean creature. But here, above all, I was pleased to see the person who had his blood taken out. He speaks well, and did this day give the Society a relation thereof in Latin, saying that he finds himself much better since, and as a new man, but he is cracked a little in his head, though he speaks very reasonably, and very well. He had but 20*s.* for his suffering it, and is to have the same again tried upon him: the first sound man that ever had it tried on him in England, and but one that we hear of in France. Saw a pretty deception of the sight by a glass with water poured into it, with a stick standing up with three balls of wax upon it, one distant from the other. How these balls did seem double and disappear one after another, mighty pretty. My Lord Anglesey told me this day that he did believe the House of Commons would, the next week, yield to the Lords; but, speaking with others this day, they conclude they will not, but that rather the King will accommodate it by committing my Lord Clarendon himself. I remember what Mr. Evelyn said, that he did believe we should soon see ourselves fall into a Commonwealth again.

December 1st. (Lord's day.) I to church: and in our pew there sat a great lady, whom I afterwards understood to be my Lady Carlisle,[2] a very fine woman indeed in person.

---

[1] Of the Royal Society.
[2] Anne, daughter of Edward, first Lord Howard of Escrick, wife to Charles, first Earl of Carlisle.

2d. The Lords' answer is come down to the Commons, that they are not satisfied in the Commons' Reasons: and so the Commons are hot, and like to sit all day upon the business what to do herein, most thinking that they will remonstrate against the Lords. Thence to Lord Crewe's, and there dined with him; where, after dinner, he took me aside and bewailed the condition of the nation, now the King and his brother are at a distance about this business of the Chancellor, and the two Houses differing. And he do believe that there are so many about the King like to be concerned and troubled by the Parliament, that they will get him to dissolve or prorogue the Parliament; and the rather, for that the King is likely, by this good husbandry of the Treasury, to get out of debt, and the Parliament is likely to give no money. Among other things, my Lord Crewe did tell me, with grief, that he hears that the King of late hath not dined nor supped with the Queen, as he used of late to do. To Westminster Hall, where my cousin Roger tells me of the high vote of the Commons this afternoon, that the proceedings of the Lords in the case of my Lord Clarendon are an obstruction to justice, and of ill precedent to future times.

3d. To Sir W. Coventry's, the first time I have seen him at his new house since he came to lodge there. He tells me of the vote for none of the House to be of the Commission for the Bill of Accounts; which he thinks is so great a disappointment to Birch and others that expected to be of it, that he thinks, could it have been foreseen, there would not have been any Bill at all. We hope it will be the better for all that are to account; it being likely that the men, being few, and not of the House, will hear reason. The main business I went about was about Gilsthrop, Sir W. Batten's clerk; who, being upon his death-bed, and now dead, hath offered to make discoveries of the disorders of the Navy and of £65,000 damage to the King: which made mighty noise in the Commons' House; and Members appointed to go to him, which they did; but nothing to the purpose got from him, but complaints of false musters, and ships being refitted with victuals and stores at Plymouth after they were fitted from other ports; but all this to no purpose, nor more than we know, and will own. But the best is, that this loggerhead should say this, that understands nothing of the Navy, nor ever would; and hath particularly blemished his master by name among us. I told Sir W. Coventry of my letter to Sir R. Brookes, and his answer to me. He advises me, in what

I write to him, to be as short as I can, and obscure, saving in things fully plain; for all that he do is to make mischief; and that the greatest wisdom in dealing with the Parliament in the world is to say little, and let them get out what they can by force: which I shall observe. He declared to me much of his mind to be ruled by his own measures, and not to go so far as many would have him to the ruin of my Lord Chancellor, and for which they do endeavour to do what they can against Sir W. Coventry. 'But,' says he, 'I have done my do in helping to get him out of the administration of things, for which he is not fit; but for his life or estate I will have nothing to say to it: besides that, my duty to my master the Duke of York is such, that I will perish before I will do anything to displease or disoblige him, where the very necessity of the kingdom do not in my judgment call me.' Home; and there met W. Batelier, who tells me the first great news, that my Lord Chancellor is fled this day, and left a paper behind him [1] for the House of Lords, telling them the reason of his retiring, complaining of a design for his ruin. But the paper I must get: only the thing at present is great, and will put the King and Commons to some new counsels certainly. Sir Richard Ford told us this evening an odd story of the baseness of the late Lord Mayor, Sir W. Bolton, in cheating the poor of the City, out of the collections made for the people that were burned, of £1800; of which he can give no account, and in which he hath forsworn himself plainly, so as the Court of Aldermen have sequestered him from their Court till he do bring in an account. He says, also, that this day hath been made appear to them that the Keeper of Newgate hath, at this day, made his house the only nursery of rogues, prostitutes, pickpockets, and thieves, in the world; where they were bred and entertained, and the whole society met: and that, for the sake of the Sheriffs, they durst not this day commit him, for fear of making him let out the prisoners, but are fain to go by artifice to deal with him. He tells me, also, speaking of the new street [2] that is to be made from Guildhall down to Cheapside, that the ground is already, most of it, bought. And tells me of one particular, of a man that hath a piece of ground lying in the very middle of the street that must be; which, when the street is cut out of it, there will remain ground enough, of each side, to build a house to front the street. He demanded £700 for

[1] This paper, which was ordered to be burnt, has been many times printed; and sometimes under the title of 'News from Dunkirk House' (see Somers's *Tracts*, vol. viii).   [2] King Street.

the ground, and to be excused paying anything for the melioration of the rest of his ground that he was to keep. The Court consented to give him £700, only not to abate him the consideration: which the man denied, but told them, and so they agreed, that he would excuse the City the £700, that he might have the benefit of the melioration without paying anything for it. So much some will get by having the City burned! Ground, by this means, that was not 4*d.* a foot before, will now, when houses are built, be worth 15*s.* a foot. But he tells me of the common standard now reckoned on between man and man, in places where there is no alteration of circumstances, but only the houses burnt: there the ground, which, with a house on it, did yield £100 a year, is now reputed worth £33 6*s.* 8*d.*; and that this is the common market-price between one man and another, made upon a good and moderate medium.

4th. I hear that the House of Lords did send down the paper which my Lord Clarendon left behind him, directed to the Lords, to be seditious and scandalous; and the Commons have voted that it be burned by the hands of the hangman, and that the King be desired to agree to it. I do hear, also, that they have desired the King to use means to stop his escape out of the nation.[1] This day Gilsthrop is buried, who hath made all the late discourse of the great discovery of £65,000, of which the King hath been wronged.

5th. This day, not for want, but for good husbandry, I sent my father, by his desire, six pair of my old shoes, which fit him, and are good; yet, methought, it was a thing against my mind to have him wear my old things.

6th. With Sir J. Minnes to the Duke of York, the first time that I have seen him, or we waited on him, since his sickness; and, blessed be God! he is not at all the worse for the small-pox, but is only a little weak yet. We did much business with him, and so parted. My Lord Anglesey told me how my Lord Northampton[2] brought in a Bill into the House of Lords yesterday, under the name of a Bill for the Honour and Privilege of the House and Mercy to my Lord Clarendon: which, he told me, he opposed, saying that he was a man accused of treason by the House of Commons; and mercy was not proper for him, having not been tried yet, and so

---

[1] A copy of the original order for the apprehension of the Earl of Clarendon, signed by the Duke of York, and directed to Sir John Bramston, is given in *The Autobiography of Sir John Bramston*, p. 257 (Camden Society).

[2] James Compton, third Earl of Northampton, Lord Lieutenant of Warwickshire, and Constable of the Tower: *ob.* 1681.

no mercy needful for him.   However, the Duke of Buckingham
and others did desire that the Bill might be read; and it was for
banishing my Lord Clarendon from all his Majesty's dominions,
and that it should be treason to have him found in any of them: the
thing is only a thing of vanity, and to insult over him.   By and by
home with Sir J. Minnes, who tells me that my Lord Clarendon did
go away in a Custom-house boat, and is now at Calais: and, I
confess, nothing seems to hang more heavy than his leaving of this
unfortunate paper behind him, that hath angered both Houses, and
hath, I think, reconciled them in that which otherwise would have
broke them in pieces.   So that I do hence, and from Sir W.
Coventry's late example and doctrine to me, learn that on these
sorts of occasions there is nothing like silence; it being seldom any
wrong to a man to say nothing, but for the most part, it is to say
anything.   Sir J. Minnes told me a story of my Lord Cottingdon,
who, wanting a son, intended to make his nephew his heir, a
country boy; but did alter his mind upon the boy's being persuaded
by another young heir, in roguery, to crow like a cock at my
Lord's table, much company being there, and the boy having a
great trick at doing that perfectly.   My Lord bade them take away
that fool from the table, and so gave over the thoughts of making
him his heir, from this piece of folly.   To White Hall to the Council chamber, where I was summoned about the business of paying
of the seamen; where I heard my Lord Anglesey put to it by Sir W.
Coventry before the King for altering the course set by the
Council; which he, like a wise man, did answer in few words, that
he had already sent to alter it according to the Council's method,
and so stopped it, whereas many words would have set the Commissioners of the Treasury on fire, who, I perceive, were prepared
for it.   Captain Cocke comes to me; and, among other discourse,
tells me that he is told that an impeachment against Sir W. Coventry
will be brought in very soon.   He tells me that even those that
are against my Lord Chancellor and the Court, in the House, do
not trust nor agree one with another.   He tells me that my Lord
Chancellor went away about ten at night, on Saturday last, at
Westminster; and took boat at Westminster, and thence by a vessel
to Calais, where he believes he now is: and that the Duke of York
and Mr. Wren knew of it, and that himself did know of it on
Sunday morning: that on Sunday his coach, and people about it,
went to Twickenham, and the world thought that he had been
there: that nothing but this unhappy paper hath undone him, and

that he doubts that this paper hath lost him everywhere: that his withdrawing do reconcile things so far as, he thinks, the heat of their fury will be over, and that all will be made well between the two [royal] brothers: that Holland do endeavour to persuade the King of France to break peace with us: that the Dutch will, without doubt, have sixty sail of ships out the next year; so knows not what will become of us, but hopes the Parliament will find money for us to have a fleet.

7th. Somebody told me this day that they hear that Thomson, with the wooden leg, and Wildman,[1] the Fifth-Monarchy man, a great creature of the Duke of Buckingham's, are in nomination to be Commissioners, among others, upon the Bill of Accounts.

8th. (Lord's day.) To White Hall, where I saw the Duchess of York, in a fine dress of second mourning for her mother,[2] being black, edged with ermine, go to make her first visit to the Queen since the Duke of York was sick; and by and by, she being returned, the Queen came and visited her. But it was pretty to observe that Sir W. Coventry and I, walking an hour and more together in the Matted Gallery, he observed, and so did I, how the Duchess, soon as she spied him, turned her head a-one side. Here he and I walked thus long, which we have not done a great while before. Our discourse was upon everything: the unhappiness of having our matters examined by people that understand them not; that it is better for us in the Navy to have men that do understand the whole, and that are not passionate; that we that have taken the most pains are called upon to answer for all crimes, while those that, like Sir W. Batten and Sir J. Minnes, did sit and do nothing, do lie still without any trouble; that, if it were to serve the King and kingdom again in a war, neither of us could do more, though upon this experience we might do better than we did; that the commanders, the gentlemen that could never be brought to order, but undid all, are now the men that find fault and abuse others; that it had been much better for the King to have given Sir J. Minnes and Sir W. Batten £1000 a year to have sat still, than to have had them in this business this war; that the serving a Prince that minds not his business is most unhappy for them that serve him well, and an

[1] Major Wildman, who had been an agitator in Cromwell's army, and had opposed his protectorship. After he regained his liberty he returned to his old habits, and was repeatedly engaged in fomenting sedition.
[2] Frances, daughter of Sir Thomas Aylesbury, Bart., Master of Requests to Charles I, second wife of Lord Chancellor Clarendon.

unhappiness so great that he declares he will never have more to do with a war, under him. That he hath papers which do flatly contradict the Duke of Albemarle's narrative, and that he hath been with the Duke of Albemarle and showed him them, to prevent his falling into another like fault; that the Duke of Albemarle seems to be able to answer them, but he thinks that the Duke of Albemarle and the Prince are contented to let their narratives sleep (they being not only contradictory in some things, as he observed about the business of the Duke of Albemarle's being to follow the Prince upon dividing the fleet, in case the enemy come out, but neither of them to be maintained in others). That the business the other night of my Lord Anglesey at the Council was happily got over for my Lord, by his dexterous silencing it, and the rest not urging it further; forasmuch as, had the Duke of Buckingham come in time enough and had got it by the end, he would have toused [1] him in it; Sir W. Coventry telling me that my Lord Anglesey did, with such impudence, maintain the quarrel against the Commons and some of the Lords, in the business of my Lord Clarendon, that he believes there are enough would be glad but of this occasion to be revenged of him. He tells me that he hears some of the Thomsons are like to be of the Commission for the Accounts, and Wildman, which he much wonders at, as having been a false fellow to everybody, and in prison most of the time since the King's coming in. But he do tell me that the House is in such a condition that nobody can tell what to make of them, and, he thinks, they were never in before; that everybody leads, and nobody follows; and that he do now think that, since a great many are defeated in their expectation of being of the Commission, now they would put it into such hands as it shall get no credit from: for, if they do look to the bottom and see the King's case, they think they are then bound to give the King money; whereas, they would be excused from that, and therefore endeavour to make this business of the Accounts to signify little. Comes Captain Cocke to me; and there he tells me, to my great satisfaction, that Sir Robert Brookes did dine with him today; and that he told him, speaking of me, that he would make me the darling of the House of Commons, so much he is satisfied concerning me. And this Cocke did tell me that I might give him thanks for it; and I do think it may do me good, for he do happen to be held a considerable person, for a young man, both for sobriety and ability.

[1] Equivalent to teased, handled roughly.

9th. Comes Sir G. Carteret to talk with me; who seems to think himself safe as to his particular, but do doubt what will become of the whole kingdom, things being so broke in pieces.   He tells me that the King himself did the other day very particularly tell the whole story of my Lord Sandwich's not following the Dutch ships, with which he is charged; and shows the reasons of it to be the only good course he could have taken, and do discourse it very knowingly.   This I am glad of, though, as the King is now, his favour, for aught I see, serves very little in stead at this day, but rather is an argument against a man; and the King do not concern himself to relieve or justify anybody, but is wholly negligent of everybody's concernment.   This morning I was troubled with my Lord Hinchingbroke's sending to borrow £200 of me; but I did answer that I had none, nor could borrow any; for I am resolved I will not be undone for anybody, though I would do much for my Lord Sandwich—for it is to answer a bill of exchange of his—but not ruin myself.   Called at Cade's, the stationer, where he tells me how my Lord Gerard is troubled for several things in the House of Commons, and in one wherein himself is concerned; and, it seems, this Lord is a very proud and wicked man, and the Parliament is likely to order him.[1]

10th. The King did send a message to the House today, that he would adjourn them on the 17th instant to February; by which time, at least, I shall have more respite to prepare things on my own behalf, and the Office, against their return.   Met Mr. Hingston,[2] the organist, walking, and I walked with him; and, asking him many questions, I do find that he can no more give an intelligible answer to a man that is not a great master in his art, than another man.   And this confirms me that it is only the want of an ingenious man that is master in music, to bring music to a certainty, and ease in composition.   I home, having finished my letter to Commissioner Middleton, who is now coming up to town from Portsmouth, to enter upon his Surveyorship.

11th. Attended the Duke of York, as we are wont, who is now grown pretty well, and goes up and down White Hall, and this night will be at the Council.   Here I met Rolt and Sir John

---

[1] *Sic* original.

[2] John Hingston, a scholar of Orlando Gibbons, after being in the service of Charles I, became organist to Cromwell for a pension of £100, and instructed his daughters in music.

Chicheley, and Harris, the player, and talked of 'Catiline,' [1] which is to be suddenly acted at the King's House; and all agree that it cannot be well done at that house, there not being good actors enough: and Burt [2] acts Cicero, which they all conclude he will not be able to do well.   The King gives them £500 for robes, there being, as they say, to be sixteen scarlet robes.   Comes Sir W. Warren to talk about some business of his and mine: and he, I find, would have me not to think that the Parliament, in the mind they are in, and having so many good offices in their view to dispose of, will leave any of the King's officers in, but will rout all, though I am likely to escape as well as any, if any can escape; and I think he is in the right, and I do look for it accordingly.   Then I away to the office, and thither comes Sir W. Pen, and he there told me what passed today with him in the Committee, by my Lord Sandwich's breaking bulk of the prizes; and it do seem to me that he hath left it pretty well understood by them, he saying that what my Lord did was done at the desire, and with the advice, of the chief officers of the fleet, and that it was no more than admirals heretofore have done in like cases; which, if it be true that he said it, is very well.

12th.   To the Duke of York's House, and saw 'The Tempest,' and the house very full.   But I could take little pleasure more than the play, from not being able to look about, for fear of being seen. Here only I saw a French lady in the pit, with a tunic, just like one of ours, only a handkercher about her neck; but this fashion for a woman did not look decent.   Thence walked to my bookseller, and he did give me a list of the twenty who were mentioned for the Commission in Parliament for the Accounts: and it is strange that of the twenty the Parliament could not think fit to choose their nine, but were fain to add three that were not in the list of the twenty, they being many of them factious people and ringleaders in the late troubles; so that Sir John Talbot did fly out and was very hot in the business of Wildman's being named, and took notice how he was entertained in the bosom of the Duke of Buckingham, a Privy Councillor; and that it was fit to be observed by the House, and punished.   The men that I know of the nine I like very well; that is, Mr. Pierrepont, Lord Brereton,[3] and Sir William

[1] A tragedy by Ben Jonson.   [2] Nicholas Burt.
[3] William, third Lord Brereton, of Leaghlin, in Ireland, M.P. for Cheshire. He disposed of his estates in that county, on account of the exigencies of the times, and his father's losses, incurred in the cause of Charles I.   He was educated at Breda, esteemed an accomplished and amiable nobleman, and was one of the founders of the Royal Society.   *Ob.* 1679.

Turner; and I do think the rest are so, too, but such as will not be able to do this business as it ought to be, to do any good with. Here I did also see their votes against my Lord Chief Justice Keeling, that his proceedings were illegal, and that he was a contemner of Magna Charta (the great preserver of our lives, freedoms, and properties), and an introduction to arbitrary government; which is very high language, and of the same sound with that in the year 1640. This day my Lord Chancellor's letter was burned at the 'Change.

13th. To Westminster, to the Parliament-door, to speak with Roger: and here I saw my Lord Keeling go into the House to the bar, to have his business heard by the whole House today; and a great crowd of people to stare upon him. Here I hear that the Lords' Bill for banishing and disabling my Lord Clarendon from bearing any office, or being in the King's dominions, and it being made felony for any to correspond with him but his own children, is brought to the Commons. But they will not agree to it, being not satisfied with that as sufficient, but will have a Bill of Attainder brought in against him: but they make use of this against the Lords, that they, that would not think there was cause enough to commit him without hearing, will have him banished without hearing. By and by comes my cousin Roger to me, he being not willing to be in the House at the business of my Lord Keeling, lest he should be called upon to complain against him for his abusing him at Cambridge, very wrongfully and shamefully, but not to his reproach, but to the Chief Justice's in the end, when all the world cried shame upon him for it. Among other news, it is now fresh that the King of Portugal [1] is deposed, and his brother made King; [2] and that my Lord Sandwich is gone from Madrid with great honour to Lisbon, to make up, at this juncture, a peace to the advantage, as the Spaniard would have it, of Spain. I wish it may be for my Lord's honour, if it be so; but it seems my Lord is in mighty estimation in Spain. After dinner comes Mr. Moore, and he and I alone a while, he telling me my Lord Sandwich's credit is like to be undone, if the bill of £200 my Lord Hinchingbroke wrote to me about be not paid tomorrow, and that, if I do not help him about it, they have no way but to let it be protested. So, finding that Creed hath supplied them with £150 in their straits, and that this is no bigger sum, I am very willing to serve my Lord, though not in this kind; but yet I will endeavour to get this done for them,

[1] Alfonso VI.   [2] Don Henrique.

and the rather because of some plate that was lodged the other day with me, by my Lady's order, which may be in part of security for my money. This do trouble me; but yet it is good luck that the sum is no bigger. With my cousin Roger to Westminster Hall, and there we met the House rising: and they have voted my Lord Chief Justice Keeling's proceedings illegal; but that, out of particular respect to him, and the mediation of a great many, they have resolved to proceed no further against him.

15th. (Lord's day.) Up, and to church, where I heard a German preach in a tone hard to be understood, but yet an extraordinary good sermon, and wholly to my great content. In the evening comes Mrs. Turner to visit us, who hath been long sick, and she sat and supped with us—her son Frank being there, now upon the point of his going to the East Indies. I did give him 'Lex Mercatoria,' [1] and my wife my old pair of tweezers, which are pretty, and my book an excellent one for him. Most of our talk was of the great discourse the world hath against my Lady Batten, for getting her husband to give her all, and disinherit his eldest son; though the truth is, the son, as they say, did play the knave with his father when time was, and the father no great matter better with him, nor with other people also.

16th. To several places, to pay what I owed. Among others, to my mercer, to pay for my fine camelott cloak, which costs me, the very stuff, almost £6; and also a velvet coat—the outside cost me above £8. And so to Westminster, where I find the House mighty busy upon a petition against my Lord Gerard, which lays heavy things to his charge, of his abusing the King in his Guards; and very hot the House is upon it.

17th. This day I do hear at White Hall that the Duke of Monmouth is sick, and in danger of the smallpox.

18th. To my goldsmith's to look after the providing of £60 for Mr. Moore, towards the answering of my Lord Sandwich's bill of exchange, he being come to be contented with my lending him £60 in part of it, which pleases me; and this, which I do do, I hope to secure out of the plate which was delivered into my custody of my Lord's, which I did get Mr. Stokes, the goldsmith, last night to weigh at my house, and there is enough to secure £100.

19th. To the office, where Commissioner Middleton first took his place at the Board as Surveyor of the Navy; and indeed I think

[1] The work of Gerard de Malynes, called *Lex Mercatoria, or The Ancient Law Merchant*. London, 1622.

will be an excellent officer, I am sure much beyond what his predecessor was. With Sir W. Pen in his coach to Guildhall, he to speak with Sheriff Gauden—I only for company; and did here look up and down this place, where I have not been before since the fire; and I see that the city are going on apace in the building of Guildhall.[1] This evening the King, by message, which he never did before, hath passed several bills, among others that for the Accounts, and for banishing my Lord Chancellor, and hath adjourned the House to February; at which I am glad, hoping in this time to get leisure to state my Tangier Accounts, and to prepare better for the Parliament's inquiries. Here I hear how the House of Lords, with great severity, if not tyranny, have proceeded against poor Carr, who only erred in the manner of the presenting his petition against my Lord Gerard, it being first printed before it was presented; which was, it seems, by Colonel Sands's[2] going into the country, into whose hands he had put it: the poor man is ordered to stand in the pillory two or three times, and to have his ears cut, and be imprisoned I know not how long.[3] But it is believed that the Commons, when they meet, will not be well pleased with it; and they have no reason, I think.

20th. To Sir W. Pen's with Sir R. Ford, and there was Sir D. Gauden, and there we only talked of sundry things; and I have found of late, by discourse, that the present sort of government is looked upon as a sort of government that we never had yet—that is to say, a King and House of Commons against the House of Lords. For so indeed it is, though neither of the two first care a fig for one another, nor the third for them both, only the Bishops are afraid of losing ground, as I believe they will. So home to my poor wife, who is in mighty pain, and her face miserably swelled so as I was frighted to see it.

21st. The Nonconformists are mighty high, and their meetings frequented and connived at: and they do expect to have their day now soon, for my Lord of Buckingham is a declared friend to them, and even to the Quakers, who had very good words the other day from the King himself. And, what is more, the Archbishop

[1] Guildhall was not destroyed by the fire, as Pepys seems to intimate.
[2] Samuel Sandys, of Ombersley, in Worcestershire, which county he then represented in Parliament. He was ancestor of the Lords Sandys, and died in 1685.
[3] The Journals of the day do not inform us that William Carr was adjudged to lose his ears. He was fined £1,000, and ordered to stand in the pillory three times; and the libel was burnt by the common hangman.

of Canterbury [1] is called no more to the Cabal,[2] nor, by the way, Sir W. Coventry; which I am sorry for, the Cabal at present being, as he says, the King, and Duke of Buckingham, and Lord Keeper, the Duke of Albemarle, and Privy Seal. The Bishops, differing from the King in the late business in the House of Lords, have caused this and what is like to follow; for everybody is encouraged nowadays to speak, and even to preach, as I have heard one of them, as bad things against them as ever in the year 1640, which is a strange change. Home to sit with my wife, who is a little better, and her cheek assuaged. I read to her out of 'The History of Algiers,' which is mighty pretty reading, and did discourse alone about my sister Pall's match, which is now on foot with one Jackson, another nephew of Mr. Phillips's, to whom the former hath left his estate.

22d. (Lord's day.) Up, and my wife, poor wretch! still in pain. To my chamber, and thither came to me Willett with an errand from her mistress, and this time I first did give her a little kiss, she being a very pretty humoured girl, and so one that I do love mightily.

23d. To the Commissioners of the Treasury, and there I had a dispute before them with Sir Stephen Fox, about our orders for money, who is very angry, but I value it not. But, Lord! to see with what folly my Lord Albemarle do speak in this business would make a man wonder at the good fortune of such a fool. I to the Exchange, and there I saw Carr stand in the pillory for the business of my Lord Gerard, which is supposed will make a hot business in the House of Commons, when they shall come to sit again, the Lords having ordered this with great injustice, as all people think, his only fault being his printing his petition before, by accident, his petition be read in the House. I hear by Creed

---

[1] Gilbert Sheldon.

[2] This use of the word, which has already occurred in the same sense (see 14th October 1665), is earlier than its application by Burnet (*History of Own Time*) in 1672, when he states, in reference to the newly formed government, that 'Cabal' proved a technical word, every letter in it being the first letter of those five—Clifford, Ashley, Buckingham, Arlington, and Lauderdale. It is obvious that the names given by Pepys do not form the word. In the *Dream of the Cabal*, anno 1672, the Cabal is made to consist of *seven* members, thus:

'Methought there met the grand Cabal of Seven
(Odd numbers, some men say, do best please Heaven).'

Burnet's words have often been mistaken. He noticed a coincidence, which many have taken to be the origin of the term.

that the Bishops of Winchester [1] and of Rochester,[2] and the Dean of the Chapel, and some other great prelates, are suspended: and a cloud upon the Archbishop ever since the late business in the House of Lords; and I believe it will be a heavy blow to the clergy. I bought a sermon of Dr. Lloyd's,[3] as well writ and as good, against the Church of Rome, as ever I read; but, Lord! how Hollyard, poor man, was taken with it. This day, at the 'Change, Creed showed me Mr. Coleman, of whom my wife hath so good an opinion, and says he is as very a rogue for women as any in the world; which did disquiet me, like a fool, and run in my mind a great while.

24th. By coach to St. James's, it being about six at night; my design being to see the ceremonies, this night being the eve of Christmas, at the Queen's chapel. I got in almost up to the rail, and with a great deal of patience stayed from nine at night to two in the morning, in a very great crowd; and there expected, but found nothing extraordinary, there being nothing but a high mass. The Queen was there, and some ladies. But, Lord! what an odd thing it was for me to be in a crowd of people, here a footman, there a beggar, here a fine lady, there a zealous poor papist, and here a Protestant, two or three together, come to see the show. I was afeard of my pocket being picked very much. Their music very good indeed, but their service, I confess, too frivolous, that there can be no zeal go along with it; and I do find by them themselves that they do run over their beads with one hand, and point, and play, and talk, and make signs with the other in the midst of their mass. But all things very rich and beautiful; and I see the papists have the wit, most of them, to bring cushions to kneel on, which I wanted, and was mighty troubled to kneel. All being done, I was sorry for my coming, and missing of what I expected; which was, to have had a child born and dressed there, and a great deal of do: but we broke up, and nothing like it done, and there I left people receiving the Sacrament: and the Queen gone, and ladies; only my Lady Castlemaine, who looked prettily in her night-clothes. So took my coach, which waited, and through Covent Garden, to set down two gentlemen and a lady, who came thither to see also, and did make mighty mirth in their talk of the folly of this religion.

[1] George Morley.   [2] John Dolben.
[3] A sermon entitled *Papists no Catholics, and Popery no Christianity*, published in 1667, by William Lloyd, who became Bishop of Lichfield and Coventry, then of St. Asaph, and lastly of Worcester, and died in 1717, aged ninety.

Drank some burnt wine at the Rose tavern door, while the constables came, and two or three bellmen went by.

25th. Being a fine, light, moonshine morning, home round the City, and stopped and dropped money at five or six places, which I was the willinger to do, it being Christmas day, and so home, and there find my wife in bed, and Jane and the maid making pies. So I to bed. Rose about nine, and to church, and there heard a dull sermon of Mr. Mills, but a great many fine people at church; and so home. Wife and girl and I alone at dinner—a good Christmas dinner. My wife reading to me 'The History of the Drummer of Mr. Mompesson,' which is a strange story of spies, and worth reading indeed. In the evening comes Mr. Pelling, and he sat and supped with us; and very good company, he reciting to us many copies of good verses of Dr. Wilde's, who writ 'Iter Boreale.'

26th. To the Swan, and by chance met Mr. Spicer and another 'Chequer clerk, and there made them drink. At my bookseller's, and there bought Mr. Harrington's works, 'Oceana,' etc., and two other books, which cost me £4. Home, and there eat a bit, and then with my wife to the King's playhouse, and there saw 'The Surprisal,' [1] which did not please me today, the actors not pleasing me; and especially Nell's acting of a serious part, which she spoils. I hear this day that Mrs. Stuart do at this day keep a great court at Somerset House with her husband, the Duke of Richmond, she being visited for her beauty's sake by people, as the Queen is, at nights; and they say also that she is likely to go to Court again, and there put my Lady Castlemaine's nose out of joint.

27th. A Committee of Tangier met, the Duke of York there: and there I did discourse over to them their condition as to money, which they were all mightily, as I could desire, satisfied with, but the Duke of Albemarle, who takes the part of the Guards against us in our supplies of money; which is an odd consideration for a dull, heavy blockhead as he is, understanding no more of either than a goose. But the ability and integrity of Sir W. Coventry in all the King's concernments I do and must admire. After the Committee up, I and Sir W. Coventry walked an hour in the gallery, talking over many businesses, and he tells me how some of his enemies at the Duke of York's had got the Duke of York's commission for the Commissioners of his estate changed, and he and Brouncker and Povy left out: that this they did do to disgrace him and impose upon him at this time, but that he, though he values

[1] A comedy by Sir Robert Howard.

not the thing, did go and tell the Duke of York what he heard, and that he did not think that he had given him any reason to do this, out of his belief that he would not be as faithful and serviceable to him as the best of those that have got him put out. Whereupon the Duke of York did say that it arose only from his not knowing whether now he would have time to regard his affairs; and that if he should, he would put him into the commission with his own hand, though the commission be passed. He answered that he had been faithful to him, and done him good service therein so long as he could attend to it; and if he had been able to have attended it more, he would not have enriched himself with such and such estates as my Lord Chancellor hath got, that did properly belong to his Royal Highness, as being forfeited to the King, and so by the King's gift given to the Duke of York. Hereupon the Duke of York did call for the commission, and hath since put him in. He tells me that the business of getting the Duchess of Richmond to Court is broke off, her husband not suffering it; and thereby great trouble is brought among the people that endeavoured it and thought they had compassed it.[1] And, Lord! to think that at this time the King should mind no other cares but these! He tells me that my Lord of Canterbury is a mighty stout man, and a man of a brave, high spirit, and cares not for this disfavour that he is under at Court, knowing that the King cannot take away his profits during his life, and therefore do not value it.

28th. With my wife and girl to the King's House, and there saw 'The Mad Couple,' which is but an ordinary play; but only Nell's and Hart's mad parts are most excellent done, but especially hers: which makes it a miracle to me, to think how ill she do any serious part, as the other day, just like a fool or changeling; and in a mad part do beyond imitation almost. It pleased us mightily to see the natural affection of a poor woman, the mother of one of the children brought on the stage: the child crying, she by force got upon the stage, and took up her child and carried it away off of the stage from Hart. Many fine faces here today. I am told today, which troubles me, that great complaint is made upon the 'Change, among our merchants, that the very Ostend little pickaroon[2]

---

[1] Considerable light is thrown upon these passages regarding the Duke and Duchess of Richmond and Archbishop Sheldon, which are here obscure, by Burnet, in the *History of his own Times*, vol. i, p. 436. 8vo edition.
[2] From the Spanish *picaron*, a rogue or villain. It must here be taken to mean privateer.

men-of-war do offer violence to our merchantmen, and search them, beat our masters, and plunder them upon pretence of carrying Frenchmen's goods.

29th. (Lord's day.) At night comes Mrs. Turner to see us; and there, among other talk, she tells me that Mr. William Pen, who is lately come over from Ireland, is a Quaker again, or some very melancholy thing; that he cares for no company, nor comes into any: which is a pleasant thing, after his being abroad so long, and his father such a hypocritical rogue, and at this time an atheist.

30th. Sir G. Carteret and I alone did talk of the ruinous condition we are in, the King being going to put out of the Council so many able men, such as my Lord Anglesey, Ashley, Hollis, Secretary Morrice (to bring in Mr. Trevor),[1] and the Archbishop of Canterbury and my Lord Bridgewater. He tells me that this is true, only the Duke of York do endeavour to hinder it, and the Duke of York himself did tell him so; that the King and the Duke of York do not in company disagree, but are friendly; but that there is a core in their hearts, he doubts, which is not to be easily removed. For these men so suffer only for their constancy to the Chancellor, or at least from the King's ill will against him: that they do now all they can to vilify the clergy, and do abuse Rochester [Dolben], and so do raise scandals, all that is possible, against other of the Bishops. He do suggest that something is intended for the Duke of Monmouth, and, it may be, against the Queen also; that we are in no manner sure against an invasion the next year; that the Duke of Buckingham do rule all now, and the Duke of York comes indeed to the Cabal, but signifies little there. That this new faction do not endure, nor the King, Sir W. Coventry; but yet that he is so useful that they cannot be without him; but that he is not now called to the Cabal. That my Lord of Buckingham, Bristol, and Arlington do seem to agree in these things; but that they do not in their hearts trust one another, but do drive several ways, all of them. In short, he do bless himself that he is no more concerned in matters now; and the hopes he hath of being at liberty, when his accounts are over, to retire into the country. That he do give over the kingdom for wholly lost. Meeting with Mr. Cooling, I with him by coach to the Wardrobe, where I never was since the fire in Hatton Garden: and he tells me that he fears that my Lord Sandwich will suffer much by Mr. Townsend's being

[1] John Trevor, knighted by Charles II, who made him Secretary of State, 1668, which office he held till his death, in 1672.

untrue to him, he being now unable to give the Commissioners of the Treasury an account of his money received by many thousands of pounds, which I am troubled for. I met with Mr. Cooling at the Temple gate after I had been at both my booksellers, and there laid out several pounds in new books now against the new year. From the 'Change, where I met with Captain Cocke, who would have borrowed money of me, but I had the grace to deny him. I with Cocke and Mr. Temple (whose wife was just now brought to bed of a boy, but he seems to be not at all taken with it, which is a strange consideration how others do rejoice to have a child born) to Sir G. Carteret's, in Lincoln's Inn Fields, and there did dine together, there being there, among other company, Mr. Attorney Montagu,[1] and his fine lady, a fine woman. After dinner I did understand from my Lady Jemimah that her brother Hinchingbroke's business was to be ended this day, as she thinks, towards his match,[2] and they do talk here of their intent to buy themselves some new clothes against the wedding, which I am very glad of. Thence with Sir Philip Carteret [3] to the King's playhouse, there to see 'Love's Cruelty,' [4] an old play, but which I have not seen before; and in the first act Orange Moll came to me, with one of our porters by my house, to tell me that Mrs. Pierce and Knipp did dine at my house today, and that I was desired to come home. So I went out presently, and by coach home, and they were gone away: so, after a very little stay with my wife, I took coach again and to the King's playhouse again, and come in the fourth act; and it proves to me a very silly play, and to everybody else, as far as I could judge. But the jest is, that here telling Moll how I had lost my journey, she told me that Mrs. Knipp was in the house, and so shows me to her; and I went to her and sat out the play, and then with her to Mrs. Manuel's, where Mrs. Pierce was, and her boy and girl; and here I did hear Mrs. Manuel and one of the Italians, her gallant, sing well. But yet I confess I am not delighted so much with it as to admire it: for, not understanding the words, I lose the benefit of the vocalities of the music, and it proves only instrumental; and therefore was more pleased to hear Knipp sing two or three little English things that I understood,

---

[1] William Montagu, afterwards Lord Chief Baron. His wife was Mary, daughter of Sir John Aubrey, Bart.

[2] With Lady Anne Boyle.

[3] Sir G. Carteret's eldest son, mentioned before, who had been knighted.

[4] A tragedy by James Shirley.

though the composition of the other, and performance, was very fine. Thence to my bookseller's and paid for the books I had bought, and away home, where I told my wife where I had been. But she was as mad as a devil, and nothing but ill words between us all the evening while we sat at cards—W. Hewer and the girl by—even to gross ill words, which I was troubled for. But I do see that I must use policy to keep her spirit down, and to give her no offence by my being with Knipp and Pierce, of which, though she will not own it, yet she is heartily jealous. At last it ended in few words and my silence, and so to supper and to bed without one word one to another. This day I did carry money out, and paid several debts. Among others my tailor and shoemaker and draper, Sir W. Turner, who begun to talk of the Commission of Accounts, wherein he is one; but though they are the greatest people that ever were in the nation as to power, and like to be our judges, yet I did never speak one word to him of desiring favour or bidding him joy in it, but did answer him to what he said, and do resolve to stand or fall by my silent preparing to answer whatever can be laid to me, and that will be my best proceeding, I think. This day I got a little rent in my new fine camelott cloak with the latch of Sir G. Carteret's door; but it is darned up at my tailor's, that it will be no great blemish to it: but it troubled me. I could not but observe that Sir Philip Carteret would fain have given me my going into a play; but yet when he came to the door he had no money to pay for himself, I having refused to accept of it for myself, but was fain. And I perceive he is known there, and do run upon the score for plays, which is a shame; but I perceive always he is in want of money. In the pit I met with Sir Ch. North,[1] formerly Mr. North, who was with my Lord at sea; and he, of his own accord, was so silly as to tell me he is married; and, for her quality (being a Lord's daughter,[2] my Lord Grey) and person and beauty and years and estate and disposition, he is the happiest man in the world. I am sure he is an ugly fellow, but a good scholar and sober gentleman, and heir to his father, now Lord North, the old Lord being dead.

[1] Charles, eldest son of Dudley, fourth Lord North. He was afterwards summoned to Parliament as Baron North and Grey of Rolleston. His mother was Anne, daughter of Sir Charles Montagu, whence his connection with Lord Sandwich.

[2] Catharine, daughter to William Grey, Lord Grey of Warke, and widow of Sir Edward Moseley. She married, thirdly, Colonel Francis Russell (see 15th November 1666), second son of Francis, fourth Earl of Bedford.

31st. To White Hall, and there waited a long time while the Duke of York was with the King in the Cabal, and there I and Creed stayed talking in the Vane Room, and I perceive all people's expectation is, what will be the issue of this great business of putting these great Lords out of the Council and power, the quarrel, I perceive, being only their standing against the will of the King in the business of the Chancellor. Anon the Duke of York comes out, and then to a Committee of Tangier, where my Lord Middleton did come today, and seems to me but a dull, heavy man; but he is a great soldier, and stout, and a needy Lord, which will still keep that poor garrison from ever coming to be worth anything to the King. There dined with me my uncle Thomas, with a mourning hatband on, for his daughter Mary. Captain Perryman did give an account, walking in the garden, that there are Irish in the town, up and down, that do labour to entice the seamen out of the nation by giving them £3 in hand and promise of 40s. per month to go into the King of France's service; which is a mighty shame, but yet I believe is true. I did advise with him about my little vessel, the Maybolt, which he says will be best for me to sell, though my employing her to Newcastle this winter and the next spring, for coals, will be a gainful trade but yet make me great trouble. Thus ends the year, with great happiness to myself and family as to health and good condition in the world, blessed be God for it! only with great trouble to my mind in reference to the public, there being but little hopes left but that the whole nation must in a very little time be lost, either by troubles at home (the Parliament being dissatisfied, and the King led into unsettled counsels by some about him, himself considering little, and divisions growing between the King and Duke of York), or else by foreign invasion, to which we must submit if any at this bad point of time should come upon us, which the King of France is well able to do. These thoughts and some cares trouble me, concerning my standing in this Office when the Committee of Parliament shall come to examine our Navy matters, which they will now shortly do. I pray God they may do the kingdom service therein, as they will have sufficient opportunity of doing it!

1668

January 1st. Dined with my Lord Crewe, with whom was Mr. Browne, Clerk of the House of Lords, and Mr. John Crewe. Here was mighty good discourse, as there is always; and among other things my Lord Crewe did turn to a place in the Life of Sir Philip Sidney, wrote by Sir Fulke Greville,[1] which do foretell the present condition of this nation in relation to the Dutch to the very degree of a prophecy; and is so remarkable that I am resolved to buy one of them, it being quite throughout a good discourse. Here they did talk much of the present cheapness of corn, even to a miracle; so as their farmers can pay no rent, but do fling up their lands and would pay in corn: but, which I did observe to my Lord, and he liked well of it, our gentry are grown so ignorant in everything of good husbandry, that they know not how to bestow this corn; which, did they understand but a little trade, they would be able to join together and know what markets there are abroad, and send it thither, and thereby ease their tenants and be able to pay themselves. They did talk much of the disgrace the Archbishop is fallen under with the King, and the rest of the Bishops also. Thence I after dinner to the Duke of York's playhouse, and there saw 'Sir Martin Mar-all,' which I have seen so often, and yet am mightily pleased with it, and think it mighty witty, and the fullest of proper matter for mirth that ever was writ; and I do clearly see that they do improve in their acting of it. Here a mighty company of citizens, 'prentices, and others; and it makes me observe that when I began first to be able to bestow a play on myself I do not remember that I saw so many by half of the ordinary 'prentices and mean people in the pit at 2s. 6d. apiece as now; I going for several years no higher than the 12d. and then the 18d. places, though I strained hard to go in when I did: so much the vanity and prodigality of the age is to be observed in this particular. Thence I to White Hall, and there walked up and down the house a while, and do hear nothing of anything done further in this

[1] This work first appeared in 1652, and was reprinted by Sir Samuel Egerton Brydges at the Lee Priory Press in 1816.

business of the change of Privy Councillors: only I hear that Sir G. Savile,[1] one of the Parliament Committee of nine for examining the Accounts, is by the King made a Lord, the Lord Halifax; which, I believe, will displease the Parliament.   By and by I met with Mr. Brisband; and having it in my mind this Christmas to do what I never can remember that I did, go to see the gaming at the groom-porter's, I having in my coming from the playhouse stepped into the two Temple halls, and there saw the dirty 'prentices and idle people playing; wherein I was mistaken, in thinking to have seen gentlemen of quality playing there, as I think it was when I was a little child, that one of my father's servants, John Bassum, I think, carried me in his arms thither.   I did tell Brisband of it, and he did lead me thither, where, after staying an hour, they begun to play at about eight at night, where to see how differently one man took his losing from another, one cursing and swearing, and another only muttering and grumbling to himself, a third without any apparent discontent at all.   To see how the dice will run good luck in one hand for half an hour together, and another have no good luck at all.   To see how easily here, where they play nothing but guineas, a £100 is won or lost.   To see two or three gentlemen come in there drunk, and putting their stock of gold together, one 22 pieces, the second 4, and the third 5 pieces; and these two play one with another, and forget how much each of them brought, but he that brought the 22 thinks that he brought no more than the rest.   To see the different humours of gamesters to change their luck when it is bad, how ceremonious they are to call for new dice, to shift their places, to alter their manner of throwing, and that with great industry, as if there was anything in it.   To see how some old gamesters, that have no money now to spend as formerly, do come and sit and look on, and among others Sir Lewis Dives,[2] who was here, and hath been a great gamester in his time.   To hear their cursing and damning to no purpose, as one man being to throw a seven if he could, and failing to do it

---

[1] Of Rufford, county Nottinghamshire, Bart.; created Lord Savile of Eland and Viscount Halifax, 1668; Earl of Halifax, 1679; and Marquis of Halifax, 1682: *ob.* 1695.

[2] Sir Lewis Dives was the son of Sir John Dives, of Bromham, in Bedfordshire, by Beatrix, daughter of Charles Walcot, Esq.   She afterwards married John Digby, first Earl of Bristol.   Sir Lewis Dives was thus half-brother to George, second Earl of Bristol, so often mentioned by Pepys.   He was an active officer in the king's army, and at one time governor of Sherborne Castle, his brother's property.

after a great many throws, cried he would be damned if ever he flung seven more while he lived, his despair of throwing it being so great, while others did it as their luck served almost every throw.   To see how persons of the best quality do here sit down and play with people of any, though meaner.   And to see how people in ordinary clothes shall come hither, and play away 100 or 200 or 300 guineas without any kind of difficulty.   And lastly, to see the formality of the groom-porter, who is their judge of all disputes in play and all quarrels that may arise therein, and how his under-officers are there to observe true play at each table and to give new dice, is a consideration I never could have thought had been in the world, had I not now seen it.   And mighty glad I am that I did see it, and it may be will find another evening before Christmas be over to see it again, when I may stay later, for their heat of play begins not till about eleven or twelve o'clock; which did give me another pretty observation of a man, that did win mighty fast when I was there.   I think he won £100 at single pieces in a little time.   While all the rest envied him his good fortune he cursed it, saying, 'It comes so early upon me, for this fortune two hours hence would be worth something to me, but then I shall have no such luck.   This kind of profane, mad entertainment they give themselves.   And so I, having enough for once, refusing to venture, though Brisband pressed me hard and tempted me with saying that no man was ever known to lose the first time, the devil being too cunning to discourage a gamester; and he offered me also to lend me ten pieces to venture, but I did refuse and so went away.

2d.   Attended the King and the Duke of York in the Duke of York's lodgings, with the rest of the officers and many of the commanders of the fleet, and some of our master shipwrights, to discourse the business of having the topmasts of ships made to lower abaft of the mainmast: a business I understand not, and so can give no good account.   But I do see that by how much greater the Council and the number of Councillors is, the more confused the issue is of their counsels; so that little was said to the purpose regularly, and but little use was made of it, they coming to a very broken conclusion upon it, to make trial in a ship or two.   From this they fell to other talk about the fleet's fighting this late war, and how the King's ships have been shattered, though the King said that the world would not have it that above ten or twenty ships in any fight did do any service, and that this hath been told

so to him himself by ignorant people. The Prince,[1] who was
there, was mightily surprised at it and seemed troubled, but the
King told him that it was only discourse of the world. But Mr.
Wren whispered me in the ear and said that the Duke of Albemarle had put it into his narrative for the House that not above
twenty-five ships fought in the engagement wherein he was, but
that he was advised to leave it out; but this he did write from sea,
I am sure, or words to that effect, and did displease many commanders, among others, Captain Batts, who the Duke of York
said was a very stout man, all the world knew; and that another
was brought into his ship that had been turned out of his place
when he was a boatswain, not long before, for being a drunkard.
This the Prince took notice of, and would have been angry, I
think, but they let their discourse fall: but the Duke of York was
earnest in it. And the Prince said to me, standing by me, 'If
they will turn out every man that will be drunk, they must turn
out all the commanders in the fleet. What is the matter if he be
drunk, so as when he comes to fight he do his work? At least, let
him be punished for his drunkenness, and not put out of his command presently.' This he spoke, very much concerned for this
idle fellow, one Greene. After this the King began to tell stories
of the cowardice of the Spaniards in Flanders when he was there
at the siege of Mardike and Dunkirk;[2] which was very pretty,
though he tells them but meanly. To Westminster Hall, and
there stayed a little; and then home, and by the way did find with
difficulty the Life of Sir Philip Sidney. And the bookseller told
me that he had sold four within this week or two, which is more
than ever he sold in all his life of them; and he could not imagine
what should be the reason of it: but I suppose it is from the same
reason of people's observing of this part therein, touching his
prophesying our present condition here in England in relation to
the Dutch, which is very remarkable. I took my wife and girl
out to the New Exchange, and there my wife bought herself a lace

---

[1] Rupert.
[2] This refers to the battle of the Dunes, 24th June 1658, when Turenne
defeated the Prince of Condé and Don Juan of Austria, who tried to relieve
Dunkirk, which the English blockaded by sea, and the French attacked by
land. It was prior to this battle that, despising the Spanish tactics, Condé
said to the young Duke of Gloucester: 'N'avez-vous jamais vu perdre une
bataille? Eh bien, vous l'allez voir.' Dunkirk surrendered on the 23rd, and
afterwards was given up to the English, with whom it remained till Charles
sold it.

for a handkercher, which I do give her, of about £3, for a new year's gift, and I did buy also a lace for a band for myself. This day my wife shows me a locket of diamonds, worth about £40, which W. Hewer do press her to accept, and hath done for a good while, out of gratitude for my kindness and hers to him. But I do not like that she should receive it, it not being honourable for me to do it; and so do desire her to force him to take it back again, he leaving it against her will yesterday with her. And she did this evening force him to take it back, at which she says he is troubled: but, however, it becomes me more to refuse it than to let her accept of it. It is generally believed that France is endeavouring a firmer league with us than the former, in order to his going on with his business against Spain the next year; which I am, and so everybody else is, I think, very glad of, for all our fear is of his invading us. This day at White Hall I overheard Sir W. Coventry propose to the King his ordering [1] of some particular thing in the Wardrobe, which was of no great value; but yet, as much as it was, it was of profit to the King and saving to his purse. The King answered to it with great indifferency, as a thing that it was no great matter whether it was done or no. Sir W. Coventry answered: 'I see Your Majesty do not remember the old English proverb, "He that will not stoop for a pin will never be worth a pound."' And so they parted, the King bidding him do as he would; which, methought, was an answer not like a King that did intend ever to do well.

4th. It seems worth remembering that this day I did hear my Lord Anglesey at the table, speaking touching this new Act for Accounts, say that the House of Lords did pass it because it was a senseless, impracticable, ineffectual, and foolish Act; and that my Lord Ashley having shown that it was so to the House of Lords, the Duke of Buckingham did stand up and told the Lords that they were beholden to my Lord Ashley, that having first commended them for a most grave and honourable assembly, he thought it fit for the House to pass this Act for Accounts because it was a foolish and simple Act: and it seems it was passed with but a few in the House, when it was intended to have met in a grand Committee upon it. And it seems that in itself it is not to be practised till after this session of Parliament, by the very words of the Act, which nobody regarded, and therefore cannot come in force yet, unless at the next meeting they do make a new Act for the bringing it

[1] i.e. putting in order.

into force sooner; which is a strange omission. But I perceive my Lord Anglesey do make a mere laughing-stock of this Act, as a thing that can do nothing considerable, for all its great noise.

5th. (Lord's day.) The business of putting out of some of the Privy Council is over, the King being at last advised to forbear it; for whereas he did design it to make room for some of the House of Commons that are against him, thereby to gratify them, it is believed that it will but so much the more fret the rest that are not provided for, and raise a new stock of enemies by them that are displeased: and it goes for a pretty saying of my Lord Anglesey's up and down the Court, that he should lately say to one of the great promoters of this putting him and others out of the Council, 'Well, and what are we to look for when we are outed? Will all things be set right in the nation?' The other said that he did believe that many things would be mended: 'But,' says my Lord, 'will you and the rest of you be contented to be hanged, if you do not redeem all our misfortunes and set all right, if the power be put into your hands?' The other answered, 'No, I would not undertake that.' 'Why, then,' says my Lord, 'I and the rest of us that you are labouring to put out will be contented to be hanged if we do not recover all that is past, if the King will put the power into our hands and adhere wholly to our advice.' Intending to go home, my Lady Carteret saw and called to me out of her window, and so would have me home with her to Lincoln's Inn Fields to dinner, and there we met with my Lord Brereton and several other strangers to dine there; and I find him a very sober and serious, able man, and was in discourse too hard for the Bishop of Chester;[1] and who, above all books lately wrote, commending the matter and style of a late book called 'The Causes of the Decay of Piety,'[2] I do resolve at his great commendation to buy it. Here dined also Sir Philip Howard, a Berkshire Howard.[3] He did take occasion to tell me at the table that I have got great ground in the Parliament by my ready answers to all that was asked me there about the business of Chatham, and they would never let me be out of employment; of which I made little but was glad to hear him, as well as others, say it. And he did say also, relating to Commissioner Pett, that he did not think that he was guilty of

[1] George Hall, who had been Archdeacon of Canterbury, consecrated Bishop of Chester, 11th May 1662: *ob.* 1668.
[2] By the author of *The Whole Duty of Man.*
[3] i.e. a son of the Earl of Berkshire.

anything like a fault, that he was either able or concerned to amend, but only the not carrying up of the ships higher, he meant; but he said three or four miles lower down, to Rochester Bridge (which is a strange piece of ignorance in a Member of Parliament); and did boldly declare that he did think the fault to lie in my Lord Middleton, who had the power of the place, to secure the boats that were made ready by Pett, and to do anything that he thought fit.   After dinner my Lord Brereton very genteely went to the organ and played a verse very handsomely.   Thence to White Hall, and there up and down the house, and on the Queen's side, to see the ladies, and there saw the Duchess of York, whom few pay the respect they used, I think, to her; but she bears all out with a very great deal of greatness; that is the truth of it.   And so, it growing night, I away home by coach.

6th. Up, leaving my wife to get herself ready and the maids to get a supper ready against night for our company; and to White Hall, and there met with Mr. Pierce, by whom I find, as I was afraid from the folly of my wife, that he understood that he and his wife was to dine at my house today, whereas it was to sup; and therefore I did go home to dinner, and there find Mr. Harris, by the like mistake, come to dine with me.   However, we did get a pretty dinner ready for him; and there he and I to discourse of many things, and I do find him a very excellent person, such as in my whole [acquaintance] I do not know another better qualified for converse, whether in things of his own trade or of other kind, a man of great understanding and observation, and very agreeable in the manner of his discourse, and civil as far as is possible.   I was mightily pleased with his company; and after dinner did take coach with him and my wife and girl to go to a play, to carry him thence to his own house.   Away to the Duke of York's House, in the pit, and so left my wife; and to Mrs. Pierce, and took her and her cousin Corbet, Knipp, and little James, and brought them to the Duke's House; and, the house being full, was forced to carry them to a box, which did cost me 20*s.*, besides oranges, which troubled me, though their company did please me.   Thence, after the play, stayed till Harris was undressed, there being acted 'The Tempest,' and so he withal, all by coach, home, where we find my house with good fires and candles ready, and our office the like, and the two Mercers, and Betty Turner, Pembleton, and W. Batelier.   And so with much pleasure we into the house, and there fell to dancing, having extraordinary music, two violins, and a bass viol and theorbo, four hands, the Duke of Buckingham's music, the best in town, sent me by Greeling, and there we set in to dancing.   By and by to my house, to a very good supper, and mighty merry, and good music playing; and after supper to dancing and singing till about twelve at night; and then we had a good sack posset for them, and an excellent cake, cost me near 20*s*., of our Jane's making, which was cut into twenty pieces, there being by this time so many of our company, by the coming in of young Goodier and some others of our neighbours, young men that could dance, hearing of our dancing; and anon comes in Mrs. Turner, the mother, and brings with her Mrs. Hollworthy, which pleased me mightily. And so to dancing again, and singing, with extraordinary great pleasure till about two in the morning, and then broke up; and Mrs. Pierce and her family and Harris and Knipp by coach home, as late as it was.   And they gone, I took Mrs. Turner and Hollworthy home to my house, and there gave wine and sweetmeats; but I find Mrs. Hollworthy but a mean woman, I think, for understanding, only a little conceited, and proud, and talking, but nothing extraordinary in person or discourse or understanding. They being gone, I paid the fiddlers £3 among the four, and so away to bed, weary and mightily pleased, and have the happiness to reflect upon it, as I do sometimes on other things, as going to a play or the like, to be the greatest real comfort that I am to expect in the world, and that it is that that we do really labour in the hopes of.   And so I do really enjoy myself, and understand that if I do not do it now I shall not hereafter, it may be, be able to pay for it, or have health to take pleasure in it, and so fill myself with vain expectation of pleasure and go without it.

7th. To the Nursery, where I never was yet:[1] but the house did not act today; and so I to the other two playhouses into the pit, to gaze up and down, and there did by this means, for nothing, see an act in 'The School of Compliments' at the Duke of York's House, and 'Henry the Fourth' at the King's House; but not liking either of the plays, I took my coach again, and home.

8th. To White Hall, and by coach home, taking up Mr. Prin

---

[1] There seem to have been, at this time, two distinct 'Nurseries for Actors,' one in Golden Lane, near the Barbican, described in Pennant's *London* as a row of low houses of singular construction; and which, according to the inscription underneath an old print in his possession, had been a nursery for the children of Henry VIII. The same author states that it was used also as a playhouse in the reign of Elizabeth and James I. The other 'Nursery' was in Hatton Garden.

at the Court gate, it raining, and setting him down at the Temple: and by the way did ask him about the manner of holding of Parliaments, and whether the number of Knights and Burgesses were always the same? And he says that the latter were not; but that, for aught he can find, they were sent up at the discretion, at first of the Sheriffs, to whom the writs are sent to send up generally the Burgesses and citizens of their county: and he do find that heretofore the Parliament-men, being paid by the country, several boroughs have complained of the Sheriffs putting them to the charge of sending up Burgesses; which is a very extraordinary thing to me that knew not this, but thought that the number had been known and always the same.

9th. Mr. Hollyard came and dined with me, and it is still mighty pleasant to hear him talk of Rome and the Pope, with what hearty hatred and zeal he talks against him. Wrote to my father about lending Anthony Joyce the money he desires; and I declare that I would do it as part of Pall's portion, and that Pall should have the use of the money till she be married, but I do propose to him to think of Mr. Cumberland rather than this Jackson that he is upon; and I confess that I have a mighty mind to have a relation so able a man, and honest, and so old an acquaintance, as Mr. Cumberland. I shall hear his answer by the next [post].

10th. To White Hall, and there to wait on the Duke of York with the rest of my brethren, which we did a little in the King's Green Room while the King was in Council. And in this room we found my Lord Bristol walking alone: which wondering at while the Council was sitting, I was answered that, as being a Catholic, he could not be of the Council; which I did not consider before. This morning there was a Persian in that country dress, with a turban, waiting to kiss the King's hand in the Vane Room, against he come out: he was a comely man as to features, and his dress, methinks, very comely. To my new bookseller's, Martin's, and there did meet with Fournier,[1] the Frenchman that hath wrote of the Sea Navigation, and I could not but buy him, and also bespoke an excellent book, which I met with there, of China.[2] The truth is, I have bought a great many books lately to a great value; but

---

[1] Pepys alludes to a book by George Fournier, a Jesuit, born at Caen in 1569, author of *L'Hydrographie*, and other nautical works.

[2] Alvarez Semedo's *History of China*, translated by a Person of Quality. London, 1655 fol.

I think to buy no more till Christmas next, and those that I have will so fill my two presses, that I must be forced to give away some or make room for them, it being my design to have no more at any time for my proper library than to fill them.　This day I received a letter from my father, and another from my cousin Roger Pepys, who have had a view of Jackson's evidences of his estate, and do mightily like of the man and his condition and estate, and do advise me to accept of the match for my sister and to finish it as soon as I can; and he do it so as, I confess, I am contented to have it done, and so give her her portion; and so I shall be eased of one care how to provide for her.

11th.　Talking with my wife in bed about Pall's business, and she do conclude to have her married here, and to be merry at it; and to have W. Hewer and Batelier and Mercer and Willett bride-men and bridesmaids, and to be very merry: and so I am glad of it, and do resolve to let it be done as soon as I can.　To the King's House, to see 'The Wildgoose Chase.' [1]　In this play I met with nothing extraordinary at all, but very dull inventions and designs. Knipp came and sat by us, and her talk pleased me a little, she telling me how Miss Davis is for certain going away from the Duke's House, the King being in love with her; and a house is taken for her, and furnishing; and she hath a ring given her already worth £600.　That the King did send several times for Nelly, and she was with him; and I am sorry for it, and can hope for no good to the State from having a Prince so devoted to his pleasure.　She told me also of a play shortly coming upon the stage of Sir Charles Sedley's, which, she thinks, will be called 'The Wandering Ladies,' [2] a comedy that, she thinks, will be most pleasant; and also another play, called 'The Duke of Lerma'; besides 'Catiline,' which she thinks, for want of the clothes which the King promised them, will not be acted for a good while.

12th. (Lord's day.)　My wife without any occasion fell to dis-course of my father's coming to live with us when my sister marries.　She declares against his coming hither, which I not presently agreeing to, she declared, if he came, she would not live with me but would shame me all over the City and Court;

[1] By Fletcher.
[2] Sedley never wrote any play with this title, or, perhaps, the name was altered.　The piece here referred to seems to be *The Mulberry Garden* (see 18th May following) which, on representation, does not seem to have an-swered Pepys's expectations.　It met, however, with success, from the notoriety or fashion of the profligate author.

which I made slight of, and so we fell very foul. And I do find she do keep very bad remembrance of my former unkindness to her and do mightily complain of her want of money and liberty, which I will rather hear and bear the complaint of than grant the contrary; and so we had very hot work a great while. But at last I did declare, as I intend, that my father shall not come and that he do not desire it. And so we parted with pretty good quiet, and went to church, where first I saw Alderman Backwell and his lady come to our church, they living in Mark Lane; and I could find in my heart to invite her to sit with us, she being a fine lady. I come in while they were singing the 119th psalm, while the sexton was gathering to his box, to which I did give 5s.

13th. With Sir W. Pen to White Hall, and there did with the rest attend the Duke of York, where nothing extraordinary; only I perceive there is nothing yet declared for the next year, what fleet shall be abroad.

14th. To my bookseller, Martin, and there did receive my book I expected of China, a most excellent book with rare cuts; and there fell into discourse with him about the burning of Paul's when the City was burned, his house being in the Church-yard. And he tells me that it took fire first upon the end of a board that, among others, was laid upon the roof instead of lead, the lead being broke off, and thence down lower and lower: but that the burning of the goods under St. Faith's arose from the goods taking fire in the Church-yard, and so got into St. Faith's church; and that they first took fire from the Draper's side, by some timber of the houses that were burned falling into the church. He says that one warehouse of books was saved under Paul's; and there were several dogs found burned among the goods in the Church-yard, and but one man, which was an old man, that said he would go and save a blanket which he had in the church, and, being weak, the fire overcame him. He says that most of the booksellers do design to fall a-building again the next year; but that the Bishop of London [1] do use them most basely, worse than any other landlords, and says he will be paid to this day the rent, or else he will not come to treat with them for the time to come; and will not, on that condition either, promise them in anything how he will use them: and, the Parliament sitting, he claims his privilege, and will not be cited before the Lord Chief Justice, as others are there, to be forced to

[1] Humphrey Henchman, who had been Bishop of Salisbury.

a fair dealing.[1]   Thence by coach to Mrs. Pierce's, where my wife is; and there they fell to discourse of the last night's work at Court, where the ladies and Duke of Monmouth and others acted 'The Indian Emperor,' wherein they told me these things most remarkable: that not any woman but the Duchess of Monmouth and Mrs. Cornwallis [2] did anything but like fools and stocks, but that these two did do most extraordinary well; that not any man did anything well but Captain O'Bryan,[3] who spoke and did well, but, above all things, did dance most incomparably.   That she did sit near the players of the Duke's House: among the rest, Miss Davis, who is the most impertinent slut, she says, in the world; and the more, now the King do show her countenance, and is reckoned his mistress, even to the scorn of the whole world, the King gazing on her, and my Lady Castlemaine being melancholy and out of humour all the play, not smiling once.   The King, it seems, hath given her a ring of £700, which she shows to everybody, and owns that the King did give it her; and he hath furnished a house in Suffolk Street most richly for her, which is a most infinite shame.   It seems she is a bastard of my Lord Berkshire, and that he hath got her for the King: but Pierce says that she is a most homely jade as ever she saw, though she dances beyond anything in the world.   She tells me that the Duchess of Richmond do not yet come to the Court, nor hath seen the King, nor will not, nor do he own his desire of seeing her, but hath used means to get her to Court, but they do not take.   I to my chamber, having a great many books brought me home from my bookbinder's, and so I to the new setting of my books against the next year, which costs me more trouble than I expected, and at it till two o'clock in the morning.

15th. Up, and to the office, where all the morning.   At noon home to dinner, and then to the office again, where we met about some business of D. Gauden's till candle-light; and then, as late as it was, I down to Redriffe, and so walked by moonlight to Deptford, where I have not been a great while.   And so walked back again, but with pleasure by the walk, and I had the sport to

[1] The claims of the owners, after the fire of London, as settled by the Commissioners, are in the British Museum.

[2] Henrietta Maria Cornwallis, whose brother Charles, third Lord Cornwallis (called *le beau* Cornwallis), afterwards became the second husband of the Duchess of Monmouth.

[3] Captain O'Bryan was probably Sir Donough O'Bryan, who married Lucia Hamilton, sister to the Comtesse de Grammont.

see two boys swear and stamp and fret for not being able to get their horse over a stile and ditch, one of them swearing and cursing most bitterly; and I would fain, in revenge, have persuaded him to have drove his horse through the ditch, by which, I believe, he would have stuck there. But the horse would not be drove, and so they were forced to go back again, and so I walked away homeward, and there reading all the evening, and so to bed. This afternoon my Lord Anglesey tells us that it is voted in Council to have a fleet of 50 ships out: but it is only a disguise for the Parliament, to get some money by; but it will not take, I believe.

16th. Lord Anglesey tells us again that a fleet is to be set out; and that it is generally, he hears, said that it is but a Spanish rhodomontado; and that he saying so just now to the Duke of Albemarle, who came to town last night, after the thing was ordered, he told him a story of two seamen: one wished all the guns of the ship were his, and that they were silver; and, says the other, 'You are a fool, for, if you can have it for wishing, why do you not wish them gold?' 'So,' says he, 'if a rhodomontado will do any good, why do you not say 100 ships?' And it is true; for the Dutch and French are said to make such preparations as 50 sail will do no good. Mightily pleased with Mr. Gibson's [1] talking, he telling me so many good stories relating to the war and practices of commanders, which I will find a time to recollect; and he will be an admirable help to my writing a history of the Navy, if ever I do. My work with my clerks till midnight was to examine my list of ships I am making for myself, and their dimensions, and to see how it agrees and differs from other lists: and I do find so great a difference between them all, that I am at a loss which to take. So little care there has been to this day to know or keep any history of the Navy.

17th. Much discourse of the duel yesterday between the Duke of Buckingham, Holmes,[2] and one Jenkins[3] on one side, and my Lord of Shrewsbury,[4] Sir John Talbot,[5] and one Bernard

---

[1] Richard Gibson, so frequently noticed by Pepys, was a clerk in the Navy office. His collection of papers relating to the Navy of England, A.D. 1650–1702, compiled, as he states, from the Admiralty books in the Navy office are in the British Museum.

[2] Sir Robert Holmes.

[3] Captain William Jenkins.

[4] Francis Talbot, eleventh Earl of Shrewsbury, who died of his wounds 16th March following.

[5] Of Lacock Abbey, Wiltshire, a Gentleman of the Privy Chamber, and

Howard[1] on the other side: and all about my Lady Shrewsbury,[2] who is at this time, and hath for a great while been, a mistress to the Duke of Buckingham. And so her husband challenged him, and they met yesterday in a close near Barn Elms, and there fought: and my Lord Shrewsbury is run through the body, from the right breast through the shoulder; and Sir John Talbot all along up one of his arms; and Jenkins killed upon the place; and the rest all, in a little measure, wounded. This will make the world think that the King hath good councillors about him, when the Duke of Buckingham, the greatest man about him, is a fellow of no more sobriety than to fight about a mistress. And this may prove a very bad accident to the Duke of Buckingham, but that my Lady Castlemaine do rule all at this time as much as ever she did, and she will, it is believed, keep all matters well with the Duke of Buckingham: though this is a time that the King will be very backward, I suppose, to appear in such a business. And it is pretty to hear how the King had some notice of this challenge a week or two ago, and did give it to my Lord General[3] to confine the Duke or take security that he should not do any such thing as fight: and the General trusted to the King that he, sending for him, would do it, and the King trusted to the General; and so, between them both, as everything else of greatest moment do, do fall between two stools. The whole House full of nothing but the talk of this business; and it is said that my Lord Shrewsbury's case is to be feared, that he may die too; and that may make it much worse for the Duke of Buckingham: and I shall not be much sorry for it, that we may have some sober man come in his room to assist in the Government. Creed tells me of Mr. Harry Howard's[4] giving the Royal Society a piece of ground next to his house to build a College on, which is a most generous act. And he tells

---

M.P. for Knaresborough. He lived to a great age, serving till after 1700. His two sons died young; and his two daughters and co-heirs: (i) Anne, married Sir John Ivory, Bart.; (ii) Barbara, married Henry Yelverton, Lord Grey de Ruthyn, and Viscount Longueville.

[1] Eighth son of Henry Frederick Howard, Earl of Arundel, and the direct ancestor of the present Duke of Norfolk.

[2] Anna Maria, daughter of Robert Brudenel, second Earl of Cardigan. She is said to have held the Duke of Buckingham's horse, in the habit of a page, while he was fighting with her husband. She married, secondly, George Rodney Bridges, son of Sir Thomas Bridges, of Keynsham, Somerset, and died 20th April 1702.

[3] The Duke of Albemarle.   [4] Afterwards Duke of Norfolk.

me he is a very fine person, and understands and speaks well; and no rigid Papist neither, but one that would not have a Protestant servant leave his religion, which he was going to do, thinking to recommend himself to his master by it; saying, that he had rather have an honest Protestant than a knavish Catholic. I was not called in to the Council; and, therefore, home, first informing myself that my Lord Hinchingbroke hath been married this week to my Lord Burlington's daughter; so that that great business is over; and I am mighty glad of it, though I am not satisfied that I have not a favour sent me, as I see Attorney Montagu and the Vice-Chamberlain have.

18th. To the 'Change, where I bought 'The Maiden Queen,' a play newly printed, which I like at the King's House so well, of Mr. Dryden's, which he himself in his preface seems to brag of, and indeed is a good play.

19th. (Lord's day.) With Captain Perryman to Redriffe, and so walked to Deptford, where I sent for Shish out of the church, to advise about my vessel, the Maybolt: and I do resolve to sell presently for anything rather than keep her longer, having already lost £100 in her value, which I was once offered and refused, and the ship left without anybody to look to her, which vexes me. Mr. Pelling tells me that my Lord Shrewsbury is likely to do well. Mr. Jessop is made Secretary to the Commissioners of Parliament for Accounts; and I am glad, and it is pretty to see that all the Cavalier party were not able to find the Parliament nine Commissioners or one Secretary fit for the business.

20th. To Drumbleby's, the pipe-maker, there to advise about the making of a flageolet to go low and soft; and he do show me a way which do do, and also a fashion of having two pipes of the same note fastened together, so as I can play on one, and then echo it upon the other, which is mighty pretty. So to my Lord Crewe's to dinner, where we hear all the good news of our making a league now with Holland against the French power coming over them or us: which is the first good act that the King hath done a great while, and done secretly and with great seeming wisdom; and is certainly good for us at this time, while we are in no condition to resist the French if they should come over hither; and then a little time of peace will give us time to lay up something, which these Commissioners of the Treasury are doing; and the world do begin to see that they will do the King's work for him, if he will let them. Here dined Mr. Case, the minister, who,

Lord! do talk just as I remember he used to preach, and did tell us a pretty story of a religious lady, Queen of Navarre;[1] and my Lord also told a good story of Mr. Newman,[2] the minister in New England, who wrote the Concordance, of his foretelling his death and preaching a funeral sermon, and at last bid the angels do their office, and died.   It seems there is great presumption that there will be a Toleration granted, so that the Presbyterians do hold up their heads; but they will hardly trust the King or the Parliament what to yield them, though most of the sober party be for some kind of allowance to be given them.   Lord Gerard is likely to meet with ill, the next sitting of Parliament, about Carr being set in the pillory; and I am glad of it; and it is mighty acceptable to the world to hear that, among other reductions, the King do reduce his Guards,[3] which do please mightily.

21st.   Comes news from Kate Joyce that if I would see her husband alive I must come presently.   So I to him, and find his breath rattled in his throat; and they did lay pigeons to his feet, and all despair of him.   It seems on Thursday last he went, sober and quiet, to Islington, and behind one of the inns, the White Lion, did fling himself into a pond, was spied by a poor woman, and got out by some people, and set on his head and got to life: and so his wife and friends sent for.   He confessed his doing the thing, being led by the Devil; and do declare his reason to be his trouble in having forgot to serve God as he ought since he came to his new employment:[4] and I believe that and the sense of his great loss by the fire did bring him to it, for he grew sick, and worse and worse to this day.   The friends that were there, being now in fear that the goods and estate would be seized on, though he lived all this while, because of his endeavouring to drown himself, my cousin did endeavour to remove what she could of plate out of the house, and desired me to take my flagons; which I did, but in great fear all the way of being seized, though there was no reason for it, he not being dead.   So, with Sir D. Gauden, to Guildhall to advise with the Town Clerk about the practice of the City and nation in this case: and he thinks it cannot be found self-

---

[1] Marguerite de Valois, Queen of Navarre, sister of Francis I of France. The 'pretty story' was doubtless from her *Heptameron*.

[2] Samuel Newman, born at Banbury and educated at Oxford.   He emigrated to New England in 1637, and died there in 1663.   His Concordance of the Bible was first published in London in 1643.

[3] One regiment of which was commanded by Lord Gerard.

[4] He kept a tavern.

murder; but if it be, it will fall, all the estate, to the King. So I to my cousin's again, where I no sooner come but find that her husband was departed. So, at their entreaty, I presently to White Hall, and there find Sir W. Coventry: and he carried me to the King, the Duke of York being with him, and there told my story which I had told him; and the King, without more ado, granted that, if it was found, the estate should be to the widow and children. I presently to each Secretary's office, and there left caveats, and so away back to my cousin's, leaving a chimney on fire at White Hall, in the King's closet, but no danger. And so, when I come thither, I find her all in sorrow, but she and the rest mightily pleased with my doing this for them; and, indeed, it was a very great courtesy, for people are looking out for the estate.

22d. At noon with my Lord Brouncker to Sir D. Gauden's, at the Victualling Office, to dinner, where I have not dined since he was Sheriff. He expected us; and a good dinner, and much good company; and a fine house, and especially two rooms, very fine, he hath built there. His lady a good lady; but my Lord led himself and me to a great absurdity in kissing all the ladies but the finest of all the company, leaving her out I know not why; and I was loth to do it, since he omitted it. Here little Chaplin [1] dined, who is like to be Sheriff the next year, and a pretty humoured little man he is, and Mr. Talents the younger, of Magdalene College, Chaplain to the Sheriff, which I was glad to see, though not much acquainted with him. Thence stole away to my cousin Kate's, and there find the Coroner's jury sitting, but they could not end it, but put off the business to Shrove Tuesday next, and so do give way to the burying of him, and that is all; but they all incline to find it a natural death, though there are mighty busy people to have it go otherwise, thinking to get his estate, but are mistaken. Thence, after sitting with her and company awhile, comforting her (though I can find she can, as all other women, cry and yet talk of other things all in a breath), home: and there to cards with my wife, Deb., and Betty Turner and Batelier, and after supper late to sing. But, Lord! how did I please myself to make Betty Turner sing, to see what a beast she is as to singing, not knowing how to sing one note in tune: but only for the experiment, I would not for 40s. hear her sing a tune—worse than my wife a thousand times, so that it do a little reconcile me to her.

[1] Afterwards Sir Francis Chaplin, knight and alderman, and lord mayor in 1687.

23d. At the office all the morning; and at noon find the Bishop of Lincoln [1] come to dine with us; and after him comes Mr. Brisband, and there mighty good company. But the Bishop a very extraordinary good-natured man, and one that is mightily pleased, as well as I am, that I live so near Buckden,[2] the seat of his bishopric, where he is like to reside: and, indeed, I am glad of it. In discourse, we think ourselves safe for this year by this league with Holland, which pleases everybody, and, they say, vexes France; insomuch that D'Estrades,[3] the French Ambassador in Holland, when he heard it, told the States that he would have them not forget that his master is at the head of 100,000 men, and is but 28 years old; which was a great speech. The Bishop tells me he thinks that the great business of Toleration will not, notwithstanding this talk, be carried this Parliament; nor for the King's taking away the Deans' and Chapters' lands to supply his wants, they signifying little to him, if he had them, for his present service. To Mrs. Turner's, where my wife and Deb. and I and Batelier spent the night, and supped, and played at cards, and very merry. She is either a very prodigal woman or richer than she would be thought, by her buying of the best things, and laying out much money in new-fashioned pewter and, among other things, a new-fashioned case for a pair of snuffers, which is very pretty; but I could never have guessed what it was for, had I not seen the snuffers in it.

24th. Carried my wife to the Temple, and then she to a play and I to St. Andrew's church, in Holborn, at the 'Quest House, where the company meets to the burial of my cousin Joyce; and here I stayed with a very great rabble of four or five hundred people of mean condition, and I stayed in the room with the kindred till ready to go to church, where there is to be a sermon of Dr. Stillingfleet,[4] and thence they carried him to St. Sepulchre's. But it being late, and, indeed, not having a black cloak to lead Kate Joyce with, or follow the corpse, I away, and saw, indeed, a very great press of people follow the corpse. I to the King's playhouse to fetch my wife, and there saw the best part of 'The Maiden Queen,' which the more I see, the more I love, and think one of the best plays I ever saw, and is certainly the best acted of anything

---

[1] Dr. William Fuller, translated from Limerick, 1667.
[2] At Brampton, in the neighbourhood of Buckden palace.
[3] Who, as we have seen, had been French ambassador in England.
[4] The rector.

ever the House did, and particularly Beck Marshall, to admiration. Found my wife and Deb., and saw many fine ladies, and sat by Colonel Reames, who understands and loves a play as well as I, and I love him for it. And so thence home; and, after being at the office, I home to supper and to bed, my eyes being very bad again with overworking with them.

25th. At noon to the 'Change with Mr. Hater, and there he and I to a tavern to meet Captain Minors, which we did, and dined; and there happened to be Mr. Prichard, a ropemaker of his acquaintance, and whom I know also and did once mistake for a fiddler which sung well, and I asked for such a song that I had heard him sing.

26th. (Lord's day.) Up, and with my wife to church, and at noon home to dinner. No strangers there; and all the afternoon and evening very late doing serious business of my Tangier accounts, and examining my East India accounts with Mr. Poynter, whom I employed all this day to transcribe it fair; and so to supper, W. Hewer with us, and the girl to comb my head till I slept, and then to bed.

27th. Mr. Povy do tell me how he is like to lose his £400 a year pension of the Duke of York, which he took in consideration of his place that was taken from him. He tells me the Duchess is a devil against him, and do now come like Queen Elizabeth, and sits with the Duke of York's Council, and sees what they do; and she crosses out this man's wages and prices as she sees fit, for saving money; but yet, he tells me, she reserves £5000 a year for her own spending; and my Lady Peterborough, by and by, tells me that the Duchess do lay up mightily jewels. Thence to my Lady Peterborough's, she desiring to speak with me. She loves to be taken dressing herself, as I always find her; and there, after a little talk, to please her, about her husband's pension, which I do not think he will ever get again, I away thence home.

28th. With W. Griffin, talking about getting a place to build a coach-house, or to hire one; for it is plainly for my benefit for saving money. To White Hall; and by and by the Duke of York comes, and we had a little meeting, Anglesey, W. Pen, and I there, and none else: and, among other things, did discourse of the want of discipline in the fleet, which the Duke of York confessed, and yet said that he, while he was there, did keep it in a good measure, but that it was now lost when he was absent; but he will endeavour to have it again. That he did tell the Prince and Duke of

Albemarle they would lose all order by making such and such commanders, which they would, because they were stout men: he told them it was a reproach to the nation, as if there were no sober men among us, that were stout, to be had.   That they did put out some men for cowards, that the Duke of York had put in but little before for stout men and would now, were he to go to sea again, entertain them in his own division, to choose: and did put in an idle fellow, Greene, who was hardly thought fit for a boatswain by him: they did put him from being a lieutenant to a Captain's place of a second-rate ship; as idle a drunken fellow, he said, as any was in the fleet.   That he will now desire the King to let him be what he is, that is, Admiral; and he will put in none but those that he hath great reason to think well of; and particularly says that, though he likes Colonel Legge well, yet his son,[1] that was, he knows not how, made a Captain after he had been but one voyage at sea, he should go to sea another apprenticeship before ever he gives him a command.   We did tell him of the many defects and disorders among the Captains, and I prayed we might do it in writing to him; which he liked, and I am glad of an opportunity of doing it.   My wife this day hears from her father and mother: they are in France, at Paris; he, poor good man! thankful for my small charities to him.   I could be willing to do something for them, were I sure not to bring them over again hither.   Coming home, my wife and I went and saw Kate Joyce, who is still in mighty sorrow, and the more from something that Dr. Stillingfleet should simply say in his sermon, of her husband's manner of dying, as killing himself.

29th.   To Sir W. Coventry.   He tells me he hath no friends in the whole Court but my Lord Keeper and Sir John Duncomb. They have reduced the charges of Ireland about £70,000 a year, and thereby cut off good profits from my Lord Lieutenant; which will make a new enemy, but he cares not.   He tells me that Townsend, of the Wardrobe, is the veriest knave and bufflehead that ever he saw in his life, and wonders how my Lord Sandwich came to trust such a fellow; and that now Reames and —— are put in to be overseers there, and do great things, and have already saved a great deal of money in the King's liveries, and buy linen so cheap, that he will have them buy the next cloth he hath, for shirts.   But then this is with ready money, which answers all. This evening come Betty Turner and the two Mercers and W.

[1] George Legge, the colonel's eldest son, in 1682 created Lord Dartmouth.

Batelier, and they had fiddlers, and danced, and kept a quarter,[1] which pleased me, though it disturbed me; but I would not be with them at all.

30th. Mr. Gibson and I and our clerks, and Mr. Clerke, the solicitor, to a little ordinary in Hercules' Pillars Alley[2]—the Crown, a poor, sorry place, where a fellow in twelve years hath gained an estate of, as he says, £600 a year, which is very strange— and there dined, and had a good dinner and very good discourse between them, old men belonging to the law. And here I first heard that my cousin Pepys, of Salisbury Court, was Marshal to my Lord Coke when he was Lord Chief Justice; which beginning of his I did not know to be so low; but so it was, it seems. When come home, I find Kate Joyce hath been there with sad news that her house stands not in the King's liberty, but the Dean of Paul's; and so, if her estate falls, it will not be in the King's power to do her any good. But I do believe this arises from somebody that hath a mind to fright her into a composition for her estate, which I advise her against; and, indeed, I do desire heartily to be able to do her service, she being, methinks, a piece of care I ought to take upon me for our fathers' and friends' sake, she being left alone, and no friend so near as me, or so able to help her.

31st. Up; and by coach, with W. Griffin with me, and our Contract-books, to Durham Yard, to the Commissioners for Accounts, the first time I ever was there; and stayed awhile before I was admitted to them. I did observe a great many people attending about complaints of seamen concerning tickets, and, among others, Mr. Carcasse and Mr. Martin, my purser. And I observe a fellow, one Collins, is there, who is employed by these Commissioners particularly to hold an office in Bishopsgate Street, or somewhat thereabouts, to receive complaints of all people about tickets: and I believe he will have work enough. Presently I was called in, where I found the whole number of Commissioners, and was there received with great respect and kindness; and did give them great satisfaction, making it my endeavour to inform them what it was they were to expect from me, and what was the duty of other people; this being my only way to preserve myself after all my pains and trouble. They did ask many questions and de- manded other books of me, which I did give them very ready and acceptable answers to: and, upon the whole, I do observe they do go about their business like men resolved to go through with it,

[1] A term for making a noise or disturbance.   [2] In Fleet Street.

and in a very good method, like men of understanding.   They have Mr. Jessop their secretary, and it is pretty to see that they are fain to find out an old-fashioned man of Cromwell's to do their business for them, as well as the Parliament to pitch upon such, for the most part, among the lowest of people that were brought into the House, for Commissioners.   I went away, giving and receiving great satisfaction: and so to White Hall, to the Commissioners of the Treasury; where, waiting some time, I there met with Colonel Birch.   And he and I fell into discourse, and I did give him thanks for his kindness to me in the Parliament-house, both before my face and behind my back.   He told me that he knew me to be a man of the old way of taking pains, and did always endeavour to do me right and prevent anything that was moved that might tend to my injury; which I was obliged to him for, and thanked him.   Thence to talk of other things and the want of money, and he told me of the general want of money in the country: that land sold for nothing, and the many pennyworths he knew of lands and houses upon them, with good titles in his country, at 16 years' purchase; 'and,' says he, 'though I am in debt, yet I have a mind to one thing, and that is a Bishop's lease'; but said, 'I will yet choose such a lease before any other, because I know they cannot stand, and then it will fall into the King's hands, and I in possession shall have an advantage by it.'   Says he, 'I know they must fall, and they are now near it, taking all the ways they can to undo themselves, and showing us the way.'   And thereupon told me a story of the present quarrel between the Bishop [1] and Dean [2] of Coventry and Lichfield, the former of whom did excommunicate the latter, and caused his excommunication to be read in the church, while he was there; and after it was read the Dean made the service be gone through with, though himself, an excommunicate, was present, which is contrary to the canon, and said he would justify the Choir therein against the Bishop.   And so they are at law in the Arches [3] about it, which is a very pretty story.   He tells me that the King is for Toleration, though the Bishops be against it, and that he do not doubt but it will be carried in Parliament; but that he fears some will stand for the tolerating of Papists with the rest; and that he knows not what to say, but rather thinks that the sober party will be without it rather than have it upon those

---

[1] John Hackett.
[2] Dr. Thomas Wood, consecrated bishop of this see in 1671.
[3] The Court of Arches.

terms; and I do believe so.   I to make a visit to Mr. Godolphin [1]
at his lodgings, who is come lately from Spain from my Lord
Sandwich, and did the other day, meeting me in White Hall, compliment me mightily, and so I did offer him this visit, but missed
him.   To my bookbinder's, and there till late at night, binding up
my second part of my Tangier accounts, and I all the while observing his working and his manner of gilding of books with great
pleasure, and so home.   This day Griffin did, in discourse in the
coach, put me in the head of the little house by our garden, where
old goodman Taylor puts his brooms and dirt, to make me a stable
of, which I shall improve, so as, I think, to be able to get me a
stable without much charge, which do please me mightily.   It is
observed, and is true, in the late fire of London, that the fire
burned just as many parish churches as there were hours from the
beginning to the end of the fire; and, next, that there were just as
many churches left standing as there were taverns left standing in
the rest of the City that was not burned, being, I think, thirteen
in all of each: which is pretty to observe.

February 1st. To the office till past two o'clock, where at the
Board some high words passed between Sir W. Pen and I, begun
by me and yielded to by him, I being in the right in finding fault
with him for his neglect of duty.   Home, my head mighty full of
business now on my hands: viz., of finishing my Tangier Accounts;
of auditing my last year's Accounts; of preparing answers to the
Commissioners of Accounts; of drawing up several important
letters to the Duke of York and the Commissioners of the Treasury;
the marrying of my sister; the building of a coach and stables
against summer; and the setting many things in the Office right;
and the drawing up a new form of Contract with the Victualler of
the Navy; and several other things, which pains, however, will go
through with.

2d. (Lord's day.) All the morning setting my books in order
in my presses for the following year: their number be much increased since the last, so as I am fain to lay by several books to make

---

[1] William Godolphin descended from a younger branch of that family,
which was afterwards ennobled in the person of Sidney, Earl Godolphin,
the great and good Lord Treasurer. William Godolphin was of Christ
Church, Oxford, and made M.A. 14th January 1661. He was afterwards
secretary to Sir H. Bennet (Lord Arlington), and M.P. for Camelford. He
was a great favourite at court, and was knighted on the 28th August 1668.
At the time of his death he was envoy in Spain, where he had become a
Roman Catholic.

room for better, being resolved to keep no more than just my presses will contain.   A very good dinner we had, of a powdered leg of pork and a loin of lamb roasted.

3d.   To the Duke of York's House, to the play, 'The Tempest,' which we have often seen, and particularly this day I took pleasure to learn the time of the seaman's dance.

4th.   To Kate Joyce's, where the jury did sit where they did before, about her husband's death, and their verdict put off for fourteen days longer at the suit of somebody under pretence of the King; but it is only to get money out of her to compound the matter.   But the truth is, something they will make out of Stillingfleet's sermon, which may trouble us, he declaring, like a fool, in his pulpit, that he did confess that his losses in the world did make him do what he did.   This vexes me, to see how foolish our Protestant divines are, while the Papists do make it the duty of confessor to be secret, or else nobody would confess their sins to them. All being put off for today, I took my leave of Kate, who is mightily troubled at it for her estate sake, not for her husband; for her sorrow for that, I perceive, is all over.

5th.   To Captain Cocke's, where he and I did discourse of our business about our prizes; and having resolved to conceal nothing but confess the truth, the truth being likely to do us most good, I to the Commissioners of Accounts, where I was forced to stay two hours before I was called in, and did take an oath to declare the truth to what they should ask me, which is a great power (I doubt more than the Act do, or as some say can, give them), to force a man to swear against himself.   And so they fell to enquire about the business of prize-goods, wherein I did answer them as well as I could, in everything the just truth, keeping myself to that.   I do perceive at last that that they do lay most like a fault to me was, that I did buy goods upon my Lord Sandwich's declaring that it was with the King's allowance, and my believing it without seeing the King's allowance, which is a thing I will own, and doubt not to justify myself in.   But what vexed me most was their having some watermen by to witness my saying that they were rogues that had betrayed my goods, which was upon some discontent with one of the watermen that I employed at Greenwich, who I did think did discover the goods sent from Rochester to the Custom-House officer; but this can do me no great harm. They were inquisitive into the minutest particulars, and had had great information; but I think that they can do me no hurt—at

the worst, more than to make me refund, if it must be known, what
profit I did make of my agreement with Captain Cocke. And yet,
though this be all, I do find so poor a spirit within me, that it
makes me almost out of my wits, and puts me to so much pain, that
I cannot think of anything, nor do anything, but vex and fret and
imagine myself undone, so that I am ashamed of myself to myself,
and do fear what would become of me if any real affliction should
come upon me. After they had done with me they called in
Captain Cocke, with whom they were shorter, and I do fear he
may answer foolishly; but I hope to preserve myself and let him
shift for himself as well as he can. Home, finding dinner done
and Mr. Cooke who came for my Lady Sandwich's plate, which I
must part with, and so endanger the losing of my money which I
lent upon my thoughts of securing myself by that plate. But it is
no great sum—but £60; and if it must be lost, better that than a
greater sum. I away back again to find a dinner anywhere else,
and so I, first, to the Ship tavern, thereby to get a sight of the pretty
mistress of the house, with whom I am not yet acquainted at all,
and I do always find her scolding, and do believe she is an ill-
natured devil, that I have no great desire to speak to her. Mr.
Moore mightily commends my Lord Hinchingbroke's match and
Lady, though he buys her £10,000 dear by the jointure and settlement his father makes her; and says that the Duke of York and
Duchess of York did come to see them in bed together on their
wedding night; and how my Lord had fifty pieces of gold taken
out of his pocket that night after he was in bed. He tells me that
an Act of Comprehension is likely to pass this Parliament, for
admitting of all persuasions in religion to the public observation
of their particular worship, but in certain places, and the persons
therein concerned to be listed of this or that Church; which, it is
thought, will do them more hurt than good and make them not
own their persuasion. He tells me that there is a pardon passed
to the Duke of Buckingham, my Lord of Shrewsbury, and the rest
for the late duel and murder; which he thinks a worse fault than
any ill use my late Lord Chancellor ever put the Great Seal to, and
will be so thought by the Parliament, for them to be pardoned
without bringing them to any trial: and that my Lord Privy Seal
therefore would not have it pass his hand, but made it go by immediate warrant; or at least they knew that he would not pass it,
and so did direct it to go by immediate warrant, that it might not
come to him. He tells me what a character my Lord Sandwich

hath sent over of Mr. Godolphin, as the worthiest man, and such a friend to him as he may be trusted in anything relating to him in the world : as one from whom, he says, he hath infallible assurances that he will remain his friend : which is very high, but indeed they say the gentleman is a fine man.

6th. Sir H. Cholmley tells me how the Parliament, which is to meet again today, are likely to fall heavy on the business of the Duke of Buckingham's pardon; and I shall be glad of it : and that the King hath put out of the Court the two Hydes,[1] my Lord Chancellor's two sons, and also the Bishops of Rochester [2] and Winchester,[3] the latter of whom should have preached before him yesterday, being Ash-Wednesday, and had his sermon ready, but was put by; which is great news.   My wife being gone before, I to the Duke of York's playhouse, where a new play of Etherege's,[4] called 'She Would if she Could'; and though I was there by two o'clock, there was 1000 people put back that could not have room in the pit; and I at last, because my wife was there, made shift to get into the 18*d.* box, and there saw.   But, Lord! how full was the house, and how silly the play, there being nothing in the world good in it, and few people pleased in it.   The King was there; but I sat mightily behind, and could see but little and hear not all. The play being done, I into the pit to look for my wife, it being dark and raining, but could not find her; and so stayed going between the two doors and through the pit an hour and a half, I think, after the play was done; the people staying there till the rain was over, and to talk with one another.   And among the rest here was the Duke of Buckingham today openly sat in the pit; and there I found him with my Lord Buckhurst and Sedley and Etherege the poet; the last of whom I did hear mightily find fault with the actors, that they were out of humour and had not their parts perfect, and that Harris did do nothing, nor could so much as sing a catch in it; and so was mightily concerned : while all the rest did, through the whole pit, blame the play as a silly, dull thing, though there was something very roguish and witty; but the design of the play, and end, mighty insipid.   At last I did find my wife, and with her was Betty Turner, Mercer, and Deb.   So I

---

[1] Lord Cornbury and Laurence Hyde.
[2] John Dolben, afterwards Archbishop of York.
[3] George Morley.
[4] Sir George Etherege, the celebrated wit and dramatic writer. He is said to have died in France, subsequently to the Revolution, having followed the fortunes of his royal master, James II.

got a coach, and a humour took us, and I carried them to Hercules' Pillars and there did give them a kind of a supper of about 7s., and very merry: and home round the town, not through the ruins, and it was pretty how the coachman by mistake drives us into the ruins from London Wall into Coleman Street, and would persuade me that I lived there. And the truth is, I did think that he and the linkman had contrived some roguery, but it proved only a mistake of the coachman; but it was a cunning place to have done us a mischief in, as any I know, to drive us out of the road into the ruins, and there stop, while nobody could be called to help us. But we come safe home.

7th. Met my cousin Roger Pepys, the Parliament meeting yesterday and adjourned to Monday next; and here he tells me that Mr. Jackson, my sister's servant,[1] is come to town and hath this day suffered a recovery on his estate, in order to the making her a settlement. There is a great trial between my Lord Gerard and Carr today, who is indicted for his life at the King's Bench for running from his colours; but all do say that my Lord Gerard, though he designs the ruin of this man, will not get anything by it. To the Commissioners of Accounts, and there presented my books, and was made to sit down, and used with much respect, otherwise than the other day, when I came to them as a criminal about the business of prizes. I sat here with them a great while, while my books were inventoried. I find these gentlemen to sit all day, and only eat a bit of bread at noon, and a glass of wine; and are resolved to go through their business with great severity and method. Met my cousin Roger again, and Mr. Jackson, who is a plain young man, handsome enough for Pall, one of no education nor discourse, but of few words, and one altogether that, I think, will please me well enough. My cousin had got me to give the odd sixth £100 presently, which I intended to keep to the birth of the first child: and let it go—I shall be eased of the care. So there parted, my mind pretty well satisfied with this plain fellow for my sister; though I shall, I see, have no pleasure nor content in him, as if he had been a man of reading and parts like Cumberland. Lord Brouncker and W. Pen and I, and with us Sir Arnold Breames, to the King's playhouse, and there saw a piece of 'Love in a Maze,' a dull, silly play, I think; and after the play home with W. Pen and his son Lowther, whom we met there.

8th. Cousin Roger and Jackson by appointment came to dine

---

[1] i.e. suitor.

with me, and Creed, and very merry, only Jackson hath few words, and I like him never the worse for it.   The great talk is of Carr's coming off in all his trials, to the disgrace of my Lord Gerard, to that degree and the ripping up of so many notorious rogueries and cheats of my Lord's, that my Lord, it is thought, will be ruined; and, above all, do show the madness of the House of Commons, who rejected the petition of this poor man by a combination of a few in the House; and, much more, the base proceedings, just the epitome of all our public managements in this age, of the House of Lords, that ordered him to stand in the pillory for those very things, without hearing and examining what he hath now, by the seeking of my Lord Gerard himself, cleared himself of in open Court, to the gaining himself the pity of all the world and shame for ever to my Lord Gerard.   To the Strand, to my bookseller's, and there bought an idle, roguish French book, which I have bought in plain binding, avoiding the buying of it better bound because I resolve, as soon as I have read it, to burn it, that it may not stand in the list of books, nor among them, to disgrace them if it should be found.   My wife well pleased with my sister's match, and designing how to be merry at their marriage.

9th. (Lord's day.) Pegg Pen [1] was brought to bed yesterday of a girl; and, among other things, if I have not already set it down, it hardly ever was remembered for such a season for the small-pox as these last two months have been, people being seen all up and down the streets, newly come out after the small-pox.

10th. Made a visit to Mr. Godolphin at his chamber; and I do find him a very pretty and able person, a man of very fine parts, and of infinite zeal to my Lord Sandwich; and one that says he is, he believes, as wise and able a person as any prince in the world hath.   He tells me that he meets with unmannerly usage by Sir Robert Southwell [2] in Portugal, who would sign with him in his negotiations there, being a forward young man: but that my Lord mastered him in that point, it being ruled for my Lord here, at a hearing of a Committee of the Council.   He says that if my Lord can compass a peace between Spain and Portugal, and hath the doing of it and the honour himself, it will be a thing of more

[1] Mrs. Lowther, here mentioned by her maiden name.

[2] He had been knighted, and sent as Envoy Extraordinary to Portugal in 1665, and went, in the same capacity, to Brussels in 1671.   He became afterwards clerk to the Privy Council, and was five times elected president of the Royal Society. *Ob.* 1702, at King's Weston in Gloucestershire, aged sixty-seven.

honour than ever any man had, and of as much advantage.   Thence
to Westminster Hall, where the Hall mighty full: and, among other
things, the House begins to sit today, and the King came.   But
before the King's coming the House of Commons met; and upon
information given them of a Bill intended to be brought in, as
common report said, for Comprehension they did mightily and
generally inveigh against it, and did vote that the King should be
desired by the House (and the message delivered by the Privy
Councillors of the House) that the laws against breakers of the
Act of Uniformity should be put in execution: and it was moved
in the House that, if any people had a mind to bring any new laws
into the House about religion, they might come, as a proposer of
new laws did in Athens, with ropes about their necks.   By and by
the King to the Lords' House, and there tells them of his league
with Holland, and the necessity of a fleet, and his debts, and, therefore, want of money; and his desire that they would think of some
way to bring in all his Protestant subjects to a right understanding
and peace one with another—meaning the Bill of Comprehension.
The Commons coming to their House, it was moved that the vote
passed this morning might be suspended, because of the King's
speech, till the House was full and called over, two days hence.
But it was denied, so furious they are against this Bill: and thereby
a great blow either given to the King or Presbyters, or, which is
the rather of the two, to the House itself, by denying a thing
desired by the King and so much desired by much the greater
part of the nation.   Whatever the consequence be, if the King
be of any stomach and heat, all do believe that he will resent
this vote.   Read over and agreed upon Pall's Deed of Settlement to our minds: she to have £600 presently, and she to be
jointured in £60 per annum; wherein I am very well satisfied.
Vexed in my mind with the variety of cares I have upon me, and
so to bed.

11th.   Comes a summons to attend the Committee of Miscarriages today, which makes me mad, that I should by my place
become the hackney of this Office, in perpetual trouble and
vexation, that need it least.   To Westminster Hall, and sent my
wife and Deb. to see 'Mustapha' acted.   Here I brought a book
to the Committee, and do find them, and particularly Sir Thomas
Clarges, mighty hot in the business of tickets, which makes me mad
to see them bite at the stone and not at the hand that flings it.
Thence to the Duke of York's playhouse, and there saw the last

act for nothing, where I never saw such good acting of any creature as Smith's part of Zanga; [1] and I do also, though Solyman was excellently acted by ——, yet want Betterton mightily. To Pemberton's [2] chamber, and did discourse all our business of the prizes; and, upon the whole, he do make it plainly appear that there is no avoiding to give these Commissioners satisfaction in everything they will ask; and that there is fear lest they may find reason to make us refund for all the extraordinary profit made by those bargains; and do make me resolve rather to declare plainly and once for all the truth of the whole, and what my profit hath been, than be forced at last to do it, and in the meantime live in pain: and with this resolution on my part I departed, with some more satisfaction of mind, though with less hopes of profit than I expected. It was pretty here to see the heaps of money upon this lawyer's table, and more to see how he had not since last night spent any time upon our business, but begun with telling us that we were not at all concerned in that Act; which was a total mistake, by his not having read over the Act at all. This morning my wife in bed told me the story of our Tom and Jane: how the rogue did first demand her consent to love and marry him, and then, with pretence of displeasing me, did slight her; but both he and she have confessed the matter to her, and she hath charged him to go on with his love to her and be true to her, which, for my love to her, because she is in love with him, I am pleased with; but otherwise I think she will have no good bargain of it. But if I do stand, I do intend to give her £50 in money and do them all the good I can in my way.

12th. To my office, where all the morning drawing up my narrative of my proceedings and concernments in the buying of prize-goods, which I am to present to the Committee for Accounts. After dinner with Mr. Jackson to find my cousin Roger Pepys, which I did in the Parliament House, where I met with him and Sir Thomas Crewe and Mr. George Montagu, who are mighty busy how to save my Lord's name from being in the Report for anything which the Committee is commanded to report to the

---

[1] The play in which Smith acted Zanga was Lord Orrery's *Mustapha*.

[2] Francis Pemberton, afterwards knighted, and made Lord Chief Justice of the King's Bench in 1679. His career was a most singular one, he having been twice removed from the Bench: perhaps he was not sufficiently pliant for those times. Roger North gives him an unfavourable character, but Evelyn speaks well of him.

House of the miscarriages of the late war. Thence with cousin Roger to his lodgings, and there sealed the writings with Jackson about my sister's marriage: and here my cousin Roger told me the pleasant passage of a fellow's bringing a bag of letters today, into the lobby of the House, where he left them and withdrew himself without observation. The bag being opened, the letters were found all of one size and directed with one hand: a letter to most of the Members of the House. The House was acquainted with it, and voted they should be brought in, and one opened by the Speaker; wherein if he found anything unfit to communicate, to propose a Committee to be chosen for it. The Speaker opening one, found it only a case with a libel in it, printed: a satire most sober and bitter as ever I read, and every letter was the same. So the House fell a-scrambling for them like boys: and my cousin Roger had one directed to him, which he lent me to read. Mr. Houblon came late to me; and going to the gate with him, I found his lady and another fine lady sitting an hour together, late at night, in their coach, while he was with me: which is so like my wife that I was mightily taken with it, though troubled for it.

13th. To the Commissioners of the Treasury, where myself alone did argue the business of the East India Company against their whole company on behalf of the King before the Lords Commissioners, and to very good effect, I think, and with reputation. That being over, the Lords and I had other things to talk about. Mr. Brisband tells me in discourse that Tom Killigrew hath a fee out of the Wardrobe for cap and bells, under the title of the King's Fool or Jester, and may revile or jeer anybody, the greatest person, without offence, by the privilege of his place. The House was called over today. This morning Sir G. Carteret came to the office to see and talk with me: and he assures me that to this day the King is the most kind man to my Lord Sandwich in the whole world; that he himself do not now mind any public business, but suffers things to go on at Court as they will, he seeing all likely to come to ruin; that this morning the Duke of York sent to him to come to make up one of a Committee of the Council for Naval Affairs; upon which, when he came, he told the Duke of York that he was none of them: which shows how things are nowadays ordered, that there should be a Committee for the Navy, and the Lord Admiral knows not the persons of it! and that Sir G. Carteret and my Lord Anglesey should be left out of it, and men wholly improper put into it. I do hear of all hands that there is a great difference at this day between my Lord Arlington and Sir W. Coventry, which I am sorry for.

14th. (Valentine's day.) Up, being called up by Mercer, who came to be my Valentine, and I did give her a guinea in gold for her Valentine's gift. There comes Roger Pepys betimes, and comes to my wife for her to be his Valentine, whose Valentine I was also, by agreement to be so to her every year; and this year I find it is likely to cost £4 or £5 in a ring for her, which she desires. I to my office, to perfect my narrative about prize-goods, and did carry it to the Commissioners of Accounts, who did receive it with great kindness and express great value of, and respect to, me: and my heart is at rest that it is lodged there in so full truth and plainness, though it may hereafter prove some loss to me. But here I do see they are entered into many inquiries about prizes, by the great attendance of commanders and others before them; which is a work I am not sorry for. Thence I away, with my head busy but my heart at pretty good ease, to the Old Exchange, and there met Mr. Houblon. I prayed him to discourse with some of the merchants that are of the Committee for Accounts, to see how they do resent my paper, and in general my particular in relation to the business of the Navy, which he hath promised to do carefully for me. Here it was a mighty pretty sight to see old Mr. Houblon, whom I never saw before, and all his sons about him, all good merchants. To visit Colonel Thomson, one of the Committee of Accounts, who, among the rest, is mighty kind to me, and is likely to mind our business more than any; and I would be glad to have a good understanding with him. Thence after dinner to White Hall, to attend the Duke of York, where I did let him know, too, the troublesome life we lead, and particularly myself, by being obliged to such attendances every day, as I am, on one Committee or other. And I do find the Duke of York himself troubled, and willing not to be troubled with occasions of having his name used among the Parliament, though he himself do declare that he did give directions to Lord Brouncker to discharge the men at Chatham by ticket, and will own it if the House call for it, but not else. Thence I attended the King and Council, and some of the rest of us, in a business to be heard about the value of a ship of one Dorrington's: and it was pretty to observe how, Sir W. Pen making use of this argument against the validity of an oath (against the King) being made by the master's mate of the ship, who was but a fellow of about 23 years of age, the master of the ship, against whom we pleaded, did say that he did think himself at that age capable of being master's mate of any ship; and do know that he, Sir W. Pen, was so himself, and in no better degree at that age himself: which word did strike Sir W. Pen dumb, and made him open his mouth no more; and I saw the King and Duke of York wink at one another at it.   This done, we into the gallery; and there I walked with several people, and among others my Lord Brouncker, who I do find under much trouble still about the business of the tickets, his very case being brought in, as is said, this day in the Report of the Miscarriages.   And he seems to lay much of it on me, which I did clear and satisfy him in, and would be glad with all my heart to serve him in, and have done it more than he hath done for himself, he not deserving the least blame, but commendations, for this.   I met with my cousin Roger Pepys and Creed, and from them understand that the Report was read today of the Miscarriages, wherein my Lord Sandwich is named about the business I mentioned this morning; but I will be at rest, for it can do him no hurt.   Our business of tickets is soundly up, and many others: so they went over them again, and spent them all the morning on the first, which is the dividing of the fleet; wherein hot work was, and that among great men, Privy Councillors, and, they say, Sir W. Coventry; but I do not much fear it, but do hope that it will show a little, of the Duke of Albemarle and the Prince to have been advisers in it.   But whereas they ordered that the King's Speech should be considered today, they took no notice of it at all, but are really come to despise the King in all possible ways of showing it.   And it was the other day a strange saying, as I am told by my cousin Roger Pepys, in the House, when it was moved that the King's Speech should be considered, that though the first part of the Speech, meaning the league that is there talked of, be the only good public thing that hath been done since the King came into England, yet it might bear with being put off to consider till Friday next, which was this day.   Secretary Morrice did this day in the House, when they talked of intelligence, say that he was allowed but £700 a year for intelligence,[1] whereas, in Cromwell's time, he [Cromwell] did allow £70,000 a year for it; and was confirmed therein by Colonel Birch, who said that thereby Cromwell carried the secrets of all the princes of Europe at his girdle.   The House is in a most broken condition: nobody adhering to anything, but reviling and finding fault, and now quite mad at

[1] Secret service money.

the Undertakers, as they are commonly called, Littleton, Lord
Vaughan, Sir R. Howard, and others that are brought over to the
Court and did undertake to get the King money; but they despise,
and will not hear, them in the House; and the Court do as much,
seeing that they cannot be useful to them, as was expected. In
short, it is plain that the King will never be able to do anything with
this Parliament; and that the only likely way to do better, for it
cannot do worse, is to break this and call another Parliament; and
some do think that it is intended. I was told tonight that my Lady
Castlemaine is so great a gamester as to have won £15,000 in one
night, and lost £25,000 in another night, at play, and hath played
£1000 and £1500 at a cast.

15th. Till midnight almost, and till I had tired my own back
and my wife's and Deb.'s, in titling of my books for the present
year, and in setting them in order; which is now done, to my very
good satisfaction, though not altogether so completely as I think
they were the last year.

16th. (Lord's day.) All the morning making a catalogue of my
books. Mr. Hollyard put in and dined with my wife and me.
His story of love and fortune, which hath been very good and very
bad in the world, well worth hearing. Much discourse about the
bad state of the Church, and how the Clergy are come to be men of
no worth in the world; and, as the world do now generally discourse, they must be reformed. And I believe the Hierarchy will in
a little time be shaken, whether they will or no, the King being
offended with them and set upon it, as I hear.

17th. All the morning getting some things more ready against
the afternoon for the Committee of Accounts, which did give me
great trouble, to see how I am forced to dance after them in one
place, and to answer Committees of Parliament in another. Great
high words in the House on Saturday last, upon the first part of
the Committee's Report about the dividing of the fleet; wherein
some would have the counsels of the King to be declared, and the
reasons of them, and who did give them; where Sir W. Coventry
laid open to them the consequences of doing that, that the King
would never have any honest and wise men ever to be of his
Council. They did here in the House talk boldly of the King's
bad counsellors, and how they all must be turned out, and many
others and better brought in. And the proceedings of the Long
Parliament in the beginning of the war were called to memory;
and the King's bad intelligence was mentioned, wherein they were

bitter against my Lord Arlington, saying, among other things, that whatever Morrice's was, who declared he had but £750 a year allowed him for intelligence, the King paid too dear for my Lord Arlington's, in giving him £10,000 and a barony for it.   Sir W. Coventry did here come to his defence, in the business of the letter that was sent to call back Prince Rupert after he was divided from the fleet, wherein great delay was objected; but he did show that he sent it at one in the morning, when the Duke of York did give him the instructions after supper that night, and did clear himself well of it: only it was laid as a fault, which I know not how he removes, of not sending it by an express, but by the ordinary post. But I think I have heard he did send it to my Lord Arlington's, and that there it lay for some hours, ; it coming not to Sir Philip Honeywood's hand at Portsmouth [1] till four in the afternoon that day, being about fifteen or sixteen hours in going.   And about this, I think, I have heard of a falling out between my Lord Arlington heretofore and W. Coventry.   Some mutterings I did hear of dissolving the Parliament; but I think there is no ground for it yet, though Oliver would have dissolved them for half the trouble and contempt these have put upon the King and his councils.   The dividing of the fleet, however, is, I hear, voted a miscarriage, and the not building a fortification at Sheerness: and I have reason every hour to expect that they will vote the like of our paying men off by ticket; and what the consequence of that will be I know not.

18th.   Walked down to the old Swan, where I find Michell building, his booth being taken down and a foundation laid for a new house, so that that street is like to be a very fine place.   So to Charing Cross stairs, and to Sir W. Coventry's, who tells me how he hath been persecuted, and how he is yet well come off in the business of the dividing of the fleet and the sending of the letter.   He expects next to be troubled about the business of bad officers in the fleet, wherein he will bid them name whom they call bad, and he will justify himself, having never disposed of any but by the Admiral's liking.   He and I did look over the list of commanders,[2] and found that we could presently recollect thirty-seven commanders that have been killed in actual service this war.   He

---

[1] Of which Sir Philip was governor.   The account of the money expended by Sir P. Honeywood on the fortifications at Portsmouth, between August 1665 and April 1667, is in the Sloane MSS., 873.

[2] A copy of the Duke of York's list of the commanders slain in the year 1666, which was given to Pepys, is in Rawlinson, A 191, fol. 108.

tells me that Sir Fr. Hollis is the main man that hath persecuted him hitherto in the business of dividing the fleet, saying vainly that the want of that letter to the Prince hath given him that that he shall remember it by to his grave, meaning the loss of his arm; when, God knows! he is as idle and insignificant a fellow as ever came into the fleet.   He tells me that in discourse he did repeat Sir Rob. Howard's words about rolling out of counsellers, that for his part he neither cared who they rolled in nor who they rolled out, by which the word is become a word of use in the House, the rolling out of officers.   I will remember what, in mirth, he said to me this morning, when upon this discourse he said, if ever there was another Dutch war they should not find a Secretary; 'Nor,' said I, 'a Clerk of the Acts, for I see the reward of it: and, thank God! I have enough of my own to buy me a good book and a good fiddle, and I have a good wife';—'Why,' says he, 'I have enough to buy me a good book, and shall not need a fiddle, because I have never a one of your good wives.'   To Westminster Hall, and there walked all the morning, and did speak with several Parliament-men—among others Birch, who is very kind to me and calls me, with great respect and kindness, a man of business, and he thinks honest, and so long will stand by me and every such man to the death.   My business was to instruct them to keep the House from falling into any mistaken vote about the business of tickets before they were better informed.   With my Lord Brouncker, who was in great pain there; and, the truth is, his business is, without reason, so ill resented by the generality of the House, that I was almost troubled to be seen to walk with him, and yet am able to justify him in all that he is in so much scandal for.   Here I did get a copy of the Report itself, about our paying off men by tickets; and am mightily glad to see it, now knowing the state of our case and what we have to answer to: so that, against Thursday, I shall be able to draw up some defence to put into some Members' hands, to inform them.   This morning the House is upon a Bill, brought in today by Sir Richard Temple, for obliging the King to call Parliaments every three years; or, if he fail, for others to be obliged to do it, and to keep him from a power of dissolving any Parliament in less than forty days after their first day of sitting, which is such a Bill as do speak very high proceedings, to the lessening of the King.   And this they will carry, and whatever else they desire, before they will give any money; and the King must have money, whatever it cost him.   Sir W. Pen and I to the

Bear, in Drury Lane, an excellent ordinary, after the French manner, but of Englishmen; and there had a good fricassee, our dinner coming to 8s., which was mighty pretty, to my great content; and thence he and I to the King's House, and there, in one of the upper boxes, saw 'Flora's Vagaries,' which is a very silly play; and the more, I being out of humour, being at a play without my wife, and she ill at home, and having no desire also to be seen, and therefore could not look about me.   I to see Kate Joyce, where I find her and her friends in great ease of mind, the jury having this day given in their verdict that her husband died of a fever.   Some opposition there was, the foreman pressing them to declare the cause of the fever, thinking thereby to obstruct it: but they did adhere to their verdict, and would give no reason; so all trouble is now over, and she safe in her estate.   Up to my wife, not owning my being at a play, and there she shows me her ring of a Turkey-stone,[1] set with little sparks of diamonds, which I am to give her as my Valentine, and I am not much troubled at it.   It will cost me near £5—she costing me but little compared with other wives, and I have not many occasions to spend money on her.

19th. With my wife out with Deb., to buy some things against my sister's wedding.   In the evening to White Hall, where I find Sir W. Coventry a great while with the Duke of York, in the King's drawing-room, they two talking together all alone, which did mightily please me.   I do hear how La Roche, a French captain, who was once prisoner here, being with his ship at Plymouth, hath played some freaks there, for which his men being beat out of the town, he hath put up a flag of defiance, and also, somewhere thereabout, did land with his men, and go a mile into the country, and did some pranks, which sounds pretty odd, to our disgrace, but we are in condition now to bear anything.   But, blessed be God! all the Court is full of good news of my Lord Sandwich's having made a peace between Spain and Portugal, which is mighty great news, and, above all, to my Lord's honour, more than anything he ever did; and yet I do fear it will not prevail to secure him in Parliament against incivilities there.

20th. The House most of the morning upon the business of not prosecuting the first victory; which they have voted one of the greatest miscarriages of the whole war, though they cannot lay the fault anywhere yet, because Harman is not come home.   Dined, and by one o'clock to the King's House: a new play, 'The Duke of

[1] Turquoise.

Lerma,' of Sir Robert Howard's: where the King and Court was; and Knipp and Nell spoke the prologue most excellently, especially Knipp, who spoke beyond any creature I ever heard. The play designed to reproach our King with his mistresses, that I was troubled for it and expected it should be interrupted; but it ended all well, which salved all.

21st. Comes to me young Captain Beckford, the slopseller, and there presents me a little purse with gold in it, it being, as he told me, for his present to me at the end of the last year. I told him I had not done him any service I knew of. He persisted, and I refused; and telling him that it was not an age to make presents in, he told me he had reason to present me with something, and desired me to accept of it, which, at his so urging me, I did. Towards Westminster, and met my Lord Brouncker and W. Pen and Sir T. Harvey in King's Street, coming away from the Parliament House; and so I to them, and to the French ordinary at the Blue Bells, in Lincoln's Inn Fields, and there dined and talked. And, among other things, they tell me how the House this day is still as backward for giving any money as ever, and do declare they will first have an account of the disposals of the last Poll-bill, and eleven months' tax; and it is pretty odd that the very first sum mentioned in the account brought in by Sir Robert Long, of the disposal of the Poll-bill money, is £5000 to my Lord Arlington for intelligence; which was mighty unseasonable, so soon after they had so much cried out against his want of intelligence. The King do also own but £250,000 or thereabouts, yet paid on the Poll-bill, and that he hath charged £350,000 upon it. This makes them mad; for that the former Poll-bill, that was so much less in its extent than the last, which took in all sexes and qualities, did come to £350,000. Upon the whole, I perceive they are like to do nothing in this matter to please the King or relieve the State, be the case never so pressing; and therefore it is thought by a great many that the King cannot be worse if he should dissolve them: but there is nobody dares advise it, nor do he consider anything himself. Thence, having dined for 20s., we to the Duke of York at White Hall, and there had our usual audience, and did little but talk of the proceedings of Parliament, wherein he is as much troubled as we; for he is not without fears that they do aim at doing him hurt. But yet he declares that he will never deny to own what orders he hath given to any man to justify him, notwithstanding their having sent to him to desire his being tender to take

upon him the doing anything of that kind. Met with Colonel
Birch and Sir John Lowther,[1] and did there in the lobby read over
what I have drawn up for our defence, wherein they own themselves mightily satisfied; and Birch, like a particular friend, do take
it upon him to defend us, and do mightily do me right in all his
discourse. Discoursed with several members, to prepare them in
our business against tomorrow. My cousin Roger Pepys showed
me Granger's written confession,[2] of his being forced by imprisonment, &c., by my Lord Gerard, most barbarously to confess his
forging of a deed in behalf of Fitton, in the great case between him
[Fitton] and my Lord Gerard; which business is under examination, and is the foulest against my Lord Gerard that ever anything
in the world was, and will, all do believe, ruin him; and I shall be
glad of it. Comes my wife to me, who hath been at Pegg Pen's
christening, which, she says, hath made a flutter and noise, but
was as mean as could be, and but little company, just like all the
rest that family do.

22d. By coach through Duck Lane, and there did buy Kircher's
Musurgia,[3] cost me 35s., a book I am mighty glad of, expecting to
find great satisfaction in it. To Westminster Hall and the lobby,
and up and down there all the morning, and the Lords' House, and
heard the Solicitor-General plead very finely, as he always do; and
this was in defence of the East India Company against a man [4] that
complains of wrong from them. And so with my wife and Mercer
and Deb., who come to the Hall to me, I away to the Bear, in
Drury Lane, and there bespoke a dish of meat; and in the meantime sat and sung with Mercer; and by and by dined with mighty
pleasure, and excellent meat, one little dish enough for us all, and
good wine, and all for 8s. To the Duke's playhouse, and there

[1] Of Lowther, in Westmorland, for which county he was Knight of the
Shire before and at the Restoration. He had been made a baronet of Nova
Scotia in 1640.
[2] Pepys here refers to the extraordinary proceedings which occurred
between Charles Lord Gerard and Alexander Fitton, of which a narrative was
published at The Hague in 1665. Granger was a witness in the cause, and
was afterwards said to be conscience-stricken from his perjury. Some notice
of this case will be found in North's *Examen*, p. 558; but the copious and
interesting note in Ormerod's *History of Cheshire*, vol. iii, p. 291, will best
satisfy the reader.
[3] *Musurgia Universalis, sive ars magna Consoni et Dissoni.* It is an elaborate
work, by the famous Jesuit, Athanasius Kircher, and was printed at Rome in
1650, in two volumes, folio.
[4] Skinner.

saw 'Albumazar,' an old play, this the second time of acting.   It
is said to have been the ground of B. Jonson's 'Alchymist'; but,
saving the ridiculousness of Angell's part, which is called Trinculo,
I do not see anything extraordinary in it, but was indeed weary of
it before it was done.[1]   The King here, and, indeed, all of us, pretty
merry at the mimic tricks of Trinculo.

23d. (Lord's day.) Up, and, being desired by a messenger from
Sir G. Carteret, I by water over to Southwark, and so walked to
the Falcon, on the Bankside, and there got another boat, and so to
Westminster, where I would have gone into the Swan.   But the
door was locked, and the girl could not let me in, and so to Wilkinson's, in King Street, and there wiped my shoes, and so to Court,
where sermon not yet done.   I met with Brisband; and he tells
me, first, that our business of tickets did come to debate yesterday,
it seems, after I was gone away, and was voted a miscarriage in
general.   He tells me that there is great looking after places upon
a presumption of a great many vacancies: and he did show me a
fellow at Court, a brother of my Lord Fanshawe's,[2] a witty but
rascally fellow, without a penny in his purse, that was asking him
what places there were in the Navy fit for him, and Brisband tells
me, in mirth, he told him the Clerk of the Acts; and I wish he had
it, so I were well and quietly rid of it.   For I am weary of this

---

[1] The comedy of *Albumazar*, in which Angell played, was originally printed
in 1615, having been performed before King James at Trinity College, Cambridge, by the gentlemen of that society, of which Tomkis, the author of the
play, was a member, on 9th March 1614.   See a long disquisition upon the
play of *Albumazar* in the *Gentlemen's Magazine*, March 1756, by which it
would seem Dryden was right, and that the piece had been only revived when
acted at Cambridge, and was written before the *Alchymist* appeared.   The
assertion of Pepys (derived from Dryden's prologue on the revival of the
comedy, in 1668) is refuted by the fact that Ben Jonson's *Alchymist* was acted
four or five years before *Albumazar* was produced—namely, in 1610.   This
play may be seen in vol. vii of the last edition of Dodsley's *Old Plays*.   Angell
was one of the original performers in Davenant's company; but early in his
career he acted, as Downes informs us, 'women's parts,' from which he was,
of course, excluded as soon as actresses were substituted.   He then seems to
have taken up broad comedy; and besides Trinculo, in *Albumazar*, we find
him performing Woodcock in Shadwell's *Sullen Lovers*, a droll part in Lord
Orrery's *Master Anthony*, and Fribble in *Epsom Wells*.
[2] Sir Thomas Fanshawe, K.B., who was created Viscount Fanshawe, of
Ireland, in 1661, died in 1665, leaving three sons: Thomas, the Lord Fanshawe
here mentioned, and Charles and Simon, who became successively the fourth
and fifth viscounts.   It is uncertain which of these two is here alluded to.
Sir Richard Fanshawe was the youngest brother of the first lord.

kind of trouble, having, I think, enough whereon to support myself. I met with Sir W. Coventry, and he and I walked awhile together in the Matted Gallery: and there he told me all the proceedings of yesterday: that the matter is found, in general, a miscarriage, but no persons named; and so there is no great matter to our prejudice yet, till, if ever, they come to particular persons. He told me Birch was very industrious to do what he could, and did, like a friend; but they were resolved to find the thing, in general, a miscarriage; and says that when we shall think fit to desire its being heard, as to our own defence, it will be granted. He tells me how he hath, with advantage, cleared himself in what concerns himself therein, by his servant Robson, which I am glad of. He tells me that there is a letter sent by conspiracy to some of the House, which he hath seen, about the manner of selling of places, which he do believe he shall be called upon tomorrow for, and thinks himself well prepared to defend himself in it; and then neither he, nor his friends for him, are afraid of anything to his prejudice. Thence by coach with Brisband to Sir G. Carteret's, in Lincoln's Inn Fields, and there dined: a good dinner and good company. And after dinner he and I alone, discoursing of my Lord Sandwich's matters; who hath, in the first business before the House, been very kindly used beyond expectation, the matter being laid by till his coming home: and old Mr. Vaughan did speak for my Lord, which I am mighty glad of. The business of the prizes is the worst that can be said, and therein I do fear something may lie hard upon him; but, against this, we must prepare the best we can for his defence. Thence with Sir G. Carteret to White Hall, where, finding a meeting of the Committee of the Council for the Navy, his Royal Highness there, and Sir W. Pen, and some of the Brethren of the Trinity House to attend, I did go in with them; and it was to be informed of the practice heretofore, for all foreign nations at enmity one with another to forbear any acts of hostility to one another in the presence of any of the King of England's ships, of which several instances were given: and it is referred to their further inquiry, in order to the giving instructions accordingly to our ships now, during the war between Spain and France. Would to God we were in the same condition as heretofore, to challenge and maintain this our dominion! Thence with W. Pen homeward, and quite through to Mile End for a little air, the days being now pretty long but the ways mighty dirty. Going back again, Sir R. Brookes overtook us coming to town; who played the jack with us all, and is a fellow that I must trust no more, he quoting me for all he hath said in this business of tickets; though I have told him nothing that either is not true or I afraid to own. But here talking, he did discourse in this style: 'We'—and 'We' all along—'will not give any money, be the pretence never so great, nay, though the enemy was in the River of Thames again, till we know what is become of the last money given'; and I do believe he do speak the mind of his fellows, and so let him.   This evening my wife did with great pleasure show me her stock of jewels, increased by the ring she hath made lately as my Valentine's gift this year, a Turkey-stone set with diamonds: and, with this and what she had, she reckons that she hath above £150 worth of jewels, of one kind or other; and I am glad of it, for it is fit the wretch should have something to content herself with.

24th. At my bookseller's, and did buy 'L'illustre Bassa'[1] in four volumes for my wife.   Meeting Dr. Gibbons,[2] he and I to see an organ at the Dean of Westminster's lodgings at the Abbey, the Bishop of Rochester's;[3] where he lives like a great prelate, his lodgings being very good; though at present under great disgrace at Court, being put by his Clerk of the Closet's place. I saw his lady,[4] of whom the *Terræ Filius*[5] of Oxford was once so merry; and two children, whereof one a very pretty little boy, like him, so fat and black.   Here I saw the organ; but it is too big for my house, and the fashion do not please me enough, and therefore I will not have it.   With my wife and Deb. to the Nursery, where none of us ever were before; the house is better and the music better than we looked for, and the acting not much worse, because I expected as bad as could be: and I was not much mistaken, for it

---

[1] *Ibrahim, ou l'illustre Bassa.*   It was the first of that almost interminable series of 'Twelve vast French romances, neatly gilt,' published by Madeleine de Scudéry.   It was printed in 1641.

[2] Christopher Gibbons, organist to the king, and of Westminster Abbey. He was admitted Doctor of Music at Oxford 1663, and died 1676.

[3] John Dolben, afterwards Archbishop of York.

[4] The Bishop of Rochester's wife was Catharine, daughter of Ralph Sheldon, of Stanton, Denbighshire, and niece of Gilbert Sheldon, Archbishop of Canterbury.   The 'pretty little boy' was her son Gilbert, who became one of the Judges of the Common Pleas in Ireland, was created a baronet by Queen Anne, and is ancestor of the present family, seated at Findon, Northamptonshire.

[5] A scholar appointed to make a satirical and jesting speech at an act in the university of Oxford.   The custom was discontinued about the beginning of the eighteenth century.

was so. However, I was pleased well to see it once, it being worth a man's seeing to discover the different ability and understanding of people, and the different growth of people's abilities by practice. Their play was a bad one, called 'Jeronimo is Mad Again,'[1] a tragedy. Here was some good company by us, who did make mighty sport at the folly of their acting, which I could not refrain from sometimes, though I was sorry for it. I was prettily served this day at the playhouse door, where, giving six shillings into the fellow's hand for three of us, the fellow by legerdemain did convey one away, and with so much grace faced me down that I did give him but five, that, though I knew the contrary, yet I was overpowered by his so grave and serious demanding the other shilling, that I could not deny him, but was forced by myself to give it him. This evening came a letter to me from Captain Allen, formerly Clerk of the Rope-yard at Chatham, who do give me notice that he hears an accusation likely to be exhibited against me of my receiving £50 of Mason, the timber merchant. The thing is, to the best of my memory, utterly false, but yet it troubles me to have my name mentioned in this business, and more to consider how I may be liable to be accused where I have indeed taken presents.

25th. Comes W. Howe to me, to advise what answer to give to the business of the prizes, wherein I did give him the best advice I could; but am sorry to see so many things, wherein I doubt it will not be prevented but Sir Roger Cuttance and Mr. Pierce will be found very much concerned in goods beyond the distribution, and I doubt my Lord Sandwich, too. I took my wife and Deb. up, and to the Nursery, and there saw them act a comedy, a pastoral, 'The Faithful Shepherd,'[2] having the curiosity to see whether they did a comedy better than a tragedy; but they do it both alike, in the meanest manner, that I was sick of it; but I shall see them no more. My wife hath bought a dressing-box and other things for her chamber and table, that cost me above £4. I do perceive, by Sir W. Warren's discourse, that the House do all they can possibly to get out of him and others what presents they have made to the officers of the Navy; but he tells me that he hath denied all, though he knows that he is forsworn as to what relates to me.

---

[1] 'Jeronimo, or, the Spanish Tragedy'; anonymous, printed in Dodsley's *Collection of Old Plays*.
[2] A pastoral comedy, from the *Pastor Fido* of Guarini, which has been frequently dramatized.

26th. After dinner comes W. Howe to tell me how he sped, who says he was used civilly, and not so many questions asked as he expected; but yet I do perceive enough to show that they do intend to know the bottom of things, and where to lay the great weight of the disposal of these East India goods, and that they intend plainly to do upon my Lord Sandwich. To Westminster Hall, where, it being now about six o'clock, I find the House just risen; and met with Sir W. Coventry and the Lieutenant of the Tower, they having sat all day; and with great difficulty have got a vote for giving the King £300,000, not to be raised by any land-tax. The sum is much smaller than I expected and than the King needs, but is grounded upon Mr. Wren's reading our estimates the other day of £270,000 to keep the fleet abroad, wherein we demanded nothing for setting and fitting of them out, which will cost almost £200,000, I do verily believe: and do believe that the King hath no cause to thank Wren for this motion. I home to Sir W. Coventry's lodgings, with him and the Lieutenant of the Tower, where also was Sir John Coventry and Sir John Duncomb and Sir Job Charleton.[1] And here a great deal of good discourse, and they seem mighty glad to have this vote passed; which I did wonder at, to see them so well satisfied with so small a sum, Sir John Duncomb swearing, as I perceive he will freely do, that it was as much as the nation could bear. Among other merry discourse about spending of money, and how much more chargeable a man's living is now than it was heretofore, Duncomb did swear that in France he did live on £100 a year with more plenty, and wine and wenches, than he believes can be done now for £200; which was pretty odd for him, being a Committee-man's son, to say. Home in Sir John Robinson's coach, and there to bed.

27th. With my wife to the King's House, to see 'The Virgin Martyr,' [2] the first time it hath been acted a great while, and it is mighty pleasant: not that the play is worth much, but it is finely acted by Beck Marshall. But that which did please me beyond anything in the whole world was the wind-music when the angel comes down, which is so sweet that it ravished me, and indeed, in a word, did wrap up my soul so that it made me really sick (just as

---

[1] M.P. for Ludlow; and in 1663 elected Speaker, which office he declined on account of ill health. He was successively King's Serjeant, Chief Justice of Chester, and a Justice of the Common Pleas; he was created a baronet 1686, and *ob.* 1697.

[2] By Massinger.

I have formerly been when in love with my wife), that neither then, nor all the evening going home, and at home, I was able to think of anything, but remained all night transported, so as I could not believe that ever any music hath that real command over the soul of a man as this did upon me: and makes me resolve to practise wind-music, and to make my wife do the like.

28th. After dinner with Sir W. Pen to White Hall, where we and the rest of us presented a great letter of the state of our want of money to his Royal Highness. I did also present a demand of mine for consideration for my travelling-charges of coach- and boat-hire during the war, which, though his Royal Highness and the company did all like of, yet, contrary to my expectation, I find him so jealous now of doing anything extraordinary, that he desired the gentlemen that they would consider it and report their minds in it to him. This did unsettle my mind a great while, not expecting this stop; but, however, I shall do as well, I know, though it causes me a little stop. But that that troubles me most, is that while we were thus together with the Duke of York comes in Mr. Wren from the House, where, he tells us, another storm hath been all this day almost against the officers of the Navy upon this complaint—that though they have made good rules for payment of tickets, yet that they have not observed them themselves, which was driven so high as to have it urged that we should presently be put out of our places: and so they have at last ordered that we shall be heard at the bar of the House upon this business on Thursday next. This did mightily trouble me and us all: but me particularly, who am least able to bear these troubles, though I have the least cause to be concerned in it. Thence, therefore, to visit Sir H. Cholmley, who hath for some time been ill of a cold; and thence walked towards Westminster and met Colonel Birch, who took me back to walk with him, and did give me an account of this day's heat against the Navy officers, and an account of his speech on our behalf, which was very good; and indeed we are much beholden to him, as I, after I parted with him, did find by my cousin Roger, whom I went to: and he and I to his lodgings. And there he did tell me the same over again; and how Birch did stand up in our defence; and that he do see that there are many desirous to have us out of the Office; and the House is so furious and passionate that he thinks nobody can be secure, let him deserve never so well. But now, he tells me, we shall have a fair hearing of the House, and, he hopes, justice of them. But, upon the whole, he do agree with me that I should hold my hand as to making any purchase of land, which I had formerly discoursed with him about, till we see a little further how matters go. He tells me that what made them so mad today, first, was several letters in the House about the Fanatics in several places, coming in great bodies, and turning people out of the churches, and there preaching themselves, and pulling the surplice over the parsons' heads. This was confirmed from several places; which makes them stark mad, especially the hectors and bravadoes of the House, who show all the zeal on this occasion.

29th. Sir G. Carteret did come to discourse about the prize business of my Lord Sandwich's, which I perceive is likely to be of great ill consequence to my Lord, the House being mighty vehement in it. We could say little but advise that his friends should labour to get it put off till he comes. We did here talk many things over, in lamentation of the present posture of affairs, and the ill condition of all people that have had anything to do under the King. They tell me how Sir Thomas Allen hath taken the Englishmen out of La Roche's ship, and taken from him an Ostend prize which La Roche had fetched out of one of our harbours; and at this day La Roche keeps upon our coasts, and had the boldness to land some men and go a mile up into the country, and there took some goods belonging to this prize out of a house there: which our King resents, and, they say, hath wrote to the King of France about; and everybody do think a war will follow; and then in what a case we shall be for want of money nobody knows. Wrote to my father, and sent him Colvill's[1] note for £600 for my sister's portion, being glad that I shall, I hope, have that business over before I am out of place; and I trust I shall be able to save a little of what I have got, for I am weary of this life.

March 1st. (Lord's day.) Up very betimes, and by coach to Sir W. Coventry's; and there, largely carrying with me all my notes and papers, did run over our whole defence in the business of tickets, in order to the answering the House on Thursday next; and I do think, unless they be set without reason to ruin us, we shall make a good defence. I find him in great anxiety, though he will not discover it, in the business of the proceedings of Parliament; and would as little as is possible have his name mentioned in our discourse to them; and particularly the business of selling

[1] The goldsmith's.

182

places is now upon his hand to defend himself in; wherein I did
help him in his defence about the flag-maker's place, which is
named in the House. We did here do the like about the complaint
of want of victuals in the fleet in the year 1666, which will lie upon
me to defend also. In lieu of a coach this year, I have got my wife
to be contented with her closet being made up this summer, and
going into the country this summer for a month or two, to my
father's: and there Mercer and Deb. and Jane shall go with her,
which I the rather do for the entertaining my wife, and preventing
of fallings out between her and my father or Deb. To Mrs.
Martin's, and here I was mightily taken with a starling which she
hath, that was the King's, which he kept in his bed-chamber, and
do whistle and talk the most and best that ever I heard anything in
my life. Spent the evening talking with W. Hewer about business
of the House, and declaring my expectation of all our being turned
out.

2d. Mr. Moore was with me, and do tell me, and so W. Hewer
tells me, he hears this morning that all the town is full of the
discourse that the officers of the Navy shall be all turned out, but
honest Sir John Minnes, who, God knows, is fitter to have been
turned out himself than any of us, doing the King more hurt by
his dotage and folly than all the rest can do by their knavery, if
they had a mind to it. This day I have the news that my sister
was married on Thursday last to Mr. Jackson; so that work is, I
hope, well over.

3d. Up betimes to work again, and then met at the office, where
to our great business of this answer to the Parliament; where to
my great vexation I find my Lord Brouncker prepared only to
excuse himself, while I, that have least reason to trouble myself, am
preparing with great pains to defend them all: and more, I perceive,
he would lodge the beginning of discharging ships by ticket upon
me. But I care not, for I believe I shall get more honour by it
when the Parliament, against my will, shall see how the whole
business of the Office was done by me. I with my clerks to
dinner, and thence presently down with Lord Brouncker, W. Pen,
T. Harvey, T. Middleton, and Mr. Tippet, who first took his
place this day at the table as a Commissioner in the room of
Commissioner Pett. Down by water to Deptford, where the
King, Queen, and Court are to see launched the new ship built
by Mr. Shish, called 'The Charles.'[1] God send her better luck

[1] Named in the *Gazette* 'Charles the Second,' and to carry 106 guns.

than the former![1]   Here some of our brethren, who went in a
boat a little before my boat, did by appointment take opportunity
of asking the King's leave that we might make full use of the want
of money in our excuse to the Parliament for the business of
tickets, and other things they will lay to our charge, all which arise
from nothing else: and this the King did readily agree to, and did
give us leave to make our full use of it.   The ship being well
launched, I back again by boat.

4th. Vexed and sickish to bed, and there slept about three
hours, but then waked, and never in so much trouble, in all my
life, of mind, thinking of the task I have upon me, and upon what
dissatisfactory grounds, and what the issue of it may be to me.

5th. With these thoughts I lay troubling myself till six o'clock,
restless, and at last getting my wife to talk to me to comfort me,
which she at last did, and made me resolve to quit my hands of
this Office, and endure the trouble no longer than till I can clear
myself of it.   So with great trouble, but yet with some ease from
this discourse with my wife, I up, and at my office, whither come
my clerks, and I did huddle the best I could some more notes for
my discourse today; and by nine o'clock was ready, and did go
down to the Old Swan, and there by boat, with T. Harvey and W.
Hewer with me, to Westminster, where I found myself come time
enough, and my brethren all ready.   But I full of thoughts and
trouble touching the issue of this day; and, to comfort myself, did
go to the Dog and drink half a pint of mulled sack, and in the
Hall [Westminster] did drink a dram of brandy at Mrs. Hewlett's;
and with the warmth of this did find myself in better order as to
courage, truly.   So we all up to the lobby; and between eleven and
twelve o'clock were called in, with the mace before us, into the
House, where a mighty full House: and we stood at the bar, namely,
Brouncker, Sir J. Minnes, Sir T. Harvey, and myself, W. Pen being
in the House as a Member.   I perceive the whole House was full,
and full of expectation of our defence what it would be, and with
great prejudice.   After the Speaker had told us the dissatisfaction
of the House, and read the Report of the Committee, I began our
defence most acceptably and smoothly, and continued at it without
any hesitation or loss, but with full scope, and all my reason free
about me, as if it had been at my own table, from that time till
past three in the afternoon; and so ended without any inter-
ruption from the Speaker; but we withdrew.   And there all my

[1] Which was captured by the Dutch in the Medway.

fellow officers, and all the world that was within hearing, did congratulate me and cry up my speech as the best thing they ever heard; and my fellow officers were overjoyed in it; and we were called in again by and by to answer only one question, touching our paying tickets to ticket-mongers; and so out. And we were in hopes to have had a vote this day in our favour, and so the generality of the House was; but my speech being so long, many had gone out to dinner and come in again half drunk; and then there are two or three that are professed enemies to us and everybody else: among others, Sir T. Littleton, Sir Thomas Lee,[1] Mr Wiles, the coxcomb whom I saw heretofore at the cock-fighting, and a few others. I say, these did rise up and speak against the coming to a vote now, the House not being full by reason of several being at dinner, but most because that the House was to attend the King this afternoon about the business of religion, wherein they pray him to put in force all the laws against Nonconformists and Papists; and this prevented it, so that they put it off to tomorrow come se'nnight. However, it is plain we have got great ground, and everybody says I have got the most honour that any could have had opportunity of getting. And so, with our hearts mightily overjoyed at this success, we all to dinner to my Lord Brouncker's—that is to say, myself, T. Harvey, and W. Pen—and there dined; and thence with Sir Anthony Morgan, who is an acquaintance of Brouncker's, a very wise man, we after dinner to the King's House, and there saw part of 'The Discontented Colonel.' To my wife, whom W. Hewer had told of my success, and she overjoyed; and, after talking awhile, I betimes to bed, having had no quiet rest a good while.

6th. Up betimes, and with Sir D. Gauden to Sir W. Coventry's chamber: where the first word he said to me was, 'Good-morrow, Mr. Pepys, that must be Speaker of the Parliament-house'; and did protest I had got honour for ever in Parliament. He said that his brother,[2] that sat by him, admires me; and another gentleman said that I could not get less than £1000 a year, if I would put on a gown and plead at the Chancery Bar; but, what pleases me most, he tells me that the Solicitor-General[3] did protest that he thought I spoke the best of any man in England. After several talks with him alone touching his own businesses, he carried me to White Hall, and there parted; and I to the Duke of York's lodgings,

---

[1] Of Hartwell, Buckinghamshire; created a baronet 1660.
[2] Henry Coventry.   [3] Sir Heneage Finch.

and find him going to the Park, it being a very fine morning, and I after him; and as soon as he saw me he told me, with great satisfaction, that I had converted a great many yesterday, and did, with great praise of me, go on with the discourse with me. And by and by overtaking the King, the King and Duke of York came to me both, and he [1] said, 'Mr. Pepys, I am very glad of your success yesterday,' and fell to talk of my well speaking, and many of the Lords there. My Lord Berkeley did cry me up for what they had heard of it; and others, Parliament-men, there about the King, did say that they never heard such a speech in their lives delivered in that manner. Progers, of the Bedchamber, swore to me afterwards before Brouncker, in the afternoon, and he did tell the King that he thought I might match the Solicitor-General. Everybody that saw me almost came to me, as Joseph Williamson and others, with such eulogies as cannot be expressed. From thence I went to Westminster Hall, where I met Mr. G. Montagu, who came to me and kissed me, and told me that he had often heretofore kissed my hands, but now he would kiss my lips: protesting that I was another Cicero, and said all the world said the same of me. Mr. Ashburnham, and every creature I met there of the Parliament, or that knew anything of the Parliament's actings, did salute me with this honour: Mr. Godolphin; Mr. Sands, who swore he would go twenty miles at any time to hear the like again, and that he never saw so many sit four hours together to hear any man in his life as there did to hear me. Mr. Chicheley, Sir John Duncomb, and everybody do say that the kingdom will ring of my abilities, and that I have done myself right for my whole life: and so Captain Cocke and others of my friends say that no man had ever such an opportunity of making his abilities known; and, that I may cite all at once, Mr. Lieutenant of the Tower did tell me that Mr. Vaughan did protest to him, and that, in his hearing, he said so to the Duke of Albemarle and afterwards to Sir W. Coventry, that he had sat twenty-six years in Parliament and never heard such a speech there before: for which the Lord God make me thankful! and that I may make use of it, not to pride and vain-glory, but that, now I have this esteem, I may do nothing that may lessen it! I spent the morning thus walking in the Hall, being complimented by everybody with admiration, and at noon stepped into the Leg with Sir William Warren, who was in the Hall, and there talked about a little of his business; and thence into the

[1] The King.

Hall a little more, and so with him by coach as far as the Temple almost, and there 'light, to follow my Lord Brouncker's coach, which I spied, and so to Madam Williams's, where I overtook him, and agreed upon meeting this afternoon. To White Hall, to wait on the Duke of York, where he again, and all the company, magnified me, and several in the Gallery: among others my Lord Gerard, who never knew me before nor spoke to me, desires his being better acquainted with me; and [said] that, at table where he was, he never heard so much said of any man as of me, in his whole life. We waited on the Duke of York, and thence into the Gallery, where the House of Lords waited the King's coming out of the Park, which he did by and by; and there, in the Vane-room, my Lord Keeper delivered a message to the King, the Lords being about him, wherein the Barons of England, from many good arguments very well expressed in the part he read out of, do demand precedence in England of all noblemen of either of the King's other two Kingdoms, be their title what it will; and did show that they were in England reputed but as Commoners, and sat in the House of Commons, and at conferences with the Lords did stand bare. It was mighty worth my hearing: but the King did say only that he would consider of it, and so dismissed them.[1] Thence with the Lieutenant of the Tower in his coach home; and there, with great pleasure, with my wife, talking and playing at cards a little—she and I, and W. Hewer and Deb.

7th. Mercer, my wife, Deb., and I to the King's playhouse, and there saw 'The Spanish Gipsies,'[2] the second time of acting, and the first that I saw it. A very silly play, only great variety of dances, and those most excellently done, especially one part by one Haynes,[3] only lately come thither from the Nursery, an under-

---

[1] The point of precedence was settled by the Act of Union. They have rank next after the peers of the like degree in England at the time of the union.

[2] *The Spanish Gipsie*, a comedy by T. Middleton and W. Rowley.

[3] Joseph Haynes: two biographies of him were printed in 1701, after his death. One of them, entitled *The Life of the Famous Comedian, Jo. Haynes, containing his Comical Exploits and Adventures, both at Home and Abroad*, 8vo, states that he had acted under Captain Bedford, 'whilst the playhouse in Hatton Garden lasted.' This must have been the 'Nursery' here alluded to by Pepys. Haynes was the first actor on record who delivered a prologue sitting on an ass. He was soon afterwards followed in this folly by Pinkethman, and, later, by Liston. Haynes seems to have been a low comedian, but good dancer. One dramatic piece is attributed to him, *A Fatal Mistake*, 4to, 1692.

standing fellow, but yet, they say, hath spent £1000 a year before he come thither.   This day my wife and I full of thoughts about Mrs. Pierce's sending me word that she and my old company, Harris and Knipp, would come and dine with us next Wednesday, how we should do—to receive or put them off, my head being at this time so full of business, and my wife in no mind to have them neither, and yet I desire it.

8th. (Lord's day.) To White Hall, where met with very many people still that did congratulate my speech the other day in the House of Commons, and I find all the world almost rings of it. With Sir W. Coventry, who I find full of care in his own business, now to defend himself against those that have a mind to choke him; and though, I believe, not for honour and for the keeping his employment, but for safety and reputation's sake, is desirous to preserve himself free from blame.   He desires me to get information against Captain Tatnell, thereby to diminish his testimony, who, it seems, hath a mind to do W. Coventry hurt: and I will do it with all my heart, for Tatnell is a very rogue.   He would be glad, too, that I could find anything proper for his taking notice against Sir F. Hollis.   To dinner with Sir G. Carteret to Lincoln's Inn Fields, where I find mighty deal of company—a solemn day for some of his and her friends,—and dine in the great dining-room above stairs, where Sir G. Carteret himself and I and his son at a little table, the great table being full of strangers.   Here my Lady Jem do promise to come and bring my Lord Hichingbroke and his lady some day this week, to dinner to me, which I am glad of. After dinner, I up with her husband, Sir Philip Carteret, to his closet, where, beyond expectation, I do find many pretty things wherein he appears to be ingenious, such as in painting, and drawing, and making of watches, and such kind of things above my expectation; though, when all is done, he is a sneak, who owns his owing me £10 for his lady two or three years ago, and yet cannot provide to pay me.

9th. By coach to White Hall, and there met Lord Brouncker: and he and I to the Commissioners of the Treasury, where I find them mighty kind to me, more, I think, than was wont.   And here I also met Colvill, the goldsmith, who tells me with great joy how the world upon the 'Change talks of me; and how several Parliament-men, viz., Boscawen[1] and Major [Lionel] Walden, of Huntingdon, who, it seems, do deal with him, do say how bravely

[1] Edward Boscawen, M.P. for Truro, ancestor of the earls of Falmouth.

I did speak, and that the House was ready to have given me thanks for it: but that, I think, is a vanity.

10th. Met Sir R. Brookes, who do mightily cry up my speech the other day, saying my fellow officers are obliged to me, as indeed they are. With Sir D. Gauden homewards, calling at Lincoln's Inn Fields; but my Lady Jemimah was not within, and so to Newgate, where he stopped to give directions to the gaoler about a Knight, one Sir Thomas Halford,[1] brought in yesterday for killing one Colonel Temple, falling out at a tavern. Home; and there comes Mr. Moore to me, who tells me that he fears my Lord Sandwich will meet with very great difficulties to go through about the prizes, it being found that he did give orders for more than the King's letter do justify; and then for the Act of Resumption, which he fears will go on and is designed only to do him hurt, which troubles me much. He tells me he believes the Parliament will not be brought to do anything in matters of religion, but will adhere to the Bishops. To supper, where I find W. Joyce and Harman come to see us, and there was also Mrs. Mercer and her two daughters, and here we were as merry as that fellow Joyce could make us with his mad talking after the old wont, which tired me. But I was mightily pleased with his singing; for the rogue hath a very good ear and a good voice. Here he stayed till he was almost drunk, and then away at about ten at night, and then all broke up.

11th. Meeting Mr. Colvill, I walked with him to his building, where he is building a fine house, where he formerly lived, in Lombard Street: and it will be a very fine street. So to Westminster; and there walked, till by and by comes Sir W. Coventry, and with him Mr. Chicheley and Mr. Andrew Newport.[2] I to dinner with them to Mr. Chicheley's, in Queen Street, in Covent Garden. A very fine house, and a man that lives in mighty great fashion, with all things in a most extraordinary manner noble and rich about him, and eats in the French fashion all; and mighty nobly served with his servants, and very civilly; that I was mightily pleased with it, and good discourse. He is a great defender of the

---

[1] Sir Thomas Halford, of Wistowe, Leicestershire, the second baronet of his race: he was born in 1638 and died in 1679, having succeeded to his grandfather's titles and estates in 1658, and had twenty-two children by his first wife, Selina, daughter of William Welby, Esq., of Denton, Lincolnshire. No other notice of the duel has been traced.

[2] A commissioner of customs. He was younger son of the first Lord Newport, of High Ercall, Salop.

Church of England, and against the Act for Comprehension, which is the work of this day about which the House is like to sit till night. After dinner with them to Westminster. About four o'clock the House rises, and hath put off the debate to this day month. In the meantime the King hath put out his proclamations this day, as the House desired, for the putting in execution the Act against Nonconformists and Papists. Here I met with Roger Pepys, who is come to town and hath been told of my performance before the House the other day, and is mighty proud of it. Captain Cocke met me here, and told me that the Speaker says he never heard such a defence made in all his life in the House, and that the Solicitor-General do commend me even to envy. I carried cousin Roger as far as the Strand, where, spying out of the coach Colonel Charles George Cocke (formerly a very great man, and my father's customer, whom I have carried clothes to, but now walks like a poor sorry sneak), he stopped, and I 'light to him. This man knew me, which I would have willingly avoided, so much pride I had, he being a man of mighty height and authority in his time, but now signifies nothing.

12th. To Gresham College, there to show myself; and was there greeted by Dr. Wilkins, Whistler, and others, as the patron of the Navy Office, and one that got great fame by my late speech to the Parliament. Here I saw a great trial of the goodness of a burning-glass, made of a new figure, not spherical (by one Smithys, I think they call him), that did burn a glove of my Lord Brouncker's, from the heat of a very little fire, which a burning-glass of the old form, very much bigger, could not do; which was mighty pretty. Then home to supper, and to talk with Mr. Pelling, who tells me what a fame I have in the City by my late performance; and upon the whole I bless God for it. I think I have, if I can keep it, done myself a great deal of repute. So by and by to bed.

13th. To fit myself for attending the Parliament again, not to make any more speeches (which, while my fame is good, I will avoid, for fear of losing of it), but only to answer to what objections will be made against us. Roger Pepys took me aside and told me how he was taken up by one of the House yesterday, for moving for going on with the King's supply of money without regard to the keeping pace therewith with the looking into miscarriages, and was told by this man privately that it did arise because he had a kinsman concerned therein; and therefore he would

prefer the safety of his kinsman to the good of the nation.   But I
did bid him be at no pain for me; for I knew of nothing but what
I was very well prepared to answer; and so I think I am.   At noon
all of us to Chatelin's, the French house in Covent Garden, to
dinner—Brouncker, J. Minnes, W. Pen, T. Harvey, and myself;
and there had a dinner cost us 8*s*. 6*d*. apiece, a base dinner, which
did not please us at all.   My head being full of tomorrow's dinner,
I to my Lord Crewe's, there to invite Sir Thomas Crewe; and
there met with my Lord Hinchingbroke and his lady, the first time
I spoke to her.   I saluted her, and she mighty civil; and, with my
Lady Jemimah, do all resolve to be very merry tomorrow at my
house.   My Lady Hinchingbroke I cannot say is a beauty, nor
ugly; but is altogether a comely lady enough, and seems very good-
humoured.   Thence home, and there find one laying of my napkins against tomorrow in figures of all sorts, which is mighty
pretty; and, it seems, it is his trade and he gets much money by it,
and do now and then furnish tables with plate and linen for a feast
at so much, which is mighty pretty, and a trade I could not have
thought of.   To Mrs. Turner, and did get her to go along with
me to the French pewterer's, and there did buy some new pewter
against tomorrow; and thence to White Hall, to have got a cook
of her acquaintance, the best in England, as she says.   But after
we had with much ado found him he could not come, nor was
Mr. Gentleman in town, whom next I would have had, nor would
Mrs. Stone let her man Lewis come, whom this man recommended
to me; so that I was at a mighty loss what in the world to do for a
cook, Philips being out of town.   Therefore, after staying here at
Westminster a great while, we back to London, and there to
Philips's, and his man directed us to Mr. Levett's, who could not
come, and he sent to two more, and they could not; so that, at last,
Levett as a great kindness did resolve he would leave his business
and come himself, which set me in great ease in my mind.

14th. Up very betimes, and with Jane to Levett's, there to
conclude upon our dinner; and thence to the pewterer's to buy a
pewter cistern,[1] which I have ever hitherto been without.   Anon
comes my company, viz., my Lord Hinchingbroke and his lady,
Sir Philip Carteret and his lady, Godolphin and my cousin Roger,
and Creed: and mighty merry.   And by and by to dinner, which
was very good and plentiful; and I should have said and Mr.

[1] A cistern was formerly part of the furniture of a well-appointed dining-
room; the plates were rinsed in it, when necessary, during the meal.

George Montagu, who came at a very little warning, which was exceeding kind of him. And there, among other things, my Lord had Sir Samuel Morland's late invention for casting up of sums of £ s. d., which is very pretty, but not very useful. Most of our discourse was of my Lord Sandwich and his family, as being all of us of the family; and with extraordinary pleasure all the afternoon thus together, eating and looking over my closet: and my Lady Hinchingbroke I find a very sweet-natured and well-disposed lady, a lover of books and pictures, and of good understanding. About five o'clock they went; and then my wife and I abroad by coach into Moorfields, only for a little air. This day I had the welcome news of our prize being come safe from Holland, so as I shall have hopes, I hope, of getting my money of my Lady Batten, or a good part of it.

15th. (Lord's day.) Walked with Sir W. Coventry into the Park, and there met the King and the Duke of York, and walked a good while with them: and here met Sir Jer. Smith, who tells me he is like to get the better of Holmes, and that when he is come to an end of that he will do Hollis's business for him in the House, for his blasphemies, which I shall be glad of. So to White Hall, and there walked with this man and that man till chapel done, and the King dined: and then Sir Thomas Clifford, the Comptroller,[1] took me with him to dinner to his lodgings, where my Lord Arlington and a great deal of good and great company; where I very civilly used by them, and had a most excellent dinner, and good discourse of Spain (Mr. Godolphin being there), particularly of the removal of the bodies of all the dead Kings of Spain that could be got together, and brought to the Pantheon[2] at the Escorial, when it was finished, and there placed before the altar, there to lie for ever; and there was a sermon made to them upon this text, 'Arida ossa, audite verbum Dei';[3] and a most eloquent sermon, as they say. Mightily pleased with a picture that W. Hewer brought, of several things painted upon a deal board, which board is so well painted that in my whole life I never was so pleased

[1] Of the Household.

[2] Panteon, a term given by the Spaniards to a Christian burial vault. Philip III began the present gorgeous chamber under the high altar, which Philip IV completed in 1654, moving in the royal bodies on 17th March.

[3] The sermon here referred to was preached by a monk of the order of St. Jerome, in 1654: part of it was translated by the Rev. Edward Clarke, who calls it the most extraordinary funeral sermon he ever met with (Southey's *Letters on the Spanish Nation*, p. 141).

or surprised with any picture, and so troubled that so good pictures should be painted upon a piece of bad deal. Even after I knew that it was not board, but only the picture of a board, I could not remove my fancy.

16th. To Westminster by water with Mr. Hater, and there, in the Hall, did walk all the morning, talking with one or other, expecting to have our business in the House; but did now a third time wait to no purpose, they being all this morning upon the business of Barker's petition about the making void the Act of Settlement in Ireland, which makes a great deal of hot work. And at last, finding by all men's opinion they could not come to our matter today, I with Sir W. Pen home, and there to dinner, where I find, by Willett's crying, that her mistress had been angry with her; but I would take no notice of it.

17th. To the Excise Office, where I met Mr. Ball, and did receive my paper I went for; and there fell in talk with him, who, being an old cavalier, do swear and curse at the present state of things, that we should be brought to this, that we must be undone and cannot be saved; that the Parliament is sitting now, and will till midnight, to find how to raise this £300,000, and he doubts they will not do it so as to be seasonable for the King: but do cry out against our great men at Court, how it is a fine thing for a Secretary of State to dance a jig, and that it was not so heretofore; and, above all, do curse my Lord of Bristol, saying the worst news that ever he heard in his life, or that the Devil could ever bring us, was this Lord's coming to prayers the other day in the House of Lords, by which he is coming about again from being a Papist, which will undo this nation; and he says he ever did say, at the King's first coming in, that this nation could not be safe while that man was alive. The House, I hear, have this day concluded upon raising £100,000 of the £300,000 by wine, and the rest by a poll-tax, and have resolved to excuse the Church, in expectation that they will do the more of themselves at this juncture. And I do hear that Sir W. Coventry did make a speech in behalf of the Clergy.

18th. Cousin Roger do still continue of the mind that there is no other way of saving this nation but by dissolving this Parliament and calling another; but there are so many about the King that will not be able to stand if a new Parliament come, that they will not persuade the King to it. To Duck Lane, and there bought Montaigne's Essays, in English. To White Hall, where we and my Lord Brouncker attended the Council, to discourse about the fitness of entering of men presently for the manning of the fleet before one ship is in condition to receive them. Sir W. Coventry did argue against it: I was wholly silent, because I saw the King, upon the earnestness of the Prince, was willing to it, crying very civilly, 'If ever you intend to man the fleet without being cheated by the Captains and pursers, you may go to bed and resolve never to have it manned.' And so it was, like other things, overruled that all volunteers should be presently entered. Then there was another great business about our signing of certificates to the Exchequer, for [prize] goods, upon the £1,250,000 Act, which the Commissioners of the Treasury did all oppose, and to the laying fault upon us. But I did then speak to the justifying what we had done, even to the angering of Duncomb and Clifford, which I was vexed at: but, for all that, I did set the Office and myself right, and went away with the victory, my Lord Keeper saying that he would not advise the Council to order us to sign more certificates. But before I began to say anything in this matter, the King and the Duke of York talking at the Council-table before all the Lords of the Committee of Miscarriages, how this entering of men before the ships could be ready would be reckoned a miscarriage, 'Why,' says the King, 'it is then but Mr. Pepys making of another speech to them'; which made all the Lords, and there were by also the Attorney- and Solicitor-General, look upon me. Thence Sir W. Pen and I, by hackney coach, to take a little air in Hyde Park, the first time that I have been there this year; and we did meet many coaches going and coming, it being mighty pleasant weather; and so, coming back again, I 'light in the Pall Mall, and there went to see Sir H. Cholmley, who continues very ill of his cold. And there came in Sir H. Yelverton, and Sir H. Cholmley commended to me his acquaintance, which the other received, but without remembering to me, or I to him, of our being school-fellows together; and I said nothing of it. But he took notice of my speech the other day at the bar of the House; and indeed I perceive he is a wise man. Here he do say that the town is full of it, that now the Parliament hath resolved upon £300,000, the King, instead of fifty, will set out but twenty-five ships, and the Dutch as many; and that Smith is to command them, who is allowed to have the better of Holmes in the late dispute, and is in good esteem in the Parliament, above the other. Thence home, and there, in favour to my eyes, stayed at home, reading the ridiculous History of my Lord Newcastle,[1] wrote by his wife, which shows her to be a mad, conceited, ridiculous woman, and he an ass to suffer her to write what she writes to him, and of him.   So to bed, my eyes being very bad; and I know not how in the world to abstain from reading.

19th. Walked all along Thames Street, which I have not done since it was burned, as far as Billingsgate; and there do see a brave street likely to be, many brave houses being built, and of them a great many by Mr. Jaggard; but the raising of the street will make it mighty fine.   I was surprised with a letter without a name to it, very well writ, in a good style, giving me notice of my cousin Kate Joyce's being likely to ruin herself by marriage, and by ill reports already abroad of her; and I do fear that this keeping of a inn may spoil her, being a young and pretty comely woman, and thought to be left well.   I did answer the letter with thanks and good liking, and am resolved to take the advice he[2] gives, and go to see her, and find out what I can : but if she will ruin herself, I cannot help it.

20th. To Kate Joyce's to speak with her; but company being with her, I only invited her to come and dine with me on Sunday next, and so away.   All the evening pricking down some things, and trying some conclusions upon my viol, in order to the inventing a better theory of music than hath yet been abroad; and I think verily I shall do it.   This day at Court I do hear that Sir W. Pen do command this summer's fleet; and Mr. Progers of the Bed-chamber, as a secret, told me that the Prince Rupert is troubled at it, and several friends of his have been with him to know the reason of it; so that he do pity Sir W. Pen, whom he hath great kindness for, that he should not at any desire of his be put to this service, and thereby make the Prince his enemy, and contract more envy from other people.

21st. To the office, and wrote my letters, and then abroad to do several things and pay what little scores I had, and among others Mrs. Martin's, and there did give 20s. to Mrs. Cregg, her landlady, who was my Valentine in the house, as well as Doll Lane.

22d. (Easter day.) Walked to the Temple, and there got a coach, and to White Hall, where spoke with several people, and find by all that Pen is to go to sea this year with the fleet; and they

[1] *The Life of William Cavendish, Duke of Newcastle,* by his duchess, of which the first edition, in folio, had just been published.

[2] i.e., the anonymous writer; but how Pepys directed the answer does not appear.

excuse the Prince's going by saying it is not a command great enough for him.   Here I met with Brisband, and, after hearing the service at the King's chapel, where I heard the Bishop of Norwich (Dr. Reynolds, the old Presbyterian) begin a very plain sermon, he and I to the Queen's chapel, and there did hear the Italians sing; and indeed their music did appear most admirable to me, beyond anything of ours: I was never so well satisfied in my life with it. So home to dinner, where Kate Joyce was, as I invited her: and after dinner she and I alone to talk about her business, as I designed; and I find her very discreet, and she assures me she neither do nor will incline to the doing anything towards marriage without my advice, and did tell me that she had many offers, and that Harman and his friends would fain have her; but he is poor, and so it will not be advisable: but that there is another, a tobacconist, one Holinshed, whom she speaks well of, to be a plain, sober man, and in good condition, that offers her very well, and submits to me by examining and enquiring after it.   If I see good, it will be best for her to marry, I think, as soon as she can—at least, to be rid of this house; for the trade will not agree with a young widow that is a little handsome.

23d.   To the tavern, and there bespoke wine for dinner; and so to Bishopsgate Street, thinking to have found a harpsicon-maker, but he is gone.   And I have a mind forthwith to have a little harpsicon made me to confirm and help me in my music notions, which my head is nowadays full of, and I do believe will come to something which is very good.   At noon come Mrs. Pierce and Mrs. Manuel, the Jew's wife, and Mrs. Corbet and Mrs. Pierce's boy and girl.   But we are defeated of Knipp by her being forced to act today, and also of Harris, which did trouble me, they being my chief guests.   However, I had an extraordinary good dinner, and the better because dressed by my own servants, and were mighty merry.   And here was Pelling by chance come and dined with me; and after sitting long at dinner I had a barge ready at Tower Wharf to take us in, and so we went all of us up as high as Barn Elms, a very fine day, and all the way sang; and Mrs. Manuel sings very finely, and is a mighty discreet, sober-carriaged woman, that both my wife and I are mightily taken with her.   At Barn Elms we walked round, and then to the barge again, and had much merry talk and good singing; and come before it was dark to the New Exchange stairs, and there landed, and walked up to Mrs. Pierce's, where we sat awhile, and then up to their dining-room. And so, having a violin and theorbo, did fall to dance, here being also Mrs. Floyd come thither, and by and by Mr. Harris. But there being so few of us that could dance, and my wife not being very well, we had not much pleasure in the dancing: there was Knipp also, by which with much pleasure we did sing a little, and so, about ten o'clock, I took coach with my wife and Deb., and so home.

24th. Comes to me Mr. Shish, to desire my appearing for him to succeed Mr. Christopher Pett, lately dead, in his place of Master-Shipwright of Deptford and Woolwich, which I do resolve to promote what I can. To White Hall, and there to the Duke of York's chamber, where I understand it is already resolved by the King and Duke of York that Shish shall have the place. From the Duke's chamber Sir W. Coventry and I to walk in the Matted Gallery; and there, among other things, he tells me of the wicked design that now is at last contriving against him, to get a petition presented from people, that the money they have paid to him for their places may be repaid them back; and that this is set on by Temple and Hollis of the Parliament, and, among other mean people in it, by Captain Tatnell: and he prays me that I will use some effectual way to sift Tatnell what he do, and who puts him on in this business, which I do undertake, and will do with all my skill for his service, being troubled that he is still under this difficulty. Thence back to White Hall, where great talk of the tumult at the other end of the town, about Moorfields, the 'prentices taking the liberty of these holidays to pull down brothels.[1] And, Lord! to see the apprehensions which this did give to all people at Court, that presently order was given for all the soldiers, horse and foot, to be in arms; and forthwith alarms were beat by drum and trumpet through Westminster, and all to their colours, and to horse, as if the French were coming into the town! So Creed, whom I met here, and I to Lincoln's Inn Fields, thinking to have gone into the fields to have seen the 'prentices; but here we found these fields full of soldiers all in a body, and my Lord Craven commanding of them, and riding up and down to give orders, like a madman. And some young men we saw brought by soldiers to the guard at White Hall, and overheard others that stood by say

---

[1] It was customary for the apprentices of the metropolis to avail themselves of their holidays, especially on Shrove Tuesday, to search after women of ill fame, and to confine them during the season of Lent. See a *Satyre against Separatists*, 1675.

that it was only for pulling down the brothels; and none of the by-standers finding fault with them, but rather of the soldiers for hindering them.   And we heard a Justice of Peace this morning say to the King that he had been endeavourng to suppress this tumult, but could not; and that, imprisoning some of them in the new prison at Clerkenwell, the rest did come and break open the prison and release them; and that they do give out that they are for pulling down the brothels, which is one of the great grievances of the nation.   To which the King made a very poor, cold, insipid answer: 'Why, why do they go to them, then?' and that was all, and had no mind to go on with the discourse.   Met Sir F. Hollis, who do still tell me that, above all things in the world, he wishes he had my tongue in his mouth, meaning since my speech in Parliament.   He took Lord Brouncker and me down to the guards, he and his company being upon the guards today; and there he did, in a handsome room to that purpose, make us drink, and did call for his bagpipes, which, with pipes of ebony tipped with silver, he did play beyond anything of that kind that ever I heard in my life; and with great pains he must have obtained it, but with pains that the instrument do not deserve at all; for, at the best, it is mighty barbarous music.   To my chamber, to prick out my song 'It is decreed,' intending to have it ready to give Mr. Harris on Thursday, when we meet, for him to sing, believing that he will do it more right than a woman that sings better, unless it were Knipp, which I cannot have opportunity to teach it to.   This evening I came home from White Hall with Sir W. Pen, who fell in talk about his going to sea this year, and the difficulties that arise to him by it, by giving offence to the Prince and occasioning envy to him, and many other things that make it a bad matter—at this time of want of money and necessaries, and bad and uneven counsels at home—for him to go abroad: and did tell me how much with the King and Duke of York he had endeavoured to be excused, desiring the Prince might be satisfied in it, who hath a mind to go; but he tells me they will not excuse him, and I believe it, and truly do judge it a piece of bad fortune to W. Pen.

25th.   Up, and walked to White Hall, there to wait on the Duke of York, which I did: and in his chamber there, first by hearing the Duke of York call me by my name, my Lord Burlington did come to me, and with great respect take notice of me and my relationship to my Lord Sandwich, and express great kindness to me; and so to talk of my Lord Sandwich's concernments.   By and by the Duke of York is ready; and I did wait for an opportunity of speaking my mind to him about Sir J. Minnes his being unable to do the King any service.   The Duke of York and all with him this morning were full of the talk of the 'prentices, who are not yet put down, though the guards and militia of the town have been in arms all this night and the night before; and the 'prentices have made fools of them, sometimes by running from them and flinging stones at them.   Some blood hath been spilt, but a great many houses pulled down; and, among others, the Duke of York was mighty merry at that of Daman Page's, the great bawd of the seamen; and the Duke of York complained merrily that he hath lost two tenants, by their houses being pulled down, who paid him for their wine licences £15 a year.   But these idle fellows have had the confidence to say that they did ill in contenting themselves in pulling down the little brothels, and did not go and pull down the great one at White Hall.   And some of them have the last night had a word among them, and it was 'Reformation and Reducement.'   This do make the courtiers ill at ease to see this spirit among people, though they think this matter will not come to much: but it speaks people's minds.   And then they do say that there are men of understanding among them, that have been of Cromwell's army: but how true that is I know not.   With my wife to the King's playhouse to see 'The Storm,' which we did, but without much pleasure, it being but a mean play compared with 'The Tempest,' at the Duke of York's House, though Knipp did act her part of grief very well.   By coach to Islington, the old house, and then home, being in fear of meeting the 'prentices, who are many of them yet, they say, abroad in the fields.

26th.   To the Duke of York's House, to see the new play, called 'The Man is the Master,' [1] where the house was, it being not one o'clock, very full.   But my wife and Deb. being there before, with Mrs. Pierce and Corbet and Betty Turner, whom my wife carried with her, they made me room; and there I sat, it costing me 8s. upon them in oranges at 6d. apiece.   By and by the King came, and we sat just under him, so that I durst not turn my back all the play.   The play is a translation out of French, and the plot Spanish, but not anything extraordinary at all in it, though translated by Sir W. Davenant; and so I found the King and his company did think meanly of it, though there was here and there

---

[1] A comedy; Sir W. Davenant's last production.   It is taken from two plays of Scarron—*Jodelet, ou Le Maître Valet* and *L'Héritière Ridicule*.

something pretty: but the most of the mirth was sorry, poor stuff of eating of sack posset and slabbering themselves, and mirth fit for clowns; the prologue but poor, and the epilogue little in it but the extraordinariness of it, it being sung by Harris and another [1] in the form of a ballad.   Thence, by agreement, we all of us to the Blue Bells, hard by, whither Mr. Pierce also goes with us, who met us at the play; and anon comes Manuel and his wife, and Knipp, and Harris, who brings with him Mr. Banister, the great master of music.   And after much difficulty in getting of music, we to dancing, and then to a supper of French dishes, which yet did not please me, and then to dance and sing; and mighty merry we were till about eleven or twelve at night, with mighty great content in all my company, and I did, as I love to do, enjoy myself.   My wife extraordinary fine today, in her flower tabby suit, bought a year and more ago, before my mother's death put her into mourning, and so not worn till this day, and everybody in love with it; and indeed she is very fine and handsome in it.   I having paid the reckoning, which come to almost £4, we parted: my company and William Batelier, who was also with us, home in a coach, round by the Wall, where we met so many stops by the watches, that it cost us much time and some trouble, and more money, to every watch, to them to drink; this being increased by the trouble the 'prentices did lately give the City, so that the militia and watches are very strict at this time; and we had like to have met with a stop for all night at the constable's watch, at Moorgate, by a prag-matical constable; but we came well home at about two in the morning.   This noon, from Mrs. Williams's, my Lord Brouncker sent to Somerset House to hear how the Duchess of Richmond do; and word was brought him that she is pretty well, but mighty full of the small-pox, by which all do conclude she will be wholly spoiled, which is the greatest instance of the uncertainty of beauty that could be in this age.   But then she hath had the benefit of it to be first married, and to have kept it so long, under the greatest temptations in the world from a King, and yet without the least imputation.   This afternoon, at the play, Sir Fr. Hollis spoke to me as a secret, and matter of confidence in me, and friendship to Sir W. Pen, who is now out of town, that it were well he were made acquainted that he finds in the House of Commons, which met this day, several motions made for the calling strictly again upon the miscarriages, and particularly in the business of the prizes,

[1] Sandford.

and the not prosecuting of the first victory, only to give an affront to Sir W. Pen, whose going to sea this year does give them matter of great dislike.

27th. To a Committee of Tangier, where I first understand that my Lord Sandwich is, in his coming back from Spain, to step over thither to see in what condition the place is, which I am glad of, hoping that he will be able to do some good there, for the good of the place which is so much out of order. To the Exchange a turn or two, only to show myself, and then home to dinner, where my wife and I had a small squabble, but I first this day tried the effect of my silence and not provoking her when she is in an ill humour; and do find it very good, for it prevents its coming to that height on both sides which used to exceed what was fit between us. So she became calm by and by, and fond; and so took coach to Hyde Park, where many coaches, but the dust so great that it was troublesome. This day at noon comes Mr. Pelling to me, and shows me the stone cut lately out of Sir Thomas Adams,[1] the old comely alderman's body, which is very large indeed, bigger I think than my fist, and weighs about twenty-five ounces: and, which is very miraculous, he never in all his life had any fit of it, but lived to a great age without pain, and died at last of something else, without any sense of this in all his life. This day Creed, at White Hall, in discourse told me what information he hath had, from very good hands, of the cowardice and ill government of Sir Jer. Smith and Sir Thomas Allen, and the repute they have both of them abroad in the Straits from their deportment when they did at several times command there; and that, above all Englishmen that ever were there, there never was any man that behaved himself like poor Charles Wager, whom the very Moors do mention with tears sometimes.

28th. Home to dinner with my clerks; and though my head full of business, yet I had a desire to end this holiday week with a play: and so, with my wife and Deb. to the King's playhouse, and there saw 'The Indian Emperor,' a very good play indeed. My people tell me that they do verily doubt that the want of men will be so great, as we must press. And if we press there will be mutinies

---

[1] Knight and baronet, and lord mayor in 1645: *ob.* 24th February 1668; *æt.* 82. The shock caused by a fall from his coach displaced the stone, and led to fatal consequences. He was a native of Wem, in Shropshire, and founded the free school there, as well as an Arabic professorship at Cambridge (*History of Wem*, 8vo, 1818).

in the town; for the seamen are said already to have threatened the pulling down of the Treasury office; and if they do once come to that, it will not be long before they come to ours.

29th. (Lord's day.) To church, and there did first find a strange Reader, who could not find in the Service-book the place for churching women, but was fain to change books with the clerk. And then a stranger preached, a seeming able man; but said in his pulpit that God did a greater work in raising of an oak tree from an acorn, than a man's body raising it at the last day from his dust, showing the possibility of the Resurrection: which was, methought, a strange saying. Comes and dines with me W. Howe and, by invitation, Mr. Harris and Mr. Banister, most extraordinary company both, the latter for music of all sorts, and the former for everything. Here we sang, and Banister played on the theorbo and afterwards on his flageolet. Harris do so commend my wife's picture of Mr. Hales's, that I shall have him draw Harris's head; and he hath also persuaded me to have Cooper draw my wife's, which though it cost £30, yet I will have done. I do hear by several that Sir W. Pen's going to sea do dislike the Parliament mightily, and that they have revived the Committee of Miscarriages to find something to prevent it; and that, he being the other day with the Duke of Albemarle to ask his opinion touching his going to sea, the Duchess overheard and came in to him, and asked W. Pen how he durst have the confidence to offer to go to sea again, to the endangering the nation, when he knew himself such a coward as he was; which, if true, is very severe.

30th. By coach to Covent Garden coffee-house, where by appointment I was to meet Harris; which I did, and also Mr. Cooper, the great painter, and Mr. Hales: and thence presently to Mr. Cooper's house [1] to see some of his work, which is all in little, but so excellent as, though I must confess I do think the colouring of the flesh to be a little forced, yet the painting is so extraordinary as I do never expect to see the like again. Here I did see Mrs. Stuart's picture as when a young maid, and now just done before her having the small-pox: and it would make a man weep to see what she was then, and what she is like to be, by people's discourse, now. Here I saw my Lord General's picture, and my Lord Arlington and Ashley's, and several others; but among the rest one Swinfen, that was secretary to my Lord Manchester, the Lord Chamberlain, with Cooling, done so admirably as I never saw

[1] In Henrietta Street, Covent Garden.

anything.   But the misery was, this fellow died in debt, and never paid Cooper for his picture; but, it being seized on by his creditors, among his other goods after his death, Cooper himself says that he did buy it and give £25 out of his purse for it, for what he was to have had but £30.   Being infinitely satisfied with this sight, and resolving that my wife shall be drawn by him when she comes out of the country, I away with Harris and Hales to the coffee-house, sending my people away, and there resolve for Hales to begin Harris's head for me, which I will be at the cost of.   To White Hall and Westminster, where I find the Parliament still boggling about the raising of this money, and everybody's mouth full now. And Mr. Wren himself tells me that the Duke of York declares to go to sea himself this year; and I perceive it is only on this occasion of distaste of the Parliament against W. Pen's going, and to prevent the Prince's: but I think it is mighty hot counsel for the Duke of York at this time to go out of the way.   But, Lord! what a pass are all our matters come to!   At noon by appointment to Cursitor's Alley, in Chancery Lane, to meet Captain Cocke and some other creditors of the Navy, and their Counsel, Pemberton, North,[1] Offly, and Charles Porter; and there dined, and talked of the business of the assignments on the Exchequer of the £1,250,000 on behalf of our creditors; and there I do perceive that the Counsel had heard of my performance in the Parliament-house lately, and did value me and what I said accordingly.   At dinner we had a great deal of good discourse about Parliament: their number being uncertain, and always at the will of the King to increase as he saw reason to erect a new borough.   But all concluded that the bane of the Parliament hath been the leaving off the old custom of the places allowing wages to those that served them in Parliament, by which they chose men that understood their business and would attend it, and they could expect an account from, which now they cannot: and so the Parliament is become a company of men unable to give account for the interest of the place they serve for.   Thence, the meeting of the Counsel with the King's Counsel this afternoon being put off by reason of the death of Serjeant Maynard's lady,[2] I to White Hall, where the Parliament was to wait on the King; and they did: and he did think fit to tell them that they might expect to be adjourned at Whitsuntide, and that they

[1] Sir Francis Pemberton and Sir Dudley North.
[2] Jane, his second wife, daughter of Cheney Selhurst, and relict of Edward Austen.

might make haste to raise their money; but this, I fear, will displease them, who did expect to sit as long as they pleased.

31st. My uncle Thomas dined with me, as he do every quarter, and I paid him his pension; and also comes Mr. Hollyard a little fuddled, and so did talk nothing but Latin, and laugh, that it was very good sport to see a sober man in such a humour, though he was not drunk to scandal. Took up my wife and Deb., and to the Park, where, being in a hackney, and they undressed, was ashamed to go into the tour,[1] but went round the park, and so with pleasure home.

April 1st. All alone to the King's House, and there sat in an upper box, to hide myself, and saw 'The Black Prince,' a very good play; but only the fancy, most of it, the same as in the rest of my Lord Orrery's plays; but the dance very stately. But I did fall asleep the former part of the play. Thence called at my bookseller's, and took Mr. Boyle's Book of Forms,[2] newly reprinted, and sent my brother my old one. Anon comes Mr. Turner to talk about the Office and his place, which, by Sir J. Minnes's age and inability, is very uncomfortable to him, as well as without profit or certainty what he shall do when Sir J. Minnes dies, which is a sad condition for a man that hath lived so long in the Office as Mr. Turner has done. But he aims to look for Mr. Ackworth's place,[3] in case he should be removed. His wife afterwards did take me into my closet and give me a cellar [4] of waters of her own distilling for my father, to be carried down with my wife and her daughter tomorrow, which was very handsome.

2d. Up, and by and by comes Betty Turner and her mother and W. Batelier, and they and Deb., to whom I did give 10s. this morning to oblige her, and also Jane; and so in two coaches set out about eight o'clock towards the carrier, there for to take coach for my father's: but I meeting my Lord Anglesey going to the office, was forced to 'light in Cheapside. To Mr. Porter's chamber, where Cocke and his Counsel, and so to the attorney's, whither the Solicitor-General came, and there their cause about their assignments on the £1,250,000 Act was argued, where all that was to be said for them was said, and so answered by the Solicitor-

---

[1] The Ring.
[2] *The Origin of Forms and Qualities, according to the Corpuscular Philosophy,* by the Honourable Robert Boyle. Oxford, 1666, 4to.
[3] At Deptford.
[4] A case for bottles. We still use the word cellaret.

General beyond what I expected, that I said not one word all my time, rather choosing to hold my tongue and so mind my reputation with the Solicitor-General, who did mightily approve of my speech in Parliament, than say anything against him to no purpose. With Lord Brouncker to the Royal Society, where they had just done; but there I was forced to subscribe to the building of a College, and did give £40; and several others did subscribe, some greater and some less sums.   But several I saw hang off: and I doubt it will spoil the Society, for it breeds faction and ill will, and becomes burdensome to some that cannot, or would not, do it. Here, to my great content, I did try the use of the Otacousticon,[1] which was only a great glass bottle broke at the bottom, putting the neck to my ear, and there I did plainly hear the dancing of the oars of the boats in the Thames to Arundel gallery window, which without it I could not in the least do, and may, I believe, be improved to a great height, which I am mighty glad of.   Thence with Lord Brouncker and several of them to the King's Head tavern by Chancery Lane, and there did drink and eat and talk. And, above the rest, I did desire of Mr. Hooke and my Lord an account of the reason of concords and discords in music, which they say is from the equality of vibrations.   But I am not satisfied in it, but will at my desire think of it more and see how far that do go to explain it.

3d. As soon as we had done with the Duke of York we did attend the Council; and were there called in, and did hear Mr. Solicitor [-General] make his report to the Council in the business of a complaint against us, for having prepared certificates on the Exchequer for the further sum of £50,000; which he did in a most excellent manner of words, but most cruelly severe against us, and so were some of the Lords Commissioners of the Treasury, as men guilty of a practice with the tradesmen, to the King's prejudice. I was unwilling to enter into a contest with them; but took advantage of two or three words last spoke, and brought it to a short issue in good words, that if we had the King's order to hold our hands, we would, which did end the matter.   And they all resolved we should have it, and so it ended; and we away, I vexed that I did not speak more in a cause so fit to be spoke in, and wherein we had so much advantage: but perhaps I might have provoked the Solicitor and the Commissioners of the Treasury, and therefore, since, I am not sorry that I

[1] Otacousticon, an instrument to facilitate hearing.

forbore.   To Duck Lane, and did here buy Descartes his little
treatise of music; and so home, and there to read a little and eat
a little, though I find that unless company invite I do not love
to spend time upon eating, and so bring emptiness and the colic.
This day I hear that Prince Rupert and Holmes do go to sea:
and by this there is a seeming friendship and peace among our
great seamen; but the devil a bit is there any love among them,
or can be.

4th. To White Hall. Took Aldgate Street in my way, and
there called upon one Hayward that makes virginals, and there did
like of a little espinette, and will have him finish it for me; for I
had a mind to a small harpsichon, but this takes up less room.   I
did dine with Sir W. Pen, where my Lady Batten did come with
desire of meeting me there: and speaking with me about the business of the £500 we demand of her for the Chest, she do protest
before God she never did see the account, but that it was, as her
husband in his lifetime did often declare to her, his expecting
£500, and that we could not deny it for his pains in that business;
and that he left her worth nothing of his own in the world, and that
therefore she could pay nothing of it, come what will come, but
that he hath left her a beggar; which I am truly sorry for, though
it is a just judgement upon people that do live so much beyond
themselves in housekeeping and vanity as they did.   I did give
her little answer, but generally words that might not trouble her.
I did attend the Duke of York, and he did carry us to the King's
lodgings: but he was asleep in his closet, so we stayed in the Green-
room, where the Duke of York did tell us what rules he had of
knowing the weather, and did now tell us we should have rain
before tomorrow, it having been a dry season for some time, and
so it did rain all night almost.   And pretty rules he hath, and told
Brouncker and me some of them, which were such as no reason
can readily be given for them.   By and by the King comes out,
and then to talk of other things: about the Quakers not swearing,
and how they do swear in the business of a late election of a Knight
of the Shire of Hertfordshire in behalf of one they have a mind to
have; and how my Lord of Pembroke [1] says he hath heard the
Quaker at the tennis-court swear to himself when he loses; and
told us what pretty notions my Lord Pembroke hath of the first
chapter of Genesis, and a great deal of such fooleries, which the
King made mighty mockery at.

[1] Philip Herbert, fifth Earl of Pembroke, and second Earl of Montgomery.

5th. (Lord's day.) To church, where I have not been a good
while.   Thence home, and dined at home, W. Hewer with me;
and after dinner he and I had a great deal of good talk touching this
Office, how it is spoiled by having so many persons in it, and so
much work that is not made the work of any one man, but of all,
and so is never done; and the best way to have it well done were to
have the whole trust in one, as myself, to set whom I pleased to
work in the several businesses of the Office, and me to be accountable for the whole, and that would do it, as I would find instruments: but this is not to be compassed.   But something I am
resolved to do about Sir J. Minnes before it be long.   Then to my
chamber again, to my music, and so to church; and then home,
and thither comes Captain Silas Taylor to me, the Storekeeper of
Harwich, where much talk, and most of it against Captaine Deane,
whom I do believe to be a high, proud fellow; but he is an active
man, and able in his way, and so I love him.   He gone, I to my
music again, and to read a little, and to sing with Mr. Pelling, who
came to see me, and so spent the evening, and then to supper and
to bed.   I hear that eight of the ringleaders in the late tumults of
the 'prentices at Easter are condemned to die.[1]

6th. The King and Duke of York themselves, in my absence,
did call for some of the Commissioners of the Treasury and give
them directions about the business of the certificates, which I,
despairing to do anything on a Sunday, and not thinking that they
would think of it themselves, did rest satisfied with, and stayed at
home all yesterday, leaving it to do something in this day.   But I
find that the King and Duke of York had been so pressing in it,
that my Lord Ashley was more forward with the doing of it this
day than I could have been.   And so I to White Hall with Alderman Backwell in his coach, with Mr. Blany, my Lord's secretary:
and there did draw up a rough draft of what order I would have,
and did carry it in, and had it read twice and approved of before my

[1] Four were executed on 9th May, namely, Thomas Limerick, Edward
Cotton, Peter Massenger, and Richard Beasley.   They were drawn, hanged,
and quartered at Tyburn, and two of their heads fixed upon London Bridge
(the *London Gazette*, No. 259).   See 'The Tryals of the London Apprentices, who were tumultuously assembled in Moore Fields, under colour of
pulling down Brothels,' 4to, London, 1668.   'It is observed,' says the
London Gazette. 'to the just vindication of the City, that none of the persons
apprehended upon the said tumult were found to be apprentices, as was given
out, but some idle persons, many of them nursed in the late Rebellion, too
readily embracing any opportunity of making their own advantages to the
disturbance of the peace, and injury of others.'

Lord Ashley and three more of the Commissioners of the Treasury, and then went up to the Council-chamber, where the Duke of York and Prince Rupert and the rest of the Committee of the Navy were sitting: and I did get some of them to read it there; and they would have had it passed presently, but Sir John Nicholas desired they would first have it approved by a full Council. And therefore a Council Extraordinary was readily summoned against the afternoon, and the Duke of York run presently to the King, as if now they were really set to mind their business, which God grant! At noon with Sir Herbert Price to Mr. George Montagu's to dinner, being invited by him in the hall, and there mightily made of, even to great trouble to me to be so commended before my face with that flattery and importunity, that I was quite troubled with it. Yet he is a fine gentleman, truly, and his lady a fine woman.[1] And, among many sons that I saw there, there was a little daughter that is mighty pretty, of which he is infinite fond, and after dinner did make her play on the guitar and sing, which she did mighty prettily, and seems to have a mighty musical soul, keeping time with most excellent spirit. Here I met with Mr. Brownlow, my old schoolfellow, who come thither, I suppose, as a suitor to one of the young ladies that were there, and a sober man he seems to be. Mr. Montagu did tell me how Mr. Vaughan in that very room did say that I was a great man and had great understanding and I know not what, which, I confess, I was a little proud of, if I may believe him. Here I do hear, as a great secret, that the King and Duke of York and Duchess and my Lady Castlemaine are now all agreed in a strict league, and all things like to go very current, and that it is not impossible to have my Lord Clarendon in time here again. But I do hear that my Lady Castlemaine is horribly vexed at the late libel,[2] the petition of the poor prostitutes about the town, whose houses were pulled down the other day. I have got one of them, and it is not very witty, but devilish severe against her and the King: and I wonder how it durst be printed and spread abroad, which shows that the times are loose, and come to a great disregard of the King or Court or Government. I to the new Cockpit by the King's Gate, and there saw the manner

[1] Elizabeth, daughter of Sir Anthony Irby.
[2] This occasioned an answer printed on a single half sheet, and entitled, *The Gracious Answer of the Most Illustrious Lady of Pleasure, the Countess of Castlem . . . . to the Poor W . . . . .' Petition.* It is signed, 'Given at our Closset, in King Street, Westminster, die Veneris, 24th April, 1668. Castlem . . . . .' Compare Evelyn, 2nd April 1668.

of it, and the mixed rabble of people that come thither, and saw two battles of cocks, wherein is no great sport, but only to consider how these creatures, without any provocation, do fight and kill one another and aim only at one another's heads. To the Park, and then to the House, and there at the door eat and drank; whither came my Lady Carnegie, of whom Creed tells me more particulars: how her Lord, finding her and the Duke of York at the King's first coming in too kind, did get it out of her that he did dishonour him; and did take the most pernicious and full piece of revenge that ever I heard of; and he at this day owns it with great glory, and looks upon the Duke of York and the world with great content, in the ampleness of his revenge. This day, in the afternoon, stepping with the Duke of York into St. James's Park, it rained; and I was forced to lend the Duke of York my cloak, which he wore through the Park.

7th. To the King's playhouse, and there saw 'The English Monsieur,' [1] sitting for privacy sake in an upper box: the play hath much mirth in it as to that particular humour. After the play done I down to Knipp, and did stay her undressing herself; and there saw the several players, men and women, go by; and pretty to see how strange they are all one to another after the play is done. Here I saw a wonderful pretty maid of her own that come to undress her, and one so pretty that she says she intends not to keep her, for fear of her being undone in her service by coming to the playhouse. Here I hear Sir W. Davenant is just now dead, and so who will succeed him in the mastership of the house is not yet known. The eldest Davenant is, it seems, gone from this house to be kept by somebody; which I am glad of, she being a very bad actor. Mrs. Knipp tells me that my Lady Castlemaine is mightily in love with Hall,[2] of their house: and he is much with her in private, and she goes to him and do give him many presents; and that the thing is most certain, and Beck Marshall only privy to it, and the means of bringing them together, which is a very odd thing; and by this means she is even with the King's love to Mrs. Davis. This done, I carried her and set her down at Mrs. Manuel's, but stayed not there myself nor went in; but straight home, and there to my letters, and so to bed.

8th. With Lord Brouncker to the Duke of York's playhouse,

---

[1] A comedy by the Honourable James Howard.
[2] Jacob Hall, the famous rope-dancer, was said to have received a salary from Lady Castlemaine.

where we saw 'The Unfortunate Lovers,' [1] no extraordinary play, methinks, and thence to Drumbleby's, and there did talk a great deal about pipes; and did buy a recorder, which I do intend to learn to play on, the sound of it being, of all sounds in the world, most pleasing to me.   She did tell me of young Captain Holmes's [2] marrying of Pegg Lowther [3] last Saturday by stealth, which I was sorry for, he being an idle rascal and proud, and worth little, I doubt; and she a mighty pretty, well-disposed lady, and good fortune.   Her mother and friends take on mightily, but the sport is, Sir Robert Holmes do seem to be mad with his brother, and will disinherit him, saying that he hath ruined himself, marrying below himself and to his disadvantage; whereas I said in this company that I had married a sister lately, with little above half that portion. So home to my chamber to be fingering my recorder and getting of the scale of music without book, which I at last see is necessary for a man that would understand music, though it be a ridiculous and troublesome way, and I know I shall be able hereafter to show the world a simpler way; but, like the old hypotheses in philosophy, it must be learnt though a man knows better.

9th. I up and down to the Duke of York's playhouse, there to see, which I did, Sir W. Davenant's corpse carried out towards Westminster, there to be buried.   Here were many coaches and six horses, and many hackneys, that made it look, methought, as if it were the burial of a poor poet.   He seemed to have many children, by five or six in the first mourning-coach, all boys.   To my office, where is come a packet from the Downs from my brother Balty, who, with Harman, are arrived there, of which this day comes the first news.   And now the Parliament will be satisfied, I suppose, about the business they have so long desired between Brouncker [4] and Harman [5] about not prosecuting the first victory.[6]

10th. (Friday.) All the morning at office.   At noon with W. Pen to Duke of York, and attended Council.   So to Duck Lane,

[1] A tragedy by Sir W. Davenant.

[2] Afterwards Sir John Holmes, governor of Usk Castle.   His grandson, Thomas, was created Lord Holmes of Kilmallock.

[3] Margaret, sister of Anthony Lowther, who had married Margaret Penn.

[4] Henry Brouncker.

[5] The proceedings against Harman will be found in the Journals of the House of Commons, 17th April 1668.

[6] Here are inserted in the *Diary* three large leaves, written on both sides, containing short notices of occurrences between the 10th and 19th of April. These entries have been deciphered, and afford a specimen of the manner in which the Memoranda for the Journal were recorded.

and there kissed bookseller's wife and bought Legend.[1]   So home,
coach.   Sailor.   Mrs. Hannam dead.   News of peace.   Conning
my gamut.

12th. (Sunday.) Dined at Brouncker's and saw the new book.

13th. (Monday.) Spent at Michell's 6*d.*; in the Folly,[2] 1*s.*;
oysters, 1*s.*; coach to W. Coventry about Mrs. Pett, 1*s.*; thence to
Commissioners of Treasury, and so to Westminster Hall by water,
6*d.*   With G. Montagu and Roger Pepys, and spoke with Birch
and Vaughan, all in trouble about the prize-business.   So with
Creed to a play.   Little laugh, 4*s.*   Thence towards the Park by
coach, 2*s.* 6*d.*

14th. By water to the Temple.   In the way read the Narrative
about prizes; and so to Lord Crewe's bed-side.   Creed and I to
the Quaker's, dined together.   The House rose about four o'clock,
and with much ado Pen got to Thursday to bring in his answer;
so my Lord escapes today.   With Godage and G. Montagu to
G. Carteret's, and there sat their dinner-time, and hear myself by
many Parliament-men mightily commended.   Thence to a play,
'Love's Cruelty.'

15th. To White Hall, to the Chapel, expecting wind music:
and to the Harp and Ball, and drank all alone.   Back, and to the
fiddling concert, and heard a practice mighty good of Grabut's.
To Westminster Hall, where all cry out that the House will be
severe with Pen; but do hope well concerning the buyers, that we
shall have no difficulty, which God grant!   Creed and I and Sir P.
Neale to the Quaker's, and there dined with a silly executor of
Bishop Juxon's and cousin Roger Pepys.   With the Duke of
York a little, but stayed not, but saw him and his lady at his pretty
little chapel, where I never was before: but silly devotion, God
knows!   To the King's playhouse, into a corner of the 18*d.* box,
and there saw 'The Maid's Tragedy,' a good play.   Coach, 1*s.*:
play and oranges, 2*s.* 6*d.*   With Sir T. Crewe, bemoaning my
Lord's folly in leaving his old interest, by which he hath now
lost all.

16th. Dined with my clerks: and merry at Sir W. Pen's crying
yesterday, as they say, to the King, that he was his martyr.   To
Westminster Hall, where I hear W. Pen is ordered to be impeached.
There spoke with many, and particularly with G. Montagu: and

[1] Probably the *Golden Legend* of Jac. de Voragine: there were several early
editions of the English version.

[2] The *Folly* was a floating house of entertainment on the Thames.

went with him and Creed to his house, where he told how Sir W.
Pen hath been severe to Lord Sandwich; but the Coventrys both
labouring to save him, by laying it on Lord Sandwich, which our
friends cry out upon, and I am silent, but do believe they did it as
the only way to save him.   It could not be carried to commit him.
It is thought the House do cool: Sir W. Coventry's being for him
provoked Sir R. Howard and his party; Court all for W. Pen.
Wrote my letters to my Lady Sandwich, and so home, where displeased to have my maid bring her brother, a countryman, to
lie there.

17th. Called up by Balty's coming, who gives me a good account
of his voyage, and pleases me well, and I hope hath got something.
This morning paid the Royal Society £1 6s.   So by coach to
White Hall: the coachman on Ludgate Hill 'lighted, and beat a
fellow with a sword.   I hear that the House is upon the business
of Harman, who, they say, takes all on himself.   Thence with
Brouncker to the King's House, and saw 'The Surprisal,' where
base singing, only Knipp,[1] who came, after her song in the clouds,
to me in the pit, and there oranges, 2s.   After the play she and I
and Rolt by coach, 6s. 6d., to Kensington, and there to the Grotto,
and had admirable pleasure with their singing, and fine ladies
listening to us: with infinite pleasure I enjoyed myself; so to the
tavern there, and did spend 16s. 6d., and the gardener 2s.   Mighty
merry, and sang all the way to the town, a most pleasant evening,
moonshine, and set them at her house in Covent Garden, and I
home.

18th. (Saturday.) Up, and my bookseller brought home books
bound—the binding comes to 17s.   Advanced to my maid
Bridget £1.   Sir W. Pen at the office, seemingly merry.   Do hear
this morning that Harman is committed by the Parliament last
night, the day he came up, which is hard; but he took all upon
himself first, and then, when a witness came in to say otherwise,
he would have retracted; and the House took it so ill, they would
commit him.   To the King's playhouse, and to the play of the
'Duke of Lerma,' 2s. 6d.   Oranges, 1s.

19th. (Sunday.) Roger Pepys and his son came, and to church
with me, where W. Pen was and did endeavour to show himself
to the church.   Roger Pepys did tell me the whole story of Harman, how he prevaricated, and hath undoubtedly been imposed
on and wheedled; and he is like the miller's man that in Richard

[1] Who played Emilia.

the Third's time was hanged for his master.[1] To walk in the Abbey with Sir John Talbot, who would fain have pumped me about the prizes, but I would not let him.

20th. Up, and busy about answer to Committee of Accounts this morning, about several questions, which vexed me, though in none I have reason to be troubled. But the business of the Flying Greyhound begins to find me some care, though in that I am wholly void of blame. To White Hall, and there hear how Brouncker is fled, which, I think, will undo him: but what good it will do Harman I know not, he hath so befouled himself; but it will be good sport to my Lord Chancellor to hear how his great enemy is fain to take the same course that he is. There met Robinson, who tells me that he fears his master, Sir W. Coventry, will this week have his business brought upon the stage again, about selling of places; which I shall be sorry for, though the less since I hear his standing up for Pen the other day to the prejudice, though not to the ruin, of my Lord Sandwich: and yet I do think what he did he did out of a principle of honesty. Meeting Sir William Hooker,[2] the Alderman, he did cry out mighty high against Sir W. Pen for his getting such an estate and giving

---

[1] The story alluded to by Pepys, which belongs not to the reign of Richard III, but to that of Edward VI, occurred during a seditious outbreak at Bodmin, Cornwall, and is thus related by Holinshed: 'At the same time, and near the same place, [Bodmin] dwelled a miller, that had been a great doer in that rebellion, for whom also Sir Anthony Kingston sought: but the miller, being thereof warned, called a good tall fellow that he had to his servant, and said unto him: "I have business to go from home; if any therefore come to ask for me, say thou art the owner of the mill, and the man for whom they shall so ask, and that thou hast kept this mill for the space of three years; but in no wise name me." The servant promised his master so to do. And shortly after, came Sir Anthony Kingston to the miller's house, and, calling for the miller, the servant came forth, and answered that he was the miller. "How long," quoth Sir Anthony, "hast thou kept this mill?" He answered: "Three years." "Well, then," said he, "come on: thou must go with me"; and caused his men to lay hands on him, and to bring him to the next tree, saying to him: "Thou hast been a busy knave, and therefore here shalt thou hang." Then cried the fellow out, and said that he was not the miller, but the miller's man. "Well, then," said Sir Anthony, "thou art a false knave, to be in two tales: therefore," said he, "hang him up"; and so incontinently hanged he was indeed. After he was dead, one that was present told Sir Anthony: "Surely, sir, this was but the miller's man."—"What then!" said he. "Could he ever have done his master better service than to hang for him?"'

[2] William Hooker, grocer. Sheriff of London in 1665, afterwards knighted, and lord mayor in 1674. His daughter was Anne, who married Sir John Lethieullier, of Sutton Place, Kent, Sheriff of London in 1674.

£15,000 with his daughter, which is more, by half, that ever he did give; but this the world believes, and so let them.

21st. Took Mrs. Turner to the King's House, and saw 'The Indian Emperor'; and after that done, took Knipp out, and to Kensington; and there walked in the garden, and then supped, and mighty merry, there being also in the house Sir Philip Howard and some company, and had a dear reckoning, but merry; and away, it being quite night, home. I hear how Sir W. Pen's impeachment was read and agreed to in the House this day, and ordered to be engrossed, and he suspended [1] the House. Harman set at liberty, and Brouncker put out of the House, and a writ for a new election,[2] and an impeachment ordered to be brought in against him, he being fled.

22d. To White Hall, and there we attended the Duke of York as usual; and I did present Mrs. Pett, the widow, and her petition to the Duke of York, for some relief from the King. Here was today a proposition made to the Duke of York by Captain Van Hemskirke for £20,000, to discover an art how to make a ship go two feet for one what any ship do now, which the King inclines to try, it costing him nothing to try; and it is referred to us to contract with the man. Then by water from the Privy Stairs to Westminster Hall; and, taking water, the King and the Duke of York were in the new buildings, and the Duke of York called to me whither I was going. And I answered aloud, 'To wait on our masters at Westminster': at which he and all the company laughed; but I was sorry and troubled for it afterwards, for fear any Parliament-man should have been there; and it will be a caution to me for the time to come. To the fishmonger's, and bought a couple of lobsters, and over to the 'sparagus garden, thinking to have met Mr. Pierce and his wife and Knipp; but met their servant coming to bring me to Chatelin's, the French house in Covent Garden: and there with music and good company, Manuel and his wife and one Swaddle, a clerk of Lord Arlington's (who dances and speaks French well, but got drunk, and was then troublesome), and here mighty merry till ten at night. This night the Duke of Monmouth and a great many blades were at Chatelin's, and I left them there, with a hackney coach attending him.

23d. At noon comes Mrs. Pierce and her daughter, and Knipp and one Mrs. Foster, and dined with me, and mighty merry; and

---

[1] From sitting as a member, pending the impeachment.
[2] At Romney, which Henry Brouncker represented.

after dinner carried them to the Tower and showed them all to be seen there, and, among other things, the crown and sceptres and rich plate, which I myself never saw before, and indeed is noble, and I mightily pleased with it. Thence by water to the Temple, and there to the Cock alehouse,[1] and drank, and eat a lobster, and sang, and mightily merry. So, almost night, I carried Mrs. Pierce home, and then Knipp and I to the Temple again and took boat, it being darkish, and to Fox-hall, it being now night, and a bonfire burning at Lambeth for the King's coronation-day. And there she and I drank; and so back and led her home, it being now ten at night; and so got a link. And, walking towards home, just at my entrance into the ruins at St. Dunstan's, I was met by two rogues with clubs, who come towards us. So I went back and walked home quite round by the Wall, and got well home, and to bed weary but pleased with my day's pleasure, but yet displeased at my expense and time I lose.

24th. I represented Mrs. Pett and her condition to Mr. Wren for his favour, which he promised. Lord Brouncker thinks the Parliament will, by their violence and delay in money matters, force the King to run any hazard and dissolve them. To Duck Lane, and there did overlook a great many of Monsieur Fouquet's[2] library, that a bookseller hath bought, and I did buy one Spanish work, 'Los Ilustres Varones.'[3] I did hear the Duke of York tell how Sir W. Pen's impeachment was brought into the House of Lords today; and he spoke with great kindness of him, and that the Lords would not commit him till they could find precedent for it, and did incline to favour him. Thence to the King's playhouse, and there saw a piece of 'Beggar's Bush,' which I have not seen some years.

25th. To the Duke of York's playhouse, and there saw 'Sir Martin Mar-all,' which, the more I see the more I like. To Westminster Hall, and there met with Roger Pepys; and he tells me that

---

[1] In Fleet Street, opposite to the Temple gate.

[2] Nicolas Fouquet, 'Surintendant des Finances' in France. Most of the great libraries contain some of his books, distinguished by his arms. He had been disgraced, and imprisoned in 1661.

[3] Probably *Los Claros Varones*, 'The Celebrated Men,' of Fernando del Pulgar, historiographer to Isabella and Ferdinand. He was ambitious to be thought the Plutarch of his nation, whence the title of his book. However, the book meant by Pepys may be *Varones ilustres del Nuevo Mundo, desenbridores, conquistadores, pacificadores de las Indias Occidentales*, by Fernando Pizarro y Orellana, printed at Madrid in 1639.

nothing hath lately passed about my Lord Sandwich, but only Sir
Robert Carr did speak hardly of him.   But it is hoped that nothing
will be done more, this meeting of Parliament, which the King did,
by a message yesterday, declare again should rise the 4th of May,
and then only adjourn for three months: and this message being
only about an adjournment, did please them mightily, for they are
desirous of their power mightily.   I home to have my hair cut by
my sister Michell and her husband, and so to bed.   This day I
did first put off my waistcoat, the weather being very hot, but yet
lay in it at night, and shall for a little time.

26th. (Lord's day.) To church, and so home, where come and
dined with me Harris, Rolt, and Banister, and one Bland, that
sings well also; and very merry, and after dinner to sing all the
afternoon.   But when all was done I did begin to think that the
pleasure of these people was not worth so often charge and cost
to me, as it hath occasioned me.   To Hales's, the painter, thinking
to have found Harris sitting there for his picture, which is drawing
for me.   But he and all this day's company and Hales were got to
the Crown tavern, at next door, and thither I to them, and stayed
a minute, leaving Captain Grant telling pretty stories of people
that have killed themselves, or been accessory to it, in revenge to
other people, and to mischief other people.   And thence with
Hales to his house, and there did see his beginning of Harris's
picture, which I think will be pretty like, and he promises a very
good picture.

27th. To Westminster Hall, and up to the Lord's House, and
there saw Sir W. Pen go into the House of Lords, where his impeachment was read to him, and he used mighty civilly, the Duke
of York being there.   And two days hence, at his desire, he is to
bring in his answer, and a day then to be appointed for his being
heard with Counsel.   Thence down into the Hall, and with Creed
and Godolphin walked; and do hear that tomorrow is appointed,
upon a motion on Friday last, to discourse the business of my
Lord Sandwich, moved by Sir R. Howard, that he should be sent
for home; and I fear it will be ordered.   Certain news come, I
hear, this day, that the Spanish Plenipotentiary in Flanders will
not agree to the peace and terms we and the Dutch have made for
him and the King of France; and by this means the face of things
may be altered, and we forced to join with the French against
Spain, which will be an odd thing.   At noon with Creed to my
Lord Crewe's, and there dined; and here was a very fine-skinned

lady dined, the daughter of my Lord Robartes, and also a fine lady, Mr. John Parkhurst his wife, that was but a boy the other day. And after dinner there comes in my Lady Robartes herself,[1] and with her Mr. Robartes's wife, that was Mrs. Bodvile, the great beauty, and a fine lady indeed. My Lord Crewe and Sir Thomas, and I and Creed all the afternoon debating of my Lord Sandwich's business against tomorrow; and thence I to the King's playhouse, and there saw most of 'The Cardinal,' a good play. To Sir W. Pen's, where I supped, and sat all the evening; and, being lighted homeward by Mrs. Markham, I blew out the candle and kissed her.

28th. By coach to Westminster Hall, and there do understand that the business of religion and the Act against Conventicles have so taken them up all this morning, and do still, that my Lord Sandwich's business is not like to come on today, which I am heartily glad of. This law against Conventicles is very severe; but Creed, whom I meet here, do tell me that, it being moved that Papists' meetings might be included, the House was divided upon it, and was carried in the negative; which will give great disgust to the people, I doubt. To the King's House, and there did see 'Love in a Maze,' wherein very good mirth of Lacy, the clown, and Wintershell,[2] the country knight, his master.

29th. To White Hall, and there do hear how Sir W. Pen hath delivered in his answer; and the Lords have sent it down to the Commons, but they have not yet read it, nor taken notice of it, so as, I believe, they will, by design, defer it till they rise, that so he, by lying under an impeachment, may be prevented in his going to sea, which will vex him and trouble the Duke of York. To the

---

[1] Isabella, daughter of Sir John Smith, of Kent. Lord Robartes's first wife was Lucy, daughter of Robert Rich, second Earl of Warwick, the mother of Robert Robartes, here mentioned, who had married Sarah, daughter and heir of John Bodvile, of Bodvile Castle, in Caernarvonshire. He died, *v.p.*, in 1681, while ambassador to Denmark, having assumed the title of Viscount Bodmin, upon his father's elevation to the earldom of Radnor, in 1679.

[2] Wintershell, or Wintersell, as his name was most likely spelt, was one of the original actors under Killigrew, at Drury Lane, and played the king in *The Humorous Lieutenant*, at the opening of that theatre. He was also Sir Amorous in Ben Jonson's *Epicene*; the king in *Henry the Fourth*, etc. Downes (*Roscius Anglicanus*) says: 'Mr. Wintersell was good in tragedy as well as in comedy, especially in Cokes, in *Bartholomew Fair*, and that the famous comedian, Nokes, came, in that part, far short of him.' He was an excellent instructor, and died in July 1679. One of his best comic parts, to the last, was Master Slender, which no less a critic than John Dennis praises highly.

Duke of York's playhouse, and there saw 'Love in a Tub'; and, after the play done I stepped up to Harris's dressing-room, where I never was, and there I observe much company come to him, and the wits, to talk after the play is done and to assign meetings. My business was to talk about going down to see the Resolution. To Westminster Hall, and there met Mr. G. Montagu, and walked and talked; who tells me that the best fence against the Parliament's present fury is delay, and recommended it to me in my friends' business and my own, if I have any; and is that that Sir W. Coventry do take, and will secure himself; that the King will deliver up all to the Parliament; and being petitioned the other day by Mr. Brouncker to protect him, with tears in his eyes the King did say he could not, and bid him shift for himself, at least till the House is up. To White Hall, and there took coach home with a stranger I let into the coach, to club with me for it, he going into London. I set him down at the lower end of Cheapside, and I home, and to Sir W. Pen's; and there, it being now about nine o'clock at night, I heard Mercer's voice, and my boy Tom, singing in the garden, which pleased me mightily, having not seen her since my wife went. And so into the garden to her and sang, and then home to supper, and mightily pleased with her company in talking and singing, and so parted.

30th. To the Dolphin tavern, there to meet our neighbours, all of the parish, this being Procession-day, to dine. And did; and much very good discourse, they being, most of them, very able merchants as any in the City: Sir Andrew Rickard, Mr. Vandeputt,[1] Sir John Frederick, Harrington, and others. They talked with Mr. Mills about the meaning of this day, and the good uses of it; and how heretofore, and yet in several places, they do whip a boy at each place they stop at in their procession. I stopped to talk with Mr. Brisband, who gives me an account of the rough usage Sir G. Carteret and his Counsel had the other day before the Commissioners of Accounts, and what I do believe we shall all of us have, in a greater degree than any he hath had yet with them, before their three years are out, which are not yet begun, nor God knows when they will, this being like to be no session of Parliament, when they now rise. Thus ends this month: my wife in the country, myself full of pleasure and expense; in some trouble for my friends and my Lord Sandwich by the Parliament, and more for my eyes, which are daily worse and worse, that I dare not write or read

[1] Was this Benjamin Vandeputt, draper, sheriff of London in 1685?

almost anything. The Parliament going in a few days to rise; myself so long without accounting now, for seven or eight months, I think, or more, that I know not what condition almost I am in, as to getting or spending for all that time, which troubles me, but I will soon do it. The kingdom in an ill state through poverty; a fleet going out, and no money to maintain it or set it out; seamen yet unpaid, and mutinous when pressed to go out again; our Office able to do little, nobody trusting us, nor we desiring any to trust us and yet have not money for anything, but only what particularly belongs to this fleet going out, and that but lamely too. The Parliament several months upon an Act for £300,000, but cannot or will not agree upon it, but do keep it back, in spite of the King's desires to hasten it, till they can obtain what they have a mind, in revenge upon some men for the late ill managements. And he is forced to submit to what they please, knowing that without it he shall have no money, and they as well, that, if they give the money, the King will suffer them to do little more. And then the business of religion do disquiet everybody, the Parliament being vehement against the Nonconformists, while the King seems to be willing to countenance them. So we are all poor and in pieces, God help us! while the peace is like to go on between Spain and France; and then the French may be apprehended able to attack us. So God help us!

May 1st. Met Sir W. Pen, who labours to have his answer to his impeachment, and sent down by the Lords' House, read by the House of Commons; but they are so busy on other matters, that he cannot, and thereby will, as he believes, by design be prevented from going to sea this year. Met my cousin Thomas Pepys of Deptford, and took some turns with him; and he is mightily troubled for this Act now passed against Conventicles, and in few words and sober do lament the condition we are in by a negligent Prince and a mad Parliament. To the King's playhouse, and there saw 'The Surprisal'; and a disorder in the pit by its raining in from the cupola at top. I understand how the Houses of Commons and Lords are like to disagree very much about the business of the East India Company and one Skinner,[1] to the latter

---

[1] The dispute here alluded to had its origin in a petition against the East India Company presented to the peers by Mr. Skinner, a merchant, which led to the memorable quarrel between the two Houses of Parliament upon a question of privilege. The particulars of the case are detailed in Lingard's *History of England*, vol. xii, p. 234, fourth edition.

of which the Lords have awarded £5000 from the former for some wrong done him heretofore; and the former appealing to the Commons, the Lords vote their petition a libel, and so there is like to follow very hot work.

2d. To Hercules' Pillars, and there dined, and thence to the Duke of York's playhouse at a little past twelve, to get a good place in the pit against the new play; and there setting a poor man to keep my place, I out, and spent an hour at Martin's, my booksellers, and so back again, where I find the House quite full. But I had my place, and by and by the King comes, and the Duke of York; and then a play begins, called 'The Sullen Lovers, or The Impertinents,' [1] having many good humours in it, but the play tedious, and no design at all in it. But a little boy, for a farce, do dance Polichinelli the best that ever anything was done in this world, by all men's report: most pleased with that, beyond anything in the world, and much beyond all the play. Thence to the King's House to see Knipp, but the play done; and so I took a hackney alone, and to the park, and there spent the evening, and to the lodge, and drank new milk. And so home to the office, ended my letters, and, to spare my eyes, home, and played on my pipes, and so to bed.

3d. (Lord's day.) To church, where I saw Sir A. Rickard, though he be under the Black Rod, by order of the Lords' House, upon the quarrel between the East India Company [2] and Skinner, which is like to come to a very great heat between the two Houses. At noon comes Mr. Mills and his wife, and Mr. Turner and his wife, by invitation to dinner, and we were mighty merry, and a very pretty dinner of my Bridget and Nell's dressing, very handsome. With Sir W. Pen to Old Street, to see Sir Thomas Teddiman, who is very ill in bed of a fever, got, I believe, by the fright the Parliament have put him into of late. Thence Pen and I to Islington, and there, at the old house, eat and drank, and merry: and there, by chance giving two pretty fat boys each of them a cake, they proved to be Captain Holland's children, whom therefore I pity. So round by Hackney home, having good discourse, Pen being very open to me in his talk, how the King ought to dissolve this Parliament when the Bill of Money is passed, they being never likely to give him more; how the King hath great opportunity of making himself popular by stopping this Act against Conventicles;

[1] A comedy by Thomas Shadwell.
[2] Of which Sir A. Rickard was president.

and how my Lord Lieutenant [1] of Ireland, if the Parliament continue, will undoubtedly fall, he having managed that place with so much self-seeking and disorder and pleasure, and some great men are designing to overthrow him, as, among the rest, my Lord Orrery; and that this will try the King mightily, he being a firm friend to my Lord Lieutenant.   So home, and to supper a little and then to bed, having stepped, after I came home, to Alderman Backwell's about business, and there talked awhile with him and his wife, a fine woman of the country, and how they had bought an estate at Buckworth, within four miles of Brampton.

4th.   To the Duke of York's House, and there saw 'The Impertinents' again, and with less pleasure than before, it being but a very contemptible play; and the pit did generally say that of it. Thence going out, Mrs. Pierce called me from the gallery, and there I took her and Mrs. Corbet by coach up and down, and took up Captain Rolt in the street; and at last, it being too late to go to the Park, I carried them to the Bear, in Drury Lane, and there did treat them with a dish of mackerel, the first I have seen this year, and another dish, and mighty merry; and so carried her home.

5th.   Creed and I to the Duke of York's playhouse; and there coming late, up to the balcony-box, where we find my Lady Castlemaine and several great ladies.   And there we sat with them, and I saw 'The Impertinents' once more, now three times, and the three only days it hath been acted.   And to see the folly how the house do this day cry up the play, more than yesterday! and I for that reason like it, I find, the better, too.   By Sir Positive At-all, I understand is meant Sir Robert Howard.   My Lady Castlemaine pretty well pleased with it; but here I sat close to her fine woman, Willson, who indeed is very handsome, but, they say, with child by the King.   I asked, and she told me this was the first time her Lady had seen it, I having a mind to say something to her.   One thing of familiarity I observed in my Lady Castlemaine: she called to one of her women, another that sat by this, for a little patch off of her face, and put it into her mouth and wetted it, and so clapped it upon her own by the side of her mouth, I suppose she feeling a pimple rising there.   Thence with Creed to Westminster Hall, and there met with cousin Roger, who tells me of the great conference this day between the Lords and Commons about the business of the East India Company, as being one of the weightiest conferences that hath ever been, and maintained as weightily.   I

[1] The Duke of Ormond.

am heartily sorry I was not there, it being upon a mighty point of the privileges of the subjects of England in regard to the authority of the House of Lords, and their being condemned by them as the Supreme Court, which, we say, ought not to be, but by appeal from other Courts. And he tells me that the Commons had much the better of them in reason and history there quoted, and believes the Lords will let it fall. To walk in the Hall, and there hear that Mrs. Martin's child, my god-daughter, is dead.

6th. I understand that my Lord St. John is meant by Mr. Woodcocke in 'The Impertinents.' This morning the House is upon the City Bill, and they say hath passed it, though I am sorry that I did not think to put somebody in mind of moving for the churches to be allotted according to the convenience of the people, and not to gratify this Bishop or that College. To Mr. Pierce's, where invited, and there was Knipp and Mrs. Foster: here dined, but a poor, sluttish dinner, as usual, and so I could not be heartily merry at it. Here saw her girl's picture, but it is mighty far short of her boy's, and not like her, neither; but it makes Hales's picture of her boy appear a good picture. To the King's playhouse, and there saw 'The Virgin Martyr,' and heard the music that I like so well, and intended to have seen Knipp, but I let her alone; and having there done, went to Mrs. Pierce's back again, where she was. And so to talk, and by and by did eat some curds and cream, and thence away home, and it being night, I did walk in the dusk up and down, round through our garden, over Tower Hill, and so through Crutched Friars, three or four times. Home to put up things against tomorrow's carrier for my wife; and, among others, a very fine salmon pie, sent me by Mr. Steventon, W. Hewer's uncle.

7th. To the Duke of York's House, and there saw 'The Man's the Master,' which proves, upon my seeing it again, a very good play. To the King's House, where going in for Knipp, the play being done, I did see Beck Marshall come dressed, off of the stage, and look mighty fine, and pretty, and noble: and also Nell, in her boy's clothes, mighty pretty. But, Lord! their confidence! and how many men do hover about them as soon as they come off the stage, and how confident they are in their talk! Here I did kiss the pretty woman newly come, called Pegg,[1] that was Sir Charles Sedley's mistress, a might pretty woman, and seems, but

---

[1] Pegg must have been Margaret Hughes, Prince Rupert's mistress, who had probably before that time lived with Sir Charles Sedley. She belonged to Killigrew's company, when first it was formed, and acted Desdemona in

is not, modest. Here took up Knipp into our coach, and all of us with her to her lodgings, and thither comes Banister with a song of hers, that he hath set in Sir Charles Sedley's play for her,[1] which is, I think, but very meanly set; but this he did, before us, teach her, and it being but a slight, silly, short air, she learnt it presently. But I did get him to prick me down the notes of the Echo in 'The Tempest,' which pleases me mightily. Here was also Haynes, the incomparable dancer of the King's House. Then we abroad to Marylebone, and there walked in the garden,[2] the first time I ever was there; and a pretty place it is.

8th. The Lords' House did sit till eleven o'clock last night about the business of difference between them and the Commons in the matter of the East India Company. To my Lord Crewe's, and there dined; where Mr. Case, the minister, a dull fellow in his talk, and all in the Presbyterian manner—a great deal of noise and a kind of religious tone, but very dull. After dinner my Lord and I together. He tells me he hears that there are great disputes like to be at Court between the factions of the two women, my Lady Castlemaine and Mrs. Stuart, who is now well again, the King having made several public visits to her, and like to come to Court: the other is to go to Berkshire House,[3] which is taken for her, and they say a Privy Seal is passed for £5000 for it. He believes all will come to ruin. Thence I to White Hall, where the Duke of York gone to the Lords' House, where there is to be a conference on the Lords' side with the Commons this afternoon, giving in their reasons, which I would have been at, but could not; for, going by direction to the Prince's chamber, there Brouncker, W. Pen, and Mr. Wren and I met, and did our business with the Duke of York. But, Lord! to see how this play [4] of Sir Positive At-all, in abuse of Sir Robert Howard, do take, all the Duke's and everybody's talk being of that, and telling more stories of him, of the like nature, that it is now the town and country talk, and, they say,

---

Othello, Theodosia in *The Mock Astrologer,* etc. This actress seems to have quitted the stage before 1670, but it is not known when or where she died. Her residence for many years was at Hammersmith, in a fine mansion, built by Sir Nicholas Crispe, which had been purchased for her by Prince Rupert.

[1] The song in Sir C. Sedley's play, *The Mulberry Garden* is 'Ah, Cloris, that I now could sit.'

[2] On the site of Manchester Square.

[3] Afterwards called from the title of Cleveland conferred on Lady Castlemaine, and preserved in the names of Cleveland Row and Cleveland Square.   [4] *The Impertinents.*

is most exactly true. The Duke of York himself said that of his playing at trap-ball is true, and told several other stories of him. Then to Brouncker's house, and there sat and talked, I asking many questions in mathematics to my Lord, which he do me the pleasure to satisfy me in.

9th. I hear that the Queen hath miscarried of a perfect child, being gone about ten weeks; which do show that she can conceive, though it be unfortunate that she cannot bring forth. We are told also that last night the Duchess of Monmouth, dancing at her lodgings, hath sprained her thigh.[1] We are told also that the House of Commons sat till five o'clock this morning upon the business of the difference between the Lords and them, resolving to do something therein before they rise, to assert their privileges. So I at noon by water to Westminster, and there find the King hath waited in the Prince's chamber these two hours, and the Houses are not ready for him, the Commons having sent this morning, after their long debate therein the last night, to the Lords, that they do think the only expedient left to preserve unity between the two Houses is that they do put a stop to any proceedings upon their late judgment against the East India Company, till their next meeting. To which the Lords returned answer, that they would return answer to them by a messenger of their own,[2] which they not presently doing, they were all inflamed, and thought it was only a trick to keep them in suspense till the King come to adjourn them. And so, rather than lose the opportunity of doing themselves right, they presently with great fury come to this vote: 'That whoever should assist in the execution of the judgment of the Lords against the Company should be held betrayers of the liberties of the people of England and of the privileges of that House.' This the Lords had notice of, and were mad at it; and so continued debating without any design to yield to the Commons, till the King came in and sent for the Commons, where the Speaker made a short but silly speech about their giving him £300,000; and then the several Bills their titles were read, and the King's assent signified in the proper terms according to the nature of the Bills, of which about three or four were public Bills, and seven or eight private ones, the additional Bills for the building of the City and the Bill against Conventicles being none of them. The King did make a short, silly speech, which he read, giving them thanks for the money, which now, he said, he did believe would be sufficient,

---

[1] She never recovered from this lameness.   [2] The usual form, at this day.

because there was peace between his neighbours (which was a
kind of a slur, methought, to the Commons), and that he was
sorry for what he heard of difference between the two Houses, but
that he hoped their recess would put them into a way of accommodation; and so adjourned them to the 9th of August, and then
recollected himself and told them the 11th, so imperfect a speaker
he is. So the Commons went to their House and forthwith
adjourned, and the Lords resumed their House, the King being
gone, and sat an hour or two after; but what they did, I cannot
tell; but everybody expected they would commit Sir Andrew
Rickard, Sir Samuel Barnardiston,[1] Mr. Boone, and Mr. Wynne,
who were all there and called in upon their knees to the bar of the
House. And Sir John Robinson I left there, endeavouring to
prevent their being committed to the Tower,[2] lest he should thereby
be forced to deny their order, because of this vote of the Commons,
whereof he is one, which is an odd case.[3] Into the King's House,
and there 'The Maid's Tragedy,' a good play, but Knipp not there;
and my head and eyes out of order, the first from my drinking
wine at dinner, and the other from my much work.

10th. (Lord's day.) Mr. Shepley came to see me, and tells me
that my Lady[4] had it in her thoughts, if she had occasion, to
borrow £100 of me, which I did not declare my opposition to,
though I doubt it will be so much lost. But, however, I will not
deny my Lady if she ask it, whatever comes of it, though it be
lost; but shall be glad that it is no bigger sum. To church, and
from church home with my Lady Pen; and I took her and Mrs.
Lowther and old Mrs. Whistler, her mother-in-law, by water with
great pleasure as far as Chelsea, and so back to Spring Garden, at
Fox-hall, and there walked and eat and drank, and so to water
again, and set down the old woman at Durham Yard:[5] and it

---

[1] Sir Samuel Barnardiston, of Brightwell Hall, Suffolk, created a baronet
11th May 1663.

[2] Of which he was governor.

[3] This 'odd case' was that of Skinner and the East India Company. According to Ralph the Commons had ordered Skinner, the plaintiff, into the
custody of the Sergeant-at-Arms, and the Lords did the same by Sir Samuel
Barnadiston, governor of the company, as likewise Sir Andrew Rickard, Mr.
Rowland Gwynn, and Mr. Christopher Boone.

[4] Lady Sandwich.

[5] So called from the palace built there, by Thomas de Hatfield, Bishop of
Durham, as the town residence for himself and his successors. It stood on the
site of the buildings afterwards called the Adelphi. The name is preserved in
Durham Street.

raining all the way, it troubled us; but, however, my cloak kept us all dry, and so home.

11th. Comes to me my cousin Sarah and my aunt Lucett, newly come out of Gloucester; and I took them home and made them drink, but they would not stay dinner, I being alone. But here they tell me that they hear that this day Kate Joyce was to be married to a man called Hollinshed, whom she indeed did once tell me of, and desired me to enquire after him. But, whatever she said of his being rich, I do fear, by her doing this without my advice, it is not as it ought to be; but, as she brews, let her bake. Took coach and called Mercer, and she and I to the Duke of York's playhouse, and there saw 'The Tempest,' and between two acts I went out to Mr. Harris, and got him to repeat to me the words of the Echo, while I writ them down, having tried in the play to have wrote them; but, having done it without looking upon my paper, I find I could not read the blacklead. But now I have got the words clear, and, in going in thither, had the pleasure to see their actors in their several dresses, especially the seamen and monster, which were very droll: so in to the play again. But there happened one thing which vexed me, which is, that the orange-woman did come in the pit and challenge me for twelve oranges which she delivered by my order at a late play, at night, in order to give to some ladies in a box, which was wholly untrue, but yet she swore it to be true. But, however, I did deny it, and did not pay her; but, for quiet, did buy 4s. worth of oranges of her at 6d. apiece. Here I saw first my Lord Ormond since his coming from Ireland, which is now about eight days. The play done, I took Mercer by water to Spring Garden; and there with great pleasure walked and eat and drank and sang, making people come about us to hear us, and two little children of one of our neighbours that happened to be there did come into our arbour, and we made them dance prettily. So by water, with great pleasure, down to the Bridge, and there landed, and took water again on the other side; and so to the Tower, and I saw her home.

12th. Lord Anglesey, in talk about the late difference between the two Houses, do tell us that he thinks the House of Lords may be in an error, at least it is possible they may, in this matter of Skinner; and did declare his judgment in the House of Lords against their proceedings therein, he having hindered 100 original causes being brought into their House, notwithstanding that he was put upon defending their proceedings. But that he is confident that the House of Commons are in the wrong in the method they take to remedy an error of the Lords; for no vote of theirs can do it, but in all like cases the Commons have done it by petition to the King, sent up to the Lords and by them agreed to, and so redressed, as they did in the Petition of Right. He says that he did tell them indeed, which is talked of, and which did vex the Commons, that the Lords were '*Judices nati et Conciliarii nati,*' but all other Judges among us are under salary, and the Commons themselves served for wages; and therefore the Lords, in reason, were the freer Judges. To Mrs. Mercer's, where I met with her two daughters and a pretty lady I never knew yet, one Mrs. Susan Gayet, a very pretty black lady, that speaks French well, and is a Catholic, and merchant's daughter, by us, and here was also Mrs. Anne Jones. I took them out, and carried them through Hackney to Kingsland, and there walked to Sir G. Whitmore's house, where I have not been many a day; and so to the old house at Islington, and eat and drank and sang, and mighty merry; and so by moonshine with infinite pleasure home, and there sang again in Mercer's garden. And so parted, I having seen a mummy in a merchant's warehouse there, all the middle of the man or woman's body black and hard. I never saw any before, and therefore it pleased me much, though an ill sight; and he did give me a little bit, and a bone of an arm, I suppose, and so home.

13th. To attend the Council about the business of Hemskirke's project of building a ship that sails two feet for one of any other ship, which the Council did agree to be put in practice, the King to give him, if it proves good, £5000 in hand and £15,000 more in seven years, which, for my part, I think a piece of folly for them to meddle with, because the secret cannot be long kept. So thence, after Council, having drunk some of the King's wine and water with Mr. Chiffinch, my Lord Brouncker, and some others, I by water to the Old Swan: so home to bed, Mrs. Turner having sat and supped with me. This morning I hear that last night Sir Thomas Teddiman, poor man! did die by a thrush in his mouth: a good man, and stout and able, and much lamented; though people do make a little mirth, and say, as I believe it did in good part, that the business of the Parliament did break his heart, or, at least, put him into this fever and disorder that caused his death.

14th. Comes Mercer, and she, to my great content, brings Mrs. Gayet, and I carried them to the King's House; but, coming too soon, we out again to the Rose tavern, and there I did give them a tankard of cool drink, the weather being very hot, and then into the playhouse again, and there saw 'The Country Captain,' a very dull play, that did give us no content, and, besides, little company there, which made it very unpleasing. Thence to the water-side at Strand bridge, and so up by water and to Fox-hall, where we walked a great while, and pleased mightily with the pleasure thereof and the company there, and then in, and eat and drank. It beginning to be dark, we to a corner and sang, that everybody got about us to hear us; and so home, where I saw them both to their doors, and, full of the content of this afternoon's pleasure, I home to bed.

15th. To a Committee for Tangier, where God knows how my Lord Bellassis's accounts passed: understood by nobody but my Lord Ashley, who, I believe, was allowed to let them go as he pleased. But here Sir H. Cholmley had his propositions read, about a greater price for his work of the Mole, or to do it upon account, which, being read, he was bid to withdraw. But, Lord! to see how unlucky a man may be by chance; for, making an unfortunate motion when they were almost tired with the other business, the Duke of York did find fault with it, and that made all the rest, that I believe he had better have given a great deal, and had nothing said to it today; whereas, I have seen other things more extravagant passed at first hearing without any difficulty. To my Lord Brouncker's, to Mrs. Williams's, and there dined, and she did show me her closet, which I was sorry to see, for fear of her expecting something from me. And here she took notice of my wife's not once coming to see her, which I am glad of; for she shall not—a prating, vain, idle woman. Thence with Lord Brouncker to Loriners' Hall,[1] by Moorgate, a hall I never heard of before, to Sir Thomas Teddiman's burial, where most people belonging to the sea were. And here we had rings: and here I do hear that some of the last words that he said were, that he had a very good King, God bless him! but that the Parliament had very ill rewarded him for all the service he had endeavoured to do them and his country; so that, for certain, this did go far towards his death. But, Lord! to see among the company the young commanders and Thomas Killigrew and others that came, how unlike a burial this was, O'Bryan taking some ballads out of his pocket, which I read, and the rest come about me to hear! and there very

[1] The Loriners, or Bit-Makers, of London, existed as a company in the reign of Henry VII; but they were not incorporated till 3rd December 1712.

merry we were all, they being new ballads. By and by the corpse went; and I, with my Lord Brouncker and Dr. Clerke and Mr. Pierce, as far as the foot of London Bridge; and there we struck off into Thames Street, the rest going to Redriffe, where he is to be buried. And we 'light at the Temple, and there parted; and I to the King's House, and there saw the last act of 'The Committee,' thinking to have seen Knipp there, but she did not act. And so to my bookseller's, and carried home some books—among others, Dr. Wilkins's 'Real Character.' [1] So home and got Mercer, and she and I in the garden singing till ten at night, and then parted with great content. The Duchess of Monmouth's hip is, I hear, now set again, after much pain. I am told also that the Countess of Shrewsbury is brought home by the Duke of Buckingham to his house, where his Duchess saying that it was not for her and the other to live together in a house, he answered, 'Why, Madam, I did think so, and therefore have ordered your coach to be ready to carry you to your father's,' [2] which was a devilish speech, but, they say, true; and my Lady Shrewsbury is there, it seems.

16th. Up, and to the office, where we sat all the morning; and at noon, home with my people to dinner, and thence to the office all the afternoon, till, my eyes weary, I did go forth by coach to the King's playhouse, and there saw the best part of 'The Sea Voyage,' [3] where Knipp did her part of sorrow very well. I afterwards to her house (but she did not come presently home), and there I did kiss her maid, who is so mighty *belle*; and I to my tailor's, and to buy me a belt for my new suit against tomorrow. And so home, and there to my office, and afterwards late walking in the garden; and so home to supper, and to bed, after Nell's cutting of my hair close, the weather being very hot.

17th. (Lord's day.) Up, and put on my new stuff-suit, with a shoulder-belt, according to the new fashion, and the bands of my vest and tunic laced with silk lace, of the colour of my suit: and so, very handsome, to church. And so home, and there I find W. Howe and a younger brother of his come to dine with me; and there comes Mercer, and brings with her Mrs. Gayet, which pleased me mightily. And here was also W. Hewer, and mighty merry;

---

[1] *An Essay towards a Real Character and a Philosophical Language, with an Alphabetical Dictionary*, London, 1668, folio, by John Wilkins, shortly afterwards made Bishop of Chester.

[2] Lord Fairfax.

[3] A comedy by Fletcher and others.

and after dinner to sing psalms. But, Lord! to hear what an excellent bass this younger brother of W. Howe's sings, even to my astonishment, and mighty pleasant. By and by Gayet goes away, being a Catholic, to her devotions, and Mercer to church: but we continuing an hour or two singing, and so parted, and I to Sir W. Pen's; and there sent for a hackney coach, and he and Lady Penn and I out to take the air. We went to Stepney, and there stopped at the Trinity House, he to talk with the servants there against tomorrow,[1] which is a great day for the choice of a new Master. Thence to Mile End, and there eat and drank, and so home; and I supped with them—that is, eat some butter and radishes, which is my excuse for my not eating any other of their victuals, which I hate because of their sluttery: and so home, and made my boy read to me part of Dr. Wilkins's new book of the 'Real Character'; and so to bed.

18th. To my Lord Bellassis, at his new house by my late Lord Treasurer's,[2] which, indeed, is mighty noble, and good pictures —indeed, not one bad one in it. Mercer came with Mrs. Horsfield and Gayet according to my desire, and then I took them up, it being almost twelve o'clock or a little more, to the King's play-house, where the doors were not then open. But presently they did open; and we in, and find many people already come in by private ways into the pit, it being the first day of Sir Charles Sedley's new play so long expected, 'The Mulberry Garden,' of whom, being so reputed a wit, all the world do expect great matters. I having sat here awhile, and eat nothing today, did slip out, getting a boy to keep my place; and to the Rose tavern, and there got half a breast of mutton, off of the spit, and dined all alone. And so to the play again, where the King and Queen by and by come, and all the Court; and the house infinitely full. But the play, when it come, though there was here and there a pretty saying, and that not very many neither, yet the whole of the play had nothing extraordinary in it at all, neither of language nor design; insomuch that the King I did not see laugh, nor pleased, from the beginning to the end, nor the company; insomuch that

[1] Trinity Monday.

[2] Probably in Bloomsbury Square, the north side of which was then occupied by Southampton House, the town residence of the late Lord Treasurer Southampton. By his daughter, Lady Rachel Wriothesley's [widow of Lord Vaughan] second marriage with William Lord Russell, Southampton House came to the Bedford family, and was afterwards known as Bedford House.

I have not been less pleased at a new play in my life, I think. And which made it the worse was, that there never was worse music played—that is, worse things composed—which made me and Captain Rolt, who happened to sit near me, mad. So away thence, very little satisfied with the play, but pleased with my company. I carried them to Kensington, to the Grotto, and there we sang to my great content, only vexed, in going in, to see a son of Sir Heneage Finch's [1] beating of a poor little dog to death, letting it lie in so much pain that made me mad to see it, till by and by the servants of the house chiding their young master, one of them come with a string, and killed the dog outright presently. Thence to Westminster palace, and there took boat and to Foxhall, where we walked, and eat and drank, and sang. But I find Mrs. Horsfield one of the veriest citizen's wives in the world, so full of little silly talk, and now and then a little slyly indecent.

19th. Pierce tells me that, for certain, Mr. Vaughan is made Lord Chief Justice, which I am glad of. He tells me, too, that since my Lord of Ormond's coming over the King begins to be mightily reclaimed, and sups every night with great pleasure with the Queen: and yet, it seems, he is mighty hot upon the Duchess of Richmond insomuch that upon Sunday was se'nnight, at night, after he had ordered his Guards and coach to be ready to carry him to the Park, he did on a sudden take a pair of oars or sculler, and all alone, or but one with him, go to Somerset House, and there, the garden-door not being open, himself clambered over the wall to make a visit to her, which is a horrid shame!

20th. Up, and with Colonel Middleton in a new coach he hath made him, very handsome, to White Hall, where the Duke having removed his lodgings for this year to St. James's, we walked thither; and there to the Council-chamber, where the Committee of the Navy sat. And here we discoursed several things: but, Lord! like fools, so as it was a shame to see things of this importance managed by a Council that understand nothing of them. And, among other things, one was about this building of a ship with Hemskirke's secret, to sail a third faster than any other ship; but he hath got Prince Rupert on his side, and by that means, I believe, will get his conditions made better than he would otherwise, or ought indeed. Having done there, Sir Richard Browne [2] took me to dinner to a new tavern, above Charing Cross, where

---

[1] Who resided at the mansion afterwards called Kensington Palace.
[2] Clerk of the Council.

some clients of his did give him a good dinner, and good company; among others one Bovy, a solicitor and lawyer and merchant all together, who hath travelled very much, did talk some things well; only he is a 'Sir Positive': but the talk of their travels over the Alps very fine. Thence walked to the King's playhouse, and saw 'The Mulberry Garden' again, and cannot be reconciled to it, but only to find here and there an independent sentence of wit, and that is all. To Hales's, and saw the beginnings of Harris's head, which I do not yet like. To the Mulberry Garden, where I never was before; and find it a very silly place, worse than Spring Garden, and but little company, only a wilderness here, that is somewhat pretty. Home, in my way going into Bishopsgate Street to bespeak places for myself and boy to go to Cambridge in the coach this week and so to Brampton to see my wife.

21st. To the office, where meets me Sir Richard Ford, who among other things congratulates me, as one or two did yesterday, on my great purchase; and he advises me rather to forbear, if it be not done, as a thing that the world will envy me in: and what is it but my cousin Tom Pepys's buying of Martin Abbey,[1] in Surrey! All the town is full of the talk of a meteor, or some fire, that did on Saturday last fly over the City at night, which do put me in mind that, being then walking in the dark an hour or more myself in the garden after I had done writing, I did see a light before me come from behind me, which made me turn back my head; and did see a sudden fire or light running in the sky, as it were towards Cheapside ward, and it vanished very quick, which did make me bethink myself what holiday it was, and took it for some rocket, though it was much brighter. And the world do make much discourse of it, their apprehensions being mighty full of the rest of the City to be burned, and the Papists to cut our throats. Which God prevent! Thence after dinner to the Temple, and there bought a new book of songs set to music by one Smith of Oxford, some songs of Mr. Cowley's. And so to Mrs. Martin's, and here she promises me her fine starling, which was the King's and speaks finely, which I shall be glad of. Meeting in the street with my cousin Alcocke, the young man, that is a good sober youth I have not seen these four or five years, newly come to town to look for employment: but I cannot serve him, though I think he deserves

---

[1] In 1668, the site of Merton, alias Martin, Priory was conveyed by Ellis Crispe to Thomas Pepys, of Hatcham Barnes, Master of the Jewel-office to Charles II and James II (Manning's *Survey*).

well. Home, and sang; and eat a dish of green peas, the first I have seen this year, given me by Mr. Gibson, extraordinary young and pretty.

22d. Comes Mr. Martin, the purser, and brings me his wife's starling, which was formerly the King's, which I am mighty proud of. To the Duke of York's House, and saw 'Sir Martin Mar-all.' The house full; and though I have seen it, I think, ten times, yet the pleasure I have is yet as great as ever. I fitted myself for my journey to Brampton tomorrow, which I fear will not be pleasant, because of the wet weather, it raining very hard all this day; but the less it troubles me, because the King and Duke of York and Court are at this day at Newmarket, at a great horse-race, and proposed great pleasure for two or three days, but are in the same wet.

23d. Up by four o'clock; and, getting my things ready, and recommending the care of my house to W. Hewer, I with my boy Tom, whom I take with me, to the Bull, in Bishopsgate Street: and there, about six, took coach, he and I and a gentleman and his man, there being another coach also with as many more, I think, in it; and so away to Bishop's Stortford. Dined, and changed horses and coach, at Mrs. Aynsworth's: but I took no knowledge of her. To dinner, and in comes Captain Forster, that do belong to my Lord Anglesey, who had been at the late horse-races at Newmarket, where the King now is, and says that they had fair weather there yesterday, though we here and at London, had nothing but rain, insomuch that the ways are mighty full of water, so as hardly to be passed. I hear Mrs. Aynsworth is going to live at London: but I believe will be mistaken in it, for it will be found better for her to be chief where she is, than to have little to do at London. After dinner to Cambridge, about nine at night; and there I met my father's horses, with a man, staying for me. But it is so late, and the waters so deep, that I durst not go tonight; but after supper to bed, and there lay very ill by reason of some drunken scholars making a noise all night, and vexed for fear that the horses should not be taken up from grass time enough for the morning. Well pleased all this journey with the conversation of him that went with me, who I think is a lawyer, and lives about Lynn, but his name I did not ask.

24th. (Lord's day.) I up at between two and three in the morning, and, calling up my boy and father's boy, set out about three o'clock; and so through the waters with very good success, though

very deep almost all the way, and got to Brampton, where most
of them in bed.   Got me ready in my new stuff clothes that I sent
down before me, and so my wife and they got ready too, while I
to my father, poor man, and walked with him up and down the
house—it raining a little, and the waters all over Portholme and
the meadows, so as no pleasure abroad.   Here I saw my brother
and sister Jackson, she growing fat, and, since being married, I
think looks comelier than before: but a mighty pert woman she is,
and I think proud, he keeping her mighty handsome, and they say
mighty fond, and are going shortly to live at Ellington of themselves, and will keep malting and grazing of cattle.   At noon
comes Mr. Phillips and dines with us, and a pretty odd-humoured
man he seems to be: but good with all men—of mighty great
methods in his eating and drinking, and will not kiss a woman since
his wife's death.   After dinner, my Lady Sandwich sending to see
whether I was come, I presently took horse, and find her and her
family at chapel: and thither I went in to them, and sat out the
sermon, where I heard Jervas Fulwood, now their chaplain, preach
a very good and seraphic kind of sermon, too good for an ordinary
congregation.   After sermon I with my Lady and my Lady
Hinchingbroke and Paulina and Lord Hinchingbroke to the
dining-room, saluting none of them, and there sat and talked an
hour or two, with great pleasure and satisfaction, to my Lady
about my Lord's matters; but I think not with that satisfaction to
her or me that it otherwise would, she knowing that she did design
tomorrow, and I remaining all the while in fear of being asked to
lend her some money, as I was afterwards, when I had taken leave
of her, by Mr. Shepley, £100, which I will not deny my Lady.

25th.   The first fair day that we have had some time.   So up,
and to walk with my father again in the garden, consulting what to
do with him and this house when Pall and her husband go away;
and I think it will be to let it, and he go live with her, though I am
against letting the house for any long time, because of having it
to retire to ourselves.   After dinner took horse, there going with
me and my boy my two brothers [1] and one Browne, whom they
call in mirth Colonel, for our guide, and also Mr. Shepley, to the
end of Huntingdon, and another gentleman who accidentally came
thither, one Mr. Castle.   And I made them drink at the Chequers,
where I observed the same tapster, Tom, that was there when I was
a little boy: and so, at the end of the town, took leave of Shepley

[1] John Pepys and Mr. Jackson.

and the other gentleman, and away to Cambridge, the waters not being now so high as before.   Here 'lighting, I took my boy and two brothers, and walked to Magdalene College.   And there into the butteries, as a stranger, and there drank of their beer, which pleased me, as the best I ever drank: and hear by the butler's man, who was son to Goody Mulliner over against the College, that we used to buy stewed prunes of, concerning the College and persons in it; and find very few, only Mr. Hollins [1] and Peachell,[2] I think, that were of my time.   Thence, giving the fellow something, away walked to Chesterton, to see our old walk, and there into the church, the bells ringing, and saw the place I used to sit in; and so to the ferry, and ferried over to the other side, and walked with great pleasure, the river being mighty high by Barnwell Abbey; and so by Jesus College to the town, and so to our quarters, and to supper.

26th. Up by four o'clock; and by the time we were ready and had eat we were called to the coach, where about six o'clock we set out, there being a man and two women of one company, ordinary people, and one lady alone, that is tolerably handsome but mighty well spoken, whom I took great pleasure in talking to, and did get her to read aloud in a book she was reading in the coach, being the King's Meditations; [3] and then the boy and I to sing, and about noon come to Bishop's Stortford, to another house than what we were at the other day, and better used.   And here I paid for the reckoning 11s., we dining together, and pretty merry; and then set out again, sleeping most part of the way, and got to Bishopsgate Street before eight o'clock, the waters being now most of them down, and we avoiding the bad way in the forest [4] by a privy way, which brought us to Hoddesden; and so to Theobalds [5] that road, which was mighty pleasant.   So home, where we find all well, and brother Balty and his wife looking to the house, she mighty fine in a new gold-laced *justaucorps*.[6]

27th. Met Mr. Sawyer [7] my old chamber-fellow; and he and I

[1] John Hollins, of Medley, in Yorkshire; admitted a Pensioner of Magdalene College, March 1651.
[2] John Peachell, afterwards Master.
[3] The prayers used by Charles I shortly before his execution.
[4] Epping Forest.
[5] The palace of Theobalds, where James I died.
[6] *Justaucorps*, a close-fitting vest, made to show the shape.
[7] Afterwards Sir Robert Sawyer, Attorney General, ancestor of the earls of Carnarvon, who inherit Highclere from him.

by water together to the Temple, he giving me an account of the
base, rude usage which he and Sir G. Carteret had lately before the
Commissioners of Accounts, where he was, as Counsel to Sir G.
Carteret; which I was sorry to hear, they behaving themselves like
most insolent and ill-mannered men.   With Sir D. Gauden to his
house, with my Lord Brouncker and Sir J. Minnes, to dinner,
where we dined very well, and much good company, among others
Dr.———, a fat man, whom by face I know as one that uses to sit
in our church, that after dinner did take me out, and walked
together, who told me that he had now newly entered into orders,
in the decay of the Church, and did think it his duty so to do,
thereby to do his part toward the support and reformation thereof;
and spoke very soberly, and said that just about the same age Dr.
Donne [1] did enter into orders.   I find him a sober gentleman, and
a man that hath seen much of the world, and I think may do good.
To see Sir W. Pen, whom I find still very ill of the gout, sitting
in his great chair, made on purpose for persons sick of that disease,
for their ease; and this very chair, he tells me, was made for my
Lady Lambert.[2]   I to drink some whey at the whey-house, and
so home, and then made the boy to read to me out of Dr. Wilkins
his 'Real Character,' and particularly about Noah's ark; where he
do give a very good account thereof, showing how few the number
of the several species of beasts and fowls were that were to be in
the ark, and that there was room enough for them and their food
and dung; which do please me mightily, and is beyond what I ever
heard of the subject.   And so to bed.

    28th.   This morning my bookseller brings me home Marcenus's
book of music,[3] which cost me £3 2s., but is a very fine book.
Met Mercer and Gayet, and took them by water, first to one of the
Neat-Houses, where walked in the garden, but nothing but a bottle
of wine to be had, though pleased with seeing the garden; and so
to Fox-hall, where with great pleasure we walked, and then to the
upper end of the further retired walk, and there sat and sang, and
brought a great many gallants and fine people about us, and, upon
the bench, we did by and by eat and drink what we had, and very
merry: and so with much pleasure to the Old Swan, and walked
with them home, and there left them.

    29th.   Received some directions from the Duke of York and the

---

    [1] John Donne, the well-known Dean of St. Paul's.
    [2] Frances, daughter of Sir William Lister, of Thornton.
    [3] Probably Mersenne's *Harmonie Universelle.*

Committee of the Navy about casting up the charge of the present summer's fleet, that so they may come within the bounds of the sum given by the Parliament. But it is pretty to see how Prince Rupert and other mad silly people are for setting out but a little fleet, there being no occasion for it; and say it will be best to save the money for better uses. But Sir G. Carteret did declare that, in wisdom, it was better to do so; but that, in obedience to the Parliament, he was for setting out the fifty sail talked on, though it spent all the money, and to little purpose; and that this was better than to leave it to the Parliament to make bad constructions of their thrift, if any trouble should happen. Thus wary the world is grown! Thence back again presently home, and did business till noon: and then to Sir G. Carteret's to dinner, with much good company, it being the King's birthday, and many healths drunk. And here I did receive another letter from my Lord Sandwich, which troubles me to see how I have neglected him, in not writing, or but once, all this time of his being abroad; and I see he takes notice, but yet gently, of it. Home, whither, by agreement, by and by comes Mercer and Gayet, and two gentlemen with them, Mr. Monteith and Pelham, the former a swaggering young handsome gentleman, the latter a sober citizen-merchant. Both sing, but the latter with great skill—the other, no skill, but a good voice and a good bass, but used to sing only tavern tunes. And so I spent all this evening till eleven at night singing with them, till I was tired of them because of the swaggering fellow, though the girl Mercer did mightily commend him before to me.

30th. Up, and put on a new summer black bombazine suit; and being come now to an agreement with my barber to keep my periwig in good order at 20s. a year, I am like to go very spruce, more than I used to do. To the King's playhouse, and there saw 'Philaster';[1] where it is pretty to see how I could remember almost all along, ever since I was a boy, Arethusa, the part which I was to have acted at Sir Robert Cooke's: and it was very pleasant to me, but more to think what a ridiculous thing it would have been for me to have acted a beautiful woman. Thence to Mr. Pierce's, and there saw Knipp also, and were merry; and here saw my little Lady Katherine Montagu come to town about her eyes, which are sore, and they think the King's evil, poor, pretty lady. To the New Exchange, and there met Harris and Rolt and one Richards, a tailor, and great company-keeper, and with these over

[1] A tragedy by Beaumont and Fletcher.

May 1668

to Fox-hall; and there fell into the company of Harry Killigrew, a rogue newly come back out of France, but still in disgrace at our Court, and young Newport and others, as very rogues as any in the town, who were ready to take hold of every woman that come by them. And so to supper in an arbour: but, Lord! their mad talk did make my heart ache! And here I first understood by their talk the meaning of the company that lately were called Ballers, Harris telling how it was by a meeting of some young blades, where he was among them, and my Lady Bennet [1] and her ladies, and their dancing naked, and all the roguish things in the world. But, Lord! what loose company was this that I was in tonight, though full of wit and worth a man's being in for once, to know the nature of it, and their manner of talk, and lives.

31st. (Lord's day.) To church. At noon I sent for Mr. Mills and his wife and daughter to dine, and they dined with me, and W. Hewer, and very good company, I being in good humour. They gone to church, comes Mr. Tempest, and he and I sang a psalm or two, and so parted. To Mrs. Pierce's, where Knipp; and she and W. Howe and Mr. Pierce and little Betty over to Fox-hall, and there walked and supped with great pleasure. Here was Mrs. Manuel also, and mighty good company, and good mirth in making W. Howe spend his six or seven shillings, and so they called him altogether 'Cully.' [2] So back, and at Somerset stairs do understand that a boy is newly drowned, washing himself there, and they cannot find his body. I hear that Mrs. Davis is quite gone from the Duke of York's House, and Gosnell comes in her room, which I am glad of. At the play at Court the other night, Mrs. Davis was there; and when she was to come to dance her jig the Queen would not stay to see it, which people do think was out of displeasure at her being the King's mistress, that she could not bear it. My Lady Castlemaine is, it seems, now mightily out of request, the King coming little to her, and thus she mighty melancholy and discontented.

---

[1] Evidently adopted as a cant expression. The woman here alluded to was a procuress well known in her day, and described in the *Tatler* (No. 84) as 'the celebrated Madam Bennet.' We further learn, from the *Spectator* (No. 266) that she was the Lady B. to whom Wycherley addressed his ironical dedication of *The Plain Dealer*, which is considered as a masterpiece of raillery.

[2] Pepys here alludes to Sir Nicholas Cully (Nokes's character) in Etherege's *Comical Revenge, or Love in a Tub.*

June 1st. To Westminster. There I met with Harris and Rolt, and carried them to the Rhenish wine-house,[1] where I have not been in a morning—nor any tavern, I think—these seven years and more. Here I did get the words of a song of Harris, that I wanted. Here also Mr. Young and Whistler by chance met us and drank with us. Alone to Fox-hall, and walked and saw young Newport and two more rogues of the town seize on two ladies, who walked with them an hour with their masks on; perhaps civil ladies, and there I left them. To Mr. Mills's, where I never was before, and here find (whom I indeed saw go in, and that did make me go thither) Mrs. Hollworthy and Mrs. Andrews, and here supped, and extraordinary merry till one in the morning, Mr. Andrews coming to us: and, mightily pleased with this night's company and mirth, I home to bed. Mrs. Turner, too, was with us.

2d. Took a coach, and called Mercer at their back door, and she brought with her Mrs. Knightly, a little, pretty, sober girl, and I carried them to Old Ford, a town by Bow where I never was before, and there walked in the fields, very pleasant, and sang: and so back again, and stopped and drank at the Gun, at Mile End, and so to the old Exchange door, and did buy them a pound of cherries, cost me 2s., and so set them down again. And so by water, it being now about nine o'clock, down to Deptford, where I have not been many a day: and to my boat again, and against the tide home. Got there by twelve, taking into my boat, for company, a man that desired a passage—a certain western bargeman, with whom I had good sport, talking of the old woman of Woolwich, and telling him the whole story.

3d. To White Hall, to the Council-chamber, where I did present the Duke of York with an account of the charge of the present fleet, to his satisfaction; and this being done, did ask his leave for my going out of town five or six days, which he did give me, saying that my diligence in the King's business was such that I ought not to be denied when my own business called me anywhither. Met Roger Pepys, who is mighty earnest for me to stay from going into the country till he goes, and to bring my people thither for some time: but I cannot, but will find another time this summer for it. To the King's House, and there saw good part of 'The Scornful Lady,' and, that done, would have taken out Knipp, but she was engaged. To my Lord Crewe's, to visit him; from whom

[1] In Cannon Row.

I learn nothing but that there hath been some controversy at the Council-table, about my Lord Sandwich's signing, where some would not have had him, in the treaty with Portugal; but all, I think, is over in it.   To Westminster, and thence to the Park, where much good company and many fine ladies; and in so handsome a hackney I was, that I believe Sir W. Coventry and others, who looked on me, did take me to be in one of my own, which I was a little troubled for.   So to the lodge, and drank a cup of new milk, and so home.   Then to bed, having laid my business with W. Hewer to go out of town Friday next, with hopes of a great deal of pleasure.

4th. Mr. Clerke, the solicitor, dined with me and my clerks. After dinner I carried and set him down at the Temple, he observing to me how St. Sepulchre's church steeple is repaired already [1] a good deal, and the Fleet Bridge is contracted for by the City to begin to be built this summer, which do please me mightily.   I to White Hall, and walked through the Park for a little air; and so back to the Council-chamber, to the Committee of the Navy, about the business of fitting the present fleet, suitable to the money given, which, as the King orders it, and by what appears, will be very little; and so, as I perceive, the Duke of York will have nothing to command, nor can intend to go abroad.   But it is pretty to see how careful these great men are to do everything so as they may answer it to the Parliament, thinking themselves safe in nothing but where the Judges, with whom they often advise, do say the matter is doubtful; and so they take upon themselves then to be the chief persons to interpret what is doubtful.   Thence home, and all the evening to set matters in order against my going to Brampton tomorrow, being resolved upon my journey and having the Duke of York's leave again today; though I do plainly see that I can very ill be spared now, there being much business, especially about this which I have attended the Council about, and I the man that am alone consulted with; and besides, my Lord Brouncker is at this time ill, and Sir W. Pen.   So things being put in order at the office, I home to do the like there; and so to bed.

5th.[2] (Friday.)   At Barnet, for milk, *6d.*   On the highway, to menders of the highway, *6d.*   Dinner at Stevenage, *5s. 6d.*

---

[1] From the damage it sustained in the fire of 1666.

[2] The Journal from this time to 17th June is contained on five leaves, inserted in the Book; and after them follow several blank pages.

6th. (Saturday.) Spent at Huntingdon with Bowles and Appleyard and Shepley, 2s.

7th. (Sunday.) My father, for money lent, and horse-hire, £1. 11s.

8th. (Monday.) Father's servants, father having in the garden told me bad stories of my wife's ill words, 14s.; one that helped at the horses, 1s.; menders of the highway, 2s. Pleasant country to Bedford, where, while they stay, I rode through the town; and a good country town; and there, drinking, 1s. We on to Newport; and there I and W. Hewer to the church, and there give the boy 1s. So to Buckingham, a good old town. Here I to see the church, which very good, and the leads, and a school in it: did give the sexton's boy 1s. A fair bridge here, with many arches: vexed at my people's making me lose so much time: reckoning, 13s. 4d. Mightily pleased with the pleasure of the ground all the day. At night to Newport Pagnell; and there a good pleasant country town, but few people in it. A very fair—and like a cathedral—church; and I saw the leads, and a vault that goes far under ground: the town, and so most of this country, well watered. Lay here well, and rose next day by four o'clock: few people in the town: and so away. Reckoning for supper, 19s. 6d.; poor, 6d. Mischance to the coach, but no time lost.

9th. (Tuesday.) We came to Oxford, a very sweet place: paid our guide £1. 2s. 6d.; barber, 2s. 6d.; book, Stonehenge,[1] 4s.; boy that showed me the colleges before dinner, 1s. To dinner; and then out with my wife and people and landlord: and to him that showed us the schools and library, 10s.; to him that showed us All Souls' College and Chicheley's picture,[2] 5s. So to see Christ Church with my wife, I seeing several others, very fine, alone before dinner, and did give the boy that went with me 1s. Strawberries, 1s. 2d. Dinner and servants, £1. 0s. 6d. After coming home from the Schools I out with the landlord to Brazenose College; to the butteries, and in the cellar find the hand of the Child of Hales,[3] ... long. Butler, 2s. Thence with coach and people to

[1] Probably Inigo Jones's *Discourse on Stonehenge*, printed in 1663; or, perhaps, *Chorea Gigantum*, of the same date, by W. Charleton.

[2] Henry Chicheley, Archbishop of Canterbury, the founder of All Souls College.

[3] John Middleton, the remarkable person here alluded to, known by the name of 'The Child of Hale,' was born in 1578, and buried in the churchyard of Hale, in Lancashire, in 1623, where his gravestone is still to be seen. About the year 1617 Sir Gilbert Ireland took him up to the court of James I, when he

Physic-garden, 1s. So to Friar Bacon's study: I up and saw it, and gave the man 1s. Bottle of sack for landlord, 2s. Oxford mighty fine place; and well seated, and cheap entertainment. At night came to Abingdon, where had been a fair of custard; and met many people and scholars going home; and there did get some pretty good music, and sang and danced till supper: 5s.

10th. (Wednesday.) Up, and walked to the Hospital: very large and fine, and pictures of founders, and the History of the Hospital; and is said to be worth £700 per annum, and that Mr. Foley [1] was here lately to see how their lands were settled; and here, in old English, the story of the occasion of it, and a rebus at the bottom.[2] So did give the poor, which they would not take but in their box, 2s. 6d. So to the inn, and paid the reckoning and servants, 13s. So forth towards Hungerford, led this good way by our landlord, one Heart, an old but very civil and well-spoken man, more than I ever heard, of his quality. He gone, we forward; and I vexed at my people's not minding the way. So come to Hungerford, where very good trouts, eels, and crayfish. Dinner: a mean town. At dinner there, 12s. Thence set out with a guide, who saw us to Newmarket Heath [3] and then left us, 3s. 6d. So all over the Plain by the sight of the steeple, the Plain high and low, to

threw the king's wrestler, and put out his thumb, by which feat he disobliged the courtiers, and was sent back, with a present of £20 from the sovereign. He returned home by Brasenose College, then full of Lancashire students, and his picture was taken, and is still preserved there. 'Middleton's hand,' observes Plot (*History of Staffordshire*, p. 297) 'measured, from the carpus to the end of his middle finger, seventeen inches, his palm was eight inches and a half broad, and his whole height nine feet three inches, wanting but six inches of the height of Goliath, if the portrait of him in Brasenose Library, drawn at length, as it is said, in his just proportion, be a true piece of him.' These dimensions appear to have been compared with the portrait at Hale, with which they exactly accorded, as did the shape of the giant's hand cut upon a stone in the college cellar, with the date affixed, to which Pepys alludes. The blank in the *Diary*, after the word Hales, was probably left for the dimensions of the hand.

[1] Thomas Foley, of Witley Court, who himself founded a hospital for sixty boys at Stourbridge, in Worcestershire.
[2] See Ashmole's *History of Berks*, vol. i, p. 127, 8vo. The following is the rebus (?) noticed by Pepys: 'V.A.B.I.N.D.O.N.R.F.I. Take the first letter of youre foure fader, with A., the worker of Wer, and I. and N. the colore of an asse; set them together, and tel me yf you can, what it is than. Richard Fannande, Irenmonger, hathe made this Tabul, and sit it here in the yere of King Henry the Sexte, XXVI^te.'
[3] Probably a mistake for East or Market Lavington, which lies in the same direction.

Salisbury, by night; but before I came to the town I saw a great fortification, and there 'light, and to it and in it; and find it prodigious, so as to fright me to be in it all alone at that time of night, it being dark. I understand, since, it to be that that is called Old Sarum.[1] Come to the George Inn, where lay in a silk bed; and very good diet. To supper; then to bed.

11th. (Thursday.) Up, and W. Hewer and I up and down the town, and find it a very brave place. The river goes through every street; and a most capacious market-place. The city great, I think greater than Oxford. But the Minster most admirable; as big, I think, and handsomer than Westminster: and a most large Close about it, and houses for the officers thereof, and a fine palace for the Bishop. So to my lodging back, and took out my wife and people to show them the town and church; but they being at prayers, we could not be shown the Choir. A very good organ; and I looked in, and saw the Bishop, my friend Dr. Ward.[2] Thence to the inn; and there not being able to hire coach-horses, and not willing to use our own, we got saddle-horses, very dear. Boy that went to look for them, 6*d.* So the three women behind W. Hewer, Murford, and our guide, and I single to Stonehenge, over the Plain and some great hills, even to fright us. Come thither, and find them as prodigious as any tales I ever heard of them, and worth going this journey to see. God knows what their use was! they are hard to tell, but yet may be told. Gave the shepherd-woman, for leading our horses, 4*d.* So back by Wilton, my Lord Pembroke's house, which we could not see, he being just coming to town; but the situation I do not like, nor the house promise much, it being in a low but rich valley. So back home; and there being 'light, we to the church, and there find them at prayers again, so could not see the Choir; but I sent the women home, and I did go in, and saw very many fine tombs, and among the rest some very ancient, of the Montagus.[3] So home to dinner; and, that being done, paid the reckoning, which was so exorbitant, and particular in rate of my horses, and 7*s.* 6*d.* for bread and beer, that I was mad, and resolve to trouble the master about it, and get something for the poor; and come away in that humour: £2 5*s.* 6*d.*

---

[1] Pepys must mean that the earthworks, more than a hundred feet in height, were prodigious and alarming, the space contained within them being only twenty-seven acres. There is undoubtedly something sublime in standing within the area, in the complete solitude and magnificence of the ramparts.

[2] Seth Ward, recently translated to Salisbury from Exeter.

[3] The Montacutes, from whom Lord Sandwich's family claimed descent.

Servants, 1s. 6d.; poor, 1s.; guide to the Stones, 2s.; poor woman in the street, 1s.; ribbons, 9d.; washwoman, 1s.; seamstress for W. Hewer, 3s.; lent W. Hewer, 2s.   Thence about six o'clock, and with a guide went over the smooth Plain indeed till night; and then, by a happy mistake, and that looked like an adventure, we were carried out of our way to a town where we would lie, since we could not go as far as we would.   And there with great diffi-culty come about ten at night to a little inn, where we were fain to go into a room where a pedlar was in bed, and made him rise; and there wife and I lay, and in a truckle-bed Betty Turner and Willett. But good beds, and the master of the house a sober, understanding man, and I had good discourse with him about this country's matters, as wool and corn and other things.   And he also merry, and made us mighty merry at supper, about manning the new ship at Bristol with none but men whose wives do master them: and it seems it is in reproach to some men of estate that are such here-abouts, that this is become common talk.   By and by to bed, glad of this mistake, because, as it seems, had we gone on as we in-tended, we could not have passed with our coach, and must have lain on the Plain all night.   This day from Salisbury I wrote by the post my excuse for not coming home, which I hope will do, for I am resolved to see the Bath, and, it may be, Bristol.

12th. (Friday.) Up, finding our beds good but lousy, which made us merry.   We set out, the reckoning and servants coming to 9s. 6d.; my guide thither, 2s.; coachman, advanced, 10s.   So rode a very good way, led to my great content by our landlord to Philip Norton, with great pleasure, being now come into Somersetshire; where my wife and Deb. mightily joyed thereat,[1] I commending the country, as indeed it deserves.   And the first town we came to was Brekington, where, stopping for something for the horses, we called two or three little boys to us, and pleased ourselves with their manner of speech.   At Philip Norton I walked to the church, and there saw a very ancient tomb of some Knight Templar, I think; and here saw the tombstone whereon there were only two heads cut, which, the story goes, and credibly, were two sisters, called the Fair Maids of Foscott, that had two bodies upward and one belly, and there lie buried.   Here is also a very fine ring of six bells, and chimes mighty tunable.   Having dined very well, 10s., we come before night to the Bath; where I presently stepped out with my landlord, and saw the baths, with

[1] They were natives of that county.

people in them. They are not so large as I expected, but yet pleasant; and the town most of stone, and clean, though the streets generally narrow. I home, and, being weary, went to bed without supper; the rest supping.

13th. (Saturday.) Up at four o'clock, being by appointment called up to the Cross Bath, where we were carried one after another, myself and wife, and Betty Turner, Willett, and W. Hewer. And by and by, though we designed to have done before company come, much company come: very fine ladies; and the manner pretty enough, only methinks it cannot be clean to go so many bodies together in the same water. Good conversation among them that are acquainted here, and stay together. Strange to see how hot the water is; and in some places, though this is the most temperate bath, the springs so hot as the feet not able to endure. But strange to see, when women and men here, that live all the season in these waters, cannot but be parboiled, and look like the creatures of the bath! Carried back, wrapped in a sheet, and in a chair home; and there one after another thus carried, I staying above two hours in the water, home to bed, sweating for an hour; and by and by comes music to play to me, extraordinary good as ever I heard at London almost, or anywhere: 5s. Up, to go to Bristol about eleven o'clock, and paying my landlord that was our guide from Chiltern, 10s., and the serjeant of the bath 10s., and the man that carried us in chairs, 3s. 6d., set out towards Bristol, and come thither, in a coach hired to spare our own horses, about two o'clock; the way bad, but country good, where set down at the Horseshoe; and there, being trimmed by a very handsome fellow, 2s., walked with my wife and people through the city, which is in every respect another London, that one can hardly know it, to stand in the country, no more than that. No carts, it standing generally on vaults, only dog-carts. So to the Three Crowns tavern I was directed; but when I came in the master told me that he had newly given over the selling of wine: it seems, grown rich. And so went to the Sun; and there Deb. going with W. Hewer and Betty Turner to see her uncle Butts, and leaving my wife with the mistress of the house, I to see the quay, which is a most large and noble place; and to see the new ship building by Bally, neither he nor Furzer [1] being in town. It will be a fine ship. Spoke with the foreman, and did give the boys that kept the cabin 2s. Walked back to the Sun, where I find Deb. come back, and with her her

[1] Daniel Furzer, Surveyor to the Navy.

uncle, a sober merchant, very good company, and so like one of
our sober, wealthy, London merchants, as pleased me mightily.
Here we dined, and much good talk with him, 7s. 6d.: a messenger
to Sir John Knight,[1] who was not at home, 6d.   Then walked with
Butts and my wife and company round the quay, and to the ship;
and he showed me the Custom-house, and made me understand
many things of the place, and led us through Marsh Street, where
our girl was born.   But, Lord! the joy that was among the old
poor people of the place to see Mrs. Willett's daughter, it seems her
mother being a brave woman and mightily beloved!   And so
brought us a back way by surprise to his house, where a substantial
good house, and well furnished; and did give us good entertainment of strawberries, a whole venison pasty, cold, and plenty of
brave wine, and above all Bristol milk:[2] where comes in another
poor woman, who, hearing that Deb. was here, did come running
hither, and with her eyes so full of tears and heart so full of joy,
that she could not speak when she come in, that it made me weep
too.   I protest that I was not able to speak to her, which I would
have done, to have diverted her tears.   Butts's wife a good woman,
and so sober and substantial as I was never more pleased anywhere.   Servant-maid, 2s.   So thence took leave, and he with us
through the city, where in walking I find the city pay him great
respect, and he the like to the meanest, which pleased me mightily.
He showed us the place where the merchants meet here, and a fine
Cross yet standing, like Cheapside.   And so to the Horseshoe,
where paid the reckoning, 2s. 6d.   We back, and by moonshine
to the Bath again about ten o'clock: bad way; and giving the coachman 1s., went all of us to bed.

14th. (Sunday.) Up, and walked up and down the town, and
saw a pretty good market-place, and many good streets, and very
fair stone houses.   And so to the great church,[3] and there saw
Bishop Montagu's[4] tomb; and, when placed, did there see many
brave people come, and, among others, two men brought in in
litters, and set down in the chancel to hear: but I did not know one
face.   Here a good organ; but a vain, pragmatical fellow preached

---

[1] Mayor of Bristol, 1663, and M.P. for that city.

[2] A sort of rum punch (milk punch), which, and turtle, were products of
the trade of Bristol with the West Indies.

[3] The abbey church.

[4] James Montagu, Bishop of Bath and Wells in 1608, and of Winchester in
1616: ob. 1618.   He was uncle to the Earl of Sandwich, whose mother was
Pepys's aunt.

a ridiculous, affected sermon, that made me angry, and some gentlemen that sat next me and sang well. So home, walking round the walls of the city, which are good, and the battlements all whole. After dinner comes Mr. Butts again to see me, and he and I to church, where the same idle fellow preached; and I slept most of the sermon. To this church again, to see it and look over the monuments, where, among others, Dr. Venner[1] and Pelling,[2] and a lady of Sir W. Waller's,[3] he lying with his face broken. My landlord did give me a good account of the antiquity of this town and Wells; and of two heads on two pillars in Wells church.

15th. (Monday.) Looked into the baths, and find the King and Queen's full of a mixed sort, of good and bad, and the Cross used almost for the gentry. So home with my wife, and did pay my guides, two women, 5s.; one man, 2s. 6d.; poor, 6d.; woman to lay my foot-cloth, 1s. So to our inn, and there eat and paid reckoning, £1. 8s. 6d.; servants, 3s.; poor, 1s.; lent the coachman, 10s. Before I took coach I went to make a boy dive in the King's bath, 1s. I paid also for my coach and a horse to Bristol, £1 1s. 6d. Took coach, and away, without any of the company of the other stage-coaches that go out of this town today; and rode all day with some trouble, for fear of being out of our way, over the Downs, where the life of the shepherds is, in fair weather only, pretty. In the afternoon come to Avebury, where, seeing great stones like those of Stonehenge standing up, I stopped, and took a countryman of that town, and he carried me and showed me a place trenched in,[4] like Old Sarum almost, with great stones pitched in it, some bigger than those of Stonehenge in figure, to my great admiration: and he told me that most people of learning, coming by, do come and view them, and that the King did so: and the Mount cast hard by is called Silbury,[5] from one King Seal buried there, as tradition says. I did give this man 1s. So took coach again, seeing one place with great high stones pitched round, which, I believe, was once some particular building, in some measure like that of

---

[1] Tobias Venner, who practised as a physician at Bath nearly half a century, and died 27th March 1660, æt. eighty-five.

[2] John Pelling, B.D., rector of Bath for thirty years.

[3] Jane, sole daughter of Sir Richard Reynell, wife of Sir William Waller, the Parliamentary General.

[4] The well-known temple of the Druids, described by Stukeley in his *Itinerary*.

[5] Of which a good description is given in *The Archæologia*, vol. xxviii, p. 402.

Stonehenge. But, about a mile off, it was prodigious to see how full the Downs are of great stones; and all along the valleys stones of considerable bigness, most of them growing certainly out of the ground so thick as to cover the ground, which makes me think the less of the wonder of Stonehenge, for hence they might undoubtedly supply themselves with stones, as well as those at Avebury. In my way did give to the poor and menders of the highway 3s. Before night come to Marlborough, and lay at the Hart; a good house, and a pretty fair town for a street or two; and what is most singular is, their houses on one side having their pent-houses supported with pillars, which makes it a good walk. All the five coaches that come this day from Bath, as well as we, were gone out of the town before six.

16th. (Tuesday.) After paying the reckoning, 14s. 4d., and servants, 2s., poor, 1s., set out; and, passing through a good part of this country of Wiltshire, saw a good house [1] of Alexander Popham's,[2] and another of my Lord Craven's,[3] I think, in Berkshire. Come to Newbury, and there dined—and music: a song of the old courtier of Queen Elizabeth's, and how he was changed upon the coming in of the King, did please me mightily, and I did cause W. Hewer to write it out. Then comes the reckoning, forced to change gold, 8s. 7d.; servants and poor, 1s. 6d. So out, and lost our way, but come into it again; and in the evening betimes come to Reading; and I to walk about the town, which is a very great one, I think bigger than Salisbury: a river runs through it in seven branches, which unite in one in one part of the town, and runs into the Thames half a mile off: one odd sign of the Broad Face. Then to my inn, and so to bed.

17th. (Wednesday.) Rose, and paying the reckoning, 12s. 6d., servants and poor, 2s. 6d.—music, the worst we have had, coming to our chamber door, but calling us by wrong names—to set out with one coach in company, and through Maidenhead, which I never saw before, to Colnbrook by noon, the way mighty good; and there dined, and fitted ourselves a little to go through London anon. Somewhat out of humour all day, reflecting on my wife's

---

[1] Littlecote House, a fine old mansion, in the parish of Ramsbury, Wiltshire. Some interest has attached to the place, as the supposed scene of the extraordinary child-murder, ascribed to William Darel, who sold Littlecote to Sir John Popham, 1587, an account of which is given in Sir Walter Scott's *Rokeby*, and Britton's *Wiltshire*, vol. iii, p. 260.

[2] M.P. for Bath.

[3] Hampstead Marshall.

neglect of things and impertinent humour got by this liberty of being from me, which she is never to be trusted with, for she is a fool. Thence pleasant way to London before night, and find all very well, to great content; and saw Sir W. Pen, who is well again. I hear of the ill news by the great fire at Barbadoes. Home, and there with my people to supper, all in pretty good humour, though I find my wife hath something in her gizzard, that only waits an opportunity of being provoked to bring up; but I will not, for my content sake, give it.

18th. I did receive a hint or two from my Lord Anglesey, as if he thought much of my taking the air as I have done; but I care not. But, whatever the matter is, I think he hath some ill will to me, or at least an opinion that I am more the servant of the Board than I am. At noon home to dinner, where my wife still in a melancholy, fusty humour, and crying, and do not tell me plainly what it is; but I by little words find that she hath heard of my going to plays and carrying people abroad every day in her absence; and that I cannot help but the storm will break out in a little time. To my Lady Peterborough's, who tells me, among other things, her Lord's good words to the Duke of York lately about my Lord Sandwich, and that the Duke of York is kind to my Lord Sandwich, which I am glad to hear: my business here was about her Lord's pension from Tangier. Here met with Povy, who tells me how hard Creed is upon him, though he did give him, about six months since, I think he said, fifty pieces in gold; and one thing there is in his accounts which I fear will touch me, but I shall help it, I hope. So my wife not speaking a word going nor coming, nor willing to go to a play, though a new one, I to the office, and did much business. At night home, where supped Mr. Turner and his wife and Betty, and Mercer and Pelling, as merry as the ill, melancholy humour that my wife was in would let us; which vexed me, but I took no notice of it, thinking that will be the best way, and let it wear away itself. After supper parted, and to bed; and my wife troubled all night, and about one o'clock goes out of the bed to the girl's bed, which did trouble me, she crying and sobbing without telling the cause. By and by she comes back to me, and still crying; I then rose, and would have sat up all night, but she would have me come to bed again; and being pretty well pacified, we to sleep.

19th. Between two and three in the morning we were waked with the maids crying out, 'Fire, fire, in Mark Lane!' So I rose and looked out, and it was dreadful; and strange apprehensions in me, and us all, of being presently burnt. So we all rose; and my care presently was to secure my gold and plate and papers, and could quickly have done it, but I went forth to see where it was. And the whole town was presently in the streets; and I found it in a new-built house that stood alone in Mincing Lane, over against the Clothworkers' Hall, which burned furiously: the house not yet quite finished, and the benefit of brick was well seen, for it burnt all inward, and fell down within itself; so no fear of doing more hurt. So homeward, and stopped at Mr. Mills's, where he and she at the door, and Mrs. Turner and Betty and Mrs. Holl-worthy, and there I stayed and talked, and up to the church leads, and saw the fire, which spent itself, till all fear over. My wife fell into her blubbering, and at length had a request to make to me, which was that she might go into France and live there out of trouble. And then all come out, that I loved pleasure and denied her any; and I find that there have been great fallings out between my father and her, whom for ever hereafter I must keep asunder, for they cannot possibly agree. And I said nothing, but, with very mild words and few, suffered her humour to spend, till we begun to be very quiet, and I think all will be over, and friends. Yesterday I heard how my Lord Ashley is like to die, having some imposthume in his breast, that he hath been fain to be cut into the body. To White Hall, where we attended the Duke of York in his closet upon our usual business. And thence out, and did see many of the Knights of the Garter, with the King and Duke of York, going into the Privy Chamber to elect the Elector of Saxony [1] in that Order, who, I did hear the Duke of York say, was a good drinker. I know not upon what score this compliment is done him. My wife and Deb. have been at the King's playhouse today, thinking to spy me there, and saw the new play, 'Evening Love,' [2] of Dryden's, which, though the world commends, she likes not. So to supper and talk, and all in good humour.

20th. My wife and I alone to the King's House and there I saw this new play my wife saw yesterday, and do not like it, it being very smutty, and nothing so good as 'The Maiden Queen,' or 'The Indian Emperor,' of Dryden's making. I was troubled at it; and my wife tells me wholly, which he confesses a little in the

[1] John George, Elector of Saxony, invested with the Garter 13th April 1668, installed by proxy, 29th May 1671, and died 1680.
[2] A comedy, the second title of which was *The Mock Astrologer*.

epilogue, taken out of the 'Illustre Bassa.' I to Mr. Povy, and there settled some business: and he thinks there will be great revolutions, and that Creed will be a great man, though a rogue, he being a man of the old strain, which will now be up again.

21st. (Lord's day.) Dined with my wife and Deb. alone, but merry and in good humour, which is, when all is done, the greatest felicity of all.

22d. With Balty to St. James's, and there presented him to Mr. Wren about his being Muster-Master this year, which will be done. So up to wait on the Duke of York, and thence, with Sir W. Coventry, walked to White Hall: good discourse about the Navy, where want of money undoes us. Thence to the coffee-house in Covent Garden; but met with nobody but Sir Philip Howard, who shamed me before the whole house there, in commendation of my speech in Parliament. To the King's playhouse, and saw an act or two of the new play, 'Evening Love,' again, but like it not. Calling this day at Herringman's,[1] he tells me Dryden do himself call it but a fifth-rate play. From thence to my Lord Brouncker's, where a Council of the Royal Society; and there heard Mr. Harry Howard's noble offers about ground for our College, and his intentions of building his own house there most nobly. My business was to meet Mr. Boyle, which I did, and discoursed about my eyes; and he did give me the best advice he could, but refers me to one Turberville,[2] of Salisbury, lately come to town, who I will go to. Thence home, where the streets full at our end of the town, removing their wine against the Act begins, which will be two days hence, to raise the price.

23d. To Dr. Turberville about my eyes, whom I met with: and

---

[1] H. Herringman, a printer and publisher in the New Exchange: see 10th August 1667, *ante*.

[2] Daubeney Turberville, of Oriel College; created M.D. at Oxford, 1660. He was a physician of some eminence, and, dying at Salisbury on 21st April 1696, aged eighty-five, he was buried in the cathedral, where his monument remains. Cassan, in his *Lives of the Bishops of Sarum*, part iii, p. 103, has reprinted an interesting account of Turberville, from the *Memoir of Bishop Seth Ward*, published in 1697, by Dr. Walter Pope. Turberville was born at Wayford, county Somerset, in 1612, and became an expert oculist; and probably Pepys received great benefit from his advice, as his vision does not appear to have failed during the many years that he lived, after discontinuing the *Diary*. The doctor died rich, and subsequently to his decease his sister Mary, inheriting all his prescriptions and knowing how to use them, practised as an oculist in London, with good reputation.

he did discourse, I thought, learnedly about them, and takes time before he did prescribe me anything, to think of it.

24th. Creed and Colonel Atkins came to me about sending coals to Tangier; and upon that most of the morning. With wife, Mercer, Deb., and W. Hewer to the Duke of York's playhouse, and there saw 'The Impertinents,' a pretty good play; and so by water to Spring Garden, and there supped, and so home, not very merry; only when we came home Mercer and I sat and sung in the garden a good while. And so to bed.

26th. At noon, with my fellow officers, to the Dolphin, at Sir G. Carteret's charge, to dinner, he having some accounts examined this morning.

27th. Dined at home, and then my wife and Deb. and I to the King's playhouse, to see 'The Indian Queen,' but do not dote upon Nan Marshall's acting therein, as the world talks of her excellence. Thence with my wife to buy some linen, £13 worth, for sheets &c., at the new shop over against the New Exchange; and the master, who is come out of London [1] since the fire, says his and other tradesmen's retail trade is so great here, and better than it was in London, that they believe they shall not return, nor the City be ever so great for retail as heretofore.

28th. (Lord's day.) Much talk of the French setting out their fleet afresh; but I hear nothing that our King is alarmed at it at all, but rather making his fleet less. [2]

29th. To Dr. Turberville's, and there did receive a direction for some physic, and also a glass of something to drop into my eyes: he gives me hopes that I may do well. Then to White Hall, where I find the Duke of York in the Council-chamber; and the Officers of the Navy were called in about Navy business, about calling in of more ships, the King of France having, as the Duke of York says, ordered his fleet to come in, notwithstanding what he had lately ordered for their staying abroad. Thence to the Chapel, it being St. Peter's day, and did hear an anthem of Silas Taylor's making: a dull, old-fashioned thing, of six and seven parts, that nobody could understand. And the Duke of York, when he came out, told me that he was a better store-keeper than anthem-maker, and that was bad enough, too. This morning

[1] To the Strand.
[2] His Majesty and Prince Rupert returned to town the day before, after viewing the fleet in the Downs and the new fortifications at Sheerness (*The London Gazette*, No. 273).

Mr. May [1] showed me the King's new buildings at White Hall, very
fine; and, among other things, his ceilings, and his houses of
office.   With my wife to the King's playhouse—'The Mulberry
Garden,' which she had not seen.

30th.   At the office all the morning: then home to dinner, where
a stinking leg of mutton, the weather being very wet and hot to
keep meat in.   Then to the office again all the afternoon: we met
about the Victualler's new contract.   And so up, and to walk all
the evening with my wife and Mrs. Turner in the garden, till
supper, about eleven at night; and so, after supper, parted, and to
bed, my eyes bad, but not worse, only weary with working.   But,
however, very melancholy under the fear of my eyes being spoiled
and not to be recovered; for I am come that I am not able to read
out a small letter, and yet my sight good for the little while I can
read, as ever it was, I think.

July 1st.   My cousin Roger dined with us, and mighty impor-
tunate for our coming down to Impington, which I think to do,
this Sturbridge Fair.   To White Hall, and so to St. James's, where
we met; and much business with the Duke of York.   And I find
the Duke of York very hot for regulations in the Navy; and, I
believe, is put on it by Sir W. Coventry; and I am glad of it.   And
particularly, he falls heavy on Chatham yard, and is vexed that
Lord Anglesey did, the other day, complain at the Council-table
of disorders in the Navy, and not to him.   So I to White Hall to
a Committee of Tangier; and there vexed with the importunity
and clamours of Alderman Backwell, for my acquittance for
money by him supplied to the garrison, before I have any order
for paying it.   So home, calling at several places—among others
the 'Change, and on Cooper, to know when my wife shall come to
sit for her picture.

2nd.   Called up by a letter from Sir W. Coventry telling me that
the Commissioners of Accounts intend to summon me about
Sir W. Warren's Hamburg contract.   All the afternoon busy to
prepare an answer to this demand; and so in the evening with my
wife and Deb. by coach to take the air, to Mile End.   And so
home, and I to bed, vexed to be put to this frequent trouble in
things we deserve best in.

3d.   To the Commissioners of Accounts at Brooke House,[2] the
first time I was ever there, and found Sir W. Turner in the chair;
and present, Lord Halifax, Thomas Gregory, Dunster, and

[1] Hugh May.   [2] In Holborn.

Osborne.[1] I long with them, and see them hot set on this matter; but I did give them proper and safe answers. Halifax, I perceive, was industrious on my side, in behalf of his uncle Coventry,[2] it being the business of Sir W. Warren. Vexed only at their denial of a copy of what I set my hand to and swore. To an alehouse: met Mr. Pierce, the surgeon, and Dr. Clerke, Waldron,[3] Turberville, my physician for the eyes, and Lower,[4] to dissect several eyes of sheep and oxen, with great pleasure, and to my great information. But strange that this Turberville should be so great a man, and yet, to this day, had seen no eyes dissected, or but once, but desired this Dr. Lower to give him the opportunity to see him dissect some.

4th. Up, and to see Sir W. Coventry and give him account of my doings yesterday, which he well liked of, and was told thereof by my Lord Halifax before; but I do perceive he is much concerned for this business. Gives me advice to write a smart letter to the Duke of York about the want of money in the Navy, and desire him to communicate it to the Commissioners of the Treasury; for he tells me he hath hot work sometimes to contend with the rest for the Navy, they being all concerned for some other part of the King's expenses, which they would prefer to this of the Navy. He showed me his closet, with his round table, for him to sit in the middle, very convenient; and I borrowed several books of him, to collect things out of about the Navy, which I have not. All the afternoon busy, till night, and then to Mile End with my wife and girl, and there drank and eat a jowl of salmon at the Rose and Crown, our old house. And so home to bed.

5th. (Lord's day.) About four in the morning took four pills of Dr. Turberville's prescribing, for my eyes, and I did get my wife to spend the morning reading of Wilkins's Real Character. At noon comes W. Hewer and Pelling, and young Michell and his wife, and dined with us, and most of the afternoon talking;

[1] Afterwards Sir Thomas Osborne, Viscount Dunblane, Earl of Danby, Marquis of Carmarthen, and Duke of Leeds. He became Lord High Treasurer and K.G.

[2] Lord Halifax's mother was Anne, sister of Sir John and Sir William Coventry, and of Harry Coventry. She married, secondly, Sir Thomas Chichele, or Chicheley, of Wimpole, in Cambridgeshire, Master of the Ordnance, which circumstance explains many allusions made by Pepys.

[3] Thomas Waldron of Balliol College; created M.D. at Oxford 1653: afterwards Physician in Ordinary to Charles II.

[4] Richard Lower, of Christ Church; admitted Bachelor of Physic at Oxford, 1665, and afterwards a celebrated physician. He died in 1691.

and then at night my wife to read again, and to supper and to bed.

6th. Attended the Duke of York, and was there by himself told how angry he was, and did declare to my Lord Anglesey, about his complaining of things of the Navy to the King in Council, and not to him. And I perceive he is mightily concerned at it, and resolved to reform things therein. Thence with Sir W. Coventry walked in the Park together a good while. He mighty kind to me: and hear many pretty stories of my Lord Chancellor's being heretofore made sport of by Peter Talbot, the priest, in his story of the death of Cardinal Balue; [1] by Lord Cottington, in his *Dolor de las Tripas*; and Tom Killigrew, in his being bred in Ram Alley, and bound 'prentice to Lord Cottington, going to Spain with £1000 and two suits of clothes. Thence to Mr. Cooper's, and there met my wife and W. Hewer and Deb.; and there my wife first sat for her picture: but he is a most admirable workman and good company. Here comes Harris, and first told us how Betterton is come again upon the stage: whereupon my wife and company to the Duke's House to see 'Henry the Fifth' while I to attend the Duke of York at the Committee of the Navy, at the Council, where some high dispute between him and W. Coventry about settling pensions upon all Flag Officers while unemployed: W. Coventry against it, and, I think, with reason. Thence I to the playhouse, and saw a piece of the play, and glad to see Betterton; and so with wife and Deb. to Spring Garden and eat a lobster. Great doings at Paris, I hear, with their triumphs for their late conquests. The Duchess of Richmond sworn last week of the Queen's Bedchamber, and the King minding little else but what he used to do—about his women.

7th. Kate Joyce come to me, but took no notice to me of her being married, but seemed mighty pale, and doubtful what to say or do, expecting, I believe, that I should begin; and not finding me beginning, said nothing, but, with trouble in her face, went away. In the evening to Unthank's; and we are fain to go round by Newgate because of Fleet Bridge being under rebuilding. Home and supped: and Mrs. Turner, the mother, comes to us, and there late, and so to bed.

8th. To Sir W. Coventry, and there discoursed of several things; and I find him much concerned in the present inquiries

---

[1] It is probable these stories in ridicule of Clarendon are nowhere recorded. Cardinal Jean Balue was the minister of Louis XI of France.

now on foot of the Commissioners of Accounts; though he reckons himself and the rest very safe, but vexed to see us liable to these troubles, in things wherein we have laboured to do best. Thence, he being to go out of town tomorrow to drink Banbury waters, I to the Duke of York to attend him about business of the Office; and find him mighty free to me, and how he is concerned to mend things in the Navy himself, and not leave it to other people. So home to dinner, and then with my wife to Cooper's, and there saw her sit; and he do extraordinary things indeed. So to White Hall; and there by and by the Duke of York comes to the Robe-chamber, and spent with us three hours till night in hearing the business of the Masters-Attendants of Chatham and the Store-keeper of Woolwich; and resolves to displace them all. So hot he is of giving proofs of his justice at this time, that it is their great fate now to come to be questioned at such a time as this.

10th. To Cooper's, and there find my wife and W. Hewer and Deb. sitting and painting; and here he do work finely, though I fear it will not be so like as I expected. But now I understand his great skill in music, his playing and setting to the French lute most excellently; and he speaks French, and indeed is an excellent man. Thence in the evening with my people in a glass hackney coach to the park, but was ashamed to be seen. So to the lodge and drank milk, and so home.

11th. To the King's playhouse, to see an old play of Shirley's, called 'Hyde Park,' the first day acted, where horses are brought upon the stage: but it is but a very moderate play, only an excellent epilogue spoke by Beck Marshall.[1]

12th. (Lord's day.) This last night Betty Michell about midnight cries out, and my wife goes to her, and she brings forth a girl, and this afternoon the child is christened, and my wife godmother again to a Betty.

13th. Walked to Duck Lane, and there to the bookseller's, at the Bible. I did there look upon and buy some books, and made way for coming again to the man. Thence to Reeves's, and there saw some, and bespoke a little perspective,[2] and was mightily pleased with seeing objects in a dark room. To Cooper's, and spent the afternoon with them; and it will be an excellent picture. Thence my people all by water to Deptford to see Balty, while I to buy my espinette, which I did now agree for, and did at Haward's meet with Mr. Thacker, and heard him play on the harpsichon, so

----

[1] Never printed.   [2] A perspective glass.

as I never heard man before, I think. So home, it being almost night, and there find in the garden Pelling, who hath brought Tempest Wallington and Pelham, to sing, and there had most excellent music late, in the dark, with great pleasure; but above all with little Wallington. This morning I was let blood, and did bleed about fourteen ounces, towards curing my eyes.

14th. This day Bosse finished his copy of my picture, which I confess I do not admire, though my wife prefers him to Browne: nor do I think it like. He does it for W. Hewer, who hath my wife's also, which I like less. This afternoon my Lady Pickering came to see us: I busy, saw her not. But how natural it is for us to slight people out of power, and for people out of power to stoop to see those that while in power they contemned!

15th. At noon is brought home the espinette I bought the other day of Haward; costs me £5. So to St. James's, where did our ordinary business with the Duke of York. So with my wife and Deb. to visit Mrs. Pierce, whom I do not now so much affect since she paints. Understand from her how my Lady Duchess of Monmouth is still lame, and likely always to be so, which is a sad chance for a young lady to get, only by trying of tricks in dancing. So home, and there Captain Dean came and spent the evening with me, to draw some finishing lines on his final draft of the Resolution, the best ship, by all report, in the world. And so to bed.

16th. I by water with my Lord Brouncker to Arundel House, to the Royal Society, and there saw the experiment of a dog's being tied through the back, about the spinal artery, and thereby made void of all motion; and the artery being loosened again, the dog recovers. Thence to Cooper's, and saw his advance on my wife's picture, which will be indeed very fine. So with her to the 'Change to buy some things, and here I first bought of the seamstress next my bookseller's, where the pretty young girl is, that will be a great beauty.

17th. To White Hall, where waited on the Duke of York, and then at the Council about the business of tickets; and I did discourse to their liking, only was too high to assert that nothing could be invented to secure the King more in the business of tickets than there is; which the Duke of Buckingham did except against, and I could have answered, but forbore; but all liked very well. The weather excessive hot, so as we were forced to lie in two beds, and I only with a sheet and rug, which is colder than ever I remember I could bear.

18th. My old acquaintance, Will Swan, to see me, who continues a factious fanatic still; and I do use him civilly, in expectation that those fellows may grow great again. Thence to the office, and then with my wife to the 'Change after having been at Cooper's and sat there for her picture, which will be a noble picture but yet I think not so like as Hales's is. They say the King of France is making a war again, in Flanders, with the King of Spain, the King of Spain refusing to give him all that he says was promised him in that treaty. Creed told me this day how when the King was at my Lord Cornwallis's,[1] when he went last to Newmarket, that being there on a Sunday, the Duke of Buckingham did in the afternoon make an obscene sermon to him out of Canticles.

19th. (Lord's day.) Come Mr. Cooper, Hales, Harris, Mr. Butler, that wrote 'Hudibras,' and Mr. Cooper's cousin Jack; and by and by come Mr. Reeves and his wife, whom I never saw before, and there we dined: a good dinner, and company that pleased me mightily, being all eminent men in their way. Spent all the afternoon in talk and mirth, and in the evening parted.

20th. To the old Exchange, to see a very noble fine lady I spied as I went through, in coming; and there took occasion to buy some gloves and admire her, and a mighty fine fair lady indeed she was. Thence idling all the afternoon. To visit my Lord Crewe, who is very sick, to great danger, by an erysipelas: the first day I heard of it. To buy a wrest for my espinette at the ironmonger's by Holborn Conduit, where the fair pretty woman is, that I have lately observed there.

21st. Went to my plate-maker's, and there spent an hour about contriving my little plates for my books of the King's four Yards.

22d. Attending at the Committee of the Navy about the old business of tickets, where the only expedient they have found is to bind the commanders and Officers by oaths. The Duke of York told me how the Duke of Buckingham, after the Council the other day, did make mirth at my position, about the sufficiency of present rules in the business of tickets; and here I took occasion to desire a private discourse with the Duke of York, and he granted it to me on Friday next. This day a falling-out between my wife and Deb., about a hood lost, which vexed me.

23d. Up, and all day long, except at dinner, at the office at work, till I was almost blind, which makes my heart sad.

24th. Up, and by water to St. James's, having, by the way,

[1] At Culford in Suffolk.

shown Symson Sir W. Coventry's chimney-pieces, in order to the making me one. And there, after the Duke of York was ready, he called me to his closet; and there I did long and largely show him the weakness of our Office, and did give him advice to call us to account for our duties, which he did take mighty well, and desired me to draw up what I would have him write to the Office. I did lay open the whole failings of the Office, and how it was his duty to fine them and to find fault with them, as Admiral, especially at this time; which he agreed to, and seemed much to rely on what I said. Attended, all of us, the Duke of York, and had the hearing of Mr. Pett's business, the Master-Shipwright at Chatham, and I believe he will be put out. But here Commissioner Middleton did, among others, show his good nature and easiness to the Masters-Attendants, by mitigating their faults, so as, I believe, they will come in again. So home, the Duke of York staying with us till almost night.

25th. At the office all the morning; and at noon, after dinner, to Cooper's, it being a very rainy day, and there saw my wife's picture go on, which will be very fine indeed. And so home again to my letters, and then to supper and to bed.

26th. (Lord's day.) Up, and all the morning, and after dinner the afternoon also, with W. Hewer in my closet, setting right my Tangier Accounts, which I have let alone these six months and more, but find them very right, and to my great comfort. So in the evening to walk with my wife, and to supper and to bed.

27th. To see my Lord Crewe, whom I find up, and did wait on him; but his face sore, but in hopes to do now very well again. Thence to Cooper's, where my wife's picture almost done, and mighty fine indeed. So over the water with my wife and Deb. and Mercer to Spring Garden, and there eat and walked; and observe how rude some of the young gallants of the town are become, to go into people's arbours where there are not men, and almost force the women; which troubled me, to see the confidence of the vice of the age. And so we away by water, with much pleasure home.

28th. With my wife and Deb. to the Duke of York's play-house, and there saw 'The Slighted Maid,' but a mean play. And thence home, there being little pleasure now in a play, the company being but little. Here we saw Gosnell, who is become very homely, and sings meanly, I think, to what I thought she did.

29th. Comes Mr. Swan, my old acquaintance, and dines with

me, and tells me for a certainty that Creed is to marry Betty Pickering, and that the thing is concluded, which I wonder at and am vexed for. I with my wife and two girls to the King's House, and saw 'The Mad Couple,' a mean play altogether, and thence to the Hyde Park, where but few coaches. So to the New Exchange, and thence by water home with much pleasure: and then to sing in the garden, my eyes for these four days being my trouble, and my heart thereby mighty sad.

30th. To White Hall. There met with Mr. May, who was giving directions about making a close way for people to go dry from the gate up into the House, to prevent their going through the galleries; which will be very good. I stayed and talked with him about the state of the King's Offices in general, and how ill he is served, and do still find him an excellent person.

31st. With Mr. Ashburnham;[1] and I made him admire my drawing a thing presently in shorthand: but, God knows! I have paid dear for it, in my eyes. To the King's House to see the first day of Lacy's 'Monsieur Ragou,'[2] now new acted. The King and Court all there, and mighty merry—a farce. Thence Sir J. Minnes giving us, like a gentleman, his coach, hearing we had some business, we to the Park, and so home. Little pleasure there, there being little company; but mightily taken with a little chariot that we saw in the street, and which we are resolved to have ours like it. The month ends mighty sadly with me, my eyes being now past all use almost; and I am mighty hot upon trying the late printed[3] experiment of paper tubes.

August 1st. My wife and Deb. and I to the King's House again, coming too late yesterday to hear the prologue, and do like the play better now than before; and indeed there is a great deal of true wit in it, more than in the common sort of plays.

2d. (Lord's day.) Up, and at home all the morning, hanging and removing of some pictures in my study and house. After dinner I and Tom, my boy, by water up to Putney, and there heard a sermon, and many fine people in the church. Thence walked to Barn Elms, and there, and going and coming, did make the boy read to me several things, being nowadays unable to read

---

[1] William Ashburnham, the cofferer.

[2] *The Old Troop; or, Monsieur Ragou,* a comedy by John Lacey, printed in 1672, 4to.

[3] An account of these tubulous spectacles is given in *The Philosophical Transactions*, vol. iii, pp. 727–31.

myself anything, for above two lines together, but my eyes grow weary.

3d. Meeting Dr. Gibbons, carried him to the Sun tavern, in King Street, and there made him and some friends of his drink; among others Captain Silas Taylor.

4th. At my Lord Arlington's, where, by Creed's being out of town, I have the trouble given me of drawing up answers to the complaints of the Turks of Algiers, and so I have all the papers put into my hand. I with my clerks sat up till two in the morning, drawing up my answers and writing them fair, which did trouble me mightily because of my eyes.

5th. Up about seven, and to White Hall, where read over my report to Lord Arlington and Berkeley, and then afterwards at the Council-board with great good liking. But, Lord! how it troubled my eyes. To the Duke of York's playhouse, and there saw 'The Guardian,' formerly the same, I find, that was called 'Cutter of Coleman Street': a silly play. And thence to Westminster Hall, where I met Fitzgerald; and with him to a tavern to consider of the instructions for Sir Thomas Allen, against his going to Algiers, he and I being designed to go down to Portsmouth by the Council's order, tomorrow morning. So I away home, and there bespeak a coach; and so home and to bed.

6th. Waked betimes, and my wife at an hour's warning is resolved to go with me, which pleases me, her readiness. But before ready comes a letter from Fitzgerald, that he is seized upon last night by an order of the General's by a file of musketeers, and kept prisoner in his chamber. The Duke of York did tell me of it today: it is about a quarrel between him and Witham, and they fear a challenge. So I to him, and sent my wife by the coach round to Lambeth. I lost my labour going to his lodgings, and he in bed: and, staying a great while for him, I at last grew impatient and would stay no longer; but to St. James's to Mr. Wren, to bid him 'God be with you!' and so over the water to Fox-hall; and there my wife and Deb. took me up, and we away to Guildford, losing our way for three or four miles about Cobham. At Guildford we dined; and I showed them the hospital there of Bishop Abbot's,[1] and his tomb in the church, which, and the rest of the tombs there, are kept mighty clean and neat, with curtains before them. So to coach again, and got to Liphook, late over Hindhead, having an old man, a guide, in the coach with us; but got

---

[1] George Abbot, Archbishop of Canterbury: *ob.* 1633.

thither with great fear of being out of our way, it being ten at night. Here good, honest people; and after supper, to bed.

7th. To coach, and with a guide to Petersfield, where I find Sir Thomas Allen and Mr. Tippet [1] come (the first about the business, the latter only in respect to me), as also Fitzgerald, who came post all last night, and newly arrived here. We four sat down presently to our business, and in an hour despatched all our talk; and did inform Sir Thomas Allen well in it, who, I perceive, in serious matters is a serious man: and tells me he wishes all we are told be true, in our defence; for he finds by all that the Turks have, to this day, been very civil to our merchantmen everywhere; and, if they would have broke with us, they never had such an opportunity over our rich merchantmen, as lately, coming out of the Straits. Then to dinner, and pretty merry: and here was Mr. Martin, the purser, who dined with us and wrote some things for us. And so took coach again back; Fitzgerald with us, whom I was pleased with all the day, with his discourse of his observations abroad, as being a great soldier and of long standing abroad, and knows all things and persons abroad very well,—I mean, the great soldiers of France and Spain and Germany,—and talks very well. Came at night to Guildford, where the Red Lion so full of people, and a wedding, that the master of the house did get us a lodging over the way at a private house, his landlord's, mighty neat and fine; and there supped, and so to bed.

8th. Met uncle Wight, whom I sent to last night, and Mr. Wight coming to see us, and I walked with them back to see my aunt at Katherine Hill, and there walked up and down the hill and places about: but a dull place, but good air, and the house dull. But here I saw my aunt, after many days not seeing her—I think, a year or two; and she walked with me to see my wife. And here, at the Red Lion, we all dined together, and pretty merry, and then parted. And we home to Fox-hall, where Fitzgerald and I 'light and by water to White Hall, where, the Duke of York being abroad, I by coach and met my wife. I hear that Colbert [2] the French Ambassador is come, and hath been at Court *incognito*. When he hath his audience, I know not.

9th. (Lord's day.) Waited on the Duke of York: and both by him and several of the Privy Council, beyond expectation, I find

[1] John Tippet, a surveyor of the Navy; afterwards knighted.
[2] Charles Colbert, Marquis de Croissy, brother of Jean Baptiste Colbert, the great minister.

that my going to Sir Thomas Allen was looked upon as a thing necessary: and I have got some advantage by it among them. To visit Lord Brouncker, and back to White Hall, where saw the Queen and ladies; and so, with Mr. Slingsby, to Mrs. Williams's, thinking to dine with Lord Brouncker there, but did not, having promised my wife to come home, though here I met Knipp, to my great content. So home; and, after dinner, I took my wife and Deb. round by Hackney, and up and down to take the air; and then home, and made visits to Mrs. Turner and Mrs. Mercer and Sir W. Pen, who is come from Epsom not well, and Sir J. Minnes, who is not well neither. And so home to supper, and to set my books a little right, and then to bed.

10th. To my Lord Arlington's house, the first time since he came thither, at Goring House, a very fine, noble place; and there he received me in sight of several Lords with great respect. I did give him an account of my journey; and here, while I waited for him a little, my Lord Orrery took notice of me, and begun discourse of hangings and of the improvement of shipping: I not thinking that he knew me, but did then discover it, with a mighty compliment of my abilities and ingenuity, which I am mighty proud of; and he do speak most excellently. To Cooper's, where I spent all the afternoon with my wife and girl, seeing him make an end of her picture, which he did to my great content, though not so great as, I confess, I expected, being not satisfied in the greatness of the resemblance, nor in the blue garment. But it is most certainly a most rare piece of work, as to the painting.[1] He hath £30 for his work—and the crystal, and case, and gold case comes to £8. 3s. 4d.; and which I sent him this night, that I might be out of his debt. Home to supper, and my wife to read a ridiculous book I bought today of the History of the Taylors' Company.[2]

11th. The Parliament met long enough to adjourn to the 10th of November next. At the office all the afternoon till night, being

---

[1] This miniature of Mrs. Pepys cannot be traced.

[2] The title of this book was: 'The Honour of the Merchant Taylors. Wherein is set forth the noble acts, valliant deeds, and heroick performances of Merchant Taylors in former ages; their honourable loves and knightly adventures, their combating of foreign enemies and glorious successes in honour of the English nation; together with their pious acts and large benevolences, their building of publick structures, especially that of Blackwell Hall, to be a market-place for the selling of woollen cloaths: Written by William Winstanley. Lond. 1668.' 8vo. With the head of Sir Ralph Blackwell, with a gold chain: arms of London on the right, and of the Merchant Taylors on the left.

mightily pleased with a trial I have made of the use of a tube-spectacle of paper, tried with my right eye.   This day I hear that, to the great joy of the Nonconformists, the time is out of the Act against them, so that they may meet: and they have declared that they will have a morning lecture [1] up again, which is pretty strange; and they are connived at by the King everywhere, I hear, in the City and country.   This afternoon my wife and Mercer and Deb. went with Pelling to see the gypsies at Lambeth,[2] and have their fortunes told; but what they did, I did not enquire.

12th.   Captain Cocke tells me that he hears for certain the Duke of York will lose the authority of an Admiral and be governed by a Committee, and all our Office changed; only they are in dispute whether I shall continue or no, which puts new thoughts in me, but I know not whether to be glad or sorry.   Home to dinner, where Pelling dines with us, and brings some partridges which are very good meat; and after dinner I and wife and Mercer and Deb. to the Duke of York's House, and saw 'Macbeth,' to our great content; and then home, where the women went to the making of my tubes.[3]   Then come Mrs. Turner and her husband to advise about their son, the chaplain, who is turned out of his ship, a sorrow for them, which I am troubled for, and do give them the best advice I can.

13th.   Up, and Greeting comes; and there he and I tried some things of Mr. Locke's for two flageolets, to my great content. And this day my wife begins again to learn of him; for I have a great mind for her to be able to play a part with me.   W. Howe dined with me, who tells me for certain that Creed is like to speed in his match with Mrs. Betty Pickering.   Here dined with me also Mr. Hollyard, who is mighty vain in his pretence to talk Latin.   So to the office again till night, very busy; and so with much content home, and made my wife sing and play on the flageolet with me, till I slept with great pleasure, in bed.

14th.   At home I find Symson putting up my new chimney-piece in our great chamber, which is very fine but will cost a great deal of money, but it is not flung away.   I with Mr. Wren, by invitation, to Sir Stephen Fox's to dinner, where the Cofferer and

---

[1] The morning lectures at Cripplegate were of great celebrity among the Puritans.   Many of them were published, forming six volumes in 4to, closely printed.   The form of lecture, it is believed, still exists.

[2] Most probably at Norwood, in the parish of Lambeth.

[3] The paper tubes for his eyes.

Sir Edward Savage; where many good stories of the antiquity and estates of many families at this day in Cheshire and that part of the kingdom, more than what is on this side, near London. My lady [Fox] dined with us: a very good lady, and a family governed so nobly and neatly as do me good to see it. Thence the Cofferer, Sir Stephen, and I to the Commissioners of the Treasury about business: and so I up to the Duke of York, who enquired for what I had promised him, about my observations of the miscarriages of our Office; and I told him he should have it next week, being glad he called for it, for I find he is concerned to do something, and to secure himself thereby, I believe. For the world is labouring to eclipse him, I doubt; I mean, the factious part of the Parliament. The Office met this afternoon as usual, and waited on him; where, among other things, he talked a great while of his intentions of going to Dover soon to be sworn as Lord Warden,[1] which is a matter of great ceremony and state. Spent the evening talking with my wife and piping, and pleased with our chimney-piece.

15th. After dinner with my wife, Mercer, and Deb. to the King's playhouse, and there saw 'Love's Mistress' revived, the thing pretty good, but full of variety of divertisement.

16th. (Lord's day.) All the morning at the office with W. Hewer, there drawing up my Report to the Duke of York, as I have promised, about the faults of this Office.

17th. To Hampstead, to speak with the Attorney-General,[2] whom we met in the fields, by his old route and house. And, after a little talk about our business of Ackworth, went and saw the Lord Wotton's[3] house[4] and garden, which is wonderful fine:

[1] Of the Cinque Ports.

[2] Sir Geoffrey Palmer, Bart. He died at his house at Hampstead, 1st May 1670.

[3] John Polyander à Kerckhoven, Lord of Heenvliet, in Holland, married Catherine, widow of Henry Lord Stanhope, eldest son of Philip, Earl of Chesterfield, who died *vitâ patris*. She was one of the four daughters and co-heirs of Thomas Lord Wotton; and her son, Charles Henry Kirkhoven, here mentioned, was created Lord Wotton, of Wotton, in Kent, in 1650, by reason of his descent, and Earl of Bellomont, in Ireland in 1680. He died without issue in 1682.

[4] Belsize House, in the parish of Hampstead, was for many years the residence of the Wood family, as lessees, under the Dean and Chapter of Westminster. When Pepys visited the place it was the chief seat of Charles Henry Kirkhoven, Lord Wotton, above-mentioned. That mansion, long since pulled down, had become, in 1720, a house of public entertainment, and was much in vogue, and continued open as late as 1745. See Lysons's *Environs* and Park's *History of Hampstead.*

too good for the house the gardens are, being, indeed, the most noble that ever I saw, and brave orange and lemon trees.   Thence to Mr. Chicheley's [1] by invitation, and there dined with Sir John, his father not coming home.   And while at dinner comes by the French Ambassador Colbert's mules, the first I ever saw, with their sumpter-clothes mighty rich, and his coaches, he being to have his entry today: but his things, though rich, are not new: supposed to be the same his brother [2] had the other day at the treaty at Aix-la-Chapelle, in Flanders.   Thence to the Duke of York's House, and there saw 'Cupid's Revenge,' [3] under the new name of 'Love Despised,' that hath something very good in it, though I like not the whole body of it.   This day the first time acted here.

18th.   Alone to the Park, but there were few coaches: among the few there were our two great beauties, my Lady Castlemaine and Richmond; the first time I saw the latter since she had the small-pox.   I had much pleasure to see them, but I thought they were strange one to another.

19th.   This week my people wash over the water, and so I little company at home.   Being busy above, a great cry I hear, and go down; and what should it be but Jane, in a fit of direct raving, which lasted half an hour.   It was beyond four or five of our strength, to keep her down; and, when all come to all, a fit of jealousy about Tom, with whom she is in love.   So at night I and my wife and W. Hewer called them to us, and there I did examine all the thing, and them, in league.   She in love, and he hath got her to promise him to marry, and he is now cold in it, so that I must rid my hands of them, which troubles me.

20th.   To work till past twelve at night, that I might get my great letter to the Duke of York ready against tomorrow, which I shall do, to my great content.

21st.   Up betimes, and with my people again to work, and finished all before noon: and then I by water to White Hall, and there did tell the Duke of York that I had done; and he hath desired me to come to him at Sunday next in the afternoon to read the letter over, by which I have more time to consider and correct it.   To St. James's; and by and by comes Monsieur Colbert, the French Ambassador, to make his first visit to the Duke of York

[1] In Great Queen Street.
[2] A mistake of Pepys's.   Colbert de Croissy, then in England, had been the French Plenipotentiary at Aix-la-Chapelle.
[3] By Beaumont and Fletcher.

and then to the Duchess: and I saw it: a silly piece of ceremony, he saying only a few formal words.   A comely man, and in a black suit and cloak of silk, which is a strange fashion, now it hath been so long left off.   This day I did first see the Duke of York's room of pictures of some Maids of Honour, done by Lely:[1] good, but not like.   Thence to Reeves's, and bought a reading-glass, and so to my bookseller's again, there to buy a Book of Martyrs,[2] which I did agree for; and so away home, and there busy very late at the correcting my great letter to the Duke of York, and so to bed.

22d. Did fall out with Sir W. Pen about his slight performance of his office; and so home to dinner, satisfied that this Office must sink or the whole Service be undone.   Pretty well at ease, my great letter being now finished to my full content; and I thank God I have opportunity of doing it, though I know it will set the Office and me by the ears for ever.   This morning Captain Cocke comes and tells me that he is now assured that it is true, what he told me the other day, that our whole Office will be turned out, only me, which, whether he says true or not, I know not, nor am much concerned, though I should be better contented to have it thus than otherwise.   To the 'Change, and thence home, and took London Bridge in my way: walking down Fish Street, and Gracious Street, to see how very fine a descent they have now made down the hill, that it is become very easy and pleasant.   Going through Leadenhall, it being market-day, I did see a woman catched, that had stole a shoulder of mutton off of a butcher's stall, and carrying it wrapped up in a cloth, in a basket.   The jade was surprised, and did not deny it, and the woman so silly as to let her go that took it, only taking the meat.

23d. (Lord's day.) To church, and heard a good sermon of Mr. Gifford's at our church, upon 'Seek ye first the kingdom of Heaven and its righteousness, and all things shall be added to you.'   A very excellent and persuasive, good and moral sermon.   He showed, like a wise man, that righteousness is a surer moral way of being rich than sin and villainy.   After dinner to the office, Mr. Gibson and I, to examine my letter to the Duke of York, which, to my great joy, I did very well by my paper tube, without pain to my eyes.   And I do mightily like what I have therein done;

[1] The set of portraits known as 'King Charles's Beauties,' formerly in Windsor Castle, but now at Hampton Court.
[2] The Book of Martyrs was Foxe's *Acts and Monuments.*

and did, according to the Duke of York's order, make haste to St. James's, and about four o'clock got thither. And there the Duke of York was ready, expecting me, and did hear it all over with extraordinary content, and did give me many and hearty thanks, and in words the most expressive tell me his sense of my good endeavours, and that he would have a care of me on all occasions; and did, with much inwardness,[1] tell me what was doing, suitable almost to what Captain Cocke tells me, of designs to make alterations in the Navy; and is most open to me in them, and with utmost confidence desires my further advice on all occasions: and he resolves to have my letter transcribed, and sent forthwith to the Office. So, with as much satisfaction as I could possibly, or did hope for, and obligation on the Duke of York's side professed to me, I away into the Park, and there met Mr. Pierce and his wife and sister and brother and a little boy, and with them to Mulberry Garden, and spent 18*s.* on them, and there left them, she being again with child, and by it the least pretty that ever I saw her. And so I away, and got a coach, and home, and there with my wife and W. Hewer talking all the evening, my mind running on the business of the Office, to see what more I can do to the rendering myself acceptable and useful to all and to the King. We to supper, and to bed.

24th. My wife is upon hanging the long chamber, where the girl lies, with the sad stuff[2] that was in the best chamber, in order to the hanging that with tapestry.

25th. Up, and by water to St. James's; and there with Mr. Wren did discourse about my great letter, which the Duke of York hath given him; and he hath set it to be transcribed by Billings, his man, whom, as he tells me, he can most confide in for secrecy, and is much pleased with it and earnest to have it be; and he and I are like to be much together in the considering how to reform the Office, and that by the Duke of York's command. Thence I, mightily pleased with this success, away to the office, where all the morning, my head full of this business. And it is pretty how Lord Brouncker this day did tell me how he hears that a design is on foot to remove us out of the Office, and proposes that we two do agree to draw up a form of a new constitution of the Office, there to provide remedies for the evils we are now under, that so we may be beforehand with the world, which I agreed to, saying nothing of my design; and, the truth is, he is the best man of them

[1] i.e. intimacy.   [2] Stuff of a sober colour.

all, and I would be glad, next myself, to save him; for, as he deserves best, so I doubt he needs his place most.

26th. In my way to the Old Swan [1] finding a great many people gathered together in Cannon Street about a man that was working in the ruins, and the ground did sink under him, and he sunk in, and was forced to be dug out again, but without hurt. It is strange to say with what speed the people employed do pull down Paul's steeple, and with what ease: it is said that it and the choir are to be taken down this year, and another church begun in the room thereof the next. Home by coach with Sir D. Gauden, who, by the way, tells me how the City do go on in several things towards the building of the public places, which I am glad to hear; and gives hope that in a few years it will be a glorious place. But we met with several stops and troubles in the way in the streets, so as makes it bad to travel in the dark now through the City. So I to Mr. Batelier's by appointment, where I find my wife and Deb. and Mercer, Mrs. Pierce and her husband, son, and daughter, and Knipp and Harris, and W. Batelier and his sister Mary and cousin Gumbleton, a good-humoured, fat young gentleman, son to the jeweller, that dances well; and here danced all night long, with a noble supper; and about two in the morning the table spread again for a noble breakfast beyond all moderation, that put me out of countenance, so much and so good. Mrs. Pierce and her people went home betimes, she being big with child; and Knipp and the rest stayed till almost three in the morning, and then broke up.

27th. Knipp home with us, and I to bed, and rose about six, mightily pleased with last night's mirth. To St. James's, and there, with Mr. Wren, did correct his copy of my letter, which the Duke of York hath signed in my very words, without alteration of a syllable. And so, pleased therewith, I to my Lord Brouncker, who I find within, but hath business, and so comes not to the office today. And so I by water to the office, where we sat all the morning; and just as the Board rises comes the Duke of York's letter, which I knowing, and the Board not being full, and desiring rather to have the Duke of York deliver it himself to us, I suppressed it for this day, my heart beginning to falsify in this business, as being doubtful of the trouble it may give me by provoking them; but, however, I am resolved to go through it, and it is too late to help it now. At noon to dinner to Captain Cocke's, where I met with Mr. Wren; my going being to tell him what I have

[1] In Upper Thames Street.

done, which he likes, and to confer with Cocke about our Office; who tells me that he is confident the design of removing our Officers do hold, but that he is sure that I am safe enough. So away home, and there met at Sir Richard Ford's with the Duke of York's Commissioners about our prizes, with whom we shall have some trouble before we make an end with them. I with my wife and W. Batelier and Deb.; carried them to Bartholomew Fair, where we saw the dancing of the ropes and nothing else, it being late.

28th. To White Hall, where the Duke of York did call me aside, and told me that he must speak with me in the afternoon, and with Mr. Wren, for that now he hath got the paper from my Lord Keeper [1] about the exceptions taken against the management of the Navy; and so we are to debate upon answering them. At noon I home with Sir W. Coventry to his house, and there dined with him, and talked freely with him; and did acquaint him with what I have done, which he is well pleased with and glad of: and do tell me that there are endeavours on foot to bring the Navy into new, but, he fears, worse hands. After much talk with great content with him I walked to the Temple, and stayed at Starky's, my bookseller's, looking over Dr. Heylin's new book of the Life of Bishop Laud [2] (a strange book of the Church history of his time) till Mr. Wren comes, and by appointment we to the Attorney-General's chamber, and there heard the witnesses in the business of Ackworth. And so with Mr. Wren to White Hall. The Duke of York fell to work with us, the Committee being gone, in the Council-chamber; and there, with his own hand, did give us his long letter, telling us that he had received several from us, and now did give us one from him, taking notice of our several doubts and failures, and desired answer to it, as he therein desired. This pleased me well; and so fell to other business, and then parted. And the Duke of York and Wren and I, it being now candle-light, into the Duke of York's closet in White Hall; and there read over this paper of my Lord Keeper's, wherein are laid down the faults of the Navy, so silly, and the remedies so ridiculous, or else the same that are now already provided, that we thought it not to need any answer, the Duke of York being able himself to do it: that so it makes us admire the confidence of these men to offer things so

[1] Sir Orlando Bridgeman.
[2] *Cyprianus Anglicus; or, The Life and Death of Archbishop Laud*, by Peter Heylin, D.D.

silly in a business of such moment.   But it is a most perfect instance of the complexion of the times, and so the Duke of York
said himself, who, I perceive, is mightily concerned in it, and do
again and again recommend it to Mr. Wren and me together, to
consider upon remedies fit to provide for him to propound to the
King before the rest of the world, and particularly the Commissioners of Accounts, who are men of understanding and order,
to find our faults, and offer remedies of their own, which I am glad
of, and will endeavour to do something in it.   So parted, and with
much difficulty, by candle-light, walked over the Matted Gallery,
as it is now with the mats and boards all taken up, so that we walked
over the rafters.   But strange to see how hard matter the plaster
of Paris is, that is there taken up, as hard as stone!   And pity to
see Holbein's work in the ceiling blotted on, and only whited
over!   My wife this day with Hales, to sit for her hand to be
mended, in her picture.

29th.   Up, and all the morning at the office, where the Duke of
York's long letter [1] was read, to their great trouble, and their sus-
pecting me to have been the writer of it.   And at noon comes, by
appointment, Harris to dine with me: and after dinner he and I to
Surgeons' Hall, where they are building it new, very fine; and there
to see their theatre, which stood all the fire, and, which was our
business, their great picture of Holbein's,[2] thinking to have bought
it, by the help of Mr. Pierce, for a little money: I did think to give
£200 for it, it being said to be worth £1000; but it is so spoiled
that I have no mind to it, and is not a pleasant, though a good
picture.   Thence carried Harris to his playhouse, where, though
four o'clock, so few people there at 'The Impertinents,' as I went

---

[1] A copy of this letter exists in the British Museum, Harl. MSS., 6003.   In
the Pepysian Collection are the following: An Inquisition, by his Royal
Highness the Duke of York when Lord High Admiral of England, into the
Management of the Navy, 1668, with his Regulations thereon, fol.   Also
Mr. Pepys's Defence of the same upon an Inquisition thereunto by Parliament,
1669, fol.

[2] It represents Henry VIII in the act of delivering their charter to the Barber
Surgeons' and Surgeons' Companies, which were united in the thirty-second
year of that king; it contains eighteen figures.   The painting is considered
to be one of Holbein's best works, and is in good preservation, though it may
have been damaged by the Great Fire, when the hall suffered so much as to
require repair.   A fine print from the picture was made by B. Baron in 1763,
and it was again engraved for Knight's *London*, which contains a very interesting account of Barber-Surgeons' Hall: the names of the persons represented
by Holbein will also be found in the *Gentleman's Magazine* for April 1789.

out; and do believe they did not act, though there was my Lord Arlington and his company there. So I out, and met my wife in a coach, and stopped her going thither to meet me; and took her and Mercer and Deb. to Bartholomew Fair, and there did see a ridiculous, obscene little stage-play, called 'Merry Andrew', a foolish thing, but seen by everybody: and so to Jacob Hall's dancing of the ropes, a thing worth seeing, and mightily followed. Writing to my father tonight not to unfurnish our house in the country for my sister, who is going to her own house, because I think I may have occasion myself to come thither; and so I do, by our being put out of the Office, which do not at all trouble me to think of.

30th. (Lord's day.) Walked to St. James's and Pall Mall, and read over, with Sir W. Coventry, my long letter to the Duke of York, and which the Duke of York hath, from mine, wrote to the Board, wherein he is mightily pleased, and I perceive do put great value upon me, and did talk very openly on all matters of State, and how some people have got the bit into their mouths, meaning the Duke of Buckingham and his party, and would likely run away with all. But what pleased me mightily was to hear the good character he did give of my Lord Falmouth for his generosity, good nature, desire of public good, and low thoughts of his own wisdom; his employing his interest in the King to do good offices to all people, without any other fault than the freedom he do learn in France of thinking himself obliged to serve his King in his pleasures: and was Sir W. Coventry's particular friend. And Sir W. Coventry do tell me very odd circumstances about the fatality of his death, which are very strange. Thence to White Hall to chapel, and heard the anthem, and did dine with the Duke of Albemarle in a dirty manner as ever. All the afternoon I sauntered up and down the house and Park. And there was a Committee for Tangier met, wherein Lord Middleton would, I think, have found fault with me for want of coals; but I slighted it, and he made nothing of it, but was thought to be drunk; and I see that he hath a mind to find fault with me and Creed, neither of us having yet applied ourselves to him about anything: but do talk of his profits and perquisites taken from him, and garrison reduced, and that it must be increased, and such things as, I fear, he will be just such another as my Lord Teviot and the rest, to ruin that place. So I to the Park, and there walk an hour or two; and in the King's garden, and saw the Queen and ladies walk, and I did steal some apples off the trees; and there did see my Lady Richmond, who is of a noble person as ever I did see, but her face worse than it was considerably by the small-pox; her sister [1] is also very handsome. Coming into the Park, and the door kept strictly, I had opportunity of handing in the little, pretty, squinting girl of the Duke of York's House, but did not make acquaintance of her; but let her go, and a little girl that was with her, to walk by themselves. So to White Hall in the evening, to the Queen's side, and there met the Duke of York; and he did tell me and Sir W. Coventry, who was with me, how the Lord Anglesey did take notice of our reading his long and sharp letter to the Board; but that it was the better, at least he said so. The Duke of York, I perceive, is earnest in it and will have good effects of it, telling Sir W. Coventry that it was a letter that might have come from the Commissioners of Accounts, but it was better it should come first from him. I met Lord Brouncker, who, I perceive, and the rest, do smell that it comes from me, but dare not find fault with it; and I am glad of it, it being my glory and defence that I did occasion and write it. So by water home; and did spend the evening with W. Hewer, telling him how we are all like to be turned out, Lord Brouncker telling me this evening that the Duke of Buckingham did, within few hours, say that he had enough to turn us all out: which I am not sorry for at all, for I know the world will judge me to go for company; and my eyes are such as I am not able to do the business of my office as I used, and would desire to do, while I am in it.

31st. To Hercules' Pillars, and there dined all alone, while I sent my shoe to have the heel fastened at Wotton's. To the Duke of York's playhouse, and saw 'Hamlet,' which we have not seen this year before, or more; and mightily pleased with it, but, above all, with Betterton, the best part, I believe, that ever man acted. Thence to the Fair, and saw 'Polichinelle,' and so home. This night lay the first night in Deb.'s chamber, which is now hung with that that hung our great chamber, and is now a very handsome room. This day Mrs. Batelier did give my wife a mighty pretty Spaniel [Flora], which she values mightily, and is pretty. But, as a new comer, I cannot be fond of her.

September 1st. To Bartholomew Fair, and there saw several sights; among others the mare that tells money, and many things

---

[1] Sophia Stuart, married to Henry Bulkeley, fourth son of Thomas, first Viscount Bulkeley, and Master of the Household to Charles II.

to admiration; and, among others, come to me when she was bid to go to him of the company that most loved a pretty wench in a corner. And this did cost me 12*d.* to the horse, which I had flung him before, and did give me occasion to kiss a mighty *belle fille* that was exceeding plain, but *fort belle.*

2d. Fast-day for the burning of London, strictly observed. Troubled with a summons, though a kind one, from Mr. Jessop, to attend the Commissioners of Accounts tomorrow.

3d. To the Commissioners of Accounts, and there was received with all possible respect, their business being only to explain the meaning of one of their late demands to us. And, this being done, away with great content, and so to my bookseller's, for Hobbes's 'Leviathan,' which is now mightily called for; and what was heretofore sold for 8*s.* I now give 24*s.* for, at the second hand, and is sold for 30*s.*, it being a book the Bishops will not let be printed again.

4th. At the office all the morning; and at noon my wife and Deb. and Mercer and W. Hewer and I to the Fair, and there, at the old house, did eat a pig, and was pretty merry, but saw no sights, my wife having a mind to see the play 'Bartholomew Fair,' with puppets. And it is an excellent play: the more I see it, the more I love the wit of it, only the business of abusing the Puritans begins to grow stale and of no use, they being the people that, at last, will be found the wisest. And here Knipp come to us, and sat with us, and thence took coach in two coaches, and losing one another, my wife and Knipp and I to Hercules' Pillars, and there supped, and I did take from her mouth the words and notes of her song of 'The Lark,' which pleases me mightily. And so set her at home, and away we home, where our company come before us. This night Knipp tells us that there is a Spanish woman lately come over, that pretends to sing as well as Mrs. Knight; both of whom I must endeavour to hear.

5th. To Mr. Hales's new house, where, I find, he hath finished my wife's hand, which is better than the other; and here I find Harris's picture, done in his habit of 'Henry the Fifth'; mighty like a player, but I do not think the picture near so good as any yet he hath made for me: however, it is pretty well.

6th. (Lord's day.) Up betimes, and got myself ready to go by water, and about nine o'clock took boat with Henry Russell to Gravesend, coming thither about one, where, at the Ship, I dined; and thither come to me Mr. Hosier, whom I went to speak with about several businesses of work that he is doing, and I would have him do of writing work for me. And I did go with him to his lodging, and there did see his wife, a pretty tolerable woman, and do find him upon an extraordinary good work of designing a method of keeping our Storekeeper's Accounts, in the Navy. Here I should have met with Mr. Wilson, but he is sick and could not come from Chatham to me. So, having done with Hosier, I took boat again the beginning of the flood, and come home by nine at night with much pleasure, it being a fine day. Going down I spent reading of the 'Five Sermons of Five Several Styles,' [1] worth comparing one with another; but I do think, when all is done, that, contrary to the design of the book, the Presbyterian style and the Independent are the best of the five sermons to be preached; and this I do, by the best of my present judgment, think. My boy was with me and read to me all day, and we sang awhile together, and so home to supper a little, and so to bed.

7th. With my Lord Brouncker (who was this day in an unusual manner merry, I believe with drink), J. Minnes, and W. Pen to Bartholomew Fair; and there saw the dancing mare again, which today I find to act much worse than the other day, she forgetting many things, which her master beat her for, and was mightily vexed; and then the dancing of the ropes, and also the little stageplay, which is very ridiculous.

8th. Up, and by water to White Hall, and to St. James's, there to talk a little with Mr. Wren about the private business we are upon in the office, where he tells me he finds that they all suspect me to be the author of the great letter, which I value not, being satisfied that it is the best thing I could ever do for myself; and so, after some discourse of this kind more, I back to the office, and there all the morning; and after dinner to it again, all the afternoon and very late, and then home to supper, where met W. Batelier and Betty Turner, and, after some talk with them, and supper, we to bed. This day I received so earnest an invitation again from

---

[1] By Abraham Wright, Fellow of St. John's College, Oxford, afterwards vicar of Oakham, who died in 1690. The title is, 'Five Sermons, in Five several Styles, or Waies of Preaching. First, in Bp. Andrews, his *way*; before the late King upon the first day of Lent. Second, in Bp. Hall's *way*; before the clergie at the author's own ordination in Christ Church, Oxford. Third, in Dr. Maine's and Mr. Cartwright's *way*; before the University at St. Marie's, Oxford. Fourth, in the Presbyterian *way*; before the Citie, at St. Paul's, London. Fifth, in the Independent *way*; never preached. . . . Printed for Edw. Archer, 1656.'

Roger Pepys, to come to Sturbridge Fair, that I resolved to let my wife go, which she shall do the next week. This day I received two letters from the Duke of Richmond about his yacht, which is newly taken into the King's service. And I am glad of it, hoping thereby to oblige him and to have occasions of seeing his noble Duchess, which I adore.

9th. To the Duke of Richmond's lodgings by his desire by letter yesterday. I find him at his lodgings in the little building in the bowling-green at White Hall, that was begun to be built by Captain Rolt. They are fine rooms. I did hope to see his lady; but she, I hear, is in the country. His business was about his yacht, and he seems a mighty good-natured man, and did presently write me a warrant for a doe from Cobham when the season comes, buck season being past. I shall make much of this acquaintance, that I may live to see his lady near. Thence to Westminster, to Sir R. Long's office:[1] and, going, met Mr. George Montagu, who talked and complimented me mightily; and long discourse I had with him, who, for news, tells me for certain that Trevor do come to be Secretary at Michaelmas, and that Morrice goes out, and, he believes, without any compensation. He tells me that now Buckingham do rule all; and the other day, in the King's journey he is now on, at Bagshot and that way, he caused Prince Rupert's horses to be turned out of an inn, and caused his own to be kept there, which the Prince complained of to the King, and the Duke of York seconded the complaint; but the King did overrule it for Buckingham, by which there are high displeasures among them; and Buckingham and Arlington rule all. To White Hall, where Brouncker, W. Pen, and I attended the Commissioners of the Treasury about the victualling contract, where high words between Sir Thomas Clifford and us, and myself more particularly, who told him that something that he said was told him about this business was a flat untruth. However, we went on to our business in the examination of the draft, and so parted, and I vexed at what happened; and I all that night as vexed that I did not sleep almost all night, which shows how unfit I am for trouble. So after a little supper and spending a little time melancholy in making a bass to the Lark's Song, I to bed.

10th. There dined with me Batelier and his wife and Mercer and my people at a good venison pasty; and after dinner I and W. Howe, who came to see me, by water to the Temple, and met our

[1] At the Exchequer, of which he was auditor.

four women, my wife, W. Batelier, Mercer, and Deb., at the Duke's playhouse, and there saw 'The Maid in the Mill,' revived— a pretty, harmless old play. I to the office, where a child is laid at Sir J. Minnes's door, as there was one heretofore. Thence to Unthank's, and 'Change, where wife did a little business while Mercer and I stayed in the coach; and, in a quarter of an hour, I taught her the whole Lark's Song perfectly, so excellent an ear she hath. Here we at Unthank's 'light, and walked them to White Hall, my wife mighty angry at it, and did give me ill words before Batelier, which vexed me; but I made no matter of it, but vexed to myself. So landed them, it being fine moonshine, at the Bear,[1] and so took water to the other side, and home. So being good friends again (my wife seeking it), by my being silent I overcoming her, we to bed.

11th. At my office all the morning, and after dinner all the afternoon shut up drawing up my defence to the Duke of York upon his great letter; which I have industriously taken this opportunity of doing for my future use. At it late, and my mind and head mighty full of it all night.

12th. To the office, where till noon, and I did see great whispering among my brethren about their replies to the Duke of York; which vexed me, though I know no occasion for it, for I have no manner of ground to fear them. At noon home to dinner, and after dinner to work all the afternoon again. At home late, and so to bed.

13th. (Lord's day.) By coach to St. James's, and met, to my wish, the Duke of York and Mr. Wren; and understand the Duke of York hath received answers from Brouncker, W. Pen, and J. Minnes: and as soon as he saw me he bid Mr. Wren read them over with me. So having no opportunity of talk with the Duke of York, and Mr. Wren some business to do, he put them into my hands like an idle companion, to take home with me before himself had read them, which do give me great opportunity of altering my answer if there was cause. After supper made my wife to read them all over, wherein she is mighty useful to me; and I find them all evasions, and in many things false, and in few to the full purpose. Little said reflective on me, though W. Pen and J. Minnes do mean me in one or two places, and J. Minnes a little more plainly would lead the Duke of York to question the exactness of my keeping my records: but all to no purpose. My mind is mightily pleased by

[1] At the foot of London Bridge, pulled down December 1761.

this, if I can but get time to have a copy taken of them for my future use; but I must return them tomorrow. So to bed.

14th. Up betimes, and walked to the Temple, and stopped, viewing the Exchange and Paul's and St. Faith's, where strange how the very sight of the stones falling from the top of the steeple do make me sea-sick! But no hurt, I hear, hath yet happened in all this work of the steeple, which is very much. So from the Temple I by coach to St. James's, where I find Sir W. Pen and Lord Anglesey, who delivered this morning his answer to the Duke of York, but I could not see it. But after being above with the Duke of York but said nothing, I down with Mr. Wren; and he and I read them all over that I had, and I expounded them to him, and did so order it that I had them home with me, so that I shall, to my heart's wish, be able to take a copy of them. After dinner I by water to White Hall; and there, with the Cofferer and Sir Stephen Fox, attended the Commissioners of the Treasury about bettering our fund; and are promised it speedily.

15th. Up mighty betimes, my wife and people, Mercer lying here all night, by three o'clock, and I about five; and they before, and I after them, to the coach in Bishopsgate Street, which was not ready to set out. So took wife and Mercer and Deb. and W. Hewer, who are all to set out this day for Cambridge, to cousin Roger Pepys's, to see Sturbridge Fair; and I showed them the Exchange, which is very finely carried on, with good dispatch. So walked back and saw them gone, there being only one man in the coach besides them; and so home to the office. To the King's playhouse to see a new play, acted but yesterday, a translation out of French by Dryden, called 'The Ladies à la Mode': [1] so mean a thing as, when they came to say it would be acted again tomorrow, both he that said it, Beeson,[2] and the pit fell a-laughing, there being this day not a quarter of the pit full.

16th. Walking it to the Temple, and in my way observe that

---

[1] No play called *The Ladies à la Mode* has been traced in 1668, or in any earlier or later year. A comedy entitled *Love à la Mode* was brought out very soon after the Restoration, but it was anonymous. Pepys is believed to be the only authority for attributing the piece to Dryden, who possibly had a hand in it, but did not print the play, on account of its ill success A comedy, named *Damoyselles à la Mode*, and printed in 1667, 8vo, is mentioned by Langbaine, p. 56, as written by Richard Flecknoe, and dedicated to the Duchess of Newcastle; but it does not appear to have ever been acted, though, in point of title and date, it comes very near what is wanted.

[2] Probably Beeston, who had been manager of the Cockpit theatre.

the Stocks [1] are now pulled quite down; and it will make the coming into Cornhill and Lombard Street mighty noble. I stopped, too, at Paul's, and there did go into St. Faith's church, and also in the body of the west part of the church; and do see a hideous sight of the walls of the church ready to fall, that I was in fear as long as I was in it: and here I saw the great vaults underneath the body of the church. No hurt, I hear, is done yet, since their going to pull down the church and steeple; but one man, one Mound, this week fell from the top of the roof of the east end, that stands next the steeple, and there broke himself all to pieces. It is pretty here to see how the late church was but a case wrought over the old church; for you may see the very old pillars standing whole within the wall of this. When I come to St. James's I find the Duke of York gone with the King to see the muster of the Guards in Hyde Park; and their Colonel, the Duke of Monmouth, to take his command this day of the King's Life-guard, by surrender of my Lord Gerard. So I took a hackney coach, and saw it all: and indeed it was mighty noble, and their firing mighty fine, and the Duke of Monmouth in mighty rich clothes, but the well-ordering of the men I understand not. Here, among a thousand coaches that were there, I saw and spoke to Mrs. Pierce: and by and by Mr. Wren hunts me out and gives me my Lord Anglesey's answer to the Duke of York's letter, where, I perceive, he do do what he can to hurt me by bidding the Duke of York call for my books: but this will do me all the right in the world, and yet I am troubled at it. So away out of the Park, and home; and there Mr. Gibson and I to dinner: and all the afternoon with him, writing over anew, and a little altering, my answer to the Duke of York, which I have not yet delivered, and so have the opportunity of doing it after seeing all their answers, though this do give me occasion to alter very little. This done, he to write it over and I to the office, where late, and then home; and he had finished it; and then he to read to me the Life of Archbishop Laud, wrote by Dr. Heylin; which is a

[1] The Stocks Market took its name from a pair of stocks erected near this spot. About 1675 Sir Robert Viner purchased an equestrian statue of John Sobieski trampling down the Turk; which, when it had undergone some necessary alteration, he erected in Stocks Market as Charles II trampling on Oliver Cromwell. The Mansion House now stands on the site. About 1737, the statue was presented to Robert Viner, the lineal representative of the convivial lord mayor, and the market transferred to the space gained by covering over the Fleet Ditch. This Fleet market has, in its turn, given place to Farringdon Street.

shrewd book, but that which I believe will do the Bishops in general no great good, but hurt, it pleads for so much Popish. This day my father's letters tell me of the death of poor Fancy in the country, big with puppies, which troubles me, as being one of my oldest acquaintances and servants. Also good Stankes is dead.

17th. At noon comes Knipp with design to dine with Lord Brouncker; but she being undressed, and there being much company, dined with me. And after dinner I out with her, and carried her to the playhouse; and in the way did give her five guineas as a fairing, I having given her nothing a great while, and her coming hither sometimes having been matter of cost to her. So to the King's playhouse, and saw 'Rollo, Duke of Normandy,'[1] which, for old acquaintance, pleased me pretty well. This evening Batelier comes to tell me that he was going down to Cambridge to my company, to see the Fair, which vexed me, and the more because I fear he do know that Knipp did dine with me today.[2]

18th. To St. James's, and there took a turn or two in the Park; and then up to the Duke of York, and there had opportunity of delivering my answer to his late letter, which he did not read, but give to Mr. Wren, as looking on it as a thing I needed not have done, but only that I might not give occasion to the rest to suspect my communication with the Duke of York against them. So now I am at rest in that matter, and shall be more when my copies are finished of their answers. To White Hall, and thither comes the Duke of York to us, where I find him somewhat sour, and particularly angry with Lord Anglesey for his not being there now nor at other times. To the King's House, and saw a piece of 'Henry the Fourth.' At the end of the play, thinking to have gone abroad with Knipp, but it was too late, and she to get her part against tomorrow, in 'The Silent Woman'; and so I only set her at home, and away home.

19th. To the King's playhouse, and there saw 'The Silent Woman,' the best comedy, I think, that ever was wrote: and sitting by Shadwell,[3] the poet, he was big with admiration of it. Here was my Lord Brouncker and W. Pen and their ladies in the box, being grown mighty kind of a sudden; but, God knows, it will last but a little while, I dare swear. Knipp did her part mighty

---

[1] By John Fletcher and others.
[2] And that he might tell Mrs. Pepys.
[3] Thomas Shadwell, the dramatic writer: *ob.* 1692.

well.[1]   And so home straight, and to write, and particularly to my cousin Roger, who, W. Hewer and my wife writes me, do use them with mighty plenty and noble entertainment: so to supper, and to bed.   All the news now is that Mr. Trevor is for certain to be Secretary in Morrice's place, which the Duke of York did himself tell me yesterday; and also that Parliament is to be adjourned to the 1st of March, which do please me well, hoping thereby to get my things in a little better order than I should have done; and the less attendances at that end of the town in winter.

20th. (Lord's day.) To church, and heard a dull sermon of Dr. Hicks, who is a suitor to Mrs. Howell, the widow of our turner of the Navy; and thence home to dinner, staying till past one o'clock for Harris, whom I invited, and to bring Shadwell the poet with him; but they came not, and so a good dinner lost through my own folly.   And so to dinner alone, having since church heard the boy read over Dryden's Reply to Sir R. Howard's Answer about his Essay of Poesy and a letter [2] in answer to that; the latter whereof is mighty silly, in behalf of Howard.   To visit Mrs. Pierce, with whom and him I stayed a little while, and do hear how the Duchess of Monmouth is at this time in great trouble of the shortness of her lame leg, which is likely to grow shorter and shorter, that she will never recover it.   So back, and walked in Gray's Inn Walks a while, but little company; and so over the fields to Clerkenwell, to see whether I could find that the fair Butlers do live there still, I seeing Frances the other day in a coach with Cary Dillon,[3] her old servant, but know not where she lives.

[1] She played the Silent Woman.
[2] 'A letter from a Gentleman to the Honourable Ed. Howard, Esq., occasioned by a Civiliz'd Epistle of Mr. Dryden's before his Second Edition of his Indian Emperour.   In the Savoy, printed by Thomas Newcomb, 1668.'   The 'Civiliz'd Epistle,' was a caustic attack on Sir Robert Howard; and the Letter is signed, 'Sir, your faithful and humble servant, R. F.'—i.e. Richard Flecknoe. —*Gentleman's Magazine* for December 1850, p. 59.
[3] Cary Dillon was the youngest son of Robert, second Earl of Roscommon, by his third wife, Anne, daughter of Sir William Stroud, of Stoake, in Somersetshire, and widow of Henry, Lord Folliott, of Ballyshannon.   He is the Colonel Dillon before mentioned by Pepys, and who had killed Colonel Giles Rawlings in a duel.   He afterwards held several posts under Charles II, and James II, and upon the death, in 1684, of his nephew, the poet, he succeeded as fifth Earl of Roscommon.   He married, not Frances Boteler, but Katherine, daughter of John Werden, of Chester, and sister of Major-General Robert Werden (before mentioned), Groom of the Bedchamber to the Duke of York, and Comptroller of his Household when king.   Lord Roscommon died 25th November 1689.

21st. To St. James's, and there the Duke of York did of his own accord come to me, and tell me that he had read, and do like of, my answers to the objections which he did give me the other day, about the Navy; and so did Sir W. Coventry too, who told me that the Duke of York had shown him them. To Southwark Fair, very dirty, and there saw the puppet show of Whittington, which was pretty to see; and how that idle thing do work upon people that see it, and even myself too! And thence to Jacob Hall's dancing on the ropes, where I saw such action as I never saw before, and mightily worth seeing; and here took acquaintance with a fellow that carried me to a tavern, whither come the music of this booth, and by and by Jacob Hall himself, with whom I had a mind to speak, to hear whether he had ever any mischief by falls in his time. He told me, 'Yes, many, but never to the breaking of a limb': he seems a mighty strong man. So, giving them a bottle or two of wine, I away with Payne, the waterman. He, seeking me at the play, did get a link to light me, and so light me to the Bear, where Bland, my waterman, waited for me with gold and other things he kept for me, to the value of £40 and more, which I had about me, for fear of my pockets being cut. So by link-light through the bridge, it being mighty dark, but still weather, and so home, where I find my draft of the Resolution come, finished, from Chatham; but will cost me, one way or other, above £12 or £13 in the board, frame, and garnishing, which is a little too much, but I will not be beholden to the King's officers that do it. This day I met Mr. Moore in the New Exchange, and had much talk of my Lord's concernments. This day also came out first the new five-pieces in gold, coined by the Guinea Company;[1] and I did get two pieces of Mr. Holder.

22d. To the office, where sitting all the morning. At noon home to dinner with my people, and so to the office again, where busy all the afternoon; and in the evening spent my time walking in the dark, in the garden, to favour my eyes, which I find nothing but ease do help. In the garden there comes to me my Lady Pen and Mrs. Turner and Markham, and we sat and talked together; and I carried them home, and there eat a bit of something, and by

---

[1] Guineas took their name from the gold brought from Guinea, by the African Company, who, as an encouragement to bring over gold to be coined, were permitted, by their charter from Charles II, to have their stamp of an elephant upon the coin. There were likewise five-pound pieces like the guinea, with the inscription upon the rim, like the crown piece.

and by comes Sir W. Pen and eat with us, and mighty merry—in appearance, at least, he being on all occasions glad to be at friendship with me, though we hate one another, and know it on both sides.   This day Mr. Wren did give me, at the Board, Commissioner Middleton's answer to the Duke of York's great letter; so that now I have all of them,

23d.   At noon comes Mr. Evelyn to me about some business with the Office; and there in discourse tells me of his loss, to the value of £500, which he hath met with in a late attempt of making of bricks upon an adventure with others, by which he presumed to have got a great deal of money: so that I see the most ingenious men may sometimes be mistaken.   To White Hall, to attend the Commissioners of the Treasury with Alderman Backwell, about £10,000 he is to lend us for Tangier; and then up to a Committee of the Council, where was the Duke of York, and they did give us, the Officers of the Navy, the proposals of the several bidders for the victualling of the Navy, for us to give our answer to, which is the best; and whether it be better to victual by commission or contract, and to bring them our answer by Friday afternoon, which is a great deal of work.

24th.   Up betimes, and Sir D. Gauden with me; and I told him all, being very desirous, for the King's sake as well as my own, that he may be kept in it.   And after consulting him I to the office about this business till night, drawing up our answer.   So home to supper and made my boy read to me awhile, and then to bed.

25th.   W. Batelier with me, who is lately come from Impington, beyond which I perceive he went not, whatever his pretence at first was; and so he tells me how well and merry all are there, and how nobly used by my cousin.   To White Hall to the Committee of the Council.   So with the Duke of York and some others to his closet, and Alderman Backwell, about a Committee of Tangier. They gone, the Duke of York did tell me how hot Clifford is for Child, and for removing of old Officers, he saying plainly tonight that though D. Gauden was a man that had done the best service that he believed any man, or any ten men, could have done, yet that it was for the King's interest not to let it lie too long in one hand, lest nobody should be able to serve him but one.   But the Duke of York did openly tell him that he was not for removing of old servants that have done well, neither in this place nor in any other place, which is very nobly said.

26th.   Could sleep but little last night, for my concernments in this business of the victualling, for Sir D. Gauden; and he comes to me, and there I did tell him all, and give him my advice, and so he away. To Charing Cross, and there into the great new ordinary,[1] by my Lord Mulgrave's[2] being led thither by Mr. Beale, one of Oliver's, and now of the King's Guards; and he sat with me while I had two grilled pigeons, very handsome and good meat, and there he and I talked of our old acquaintances, W. Clerke and others, he being a very civil man, and so parted. To White Hall, and there attended the King and Council. I present, and then withdrew; and they spent two hours at least afterwards about it and at last rose; and, to my great content, the Duke of York, at coming out, told me that it was carried for D. Gauden at 6*d.*, 8*d.*, and 8¾*d.*; but with great difficulty, I understand, both from him and others, so much that Sir Edward Walker told me that he prays to God he may never live to need to plead his merit, for D. Gauden's sake; for that it hath stood him in no stead in this business at all, though both he and all the world that speaks of him speaks of him as the most deserving man of any servant of the King's, of the whole nation, and so I think he is: but it is done, and my heart is glad at it. To my house, where D. Gauden did talk a little: and he do mightily acknowledge my kindness to him, and I know I have done the King and myself good service in it. This noon I went to my Lady Peterborough's house, and talked with her about the money due to her Lord; and it gives me great trouble, her importunity and impertinency about it. This afternoon at Court I met with Lord Hinchingbroke, newly come out of the country, who tells me that Creed's business[3] with Mrs. Pickering will do, which I am neither troubled nor glad at.

27th. (Lord's day.) To White Hall, calling in at Somerset House Chapel, and there did hear a little mass: and so to White Hall; and there, the King being gone to chapel, I to walk all the morning in the Park, where I met Mr. Wren; and he and I walked together in the Pall Mall, it being most summer weather that ever was seen. And here talking of several things: of the corruption of the Court, and how unfit it is for ingenuous men, and himself particularly, to live in it, where a man cannot live but he must

---

[1] The Swan tavern.
[2] John Sheffield, third Earl of Mulgrave, afterwards created Marquis and Duke of Normanby and Buckinghamshire. He was succeeded by his only son, Edmund, with whom all the honours became extinct, in 1737.
[3] Their marriage, which took place soon after.

spend money, and cannot get it suitably without breach of his honour. And he did thereupon tell me of the basest thing of my Lord Berkeley that ever was heard of any man, which was this: how the Duke of York's Commissioners do let his wine licences at a bad rate, and being offered a better, they did persuade the Duke of York to give some satisfaction to the former to quit it, and let it to the latter; which being done, my Lord Berkeley did make the bargain for the former to have £1500 a year to quit it; whereof, since, it is come to light that they were to have but £800 and himself £700, which the Duke of York hath ever since for some years paid, though the second bargain hath been broken, and the Duke of York lost by it, half of what the first was. He told me that there hath been a seeming accommodation between the Duke of York and the Duke of Buckingham and Lord Arlington, the two latter desiring it; but yet that there is not true agreement between them, but they do labour to bring in all new creatures into play, and the Duke of York do oppose it. Thence, he gone, I to the Queen's Chapel, and there heard some good singing; and so to White Hall, and saw the King and Queen at dinner. And thence with Sir Stephen Fox to dinner, and the Cofferer with us; and there mighty kind usage and good discourse. Thence spent all the afternoon walking in the Park, and then in the evening at Court, on the Queen's side; and there met Mr. Godolphin, who tells me that the news is true we heard yesterday, of my Lord Sandwich's being come to Mount's Bay, in Cornwall. This night, in the Queen's drawing-room, my Lord Brouncker told me the difference that is now between the three Ambassadors here, the Venetian,[1] French,[2] and Spaniard:[3] the third not being willing to make a visit to the first, because he would not receive him at the door; who is willing to give him as much respect as he did to the French, who was used no otherwise, and who refuses now to take more of him, upon being desired thereto, in order to the making an accommodation in this matter.

28th. Knipp's maid comes to me, to tell me that the women's day [4] at the playhouse is today, and that therefore I must be there to increase their profit. I did give the pretty maid Betty, that comes to me, half-a-crown for coming, and had a kiss or two— *elle* being mighty *jolie*. By water to St. James's, and there had good opportunity of speaking with the Duke of York, who desires

---

[1] Pietro Mocenigo.   [2] Charles Colbert.
[3] Conde de Dona.   [4] Their benefit.

me again, talking on that matter, to prepare something for him to do for the better managing of our Office, telling me that, my Lord Keeper and he talking about it yesterday, my Lord Keeper did advise him to do so, it being better to come from him than otherwise; which I have promised to do.   Thence to my Lord Burlington's house, the first time I ever was there, it being the house built by Sir John Denham, next to Clarendon House; and here I visited my Lord Hinchingbroke and his lady.   Mr. Sidney Montagu being last night come to town unexpectedly from Mount's Bay, where he left my Lord well, eight days since, so as we now hourly expect to hear of his arrival at Portsmouth. Sidney is mighty grown; and I am glad I am here to see him at his first coming, though it cost me dear, for here I come to be necessitated to supply them with £500 for my Lord.[1]   He sent him up with a declaration to his friends, of the necessity of his being presently supplied with £2000; but I do not think he will get £1000.   However, I think it becomes my duty to my Lord to do something extraordinary in this, and the rather because I have been remiss in writing to him during this voyage, more than ever I did in my life, and more indeed than was fit for me.   By and by comes Sir W. Godolphin to see Mr. Sidney, who, I perceive, is much dissatisfied that he should come to town last night and not yet be with my Lord Arlington, who, and all the town, hear of his being come: and he did, it seems, take notice of it to Godolphin this morning, so that I perceive this remissness in affairs do continue in my Lord's managements still, which I am sorry for; but, above all, to see in what a condition my Lord is for money, that I dare swear he do not know where to take up £500 of any man in England at this time, upon his word, but of myself, as I believe by the sequel hereof it will appear.   Here I first saw and saluted my Lady Burlington,[2] a very fine-speaking lady and a good woman, but old, and not handsome; but a brave woman in her parts. Here my Lady Hinchingbroke tells me that she hath bought most of the wedding-clothes for Mrs. Pickering, so that the thing [3] is gone through and will soon be ended; which I wonder at, but let them do as they will.   Here I also, standing by a candle that was

---

[1] See Pepys's letter to Lord Sandwich on this subject, in the Correspondence, 29th September 1668.

[2] Elizabeth, sole daughter and heir to Henry Clifford, Earl of Cumberland, wife of Richard Boyle, first Earl of Burlington.

[3] The marriage with Creed.

brought for sealing a letter, do set my periwig afire, which made
such an odd noise, nobody could tell what it was till they saw the
flame, my back being to the candle.   To my vintner's, and there
did only look upon his wife, which is mighty handsome; and so to
my glove and ribbon shop, in Fenchurch Street, and did the like
there.   And there, stopping against the door of the shop, saw
Mrs. Horsfall, now a widow, in a coach: I to her, and shook her
by the hand, and so she away; and I by coach to the King's playhouse, and there saw 'The City Match,' [1] not acted these thirty
years, and but a silly play: the King and Court there; the house,
for the women's sake, mighty full.   So I to White Hall, and there
all the evening on the Queen's side; and it being a most summer-
like day and a fine warm evening, the Italians came in a barge under
the leads, before the Queen's drawing-room; and so the Queen
and ladies went out and heard them for almost an hour: and the
singing was indeed very good together; but yet there was but one
voice that alone did appear considerable, and that was Signor
Joanni.[2]   This done, by and by they went in: and here I saw Mr.
Sidney Montagu kiss the Queen's hand, who was mighty kind to
him, and the ladies looked mightily on him; and the King came by
and by, and did talk to him.   So I away by coach with Alderman
Backwell home, who is mighty kind to me, more than ordinary,
in his expressions.   But I do hear this day what troubles me, that
Sir W. Coventry is quite out of play, the King seldom speaking to
him; and that there is a design of making a Lord Treasurer, and
that my Lord Arlington shall be the man; but I cannot believe it.
But yet the Duke of Buckingham hath it in his mind, and those
with him, to make a thorough alteration in things, and, among the
rest, Coventry to be out.   The Duke of York did this day tell
me how hot the whole party was in the business of Gauden; and
particularly, my Lord Anglesey tells me, the Duke of Buckingham
for Child against Gauden; but the Duke of York did stand
stoutly to it.

29th. (Tuesday. Michaelmas day.) Up, and to the Office,
where all the morning.

* * * * *

October 11th.[3] To church, where I find Parson Mills come to

---

[1] A comedy by Jasper Maine, D.D.   [2] Probably Giovanni B. Draghi.
[3] In this part of the *Diary* no entry occurs for thirteen days, though there
are several pages left blank.   During the interval Pepys went into the country,
as he subsequently mentions his having been at Saxham, in Suffolk, during

town and preached, and the church full, most people being now come home to town, though the season of year is as good as summer in all respects. At noon dined at home with my wife, all alone. At night comes Mr. Turner and his wife, and there they tell me that Mr. Harper is dead at Deptford, and so now all his and my care is how to secure his being Storekeeper in his stead. And here they and their daughter, and a kinswoman that come along with them, did sup with me, and pretty merry.

12th. Up, and with Mr. Turner to White Hall, to enquire when the Duke of York will be in town, in order to Mr. Turner's going down to Audley End[1] about his place; and here I met in St. James's Park with one that told me that the Duke of York would be in town tomorrow. I did stop my intentions of going to the Court, also this day, about securing Mr. Turner's place of Petty Purveyor to Mr. Hater. Meeting a gentleman of my Lord Middleton's looking for me about the payment of the £1000 lately ordered to his Lord in advance of his pay, which shall arise upon his going Governor to Tangier, I did go to his Lord's lodgings, and there spoke the first time with him, and find him a shrewd man, but a drinking man, I think, as the world says; but a man that hath seen much of the world, and is a Scot. I offered him my service, though I can do him little; but he sends his man home with me, where I made him stay till I had gone to Sir W. Pen to bespeak him about Mr. Hater, who, contrary to my fears, did appear very friendly, to my great content; for I was afraid of his appearing for his man Burroughs. But he did not; but did declare to me afterwards his intentions to desire an excuse in his own business, to be eased of the business of Comptroller, his health not giving him power to stay always in town, but he must go into the country. Home, where I find Sir H. Cholmley come to town, and now come hither to see me: and he is a man that I love mightily, as being, of a gentleman, the most industrious that ever I saw. He stayed with me awhile talking, and telling me his obligations to my

---

the king's visit to Lord Crofts, which took place at this time (see 23rd October, post). He might also probably have gone to Impington, to fetch his wife, whom we find dining at her home on the 11th October. At all events, the pages left blank were never filled up.

[1] Her Majesty, attended by several ladies of the Court, left Whitehall for Audley End on the 6th October, where His Majesty was expected, after having divertised himself at Newmarket. The Court remained at Audley End till the 14th (*The London Gazette*, No. 302).

Lord Sandwich, which I was glad of; and that the Duke of Buckingham is now chief of all men in this kingdom, which I knew before; and that he do think the Parliament will hardly ever meet again, which is a great many men's thoughts, and I shall not be sorry for it. I home, and there to dinner, and Mr. Pelling with us; and thence my wife and Mercer and W. Hewer and Deb. to the King's playhouse, and afterwards by water with them, and there we did hear the eunuch, who, it seems, is a Frenchman, but long bred in Italy, sing, which I seemed to take as new to me, though I saw him on Saturday last but said nothing of it; but such action and singing I could never have imagined to have heard, and do make good whatever Tom Hill used to tell me. Here we met with Mr. Batelier and his sister, and so they home with us in two coaches, and there at my house stayed and supped. And this night my bookseller, Shrewsbury, comes and brings my books of Martyrs, and I did pay him for them, and did this night make the young women before supper to open all the volumes for me. Read a ridiculous nonsensical book set out by Will. Pen [1] for the Quakers; but so full of nothing but nonsense, that I was ashamed to read in it.

13th. With my Lord Brouncker, and did get his ready assent to T. Hater's having of Mr. Turner's place, and so Sir J. Minnes's also: but, when we come to sit down at the Board, comes to us Mr. Wren this day to town, and tells me that James Southern do petition the Duke of York for the Storekeeper's place of Deptford, which did trouble me much, and also the Board, though, upon discourse after he was gone, we did resolve to move hard for our clerks, and that places of preferment may go according to seniority and merit. After doing some business I with Mr. Turner to the Duke of Albemarle's at night; and there did speak to him about his appearing to Mr. Wren as a friend to Mr. Turner, which he did take kindly from me; and so away thence, well pleased with what we had now done, and so I with him home, stopping at my Lord Brouncker's and getting his hand to a letter I wrote to the Duke of York for T. Hater. At my Lord Middleton's, to give him an

[1] Penn's first work, entitled 'Truth exalted, in a short but sure testimony against all those religions, faiths, and worships, that have been formed and followed, in the darkness of apostacy; and for that glorious light which is now risen, and shines forth, in the life and doctrine of the despised Quakers . . . by W. Penn, whom divine love constrains, in holy contempt, to trample on Egypt's glory, not fearing the King's wrath, having beheld the Majesty of Him who is invisible.'

account of what I had done this day with his man at Alderman
Backwell's, about the getting of his £1000 paid; and here he did
take occasion to discourse about the business of the Dutch war,
which, he says, he was always an enemy to; and did discourse well
of it, I saying little, but pleased to hear him talk and to see how
some men may by age come to know much, and yet by their
drinking and other pleasures render themselves not very considerable. I did this day find by discourse with somebody that
this nobleman was the great Major-General Middleton that was of
the Scots army in the beginning of the late war against the King.

14th. To White Hall, and there walked to St. James's, where I
find the Court mighty full, it being the Duke of York's birthday;
and he mighty fine, and all the music, one after another, to my
great content. Here I met with Sir H. Cholmley; and he and I to
walk, and to my Lord Berkeley's new house, there to see a new
experiment of a cart, which, by having two little wheels fastened
to the axle-tree, is said to make it go with half the ease and more,
than another cart; but we did not see the trial made. To St.
James's, and there met my brethren; but the Duke of York being
gone out, and tonight being a play there, and a great festival, we
would not stay, but went all of us to the King's playhouse, and
there saw 'The Faithful Shepherdess' again, that we might hear
the French eunuch sing, which we did, to our great content, though
I do admire his action as much as his singing, being both beyond
all I ever saw or heard.

15th. After dinner my wife and I and Deb. out by coach to the
upholsterer's in Long Lane, Alderman Reeves's, and then to
Alderman Crow's, to see variety of hangings, and were mightily
pleased therewith; and at last I think we shall pitch upon the best
suit of Apostles, where three pieces for my room will come to
almost £80. So home. This day at the Board comes unex-
pected the warrants from the Duke of York for Mr. Turner and
Hater, for the places they desire, which contents me mightily.

16th. I took my wife by coach, and Deb., and showed her Mr.
Wren's hangings and bed at St. James's, and Sir W. Coventry's
in the Pall Mall, for our satisfaction in what we are going to buy.
And so by Mr. Crow's, home, about his hangings, and do pitch
upon buying his second suit of Apostles—the whole suit, which
comes to £83; and this we think the best for us, having now the
whole suit, to answer any other rooms or service. With Mr.
Hater by water to St. James's: there Mr. Hater to give Mr. Wren

thanks for his kindness about his place that he hath lately granted him, of Petty Purveyor of petty missions, upon the removal of Mr. Turner to be Storekeeper at Deptford on the death of Harper. To my aunt Wight's, the first time, I think, these two years; and there mighty kindly used, and had a barrel of oysters, and so to look up and down their house, they having hung a room since I was there, but with hangings not fit to be seen with mine, which I find all come home tonight.

17th. Late home, and there with much pleasure getting Mr. Gibbs, that writes well, to write the name upon my new draft of the Resolution; and so set it up, and altered the situation of some of my pictures in my closet, to my extraordinary content. Mr. Moore and Seymour were with me this afternoon, who tell me that my Lord Sandwich was received mighty kindly by the King, and is in exceeding great esteem with him and the rest about him; but I doubt it will be hard for him to please both the King and the Duke of York, which I shall be sorry for.   Mr. Moore tells me the sad condition my Lord is in, in his estate and debts; and the way he now lives in, so high, and so many vain servants about him, that he must be ruined if he do not take up, which, by the grace of God, I will put him upon when I come to see him.

18th. With Lord Brouncker to Lincoln's Inn, and Mr. Ball, to visit Dr. Wilkins, now newly Bishop of Chester: and he received us mighty kindly, and had most excellent discourse from him about his Book of Real Character: and so I with Lord Brouncker to White Hall, and there saw the Queen and some ladies.

19th. With my wife and Deb. and Mr. Harman, the upholsterer, and carried them to take measure of Mr. Wren's bed in St. James's, I being resolved to have just such another made me.   To the Duke of York's playhouse, and there saw, the first time acted, 'The Queen of Aragon,' [1] an old Blackfriars' play, but an admirable one, so good that I am astonished at it, and wonder where it hath lain asleep all this while, that I have never heard of it before.   Here met W. Batelier and Mrs. Hunt, Deb.'s aunt; and saw her home—a very witty woman, and one that knows this play and understands a play mighty well.   Left at her home in Jewin Street, and we home and to supper; and my wife to read to me, and so to bed.

20th. This day a new girl came to us in the room of Nell, who is lately, about four days since, gone away, being grown lazy and

---

[1] A tragi-comedy by William Habington.   Upon its revival the prologue and epilogue were written by Butler, the author of *Hudibras*.

proud. This girl to stay only till we have a boy, which I intend to keep when I have a coach, which I am now about. At this time my wife and I mighty busy laying out money in dressing up our best chamber, and thinking of a coach and coachman and horses, &c.; and the more because of Creed's being now married to Mrs. Pickering, a thing I could never have expected, but it is done about seven or ten days since. I walked out to look for a coach, and saw many; and did light on one for which I bid £50, which do please me mightily.

21st. At noon to dinner to Mr. Batelier's, his mother coming this day a-housewarming to him, and several friends of his, to which he invited us. Here mighty merry, and his mother the same: I heretofore took her for a gentlewoman, and understanding. I rose from table before the rest, because under an obligation to go to my Lord Brouncker's, where to meet several gentlemen of the Royal Society, to go and make a visit to the French Ambassador, Colbert, at Leicester House, he having endeavoured to make one or two to my Lord Brouncker, as our President, but he was not within. But I came too late, they being gone before: so I followed to Leicester House; [1] but they are gone in and up before me. And so I away to the New Exchange, and there stayed for my wife, and she come, we to Cow Lane, and there I showed her the coach which I pitch on, and she is out of herself for joy almost. But the man not within, so did nothing more towards an agreement, but to Mr. Crow's about a bed, to have his advice. *Memorandum:* that from Crow's, we went back to Charing Cross, and there left my people at their tailor's, while I to my Lord Sandwich's lodgings, who came to town the last night, and is come thither to lie: and met with him within, and among others my new cousin Creed, who looks mighty soberly; and he and I saluted one another with mighty gravity, till we came to a little more freedom of talk about it. But here I hear that Sir Gilbert Pickering is lately dead, about three days since, which makes some sorrow there, though not much, because of his being long expected to die, having been in a lethargy long. So waited on my Lord to Court, and there stayed and saw the ladies awhile: and thence to my wife, and took them up; and so home, and to supper and bed.

22d. Up, and W. Batelier's Frenchman, a periwig-maker, comes and brings me a new one, which I liked and paid him for: a mighty genteel fellow. To Crow's, and there did see some more

[1] It occupied the north side of the present Leicester Square.

beds; and we shall, I think, pitch upon a camelott one when all is done. Thence to Arundel House, where the first time we [1] have met since the vacation, and not much company: but here much good discourse, and afterwards my Lord and others and I to the Devil tavern,[2] and there eat and drank, and so home by coach; and there found my uncle Wight and aunt, and Woolly and his wife, and there supped, and mighty merry. And anon they gone, and Mrs. Turner stayed, who was there also to talk of her husband's business; and the truth is, I was the less pleased to talk with her, for that she hath not yet owned, in any fit manner of thanks, my late and principal service to her husband about his place, which I alone ought to have been thanked for, if they know as much as I do. But let it go: if they do not own it, I shall have it in my hand to teach them to do it. This day word came for all the principal officers to bring the Commissioners of Accounts their patents, which I did in the afternoon by leaving it at their office, but am troubled at what should be their design therein.

23d. Up, and plasterers at work, and painters, about my house. To my Lord Sandwich's, where I find my Lord within, but busy, private; and so I stayed a little talking with the young gentlemen: and so away with Mr. Pierce, the surgeon, towards Tyburn, to see the people executed; but come too late, it being done—two men and a woman hanged. In the afternoon comes my cousin, Sidney Pickering,[3] to bring my wife and me his sister's favour for her wedding, which is kindly done. Pierce do tell me, among other news, the late frolic and debauchery of Sir Charles Sedley and Buckhurst, running up and down all the night, almost naked, through the streets; and at last fighting, and being beat up by the watch and clapped up all night. And how the King takes their parts, and my Lord Chief Justice Keeling hath laid the constable by the heels to answer it next Sessions, which is a horrid shame. How the King and these gentlemen did make the fiddlers of Thetford, this last progress, to sing them all the obscene songs they could think of. How Sir W. Coventry was brought the other day to the Duchess of York by the Duke, to kiss her hand, and did acknowledge his unhappiness to occasion her so much sorrow, declaring his intentions in it, and praying her pardon; which she did give him upon his promise to make good his pretences of innocence to her family by his faithfulness to his Master, the Duke of York. That the Duke of Buckingham is now all in all, and

[1] The Royal Society.   [2] In Fleet Street.   [3] Mrs. Creed's brother.

293

will ruin Coventry, if he can: and that Coventry do now rest wholly upon the Duke of York for his standing, which is a great turn. He tells me that my Lady Castlemaine, however, is a mortal enemy to the Duke of Buckingham, which I understand not; but, it seems, she is disgusted with his greatness and his ill usage of her. That the King was drunk at Saxham [1] with Sedley, Buckhurst, &c., the night that my Lord Arlington came thither, and would not give him audience, or could not: which is true, for it was the night that I was there, and saw the King go up to his chamber, and was told that the King had been drinking. He tells me, too, that the Duke of York did the next day chide Bab. May for his occasioning the King's giving himself up to these gentlemen, to the neglecting of my Lord Arlington: to which he answered merrily that there was no man in England that had a head to lose durst do what they do every day with the King, and asked the Duke of York's pardon: which is a sign of a mad world; God bless us out of it!

24th. This morning comes to me the coachmaker, and agreed with me for £53, and to stand to the courtesy of what more I should give him upon the finishing of the coach: he is likely, also, to fit me with a coachman. Lord Brouncker tells me that the making Sir J. Minnes a bare Commissioner [2] is now in doing, which I am glad of, but he speaks of two new Commissioners, which I do not believe.

25th. (Lord's day.) Up, and discoursing with my wife about our house and many new things we are doing of, and so to church I, and there find Jack Fenn come, and his wife, a pretty black woman: I never saw her before, nor took notice of her now. At night W. Batelier comes and sups with us; and after supper to have my head combed by Deb., which occasioned the greatest sorrow to me that ever I knew in this world; for my wife, coming up suddenly, did find me embracing the girl. I was at a wonderful loss upon it, and I endeavoured to put it off; but my wife was struck mute and grew angry, and, as her reason came to her, grew quite out of order: and I to say little, but to bed, and my wife said

---

[1] Saxham, near Bury St. Edmunds, then the seat of William Baron Crofts. 'My last told your Grace I was going into the country to pass my Christmas at my Lord Crofts'; and when I tell you that the Duke of Bucks and George Potter were there, you will not doubt but we passed it merrily.'—Lord Arlington to the Duke of Ormond, Oxford, 9th January 1666 (*Miscellanea Aulica*, p. 371).

[2] On his relinquishing his other office of Comptroller of the Navy.

little also, but could not sleep all night, but about two in the morning waked me and cried, and fell to tell me as a great secret that she was a Roman Catholic and had received the Holy Sacrament; which troubled me, but I took no notice of it, but she went on from one thing to another till at last it appeared plainly her trouble was at what she saw. But after her much crying and reproaching me with inconstancy, I did give her no provocation, but did promise all fair usage to her, and love, till at last she seemed to be at ease, and so toward morning a little sleep.

26th. I was obliged to attend the Duke of York, thinking to have had a meeting of Tangier today, but had not; but he did take me and Mr. Wren into his closet, and there did press me to prepare what I had to say upon the answers of my fellow officers to his great letter, which I promised to do against his coming to town again, the next week: and so to other discourse, finding plainly that he is in trouble, and apprehensions of the Reformers, and would be found to do what he can towards reforming, himself. And so thence to my Lord Sandwich's, where, after long stay, he being in talk with others privately, I to him; and there he, taking physic and keeping his chamber, I had an hour's talk with him about the ill posture of things at this time while the King gives countenance to Sir Charles Sedley and Lord Buckhurst. He tells me that he thinks his matters do stand well with the King, and hopes to have dispatch to his mind; but I doubt it, and do see that he do fear it, too. He told me of my Lady Carteret's trouble about my writing of that letter of the Duke of York's lately to the Office, which I did not own, but declared to be of no injury to Sir G. Carteret, and that I would write a letter to him to satisfy him therein. But this I am in pain how to do without doing myself wrong, and the end I had, of preparing a justification to myself hereafter, when the faults of the Navy come to be found out: however, I will do it in the best manner I can. Thence by coach home and to dinner, finding my wife mightily discontented. All the evening busy, and my wife full of trouble in her looks; and anon to bed, where about midnight she wakes me, and there falls foul of me again, and, upon her pressing me, I did offer to give her under my hand that I would never see Mrs. Pierce more nor Knipp, but did promise her particular demonstrations of my true love to her, owning some indiscretions in what I did, but that there was no harm in it. She at last, upon these promises, was quiet, and very kind we were, and so to sleep.

27th. This evening Mr. Spong come, and sat late with me, and first told me of the instrument called a parallelogram,[1] which I must have one of, showing me his practice thereon, by a map of England.

28th. By coach with Mr. Gibson to Chancery Lane, and there made oath before a Master in Chancery to my Tangier account of fees; and so to White Hall, where, by and by, a Committee met, my Lord Sandwich there, but his report was not received, it being late, but only a little business done about the supplying the place with victuals. But I did get, to my great content, my account allowed of fees, with great applause by my Lord Ashley and Sir W. Pen. Thence home, calling at one or two places; and there about our workmen, who are at work upon my wife's closet and other parts of my house, that we are all in dirt.

29th. Mr. Wren first tells us of the order from the King, come last night to the Duke of York, for signifying his pleasure to the Solicitor-General for drawing up a Commission for suspending of my Lord Anglesey,[2] and putting in Sir Thomas Littleton and Sir Thomas Osborne,[3] the former a creature of Arlington's, and the latter of the Duke of Buckingham's, during the suspension. The Duke of York was forced to obey, and did grant it, he being to go to Newmarket this day with the King, and so the King pressed for it. But Mr. Wren do own that the Duke of York is the most wounded in this, in the world, for it is done and concluded without his privity, after his appearing for Lord Anglesey, and that it is plain that they do aim to bring the Admiralty into Commission too, and lessen the Duke of York. This do put strange apprehensions into all our Board; only I think I am

[1] Now generally called pantograph. It is an instrument, by means of which persons having no skill in drawing may copy designs, prints, etc., in any proportion.

[2] See, in *Memoirs relating to the Navy*, 8vo, 1729, two warrants of 18th October 1668 and 20th October 1668, addressed by the Duke of York to Sir Heneage Finch, the Solicitor-General. The former directs him to prepare a warrant for his suspension, and the second to prepare a Bill for the royal signature, constituting and appointing Sir Thomas Osborne and Sir Thomas Littleton to the office of Treasurer of the Navy, hitherto filled by Lord Anglesey.

[3] Eldest son of Sir Edward Osborne, Bart.; made a Privy Councillor 1673, and soon after constituted Lord High Treasurer, and elected K.G. in 1677. He was created Baron Osborne of Kiveton and Viscount Latimer of Danby 1673, Earl of Danby 1674, Viscount Dunblaine, in Scotland, in 1675, Marquis of Carmarthen 1689, and Duke of Leeds 1694. *Ob.* 1712, *æt. suæ* 81.

the least troubled at it, for I care not at all for it, but my Lord Brouncker and Pen do seem to think much of it.

30th. Up betimes, and Mr. Povy comes to even accounts with me, which we did, and then fell to other talk. He tells, in short, how the King is made a child of by Buckingham and Arlington, to the lessening of the Duke of York, whom they cannot suffer to be great for fear of my Lord Chancellor's return, which, therefore, they make the King violent against. That he believes it is impossible these two great men can hold together long: or, at least, that the ambition of the former is so great, that he will endeavour to master all, and bring into play as many as he can. That Anglesey will not lose his place easily, but will contend in law with whoever comes to execute it. That the Duke of York, in all things but in his amours, is led by the nose by his wife. That Sir W. Coventry is now, by the Duke of York, made friends with the Duchess, and that he is often there, and waits on her. That he do believe that these present great men will break in time, and that Sir W. Coventry will be a great man again; for he do labour to have nothing to do in matters of the State, and is so useful to the side that he is on, that he will stand, though at present he is quite out of play. That my Lady Castlemaine hates the Duke of Buckingham. That the Duke of York hath expressed himself very kind to my Lord Sandwich, which I am mighty glad of. That we are to expect more changes if these men stand. This done, he and I to talk of my coach, and I got him to go see it, where he finds most infinite fault with it, both as to being out of fashion and heavy, with so good reason, that I am mightily glad of his having corrected me in it; and so I do resolve to have one of his build, and with his advice, both in coach and horses, he being the fittest man in the world for it.

31st. This day my Lord Anglesey was at the office, and do seem to make nothing of this business of his suspension, resolving to bring it into the Council, where he seems not to doubt to have right, he standing upon his defence and patent, and hath put in his caveats to the several Offices: so, as soon as the King comes back,[1] which will be on Tuesday next, he will bring it into the Council. Thus ends this month with some quiet to my mind after the greatest falling out with my poor wife, and through my folly, that ever I had; and I have reason to be sorry and ashamed of it, and more to be troubled for the poor girl's sake. This day Roger

---

[1] From Newmarket.

Pepys and his son Talbot, newly come to town, come and dined with me, and mighty glad I am to see them.

November 1st. (Lord's day.) This noon Mr. Povy sent his coach for my wife and I to see, which we like mightily, and will endeavour to have him get us just such another.

2d. Up, and a cold morning, by water through bridge without a cloak, and there to Mr. Wren at his chamber at White Hall, the first time of his coming thither this year, the Duchess coming thither tonight. To visit Creed at his chamber, but his wife not come thither yet, nor do he tell me where she is, though she be in town, at Stepney, at Atkins's.[1] To Mr. Povy's about a coach, but there I find my Lords Sandwich, Peterborough, and Hinching-broke, Charles Harbord, and Sidney Montagu; and there I was stopped, and dined mighty nobly at a good table, with one little dish at a time upon it, but mighty merry. I was glad to see it: but sorry, methought, to see my Lord have so little reason to be merry, and yet glad, for his sake, to have him cheerful. After dinner up, and looked up and down the house, and so to the cellar: and thence I slipped away without taking leave. This day I went, by Mr. Povy's direction, to a coach-maker near him, for a coach just like his, but it was sold this very morning.

3d. All the morning at the office. At noon to dinner, and then to the office busy till twelve at night, without much pain to my eyes; but I did not use them to read or write, and so held out very well. So home, and there to supper; and I observed my wife to eye my eyes, whether I did ever look upon Deb., which I could not but do now and then. And my wife did tell me in bed, by the by, of my looking on other people, and that the only way is to put things out of sight; and this I know she means by Deb., for she tells me her aunt was here on Monday, and she did tell her of her desire of parting with Deb., but in such kind terms on both sides, that my wife is mightily taken with it. I see it will be, and it is but necessary; and therefore, though it cannot but grieve me, yet I must bring my mind to give way to it. We had a great deal of do this day at the office about Clutterbuck, I declaring my dissent against the whole Board's proceedings, and I believe I shall go near to show W. Pen a very knave in it, whatever I find my Lord Brouncker.

4th. To White Hall; and there I find the King and Duke of York came the last night, and everybody's mouth full of my Lord

[1] Colonel Atkins.

298

Anglesey's suspension being sealed, which it was, it seems, yesterday; so that he is prevented in his remedy at the Council. And, it seems, the two new Treasurers did kiss the King's hand this morning, brought in by my Lord Arlington. They walked up and down together in the Court this day, and several people joyed them; but I avoided it, that I might not be seen to look either way. This day also I hear that my Lord Ormond is to be declared in Council no more Deputy Governor of Ireland, his commission being expired: and the King is prevailed with to take it out of his hands; which people do mightily admire, saying that he is the greatest subject of any prince in Christendom, and hath more acres of land than any, and hath done more for his Prince than ever any yet did. But all will not do; he must down, it seems, the Duke of Buckingham carrying all before him. But that that troubles me most is that they begin to talk that the Duke of York's regiment is ordered to be disbanded; and more, that undoubtedly his Admiralty will follow: which do shake me mightily, and I fear will have ill consequences in the nation, for these counsels are very mad. The Duke of York do, by all men's report, carry himself wonderful submissive to the King, in the most humble manner in the world: but yet, it seems, nothing must be spared that tends to the keeping out the Chancellor, and that is the reason of all this. The great discourse now is that the Parliament shall be dissolved and another called, which shall give the King the Dean and Chapter lands; and that will put him out of debt. And it is said that Buckingham do knowingly meet daily with Wildman and other Commonwealthmen; and that when he is with them he makes the King believe that he is with his wenches; and something looks like the Parliament's being dissolved, by Harry Brouncker's being now come back and appearing this day the first time at White Hall; but he hath not been yet with the King, but is secure that he shall be well received, I hear. God bless us, when such men as he shall be restored! But that that pleases me most is, that several do tell me that Pen is to be removed, and others that he hath resigned his place; and particularly Spragg tells me for certain that he hath resigned it, and is become a partner with Gauden in the Victualling: in which I think he hath done a very cunning thing. But I am sure I am glad of it, and it will be well for the King to have him out of this Office. Sir John Talbot talks mighty high for my Lord of Ormond, and I perceive this family of the Talbots hath been raised by my Lord. This evening my wife and I talking of our being put out of the Office, and my going to live at Deptford at her brother's, till I can clear accounts and rid my hands of the town, which will take me a year or more; and I do think it will be best for me to do so, in order to our living cheap and out of sight.

5th. The Duke of York did call me and Mr. Wren; and my paper, that I have lately taken pains to draw up, was read, and the Duke of York pleased therewith; and we did all along conclude upon answers to my mind for the Board, and that which, if put in execution, will do the King's business. But I do now more and more perceive the Duke of York's trouble, and that he do lie under great weight of mind from the Duke of Buckingham's carrying things against him; and particularly when I advised that he would use his interest that a seaman might come into the room of Sir W. Pen (who is now declared to be gone from us to that of the Victualling), and did show how the Office would now be left without one seaman in it, but the Surveyor and the Comptroller, who is so old as to be able to do nothing, he told me plainly that I knew his mind well enough as to seamen, but that it must be as others will. And Wren did tell it me, as a secret, that when the Duke of York did first tell the King about Sir W. Pen's leaving of the place, and did move the King that either Captain Cox or Sir Jer. Smith might succeed him, the King did tell him that was a matter fit to be considered of, and would not agree to either presently: and so the Duke of York could not prevail for either, nor knows who it shall be. The Duke did tell me himself that if he had not carried it privately when first he mentioned Pen's leaving his place to the King, it had not been done; for the Duke of Buckingham and those of his party do cry out upon it, as a strange thing to trust such a thing into the hands of one that stands accused in Parliament: and that they have so far prevailed upon the King that he would not have him named in the Council, but only take his name to the Board. But I think he said that only D. Gauden's name shall go in the patent; at least, at the time when Sir Richard Browne[1] asked the King the names of D. Gauden's security, the King told him it was not yet necessary for him to declare them. And by and by, when the Duke of York and we had done, Wren brought into the closet Captain Cox and James Temple about business of the Guinea Company; and talking something of the Duke of Buckingham's concernment therein, says the Duke of York, 'I shall give the Devil his due, as they say, the Duke of

[1] As Clerk of the Council.

Buckingham hath paid in his money to the Company,' or something of that kind, wherein he would do right to him. The Duke of York told me how these people do begin to cast dirt upon the business that passed the Council lately, touching Supernumeraries, as passed by virtue of his authority there, there being not liberty for any man to withstand what the Duke of York advises there; which, he told me, they bring only as an argument to insinuate the putting of the Admiralty into Commission, which by all men's discourse is now designed, and I perceive the same by him. This being done, and going from him, I up and down the house to hear news: and there everybody's mouth full of changes; and, among others, the Duke of York's regiment of Guards, that was raised during the late war at sea, is to be disbanded: and also that this day the King do intend to declare that the Duke of Ormond is no more Deputy of Ireland, but that he will put it into Commission. This day our new Treasurers did kiss the King's hand, who complimented them, as they say, very highly—that he had for a long time been abused in his Treasurer and that he was now safe in their hands. I saw them walk up and down the Court together all this morning; the first time I ever saw Osborne, who is a comely gentleman. This day I was told that my Lord Anglesey did deliver a petition on Wednesday in Council to the King, laying open that whereas he had heard that his Majesty had made such a disposal of his place, which he had formerly granted him for life upon a valuable consideration, and that without anything laid to his charge and during a Parliament's sessions, he prayed that his Majesty would be pleased to let his case be heard before the Council and the Judges of the land, who were his proper counsel in all matters of right. To which, I am told, the King, after my Lord's being withdrawn, concluded upon his giving him an answer some few days hence; and so he was called in and told so. At the Treasurer's, Sir Thomas Clifford, where I did eat some oysters; which while we were at, in comes my Lord Keeper and much company; and so I thought it best to withdraw. And so away, and to the Swede's Agent's,[1] and there met Mr. Povy, where the Agent would have me stay and dine, there being only them and Joseph Williamson and Sir Thomas Clayton;[2] but what he is I know not.

---

[1] Sir J. B. Leyenburg.

[2] Thomas Clayton, M.D., Professor of Physic, and Anatomy Lecturer at Oxford, for which university he was returned to serve in Parliament in 1660, and afterwards knighted, and made warden of Merton College.

Here much extraordinary noble discourse of foreign princes, and particularly the greatness of the King of France, and of his being fallen into the right way of making the kingdom great. I was mightily pleased with this company and their discourse. With Mr. Povy spent all the afternoon going up and down among the coachmakers in Cow Lane, and did see several, and at last did pitch upon a little chariot, whose body was framed but not covered, at the widow's that made Mr. Lowther's fine coach; and we are mightily pleased with it, it being light, and will be very genteel and sober: to be covered with leather, but yet will hold four. Being much satisfied with this, I carried him to White Hall. Home, where I give my wife a good account of my day's work.

6th. Up, and presently my wife up with me, which she professedly now do every day to dress me, that I may not see Willett, and, do I move, whether I cast my eye upon her. To see Roger Pepys at his lodgings, next door to Arundel House, a barber's; and there I did see a book which my Lord Sandwich hath promised one to me of, 'A Description of the Escorial in Spain';[1] which I have a great desire to have, though I took it for a finer book when he promised it me. Home, with my mind troubled and finding no content, my wife being still troubled.

7th. This afternoon I did go out towards Sir D. Gauden's, thinking to have bespoke a place for my coach and horses, when I have them, at the Victualling Office; but find the way so bad and long that I returned, and looked up and down for places elsewhere, in an inn, which I hope to get with more convenience than there.

8th. (Lord's day.) Up, and at my chamber all the morning, setting my papers to rights, with my boy; and so to dinner at noon.

[1] The book alluded to by Pepys is that of the Father Francisco de los Santos, first printed at Madrid in 1657, and entitled *Descripcion breve del Monasterio de S. Lorenzo el Real del Escorial, unica maravilla del mundo.* It is in folio, and has some plates; but Pepys might well express his disappointment, for the appearance of the volume does not answer to the magnificence of the subject. About the time when Pepys wrote, or soon after, the Escorial received some damage by fire, and was even said to be totally destroyed; and in that belief, an abstract of Father Francisco's work was published in 1671, purporting to be 'translated into English by a servant of the Earl of Sandwich.' That a great amount of damage was really done, is proved by the title of the third edition of the work, printed in Madrid in 1681, which says that the Escorial was rebuilt, after the fire, by Charles II; and Santos, then alive, asserts the same, in his dedication to that king, comparing him to the restorers of Solomon's Temple.

9th. The Duke of York told me that Sir W. Pen had been with him this morning, to ask whether it would be fit for him to sit at the office now, because of his resolution to be gone and to become concerned in the Victualling. The Duke of York answered, 'Yes, till his contract was signed.' Thence I to Lord Sandwich's, and there to see him; but was made to stay very long, as his best friends are, and when I came to him had little pleasure, his head being full of his own business, I think. Thence to White Hall with him, to a Committee of Tangier: a day appointed for him to give an account of Tangier, and what he did and found there, which, though he had admirable matter for it, and his doings there were good and would have afforded a noble account, yet he did it with a mind so low and mean, and delivered in so poor a manner, that it appeared nothing at all, nor anybody seemed to value it; whereas, he might have shown himself to have merited extraordinary thanks, and been held to have done a very great service; whereas now, all that cost the King hath been at for his journey through Spain thither seems to be almost lost. After we were up Creed and I walked together, and did talk a good while of the weak report my Lord made, and were troubled for it, I fearing that either his mind and judgment are depressed, or that he do it out of his great neglect, and so that he do all the rest of his affairs accordingly. I stayed about the Court a little while, and then to look for a dinner and had it at Hercules' Pillars, very late, all alone, costing me 10d.

11th. To the office, where, by a special desire, the new Treasurers came, and there did show their Patent, and the Great Seal for the suspension of my Lord Anglesey; and here did sit and discourse of the business of the Office; and brought Mr. Hutchinson with them, who, I hear, is to be their Paymaster, in the room of Mr. Waith. For it seems they do turn out every servant that belongs to the present Treasurer: and so for Fenn do bring in Mr. Littleton, Sir Thomas's brother, and oust all the rest. But Mr. Hutchinson do already see that his work now will be another kind of thing than before, as to the trouble of it. They gone (and indeed they appear, both of them, very intelligent men), I home to dinner. Then by coach to my cousin Roger Pepys, who did, at my last being with him this day se'nnight, move me as to the supplying him with £500 this term, and £500 the next, for two years, upon a mortgage (he having that sum to pay, a debt left him by his father), which I did agree to, trusting to his honesty and ability, and am resolved to do it for him, that I may not have all I have lie in the King's hands.

12th. Up, and my wife with me as heretofore, and so I to the office, and at noon to dinner, and Mr. Wayth with me. So having dined we parted, and to my wife and to sit with her a little, and then called her and Willett to my chamber and there did, with tears in my eyes (which I could not help), discharge her and advise her to be gone as soon as she could, and never to see me, or let me see her, more; which she took with tears too. Thence, parting kindly with my wife, I away by coach to my cousin Roger, according as by mistake, which the trouble of my mind for some days has occasioned, is set down in yesterday's notes. And so back again, and with Mr. Gibson late at my chamber, making an end of my draft of a letter for the Duke of York, in answer to the answers of this Office, which I have now done to my mind, so as, if the Duke likes it, will, I think, put an end to a great deal of the faults of this Office, as well as my trouble for them. So to bed.

13th. Up, and with Sir W. Pen by coach to White Hall, where to the Duke of York, and there did our usual business; and thence I to the Commissioners of the Treasury, where I stayed, and heard an excellent case argued between my Lord Gerard and the Town of Newcastle, about a piece of ground which that Lord hath got a grant of under the Exchequer Seal, which they were endeavouring to get of the King under the Great Seal. I liked mightily the Counsel for the town, Shafto,[1] their Recorder, and Mr. Offly. But I was troubled, and so were the Lords, to hear my Lord fly out against their great pretence of merit from the King, for their sufferings and loyalty; telling them that they might thank him for that repute which they have for their loyalty, for that it was he that forced them to be so, against their wills, when he was there: and, moreover, did offer a paper to the Lords to read from the Town, sent in 1648; but the Lords would not read it, but I believe it was something about bringing the King to trial, or some such thing, in that year. Thence I to the Three Tuns tavern, by Charing Cross, and there dined with W. Pen, Sir J. Minnes, and Commissioner Middleton; and as merry as my mind could be, that hath so much trouble upon it. And thence to White Hall, and there stayed in Mr. Wren's chamber with him, reading over my draft of

---

[1] Robert Shafto, knighted 26th June 1670. He died in 1704, and was buried in St. Nicholas's Church, Newcastle. He married Katharine, daughter and coheir of Sir Thomas Widrington, of the Grange, Yorkshire.

a letter, which Mr. Gibson then attended me with; and there he did like all, but doubted whether it would be necessary for the Duke to write in so sharp a style to the Office as I had drawn it in; which I yield to him, to consider the present posture of the times and the Duke of York, and whether it were not better to err on that hand than the other.   He told me that he did not think it was necessary for the Duke of York to do so, and that it would not suit so well with his nature nor greatness; which last, perhaps, is true, but then do too truly show the effects of having Princes in places where order and discipline should be.   I left it to him to do as the Duke of York pleases, and so fell to other talk, and with great freedom, of public things; and he told me, upon my several inquiries to that purpose, that he did believe it was not yet resolved whether the Parliament should ever meet more or no, the three great rulers of things now standing thus: The Duke of Buckingham is absolutely against their meeting, as moved thereto by his people that he advises with, the people of the late times, who do never expect to have anything done by this Parliament for their religion, and who do propose that by the sale of the Church lands they shall be able to put the King out of debt.   My Lord Keeper is utterly against putting away this and choosing another Parliament, lest they prove worse than this, and will make all the King's friends and the King himself in a desperate condition.   My Lord Arlington knows not which is best for him, being to seek whether this or the next will use him worst.   He tells me that he believes that it is intended to call this Parliament, and try them for a sum of money; and, if they do not like it, then to send them going, and call another, who will, at the ruin of the Church perhaps, please the King with what he will have for a time.   And he tells me, therefore, that he do believe that this policy will be endeavoured by the Church and their friends—to seem to promise the King money when it shall be propounded, but make the King and these great men buy it dear before they have it.   He tells me that he is really persuaded that the design of the Duke of Buckingham is by bringing the state into such a condition as, if the King do die without issue, it shall, upon his death, break into pieces again; and so put by the Duke of York, whom they have disobliged, they know, to that degree, as to despair of his pardon.   He tells me that there is no way to rule the King but by briskness, which the Duke of Buckingham hath above all men; and that the Duke of York having it not, his best way is what he practises, that is to say, a good temper, which will support him till the Duke of Buckingham and Lord Arlington fall out, which cannot be long first, the former knowing that the latter did, in the time of the Chancellor, endeavour with the Chancellor to hang him at that time when he was proclaimed against. And here, by the by, he told me that the Duke of Buckingham did, by his friends, treat with my Lord Chancellor, by the mediation of Matt. Wren and Clifford, to fall in with my Lord Chancellor; which, he tells me, he did advise my Lord Chancellor to accept of, as that that, with his own interest and the Duke of York's, would undoubtedly have secured all to him and his family; but that my Lord Chancellor was a man not to be advised, thinking himself too high to be counselled: and so all is come to nothing; for by that means the Duke of Buckingham became desperate, and was forced to fall in with Arlington, to the Chancellor's ruin. Thence I home, and there to talk with great pleasure all the evening with my wife, who tells me that Deb. has been abroad today and says she has got a place to go to, so as she will be gone tomorrow morning. My wife told me she would not have me to see her or give her her wages; and so I did give my wife £10 for her year and half a quarter's wages. And so to bed, and there, blessed be God! we did sleep well and with peace, which I had not done in now almost twenty nights together. This morning, at the Treasury-chamber, I did meet Jack Fenn, and there he did show me my Lord Anglesey's petition and the King's answer: the former good and stout, as I before did hear it, but the latter short and weak, saying that he was not, by what the King had done, hindered from taking the benefit of the law, and that the reason he had to suspect his mismanagement of his money in Ireland, did make him think it unfit to trust him with his Treasury in England, till he was satisfied in the former.

14th. Up, and my wife rose presently, and would not let me be out of her sight, and went down before me into the kitchen, and came up and told me she was in the kitchen, and therefore would have me go round the other way. Which she repeating, and I vexed at it, answered her a little angrily: upon which she instantly flew into a rage, calling me dog and rogue, and that I had a rotten heart. All which, knowing that I deserved it, I bore with, and word being brought presently up that she was gone away by coach with her things, my wife was friends, and so all quiet. And I to the office with my heart sad, and troubled to see how my wife is by this means likely for ever to have her hand over me, that I shall ever be a slave to her—that is to say, only in matters of pleasure; but in other things she will make it her business, I know, to please me and to keep me right to her, which I will labour to be, indeed, for she deserves it of me. At the office all the morning, and merry at noon, at dinner; and after dinner to the office, where all the afternoon, doing much business, late.

15th. (Lord's day.) After dinner, W. Howe to tell me what hath happened between him and the Commissioners of late, who are hot again, more than ever, about my Lord Sandwich's business of prizes; which I am troubled for, and the more because of the great security and neglect with which, I think, my Lord do look upon this matter, that may yet, for aught I know, undo him. I in the evening to my office again to make an end of my journal, and so to supper and to bed with my mind pretty quiet.

16th. I did call at Martin's, my bookseller's, and there bought 'Cassandra,' [1] and some other French books for my wife's closet, and so home, having eat nothing but two pennyworths of oysters, opened for me by a woman in the Strand.

17th. To the office all the morning, where the new Treasurers come, their second time, and before they sat down did discourse with the Board, and particularly my Lord Brouncker, about their place, [2] which they challenge, as having been heretofore due and given to their predecessor; which, at last, my Lord did own hath been given him only out of courtesy to his quality, and that he did not take it as of right at the Board: so they, for the present, sat down, and did give him the place, but, I think, with an intent to have the Duke of York's directions about it. My wife and maids busy now, to make clean the house above stairs, the upholsterers having done there, in her closet and the blue room, and they are mighty pretty.

19th. At the office all the morning. At noon, running upstairs to see the upholsterers, who are at work upon hanging my best room and setting up my new bed, I found my wife sitting sad in the dining-room: which enquiring into the reason of, she begun to call me all the false, rotten-hearted rogues in the world, letting me understand that I was with Deb. yesterday, which, thinking it impossible ever for her to understand, I did for a while deny; but

---

[1] A romance by Gualtier de Costes, Seigneur de la Calprenède. It had been recently translated into English by Sir Charles Cotterell, noticed 8th September 1667.

[2] i.e. precedence.

at last, for the ease of my mind and hers, and for ever to discharge my heart of this wicked business, I did confess all, and I did endure the sorrow of her threats and vows and curses all the afternoon. And, what was worse, she swore by all that was good that she would be gone herself this very night from me, and did there demand three or four hundred pounds of me to buy my peace, or else protested that she would make all the world know of it.   So with most perfect confusion of face and heart, and sorrow and shame, and the greatest agony in the world, I did pass this afternoon, fearing that it will never have an end.   But at last I did call for W. Hewer, who I was forced to make privy now to all; and the poor fellow did cry like a child and obtained what I could not, that she would be pacified upon condition that I would give it under my hand never to see or speak with Deb. while I live, as I did before with Pierce and Knipp.   So before it was late, there was, beyond my hopes as well as desert, a durable peace: and so to supper, and pretty kind words, and so with some rest spent the night in bed, being most absolutely resolved, if ever I can master this bout, never to give her occasion while I live of more trouble of this or any other kind, there being no curse in the world so great as this of the differences between myself and her.   And therefore I do, by the grace of God, promise never to offend her more; and did this night begin to pray to God upon my knees alone in my chamber, which God knows I cannot yet do heartily; but I hope God will give me the grace more and more every day to fear Him and to be true to my poor wife.

20th.   This morning up with mighty kind words between my poor wife and I.   And so to White Hall by water, W. Hewer with me, who is to go with me everywhere until my wife be in condition to go out along with me herself; for she do plainly declare that she dare not trust me out alone, and therefore made it a piece of our league that I should alway take somebody with me, or her herself, which I am mighty willing to do, being, by the grace of God, never to do her wrong more.   We landed at the Temple, and then I did bid him call at my cousin Roger Pepys's lodgings; and so to White Hall, in my way I telling him plainly and truly my resolutions, if I can get over this evil, never to give new occasion for it. He is, I think, so honest and true a servant to us both, and one that loves us, that I was not much troubled at his being privy to all this, but rejoiced in my heart that I had him to assist in the making us friends, which he did truly and heartily and with good

success. At White Hall with the Duke of York, doing our
ordinary business with him, here being also, the first time, the new
Treasurers. And so I took him into St. James's Park, and there
I did enter into more talk about my wife and myself: and he did
give me great assurance of several particular cases to which my
wife had from time to time made him privy of her loyalty and
truth to me after many and great temptations; and I believe them
truly. I did also discourse the unfitness of my leaving of my
employment now in many respects to go into the country, as my
wife desires; but that I would labour to fit myself for it, which he
thoroughly understands and do agree with me in it. And so,
hoping to get over this trouble, we about our business to Westminster Hall to meet Roger Pepys, which I did, and did there discourse of the business of lending him £500 to answer some occasions of his, which I believe to be safe enough. And away by
coach home, calling on my coachmaker by the way, where I like
my little coach mightily. But when I came home, hoping for a
further degree of peace and quiet, I found my wife upon her bed
in a horrible rage afresh, calling me all the bitter names: and,
rising, did fall to revile me in the bitterest manner in the world,
and could not refrain to strike me and pull my hair, which I
resolved to bear with, and had good reason to bear it. So I by
silence and weeping did prevail with her a little to be quiet, and she
would not eat her dinner without me. But yet by and by into a
raging fit she fell again, worse than before, that she would slit the
girl's nose: and at last W. Hewer came in and came up, who did
allay her fury, I flinging myself in a sad, desperate condition upon
the bed in the blue room, and there lay while they spoke together.
And at last it came to this, that if I would write to Deb. that I
hated her and would never see her more, she would believe me and
trust in me; which I did agree to. So from that minute my wife
begun to be kind to me, and we to kiss and be friends, and so continued all the evening, and fell to talk of other matters with great
comfort. This evening comes Mr. Billup to me, to read over
Mr. Wren's alterations of my draft of a letter for the Duke of
York to sign to the Board; which I like mighty well, they being
not considerable, only in mollifying some hard terms which I had
thought fit to put in. From this to other discourse; and do find
that the Duke of York and his master, Mr. Wren, do look upon
this service of mine as a very seasonable service to the Duke,
as that which he will have to show to his enemies in his own

justification, of his care of the King's business. And I am sure
I am heartily glad of it, both for the King's sake and the
Duke of York's, and my own also; for, if I continue here, my
work by this means will be the less, and my share in the blame
also.

21st. At the office all the morning; and after dinner abroad with
W. Hewer to my Lord Ashley's, where my Lord Berkeley and
Sir Thomas Ingram met upon Mr. Povy's account, where I was
in great pain about that part of his account wherein I am concerned, above £150, I think; and Creed hath declared himself
dissatisfied with it, so far as to desire to cut his *Examinatur* out
of the paper, as the only condition in which he would be silent
in it. This Povy had the wit to yield to; and so, when it come to
be enquired into, I did avouch the truth of the account as to that
particular, of my own knowledge, and so it went over as a thing
good and just—as, indeed, in the bottom of it, it is; though in
strictness, perhaps, it would not so well be understood. The
Committee rising, I, with my mind much satisfied herein, away
by coach home, setting Creed into Southampton Buildings, and so
home; and there ended my letters, and then home to my wife,
where I find my house clean now, from top to bottom, so as I have
not seen it many a day, and to the full satisfaction of my mind that
I am now at peace as to my poor wife, as to the dirtiness of my
house, and as to seeing an end, in a great measure, to my present
great disbursements upon my house and coach and horses.

22d. (Lord's day.) My wife and I lay long, with mighty content;
and so rose, and she spent the whole day making herself clean, after
four or five weeks being in continued dirt; and I knocking up nails
and making little settlements in my house till noon, and then eat a
bit of meat in the kitchen, I all alone. And so to the office, to set
down my journal, for some days leaving it imperfect, the matter
being mighty grievous to me, and my mind, from the nature of it;
and so in, to solace myself with my wife, whom I got to read to me,
and so W. Hewer, and the boy; and so, after supper, to bed. This
day my boy's livery is come home, the first I ever had, of green
lined with red, and it likes me well enough.

23d. Up, and called upon by W. Howe, who went, with W.
Hewer with me, by water to the Temple; his business was to have
my advice about a place he is going to buy—the Clerk of the
Patent's place, which I understand not, and so could say little to
him. To visit my Lord Sandwich, who is now so reserved, or

moped rather, I think, with his own business, that he bids welcome
to no man, I think, to his satisfaction. However, I bear with it,
being willing to give him as little trouble as I can, and to receive
as little from him, wishing only that I had my money in my purse,
that I have lent him; but, however, I show no discontent at all.
I met with Mr. Povy, who tells me that this discourse which I told
him of, of the Duke of Monmouth being made Prince of Wales,
hath nothing in it; though he thinks there are all the endeavours
used in the world to overthrow the Duke of York. He would
not have me doubt of my safety in the Navy, which I am doubtful
of from the reports of a general removal; but he will endeavour to
inform me what he can gather from my Lord Arlington. That he
do think that the Duke of Buckingham hath a mind rather to overthrow all the Kingdom and bring in a Commonwealth, wherein he
may think to be General of their Army, or to make himself King,
which, he believes, he may be led to by some advice he hath had
with conjurers, which he do affect. Thence with W. Hewer, who
goes up and down with me like a gaoler, but yet with great love
and to my great good liking, it being my desire above all things
to please my wife therein. I took my wife and boy to Hercules'
Pillars, and there dined, and thence to our upholsterer's, about some
things more to buy; and so to see our coach, and so to the looking-
glass man's by the New Exchange, and so to buy a picture for our
blue chamber chimney, and so home; and there I made my boy to
read to me most of the night, to get through the Life of the Archbishop of Canterbury. At supper comes Mary Batelier, and with
us all the evening, prettily talking, and very innocent company
she is; and she gone, we with much content to bed, and to sleep,
with mighty rest all night.

24th. Up, and at the office all the morning, and at noon home
to dinner, where Mr. Gentleman, the cook, and an old woman, his
third or fourth wife, come and dined with us, to enquire about a
ticket of his son's, that is dead; and after dinner, I with Mr. Hosier
to my closet, to discourse of the business of balancing Storekeepers' accounts, which he hath taken great pains in reducing to
a method to my great satisfaction, and I shall be glad, for both the
King's sake and his, that the thing may be put in practice, and will
do my part to promote it. That done, he gone, I to the office,
where busy till night; and then with comfort to sit with my wife,
and get her to read to me, and so to supper, and to bed with my
mind at mighty ease.

25th. By coach with W. Hewer to see Sir W. Coventry; but he gone out, I to White Hall, and there waited on Lord Sandwich, which I have little encouragement to do, because of the difficulty of seeing him and the little he hath to say to me when I do see him, or to anybody else but his own idle people about him, Sir Charles Harbord, &c.   Thence walked with him to White Hall, where to the Duke of York; and there the Duke and Wren and I by appointment in his closet, to read over our letter to the Office, which he heard, and signed it, and it is to my mind, Mr. Wren having made it somewhat sweeter to the Board, and yet with all the advice fully, that I did draw it up with.   The Duke said little more to us now, his head being full of other business; but I do see that he do continue to put a value upon my advice.   And so Mr. Wren and I to his chamber, and there talked: and he seems to hope that these people, the Duke of Buckingham and Arlington, will run themselves off of their legs, they being forced to be always putting the King upon one idle thing or other, against the easiness of his nature, which he will never be able to bear nor they to keep him to, and so will lose themselves.   And, for instance of their little progress, he tells me that my Lord of Ormond is like yet to carry it, and to continue in his command in Ireland; at least, they cannot get the better of him yet.   But he tells me that the Keeper [1] is wrought upon, as they say, to give his opinion for the dissolving of the Parliament, which, he thinks, will undo him in the eyes of the people.   He do not seem to own the hearing or fearing of anything to be done in the Admiralty to the lessening of the Duke of York, though he hears now the town-talk is full of it.   Thence I by coach home, and there find my cousin Roger come to dine with me, and to seal his mortgage for the £500 I lend him; but he and I first walked to the 'Change, there to look for my uncle Wight, and get him to dinner with us.   So home, buying a barrel of oysters at my old oyster-woman's in Gracious Street, but over the way to where she kept her shop before.   Merry at dinner; and the money not being ready, I carried Roger Pepys to Holborn Conduit, and there left him going to Stradwick's,[2] whom we avoided to see, because of our long absence, and my wife and I to the Duke of York's House, to see 'The Duchess of Malfi,' a sorry play, and sat with little pleasure for fear of my wife's seeing me look about; and so I was uneasy all the while.   This evening, to my

[1] Lord Keeper, Sir Orlando Bridgeman.
[2] Pepys's cousin, Thomas Stradwick.

great content, I got Sir Richard Ford to give me leave to set my coach in his yard.

26th. At the office all the morning, where I was to have delivered the Duke of York's letter of advice to the Board, in answer to our several answers to his great letter; but Lord Brouncker not being there, and doubtful to deliver it before the New Treasurer, I forbore it till the next sitting. So home at noon to dinner, where I find Mr. Pierce and his wife: but I was forced to show very little pleasure in her being there, because of my vow to my wife, and therefore was glad of a very bad occasion for my being really troubled, which is, at W. Hewer's losing of a tally of £1000, which I sent him this day to receive of the Commissioners of Excise.

27th. Up, and with W. Hewer to see Sir W. Coventry, but missed him again by coming too late, the man of all the world that I am resolved to preserve an interest in. Thence to White Hall, and there at our usual waiting on the Duke of York; and, that being done, I away to the Exchequer to give a stop and take some advice about my lost tally, wherein I shall have some remedy, with trouble. So home, and there find Mr. Povy by appointment to dine with me; and much pleasant discourse with him, and some serious: and he tells me that he would, by all means, have me get to be a Parliament-man the next Parliament. By and by comes my cousin Roger, and dines with us, and after dinner did seal his mortgage, wherein I do wholly rely on his honesty, not having so much as read over what he hath given me for it, nor minded it, but do trust to his integrity therein.

28th. All the morning at the office, where, while I was sitting, one comes and tells me that my coach is come. So I was forced to go out, and to Sir Richard Ford's, where I spoke to him, and he is very willing to have it brought in and stand there; and so I ordered it, to my great content, it being mighty pretty, only the horses do not please me, and therefore resolve to have better. This day I presented to the Board the Duke of York's letter, which, I perceive, troubled Sir W. Pen, he declaring himself meant in that part that concerned excuse by sickness; but I do not care, but am mightily glad that it is done, and now I shall begin to be at pretty good ease in the Office. This morning, to my great content, W. Hewer tells me that a porter is come, who found my tally in Holborn, and brings it him, for which he gives him 20s.

29th. (Lord's day.) Lay long in bed with pleasure with my wife, with whom I have now a great deal of content; and my mind is in other things also mightily more at ease, and I do mind my business better than ever and am more at peace, and trust in God I shall ever be so, though I cannot yet get my mind off from thinking now and then of Deb. But I do, ever since my promise a while since to my wife, pray to God by myself in my chamber every night, and will endeavour to get my wife to do the like with me ere long. But am much in fear of what she has lately frighted me about her being a Catholic; and I dare not, therefore, move her to go to church, for fear she should deny me; but this morning, of her own accord, she spoke of going to church the next Sunday, which pleases me mightily. This morning my coachman's clothes come home, and I like the livery mightily. All the morning in my chamber, and dined with my wife, and got her to read to me in the afternoon till Sir W. Warren, by appointment, comes to me, who spent two hours, or three, with me, about his accounts of Gothenburg,[1] which are so confounded, I doubt they will hardly ever pass without my doing something, which he desires of me, and which, partly from fear and partly from unwillingness to wrong the King and partly from its being of no profit to me, I am backward to give way to, though the poor man do indeed deserve to be rid of this trouble that he hath lain so long under from the negligence of this Board. He tells me, as soon as he saw my coach yesterday, he wished that the owner might not contract envy by it;[2] but I told him it was now manifestly for my profit to keep a coach, and that, after employments like mine for eight years, it were hard if I could not be thought to be justly able to do that. To supper, and so my wife to read, and made an end of the Life of Archbishop Laud, which is worth reading, as informing a

[1] Probably for timber.
[2] Though Pepys prided himself not a little upon becoming possessed of a carriage, the acquisition was regarded with envy and jealousy by his enemies, as will appear by the following extract from the scurrilous pamphlet in which Pepys and Hewer are severely handled. 'There is one thing more you must be mighty sorry for with all speed. Your presumption in your coach, in which you daily ride, as if you had been son and heir to the great Emperor Neptune, or as if you had been infallibly to have succeeded him in his Government of the Ocean, all which was presumption in the highest degree. First you had upon the fore part of your chariot, tempestuous waves and wrecks of ships; on your left hand, forts and great guns, and ships a fighting; on your right hand was a fair harbour and galleys riding, with their flags and pennants spread, kindly saluting each other, just like P[epys] and H[ewer]. Behind it were high curled waves and ships a sinking, and here and there an appearance of some bits of land.'

man plainly in the posture of the Church, and how the things of it were managed with the same self-interest and design that every other thing is, and have succeeded accordingly.

30th. With W. Hewer, who is my guard, to White Hall, to a Committee of Tangier, where the business of Mr. Lanyon took up all the morning; and, poor man! he did manage his business with so much folly, and ill fortune to boot, that the Board, before his coming in inclining of their own accord to lay his cause aside and leave it to the law, he pressed that we would hear it, and it ended to the making him appear a very knave, as well as it did to me a fool also, which I was sorry for. Thence by water, Mr. Povy, Creed, and I, to Arundel House, and there I did see them choosing their Council, it being St. Andrew's day; and I had his cross set on my hat, as the rest had, and cost me 2s. My wife, after dinner, went the first time abroad in her coach, calling on Roger Pepys and visiting Mrs. Creed and my cousin Turner. Thus ended this month, with very good content, that hath been the most sad to my heart and the most expenseful to my purse on things of pleasure (having furnished my wife's closet and the best chamber, and a coach and horses) that ever I knew in the world; and I am put into the greatest condition of outward state that ever I was in, or hoped ever to be, or desired: and this at a time when we do daily expect great changes in this Office; and by all reports we must, all of us, turn out. But my eyes are come to that condition that I am not able to work; and therefore that, and my wife's desire, make me have no manner of trouble in my thoughts about it. So God do His will in it!

December 1st. This day I hear of poor Mr. Clerke, the solicitor, being dead of a cold, after being not above two days ill, which troubles me mightily, poor man!

2d. Abroad with W. Hewer, thinking to have found Mr. Wren at Captain Cox's to have spoke something to him about doing a favour for Will's uncle Steventon, but missed him. And so back again, and abroad with my wife, the first time that ever I rode in my own coach, which do make my heart rejoice, and praise God, and pray him to bless it to me and continue it. So she and I to the King's playhouse, and there saw 'The Usurper,' a pretty good play, in all but what is designed to resemble Cromwell and Hugh Peters, which is mighty silly. The play done, we to White Hall, where my wife stayed while I up to the Duchess's and Queen's side, to speak with the Duke of York: and here saw all the ladies, and heard the silly discourse of the King, with his people about him, telling a story of my Lord Rochester's having of his clothes stole while he was with a wench; and his gold all gone, but his clothes found afterwards, stuffed into a feather bed by the wench that stole them.   I spoke with the Duke of York, just as he was set down to supper with the King, about our sending of victuals to Sir Thomas Allen's fleet hence to Cales [Cadiz], to meet him. Today I hear that Mr. Ackworth's cause went for him at Guildhall, against his hosiers, which I am well enough pleased with.

3d. Mr. Wren gives me but small hopes of the favour I hoped to get for Mr. Steventon, Will's uncle, of having leave, being upon the point of death, to surrender his place, which do trouble me, but I will do what I can.   To the office, Sir Jer. Smith with me, who is a silly, prating, talking man; but he tells me what he hears— that Holmes and Spragg now rule all with the Duke of Buckingham, as to sea-business, and will be great men: but he do prophesy what will be the fruit of it; so I do.   So to the office, where we sat all the morning; and at noon home to dinner, and then abroad again with my wife to the Duke of York's playhouse, and saw 'The Unfortunate Lovers'; a mean play, I think, but some parts very good, and excellently acted.   We sat under the boxes, and saw the fine ladies: among others my Lady Carnegie, who is most devilishly painted.   And so home, it being mighty pleasure to go alone with my poor wife in a coach of our own to a play, and makes us appear mighty great, I think, in the world; at least, greater than ever I could, or my friends for me, have once expected; or, I think, than ever any of my family ever yet lived, in my memory, but my cousin Pepys in Salisbury Court.

4th. Did wait as usual upon the Duke of York, where, upon discoursing something touching the Ticket Office, which by letter the Board did give the Duke of York their advice to be put upon Lord Brouncker, Sir J. Minnes did foolishly rise up and complain of the Office, and his being made nothing of; and this before Sir Thomas Littleton, who would be glad of this difference among us; which did trouble me mightily, and therefore I did forbear to say what I otherwise would have thought fit for me to say on this occasion, upon so impertinent a speech as this doting fool made— but, I say, I let it alone, and contented myself that it went as I advised, as to the Duke of York's judgment, in the thing disputed. Home, where by invitation I find my aunt Wight, who looked over all our house and is mighty pleased with it; and indeed it is

now mighty handsome, and rich in furniture.   I carried my wife
and her to Smithfield, where they sit in the coach while Mr.
Pickering, who meets me at Smithfield, and I and W. Hewer and a
friend of his, a jockey, did go about to see several pairs of horses
for my coach; but it was late, and we agreed on none, but left it
to another time: but here I do see instances of a piece of craft and
cunning that I never dreamed of, concerning the buying and
choosing of horses.   So Mr. Pickering, to whom I am much
beholden for his kindness herein, and I parted; and I with my
people home.   To the office, where vexed to see how ill all the
Comptroller's business is likely to go, as long as ever Sir J. Minnes
lives; and so troubled I was, that I thought it a good occasion for
me to give my thoughts of it in writing, and therefore wrote a letter
at the Board, by the help of a tube, to Lord Brouncker, and did
give it him, which I kept a copy of, and it may be of use to me
hereafter to show in this matter.   This being done, I home to my
aunt, who supped with us, and my uncle also: and a good-
humoured woman she is, so that I think we shall keep her acquaintance; but mighty proud she is of her wedding-ring, being lately
set with diamonds, cost her about £12: and I did commend it
mightily to her, but do not think it very suitable for one of our
quality.

5th.   Up after a little talk with my wife, which troubled me, she
being, ever since our late difference, mighty watchful of my sleep
and dreams, and will not be persuaded that I do not dream of Deb.,
and do tell me that I speak in my dreams and that this night I did
cry 'Huzzy,' and it must be she; and now and then I start otherwise
than I used to do; which I know not, for I do not know that I
dream of her more than usual, though I cannot deny that my
thoughts waking do run now and then against my will and judgment upon her, for that only is wanting to undo me, being now in
every other thing as to my mind most happy, and may still be so
but for my own fault if I be catched loving anybody but my wife
again.   No news stirring, but that my Lord of Ormond is likely
to go to Ireland again, which do show that the Duke of Buckingham do not rule all so absolutely; and that, however, we shall
speedily have more changes in the Navy; and it is certain that the
Nonconformists do now preach openly in houses, in many places,
and among others the house that was heretofore Sir G. Carteret's,
in Leadenhall Street, and have ready access to the King.   And
now the great dispute is whether this Parliament or another; and

my great design, if I continue in the Navy, is to get myself to be a Parliament-man.

6th. (Lord's day.) Up, and with my wife to church; which pleases me mightily, I being full of fear that she would never go to church again, after she had declared to me that she was a Roman Catholic. But though I do verily think she fears God, and is truly and sincerely righteous, yet I do see she is not so strictly a Catholic as not to go to church with me, which pleases me mightily. Here Mills made a lazy sermon upon Moses' meekness. With my wife and W. Hewer talking over the business of the Office, and particularly my own office, how I will make it, and it will become in a little time an office of ease, and not slavery as it hath for so many years been.

7th. Up by candle-light, and with W. Hewer did walk it very well to Sir W. Coventry, and there alone with him an hour talking of the Navy, which he pities, but says that he hath no more mind to be found meddling with the Navy, lest it should do it hurt, as well as him. So to talk of general things: and telling him that, with all these doings, he, I thanked God, stood yet, he told me, Yes, but that he thought his continuing in did arise from his enemies my Lord of Buckingham and Arlington's seeing that he cared so little if he was out; and he do protest to me that he is as weary of the Treasury as ever he was of the Navy. He tells me that he do believe that their heat is over almost, as to the Navy, there being now none left of the old stock but my Lord Brouncker, J. Minnes, who is ready to leave the world, and myself. But he tells me that he do foresee very great wants and great disorders by reason thereof, insomuch as he is represented to the King by his enemies as a melancholy man, and one that is still prophesying ill events, so as the King called him Visionaire, which being told him, he said he answered the party that, whatever he foresaw, he was not afraid as to himself of anything, nor particularly of my Lord Arlington so much as the Duke of Buckingham hath been, nor of the Duke of Buckingham so much as my Lord Arlington at this time is. But he tells me that he hath been always looked upon as a melancholy man, whereas others that would please the King do make him believe that all is safe: and so he hath heard my Lord Chancellor openly say to the King that he was now a glorious prince, and in a glorious condition, because of some one accident that hath happened, or some one rut that hath been removed; 'when,' says Sir W. Coventry, 'they reckoned their one good meal, without considering that there was nothing left in the cupboard for tomorrow.' After this discourse, to my Lord Sandwich's, and took a quarter of an hour's walk in the garden with him, which I have not done for so much time with him since his coming into England; and talking of his own condition, and particularly of the world's talk of his going to Tangier. I find, if his conditions can be made profitable and safe as to money, he would go, but not else; but, however, will seem not averse to it, because of facilitating his other accounts now depending, which he finds hard to get through, but yet hath some hopes, the King, he says, speaking very kindly to him.

8th. Up, and Sir H. Cholmley betimes with me, about some accounts and moneys due to him; and he gone, I to the office, where sat all the morning. And here, among other things, breaks out the storm W. Hewer and I have long expected from the Surveyor,[1] about W. Hewer's conspiring to get a contract, to the burdening of the stores with kerseys and cottons, of which he hath often complained, and lately more than ever. And now he did it by a most scandalous letter to the Board, reflecting on my office: and, by discourse, it fell to such high words between him and me as can hardly ever be forgot, I declaring I would believe W. Hewer as soon as him, and laying the fault, if there be any, upon himself; he, on the other hand, vilifying of my word and W. Hewer's, calling him knave, and that if he were his clerk he should lose his ears. At last I closed the business for this morning with making the thing ridiculous, as it is, and he swearing that the King should have right in it, or he would lose his place. The office was cleared of all but ourselves and W. Hewer; but, however, the world did by the beginning see what it meant, and it will, I believe, come to high terms between us, which I am sorry for, to have any blemish laid upon me or mine at this time, though never so unjustly, for fear of giving occasion to my real discredit: and therefore I was not only all the rest of the morning vexed, but so went home to dinner, where my wife tells me of my Lord Orrery's new play 'Tryphon,'[2] at the Duke of York's House, which, however, I would see, and therefore put a bit of meat in our mouths, and went thither, where, with much ado, at half-past one, we got into a blind hole in the 18*d*. place, above stairs, where we could not hear well.

---

[1] Colonel Middleton.
[2] This tragedy, taken from the first book of Maccabees, was performed with great success.

The house infinite full, but the prologue most silly, and the play, though admirable, yet no pleasure almost in it, because just the very same design and words and sense and plot as every one of his plays have, any one of which alone would be held admirable, whereas so many of the same design and fancy do but dull one another; and this, I perceive, is the sense of everybody else, as well as myself, who therefore showed but little pleasure in it.   So home, mighty hot, and my mind mightily out of order, so as I could not eat my supper, or sleep almost all night, though I spent till twelve at night with W. Hewer to consider of our business: and we find it not only most free from any blame of our side, but so horrid scandalous on the other, to make so groundless a complaint, and one so shameful to him, that it could not but let me see that there is no need of my being troubled; but such is the weakness of my nature, that I could not help it, which vexes me, showing me how unable I am to live with difficulties.

9th.   To the office, but did little there, my mind being still uneasy, though more and more satisfied that there is no occasion for it.   But abroad with my wife to the Temple, where I met with Auditor Wood's clerk and did some business with him, and so to see Mr. Spong, and found him out by Southampton Market,[1] and there carried my wife, and up to his chamber, a bye place, but with a good prospect of the fields.   And there I had most infinite pleasure, not only with his ingenuity in general, but in particular with his showing me the use of the parallelogram, by which he drew in a quarter of an hour before me, in little, from a great, a most neat map of England—that is, all the outlines, which gives me infinite pleasure, and foresight of pleasure I shall have with it; and therefore desire to have that which I have bespoke made. Many other pretty things he showed us, and did give me a glass bubble,[2] to try the strength of liquors with.   This done, and having spent 6d. in ale in the coach, at the door of the Bull inn, with the innocent master of the house, a Yorkshireman, for his letting us go through his house, we away to Hercules' Pillars, and there eat a bit of meat: and so, with all speed, back to the Duke of York's House, where mighty full again; but we come time enough to have a good place in the pit, and did hear this new play again, where,

---

[1] Better known as Bloomsbury Market; but since (1851–3) swallowed up in New Oxford Street.

[2] This seems to be Mr. Boyle's hydrometer, described in the *Philosophical Transactions* of the time.

though I better understood it than before, yet my sense of it and pleasure was just the same as yesterday, and no more, nor anybody else's about us. So took our coach and home, having now little pleasure to look about me to see the fine faces, for fear of displeasing my wife, whom I take great comfort now, more than ever, in pleasing; and it is a real joy to me. So home, and to my office, where spent an hour or two; and so home to my wife, to supper and talk, and so to bed.

10th. Up, and to the office, where busy all the morning: Middleton not there, so no words or looks of him. At noon, home to dinner; and so to the office, and there all the afternoon busy; and at night W. Hewer home with me, and we think we have got matter enough to make Middleton appear a coxcomb. But it troubled me to have Sir W. Warren meet me at night, going out of the office home, and tell me that Middleton do intend to complain to the Duke of York: but, upon consideration of the business, I did go to bed satisfied that it was best for me that he should; and so my trouble was over, and to bed, and slept well.

11th. Up, and with W. Hewer by water to Somerset House; and there I to my Lord Brouncker, before he went forth to the Duke of York, and there told him my confidence that I should make Middleton appear a fool, and that it was, I thought, best for me to complain of the wrong he hath done; but brought it about that my Lord desired me I would forbear, and promised that he would prevent Middleton till I had given in my answer to the Board, which I desired. And so away to White Hall, and there did our usual attendance: and no word spoke before the Duke of York by Middleton at all; at which I was glad to my heart, because by this means I have time to draw up my answer to my mind. With W. Hewer by coach to Smithfield, but met not Mr. Pickering, he being not come, and so Will and I to a cook's shop in Aldersgate Street, and dined well for 19½d., upon roast beef; and so, having dined, we back to Smithfield, and there met Pickering, and up and down all the afternoon about horses, and did see the knaveries and tricks of jockeys. Here I met W. Joyce, who troubled me with his impertinencies a great while, and the like Mr. Knipp, who, it seems, is a kind of a jockey, and would fain have been doing something for me, but I avoided him, and the more for fear of being troubled thereby with his wife, whom I dare not see for my vow to my wife. At last concluded upon giving £50 for a fine pair of black horses we saw this day se'nnight; and so set Mr.

Pickering down near his house, whom I am much beholden to for his care herein, and he hath admirable skill, I perceive, in this business. And so home.

12th. I hear this day that there is fallen down a new house, not quite finished, in Lombard Street, and that there have been several so, they making use of bad mortar and bricks; but no hurt yet, as God hath ordered it. This day was brought home my pair of black coach-horses, the first I ever was master of, a fine pair!

13th. (Lord's day.) Up, and with W. Hewer to the office, where all the morning; and then home to a little dinner, and presently to it again till twelve at night, drawing up my answer to Middleton. So to bed, weary with walking in my office dictating to him.

14th. To a Committee of Tangier, where, among other things, a silly account of a falling out between Norwood,[1] at Tangier, and Mr. Bland, the mayor, who is fled to Cales [Cadiz]. His complaint is ill worded, and the other's defence the most ridiculous that ever I saw; and so everybody else that was there thought it. But never did I see so great an instance of the use of grammar and knowledge how to tell a man's tale as this day, Bland having spoiled his business by ill telling it, who had work to have made himself notorious by his mastering Norwood, his enemy, if he had known how to have used it. To dinner by a hackney, my coachman being this day about breaking of my horses to the coach, they having never yet drawn. This day, I hear, and am glad, that the King hath prorogued the Parliament to October next; and, among other reasons, it will give me time to go to France, I hope.

15th. Up, and to the office, where sat all the morning, and the new Treasurers there; and, for my life, I cannot keep Sir J. Minnes and others of the Board from showing our weakness, to the dishonour of the Board, though I am not concerned: but it do vex me to the heart to have it before these people, that would be glad to find out all our weaknesses.

18th. To Lord Brouncker, and got him to read over my paper, who owns most absolute content in it, and the advantage I have in it, and the folly of the Surveyor. At noon home to dinner; and then to Brooke House, and there spoke with Colonel Thomson, I by order carrying the Commissioners of Accounts our Contract-books, from the beginning to the end of the late war. I found him finding of errors in a ship's book, where he showed me many,

----

[1] Colonel Norwood, the deputy governor.

which must end in the ruin, I doubt, of the Comptroller, who found them not out in the pay of the ship, or the whole Office. To the office, and after some other business done, we fell to mine. The Surveyor began to be a little brisk at the beginning; but when I came to the point to touch him, which I had all the advantages in the world to do, he became as calm as a lamb, and owned, as the whole Board did, their satisfaction, and cried excuse: and so all made friends, and their acknowledgment put into writing and delivered into Sir J. Minnes's hand, to be kept there for the use of the Board, or me, when I shall call for it; they desiring it might be so, that I might not make use of it to the prejudice of the Surveyor, whom I had an advantage over, by his extraordinary folly in this matter. So Middleton desiring to be friends, I forgave him; and all mighty quiet, and fell to talk of other stories, and there stayed, all of us, till nine or ten at night, more than ever we did in our lives before, together. And so home, where I have a new fight to fight with my wife, who is under new trouble by some news she has heard of Deb.'s being mighty fine and gives out that she has a friend that gives her money: and this my wife believes to be me, and poor wretch! I cannot blame her, and therefore she run into me extreme. But I did pacify all, and were mighty good friends; and to bed, and I hope it will be our last struggle from this business.

19th. My wife and I by hackney to the King's playhouse, and there, the pit being full, sat in the box above, and saw 'Catiline's Conspiracy,' [1] yesterday being the first day: a play of much good sense and words to read, but that do appear the worst upon the stage, I mean the least diverting, that ever I saw any, though most fine in clothes; and a fine scene of the Senate, and of a fight, as ever I saw in my life. We sat next to Betty Hall, that did belong to this house, and was Sir Philip Howard's mistress: a mighty pretty wench, though my wife will not think so; and I dare neither commend, nor be seen to look upon her or any other, for fear of offending her. So, our own coach coming for us, home, and to end letters, and my wife to read to me out of 'The Siege of Rhodes,' and so to supper, and to bed.

20th. (Lord's day.) With my wife to church, and then home, and there found W. Joyce come to dine with me, as troublesome a talking coxcomb as ever he was, and yet once in a year I like him well enough. In the afternoon my wife and W. Hewer and I to

[1] By Stephen Gosson. It was never printed.

White Hall, where they stayed till I had been with the Duke of York, with the rest of us of the Office, and did a little business. And then the Duke of York in good humour did fall to tell us many fine stories of the wars in Flanders, and how the Spaniards are the best disciplined foot in the world: will refuse no extraordinary service if commanded, but scorn to be paid for it as in other countries, though at the same time they will beg in the streets; not a soldier will carry you a cloak-bag for money for the world, though he will beg a penny, and will do the thing, if commanded by his Commander. That, in the citadel of Antwerp, a soldier hath not a liberty of begging till he hath served three years. They will cry out against their King and commanders and generals, none like them in the world, and yet will not hear a stranger say a word of them but they will cut his throat. That, upon a time, some of the commanders of their army exclaiming against their generals, and particularly the Marquis de Caranen,[1] the confessor of the Marquis coming by and hearing them, he stops and gravely tells them that the three great trades of the world are the lawyers, who govern the world, the churchmen, who enjoy the world, and a sort of fellows whom they call soldiers, who make it their work to defend the world. He told us too, that Turenne being now become a Catholic,[2] he is likely to get over the head of Colbert,[3] their interests being contrary; the latter to promote trade and the sea (which, says the Duke of York, is that we have most cause to fear), and Turenne to employ the King and his forces by land, to increase his conquests. W. Hewer tells me today that he hears that the King of France hath declared in print that he do intend this next summer to forbid his commanders to strike to us, but that both we and the Dutch shall strike to him; and that he hath made his Captains swear already that they will observe it: which is a great thing if he do it, as I know nothing to hinder him.

21st. My own coach carrying me and my boy Tom (who goes

---

[1] Luis de Benavides Carillo y Toledo, Marques de Caracena, one of the most eminent of the Spanish generals. He had been Commander of the Spanish cavalry in Flanders; and was afterwards Governor of Milan, and employed in the wars of Italy. He died in 1668.

[2] Henri, Vicomte de Turenne, the celebrated general. In 1666, after the death of his wife, Charlotte, heiress of the Duc de la Force, who, like himself, had been a Huguenot, and whose influence had retained him in that communion, Turenne became a Roman Catholic.

[3] Jean Baptiste Colbert, the great minister.

with me in the room of W. Hewer, who could not, and I dare not go alone), to the Temple, the first time my fine horses ever carried me, and I am mighty proud of them. So home, and there dined with my wife and my people: and then she and W. Hewer and I out with our coach, but the old horses, not daring yet to use the others too much, but only to enter them. Went into Holborn, and there saw the woman that is to be seen with a beard. She is a little plain woman, a Dane: her name, Ursula Dyan; about forty years old; her voice like a little girl's; with a beard as much as any man I ever saw, black almost, and grizzly; it began to grow at about seven years old, and was shaved not above seven months ago, and is now so big as any man's almost that ever I saw; I say, bushy and thick. It was a strange sight to me, I confess, and what pleased me mightily. Thence to the Duke's playhouse, and saw 'Macbeth.' The King and Court there; and we sat just under them and my Lady Castlemaine, and close to a woman that comes into the pit, a kind of a loose gossip, that pretends to be like her, and is so, something. And my wife, by my troth, appeared, I think, as pretty as any of them: I never thought so much before, and so did Talbot and W. Hewer, as I heard they said to one another. The King and Duke of York minded me, and smiled upon me, at the handsome woman near me: but it vexed me to see Moll Davis, in the box over the King's and my Lady Castlemaine's, look down upon the King, and he up to her; and so did my Lady Castlemaine once, to see who it was: but when she saw Moll Davis, she looked like fire; which troubled me.

23d. Discoursed with Sir John Bankes, who thinks this prorogation will please all but the Parliament itself, which will, if ever they meet, be vexed at Buckingham, who yet governs all. He says the Nonconformists are glad of it, and, he believes, will get the upper hand in a little time, for the King must trust to them or nobody; and he thinks the King will be forced to it. He says that Sir D. Gauden is mightily troubled at Pen's being put upon him by the Duke of York,[1] and that he believes he will get clear of it, which, though it will trouble me to have Pen still at the office, yet I shall think D. Gauden do well in it, and what I would advise him to, because I love him. So home to dinner, and then with my wife alone abroad, with our new horses, the beautifullest almost that ever I saw, and the first time they ever carried her and me, but once; but we are mighty proud of them. To her tailor's, and so

[1] As his partner, in the contract for victualling the Navy.

to the 'Change, and laid out three or four pounds in lace, for her and me.   And so home, and there I up to my Lord Brouncker at his lodgings; and sat with him an hour on purpose to talk over the wretched state of this Office at present, according to the present hands it is made up of; wherein he do fully concur with me, and that it is our part not only to prepare for defending it and ourselves against the consequences of it, but to take the best ways we can to make it known to the Duke of York; for, till Sir J. Minnes be removed, and a sufficient man brought into W. Pen's place when he is gone, it is impossible for this Office ever to support itself.

24th. A cold day.   Up, and to the office, where all the morning alone, nobody meeting, being the eve of Christmas.   At noon home to dinner, and then at the office busy all the afternoon, and at night home.

25th. (Christmas day.) I to church, where Alderman Backwell coming in late, I beckoned to his lady to come up to us, who did, with another lady; and after sermon, I led her down through the church to her husband and coach, a noble, fine woman, and a good one, and one my wife shall be acquainted with.   So home, and to dinner alone with my wife, who, poor wretch, sat undressed all day, till ten at night, altering and lacing of a noble petticoat: while I by her, making the boy read to me the Life of Julius Cæsar,[1] and Descartes's book of Music [2]—the latter of which I understand not, nor think he did well that writ it, though a most learned man.   Then, after supper, I made the boy play upon his lute, which I have not done before, since he came to me; and so, my mind in mighty content, we to bed.

26th. Lay long with pleasure, prating with my wife, and then up, and I a little at the office and my head busy setting some papers and accounts to rights, which, being long neglected because of my eyes, will take me up much time and care to do: but it must be done.   At noon to dinner, and then abroad with my wife to a play, at the Duke of York's House, the house full of ordinary citizens.   The play was 'Women Pleased,' [3] which we had never

[1] The *Life of Julius Cæsar, with an Account of his Medals.*   By Clement Edmonds, fol., London, 1655.

[2] *Musicæ Compendium,* by René des Cartes, Amsterdam, 1617; rendered into English: London, 1653, 4to.   The translator, whose name did not appear on the title, was William, Viscount Brouncker, Pepys's colleague, who proved his knowledge of music by the performance.

[3] A tragi-comedy by Fletcher: fol., 1647; 8vo, 1778.

seen before; and, though but indifferent, yet there is a good design for a good play.

27th. (Lord's day.) Saw the King at chapel; but stayed not to hear anything, but went to walk in the Park with W. Hewer; and there, among others, met with Sir G. Downing, and walked with him an hour, talking of business, and how the late war was managed, there being nobody to take care of it: and he telling, when he was in Holland, what he offered the King to do, if he might have power, and then, upon the least word, perhaps of a woman, to the King, he was contradicted again, and particularly to the loss of all that we lost in Guinea. He told me that he had so good spies, that he hath had the keys taken out of De Witt's [1] pocket when he was a-bed, and his closet opened, and papers brought to him and left in his hands for an hour, and carried back and laid in the place again, and keys put into De Witt's pocket again. He says he hath always had their most private debates, that have been but between two or three of the chief of them, brought to him in an hour after, and an hour after that hath sent word thereof to the King, but nobody here regarded them. But he tells me the sad news, that he is out of all expectations that ever the debts of the Navy will be paid, if the Parliament do not enable the King to do it by money; all they can hope for to do out of the King's revenue being but to keep our wheels a-going on present services, and, if they can, to cut off the growing interest: which is a sad story, and grieves me to the heart. So home, my coach coming for me; and there find Balty and Mr. Howe, who dined with me. And there my wife and I fell out a little about the foulness of the linen of the table, but were friends presently: but she cried, poor heart! which I was troubled for, though I did not give her one hard word.

28th. Called up by drums and trumpets, these things and boxes having cost me much money this Christmas already, and will do more. My wife down by water to see her mother, and at night home and tells me how much her mother prays for me and is troubled for my eyes; and I am glad to have friendship with them, and believe they are truly glad to see their daughter come to live so well as she do.

[1] The celebrated John de Witt, Grand Pensionary of Holland, who, a few years afterwards, was massacred, with his brother Cornelius, by the Dutch mob, enraged at their opposition to the elevation of William of Orange to the Stadtholdership, when the States were overrun by the French army, and the Dutch fleets beaten at sea by the English.

29th. Up, and at the office all the morning, and at noon to dinner, and there, by a pleasant mistake, find my uncle and aunt Wight and three more of their company come to dine with me today, thinking that they had been invited, which they were not; but yet we did give them a pretty good dinner, and mighty merry at the mistake. They sat most of the afternoon with us, and then parted; and my wife and I out, thinking to have gone to a play, but it was too far begun, and so to the 'Change, and there she and I bought several things, and so home, with much pleasure, talking, and then to reading, and so to supper and to bed.

30th. Up, and vexed a little to be forced to pay 40s. for a glass of my coach, which was broke the other day, nobody knows how, within the door, while it was down; but I do doubt that I did break it myself with my knees. After dinner, my wife and I to the Duke's playhouse, and there did see 'King Harry the Eighth'; and was mightily pleased, better than I ever expected, with the history and shows of it. We happened to sit by Mr. Andrews, our neighbour, and his wife, who talked so fondly to his little boy. Thence my wife and I to the 'Change; but, in going, our near horse did fling himself, kicking of the coachbox over the pole; and a great deal of trouble it was to get him right again, and we forced to 'light, and in great fear of spoiling the horse, but there was no hurt. Blessed be God! the year ends, after some late very great sorrow with my wife by my folly; yet ends, I say, with great mutual peace and content, and likely to last so by my care, who am resolved to enjoy the sweet of it which I now possess by never giving her like cause of trouble.

1669

January 1st. Presented from Captain Beckford, with a noble silver warming-pan, which I am doubtful whether to take or no. With W. Hewer to the cabinet-shops, to look out, and did agree for, a cabinet to give my wife for a New-year's gift; and I did buy one cost me £11, which is very pretty, of walnut tree. To the Old Exchange, and met my uncle Wight; and there walked, and met with the Houblons, and talked with them—gentlemen whom

I honour mightily. And so to my uncle's and met my wife; and there, with W. Hewer, we dined with our family, and had a very good dinner, and pretty merry: and after dinner, my wife and I with our coach to the King's playhouse, and there in a box saw 'The Maiden Queen.' Knipp looked upon us, but I durst not show her any countenance; and, as well as I could carry myself, I found my wife uneasy there, poor wretch! Therefore I shall avoid that house as much as I can. So back to my aunt's, and there supped and talked, and stayed pretty late, it being dry and moonshine, and so walked home, and to bed in very good humour.

2d. Home to dinner, where I find my cabinet, and paid for it, and it pleases me and my wife well.

3d. (Lord's day.) Busy all the morning, getting rooms and dinner ready for my guests, which were my uncle and aunt Wight, and two of their cousins, and an old woman, and Mr. Mills and his wife; and a good dinner, and all our plate out, and mighty fine and merry, only I a little vexed at burning a new table-cloth myself with one of my trencher-salts. Dinner done, I out with W. Hewer and Mr. Spong, who by accident came to dine with me, and good talk with him: to White Hall by coach, and there left him. Up and down the house till the evening, hearing how the King do intend [1] this frosty weather, it being this day the first, and very hard frost, that hath come this year, and very cold it is. So home, and to supper and read; and there my wife and I treating about coming to an allowance to her for clothes; and there I, out of my natural backwardness, did hang off, which vexed her and did occasion some discontented talk in bed, when we went to bed, and also in the morning; but I did recover all.

4th. Lay long talking with my wife, and did of my own accord come to an allowance of her of £30 a year for all expenses, clothes and everything, which she was mightily pleased with, it being more than ever she asked or expected, and so rose with much content. W. Hewer and I went and saw the great tall woman that is to be seen, who is but twenty-one years old, and I do easily stand under her arms.[2] Then, going further, The. Turner called

---

[1] This sentence is imperfect.

[2] Evelyn saw her, 29th January 1669. She was born in the Low Countries, and stood, at the age of twenty-one, according to Evelyn, six feet ten inches high; yet Pepys, 8th February 1669, makes her height six feet five inches.

me, out of her coach, where her mother, &c., was, and invited me by all means to dine with them at my cousin Roger's mistress's, the widow Dickenson. So I went to them afterwards, and dined with them, and mighty handsomely treated, and she a wonderful merry, good-humoured, fat, but plain woman, but I believe a very good woman, and mighty civil to me. Mrs. Turner,[1] the mother,[2] and Mrs. Dyke[3] and The. and Betty was the company, and a gentleman of their acquaintance. Betty I did long to see, and she is indifferent pretty, but not what the world did speak of her; but I am mighty glad to have one so pretty of our kindred. After dinner I walked with them, to show them the great woman, which they admire, as well they may; and back with them, and left them. And I to White Hall, where a Committee of Tangier met; and I did receive an instance of the Duke of York's kindness to me, and the whole Committee, that they would not order anything about the Treasury for the Corporation now in establishing, without my assent, and considering whether it would be to my wrong or no. Thence up and down the house, and to the Duke of York's side, and there in the Duchess's presence; and was mightily complimented by my Lady Peterborough, in my Lord Sandwich's presence, whom she engaged to thank me for my kindness to her and her Lord. By and by I met my Lord Brouncker; and he and I to the Duke of York alone, and discoursed over the carriage of the present Treasurers, in opposition to, or at least independency of, the Duke of York or our Board, which the Duke of York is sensible of, and all remember, I believe; for they do carry themselves very respectlessly of him and us. We also declared our minds together to the Duke of York about Sir John Minnes's incapacity to do any service in the Office, and that it is but to betray the King to have any business of trust committed to his weakness. So that the Duke of York was very sensible of it, and he promised to speak to the King about it. To supper, and put into writing, in merry terms, an agreement between my wife and me about the £30 a year, and so to bed. This was done under both our hands merrily, and put into W. Hewer's to keep.

5th. The frost and cold continuing. At noon home with my people to dinner, and in the evening comes Creed to me, and tells me his wife is at my house. So I in, and spent an hour with them,

[1] Jane, the wife of Serjeant John Turner.
[2] Anne Pepys, who married Terry Walpole, of South Creake.
[3] Elizabeth, married to Thomas Dyke.

the first time she hath been here, or I have seen her, since she was married. She is not over-handsome, though a good lady, and one I love. So after some pleasant discourse, they gone, I to the office again.

6th. (Twelfth day.) Up, and to look after things against dinner today for my guests; and then to the office to write down my journal for five or six days backward, and so home. At noon comes Mrs. Turner and Dyke, and Mrs. Dickenson, and then comes The. and Betty Turner, the latter of which is a very pretty girl; and then Creed and his wife, whom I sent for, by my coach. These were my guests, and Mrs. Turner's friend, whom I saw the other day, Mr. Wicken. And very merry we were at dinner, and so all the afternoon, talking and looking up and down my house; and in the evening I did bring out my cake—a noble cake—and there cut it into pieces, with wine and good drink: and after a new fashion, to prevent spoiling the cake, did put so many titles into a hat, and so drew cuts: and I was the Queen, and The. Turner King; Creed Sir Martin Mar-all, and Betty Mrs. Millicent. And so we were mighty merry till it was midnight; and, being moonshine and fine frost, they went home, I lending some of them my coach to help to carry them.

7th. My wife and I to the King's playhouse, and there saw 'The Island Princess,' [1] the first time I ever saw it; and it is a pretty good play, many good things being in it, and a good scene of a town on fire. We sat in an upper box, and the jade Nell came and sat in the next box: a bold merry slut, who lay laughing there upon people, and with a comrade of hers of the Duke's House, that came in to see the play.

8th. Up, and with Colonel Middleton, in his coach, and Mr. Tippet to White Hall; and there attended the Duke of York with the rest, where the Duke was mighty plain with the Treasurers, according to the advice my Lord Brouncker and I did give him the other night; and he did it fully, and so as, I believe, will make the Treasurers careful of themselves, unless they do resolve upon defying the Duke of York. At the Treasury-chamber, where I alone did manage the business of the Leopard against the whole Committee of the East India Company, with Mr. Blackburne with them; and to the silencing of them all, to my no great content.

[1] A tragi-comedy by Fletcher; reprinted in 1669 (4to), 'as it is acted at the Theatre Royal by His Majesty's servants. With the alterations and new additional scenes.'

Home to my wife's chamber, my people having laid the cloth, and got the rooms all clean above stairs for our dinner tomorrow.

9th. At noon my Lord Brouncker, Mr. Wren, Joseph Williamson, and Captain Cocke dined with me; and, being newly sat down, comes in, by invitation of Williamson's, the Lieutenant of the Tower, and he brings in with him young Mr. Whore, whose father, of the Tower, I know. And here I had a neat dinner, and all in so good manner and fashion, and with so good company and everything to my mind, as I never had more in my life—the company being to my heart's content, and they all well pleased. So continued, looking over my books and closet till the evening. To bed with my mind mightily pleased with this day's management, as one of the days of my life of fullest content.

10th. (Lord's day.) Accidentally talking of our maids before we rose, I said a little word that did give occasion to my wife to fall out; and she did most excessively, almost all the morning, but ended most perfect good friends; but the thoughts of the unquiet which her ripping up of old faults will give me, did make me melancholy all day long.

11th. With W. Hewer, my guard, to White Hall, where no Committee of Tangier sat; so up and down the house talking with this and that man, and so to the 'Change and there did a little business, and so home to dinner. And then abroad with my wife to the King's playhouse, and there saw 'The Jovial Crew'; but ill acted to what it was heretofore, in Clun's time, and when Lacy could dance. Thence to the New Exchange to buy some things; and, among others, my wife did give me my pair of gloves, which, by contract, she is to give me in her £30 a year. Here Mrs. Smith[1] tells of the great murder thereabouts on Saturday last, of one Captain Bumbridge[2] by one Symons, both of her acquaintance, and hectors that were at play, and in drink: the former is killed, and is kinsman to my Lord of Ormond, which made him speak of it with so much passion. So home; and there all the evening, and made Tom to prick down some little conceits and notions of mine in music, which do mightily encourage me to spend some more thoughts about it; for I fancy, upon good reason, that I am in the right way of unfolding the mystery of this matter better than ever yet.

12th. Up, and to the office, where, by occasion of a message from the Treasurers that their Board found fault with Commissioner

[1] Pepys's pretty seamstress.   [2] Or Bainbridge.

Middleton, I went up from our Board to the Lords of the Treasury, and there did dispute the business, it being about the matter of paying a little money to Chatham Yard; wherein I find the Treasurers mighty supple, and I believe we shall bring them to reason, though they begun mighty upon us, as if we had no power of directing them, but they us. Thence back presently home to dinner, where I discern my wife to have been in pain about where I have been, but said nothing to me, but I believe did send W. Hewer to seek me: but I take no notice of it, but am vexed. So to dinner with my people, and then to the office, where all the afternoon, and did much business, and at it late, and so home to supper and to bed. This day meeting Mr. Pierce at White Hall, he tells me that his boy hath a great mind to see me, and is going to school again: and Dr. Clerke, being by, do tell me that he is a fine boy; but I durst not answer anything, because I durst not invite him to my house, for fear of my wife; and therefore, to my great trouble, was forced to neglect that discourse. Mr. Pierce, I asking him whither he was going, told me as a great secret that he was going to his master's mistress, Mrs. Churchill,[1] with some physic; meaning, I suppose, that she is with child. This evening I observed my wife mighty dull, and I myself was not mighty fond, because of some hard words she did give me at noon out of a jealousy at my being abroad this morning, which, God knows, it was upon the business of the Office unexpectedly: but I to bed, not thinking but she would come after me. But waking by and by out of a slumber, which I usually fall into presently after my coming into the bed, I found she did not prepare to come to bed, but got fresh candles, and more wood for her fire, it being mighty cold, too. At this being troubled, I after a while prayed her to come to bed; so, after an hour or two, she silent, and I now and then praying her to come to bed, she fell out into a fury, that I was a rogue and false to her. I did, as I might truly, deny it, and was mightily troubled, but all would not serve. At last, about one o'clock, she came to my side of the bed and drew my curtain open, and with the tongs red hot at the end made as if she did design to pinch me with them: at which, in dismay, I rose up, and with a few words

---

[1] Arabella Churchill, sister to John Duke of Marlborough, and one of the maids of honour to the Duchess of York. James Duke of Berwick and three other children were the fruits of this intrigue. She married subsequently Colonel Godfrey, Comptroller of the Household, and died 1730, aged eighty-two.

she laid them down, and did by little and little, very sillily, let all the discourse fall; and about two, but with much seeming difficulty, came to bed, and there lay well all night, and long in bed talking together with much pleasure, it being, I know, nothing but her doubt of my going out yesterday without telling her of my going, which did vex her, poor wretch! last night; and I cannot blame her jealousy, though it do vex me to the heart.

13th. Home, after visiting my Lady Peterborough, and there by invitation find Mr. Povy, and there was also Talbot Pepys, newly come from Impington, and dined with me. After dinner I and my wife and Talbot towards the Temple, and there to the King's playhouse, and there saw, I think, 'The Maiden Queen.' This day come home the instrument I have so long longed for, the parallelogram.

15th. To Sir W. Coventry, where with him a good while in his chamber, talking of the great factions at Court at this day, even to the sober engaging of great persons, and differences, and making the King cheap and ridiculous. It is about my Lady Harvey's being offended at Doll Common's acting of Sempronia,[1] to imitate her, for which she got my Lord Chamberlain, her kinsman, to imprison Doll: upon which my Lady Castlemaine made the King to release her, and to order her to act it again, worse than ever, the other day, where the King himself was; and since it was acted again, and my Lady Harvey provided people to hiss her and fling oranges at her: but it seems the heat is come to a great height, and real troubles at Court about it. Through the Park, where I met

---

[1] The following cast of parts in *The Alchymist*, as acted by the king's company, and given by Downes, in his *Roscius Anglicanus*, furnishes a clue to the actress described here, and in a former passage, as 'Doll Common':

Subtle	Mr. Clun
Face	Major Mohun
Sir E. Mammon . . .	Mr. Cartwright
Surly	Mr. Burt
Ananias	Mr. Lacy
Wholesome	Mr. Bateman
Doll Common	*Mrs. Corey*
Dame Plyant	Mrs. Rutter

The identity, however, is placed beyond doubt, by a reference to 'Catiline's Conspiracy,' where we find Mrs. Corey acting the part of Sempronia, in which 'Doll Common,' as Pepys styles her, gave offence, by imitating Lady Harvey, and, consequently, was sent to prison. We may add, that Mrs. Corey's name stands first in the list of female performers in the king's company, under Killigrew: see *Roscius Anglicanus*, 1708.

the King and the Duke of York, and so walked with them; and I
did give the Duke of York thanks for his favour to me yesterday,
at the Committee of Tangier, in my absence, where some business
was brought forward which the Duke of York would not suffer
to go on without my presence at the debate. And he answered
me just thus: that he ought to have a care of him that do the
King's business in the manner that I do, and words of more force
than that. Then down with Lord Brouncker to Sir R. Murray,
into the King's little elaboratory under his closet, a pretty place;
and there saw a great many chemical glasses and things, but understood none of them. With my wife at my cousin Turner's, where
I stayed and sat a while, and carried The. and my wife to the Duke
of York's House, to 'Macbeth,' and myself to White Hall, to the
Lords of the Treasury, about Tangier business; and there was by
at much merry discourse between them and my Lord Anglesey,
who made sport of our new Treasurers, and called them his
deputies, and much of that kind. And having done my own
business, I away back, and carried my cousin Turner and sister
Dyke to a friend's house, where they sup, in Lincoln's Inn Fields;
and I to the Duke of York's House, and so carried The. thither,
and so home with my wife. This day The. Turner showed me at
the play my Lady Portman,[1] who was grown out of my knowledge.

16th. This morning Creed, and in the afternoon comes Povy,
to advise with me about my answer to the Lords Commissioners
of Tangier, about the propositions for the Treasurership there,
which I am not much concerned for. But the latter, talking of
public things, told me, as Mr. Wren also did, that the Parliament
is likely to meet again, the King being frighted with what the
Speaker hath put him in mind of—his promise not to prorogue,
but only to adjourn them. They speak mighty freely of the folly
of the King in this foolish woman's business, of my Lady Harvey.
Povy tells me that Sir W. Coventry was with the King alone an
hour this day; and that my Lady Castlemaine is now in a higher
command over the King than ever—not as a mistress, for she
scorns him, but as a tyrant, to command him: and says that the
Duchess of York and the Duke of York are mighty great with her,
which is a great interest to my Lord Chancellor's [2] family; and that

[1] Elizabeth, daughter of Sir John Cutler (by his second wife), married to
Sir William Portman, K.B., who was the third and last baronet of his family.
Pepys could have known neither of his former wives.
[2] Clarendon, whom Pepys mentions by his former office.

they do agree to hinder all they can the proceedings of the Duke of Buckingham and Arlington. And so we are in the old mad condition, or rather worse than any, no man knowing what the French intend to do the next summer.

17th. (Lord's day.) After church, home, and thither comes Mrs. Batelier and her two daughters to dinner with us, and W. Hewer and his mother and Mr. Spong. We were very civilly merry, and Mrs. Batelier a very discreet woman, but mighty fond in the stories she tells of her son Will. After dinner Mr. Spong and I to my closet, there to try my instrument parallelogram, which do mighty well, to my full content, but only a little stiff, as being new. Thence taking leave of my guests, to White Hall, and there parting with Spong, a man that I mightily love for his plainness and ingenuity, spoke with my Lords Bellassis and Peterborough about the business now in dispute, about my deputing a Treasurer to pay the garrison at Tangier, which I would avoid and not be accountable, and they will serve me therein. Here I met Hugh May, and he brings me to the knowledge of Sir Henry Capel,[1] a Member of Parliament, and brother of my Lord of Essex,[2] who hath a great value, it seems, for me; and they appoint a day to come and dine with me, and see my books and papers of the Office, which I shall be glad to show them and have opportunity to satisfy them therein. Here all the discourse is that now the King is of opinion to have the Parliament called, notwithstanding his late resolutions for proroguing them; so unstable are his councils, and those about him.

18th. To Sir W. Coventry's, and there discoursed the business of my Treasurer's place, at Tangier, wherein he consents to my desire, and concurs therein, which I am glad of, that I may not be accountable for a man so far off. And so I to my Lord Sandwich's, and there walk with him through the garden, to White Hall, where he tells me what he hath done about this Treasurer's place, and I perceive the whole thing did proceed from him: that finding it would be best to have the Governor have nothing to do with the

[1] Henry, second son of Arthur, first Baron Capel of Hadham, and himself elevated to the peerage in 1692, by the title of Lord Capel of Tewkesbury, for which town he had served in Parliament. He had been created K.B. at the coronation of Charles II, and was a leading member of the House of Commons; and in 1679 appointed First Commissioner of the Admiralty. At the time of his death at Dublin Castle, 30th May 1696, he was Lord Deputy of Ireland. He left no issue.

[2] Which title had been revived for the Capel family in 1661.

pay of the garrison, he did propose to the Duke of York alone that a paymaster should be there; and that, being desirous to do a courtesy to Sir Charles Harbord and to prevent the Duke of York's looking out for anybody else, he did name him to the Duke of York. That when he came the other day to move this to the Board of Tangier the Duke of York, it seems, did readily reply that it was fit to have Mr. Pepys satisfied therein first, and that it was not good to make places for persons. This my Lord in great confidence tells me, that he do take very ill from the Duke of York, though nobody knew the meaning of these words but him; and that he did take no notice of them, but bit his lip, being satisfied that the Duke of York's care of me was as desirable to him as it could be to serve Sir Charles Harbord: and did seem industrious to let me see that he was glad that the Duke of York and he might come to contend who shall be the kindest to me, which I owned as his great love, and so I hope and believe it is, though my Lord did go a little too far in this business, to move it so far, without consulting me. But I took no notice of that, but was glad to see this competition come about, that my Lord Sandwich is apparently jealous of my thinking that the Duke of York do mean me more kindness than him. So we walked together, and I took this occasion to invite him to dinner to my house, and he readily appointed Friday next, which I shall be glad to have over to his content, he having never yet eat a bit of my bread. Thence to the Duke of York on the King's side, and so away; and meeting Mr. Sidney Montagu and Sheres,[1] a small invitation served their turn to carry them to London, where I paid Sheres his £100, given him for his pains in drawing the plate of Tangier fortifications. Home to my house to dinner, where I had a pretty handsome sudden dinner, and all well pleased; and thence we three and my wife to the Duke of York's playhouse, and there saw 'The Wits,' a medley of things, but some similes mighty good, though ill mixed. At White Hall, and there, in the Queen's withdrawing-room, invited my Lord Peterborough to dine with me, with my Lord Sandwich, who readily accepted it. To the Pope's Head tavern, there to see the fine painted room which Rogerson told me of, of his doing; but I do not like it at all, though it be good for such a public room.

---

[1] H. Sheeres was afterwards employed under Lord Dartmouth, as an engineer, in blowing up the works at Tangier, in 1683. He had previously been one of Lord Sandwich's suite in the embassy to Spain. He was knighted in 1685 and died in 1710.

19th. At noon eat a mouthful, and so with my wife to Madam Turner's, and find her gone, but The. stayed for us; and so to the King's House to see 'Horace';[1] this the third day of its acting— a silly tragedy, but Lacy hath made a farce of several dances— between each act one,—but his words are but silly, and invention not extraordinary as to the dances; only some Dutchmen come out of the mouth and tail of a Hamburg sow. Thence, not much pleased with the play, set them at home in the Strand; and my wife and I home, and there to do a little business at the office, and so home to supper and to bed.

20th. Up, and my wife and I and W. Hewer to White Hall, where she set us down; and there I spoke with my Lord Peterborough, to tell him of the day for his dining with me, being altered by my Lord Sandwich from Friday to Saturday next. Heard at the Council Board the City, by their single counsel Symson, and the Company of Strangers Merchants,[2] debate the business of water-bailage, a tax demanded upon all goods, by the City, imported and exported, which these Merchants oppose, and demanding leave to try the justice of the City's demand by a *Quo warranto*, which the City opposed, the Merchants did quite lay the City on their backs with great triumph, the City's cause being apparently too weak. But here I observed Mr. Gold,[3] the merchant, to speak very well, and very sharply against the City. To the Duke of York's House, and saw 'Twelfth Night' as it is now revived, but, I think, one of the weakest plays that ever I saw on the stage. This afternoon, before the play, I called with my wife at Dankers's,[4] the great landscape-painter, by Mr. Povy's advice; and have bespoke him to come to take measure of my dining-room panels.

---

[1] There were two translations, about this period, of the *Horace* of P. Corneille; one by Charles Cotton; the other, which was performed at court, by Katherine Philips, the fifth act being added by Sir John Denham. Pepys saw Mrs. Philips's translation, as did Evelyn. See Evelyn's *Diary*, under 5th February 1669.

[2] An account of the Merchants Strangers from their settlement, in the reign of Richard III to that of Charles II, is given in Seymour's *Survey of London*, vol. ii, pp. 473–82.

[3] Edward Gold, a native of Devonshire, living at Highgate, who married Elizabeth, daughter of Richard Gower, of that place. Their names occur amongst those of the governors of Sir Roger Cholmeley's Grammar School in Highgate.

[4] Henry Danckerts, born at The Hague, employed by Charles II to paint views of his seaports and palaces. He followed his profession for some years in London.

There I met with the pretty daughter of the coal-seller's, that lived in Cheapside, and now in Covent Garden, who hath her picture drawn here, but very poorly; but she is a pretty woman, and now, I perceive, married, a very pretty black woman. Home, my wife letting fall some words of her observing my eyes to be mightily employed in the playhouse, meaning upon women, which did vex me; but, however, when we come home, we were good friends; and so to read, and to supper, and so to bed.

21st. To a Committee of Tangier. Thence in my own coach home, where I find Madam Turner, Dyke, and The.; and had a good dinner for them, and merry; and so carried them to the Duke of York's House, all but Dyke, who went away on other business, and there saw 'The Tempest'; but it is but ill done by Gosnell, in lieu of Moll Davis. Thence set them at home, and my wife and I to the 'Change, and so home, where my wife mighty dogged, and I vexed to see it, being mightily troubled of late at her being out of humour, for fear of her discovering any new matter of offence against me, though I am conscious of none; but I do hate to be unquiet at home. So, late up, silent, and not supping, but hearing her utter some words of discontent to me with silence, and so to bed, weeping to myself for grief, which she discerning, came to bed, and mighty kind. And so with great joy on both sides to sleep.

22d. To the Exchange, calling at several places on occasions relating to my feast tomorrow, on which my mind is now set: as how to get a new looking-glass for my dining-room, and some pewter, and good wine, against tomorrow; and so home, where I had the looking-glass set up, cost me £6. 7s. 6d. At the 'Change I met with Mr. Dankers, with whom I was on Wednesday; and he took measure of my panels in my dining-room, where, in the four, I intend to have the four houses of the King, White Hall, Hampton Court, Greenwich, and Windsor. Mightily pleased with the fellow that came to lay the cloth and fold the napkins, which I like so well, as that I am resolved to give him 40s. to teach my wife to do it. So to supper, with much kindness between me and my wife, which nowadays is all my care, and so to bed.

23d. To the office till noon, when word brought me that my Lord Sandwich was come; so I presently rose, and there I found my Lords Sandwich, Peterborough, and Sir Charles Harbord: and presently after them comes my Lord Hinchingbroke, Mr. Sidney,[1]

[1] Sidney Montagu.

and Sir William Godolphin. And after greeting them, and some time spent in talk, dinner was brought up, one dish after another, but a dish at a time, but all so good; but, above all things, the variety of wines, and excellent of their kind, I had for them, and all in so good order, that they were mightily pleased, and myself full of content at it: and indeed it was, of a dinner of about six or eight dishes, as noble as any man need to have, I think; at least, all was done in the noblest manner that ever I had any, and I have rarely seen in my life better anywhere else, even at the Court. After dinner my Lords to cards, and the rest of us sitting about them and talking, and looking on my books and pictures and my wife's drawings, which they commended mightily; and mighty merry all day long, with exceeding great content; and so till seven at night, and so took their leaves, it being dark and foul weather. Thus was this entertainment over, the best of its kind and the fullest of honour and content to me that ever I had in my life: and I shall not easily have so good again. The truth is, I have some fear that I am more behind-hand in the world for these last two years, since I have not, or for some time could not, look after my accounts, which do a little allay my pleasure. But I do trust in God that I am pretty well yet, and resolve in a very little time to look into my accounts and see how they stand.

24th. (Lord's day.) An order brought me in bed for the principal Officers to attend the King at my Lord Keeper's this afternoon, it being resolved late the last night; and, by the warrant, I find my Lord Keeper did not then know the cause of it, the messenger being ordered to call upon him, to tell it him by the way as he came to us. So I up, and to my office to set down my journal for yesterday, and so home, and with my wife to church, and then home and to dinner; and after dinner out with my wife by coach to cousin Turner's, where she and The. gone to church, but I left my wife with Mrs. Dyke and Joyce Norton, whom I have not seen till now since their coming to town: she has become an old woman, and with as cunning a look as ever. I to White Hall; and here I met Will. Batelier, newly come post from France, his boots all dirty. He brought letters to the King, and I glad to see him, it having been reported that he was drowned for some days past. By and by the King comes out, and so I took coach, and followed his coaches to my Lord Keeper's, at Essex House,[1] where I never

[1] Essex House, where Robert Devereux, third earl of that name, died, in 1646, when Pepys was fourteen years old, stood formerly on the site of Essex

was before, since I saw my old Lord Essex lie in state when he was dead: a large, but ugly house.   Here all the Officers of the Navy attended, and by and by were called in to the King and Cabinet, where my Lord, who was ill, did lie upon the bed, as my old Lord Treasurer, or Chancellor, heretofore used to do; and the business was to know in what time all the King's ships might be repaired, fit for service.   The Surveyor answered, in two years, and not sooner.   I did give them hopes that, with supplies of money suitable, we might have them all fit for sea some part of the summer after this.   Then they demanded in what time we could set out forty ships.   It was answered, as they might be chosen of the newest and most ready, we could, with money, get forty ready against May.   The King seemed mighty full that we should have money to do all that we desired, and satisfied that without it nothing could be done; and so, without determining anything, we were dismissed; and I doubt all will end in some little fleet this year, and that of hired merchantmen, which would indeed be cheaper to the King, and have many conveniencies attending it, more than to fit out the King's own.   And this, I perceive, is designed, springing from Sir W. Coventry's counsel; and the King and most of the Lords, I perceive, full of it, to get the King's fleet all at once in condition for service.   Thence with Mr. Wren in his coach, for discourse' sake: and he told me how the business of the Parliament is wholly laid aside, it being overruled now that they shall not meet, but must be prorogued, upon this argument chiefly, that all the differences between the two Houses and things on foot that were matters of difference and discontent may be laid aside, and must begin again, if ever the House shall have a mind to pursue them.   Here he set me down, and I to my cousin Turner, and stayed and talked a little; and so took my wife, and home, and there to make her read, and then to supper and to bed.   At supper came W. Batelier and supped with us, and told us many pretty things of France, and the greatness of the present King.

25th. My wife showed me many excellent prints of Nanteuil's [1] and others, which W. Batelier hath, at my desire, brought me out of France, of the King and Colbert and others, most excellent, to

---

Street and Devereux Court, near the Temple.   It had belonged, in the reign of Elizabeth, to the Earl of Leicester, who left it to the second Earl of Essex, father of the parliamentary general here mentioned.

[1] Robert Nanteuil, the celebrated French engraver, a native of Rheims. He died at Paris in 1678.

my great content. But he hath also brought a great many gloves perfumed, of several sorts; but all too big by half for her, and yet she will have two or three dozen of them, which vexed me and made me angry. So she at last, to please me, did come to take what alone I thought fit, which pleased me.

26th. To the office, and then to White Hall, leaving my wife at Unthank's; and I to the Secretary's chamber, where I was, by particular order, this day summoned to attend, as I find Sir D. Gauden also was. And here was the King and the Cabinet met. and being called in among the rest, I find my Lord Privy Seal, whom I never before knew to be in so much play as to be of the Cabinet. The business is, that the Algerines have broke the peace with us by taking some Spaniards and goods out of an English ship which had the Duke of York's pass, of which advice came this day; and the King is resolved to stop Sir Thomas Allen's fleet from coming home till he hath amends made him for this affront, and therefore sent for us to advise about victuals to be sent to that fleet, and some more ships; wherein I answered them to what they demanded of me, which was but some few mean things: but I see that on all these occasions they seem to rely most upon me. Home, and there I find W. Batelier hath also sent the books which I made him bring me out of France. Among others, L'Estat de France,[1] Marnix, &c., to my great content; and so I was well pleased with them as also one or two printed music-books of songs, but my eyes are now too much out of tune to look upon them with any pleasure.

27th. To my cousin Turner's, where I find Roger Pepys come last night to town, and here is his mistress, Mrs. Dickenson; and by and by comes in Mr. Turner, a worthy, sober, serious man—I honour him mightily. And there we dined, having but an ordinary dinner; and so, after dinner, she, and I and Roger and his mistress to the Duke of York's playhouse, and there saw 'The Five Hours' Adventure,' which hath not been acted a good while before, but once, and is a most excellent play, I must confess.

28th. Going home to supper with my wife, and to get her to read to me, I did find that Mr. Sheres hath, beyond his promise, not only got me a candlestick made me after a form he remembers to have seen in Spain, for keeping the light from one's eyes, but hath

[1] *Résolutions Politiques, ou Maximes d'État*, par Jean de Marnix, Baron de Potes: Bruxelles, 1612, fol. There were two later editions of this work printed at Rouen.

got it done in silver very neat, and designs to give it me in thanks for my paying him his £100 in money for his service at Tangier, which was ordered him; but I do intend to force him to make me pay for it. But I yet, without his direction, cannot tell how it is to be made use of.

29th. To the Duke of York, where I did give a severe account of our proceedings, and what we found, in the business of Sir W. Jenings's demand of Supernumeraries. I thought it a good occasion to make an example of him, for he is a proud, idle fellow. And it did meet with the Duke of York's acceptance and well-liking; and he did call him in after I had done, and did not only give him a soft rebuke, but condemns him to pay both their victuals and wages, or right himself of the purser. This I was glad of, and so were all the rest of us, though I know I have made myself an immortal enemy by it. My aunt Wight and her husband came presently, and so to dinner; and after dinner Roger and I and my wife and aunt to see Mr. Cole: but [neither] he nor his wife was within, but we looked upon his picture of Cleopatra, which I went principally to see, being so much commended by my wife and aunt; but I find it a base copy of a good original, that vexed me to hear so much commended. Thence to see Creed's wife, where both of them within; and here met Mr. Bland, newly come from Cales [Cadiz], after his differences with Norwood. I think him a foolish, light-headed man; but certainly he hath been abused in this matter by Colonel Norwood. Here Creed showed me a copy of some propositions which Bland and others, in the name of the Corporation of Tangier, did present to Norwood for his opinion in, in order to the King's service, which were drawn up very humbly and were really good things; but his answer to them was in the most proud, carping, insolent, and ironically profane style, that ever I saw in my life, so as I shall never think the place can do well while he is there. Hence, after some talk and Creed's telling us that he is upon taking the next house to his present lodgings, which is next to that which my cousin Tom Pepys once lived in, in Newport Street, in Covent Garden; and is in a good place, and then, I suppose, he will keep his coach. So, setting Roger down at the Temple, who tells me that he is now concluded in all matters with his widow, we home, and there hired my wife to make an end of Boyle's Book of Forms, tonight and tomorrow; and so fell to read and sup, and then to bed. This day Mr. Ned Pickering brought his lady to see my wife, in acknowledgement of a little present of oranges and olives which I sent her for his kindness to me in the buying of my horses, which was very civil. She is old, but hath, I believe, been a pretty comely woman.

30th. Lay long in bed, it being a fast-day for the murder of the late King; and so up and to church, where Dr. Hicks made a dull sermon; and so home, and W. Batelier and Balty dined with us, and I spent all the afternoon with my wife and W. Batelier talking, and then making them read, and particularly made an end of Mr. Boyle's Book of Forms, which I am glad to have over. W. Batelier then fell to read a French discourse, which he hath brought over with him for me, to invite the people of France to apply themselves to Navigation, which it do very well, and is certainly their interest, and what will undo us in a few years, if the King of France goes on to fit up his Navy and increase it and his trace, as he hath begun. After supper my wife begun another book I lately bought, called 'The State of England,' [1] which promises well and is worth reading.

31st. (Lord's day.) To church, and there did hear the Doctor that is lately turned Divine, Dr. Waterhouse.[2] He preaches in a devout manner, not elegant nor very persuasive, but seems to mean well, and that he would preach holily; and was mighty passionate against people that make a scoff of religion. And the truth is, I did observe Mrs. Hollworthy smile often, and many others of the parish, who, I perceive, have known him, and were in mighty expectation of hearing him preach, but could not forbear smiling, and she particularly on me, and I on her. So home to dinner: and before dinner to my office, to set down my journal for this week, and then home to dinner; and after dinner to get my wife and boy, one after another, to read to me; and so spent the afternoon and the evening, and so after supper to bed. And thus endeth this month, with many different days of sadness and mirth, from differences between me and my wife; but this night we are at present very kind. And so ends this month.

February 1st. Up, and by water from the Tower to White Hall, the first time that I have gone to that end of the town by water for two or three months, I think, since I kept a coach, which

<hr />

[1] *Angliæ Notitiæ*, 1669, etc., by Edward Chamberlayne, LL.D.

[2] A. Wood, *Fasti*, vol. iv, p. 163 (Bliss), mentions that John Waterhouse of Trinity College, Cambridge, was created M.D. by virtue of letters from Oliver Cromwell in 1650, and went over to Ireland as physician to the army, where he discharged his duties with ability and diligence.

God send propitious to me; but it is a very great convenience. Meeting Mr. Povy, he and I away to Dankers's, to speak something touching the pictures I am getting him to make for me.   And thence he carried me to Mr. Streater's,[1] the famous history-painter, over the way, whom I have often heard of but did never see him before.   And there I found him and Dr. Wren [2] and several Virtuosos looking upon the paintings which he is making for the new Theatre at Oxford: and, indeed, they look as if they would be very fine, and the rest think better than those of Rubens in the Banqueting-house at White Hall, but I do not so fully think so. But they will certainly be very noble; and I am mightily pleased to have the fortune to see this man and his work, which is very famous; and he a very civil little man, and lame, but lives very handsomely.   So thence to my Lord Bellassis, and met him within: my business only to see a chimney-piece of Dankers's doing, in distemper, with egg to keep off the glaring of the light, which I must have done for my room: and indeed it is pretty, but, I must confess, I do think it is not altogether so beautiful as the oil pictures; but I will have some of one and some of another.   So to the King's playhouse, thinking to have seen 'The Heiress,' [3] first acted on Saturday last; but when we come thither we find no play there; Kynaston, that did act a part therein in abuse to Sir Charles Sedley, being last night exceedingly beaten with sticks by two or three that saluted him, so as he is mightily bruised and forced to keep his bed.[4]   So we to the Duke of York's playhouse, and there

[1] Robert Streater, appointed serjeant-painter at the Restoration: *ob.* 1680.

[2] Afterwards Sir Christopher Wren.

[3] *The Heiress* does not appear in the list of the Duke of Newcastle's works, nor has any play of that name and date been traced.   At the same time, it is to be observed that 'heir' was formerly used for 'heiress'; and such is the case in May's play of *The Heir*, in vol. viii of the last edition of Dodsley's *Old Plays*.

[4] The story about the caning of Kynaston has been preserved by Oldys, and copied by Malone, who tells us that Kynaston was vain of his personal resemblance to Sir C. Sedley, and dressed exactly like him.   Sedley, to revenge this insult, hired a bravo to chastise him in St. James's Park, under the pretext that he mistook him for the baronet.   According to Pepys, it would seem that the imitation was made in the play of *The Heiress*, which is very likely; and perhaps for this he got another beating, or it might be the same, and that in which the story, the scene of which is laid in the park, originated.   It is worth remarking, on the authority of Mr. Genest, the compiler of *Some Account of the English Stage from 1660 to 1830*, that Sir C. Sedley expressly introduced the incident of the beating of one man for another, owing to similarity of dress and appearance, into his comedy of *The Mulberry Garden*, which seems to have been first acted 16th May 1668, some time before the date Pepys assigns to the caning of Kynaston, 1st February 1669.

saw 'She Would if She Could.' This day, going to the play, The. Turner met us, and carried us to her mother at my Lady Mordaunt's; and I did carry both mother and daughter with us to the Duke of York's playhouse next door.

2d. To dinner at noon, where I find Mr. Sheres; and there made a short dinner, and carried him with us to the King's playhouse, where 'The Heiress,' notwithstanding Kynaston's being beaten, is acted: and they say the King is very angry with Sir Charles Sedley for his being beaten, but he do deny it. But his part is done by Beeston, who is fain to read it out of a book all the while, and thereby spoils the part, and almost the play, it being one of the best parts in it; and though the design is, in the first conception of it, pretty good, yet it is but an indifferent play, wrote, they say, by my Lord Newcastle. But it was pleasant to see Beeston come in with others, supposing it to be dark, and yet he is forced to read his part by the light of the candles: and this I observing to a gentleman that sat by me, he was mightily pleased therewith, and spread it up and down. But that that pleased me most in the play is the first song that Knipp sings, she singing three or four; and, indeed, it was very finely sung, so as to make the whole house clap her. Thence carried Sheres to White Hall, and there I stepped in and looked out Mr. May, who tells me that he and his company cannot come to dine with me tomorrow, whom I expected only to come to see the manner of our office and books, at which I was not very much displeased, having much business at the office. My wife in mighty ill humour all night, and in the morning I found it to be from her observing Knipp to wink and smile on me, and she says I smiled on her; and, poor wretch! I did perceive that she did, and do on all such occasions, mind my eyes. I did with much difficulty pacify her, and we were friends, she desiring that hereafter, at that house, we might always sit either above in a box, or, if there be no room, close up to the lower boxes.

3d. Up, and to the office till noon, and then home to a little dinner, and thither again till night, mighty busy, to my great content, doing a great deal of business, and so home to supper and to bed. I finding this day that I may be able to do a great deal of business by dictating, if I do not read myself, or write, without spoiling my eyes, I being very well in my eyes after a great day's work.

4th. After dinner comes Mr. Spong to see me, and brings me my parallelogram in better order than before, and two or three drafts of the port of Brest to my great content, and I did call Mr. Gibson to take notice of it who is very much pleased therewith; and it seems this parallelogram is not, as Mr. Sheres would the other day have persuaded me, the same as a protractor,[1] which do so much the more make me value it, but of itself it is a most useful instrument. Thence out with my wife and him, and carried him to an instrument-maker's shop, in Chancery Lane, that was once a 'prentice of Greatorex's. But the master was not within, and there Gibson showed me a parallelogram in brass, which I like so well that I will buy, and therefore bid it be made clean and fit for me. And so to my cousin Turner's, and there just spoke with The., the mother not being at home; and so to the New Exchange, and thence home to my letters; and so to supper and to bed. This morning I made a slip from the office to White Hall, expecting Povy's business at a Committee of Tangier, at which I would be, but it did not meet, and so I presently back.

5th. Betimes to Sir W. Coventry's, meaning by my visit to keep fresh my interest in him; and he tells me how it hath been talked that he was to go one of the Commissioners to Ireland, which he was resolved never to do unless directly commanded: for that to go thither while the Chief Secretary of State was his professed enemy was to undo himself; and therefore it were better for him to venture being unhappy here, than to go further off to be undone by some obscure instructions, or whatever other way of mischief his enemy should cut out for him. He mighty kind to me, and so parted. Thence home, calling in two or three places—among others, Dankers's, where I find him beginning of a piece for me, of Greenwich, which will please me well. And so home to dinner, and very busy all the afternoon, and so at night home to supper and to bed.

6th. To the King's playhouse, and there—in an upper box, where come in Colonel Poynton [2] and Doll Stacey, who is very

---

[1] An instrument used in surveying, by which the angles are taken.

[1] Probably Boynton. Sir Matthew Boynton, of Barneston, in Yorkshire, was created a baronet in 1618. He had seven sons, one of whom, Colonel Boynton, having embraced, like his father, the cause of the Parliament, took Sir John Hotham prisoner at York. Sir Matthew died in 1646. His eldest son became Sir Francis Boynton; the second, Matthew, was slain at Wigan, before the advance of Charles II to Worcester: he left two daughters, one of whom, Katharine, the maid of honour, who figures in Grammont, married Richard Talbot, afterwards Duke of Tyrconnel; the other married Wentworth, Earl of Roscommon. The remaining five sons, Marmaduke, John, Gustavus,

fine, and, by her wedding-ring, I suppose he hath married her at last—did see 'The Moor of Venice': but ill acted in most parts, Mohun, which did a little surprise me, not acting Iago's part by much so well as Clun used to do: nor another Hart's, which was Cassio's; nor, indeed, Burt doing the Moor's so well as I once thought he did.   Thence home, and just at Holborn Conduit the bolt broke, that holds the fore-wheels to the perch, and so the horses went away with them and left the coachman and us; but, being near our coach-maker's, and we staying in a little iron-monger's shop, we were presently supplied with another.

7th. (Lord's day.) My wife mighty peevish in the morning about my lying unquietly a'nights, and she will have it that it is a late practice from my evil thoughts in my dreams, and mightily she is troubled about it; but all blew over, and I up, and to church, and so home to dinner, where my wife in a worse fit, which lasted all the afternoon, and shut herself up in her closet, and I mightily grieved and vexed, and could not get her to tell me what ailed her, or to let me into her closet: but at last she did, where I found her crying on the ground, and could not please her; but at last find that she did plainly expound it to me.   It was that she did believe me false to her with Jane, and did rip up three or four silly circumstances of her not rising till I come out of my chamber, and her letting me thereby see her dressing herself, and that I must needs go into her chamber; which was so silly, and so far from truth, that I could not be troubled at it, though I could not wonder at her being troubled, if she had these thoughts.   At last I did give her such satisfaction, that we were mighty good friends.

8th. Up, and dressed myself; and by coach with W. Hewer and my wife to White Hall, where she set us down; and in the way our little boy, at Martin my bookseller's shop, going to 'light, did fall down; and, had he not been a most nimble boy (I saw how he did it, and was mightily pleased with him for it), he had been run over by the coach.   To visit my Lord Sandwich; and there, while my Lord was dressing himself, did see a young Spaniard, that he hath brought over with him, dance, which he is admired for, as the best dancer in Spain; and indeed he do with mighty mastery, but I do not like his dancing as well as the English, though my Lord

Cornelius, Charles, all died unmarried.   One of the sons must have been the Colonel Boynton who took Sir John Hotham prisoner, and in all probability he is the same who is here mentioned in connection with Doll Stacey.   Pepys only *supposes* he had married her.

commends it mightily. But I will have him to my house, and show it my wife. Here I met with Mr. Moore, who tells me the state of my Lord's accounts of his embassy, which I find not so good as I thought: for, though it be passed the King and his Cabal, the Committee for Foreign Affairs, as they are called, yet they have cut off from £19,000 full £8000, and have now sent it to the Lords of the Treasury, who, though the Committee have allowed the rest, yet they are not obliged to abide by it. So that I do fear this account may yet be long ere it be passed—much more ere that sum be paid: I am sorry for the family, and not a little for what it owes me. To my wife, and in our way home did show her the tall woman, in Holborn, which I have seen before; and I measured her, and she is, without shoes, just six feet five inches high, and they say not above twenty-one years old. Thence home, and there to dinner, and my wife in a wonderful ill humour; and after dinner I stayed with her alone, being not able to endure this life, and we fell to some angry words together; but by and by were mighty good friends, she telling me plain it was about Jane, which I made a matter of mirth at; but at last did call up Jane, and confirm her mistress's directions for her being gone at Easter, which I find the wench willing to be, but directly prays that Tom might go with her, which I promised, and was but what I designed; and she being thus spoke with and gone, my wife and I good friends, I having promised, and I will perform it, never to give her for the time to come ground of new trouble. This day I was told by Mr. Wren that Captain Cox, Master-Attendant at Deptford, is to be one of us very soon, he and Tippet being to take their turns for Chatham and Portsmouth, which choice I like well enough; and Captain Annesley is to come in his room at Deptford. This morning also, going to visit Roger Pepys, at the potticary's in King's Street, he tells me that Roger is gone to his wife's, so that they have been married, as he tells me, ever since the middle of last week: it was his design, upon good reasons, to make no noise of it, but I am well enough contented that it is over.

9th. To the King's playhouse, and there saw 'The Island Princess,' which I like mighty well, as an excellent play: and here we find Kynaston to be well enough to act again, which he do very well after his beating by Sir Charles Sedley's appointment.

10th. To White Hall, where the Duke of York was gone a-hunting; and so to the plasterer's at Charing Cross, that casts heads and bodies in plaster: and there I had my whole face done.

But I was vexed first to be forced to daub all my face over with pomatum: but it was pretty to feel how soft and easily it is done on the face, and by and by, by degrees, how hard it becomes, that you cannot break it, and sits so close, that you cannot pull it off, and yet so easy that it is as soft as a pillow, so safe is everything where many parts of the body do bear alike. Thus was the mould made; but when it came off there was little pleasure in it as it looks in the mould, nor any resemblance, whatever there will be in the figure when I come to see it cast off. To White Hall, where I stayed till the Duke of York came from hunting, which he did by and by, and, when dressed, did come out to dinner; and there I waited. Here he dined, and did mightily magnify his sauce, which he did then eat with everything, and said it was the best universal sauce in the world, it being taught him by the Spanish Ambassador:[1] made of some parsley and a dry toast beat in a mortar together with vinegar, salt, and a little pepper. He eats it with flesh or fowl or fish. And then he did now mightily commend some new sort of wine lately found out, called Navarre wine, which I tasted, and is, I think, good wine: but I did like better the notion of the sauce, and by and by did taste it, and liked it mightily. After dinner I did what I went for, which was to get his consent that Balty might hold his Muster-Master's place by deputy in his new employment which I design for him, about the Storekeeper's accounts; which the Duke of York did grant me, and I was mightily glad of it. Home, and there I find Povy and W. Batelier, by appointment, met to talk of some merchandise of wine and linen; but I do not like of their troubling my house to meet in, having no mind to their pretences of having their rendezvous here.

11th. Heard that the last night Colonel Middleton's wife died, a woman I never saw since she come hither, having never been within their house since.

12th. To wait on the Duke of York, with the rest of us, at the Robes, where the Duke of York did tell us that the King would have us prepare a draft of the present administration of the Navy, and what it was in the late times, in order to his being able to distinguish between the good and the bad; which I shall do, but to do it well will give me a great deal of trouble. Here we showed him Sir J. Minnes's propositions about balancing Storekeepers' accounts; and I did show him Hosier's, which did please him mightily, and he will have it showed the Council and King anon,

[1] The Conde de Dona.

to be put in practice.   Thence to the Treasurer's; and I and Sir J.
Minnes and Mr. Tippet down to the Lords Commissioners of the
Treasury, and there had a hot debate from Sir Thomas Clifford
and my Lord Ashley, the latter of whom, I hear, is turning about
as fast as he can to the Duke of Buckingham's side, being in danger,
it seems, of being otherwise out of play, which would not be convenient for him against Sir W. Coventry and Sir J. Duncomb, who
did uphold our Office against an accusation of our Treasurers, who
told the Lords that they found that we had run the King in debt
£50,000 or more, more than the money appointed for the year
would defray; which they declared like fools, and with design to
hurt us, though the thing is in itself ridiculous.   But my Lord
Ashley and Clifford did most horribly cry out against the want of
method in the Office.   At last it came that it should be put in
writing what they had to object; but I was devilish mad at it, to
see us thus wounded by our own members.   My wife and I to
Hercules' Pillars, and there dined; and there coming a Frenchman
by with his Show, we did make him show it us, which he did just
as Lacy acts it, which made it mighty pleasant to me.   Away, and
to Dankers's, and there saw our picture of Greenwich in doing,
which is mighty pretty.   Attended with Lord Brouncker the King
and Council, about the proposition of balancing Storekeepers'
accounts; and there presented Hosier's book, and it was mighty
well resented [1] and approved of.   So the Council being up, we to
the Queen's side with the King and Duke of York: and the Duke
of York did take me out to talk of our Treasurers, whom he is
mighty angry with; and I perceive he is mighty desirous to bring
in as many good motions of profit and reformation in the Navy as
he can before the Treasurers do light upon them, they being
desirous, it seems, to be thought the great reformers: and the Duke
of York do well.   But to my great joy he is mighty open to me in
everything; and by this means I know his whole mind, and shall
be able to secure myself, if he stands.   Here tonight I understand,
by my Lord Brouncker, that at last it is concluded on by the King
and Buckingham that my Lord of Ormond shall not hold his
government of Ireland, which is a great stroke, to show the power
of Buckingham and the poor spirit of the King, and little hold that
any man can have of him.   I and my wife called at my cousin
Turner's, and there met our new cousin Pepys, Mrs. Dickenson,
and Bab. and Betty come yesterday to town, poor girls, whom we

[1] Resent, to take *well* or ill.—Johnson.

have reason to love, and mighty glad we are to see them.   And there stayed a little, being also mightily pleased to see Betty Turner, who is now in town, and her brothers Charles and Will, being come from school to see their father.   And there talked a while, and so home, and there Pelling hath got W. Pen's book against the Trinity.[1]   I got my wife to read it to me; and I find it so well writ as, I think, it is too good for him ever to have writ it; and it is a serious sort of book, and not fit for everybody to read.

14th. (Lord's day.) Up, and by coach to Sir W. Coventry: and there he tells me he takes no care for anything more than in the Treasury; and that, that being done, he goes to cards and other delights, as plays, and in the summer-time to bowls.   But here he did show me two or three old books of the Navy, of my Lord Northumberland's [2] times, which he hath taken many good notes out of, for justifying the Duke of York and us in many things, wherein, perhaps, precedents will be necessary to produce.   W. Hewer and I to White Hall, where the Duke of York expected me; and in his closet Wren and I.   He did tell me how the King hath been acquainted with the Treasurers' [3] discourse at the Lords Commissioners of the Treasury the other day, and is dissatisfied with our running him in debt, which I removed: and he did carry me to the King, and I did satisfy him also; but his satisfaction is nothing worth, it being easily got and easily removed; but I do purpose to put in writing that which shall make the Treasurers ashamed.   But the Duke of York is horrid angry against them; and he hath cause, for they do work all they can to bring dishonour upon his management, as do plainly appear in all they do.   Having done with the Duke of York, who do repose all in me, I with Mr. Wren to his chamber to talk: where he observed that these people are all of them a broken sort of people, that have not much to lose, and therefore will venture all to make their fortunes better: that Sir Thomas Osborne is a beggar, having 11 or £1200 a year, but owes above £10,000.   The Duke of Buckingham's condition is shortly this: that he hath about £19,600 a year, of which he pays away about £7000 a year in interest, about £2000 in fee-farm rents

---

[1] Entitled *The Sandy Foundation Shaken*.   It caused him to be imprisoned in the Tower. 'Aug. 4, 1669. Young Penn, who wrote the blasphemous book, is delivered to his father to be transported.'—Letter to Sir John Birkenhead, quoted by Bishop Kennett in his MS. Collections, vol. lxxxix, p. 477.

[2] Algernon Percy, tenth Earl of Northumberland, Lord High Admiral to Charles I.

[3] Of the Navy.

to the King, about £6000 in wages and pensions, and the rest to live upon, and pay taxes for the whole. Wren says that for the Duke of York to stir in this matter, as his quality might justify, would but make all things worse, and that therefore he must bend and suffer all till time works it out: that he fears they will sacrifice the Church, and that the King will take anything, and so he will hold up his head a little longer, and then break in pieces. But Sir W. Coventry did today mightily magnify my late Lord Treasurer,[1] for a wise and solid, though infirm man: and, among other things, that when he hath said it was impossible in nature to find this or that sum of money, and my Lord Chancellor[2] hath made sport of it, and told the King that when my Lord hath said it was impossible, yet he hath made shift to find it, and that was by Sir G. Carteret's getting credit, my Lord did once in his hearing say thus, which he magnifies as a great saying—that impossible would be found impossible at last; meaning that the King would run himself out beyond all his credit and funds, and then we should too late find it impossible; which is, he says, now come to pass.

15th. Up, and with Tom to White Hall; and there at a Committee of Tangier, where a great instance of what a man may lose by the neglect of a friend: Povy never had such an opportunity of passing his accounts, the Duke of York being there, and everybody well disposed and in expectation of them; but my Lord Ashley, on whom he relied, and for whose sake this day was pitched on, that he might be sure to be there among the rest of his friends, stayed too long, till the Duke of York and his company thought unfit to stay longer: and so the day lost, and God knows when he will have so good a one again as long as he lives. And this was the man of the whole company that he hath made the most interest to gain, and now most depended upon him. To the plasterer's, and there saw the figure of my face taken from the mould: and it is most admirably like, and I will have another made before I take it away. To my cousin Turner's, where having the last night been told by her that she had drawn me for her Valentine, I did this day call at the New Exchange, and bought her a pair of green silk stockings and garters and shoe-strings, and two pair of jessimy gloves, all coming to about 28*s.*, and did give them to her this noon. At the 'Change I did at my bookseller's shop accidentally fall into talk with Sir Samuel Tuke[3] about trees and Mr. Evelyn's garden;

---

[1] Southampton.   [2] Clarendon.

[3] Sir Samuel Tuke, of Cressing Temple, Essex, Bart., was a colonel in

and I do find him, I think, a little conceited, but a man of very fine discourse as any I ever heard almost, which I was mighty glad of. After dinner my wife and I endeavoured to make a visit to Ned Pickering; but he not at home, nor his lady, and therefore back again, and took up my cousin Turner, and to my cousin Roger's lodgings, and there find him pretty well again, and his wife mighty kind and merry, and did make mighty much of us, and I believe he is married to a very good woman. Here was also Bab. and Betty, who have not their clothes yet, and therefore cannot go out, otherwise I would have had them abroad tomorrow; but the poor girls mighty kind to us, and we must show them kindness also. In Suffolk Street lives Moll Davis; and we did see her coach come for her to her door, a mighty pretty fine coach. To White Hall, and there, by means of Mr. Cooling, did get into the play, the only one we have seen this winter: it was 'The Five Hours' Adventure'; but I sat so far I could not hear well, nor was there any pretty woman that I did see, but my wife, who sat in my Lady Fox's pew, with her. The house very full; and late before done, so that it was past eleven before we got home.

16th. Home, where I find some things of W. Batelier's come out of France, among which some clothes for my wife, wherein she is likely to lead me to the expense of so much money as vexed me; but I seemed so, more than I at this time was, only to prevent her taking too much. But I was mightily pleased with another picture of the King of France's head, of Nanteuil's, bigger than the other which he brought over. And so to the office, where busy all the afternoon, though my eyes mighty bad with the light of the candles last night, which was so great as to make my eyes sore all this day, and do teach me, by a manifest experiment, that it is only too much light that do make my eyes sore. Nevertheless, with the help of my tube, and being desirous of easing my mind of five or six days' journal, I did venture to write it down from ever since this day se'nnight, and I think without hurting my eyes any more than they were before, which was very much, and so home to supper and to bed.

17th. The King dining yesterday at the Dutch Ambassador's, after dinner they drank and were pretty merry; and among the

Charles I's army, and cousin to John Evelyn. He died at Somerset House, January 1674. We have seen that he was the translator of *The Adventures of Five Hours*. He was a Roman Catholic, and there is a life of him in Dodd's *Church History*.

rest of the King's company there was that worthy fellow my Lord of Rochester and Tom Killigrew, whose mirth and raillery offended the former so much, that he did give Tom Killigrew a box on the ear in the King's presence, which do give much offence to the people here at Court, to see how cheap the King makes himself; and the more for that the King hath not only passed by the thing, and pardoned it to Rochester already, but this very morning the King did publicly walk up and down, and Rochester I saw with him as free as ever, to the King's everlasting shame, to have so idle a rogue his companion.[1] How Tom Killigrew takes it I do not hear. I do also this day hear that my Lord Privy Seal do accept to go Lieutenant into Ireland; but whether it be true or no I cannot tell. To Colonel Middleton's, to the burial of his wife, where we were all invited, and much more company, and had each of us a ring: and so towards evening to our church, where there was a sermon preached by Mills, and so home. At church there was my Lord Brouncker and Mrs. Williams in our pew, the first time they were ever there or that I knew that either of them would go to church. Comes Castle to me, to desire me to go to Mr. Pedley this night, he being to go out of town tomorrow morning, which I therefore did, by hackney coach, first going to White Hall to meet with Sir W. Coventry, but missed him. But here I had a pleasant rencontre of a lady in mourning, that, by the little light I had, seemed handsome. I passing by her, did observe she looked back again and again upon me, I suffering her to go before, and it being now dusk. She went into the little passage towards the Privy Water-gate, and I followed, but missed her; but coming back again, I observed she returned, and went to go out of the Court. I followed her, and took occasion, in the new passage now built, where the walk is to be, to take her by the hand, to lead her through, which she willingly accepted; and I led her to the Great Gate, and there left her, she telling me of her own accord that she was going as far as Charing Cross; but my boy was at the Gate, and so I durst not go out with her. So to Lincoln's Inn, where to Mr. Pedley, with whom I spoke and did my business presently: and I find him a man of good language, and mighty civil, and I believe very upright: and so home, where W. Batelier was, and supped with us, and I did reckon this night what I owed him; and I do find that the things my wife, of her own head, hath

[1] Rochester was not yet twenty-one years old, whilst Charles was of the mature age of thirty-eight.

taken, together with my own, which comes not to above £5, comes to about £22. But it is the last, and so I am the better contented; and they are things that are not trifles, but clothes, gloves, shoes, hoods, &c. So after supper to bed.

18th. To the office, and at noon home, expecting to have this day seen Bab. and Betty Pepys here, but they came not; and so, after dinner, my wife and I to the Duke of York's House, to a play, and there saw 'The Mad Lover,' which do not please me so well as it used to do, only Betterton's part still pleases me. But here who should we have come to us but Bab. and Betty and Talbot, the first play they were yet at; and going to see us, and hearing by my boy, whom I sent to them, that we were here, they came to us hither, and happened all of us to sit by my cousin Turner and The. We carried them home first, and then took Bab. and Betty to our house, where they lay and supped, and pretty merry, and very fine with their new clothes, and good comely girls they are enough, and very glad I am of their being with us, though I would very well have been contented to be without the charge. So they to bed.

19th. Up, and after seeing the girls, who lodged in our bed with their maid Martha, who hath been their father's maid these twenty years and more, I to the office while the young people went to see Bedlam.[1] This morning, among other things, talking with Sir W. Coventry, I did propose to him my putting into serve in Parliament, if there should, as the world begins to expect, be a new one chose: he likes it mightily, both for the King's and Service's sake, and the Duke of York's, and will propound it to the Duke of York: and I confess, if there be one, I would be glad to be in.

20th. After dinner with my wife and my two girls to the Duke of York's House, and there saw 'The Grateful Servant,'[2] a pretty good play, and which I have forgot that ever I did see. And thence with them to Mrs. Grotier's, the Queen's tire-woman, for a pair of locks for my wife; she is an oldish French woman, but with a pretty hand as most I have seen; and so home.

21st. (Lord's day.) With my wife and two girls to church, they very fine; and so home, where comes my cousin Roger and his wife, I having sent for them, to dine with us. And there comes in by chance also Mr. Shepley, who is come to town with my Lady Paulina, who is desperately sick and is gone to Chelsea, to the old

[1] Then in Bishopsgate Without.
[2] A comedy by James Shirley.

house where my Lord himself was once sick, where I doubt my
Lord means to visit her, more for young Mrs. Beck's sake than for
hers. Here we dined, with W. Batelier and W. Hewer with us,
these two girls making it necessary that they be always with us, for
I am not company light enough to be always merry with them: and
so sat talking all the afternoon, and then Shepley went away first,
and then my cousin Roger and his wife.

22d. After dinner, with my wife in her morning gown, and the
two girls dressed, to Unthank's, where my wife dresses herself,
having her gown this day laced, and a new petticoat; and so is
indeed very fine. In the evening I do carry them to White Hall,
and there did without much trouble get into the playhouse, there
in a good place among the Ladies of Honour, and myself also sat
in the pit; and then by and by came the King and Queen, and they
began 'Bartholomew Fair.' But I like no play here so well as at
the common playhouse; besides that, my eyes being very ill since
last Sunday and this day se'nnight, I was in mighty pain to defend
myself now from the light of the candles. After the play done
we met with W. Batelier and W. Hewer and Talbot Pepys, and
they followed us in a hackney coach: and we all stopped at Hercules'
Pillars; and there I did give them the best supper I could, and pretty
merry; and so home between eleven and twelve at night.

23d. Up; and to the office, where all the morning, and then
home and put a mouthful of victuals in my mouth; and by a hackney coach followed my wife and the girls, who are gone by eleven
o'clock, thinking to have seen a new play at the Duke of York's
House. But I do find them staying at my tailor's, the play not
being today; and therefore I took them to Westminster Abbey,
and there did show them all the tombs very finely, having one with
us alone, there being other company this day to see the tombs, it
being Shrove Tuesday. And here we did see, by particular
favour, the body of Queen Katherine of Valois; and I had the
upper part of her body in my hands, and I did kiss her mouth,
reflecting upon it that I did kiss a Queen, and that this was my
birthday, thirty-six years old, that I did kiss a Queen.[1] But here
this man, who seems to understand well, tells me that the saying is
not true that she was never buried, for she was buried; only, when

[1] The story told Pepys in Westminster Abbey appears to have been correct;
for Neale informs us (*History of Westminster Abbey*, vol. ii, p. 88), that near
the south side of Henry V's tomb there was formerly a wooden chest, or
coffin, wherein part of the skeleton and parched body of Katherine de Valois,

Henry the Seventh built his chapel, she was taken up and laid in this wooden coffin; but I did there see that, in it, the body was buried in a leaden one which remains under the body to this day. Thence to the Duke of York's playhouse, and there, finding the play begun, we homeward to the Glass House,[1] and there showed my cousins the making of glass, and had several things made with great content: and, among others, I had one or two singing-glasses made, which make an echo to the voice, the first that ever I saw; but so thin, that the very breath broke one or two of them. Thence to Mr. Batelier's, where we supped and had a good supper, and here was Mr. Gumbleton: and after supper some fiddles, and so to dance; but my eyes were so out of order, that I had little pleasure this night at all, though I was glad to see the rest merry.

24th. I to the office, and at night my wife sends for me to W. Hewer's lodging, where I find two best chambers of his so finely furnished, and all so rich and neat, that I was mightily pleased with him and them: and here only my wife and I and the two girls, and had a mighty neat dish of custards and tarts, and good drink and talk. And so away home to bed, with infinite content at this his treat; for it was mighty pretty, and everything mighty rich.

25th. To the Duke of York's House, and there before one, but the house infinite full; where by and by the King and Court came, it being a new play, or an old one new vamped, by Shadwell, called 'The Royal Shepherdess';[2] but the silliest for words and design and everything that ever I saw in my whole life, there being nothing in the world pleasing in it, but a good martial dance of pikemen, where Harris and another do handle their pikes in a dance to admiration; but I was never less satisfied with a play in my life.

26th. Was forced to send my excuse to the Duke of York for

---

his queen (from the waist upwards) was to be seen. She was interred in January 1437 in the Chapel of Our Lady, at the east end of this church; but when that building was pulled down by her grandson, Henry VII, her coffin was found to be decayed, and her body was taken up and placed in a chest near her first husband's tomb. 'There,' says Dart, 'it hath ever since continued to be seen, the bones being firmly united, and thinly clothed with flesh, like scrapings of tanned leather.' It was at length removed from the public gaze, into St. Nicholas's Chapel, and finally deposited under the monument of Sir George Villiers, when the vault was made for the remains of Elizabeth Percy, Duchess of Northumberland, in December 1776.

[1] In Blackfriars.
[2] A tragi-comedy, altered by Thomas Shadwell from a comedy written by Mr. Fountain, called *The Rewards of Virtue*.

my not attending him this day because of my cold, and was the less troubled because I was thereby out of the way to offer my proposals about pursers till the Surveyor had delivered his notions. Though I could not speak, yet I went with my wife and girls to the King's playhouse, and saw 'The Faithful Shepherdess.' But, Lord! what an empty house, there not being, as I could tell the people, so many as to make up above £10 in the whole house! The being of a new play at the other house, I suppose, being the cause, though it be so silly a play that I wonder how there should be enough people to go thither two days together and not leave more to fill this house. The emptiness of the house took away our pleasure a great deal, though I liked it the better; for I plainly discern the music is the better by how much the house the emptier. Thence home, and again to W. Hewer's, and had a pretty little treat, and spent an hour or two, my voice being wholly taken away with my cold, and so home and to bed.

28th. (Lord's day.) Up, and got my wife to read to me a copy of what the Surveyor offered to the Duke of York on Friday, he himself putting it into my hands to read. But, Lord! it is a poor, silly thing ever to think to bring it in practice in the King's Navy. It is to have the Captains to account for all stores and victuals; but upon so silly grounds, to my thinking, and ignorance of the present instructions of Officers, that I am ashamed to hear it. However, I do take a copy of it for my future use and answering; and so to church, where, God forgive me! I did most of the time gaze on the fine milliner's wife, in Fenchurch Street, who was at our church today; and so home to dinner. After dinner to write down my journal; and then abroad by coach with my cousins, to their father's, where we are kindly received, but he is in great pain for his man Arthur, who, he fears, is now dead, having been desperate sick, and speaks so much of him that my cousin his wife and I did make mirth of it, and call him Arthur O'Bradley.[1] After staying here a little, and eat and drank, and she give me some gingerbread made in cakes, like chocolate, very good, made by a friend, I carried him and her to my cousin Turner's, where we stayed, expecting her coming from church; but she coming not, I went to her husband's chamber in the Temple, and thence fetched her. After talking there awhile, and agreeing to be all merry at my house on Tuesday next, I away home, and there spent the evening talking and reading with my wife and Mr. Pelling.

[1] This was an allusion to the old and popular ballad of Arthur O'Bradley.

March 1st. I do hear that my Lady Paulina Montagu did die yesterday; at which I went to my Lord's lodgings, but he is shut up with sorrow, and so not to be spoken with: and therefore I returned, and to Westminster Hall, where I have not been, I think, in some months. And here the Hall was very full, the King having, by Commission to some Lords, this day prorogued the Parliament till the 19th of October next: at which I am glad, hoping to have time to go over to France this year. But I was most of all surprised this morning by my Lord Bellasis, who, by appointment, met me at Auditor Wood's, at the Temple, and tells me of a duel designed between the Duke of Buckingham and my Lord Halifax or Sir W. Coventry, the challenge being carried by Harry Savile,[1] but prevented by my Lord Arlington, and the King told of it; and this was all the discourse at Court this day. But I meeting Sir W. Coventry in the Duke of York's chamber, he would not own it to me, but told me he was a man of too much peace to meddle with fighting, and so it rested: but the talk is full in the town of the business. Thence, having walked some turns with my cousin Pepys, and most people, by their discourse, believing that this Parliament will never sit more, I away to several places to look after things against tomorrow's feast, and so home to dinner. And thence, after noon, my wife and I out by hackney coach, and spent the afternoon in several places, doing several things at the 'Change and elsewhere against tomorrow; and, among others, I did bring home a piece of my face cast in plaster, for to make a vizard upon for my eyes. And so home, where W. Batelier came and sat with us; and there, after many doubts, did resolve to go on with our feast and dancing tomorrow; and so after supper left the maids to make clean the house and to lay the cloth and other things against tomorrow, and so to bed.

2d. Home, and there I find my company come, namely, Madam Turner, Dyke, The. and Betty Turner, and Mr. Bellwood, formerly their father's clerk, but now set up for himself—a conceited, silly fellow, but one they make mightily of—my cousin Roger Pepys and his wife and two daughters. I had a noble dinner for them, as I almost ever had, and mighty merry, and particularly myself pleased with looking on Betty Turner, who is mighty pretty.

---

[1] Henry Savile was a younger son of Sir William Savile, Bart., of Thornhill in Yorkshire, by Anne, daughter of Thomas, first Lord Coventry, and sister to Sir William Coventry. He became vice-chamberlain to Charles II, and served in Parliament for Newark. He died *s.p.*

After dinner we fell one to one talk and another to another, and looking over my house and closet and things; and The. Turner to write a letter to a lady in the country, in which I did now and then put in half a dozen words, and sometimes five or six lines, and then she as much, and made up a long and good letter, she being mighty witty really, though troublesome-humoured with it. And thus till night, that our music came, and the office ready and candles, and also W. Batelier and his sister Susan came, and also Will. Howe and two gentlemen more, strangers, which, at my request yesterday, he did bring to dance, called Mr. Ireton and Mr. Starkey. We fell to dancing, and continued, only with intermission for a good supper, till two in the morning, the music being Greeting, and another most excellent violin, and theorbo, the best in town. And so with mighty mirth and pleased with their dancing of jigs afterwards several of them, and among others Betty Turner, who did it mighty prettily; and, lastly, W. Batelier's 'Blackmore and Blackmore Mad'; and then to a country dance again, and so broke up with extraordinary pleasure, as being one of the days and nights of my life spent with the greatest content, and that which I can but hope to repeat again a few times in my whole life. This done, we parted, the strangers home, and I did lodge my cousin Pepys and his wife in our blue chamber. My cousin Turner, her sister, and The. in our best chamber; Bab., Betty, and Betty Turner in our own chamber; and myself and my wife in the maid's bed, which is very good. Our maids in the coachman's bed, the coachman with the boy in his settle-bed,[1] and Tom where he uses to lie. And so I did, to my great content, lodge at once in my house, with the greatest ease, fifteen, and eight of them strangers of quality. My wife this day put on first her French gown, called a Sac,[2] which becomes her very well, brought her over by W. Batelier.

3d. To my guests, and got them to breakfast, and then parted by coaches; and I did, in mine, carry my she-cousin Pepys and her daughters home, and there left them. To White Hall, where W. Hewer met me; and he and I took a turn in St. James's Park, and in the Mall did meet Sir W. Coventry and Sir J. Duncomb, and did speak with them about some business before the Lords of the Treasury: but I did find them more than usually busy, though I knew not then the reason of it, but I guessed it by what followed next day. Thence to Dankers's, the painter's, and there saw my picture of Greenwich finished to my very good content, though

[1] A folding bed.   [2] Which remained in fashion till a much later date.

this manner of distemper do make the figures not so pleasing as in oil. To the Duke of York's playhouse, and there saw an old play, the first time acted these forty years, called 'The Lady's Trial,'[1] acted only by the young people of the house; but the house very full. To the New Exchange, and so called at my cousin Turner's; and there, meeting Mr. Bellwood, did hear how my Lord Mayor,[2] being invited this day to dinner at the Reader's at the Temple, and endeavouring to carry his sword up,[3] the students did pull it down, and forced him to go and stay all the day in a private Councillor's chamber, until the Reader himself could get the young gentlemen to dinner; and then my Lord Mayor did retreat out of the Temple by stealth, with his sword up. This do make great heat among the students; and my Lord Mayor did send to the King, and also I hear that Sir Richard Browne did cause the drums to beat for the train-bands; but all is over, only I hear that the students do resolve to try the Charter of the City.[4] So we home, and betimes to bed, and slept well all night.

4th. To White Hall, where in the first court I did meet Sir Jeremy Smith, who did tell me that Sir W. Coventry was just now sent to the Tower about the business of his challenging the Duke of Buckingham, and so was also Harry Savile to the Gate-house;[5] which, as he is a gentleman, and of the Duke of York's bed-chamber, I heard afterwards that the Duke of York is mightily incensed at it, and do appear very high to the King that he might

---

[1] A tragedy by John Ford.   [2] Sir William Peake, clothworker.
[3] As a symbol of his authority.
[4] The only printed notice of the dispute between the Temple and the City occurs in Pearce's *History of the Inns of Court and Chancery*, 8vo, 1848, p. 236: 'The Lord Mayor (Sir W. Turner) complained to the King, and on the 7th April 1669, the case was heard before his Majesty in Council. The ring-leaders, Mr. Hodges, Mr. Wynn, and Mr. Monday, appeared at the Board, attended by counsel, who were heard on their behalf. Upon consideration, it appearing to the King that the matter very much depended upon the right and privilege of bearing up the Lord Mayor's sword within the Temple, which, by order of Council on the 24th March, in the same year, had been left to be decided by due course of law, his Majesty thought fit to suspend the declaration of his pleasure thereupon, until the said right and privilege should be determined at law.' Mr. Tyrrel, the City Remembrancer, has obligingly communicated the only two entries relating to the business, existing in the Corporation records: the first is an order, dated 23rd March 1668, for the Lord Mayor, aldermen, etc., to attend the Council on the following day; and the other directs the Chamberlain to pay the Town Clerk £23 14s. 6d., by him disbursed for counsel, about the business of the Temple, etc.
[5] At Westminster.

not be sent thither, but to the Tower, this being done only in contempt to him. This news of Sir W. Coventry did strike me to the heart, and with reason, for by this and my Lord of Ormond's business I do doubt that the Duke of Buckingham will be so flushed, that he will not stop at anything, but be forced to do anything now, as thinking it not safe to end here; and, Sir W. Coventry being gone, the King will have no good counsellor left, nor the Duke of York any sure friend to stick to him; nor any good man will remain to advise what is good. This, therefore, do heartily trouble me as anything that ever I heard. So up into the house, and met with several people; but the Committee did not meet: and the whole house I find full of this business of Sir W. Coventry's, and most men very sensible of the cause and effects of it. So, meeting with my Lord Bellassis, he told me the particulars of this matter: that it arises about a quarrel which Sir W. Coventry had with the Duke of Buckingham about a design between the Duke and Sir Robert Howard to bring him into a play at the King's House, which W. Coventry not enduring, did by H. Savile send a letter to the Duke of Buckingham that he had a desire to speak with him. Upon which, the Duke of Buckingham did bid Holmes, his champion ever since my Lord Shrewsbury's business, go to him to do the business; but H. Savile would not tell it to any but himself, and therefore did go presently to the Duke of Buckingham, and told him that his uncle Coventry was a person of honour and was sensible of his Grace's liberty taken of abusing him, and that he had a desire of satisfaction, and would fight with him. But that here they were interrupted by my Lord Chamberlain's coming in, who was commanded to go to bid the Duke of Buckingham to come to the King, Holmes having discovered it. He told me that the King did last night at the Council ask the Duke of Buckingham, upon his honour, whether he had received any challenge from W. Coventry; which he confessed that he had: and then the King asking W. Coventry, he told him that he did not own what the Duke of Buckingham had said, though it was not fit for him to give him a direct contradiction. But being by the King put upon declaring the truth upon his honour, he answered that he had understood that many hard questions had upon this business been moved to some lawyers, and that therefore he was unwilling to declare anything that might, from his own mouth, render him obnoxious to his Majesty's displeasure, and therefore prayed to be excused; which the King did

think fit to interpret to be a confession, and so gave warrant that
night for his commitment to the Tower. Being very much
troubled at this, I away by coach homewards, and directly to the
Tower, where I find him in one Mr. Bennet's house, son to Major
Bailey, one of the Officers of the Ordnance, in the Brick Tower,
where I find him busy with my Lord Halifax and his brother. So
I would not stay to interrupt them, but only to give him comfort
and offer my service to him, which he kindly and cheerfully
received, only owning his being troubled for the King his master's
displeasure, which, I suppose, is the ordinary form and will of
persons in this condition. And so I parted with great content
that I had so earlily seen him there; and so going out, did meet Sir
Jer. Smith going to meet me, who had newly been with Sir W.
Coventry. And so he and I by water to Redriffe, and so walked
to Deptford, where I have not been, I think, these twelve months.
And there to the Treasurer's house, where the Duke of York is,
and his Duchess; and there we find them at dinner in the great
room, unhung, and there was with them my Lady Duchess of
Monmouth, the Countess of Falmouth, Castlemaine, Henrietta
Hyde[1] (my Lady Hinchingbroke's sister), and my Lady Peter-
borough. And after dinner Sir Jer. Smith and I were invited down
to dinner with some of the Maids of Honour, namely, Mrs. Ogle,[2]
Blague,[3] and Howard,[4] which did me good to have the honour to
dine with and look on them; and the Mother of the Maids,[5] and
Mrs. Howard,[6] the mother of the Maid of Honour of that name, and

[1] Henrietta, fifth daughter to the Earl of Burlington, married Laurence
Hyde, afterwards created Earl of Rochester.

[2] Anne Ogle, daughter of Thomas Ogle, of Pinchbeck in Lincolnshire.
She was afterwards the first wife of Craven Howard.

[3] Margaret Blagge, or Blague, daughter of Colonel Blague, and afterwards
wife of Sidney Godolphin.

[4] Dorothy, the elder daughter of Mrs. Howard. She afterwards married
Colonel James Graham, of Levens, Keeper of the Privy Purse of the Duke of
York. Their daughter, Katherine Graham, married her cousin, Henry
Bowes Howard, fourth Earl of Berkshire, and eleventh Earl of Suffolk.

[5] The 'mother of the maid' in the Court of Queen Catherine was Bridget,
Lady Sanderson, daughter of Sir Edward Tyrrell, Knight, and wife of Sir
William Sanderson, Gentleman of the Privy Chamber. It is possible, however, that someone filled the like office in the household of the Duchess
of York.

[6] Elizabeth, daughter of Lowthiel, Lord Dundas, wife of William Howard,
fourth son of the first Earl of Berkshire. Her son, Craven Howard, married,
first, Anne Ogle, mentioned above, and secondly, Mary, daughter of George
Bower, of Elford, in Staffordshire, by whom he had Henry Bowes Howard,
who married Katherine Graham.

the Duke's housekeeper here. Here was also Monsieur Blanquefort,[1] Sir Richard Powle,[2] Colonel Villiers,[3] Sir Jonathan Trelawny,[4] and others. And here drank most excellent and great variety and plenty of wines, more than I have drank at once these seven years, but yet did me no great hurt. Having dined very merrily, and understanding by Blancfort how angry the Duke of York was about their offering to send Savile to the Gate-house among the rogues; and then, observing how this company, both the ladies and all, are of a gang, and did drink a health to the union of the two brothers, and talking of others as their enemies, they parted, and so we up; and there I did find the Duke of York and Duchess with all the great ladies sitting upon a carpet, on the ground, there being no chairs, playing at 'I love my love with an A because he is so and so, and I hate him with an A because of this and that': and some of them, but particularly the Duchess herself and my Lady Castlemaine, were very witty. This done, they took barge, and I with Sir J. Smith to Captain Cox's; and there to talk, and left them and other company to drink while I slunk out to Bagwell's; and there saw her and her mother and our late maid Nell, who cried for joy to see me. So to Cox's, and thence walked with Sir J. Smith back to Redriffe; and so by water home, and there my wife mighty angry for my absence, and fell mightily out, but not being certain of anything, but thinks only that Pierce or Knipp was there, and did ask me, and, I perceive, the boy, many questions. But I did answer her; and so, after much ado, did go to bed and lie quiet all night. But she had another bout with me in the morning, but I did make shift to quiet her, but yet she was not fully satisfied, poor wretch! in her mind, and thinks much at my taking so much pleasure without her, which, indeed, is a fault, though I did not design or foresee it when I went.

5th. After dinner, I to the Tower, where I find Sir W. Coventry with abundance of company with him: and, after sitting awhile and

[1] In 1677 he succeeded to the titles and estates of his father-in-law, Sir George Sondes, who, in April 1676, was created Earl of Feversham and Viscount Sondes. As Earl of Feversham, Blanquefort became of great importance during the short but eventful reign of James II. He died in 1709, *s.p.*

[2] Sir Richard Powle, of Shottesbrooke, Berkshire, Master of the Horse to the Duchess of York.

[3] Edward Villiers, Master of the Robes, and Groom of the Bedchamber to the Duke of York. He was afterwards knighted, and is the direct ancestor of the earls of Jersey.

[4] The second baronet of his family, and father of the Bishop of Winchester, of the same names.

hearing some merry discourse, (and, among others, of Mr. Brouncker's being this day summoned to Sir William Morton,[1] one of the Judges, to give in security for his good behaviour upon his words the other day to Sir John Morton,[2] a Parliament-man, at White Hall, who had heretofore spoke very highly against Brouncker in the House), I away, and to Aldgate. Walked forward towards Whitechapel till my wife overtook me with the coach, it being a mighty fine afternoon; and there we went the first time out of town with our coach and horses, and went as far as Bow, the spring beginning a little now to appear, though the way be dirty; and so, with great pleasure, with the fore part of our coach up, we spent the afternoon. And so in the evening home, and there busy at the office awhile, and so to bed, mightily pleased with being at peace with my poor wife, and with the pleasure we may hope to have with our coach this summer when the weather comes to be good.

6th. Before the office, I stepped to Sir W. Coventry at the Tower, and there had a great deal of discourse with him: among others, of the King's putting him out of the Council yesterday, with which he is well contented, as with what else they can strip him of, he telling me, and so hath long done, that he is weary and surfeited of business; but he joins with me in his fears that all will go to naught, as matters are now managed. He told me the matter of the play that was intended for his abuse, wherein they foolishly and sillily bring in two tables like that which he hath made, with a round hole in the middle, in his closet, to turn himself in; and he is to be in one of them as master, and Sir J. Duncomb in the other as his man or imitator: and their discourse in those tables about the disposing of their books and papers very foolish. But that that he is offended with, is his being made so contemptible, as that any should dare to make a gentleman a subject for the mirth of the world: and that therefore he had told Tom Killigrew that he should tell his actors, whoever they were, that did offer at anything like representing him, that he would not complain to my Lord Chamberlain, which was too weak, nor get him beaten, as Sir Charles Sedley is said to have done, but that he would cause his nose to be cut. He told me how that the Duke of Buckingham

---

[1] Made a Justice of the King's Bench 1665: *ob.* 1672.
[2] Sir John Morton, of Milborne St. Andrews, Dorsetshire, the second baronet of his family, then serving as burgess for Poole, and afterwards for Melcombe Regis. He died in 1698, *æt.* 71, *M.I.*

did himself, some time since, desire to join with him, of all men in England, and did bid him propound to himself to be Chief Minister of State, saying that he would bring it about, but that he refused to have anything to do with any faction; and that the Duke of Buckingham did, within these few days, say that, of all men in England, he would have chosen Sir W. Coventry to have joined entire with. He tells me that he fears their prevailing against the Duke of York; and that their violence will force them to it, as being already beyond his pardon. He repeated to me many examples of challenging of Privy Councillors and others, but never any proceeded against with that severity which he is, it never amounting with others to more than a little confinement. He tells me of his being weary of the Treasury, and of the folly, ambition, and desire of popularity of Sir Thomas Clifford, and yet the rudeness of his tongue and passions when angry. This day my wife made it appear to me that my late entertainment this week cost me above £12, an expense which I am almost ashamed of, though it is but once in a great while, and is the end for which, in the most part, we live, to have such a merry day once or twice in a man's life.

7th. (Lord's day.) To the Tower, to see Sir W. Coventry, who had H. Jermyn and a great many more with him, and more, while I was there, came in; so that I do hear that there was not less than sixty coaches there yesterday and the other day; which I hear also that there is great exception taken at by the King and the Duke of Buckingham, but it cannot be helped. To Suffolk Street, to see my cousin Pepys, but neither the old nor young at home. I to White Hall, and there hear that there are letters come from Sir Thomas Allen, that he hath made some kind of peace with Algiers; upon which the King and Duke of York, being to go out of town tomorrow, are met at my Lord Arlington's. So I there, and by Mr. Wren was desired to stay to see if there were occasion for their speaking with me, which I did, walking without with Charles Porter, talking of a great many things: and I perceive all the world is against the Duke of Buckingham's acting thus high, and do prophesy nothing but ruin from it. But he do well observe that the Church lands cannot certainly come to much, if the King shall be persuaded to take them, they being leased out for long leases. By and by, after two hours' stay, the Council rose, having, as Wren tells me, resolved upon sending six ships to the Straits forthwith, not being contented with the peace upon the terms they demand, which are that all our ships, where any Turks or Moors shall be found slaves, shall be prizes, which will imply that they must be searched. I hear that tomorrow the King and Duke of York set out for Newmarket, by three in the morning, to some foot- and horse-races, to be abroad ten or twelve days. So I away without seeing the Duke of York; but Mr. Wren showed me the Order of Council about the balancing the Storekeeper's accounts, which passed the Council in the very terms I drew it, only I did put in my name as he that presented the book of Hosier's preparing, and that is left out—I mean, my name—which is no great matter.

8th. To White Hall, from whence the King and the Duke of York went by three in the morning, and had the misfortune to be overset with the Duke of York, the Duke of Monmouth, and the Prince at the King's Gate in Holborn; and the King all dirty, but no hurt. How it came to pass I know not, but only it was dark, and the torches did not, they say, light the coach as they should do. I thought this morning to have seen my Lord Sandwich before he went out of town, but I came half an hour too late; which troubles me, I having not seen him since my Lady Pall died. W. Hewer and I to the Harp and Ball to drink my morning draught, and there met with King, the Parliament-man, with whom I had some im- pertinent talk. And so to the Privy Seal office, to examine what records I could find there, for my help in the great business I am put upon of defending the present constitution of the Navy: but there could not have liberty without order from him that is in present waiting, Mr. Bickerstaffe, who is out of town. Met Mr. Moore, and I find him the same discontented poor man as ever. He tells me that Mr. Shepley is upon being turned away from my Lord's family, and another sent down, which I am sorry for; but his age and good fellowship have almost made him fit for nothing. With my wife to the King's playhouse, and there saw 'The Mock Astrologer,' which I have often seen, and but an ordinary play; and so to my cousin Turner's, where we met Roger Pepys, his wife, and two daughters, and then home. There my wife to read to me, my eyes being sensibly hurt by the too great lights of the playhouse.

9th. Up, and to the Tower; and there find Sir W. Coventry alone, writing down his journal, which, he tells me, he now keeps of the material things. Upon which I told him, and he is the only man I ever told it to, I think, that I kept it most strictly these eight or ten years; and I am sorry almost that I told it him, it not being necessary, nor may be convenient to have it known. Here he showed me the petition he had sent to the King by my Lord

Keeper, which was not to desire any admittance to employment, but submitting himself therein humbly to his Majesty; but prayed the removal of his displeasure, and that he might be set free. He tells me that my Lord Keeper did acquaint the King with the substance of it, not showing him the petition; who answered that he was disposing of his employments, and when that was done he might be led to discharge him: and this is what he expects and what he seems to desire. But by this discourse he was pleased to take occasion to show me and read to me his account, which he hath kept by him under his own hand, of all his discourse and the King's answers to him upon the great business of my Lord Clarendon, and how he had first moved the Duke of York with it twice, at good distance, one after another, but without success; showing me thereby the simplicity and reasons of his so doing, and the manner of it; and the King's accepting it, telling him that he was not satisfied in his management, and did discover some dissatisfaction against him for his opposing the laying aside of my Lord Treasurer, at Oxford, which was a secret the King had not discovered. And really I was mighty proud to be privy to this great transaction, it giving me great conviction of the noble nature and ends of Sir W. Coventry in it, and considerations in general of the consequences of great men's actions, and the uncertainty of their estates, and other very serious considerations. To the office, where we sat all the morning, and after dinner by coach to my cousin Turner's, thinking to have taken up the young ladies; but The. was let blood today, and so my wife and I towards the King's playhouse, and by the way found Betty Turner and Bab. and Betty Pepys staying for us; and so took them all to see 'Claracilla,' which do not please me almost at all, though there are some good things in it. And so to my cousin Turner's, and there find my Lady Mordaunt and her sister Johnson; and by and by comes in a gentleman, Mr. Overbury, a pleasant man who plays most excellently on the flageolet, a little one that sounded as low as one of mine, and mighty pretty. Hence with my wife and Bab. and Betty Pepys and W. Hewer, whom I carried all this day with me, to my cousin Stradwick's, where I have not been ever since my brother Tom died, there being some difference between my father and them upon the account of my cousin Scott: and I glad of this opportunity of seeing them, they being good and substantial people, and kind. Here met my cousin Roger and his wife, and my cousin Turner, and here, which I never did before, I drank a glass (of a pint, I believe) at one draught, of the juice of oranges, of whose peel they make comfits; and here they drink the juice as wine, with sugar, and it is very fine drink; but, it being new, I was doubtful whether it might not do me hurt. Having stayed awhile, my wife and I back with my cousin Turner, &c., to her house. There we took our leaves of my cousin Pepys, who goes with his wife and two daughters for Impington tomorrow. They are very good people, and people I love and am obliged to, and shall have great pleasure in their friendship, and particularly in hers, she being an understanding and good woman.

10th. By hackney coach to Auditor Beale's office, in Holborn, to look for records of the Navy, but he was out of the way, and so forced to go next to White Hall, to the Privy Seal; and, after staying a little there, then to Westminster, where, at the Exchequer, I met with Mr. Newport and Major Halsey. And, after doing a little business with Mr. Burges, we by water to White Hall, where I made a little stop: and so with them by coach to Temple Bar, where, at the Sugar Loaf, we dined. And there comes a companion of theirs, Colonel Vernon, I think they called him, a merry good fellow, and one that was very plain in cursing the Duke of Buckingham and discoursing of his designs to ruin us, and that ruin must follow his counsels, and that we are an undone people. To which the others concurred, but not so plain, but all vexed at Sir W. Coventry's being laid aside: but Vernon is concerned, I perceive, for my Lord Ormond's being laid aside; but their company, being all old cavaliers, were very pleasant to hear how they swear and talk. But Halsey, to my content, tells me that my Lord Duke of Albemarle says that, W. Coventry being gone, nothing will be well done at the Treasury, and I believe it; but they do all talk as that Duncomb, upon some pretence or other, must follow him. Thence to the Privy Seal at White Hall, where, with W. Hewer and Mr. Gibson, I spent the afternoon till evening looking over the books there; and did find several things to my purpose, though few of those I designed to find, the books being kept there in no method at all. Having done there, we by water home, and there I find my cousin Turner and her two daughters come to see us; and there, after talking a little, I had my coach ready, and they going home, my wife and I out to Whitechapel to take a little air, though yet the dirtiness of the road do prevent most of the pleasure which we hoped to have from this tour. So home, and my wife to read to me till supper, and to bed.

11th. Up, and to Sir W. Coventry, to the Tower, who tells me that he hears that the Commission is gone down to the King, with a blank to fill for his place in the Treasury: and he believes it will be filled with one of our Treasurers of the Navy; but which he knows not, but he believes it will be Osborne. We walked down to the Stone Walk, which is called, it seems, my Lord of Northumberland's walk,[1] being paved by someone of that title that was prisoner there: and at the end of it there is a piece of iron upon the wall with his arms upon it, and holes to put in a peg for every turn they make upon that walk. So away to the office, where busy all the morning, and so to dinner, and so very busy all the afternoon at my office, late; and then home tired, to supper with content with my wife, and so to bed, she pleasing me, though I dare not own it, that she hath hired a chambermaid; but she, after many commendations, told me that she had one great fault, and that was that she was very handsome, at which I made nothing, but let her go on; but many times tonight she took occasion to discourse of her handsomeness and the danger she was in, by taking her, and that she did doubt yet whether it would be fit for her to take her. But I did assure her of my resolution to have nothing to do with her maids, though in myself I was glad to have the content to have a handsome one to look on.

12th. With W. Hewer to his office, and there with great content spent all the morning looking over the Navy accounts of several years, and the several patents of the Treasurers. At noon I ended there, to my great content, and giving the clerks there 20s. for their trouble, and having sent for W. Howe to discourse with him about the Patent Office records, wherein I remembered his brother to be concerned, I took him in my coach with W. Hewer and myself towards Westminster; and there he carried me to Nott's, the famous bookbinder, that bound for my Lord Chancellor's library: and here I did take occasion for curiosity to bespeak a book to be bound, only that I might have one of his binding. To Gray's Inn, and, at the next door, at a cook's shop of Howe's acquaintance, we bespoke dinner, it being now two o'clock; and in the meantime he carried us into Gray's Inn, to his chamber, where I never was before; and it is very pretty, and little, and neat, as he was always.

[1] No trace of this is to be found in Bayley's *History of the Tower*. Henry, the ninth earl, called the Wizard Earl, was confined in the Tower from 1605 to 1621, and the walk was probably constructed for his use during that long imprisonment.

And so, after a little stay and looking over a book or two there, we carried a piece of my Lord Coke [1] with us, and to our dinner, where, after dinner, he read at my desire a chapter in my Lord Coke about perjury, wherein I did learn a good deal touching oaths; and so away to the Patent Office, in Chancery Lane, where his brother Jack, being newly broke by running in debt and growing an idle rogue, he is forced to hide himself, and W. Howe do look after the office. Here I did set a clerk to look out some things for me in their books while W. Hewer and I to the Crown Office, [2] where we met with several good things that I most wanted, and did take short notes of the dockets, and so back to the Patent Office, and did the like there, and by candle-light ended. And so home, where, thinking to meet my wife with content after my pains all this day, I find her in her closet, alone in the dark, in a hot fit of railing against me, upon some news she has this day heard of Deb.'s living very fine, and with black spots, and speaking ill words of her mistress; which with good reason might vex her, and the baggage is to blame; but, God knows, I know nothing of her, nor what she do. But, what with my high words, and slighting, I did at last bring her to very good and kind terms, poor heart! And I was heartily glad of it, for I do see there is no man can be happier than myself, if I will, with her. But in her fit she did tell me what vexed me all the night, that this had put her upon putting off her handsome maid and hiring another that was full of the small-pox, which did mightily vex me, though I said nothing and do still. So down to supper, and she to read to me, and then with all possible kindness to bed.

13rh. Up, and to the Tower, to see Sir W. Coventry, and with him talking of business of the Navy all alone an hour, he taking physic. And so away to the office, where all the morning, and then home to dinner with my people, and so to the office again, and there all the afternoon till night, when comes, by mistake, my cousin Turner and her two daughters, which love such freaks, to eat some anchovies and ham of bacon with me, instead of noon, at dinner, when I expected them. But, however, I had done my business before they come, and so was in good humour enough to be with them, and so home to them to supper, being pleased to see Betty Turner, which hath something mighty pretty. But that which put me in good humour, both at noon and night, is the fancy that I am this day made a Captain of one of the King's ships,

[1] Coke's *Institutes*.   [2] In the Temple.

Mr. Wren having this day sent me the Duke of York's commission to be Captain of the Jerzy, in order to my being of a Court-martial for examining the loss of the Defiance, and other things; which do give me occasion of much mirth, and may be of some use to me: at least I shall get a little money for the time I have it, it being designed that I must really be a Captain to be able to sit in this Court. They stayed till about eight at night, and then away, and my wife to read to me, and then to bed in mighty good humour, but for my eyes.

14th. (Lord's day.) With my wife to church, where I did see my milliner's wife come again, which pleased me; but I durst not be seen to mind her, for fear of my wife's seeing me, though the woman I did never speak twenty words to, and that but only in her husband's shop. But so fearful I am of discontenting my wife or giving her cause of jealousy. But here we heard a most excellent good sermon of Mr. Gifford's,[1] upon the righteousness of Scribes and Pharisees. To write down my journal for the last week, my eyes being very bad, and therefore I forced to find a way to use by turns with my tube, one after another. This night I did tell Tom my resolution not to keep him after Jane was gone, but shall do well by him, which pleases him: and I think he will presently marry her and go away out of my house with her.

15th. Up, and by water with W. Hewer to the Temple; and thence to the Rolls, where I made inquiry for several rolls, and was soon informed in the manner of it: and so spent the whole morning with W. Hewer, he taking little notes in shorthand, while I hired a clerk there to read to me about twelve or more several rolls which I did call for: and it was great pleasure to me to see the method wherein their rolls are kept, that when the Master of the Office, one Mr. Case, do call for them, who is a man that I have heretofore known by coming to my Lord of Sandwich's, he did most readily turn to them. At noon they shut up, and W. Hewer and I did walk to the Cock, at the end of Suffolk Street, where I never was, a great ordinary, mightily cried up, and there bespoke a pullet; which while dressing he and I walked into St. James's Park, and thence back and dined very handsome, with a good soup and a pullet, for 4s. 6d. the whole. Thence back to the Rolls, and did a little more business: and so by water to White Hall, whither I went to speak with Mr. Williamson, that if he hath any papers relating

[1] George Gifford, A.M., appointed, in 1661, rector of St. Dunstan's in the East: *ob.* 1686.

to the Navy I might see them, which he promises me: and so by water home, with great content for what I have this day found, having got almost as much as I desire of the history of the Navy from 1618 to 1642, when the King and Parliament fell out.

16th. Visited Sir W. Coventry at the Tower, and walked with him upon the Stone Walk alone, till other company came to him, and had very good discourse with him. My wife and Jane gone abroad, and Tom, in order to their buying of things for their wedding, which, upon my discourse last night, is now resolved to be done upon the 26th of this month, the day of my solemnity for my cutting of the stone, when my cousin Turner must be with us. My wife, therefore, not at dinner; and comes to me Mr. Evelyn of Deptford, a worthy good man, and dined with me, but a bad dinner; who is grieved for, and speaks openly to me his thoughts of, the times and our ruin approaching; and all by the folly of the King. His business to me was about some ground of his at Deptford, next to the King's yard: and after dinner we parted. To Woolwich, where I saw, but did not go on board, my ship the Jerzy, she lying at the wharf under repair. But my business was to speak with Ackworth about some old things and passages in the Navy, for my information therein, in order to my great business now of stating the history of the Navy. This I did; and upon the whole do find that the late times, in all their management, were not more husbandly than we; and other things of good content to me. Thence to Greenwich by water, and there landed at the King's house,[1] which goes on slow, but is very pretty. I to the Park, there to see the prospect of the hill, to judge of Dankers's picture which he hath made thereof for me, and I do like it very well: and it is a very pretty place. Thence to Deptford, but stayed not, Unthwayte being out of the way: and so home, and then to the King's tavern, Morrice's, and stayed till W. Hewer fetched his uncle Blackburne by appointment to me, to discourse of the business of the Navy in the late times; and he did do it, by giving me a most exact account in writing of the several turns in the Admiralty and Navy, and of the persons employed therein, from

---

[1] The old palace at Greenwich had just been pulled down, and a new building commenced by Charles II, only one wing of which was completed, at the expense of £36,000, under the auspices of Webb, Inigo Jones's kinsman and executor. In 1694 the unfinished edifice was granted by William and Mary to trustees, for the use and service of a naval hospital; and it has been repeatedly enlarged and improved, till it has arrived at its present splendour.

the beginning of the King's leaving the Parliament, to his son's coming in, to my great content; and now I am fully informed in all I at present desire. We fell to other talk: and I find by him that the Bishops must certainly fall, and their hierarchy; these people [1] have got so much ground upon the King and kingdom as is not to be got again from them: and the Bishops do well deserve it. But it is all the talk, I find, that Dr. Wilkins, my friend, the Bishop of Chester, shall be removed to Winchester and be Lord Treasurer.[2] Though this be foolish talk, yet I do gather that he is a mighty rising man, as being a Latitudinarian, and the Duke of Buckingham his great friend.

17th. Up, and by water to see Mr. Wren, and then Mr. Williamson, who did show me the very original books of propositions made by the Commissioners for the Navy in 1618, to my great content; but no other Navy papers he could now show me. Home, and took my wife by a hackney to the King's playhouse, and saw 'The Coxcomb,' [3] the first time acted, but an old play and a silly one, being acted only by the young people.

18th. Up, and to see Sir W. Coventry, and walked with him a good while in the Stone Walk: and brave discourse about my Lord Chancellor and his ill managements and mistakes, and several things of the Navy. Home to dinner, where my wife mighty finely dressed, by a maid that she hath taken and is to come to her when Jane goes; and the same she the other day told me of, to be so handsome. I therefore longed to see her, but did not till after dinner, that my wife and I going by coach, she went with us to Holborn, where we set her down. She is a mighty proper maid, and pretty comely, but so so; but hath a most pleasing tone of voice, and speaks handsomely, but hath most great hands, and I believe ugly; but very well dressed, and good clothes, and that otherwise I believe will please me well enough. Thence to visit Ned Pickering and his lady and Creed and his wife, but the former abroad, and the latter out of town, gone to my Lady Pickering's, in Northamptonshire, upon occasion of the late death of their brother Oliver Pickering, a youth, that is dead of the small-pox. So my wife and I to Dankers's, to see the pictures; and thence to Hyde Park, the first time we were there this year, or ever, in our

[1] The anti-church party.
[2] The report could hardly have been believed, considering his connection with Oliver Cromwell.
[3] A comedy by Beaumont and Fletcher.

own coach, where with mighty pride rode up and down, and many coaches there; and I thought our horses and coach as pretty as any there, and observed so to be by others. Here stayed till night, and so home.

19th. Sir Thomas Clifford did speak to me, as desirous that I would some time come and confer with him about the Navy, which I am glad of, but will take the direction of the Duke of York before I do it, though I would be glad to do something to secure myself, if I could, in my employment. Thence to the plasterer's, and took my face and my Lord Duke of Albemarle's home with me by coach, they being done to my mind; and mighty glad I am of understanding this way of having the pictures of any friends. After dinner, with Commissioner Middleton and Kempthorne [1] to a Court-martial, to which, by virtue of my late Captainship, I am called, the first I was ever at; where many Commanders, and Kempthorne president. Here was tried a difference between Sir L. van Hemskirke, the Dutch Captain who commands the Nonsuch, built by his direction, and his Lieutenant; a drunken kind of silly business. We ordered the Lieutenant to ask him pardon, and have resolved to lay before the Duke of York what concerns the Captain, which was striking of his Lieutenant and challenging him to fight, which comes not within any article of the laws martial. But upon discourse the other day with Sir W. Coventry I did advise Middleton, and he and I did forbear to give judgment; but after the debate did withdraw into another cabin, the Court being held in one of the yachts which was on purpose brought up over against St. Katharine's, it being to be feared that this precedent of our being made Captains in order to the trying of the loss of the Defiance, wherein we are the proper persons to enquire into the want of instructions while ships to lie in harbour, might be hereafter made of evil use, by putting the Duke of Buckingham or any of these rude fellows that now are uppermost to make packed Courts, by Captains made on purpose to serve their turns. The other cause was of the loss of the Providence at Tangier, where the Captain's being by chance on shore may prove very inconvenient to him, for example's sake, though the man be a good man, and one whom, for Norwood's sake, I would be kind to; but I will not offer anything to the excusing such a miscarriage. He is at present confined till he can bring better proofs on his

[1] Sir John Kempthorne, a Commissioner of the Navy under Charles II, and admiral of a fleet in the Narrow Seas, 1677–8 (Pepys's *Signs Manual*).

behalf of the reasons of his being on shore.   So Middleton and I
away to the office; and there I late busy, making my people, as I
have done lately, to read Mr. Holland's [1] Discourse of the Navy,
and what other things I can get to inform me fully in all; and here
late, about eight at night, comes Mr. Wren to me, who had been
at the Tower to visit Sir W. Coventry.   He came only to see how
matters go, and tells me, as a secret, that last night the Duke of
York's closet was broken open, and his cabinets, and shut again,
one of them; that the rogue that did it hath left plate and a watch
behind him, and therefore they fear that it was only for papers,
which looks like a very malicious business in design, to hurt the
Duke of York: but they cannot know that till the Duke of York
comes to town about the papers, and therefore make no words
of it.   He gone, I to work again, and then to supper at home,
and to bed.

20th.   Up, and to the Tower, to Sir W. Coventry, and there
walked with him alone on the Stone Walk, till company came to
him; and there about the business of the Navy discoursed with
him, and about my Lord Chancellor and Treasurer: that they were
against the war with the Dutch at first, declaring as wise men and
statesmen, at first to the King, that they thought it fit to have a
war with them at some time or other, but that it ought not to be
till we found the Crowns of Spain and France together by the
ears, the want of which did ruin our war.   But then he told me
that a great while before the war my Lord Chancellor did speak of
a war with some heat, as a thing to be desired, and did it upon a
belief that he could with his own speeches make the Parliament
give what money he pleased, and do what he would, or would make
the King desire; but he found himself soon deceived of the Parliament, they having a long time before his removal been cloyed with
his speeches and good words, and being come to hate him.   Sir
W. Coventry did tell me it as the wisest thing that ever was said
to the King by any statesman of his time, and it was by my Lord

[1] John Holland, Paymaster to the Treasurer of the Navy, mentioned before
(see vol. i, 30th November 1660).   A copy of this work, which has never
been printed, is amongst Sir Hans Sloane's MSS., and another, in connection
with papers relative to the navy, formerly belonging to Sir George Duckett,
both in the British Museum.   In the Pepysian collection, No. 113, are Two
Discourses of Mr. Holland's touching the Government of the Navy: one
under the Earl of Northumberland in 1638, probably perused by Pepys, 14th
February, *ante*, and 18th April, *post*; the other during the Rebellion, 1659,
2 vols., fol.

Treasurer that is dead, whom I find he takes for a very great statesman—that when the King did show himself forward for passing the Act of Indemnity, he did advise the King that he would hold his hand in doing it till he had got his power restored, that had been diminished by the late times, and his revenue settled in such a manner as he might depend on himself, without resting upon Parliaments, and then pass it. But my Lord Chancellor, who thought he could have the command of Parliaments for ever, because for the King's sake they were awhile willing to grant all the King desired, did press for its being done; and so it was, and the King from that time able to do nothing with the Parliament almost. Mightily pleased with the news brought me tonight, that the King and Duke of York are come back this afternoon, and no sooner come but a warrant was sent to the Tower for the releasing Sir W. Coventry; which do put me in some hopes that there may be, in this absence, some accommodation made between the Duke of York and the Duke of Buckingham and Lord Arlington.

21st. (Lord's day.) By water over to Southwark; and then, not getting a boat, I forced to walk to Stangate; [1] and so over to White Hall in a scull; where to the Duke of York's dressing-room, and there met Harry Savile, and do understand that Sir W. Coventry is come to his house last night. I understand by Mr. Wren that his friends having, by Secretary Trevor and my Lord Keeper, applied to the King upon his first coming home, and a promise made that he should be discharged this day, my Lord Arlington did anticipate them by sending a warrant presently for his discharge, which looks a little like kindness, or a desire of it; which God send! though I fear the contrary. However, my heart is glad that he is out. Thence up and down the House. Met Mr. May, who tells me the story of his being put by Sir John Denham's place, of Surveyor of the King's Works, who, it seems, is lately dead, by the unkindness of the Duke of Buckingham, who hath brought in Dr. Wren: [2] though, he tells me, he hath been his servant for twenty years together, in all his wants and dangers, saving him from want of bread by his care and management, and with a promise of having his help in his advancement, and an engagement under his hand for £1000 not yet paid, and yet the Duke of Buckingham is so ungrateful as to put him by: which is an ill thing, though Dr. Wren is a worthy man. But he tells me that the King is kind to him, and

[1] Near Lambeth.   [2] Sir Christopher.

hath promised him a pension of £300 a year out of the Works; which will be of more content to him than the place which, under their present wants of money, is a place that disobliges most people, being not able to do what they desire to their lodgings. Here meeting with Sir H. Cholmley and Povy, they tell me that my Lord Middleton is resolved in the Cabal that he shall not go to Tangier; and that Sir Edward Harley, whom I know not, is propounded to go, who was Governor of Dunkirk, and, they say, a most worthy brave man, which I shall be very glad of. W. Howe comes to dine with me, and after dinner propounds to me my lending him £500 to help him to purchase a place—the Master of the Patent Office—of Sir Richard Piggott. I did give him a civil answer, but shall think twice of it; and the more, because of the changes we are like to have in the Navy, which will make it fit for me to divide the little I have left more than I have done, God knowing what my condition is, I having not attended, and now not being able to examine what my state is, of my accounts, and being in the world, which troubles me mightily. News lately come of the Algerines taking £13,000 in money out of one of our Company's East India ships, outward bound, which will certainly make the war last; which I am sorry for, being so poor as we are, and broken in pieces. Pelling comes to see and sup with us, and I find that he is assisting my wife in getting a licence to our young people to be married this Lent, which is resolved shall be done upon Friday next, my great day, or feast, for my being cut of the stone.

22d. Up, and by water with W. Hewer to White Hall, there to attend the Lords of the Treasury; but before they sat I did make a step to see Sir W. Coventry at his house, where, I bless God! he is come again. But in my way I met him, and so he took me into his coach and carried me to White Hall, and there set me down where he ought not—at least, he hath not yet leave—to come, nor hath thought fit yet to ask it, hearing that Harry Savile is not only denied to kiss the King's hand, but the King, being asked it by the Duke of York, did deny it, and directed that the Duke shall not receive him to wait upon him in his chamber till further orders. Sir W. Coventry told me that he was going to visit Sir John Trevor, who hath been kind to him: and he showed me a long list of all his friends that he must this week make visits to, that came to visit him in the Tower; and seems mighty well satisfied with his being out of business, but I hope he will not long be so;

at least, I do believe that all must go to rack, if the King do not come to see the want of such a servant.   Thence to the Treasury Chamber, and there all the morning, to my great grief, put to do Sir G. Downing's work of dividing the Customs for this year between the Navy, the Ordnance, and Tangier: but it did so trouble my eyes, that I had rather have given £20 than have had it to do; but I did thereby oblige Sir Thomas Clifford and Sir J. Duncomb, and so am glad of the opportunity to recommend myself to the former, for the latter I need not, he loving me well already. At it till noon, here being several of my brethren with me, but doing nothing, but I all.   But this day I did also represent to our Treasurers, which was read here, a state of the charge of the Navy, and what the expense of it this year would likely be; which is done so as it will appear well done, and to my honour, for so the Lords did take it: and I oblige the Treasurers by doing it at their request. With W. Hewer at noon to Unthank's, where my wife stays for me; and so to the Cock, where there was no room, and thence to King Street, to several cook's shops, where nothing to be had; and at last to the corner shop, going down Ivy Lane, by my Lord of Salisbury's, and there got a good dinner, my wife and W. Hewer and I; and after dinner she, with her coach, home; and he and I to look over my papers for the East India Company against the afternoon: which done, I with them to White Hall, and there to the Treasury Chamber, where the East India Company and three Councillors pleaded against me alone for three or four hours, till seven at night, before the Lords; and the Lords did give me the conquest on behalf of the King, but could not come to any conclusion, the Company being stiff: and so I think we shall go to law with them.   This done, and my eyes mighty bad with this day's work, I to Mr. Wren's, and then up to the Duke of York, and there with Mr. Wren did propound to him my going to Chatham tomorrow with Commissioner Middleton, and so this week to make the pay there and examine the business of the Defiance being lost, and other businesses, which I did the rather, that I might be out of the way at the wedding, and be at a little liberty myself for a day or two, to find a little pleasure and give my eyes a little ease.   The Duke of York mightily satisfied with it; and so away home, where my wife troubled at my being so late abroad, poor woman! though never more busy, but I satisfied her; and so begun to put things in order for my journey tomorrow, and so after supper to bed.

23d. I took coach with Commissioner Middleton, Captain Tinker, and Mr. Hutchinson, and out towards Chatham, and dined at Dartford, where we stayed an hour or two, it being a cold day; and so on, and got to Chatham just at night, with very good discourse by the way, but mostly of matters of religion, wherein Hutchinson his vein lies. After supper we fell to talk of spirits and apparitions, whereupon many pretty, particular stories were told, so as to make me almost afraid to be alone, but for shame I could not help it: and so to bed, and being sleepy, fell soon to rest, and so rested well.

24th. To the Hill House, and there did give order for a coach to be made ready; and got Mr. Gibson, whom I carried with me, to go with me and Mr. Coney, the surgeon, towards Maidstone, which I had a mighty mind to see, and took occasion, in my way, at St. Margett's, to pretend to call to see Captain Allen, to see whether Mrs. Jewkes, his daughter, was there; and there his wife come to the door, he being at London, and, through a window I spied Jewkes, but took no notice of her, but made excuse till night, and then promised to come and see Mrs. Allen again. A mighty cold and windy but clear day and had the pleasure of seeing the Medway running, winding up and down mightily, and a very fine country; and I went a little out of the way to have visited Sir John Bankes, but he at London; but here I had a sight of his seat and house,[1] the outside, which is an old abbey just like Hinchingbroke, and as good at least, and mighty finely placed by the river; and he keeps the grounds about it and walls and the house very handsome: I was mightily pleased with the sight of it. Thence to Maidstone, which I had a mighty mind to see, having never been there; and walked all up and down the town, and up to the top of the steeple, and had a noble view, and then down again: and in the town did see an old man beating of flax, and did step into the barn and give him money, and saw that piece of husbandry which I never saw, and it is very pretty: in the street also I did buy and send to our inn, the Bell, a dish of fresh fish. And so, having walked all round the town, and found it very pretty, as most towns I ever saw, though not very big, and people of good fashion in it, we to our inn, and had a good dinner; and a barber came to me, and there trimmed me, that I might be clean against night, to go to Mrs. Allen. And so, staying till four o'clock, we set out, I alone in the coach going and coming: and in our way back I 'light out of the

[1] The Friary, Aylesford.

way to see a Saxon monument,[1] as they say, of a King, which is of
three stones standing upright, and a great round one lying on
them, of great bigness, although not so big as those on Salisbury
Plain; but certainly it is a thing of great antiquity, and I am mightily
glad to see it; it is near to Aylesford, where Sir John Bankes lives.
So homeward to Chatham, to Captain Allen's, and there 'light,
and sent the coach and Gibson home, and I and Coney stayed; and
there comes to us Mrs. Jewkes, who is a very fine, proper lady, as
most I know, and well dressed.   Here was also a gentleman, one
Major Manley,[2] and his wife, neighbours; and here we stayed, and
drank, and talked, and sat.   Coney and he to play, while Mrs.
Jewkes and I to talk, and there had all our old stories up, and there
I had the liberty to salute her often; and she mighty free in kindness
to me, and had there been time, I might have carried her to Cobham, as she, upon my pressing it, was very willing to go.   Here
was a pretty cousin of hers come into supper also, of a great
fortune, daughter-in-law to this Manley, mighty pretty, but had
now such a cold, she could not speak.   Here stayed till almost
twelve at night, and then with a lanthorn from thence walked over
the fields, as dark as pitch, and mighty cold and snow, to Chatham,
and Mr. Coney with great kindness to me; and there all in bed
before I came home, and so I presently to bed.

25th.   Up, and by and by, about eight o'clock, came Rear-
Admiral Kempthorne and seven Captains more, by the Duke of
York's order, as we expected, to hold the Court-martial about
the loss of the Defiance; and so presently we by boat to the
Charles, which lies over against Upnor Castle; and there I did
manage the business, the Duke of York having, by special order,
directed them to take the assistance of Commissioner Middleton
and me, forasmuch as there might be need of advice in what relates
to the government of the ships in harbour.   And so I did lay the
law open to them, and rattle the Master-Attendants out of their
wits almost; and made the trial last till seven at night, not eating a
bit all the day; only when he had done examination, and I given

---

[1] This is the ancient monument called Kit's Coty House, supposed to be
the burial-place of Catigern, who fell in command of the Britons, in a san-
guinary but successful conflict against the Saxons, under Hengist and Horsa.
It stands on the downs, about one mile north-east of Aylesford church.   See
Stukeley's *Itinerarium*, in which are two views of the monument, and Hasted's
History of Kent, vol. ii, p. 177.

[2] John Manley, M.P. for Bridport: he married Margaret, daughter of the
unfortunate Isaak Dorislaus.

my thoughts that the neglect of the gunner of the ship was as great as I thought any neglect could be, which might by the law deserve death, but Commissioner Middleton did declare that he was against giving the sentence of death, we withdrew, as not being of the Court, and so left them to do what they pleased. And while they were debating it the boatswain of the ship did bring us out of the kettle a piece of hot salt beef, and some brown bread and brandy; and there we did make a little meal, but so good as I never would desire to eat better meat while I live, only I would have cleaner dishes. By and by they had done, and called us down from the quarter-deck; and there we find they do sentence that the gunner of the Defiance should stand upon the Charles three hours, with his fault writ upon his breast and with a halter about his neck, and so be made incapable of any service. The truth is, the man do seem, and is, I believe, a good man; but his neglect, in trusting a girl to carry fire into his cabin, is not to be pardoned. This being done, we took boat and home; and there a good supper was ready for us, which should have been our dinner. The Captains, desirous to be at London, went away presently for Gravesend, to get thither by this night's tide; and so we to supper, having been a great snowy and mighty cold, foul day; and so after supper to bed.

26th. Up, and with Middleton all the morning at the Dock, looking over the storehouses and Commissioner Pett's house, in order to Captain Cox's coming to live there in his stead, as Commissioner. But it is a mighty pretty house, and pretty to see how everything is said to be out of repair for this new man, though £10 would put it into as good condition in everything, as it ever was in, so free everybody is of the King's money! And so to dinner at the Hill House; and after dinner, till eight at night, close, Middleton and I, examining the business of Mr. Pett about selling a boat, and we find him a very knave; and some other quarrels of his, wherein, to justify himself, he hath made complaints of others. This being done, we to supper, and so to talk, Commissioner Middleton being mighty good company upon a journey. And so to bed, thinking how merry my people are at this time, Tom and Jane being to have been married this day, it being also my feast for my being cut of the stone, but how many years I do not remember, but I think it to be about ten or eleven.

27th. After drinking a little buttered ale, Hutchinson and I took coach, and, exceedingly merry in talk, to Dartford: Middleton

finding stories of his own life at Barbadoes, and up and down at
Venice, and elsewhere, that are mighty pretty and worth hearing;
and he is a strange good companion, and droll upon the road, more
than ever I could have thought to have been in him.   Took coach
again, and got home about six at night, it being all the morning as
cold, snowy, windy, and rainy day, as any in the whole winter
past, but pretty clear in the afternoon.   I find all well, but my wife
abroad with Jane, who was married yesterday.   By and by my
wife comes, and there I hear how merry they were yesterday, and
I am glad at it, they being married, it seems, very handsomely at
Islington; and dined at the old house, and lay in our blue chamber,
with much company, and wonderful merry: The. Turner and
Mary Batelier bridesmaids, and Talbot Pepys and W. Hewer
bridesmen.

28th. (Lord's day.) To the office with Tom, who looks mighty
smug upon his marriage, as Jane also do, both of whom I did give
joy, and so Tom and I to work at the office all the morning till
dinner, and then dined, W. Batelier with us; and so after dinner to
work again, and sent for Gibson, and kept him also till eight at
night doing much business.   And so, that being done and my
journal writ, my eyes being very bad, and every day worse and
worse, I home: but I find it most certain that strong drinks do make
my eyes sore, as they have done heretofore always; for, when I
was in the country, when my eyes were at the best, their strong
beer would make my eyes sore.   So home to supper, and by and by
to bed.

29th. Up, and by water to White Hall; and there to the Duke
of York, to show myself, after my journey to Chatham, but did no
business today with him: only after gone from him.   I to Sir T.
Clifford's; and there, after an hour's waiting, he being alone in his
closet, I did speak with him and give him the account he gave me
to draw up, and he did like it very well.   And then fell to talk of
the business of the Navy: and giving me good words, did fall foul
of the constitution of the Board, and then did discover his thoughts,
that Sir J. Minnes was too old, and so was Colonel Middleton, and
that my Lord Brouncker did mind his mathematics too much.   I
did not give much encouragement to that of finding fault with my
fellow officers, but did stand up for the constitution, and did say
that what faults there were in our Office would be found not to
arise from the constitution, but from the failures of the officers in
whose hands it was.   This he did seem to give good ear to; but

did give me of myself very good words, which pleased me well, though I shall not build upon them anything. Thence home; and after dinner by water with Tom down to Greenwich, he reading to me all the way, coming and going, my collections out of the Duke of York's old manuscript of the Navy, which I have bound up and do please me mightily. At Greenwich I came to Captain Cocke's, where the house full of company, at the burial of James Temple, who, it seems, hath been dead these five days: here I had a very good ring, which I did give my wife as soon as I came home. I spent my time there walking in the garden, talking with James Pierce, who tells me that he is certain that the Duke of Buckingham had been with his wenches all the time that he was absent, which was all the last week, nobody knowing where he was. The great talk is of the King's being hot of late against Conventicles, and to see whether the Duke of Buckingham's being returned will turn the King, which will make him very popular; and some think it is his plot to make the King thus, to show his power in the making him change his mind. But Pierce did tell me that the King did certainly say that he that took one stone from the Church did take two from his Crown. By and by the corpse came out; and I, with Sir Richard Browne and Mr. Evelyn, in their coach, to the church, where Mr. Plume preached. I, in the midst of the sermon, did go out, and walked all alone round to Deptford; and so to the King's Yard, and there my boat by order met me, and home. This day my new chambermaid, that comes in the room of Jane, is come, Jane and Tom lying at their own lodging this night: the new maid's name is Matt, a proper and very comely maid. This day also our cook-maid Bridget went away, which I was sorry for; but, just at her going, she was found to be a thief, and so I was the less troubled for it; but now our whole house will, in a manner, be new, which, since Jane is gone, I am not at all sorry for, for my late differences with my wife about poor Deb. will not be remembered.

30th. Up, and to Sir W. Coventry, to see and discourse with him; and he tells me that he hath lately been with my Lord Keeper, and had much discourse about the Navy: and particularly he tells me that he finds they are divided touching me and my Lord Brouncker: some are for removing, and some for keeping us. He told my Lord Keeper that it would cost the King £10,000 before he had made another as fit to serve him in the Navy as I am; which though I believe it is true, yet I am much pleased to have that character given me by Sir W. Coventry, whatever be the success of it. But I perceive they do think that I know too much and shall impose upon whomever shall come next, and therefore must be removed, though he tells me that Sir T. Clifford is inclined well enough to me, and Sir T. Osborne, by what I have lately done, I suppose. This news is but what I ought not to be much troubled for, considering my incapacity, in regard to my eyes, to continue long at this work. To the office, where all the morning; and Sir W. Pen, the first time that he hath been here since his being last sick, which I think is two or three months; and I think will be the last that he will be here as one of the Board, he now inviting us all to dine with him, as a parting dinner, on Thursday next, which I am glad of, I am sure; for he is a very villain.

31st. Up, and by water to Sir W. Coventry's, there to talk with him about business of the Navy, and received from him direction what to advise the Duke of York at this time, which was, to submit and give way to the King's naming a man or two that the people about him have a mind should be brought into the Navy, and perhaps that may stop their fury in running further against the whole; and this, he believes, will do it. After much discourse with him I walked out with him into St. James's Park, where, being afraid to be seen with him, he having not leave yet to kiss the King's hand, but notice taken, as I hear, of all that go to him, I did make the pretence of my attending the Tangier Committee to take my leave, though to serve him I should, I think, stick at nothing. At the Committee, this morning, my Lord Middleton declares at last his being ready to go, as soon as ever money can be made ready to pay the garrison : and so I have orders to get money, but how soon I know not. Thence home, and there find Mr. Sheres, of whom I find my wife of late to talk with mighty kindness; and particularly he hath shown himself to be a poet, and that she do mightily value him for. He did not stay to dine with us, but we to dinner; and then, in the afternoon, my wife being very well dressed by her new maid, we abroad to make a visit to Mrs. Pickering; but she abroad again, and so we never yet saw her. Thence to Dankers's, and there saw our pictures which are in doing; and I did choose a view of Rome, instead of Hampton Court; and mightily pleased I shall be in them. Here were Sir Charles Cotterell and his son bespeaking something: both ingenious men, I hear. Thence my wife and I to the Park; and pretty store of company; and so home with great content. And so ends the month, my mind in pretty good content for all things, but the designs on foot to bring alterations in the Office, which trouble me.

April 1st. Up, and with Colonel Middleton, at the desire of Rear-Admiral Kempthorne, the president, for our assisting them, to the Court-martial on board a yacht in the river here, to try the business of the Purser's complaints, Baker against Trevanion, his Commander, of the Dartmouth. But, Lord! to see what wretched doings there were among all the Commanders to ruin the purser, and defend the Captain in all his rogueries, be it to the prejudice of the King or Purser, no good man could bear! I confess I was pretty high, which the young gentlemen Commanders did not like; and Middleton did the same. But could not bring it to any issue this day, sitting till two o'clock; and therefore we being sent for, went to Sir W. Pen's by invitation to dine; where my wife was, and my Lord Brouncker and his mistress, and Sir J. Minnes and his niece: and here a bad dinner and little mirth, I being little pleased with my host. However, I make myself sociable; and so after dinner my wife and I with my Lord Brouncker and his mistress, who set us down at my cousin Turner's, and there we stayed awhile and talked: and particularly here we met with Dr. Ball, the parson of the Temple, who did tell me a great many pretty stories about the manner of the parsons being paid for their preaching at Paul's heretofore and now, and the ground of the lecture, and for the names of the founders thereof, which were many, at some 5s., some 6s. per annum towards it: and had their names read in the pulpit every sermon among those holy persons that the Church do order a collect for, giving God thanks for.

2d. Up, and by water to White Hall, and there with the Office attended the Duke of York; and so with W. Hewer to the Cock, and there he and I dined alone with great content, he reading to me, for my memory sake, my late collection of the history of the Navy, that I might represent the same by and by to the Duke of York. And so after dinner he and I to White Hall, and there to the Duke of York's lodgings, whither he, by and by, by his appointment came: and alone with him an hour in his closet, telling him mine and Sir W. Coventry's advice touching the present posture of the Navy, as the Duke of Buckingham and the rest do now labour to make changes therein; and that it were best for him to suffer the King to be satisfied with the bringing in of a man or two whom they desire.   I did also give the Duke of York a short account of the history of the Navy, as to our Office, wherewith he was very well satisfied: but I do find that he is pretty stiff against their bringing in of men against his mind, as the Treasurers were, and particularly against Child's[1] coming in, because he is a merchant.   After much discourse with him we parted; and he to the Council, while I stayed waiting for his telling me when I should be ready to give him a written account of the administration of the Navy, which caused me to wait the whole afternoon, till night. In the meantime, stepping to the Duchess of York's side to speak with Lady Peterborough, I did see the young Duchess,[2] a little child in hanging sleeves, dance most finely, so as almost to ravish me, her ears were so good: taught by a Frenchman that did heretofore teach the King and all the King's children and the Queen-mother herself, who do still dance well.   Thence to the Council door, and Mr. Chiffinch took me into the back stairs, and there with his friend, Mr. Fowkes, for whom he is very solicitous in some things depending in this Office, he did make me, with some others that he took in (among others, Alderman Backwell), eat a pickled herring, the largest I ever saw, and drink variety of wines till I was almost merry.   But I did keep in good time; and so, after the Council was up, I home, and there find my wife not yet come from Deptford, where she hath been all this day to see her mother.   This night I did bring home from the King's potticary's, in White Hall, by Mr. Cooling's direction, a water that he says is mighty good for his eyes.   I pray God it may do me good; but, by his description, his disease was the same as mine, and this do encourage me to use it.

3d. Up, and to the Council of War again with Middleton: and the proceedings of the Commanders so devilishly bad, and so professedly partial to the Captain, that I could endure it no longer, but took occasion to pretend business at the office, and away, and Colonel Middleton with me, who was of the same mind, and resolved to declare our minds freely to the Duke of York about it.

4th. (Lord's day.) Up, and to church, where Alderman Backwell's wife, by invitation with my head, came up with her mother, and sat with us; and after sermon I did walk with them home, and there left them, and home to dinner.   After dinner with Sir J. Minnes and T. Middleton to White Hall, by appointment; and at

[1] Afterwards Sir Josiah Child.
[2] The Princess Mary, afterwards Queen of England.

my Lord Arlington's the Office did attend the King and Cabal, to discourse of the further quantity of victuals fit to be declared for, which was 2000 men for six months; and so home without more ado or stay there, hearing no news but that Sir Thomas Allen is to be expected every hour at home with his fleet, or news of his being gone back to Algier. The Queen-mother hath been of late mighty ill, and some fears of her death.

5th. With Creed, walking in the garden and talking about our Office and Child's coming in to be a Commissioner; and, being his friend, I did think he might do me a kindness to learn of him what the Duke of Buckingham and the faction do design touching me, and to instil good words concerning me, which he says, and I believe he will: and it is but necessary; for I have not a mind indeed at this time to be put out of my office, if I can make any shift that is honourable to keep it; but I will not do it by deserting the Duke of York. At noon by appointment comes Mr. Sheres, and he and I to Unthank's, where my wife stays for us in our coach, and Betty Turner with her; and we to the Mulberry Garden, where Sheres is to treat us with a Spanish Olio,[1] by a cook of his acquaintance that is there, that was with my Lord in Spain. And without any other company he did do it, and mighty nobly; and the Olio was indeed a very noble dish, such as I never saw better, or any more of. This, and the discourse he did give us of Spain, and description of the Escorial, was a fine treat. So we left other good things, that would keep till night, for a collation: and, with much content, took coach again, and went five or six miles towards Brentford, where the Prince of Tuscany,[2] who comes into England only to spend money and see our country, comes into the town today, and is much expected; and we met him, but the coach passing by apace, we could not see much of him, but he seems a very jolly and good comely man. By the way we overtook Captain Ferrers upon his fine Spanish horse, and he is a fine horse indeed; but not so good, I think, as I have seen some. He did ride by us most of the way, and with us to the Park, and there left us, where we passed the evening; and meeting The. Turner, Talbot, W. Batelier, and his sister, in a coach, we anon took them with us to the Mulberry Garden; and there, after a walk, to supper upon what was left at

[1] Oleo, or olio, a savoury dish composed of a great variety of ingredients, as meat, herbs, etc.
[2] Cosimo de' Medici, who succeeded his father Ferdinand in the dukedom of Tuscany, 1670.

noon: and very good, only Mr. Sheres being taken suddenly ill for a while did spoil our mirth; but by and by was well again, and we mighty merry. And so broke up, and left him at Charing Cross, and so calling only at my cousin Turner's, away home, mightily pleased with the day's work. This day come another new maid, for a middle-maid, but her name I know not yet; and for a cook-maid we have, ever since Bridget went, used a blackmoor of Mr. Batelier's, Doll, who dresses our meat mighty well, and we mightily pleased with her.

6th. To Mr. Batelier's to dinner, where my cousin Turner and both her daughters, and Talbot Pepys and my wife, and a mighty fine dinner. They at dinner before I come; and when I had dined I away home, and thence to White Hall, where the Board waited on the Duke of York; and Middleton and I did in plain terms acquaint him what we thought and had observed in the late Court-martial, which the Duke did give ear to; and though he thinks not fit to revoke what is already done in this case by a Court-martial, yet it shall bring forth some good laws in the behaviour of Captains to their under officers for the time to come. Thence home, and after a while at the office, came home my wife, who hath been at Batelier's late, and dancing with the company, at which I seemed a little troubled, not being sent for myself, but I was not so much so, but went to bed well enough pleased.

7th. By coach to my cousin Turner's, and invited them to dine at the Cock today with my wife and me; and so to the Lords of the Treasury, where all the morning, and settled matters to their liking about the assignments on the Customs, between the Navy Office and Victualler, and to that end spent most of the morning there with D. Gauden. I to the New Exchange, to talk with Betty,[1] my little seamstress; and so to Mrs. Turner's, to call them to dinner, but my wife not come, I back again, and was overtaken by a porter with a message from my wife that she was ill and could not come to us: so I back again to Mrs. Turner's, and find them gone; and so back again to the Cock, and there find Mrs. Turner, Betty, and Talbot Pepys, and they dined with myself, Sir D. Gauden, and Gibson, and mighty merry, this house being famous for good meat, and particularly pease-porridge. After dinner broke up, and they away; and I to the Council Chamber, and there heard the great complaint of the City tried against the gentlemen of the Temple, for the late riot, as they would have it, when

[1] Betty Smith.

my Lord Mayor was there. But upon hearing the whole business,
the City was certainly to blame to charge them in this manner as
with a riot: but the King and Council did forbear to determine
anything in it till the other business of the title and privilege be
decided, which is now under dispute at law between them, whether
the Temple be within the liberty of the City or no. But I was
sorry to see the City so ill advised as to complain in a thing where
their proofs were so weak. Thence to my cousin Turner's, and
thence with her and her daughters and her sister Turner, I carrying
Betty in my lap, to Talbot's chamber at the Temple, where, by
agreement, the poor rogue had a pretty dish of anchovies and
sweetmeats for them; and hither came Mr. Eden,[1] who was in his
mistress's disfavour ever since the other night that he came in
thither fuddled, when we were there. But I did make them
friends by my buffoonery, and bringing up a way of spelling their
names, and making Theophila spell Lambton, which she would
have to be the name of Mr. Eden's mistress, and mighty merry we
were till late. This day I do hear that Betty Turner is to be left at
school at Hackney, which I am mightily pleased with; for then I
shall, now and then, see her. She is pretty, and a girl for that,
and her relations, I love.

8th. Up, and to White Hall, to the King's side, to find Sir T.
Clifford, where the Duke of York came and found me, which I was
sorry for, for fear he should think I was making friends on that
side. But I did put it off the best I could, my being there: and so,
by and by, had opportunity alone to show Sir T. Clifford the fair
account I had drawn up of the Customs, which he liked, and
seemed mightily pleased with me; and so away to the Excise Office,
to do a little business there, and so to the office, where all the
morning. With my wife by coach to Islington, to pay what we
owe there for the late dinner at Jane's wedding; and so round by
Kingsland and Hogsden[2] home, pleased with my wife's singing
with me by the way. Going through Smithfield I did see a coach
run over a coachman's neck, and stand upon it, and yet the man
rose up and was well after it, which I thought a wonder.

9th. Up, and by water to White Hall, and there, with the Board,

[1] Robert Eden, of West Auckland, Durham, which county he represented
in Parliament for many years, married the lady here alluded to, Margaret,
daughter and heir of John Lambton. He was created a baronet 13th
November 1672, and died in 1720, his wife surviving till 1730.
[2] *Hodiè* Hoxton.

attended the Duke of York, and Sir Thomas Allen with us (who came to town yesterday); and it is resolved another fleet shall go to the Straits forthwith, and he command it. But his coming home is mighty hardly talked on by the merchants, for leaving their ships there to the mercy of the Turks: but of this more in my White Book. To the Excise Office, and to several places: among others, to Mr. Faithorne's, to have seen an instrument which he was said to have, for drawing perspectives, but he had it not; but here I did see his workhouse, and the best things of his doing he had by him.

10th. After dinner comes Mr. Seymour to visit me, a talking fellow: but I hear by him that Captain Trevanion do give it out everywhere that I did overrule the whole Court-martial against him so long as I was there; and perhaps I may receive, at this time, some wrong by it: but I care not, for what I did was out of my desire to do justice.

11th. (Easter-day.) Up, and to church, where Alderman Back-well's lady and mother and boy and another gentlewoman did come and sit in our pew; but no women of our own there, and so there was room enough. Our parson made a dull sermon, and so home to dinner; and after dinner my wife and I by coach, and Balty with us, to Loten,[1] the landscape-drawer, a Dutchman, living in St. James's market, but there saw no good pictures. But by accident he did direct us to a painter that was then in the house with him, a Dutchman, newly come over, one Verelst,[2] who took us to his lodging close by, and did show us a little flower-pot of his drawing, the finest thing that ever, I think, I saw in my life; the drops of dew hanging on the leaves, so as I was forced, again and again, to put my finger to it, to feel whether my eyes were deceived or no. He do ask £70 for it: I had the vanity to bid him £20; but a better picture I never saw in my whole life; and it is worth going twenty miles to see it. Thence, leaving Balty there, I took my wife to St. James's, and there carried her to the Queen's chapel, the first time I ever did it; and heard excellent music, but not so good as by accident I did hear there yesterday, as I went through the Park from White Hall to see Sir W. Coventry, which I have forgot to set down in my journal yesterday. And going out of the chapel,

---

[1] John Loten, a landscape painter, long established in London, where he died 1681.

[2] Simon Verelst, a Dutch flower-painter, who practised his art with much success in England about this time.

I did see the Prince of Tuscany come out, a comely, black, fat man, in a mourning suit; and my wife and I did see him this afternoon through a window in this chapel.   All that Sir W. Coventry yesterday did tell me new was that the King would not yet give him leave to come to kiss his hand; and he do believe that he will not in a great while do it, till those about him shall see fit, which I am sorry for.   Thence to the Park, my wife and I; and here Sir W. Coventry did first see me and my wife in a coach of our own; and so did also this night the Duke of York, who did eye my wife mightily.   But I begin to doubt that my being so much seen in my own coach at this time may be observed to my prejudice; but I must venture it now.   So home, and so set down my journal, with the help of my left eye through my tube, for fourteen days past; which is so much as, I hope, I shall not run in arrear again, but the badness of my eyes do force me to it.

12th.   The whole Office attended the Duke of York at his meeting with Sir Thomas Allen and several flag-officers, to consider of the manner of managing the war with Algiers; and, it being a thing I was wholly silent in, I did only observe; and find that their manner of discourse on this weighty affair was very mean and disorderly, the Duke of York himself being the man that I thought spoke most to the purpose.   Meeting Mr. Sheres, took him to see the fine flower-pot I saw yesterday, and did again offer £20 for it; but he [Verelst] insists upon £50.   By and by to my wife at Unthank's, and with her was Jane, and so to the Cock, where they and I and Sheres and Tom dined, my wife having a great desire to eat of their soup made of pease.   By water to the Bear Garden, and there happened to sit by Sir Frecheville Hollis, who is still full of his vainglorious and profane talk.   Here we saw a prize fought between a soldier and a country fellow, one Warrell, who promised the least in his looks, and performed the most of valour in his boldness and evenness of mind, and smiles in all he did, that ever I saw; and we were all both deceived and infinitely taken with him. He did soundly beat the soldier, and cut him over the head. Thence back to White Hall, mightily pleased, all of us, with this sight, and particularly this fellow, as a most extraordinary man for his temper and evenness in fighting.   Home, and after sitting a while, thrumming upon my viol and singing, I to bed, and left my wife to do something to a waistcoat and petticoat she is to wear tomorrow.   This evening, coming home, we overtook Alderman Backwell's coach and his lady, and followed them to their house, and there made them the first visit, where they received us with extraordinary civility, and owning the obligation. But I do, contrary to my expectation, find her something a proud and vain-glorious woman, in telling the number of her servants and family and expenses: he is also so, but he was ever of that strain. But here he showed me the model of his houses that he is going to build in Cornhill and Lombard Street; but he hath purchased so much there, that it looks like a little town, and must have cost him a great deal of money.

13th. At the office a good while, and then, my wife going down the river to spend the day with her mother at Deptford, I abroad: and first to the milliners in Fenchurch Street; and there I bought a pair of gloves and fell to talk, and found so much freedom that I stayed therein the best part of the morning with great pleasure, it being a holiday; and then against my will away and to the 'Change, where I left W. Hewer, and I by hackney coach to the Spital, and heard a piece of a dull sermon to my Lord Mayor and Aldermen, and thence saw them all take horse and ride away, which I have not seen together many a day; their wives also went in their coaches; and, indeed, the sight was mighty pleasing. Thence took occasion to go back to a milliner's in Fenchurch Street, whose name I understand to be Clerke; and there, her husband inviting me up to the balcony to see the Show go by to dinner at Cloth-worker's-Hall, I did go up, and there saw it go by: and then, there being a good piece of cold roast beef upon the table, one Margetts (a young merchant that lodges there and is likely to marry a sister of hers) and I stayed and eat, and had much good conversation with her, who hath the vanity to talk of her great friends and father, one Wingate, near Welwyn,[1] that hath been a Parliament man. Here also was Stapely, the rope-merchant, and dined with us; and after spending most of the afternoon also, I away home; and by water to White Hall to look, among other things, for Mr. May, to unbespeak his dining with me tomorrow. Home by water, and there I find Talbot Pepys and Mrs. Turner and Betty come to invite us to dinner on Thursday; and, after drinking, saw them to the waterside. So home to supper, where very sparing in my discourse, not giving occasion of inquiry where I have been today, or what I have done. And so without any trouble tonight, more than my fear, we to bed.

14th. Up, and with W. Hewer to White Hall, and there I did

[1] Edward Wingate represented St. Albans in the Long Parliament.

speak with the Duke of York, the Council sitting in the morning; and it was to direct me to have my business ready of the Administration of the Office against Saturday next, when the King would have a hearing of it. To the Duke of York's playhouse, and there saw 'The Impertinents,' a play which pleases me well still; but it is with great trouble that I now see a play, because of my eyes, the light of the candles making it very troublesome to me. After the play to Creed's, and there find him and his wife together alone in their new house, where I never was before: and a pretty house it is, but I do not see that they intend to keep any coach. Here they treat us like strangers, quite according to the fashion—nothing to drink or eat, which is a thing that will spoil our ever having any acquaintance with them; for we do continue the old freedom and kindness of England to all our friends. They do here talk mightily of my Lady Paulina making a very good end, and being mighty religious in her lifetime; and she hath left many good notes of sermons and religion, wrote with her own hand, which nobody ever knew of; which I am glad of: but she was always a peevish lady.

15th. To my cousin Turner's, where I find they are gone all to dinner to Povy's, and thither I, and there they were all, and W. Batelier and his sister, and had dined; but I had good things brought me, and then all up and down the house, and mightily pleased to see the fine rooms: but the truth is there are so many bad pictures that do make the good ones lose much of the pleasure in seeing them. The. and Betty Turner in new flowered tabby gowns, and so we were pretty merry. So, about five or six o'clock, away, and I took my wife and the two Bateliers, and carried them homeward; and W. Batelier 'lighting, I carried the women round by Islington, and so down Bishopsgate Street home, and there to talk and sup, and then to bed.

16th. My wife being gone abroad with W. Hewer, to see the new play today, at the Duke of York's House, 'Guzman,' I dined alone with my people, and in the afternoon away by coach to White Hall; and there the Office attended the Duke of York. And being despatched pretty soon, and told that we should not wait on the King, as intended, till Sunday, I thence presently to the Duke of York's playhouse, and there, in the 18*d.* seat, did get room to see almost three acts of the play; but it seemed to me but very ordinary. After the play done I into the pit, and there find my wife and W. Hewer; and Sheres got to them, which, so jealous is my nature, did trouble me, though my judgment tells me there is no hurt in it on either side. But here I did meet with Shadwell, the poet, who, to my great wonder, do tell me that my Lord of [Orrery] did write this play, trying what he could do in comedy, since his heroic plays could do no more wonders. This do trouble me: for it is as mean a thing, and so he says, as hath been upon the stage a great while; and Harris, who hath no part in it, did come to me, and told me in discourse that he was glad of it, it being a play that will not take.

17th. At noon home to dinner, and there find Mr. Pierce, the surgeon, and he dined with us; and there hearing that 'The Alchemist' was acted, we did go, and took him with us to the King's House; and it is still a good play, having not been acted for two or three years before; but I do miss Clun for the Doctor. To Sir W. Coventry's, reading over first my draft of the Administration of the Navy, which he do like very well; and so fell to talk of his late disgrace, and how basely and in what a mean manner the Duke of Buckingham hath proceeded against him—not like a man of honour. He tells me that the King will not give other answer about his coming to kiss his hands than 'Not yet.' But he says that this that he desires, of kissing the King's hand, is only to show to the world that he is not discontented, and not in any desire to come again into play, though I do perceive that he speaks this with less earnestness than heretofore: and this, it may be, is, from what he told me lately, that the King is offended at what is talked, that he hath declared himself desirous not to have to do with any employment more. But he do tell me that the leisure he hath yet had do not at all begin to be burdensome to him, he knowing how to spend his time with content to himself; and that he hopes shortly to contract his expense, so as that he shall not be under any straits in that respect neither; and so seems to be in very good condition of content. Thence I away over the Park, it being now night, to White Hall: and there, in the Duchess's chamber, do find the Duke of York; and, upon my offer to speak with him, he did come to me and withdrew to his closet, and there did hear and approve my paper of the Administration of the Navy, only did bid me alter these words, 'upon the rupture between the late King and the Parliament' to these, 'the beginning of the late Rebellion'; giving it me as but reason to show that it was through the Rebellion that the Navy was put out of its old good course, into that of a Commission. Having done this we fell to other

talk, he with great confidence telling me how matters go among
our adversaries in reference to the Navy, and that he thinks they
do begin to flag; but then, beginning to talk in general of the
excellency of old constitutions, he did bring out of his cabinet,
and made me read it, an extract out of a book of my late Lord of
Northumberland's, so prophetic of the business of Chatham, as is
almost miraculous.[1]   I did desire, and he did give it me to copy
out, which pleased me mightily.

18th. (Lord's day.) To my office again, to examine the fair
draft; and so, borrowing Sir J. Minnes's coach, he going with
Colonel Middleton, I to White Hall, where we all met and did sign
it; and then to my Lord Arlington's, where the King, and the
Duke of York, and Prince Rupert, as also Ormond and the two
Secretaries, with my Lord Ashley and Sir T. Clifford, were.   And
there, by and by being called in, Mr. Williamson did read over our
paper, which was in a letter to the Duke of York, bound up in a
book with the Duke of York's Book of Instructions.   He read it
well; and, after read, we were bid to withdraw, nothing being at
all said to it.   And by and by we were called in again, and nothing
said to that business; but another begun, about the state of this
year's action and our wants of money, as I had stated the same
lately to our Treasurers; which I was bid, and did largely, and
with great content, open.   And having so done, we all withdrew,
and left them to debate our supply of money; to which, being called
in, and referred to attend on the Lords of the Treasury, we all
departed.   And I only stayed in the House till the Council rose;
and then to the Duke of York, in the Duchess's chamber, where
he told me that the book was there left with my Lord Arlington,
for any of the Lords to view that had a mind, and to prepare and
present to the King what they had to say in writing, to any part of
it, which is all we can desire, and so that rested.   The Duke of
York then went to other talk; and by and by comes the Prince of
Tuscany to visit him, and the Duchess; and I find that he do still
remain incognito, and so intends to do all the time he stays here,

---

[1] Most probably John Holland's report on the state of the defences of the
Navy, made to Algernon Earl of Northumberland, in 1638, when Lord High
Admiral.   See note at 19th March, *ante*.   A copy of the paper here alluded to
is in Rawlinson, A 195, fol. 124.   It was an extract from an old book formerly in the library at Petworth, and written by Sir William Monson, the well-
known English admiral, who died in 1643.   He was the author of several
naval tracts, all of which are printed in Churchill's *Voyages*, and the passage quoted by Pepys will be found at p. 421 of vol. iii.

for avoiding trouble to the King and himself, and expense also to both. Thence I to White Hall Gate, thinking to have found Sir J. Minnes's coach staying for me; but not being there, and this being the first day of rain we have had many a day, the streets being as dusty as in summer, I forced to walk to my cousin Turner's; and there, having kissed and taken leave of Betty, who goes to Putney to school tomorrow, I walked through the rain to the Temple, and there, with much ado, got a coach, and so home.

19th. Up, and with Tom, whom, with his wife, I and my wife had this morning taken occasion to tell that I did intend to give him £40 for himself and £20 to his wife, towards their setting out in the world, and that my wife would give her £20 more, that she might have as much to begin with as he, by coach to White Hall. After dinner out again, and, calling about my coach, which was at the coachmaker's, and hath been for these two or three days, to be new painted, and the window-frames gilt against next May-day, went on with my hackney to White Hall.

20th. Up, and to the office, and my wife abroad with Mary Batelier, with our own coach, but borrowed Sir J. Minnes's coach-man, that so our own might stay at home to attend at dinner; our family being mightily disordered by our little boy's falling sick the last night, and we fear it will prove the small-pox. At noon comes my guest, Mr. Hugh May, and with him Sir Henry Capell, my old Lord Capell's son, and Mr. Parker; and I had a pretty dinner for them; and both before and after dinner had excellent discourse; and showed them my closet and my office, and the method of it, to their great content; and more extraordinary, manly discourse and opportunity of showing myself, and learning from others, I have not, in ordinary discourse, had in my life, they being all persons of worth, but especially Sir H. Capell, whose being a Parliament-man, and hearing my discourse in the Parliament-house, hath, as May tells me, given him a long desire to know and discourse with me. In the afternoon we walked to the Old Artillery Ground [1] near the Spitalfields, where I never was before, but now, by Captain Deane's invitation, did go to see his new gun

---

[1] Teasel Close, in Bishopsgate Street, where some land had been granted to the gunners of the Tower for the practice of great and small ordnance, by William, last prior of St. Mary Spittle. It was long called the Artillery Garden; but ultimately it was found too small, and disused. Artillery Lane was built on its site.

tried, this being the place where the Officers of the Ordnance do try all their great guns; and when we came, did find that the trial had been made; and they going away with extraordinary report of the proof of his gun, which, from the shortness and bigness, they do call Punchinello. But I desired Colonel Legg to stay and give us a sight of her performance, which he did, and there, in short, against a gun more than as long and as heavy again, and charged with as much powder again, she carried the same bullet as strong to the mark, and nearer and above the mark at a point blank than theirs, and is more easily managed, and recoils no more than that, which is a thing so extraordinary as to be admired for the happiness of his invention, and to the great regret of the old Gunners and Officers of the Ordnance that were there, only Colonel Legg did do her much right in his report of her. And so, having seen this great and first experiment, we all parted, I seeing my guests into a hackney coach, and myself, with Captain Deane, taking a hackney coach, did go out towards Bow, and went as far as Stratford, and all the way talking of this invention, and he offering me a third of the profit of it; which, for aught I know, or do at present think, may prove matter considerable to us: for either the King will give him a reward for it, if he keeps it to himself, or he will give us a patent to make our profit of it; and no doubt but it will be of profit to merchantmen and others, to have guns of the same force at half the charge. This was our talk: and then to talk of other things of the Navy in general; and among other things he did tell me that he do hear how the Duke of Buckingham hath a spite at me, which I knew before, but value it not: and he tells me that Sir T. Allen is not my friend; but for all this I am not much troubled, for I know myself so useful that, as I believe, they will not part with me; so I thank God my condition is such that I can retire and be able to live with comfort, though not with abundance. Thus we spent the evening with extraordinary good discourse, to my great content: and so home to the office, and then home, where my wife do come home, and I vexed at her staying out so late. But she tells me she hath been at home with Mr. Batelier a good while. So I made nothing of it, but to supper and to bed.

21st. Up, and with my own coach as far as the Temple; and thence sent it to my cousin Turner, who, to ease her own horses, that are going with her out of town, do borrow mine. To Auditor Wood's, and met my Lord Bellassis upon some business of his accounts. Attended the Duke of York a little, being the first time of my waiting on him at St. James's this summer, whither he is now newly gone; and thence walked to White Hall; and so, by and by, to the Council Chamber, and heard a remarkable cause pleaded between the Farmers of the Excise of Wiltshire, in complaint against the Justices of Peace of Salisbury: and Sir H. Finch was for the former. But, Lord! to see how he did with his admirable eloquence order the matter, is not to be conceived almost; so pleasant a thing it is to hear him plead. By and by comes my cousin Turner and The. and Joyce, in their riding-clothes, they being come from their lodgings to her husband's chamber at the Temple, and there do lie and propose to go out of town on Friday next; and here I had a good dinner for them. After dinner by water to White Hall, where the Duke of York did meet our Office, and went with us to the Lords Commissioners of the Treasury; and there we did go over all the business of the state I had drawn up, of this year's action and expense, which I did do to their satisfaction, and convincing them of the necessity of providing more money, if possible, for us. Thence the Duke of York being gone, I did there stay walking with Sir H. Cholmley in the Court, talking of news; where he told me that now the great design of the Duke of Buckingham is to prevent the meeting, since he cannot bring about with the King the dissolving, of this Parliament, that the King may not need it; and therefore my Lord St. Albans is hourly expected with great offers of a million of money, to buy our breach with the Dutch; and this, they do think, may tempt the King to take the money, and thereby be out of a necessity of calling the Parliament again, which these people dare not suffer to meet again: but this he doubts, and so do I, that it will be the ruin of the nation if we fall out with Holland. My boy comes to tell me that his mistress was at the Gate with the coach, whither I went, and there and my wife and the whole company. So she and Mrs. Turner and The. and Talbot in mine; and Joyce, W. Batelier, and I, in a hackney, to Hyde Park, where I was ashamed to be seen; but mightily pleased, though troubled, with a drunken coachman that did not remember when we come to 'light, where it was that he took us up; but said at Hammersmith, and thither he was carrying of us when we come first out of the Park. So I carried them all to Hercules' Pillars, and there did treat them: and so, about ten at night, parted, and my wife and I and W. Batelier home; and he gone, we to bed.

22d. Up, and to the office, where all the morning. At noon

home to dinner, and Captain Deane with us; and very good discourse, and particularly about my getting a book for him to draw up his whole theory of shipping, which, at my desire, he hath gone far in, and hath shown me what he hath done therein, to admiration. I did give him a parallelogram, which he is mightily taken with; and so after dinner to the office, where all the afternoon till night late, and then home. Vexed at my wife's not being come home, she being gone again abroad with M. Batelier, and come not home till ten at night, which vexed me, so that I to bed, and lay in pain awake till past one, and then to sleep.

23d. Going to rise without saying anything, my wife stopped me; and, after a little angry talk, did tell me how she spent all yesterday with M. Batelier and her sweetheart, and seeing a play at the New Nursery, which is set up at the house in Lincoln's Inn Fields, which was formerly the King's house. To the Council-Chamber, and heard two or three causes; among others, that of the complaint of Sir Philip Howard and Watson, the inventors, as they pretend, of the business of varnishing and lacquer-work, against the Company of Painters, who take upon them to do the same thing; where I saw a great instance of the weakness of a young Counsel not used to such an audience, against the Solicitor-General and two more able Counsel used to it. Though he had the right of his side, and did prevail for what he pretended to against the rest, yet it was with much disadvantage and hazard. Here I also heard Mr. Papillon [1] make his defence to the King, against some complaints of the Farmers of Excise; but it was so weak, and done only by his own seeking, that it was to his injury more than profit, and made his case the worse, being ill managed, and in a cause against the King. By agreement met my wife, and with her to the Cock, and did give her a dinner. Thence to the King's playhouse, and saw 'The Generous Portugals,' [2] a play that pleases me better and better every time we see it; and, I thank God! it did not trouble my eyes so much as I was afraid it would. Here, by, accident, we met Mr. Sheres, and yet I could not but be troubled

---

[1] Thomas Papillon, Esq., of Lubenham in Leicestershire, who purchased the manor of Acrise, in Kent, in 1666. He was an eminent merchant of London, and Master of the Mercers' Company in 1698; and was M.P. for Dover, 1689–95, and for London 1695–1700. The case of Mr. Papillon related to a petition of the Company of Wine Merchants, concerning Brandy, alias Strong Water, against the Farmer of Excise.

[2] This play has not been traced.

because my wife do so delight to talk of him, and to see him. Nevertheless, we took him with us to our mercer's, and to the Exchange, and he helped me to choose a summer-suit of coloured camelott, coat and breeches, and a flowered tabby coat very rich; and so home, where he took his leave, and down to Greenwich, where he hath some friends; and I to see Colonel Middleton, who hath been ill for a day or two, or three; and so home to supper, and to bed.

24th. Mr. Sheres dining with us by agreement; and my wife, which troubled me, mighty careful to have a handsome dinner for him; but yet I see no reason to be troubled at it, he being a very civil and worthy man, I think; but only it do seem to imply some little neglect of me. After dinner to the King's House, and there saw 'The General' [1] revived—a good play, that pleases me well, and thence, our coach coming for us, we parted and home. Well pleased tonight to have Lead, the vizard-maker, bring me home my vizard, with a tube fastened in it, which, I think, will do my business, at least in a great measure, for the easing of my eyes.

25th. (Lord's day.) Up, and to my office awhile, and thither comes Lead with my vizard, with a tube fastened within both eyes; which, with the help which he prompts me to, of a glass in the tube, do content me mightily. To church, where a stranger made a dull sermon, but I mightily pleased to look upon Mr. Buckworth's little pretty daughters. W. Howe came and dined with us; and then I to my office, he being gone, to write down my journal for the last twelve days: and did it with the help of my vizard and tube fixed to it, and do find it mighty manageable, but how helpful to my eyes this trial will show me. So abroad with my wife, in the afternoon, to the Park, where very much company, and the weather very pleasant. I carried my wife to the Lodge, the first time this year, and there in our coach eat a cheesecake and drank a tankard of milk. I showed her this day also first the Prince of Tuscany, who was in the Park, and many very fine ladies.

26th. To Lilly's, the varnisher, who is lately dead, and his wife and brother keep up the trade, and there I left my French prints to be put on boards: and, while I was there a fire burst out in a chimney of a house over against his house, but it was with a gun quickly put out. So home, calling at the laceman's for some lace for my new suit, and at my tailor's, and Mr. Sheres dined with us, who came hither today to teach my wife the rules of the perspective;

[1] By James Shirley.

but I think, upon trial, he thinks it too hard to teach her, being ignorant of the principle of lines. After dinner comes Colonel Macnachan, one that I see often at Court, a Scotchman, but know him not; only he brings me a letter from my Lord Middleton, who, he says, is in great distress for £500 to relieve my Lord Morton [1] with, but upon what account I know not; and he would have me advance it without order upon his pay for Tangier, which I was astonished at, but had the grace to deny him with an excuse. And so he went away, leaving me a little troubled that I was thus driven, on a sudden, to do anything herein; but Creed coming just now to see me, he approves of what I have done. And then to talk of general matters, and, by and by, Sheres being gone, my wife and he and I out, and I set him down at Temple Bar, and myself and wife went down the Temple upon seeming business, only to put him off; and to the 'Change, about things for her; and here, at Mrs. Burnett's shop, I am told by Betty, who was all undressed, of a great fire happened in Durham Yard last night, burning the house of one Lady Hungerford,[2] who was to come to town to it this night; and so the house is burned, new furnished, by carelessness of the girl sent to take off a candle from a bunch of candles, which she did by burning it off, and left the rest, as is supposed, on fire. The King and Court were here, it seems, and stopped the fire by blowing up of the next house. The King and Court went out of town to Newmarket this morning betimes, for a week. This night I did call at the coachmaker's, and do resolve upon having the standards of my coach gilt with this new sort of varnish, which will come but to 40s.; and, contrary to my expectation, the doing of the biggest coach all over comes not to above £6, which is [not] very much.

27th. Up and to the office, where all the morning. At noon home to dinner, and then to the office again, where all the afternoon busy till late, and then home, and got my wife to read to me in the Nepotism,[3] which is very pleasant, and so to supper and to bed.

[1] William Douglas, ninth Earl of Morton, who had married Lord Middleton's daughter Grizel.

[2] Margaret, daughter and co-heir of William Halliday, alderman of London, widow of Sir Edward Hungerford, of Black Bourton, Oxfordshire, who died, *s.p.*, 1648. She survived till 1673. The house burned down was replaced by Hungerford Market, eventually the site of Charing Cross railway station.

[3] The work here mentioned is a French translation, published in 1669, of a bitter satire against the Court of Rome, written in Italian, and as some say, by Gregorio Leti. It was first printed in 1667, without the name of place or

This afternoon was brought to me a fresh *Distringas* upon the score of the Tangier accounts, which vexes me though I will not turn to my wrong.

28th. Up, and was called upon by Sir H. Cholmley to discourse about some accounts of his, of Tangier; and then to other talk: and I find by him that it is brought almost to effect (through the late endeavours of the Duke of York and Duchess, the Queen-mother, and my Lord St. Albans, together with some of the contrary faction, as my Lord Arlington), that for a sum of money we shall enter into a league with the King of France, wherein, he says, my Lord Chancellor [1] is also concerned; and that he believes that, in the doing hereof, it is meant that he [Clarendon] shall come in again, and that this sum of money will so help the King as that he will not need the Parliament; and that, in that regard, it will be forwarded by the Duke of Buckingham and his faction, who dread the Parliament. But hereby we must leave the Dutch, and that I doubt will undo us; and Sir H. Cholmley says he finds W. Coventry do think the like. My Lady Castlemaine is instrumental in this matter, and, he says, never more great with the King than she is now. But this is a thing that will make the Parliament and Kingdom mad, and will turn to our ruin: for with this money the King shall wanton away his time in pleasures, and think nothing of the main till it be too late. This morning Mr. Sheres sent me, in two volumes, Marian his History of Spain,[2] in Spanish, an excellent book; and I am much obliged to him for it.

29th. Up, and to the office, where all the morning, and at noon dined at home: and then to the office again, there to dispatch as much business as I could, that I might be at liberty tomorrow to look after many things that I have to do against May-day.

30th. Up, and by coach to the coachmaker's: and there I do

---

printer, but it is from the press of the Elzevirs. The scope of the work will be well understood by the title: 'Il Nipotismo di Roma, o vero relatione delle ragioni che muovono i Pontefici all' aggrandimento de' Nipoti: del bene e male che hanno portato alla Chiesa dopo Sixto IV, sino al presente: delle difficoltà che incontrano i ministri de' Principi nel trattare con loro, ed insieme col rimedio opportuno per liberarsi da tali difficoltà, e della causa perche le famiglie de' Pontefici non sono durate lungo tempo in grandezza.' From this work the word nepotism is derived, and is applied to the bad practice of statesmen, when in power, providing lucrative places for their relations.

[1] Clarendon, then an exile in France.

[2] *Historiæ de Rebus Hispaniæ Libri XX.* By Juan Mariana; first printed at Toledo in 1592. The Spanish version is best known.

find a great many ladies sitting in the body of a coach that must be ended by tomorrow: they were my Lady Marquess of Winchester,[1] Bellassis,[2] and other great ladies, eating of bread and butter and drinking ale. I to my coach, which is silvered over, but no varnish yet laid on, so I put it in a way of doing; and myself about other business, and particularly to see Sir W. Coventry, with whom I talked a good while to my great content; and so to other places—among others to my tailor's: and then to the beltmaker's, where my belt cost me 55s. of the colour of my new suit; and here, understanding that the mistress of the house, an oldish woman in a hat, hath some water good for the eyes, she did dress me, making my eyes smart most horribly, and did give me a little glass of it, which I will use, and hope it will do me good. So to the cutler's, and there did give Tom, who was with me all day, a sword cost me 12s. and a belt of my own; and sent my own silver-hilt sword a-gilding against tomorrow. This morning I did visit Mr. Oldenburgh,[3] and did see the instrument for perspective made by Dr. Wren,[4] of which I have one making by Browne; and the sight of this do please me mightily. At noon my wife came to me at my tailor's, and I sent her home, and myself and Tom dined at Hercules' Pillars; and so about our business again, and particularly to Lilly's, the varnisher, about my prints, whereof some of them are pasted upon the boards, and to my full content. Thence to the framemaker's, one Norris, in Long Acre, who showed me several forms of frames, which were pretty, in little bits of mouldings, to choose patterns by. This done, I to my coachmaker's, and there vexed to see nothing yet done to my coach, at three in the afternoon; but I set it in doing, and stood by till eight at night, and saw the painter varnish it, which is pretty to see how every doing it over do make it more and more yellow: and it dries as fast in the sun as it can be laid on almost; and most coaches are, nowadays, done so, and it is very pretty when laid on well, and not too pale, as some are,

---

[1] Isabella, daughter of William Howard, Viscount Stafford, third wife to John Paulet, fifth Marquis of Winchester.

[2] John Lord Belasyse was thrice married: first, to Jane, daughter of Sir Robert Boteler, of Woodhall, Hertfordshire; secondly, to Ann, daughter of Sir Robert Crane, of Chilton, Suffolk; thirdly, to Lady Anne Paulet, daughter of the above-named Marquis of Winchester (by his second wife, Lady Honora de Burgh); and who is the person referred to by Pepys.

[3] Henry Oldenburgh, secretary of the Royal Society.

[4] A description of an instrument invented many years before by Dr. Christopher Wren, for drawing the outlines of any object in perspective, is given in the *Abridgment of Philosophical Transactions*, vol. i, p. 325 (1669).

even to show the silver. Here I did make the workmen drink, and saw my coach cleaned and oiled; and, staying among poor people there in the alley, did hear them call their fat child Punch, which pleased me mightily, that word being become a word of common use for all that is thick and short.[1] At night home, and there find my wife hath been making herself clean against to-morrow; and, late as it was, I did send my coachman and horses to fetch home the coach tonight, and so we to supper, myself most weary with walking and standing so much, to see all things fine against tomorrow, and so to bed. Meeting with Mr. Sheres, to several places, and, among others, to buy a periwig, but I bought none; and also to Dankers's, where he was about my picture of Windsor, which is mighty pretty, and so will the prospect of Rome be.

May 1st. Up betimes. Called by my tailor, and there first put on a summer suit this year; but it was not my fine one of flowered tabby vest, and coloured camelott tunic, because it was too fine with the gold lace at the bands, that I was afraid to be seen in it; but put on the stuff suit I made the last year, which is now repaired; and so did go to the office in it, and sat all the morning, the day looking as if it would be foul. At noon home to dinner, and there find my wife extraordinary fine, with her flowered tabby gown that she made two years ago, now laced exceeding pretty; and, indeed, was fine all over; and mighty earnest to go, though the day was very lowering; and she would have me put on my fine suit, which I did. And so anon we went alone through the town with our new liveries of serge, and the horses' manes and tails tied with red ribbons, and the standards gilt with varnish, and all clean, and green reins, that people did mightily look upon us; and, the truth is, I did not see any coach more pretty, though more gay, than ours, all the day. But we set out, out of humour—I because Betty, whom I expected, was not come to go with us; and my wife that I would sit on the same seat with her, which she likes not, being so fine: and she then expected to meet Sheres, which we did in the Pall Mall, and, against my will, I was forced to take him into the coach, but was sullen all day almost, and little complaisant: the day being unpleasing, though the Park full of coaches, but

[1] '*Puncheon*, the vessel, French *poinçon*, perhaps so-called from the pointed form of the staves; the vessel bellying out in the middle, and tapering towards each end: and hence *punch* (i.e. the large belly) became applied, as Pepys records, to anything thick or short.'—Richardson's *Dictionary*.

dusty and windy and cold, and now and then a little dribbling of rain; and, what made it worse, there was so many hackney coaches as spoiled the sight of the gentlemen's; and so we had little pleasure. But here was W. Batelier and his sister in a borrowed coach by themselves, and I took them, and we to the lodge; and at the door did give them a syllabub and other things, cost me 12*s.*, and pretty merry. And so back to the coaches, and there till the evening, and then home, leaving Mr. Sheres at St. James's Gate, where he took leave of us for altogether, he being this night to set out for Portsmouth post, in his way to Tangier, which troubled my wife mightily, who is mighty, though not, I think, too fond of him. But she was out of humour all the evening, and I vexed at her for it; and she did not rest almost all the night, so as I was forced to take her and hug her to put her to rest.

2d. (Lord's day.) Up, and by water to White Hall, and there visited my Lord Sandwich, who, after about two months' absence at Hinchingbroke, came to town last night. I saw him, and he was very kind; and I am glad he is so, I having not wrote to him all the time, my eyes indeed not letting me. Here with Sir Charles Harbord and my Lord Hinchingbroke and Sidney, and we looked upon the picture of Tangier designed by Charles Harbord and drawn by Dankers, which my Lord Sandwich admires as being the truest picture that ever he saw in his life: and it is indeed very pretty, and I will be at the cost of having one of them. Thence with them to White Hall, and there walked out the sermon with one or other; and then saw the Duke of York, and he talked to me a little; and so away back by water home. After dinner got my wife to read, and then by coach, she and I, to the Park, and there spent the evening with much pleasure, it proving clear after a little shower, and we mighty fine as yesterday, and people mightily pleased with our coach, as I perceive; but I had not on my fine suit, being really afraid to wear it, it being so fine with the gold lace, though not gay. So home to supper, and my wife to read my 'Nepotism,' and then to bed.

3d. Up, and by coach to my Lord Brouncker's, where Sir G. Carteret did meet Sir J. Minnes and me to discourse upon Mr. Dering's business, who was directed, in the time of the war, to provide provisions at Hamburg by Sir G. Carteret's direction; and now Sir G. Carteret is afraid to own it, it being done without written order. But by our meeting we do all begin to recollect enough to preserve Mr. Dering, which I think, poor, silly man! I shall be glad of, it being too much he should suffer for endeavouring to serve us. Thence to St. James's, where the Duke of York was playing in the Pall Mall; and so he called me to him most part of the time that he played, which was an hour, and talked alone to me; and, among other things, tells me how the King will not yet be got to name anybody in the room of Pen, but puts it off for three or four days: from whence he do collect that they are brewing something for the Navy, but what he knows not; but I perceive is vexed that things should go so, and he hath reason. For he told me that it is likely they will do in this as in other things—resolve first and consider it and the fitness of it afterwards. Thence to White Hall and met with Creed, and I took him to the Harp and Balls, and there drank a cup of ale and discoursed of matters. And I perceive by him that he makes no doubt but that all will turn to the old religion, for these people cannot hold things in their hands, nor prevent its coming to that; and by his discourse he fits himself for it, and would have my Lord Sandwich do so, too, and me. After a little talk with him, and particularly about the ruinous condition of Tangier, which I have a great mind to lay before the Duke of York before it be too late (but dare not, because of his great kindness to Lord Middleton), we parted, and I homeward; but called at Povy's, and there he stopped me to dinner, there being Mr. Williamson, the Lieutenant of the Tower,[1] Mr. Child, and several others. And after dinner Povy and I together to talk of Tangier; and he would have me move the Duke of York in it, for it concerns him particularly, more than any, as being the head of us; and I do think to do it.

4th. Walked with my wife in the garden, and my Lord Brouncker with us, who is newly come to W. Pen's lodgings; and by and by comes Mr. Hooke; and my Lord and he and I into my Lord's lodgings, and there discoursed of many fine things in philosophy, to my great content.

5th. Up, and thought to have gone with Lord Brouncker to Mr. Hooke this morning betimes; but my Lord is taken ill of the gout, and says his new lodgings have infected him, he never having any symptom of it till now. So walked to Gresham College, to tell Hooke that my Lord could not come; and so left word, he being abroad. To St. James's, and thence, with the Duke of York, to White Hall, where the Board waited on him all the morning: and so at noon with Sir Thomas Allen and Sir

[1] Sir John Robinson.

Edward Scott and Lord Carlingford to the Spanish Ambassador's, where I dined the first time. The Olio not so good as Sheres's. There was at the table himself and a Spanish countess, a good, comely, and witty lady—three Fathers and us. Discourse good and pleasant. And here was an Oxford scholar in a Doctor of Laws gown, sent from the College where the Ambassador lay when the Court was there, to salute him before his return to Spain. This man, though a gentle sort of scholar, yet sat like a fool for want of French or Spanish, but knew only Latin, which he spoke like an Englishman to one of the Fathers. And by and by he and I to talk, and the company very merry at my defending Cambridge against Oxford: and I made much use of my French and Spanish here, to my great content. But the dinner not extraordinary at all, either for quantity or quality. Thence home to my wife, and she read to me the Epistle of Cassandra, which is very good indeed; and the better to her, because recommended by Sheres. So to supper, and to bed.

6th. Up, and by coach to Sir W. Coventry's, but he gone out. I by water back to the office, and there all the morning; then to dinner, and then to the office again, and anon with my wife by coach to take the air, it being a noble day, as far as the Green Man,[1] mightily pleased with our journey and our condition of doing it in our own coach. And so home, and to walk in the garden, and so to supper and to bed, my eyes being bad with writing my journal, part of it, tonight.

7th. Up, and by coach to Sir W. Coventry's; and there to talk with him a great deal with great content; and so to the Duke of York, having a great mind to speak to him about Tangier; but, when I came to it, his interest for my Lord Middleton is such that I dared not. I passed by Guildhall, which is almost finished, and saw a poor labourer carried by, I think dead with a fall, as many there are, I hear. To see my Lord Brouncker, who is a little ill of the gout; and there Madam Williams told me that she heard that my wife was going into France this year, which I did not deny, if I can get time, and I pray God I may. But I wondering how she come to know it, she tells me a woman that my wife spoke to for a maid did tell her so, and that a lady that desires to go thither would be glad to go in her company. Thence with my wife abroad with our coach, most pleasant weather; and to Hackney, and into the marshes, where I never was before, and thence round about to

[1] Probably on Stroud Green.

Old Ford and Bow. And coming through the latter home, there being some young gentlewomen at a door, and I seeming not to know who they were, my wife's jealousy told me presently that I knew well enough it was the place where Deb. dwelt: which made me answer very angrily that it was false, as it was, and I carried her back again to see the place, and it proved not. So I continued out of humour a good while at it, she being willing to be friends; so I was by and by, saying no more of it. So home, and there met with a letter from Captain Silas Taylor, and with it his written copy of a play that he hath wrote, and intends to have acted. It is called 'The Serenade, or Disappointment,' which I will read, not believing he can make any good of that kind. He did once offer to show Harris it, but Harris told him that he would judge by one act whether it were good or no, which is indeed a foolish saying, and we see them out themselves in the choice of a play after they have read the whole, it being sometimes not fit to act above three times; nay, and some that have been refused at one house is found a good one at the other. This made Taylor say he would not show it him, but is angry, and hath carried it to the other house, and he thinks it will be acted there, though he tells me they are not yet agreed upon it. But I will find time to get it read to me, and I did get my wife to begin a little tonight in the garden, but not so much as I could make my judgment of it.

8th. Up, and to the office, and there comes Lead to me, and at last my vizards are done, and glasses got to put in and out as I will; and I think I have brought it to the utmost, both for easiness of using and benefit, that I can; and so I paid him 15*s.* for what he hath done now last, in the finishing them, and they, I hope, will do me a great deal of ease. At the office all the morning, and this day, the first time, did alter my side of the table, after above eight years sitting on that next the fire. But now I am not able to bear the light of the windows in my eyes, I do go there, and I did sit with much more content than I had done on the other side for a great while, and in winter the fire will not trouble my back. After dinner, all the afternoon, within with Mr. Hater, Gibson, and W. Hewer, reading over and drawing up new things in the Instructions of Commanders, which will be good, and I hope to get them confirmed by the Duke of York, though I perceive nothing will effectually perfect them but to look over the whole body of the Instructions, of all the officers of a ship, and make them all perfect together. This being done, comes my bookseller, and brings me home my collection of papers about my Address to the Duke of York in August, bound, which makes me glad, it being that which shall do me more right many years hence than, perhaps, all I ever did in my life: and therefore I do, both for my own and the King's sake, value it much. By and by also comes Browne, the mathematical instrument-maker, and brings me home my instrument for perspective, made according to the description of Dr. Wren's, in the late Transactions; and he hath made it, I think, very well, and that that I believe will do the thing, and therein gives me great content; but I have, I fear, all the content that must be received by my eyes, which are almost lost.

9th. (Lord's day.) Up; and, after dressing in my best suit with gold trimming, to the office; and, when church-time, to church with my wife. Dr. Mills preached a dull sermon, and so we home to dinner; and thence by coach to St. Andrew's, Holborn, thinking to have heard Dr. Stillingfleet preach, but we could not get a place: and so to St. Margaret's, Westminster, and there heard a sermon, and did get a place, the first we have heard there these many years. Thence towards the Park, but too soon to go in, so went on to Knightsbridge, and there eat and drank at the World's End, where we had good things, and then back to the Park, and there till night, being fine weather, and much company, and so home. This day I first left off both my waistcoats by day, and my waistcoat by night, it being very hot weather, so hot as to make me break out here and there in my hands, which vexes me to see, but is good for me.

10th. Troubled about three in the morning with my wife's calling her maid up, and rising herself, to go with her coach abroad, to gather May-dew, which she did, and I troubled for it, for fear of any hurt, going abroad so betimes, happening to her; but I to sleep again, and she came home about six. To White Hall, where the Duke of York met the Office, and there discoursed of several things, particularly the Instructions of Commanders of ships. But here happened by chance a discourse of the Council of Trade, against which the Duke of York is mightily displeased, and particularly Mr. Child, against whom he speaking hardly, Captain Cox did second the Duke of York, by saying that he was talked of for an unfair dealer with masters of ships, about freight: to which Sir T. Littleton very hotly and foolishly replied presently, that he never heard any honest man speak ill of Child; to which the Duke of York did make a smart reply, and was angry; so as I was sorry to hear it come so far, and that I, by seeming to assent to Cox, might be observed too much by Littleton, though I said nothing aloud, for this must breed great heart-burnings. After this meeting done, the Duke of York took the Treasurers into his closet to chide them, as Mr. Wren tells me; for that my Lord Keeper did last night at the Council say, when nobody was ready to say anything against the constitution of the Navy, that he did believe the Treasurers of the Navy had something to say, which was very foul on their part, to be parties against us. They being gone, Mr. Wren and I took boat, thinking to dine with my Lord of Canterbury; but when we came to Lambeth the gate was shut, which is strictly done at twelve o'clock, and nobody comes in afterwards; so we lost our labour, and therefore back to White Hall, and thence walked to my Lord Crewe, whom I have not seen since he was sick, which is eight months ago, I think, and there dined with him: he is mightily broke. A stranger, a country gentleman, was with him: and he pleased with my discourse accidentally about the decay of gentlemen's families in the country, telling us that the old rule was that a family might remain fifty miles from London one hundred years, one hundred miles from London two hundred years, and so farther or nearer London more or less years. He also told us that he hath heard his father say that in his time it was so rare for a country gentleman to come to London, that when he did come he used to make his will before he set out. Thence to St. James's, and there met the Duke of York, who told me, with great content, that he did now think he should master our adversaries, for that the King did tell him that he was satisfied in the constitution of the Navy, but that it was well to give these people leave to object against it, which they having not done, he did give order to give warrant to the Duke of York to direct Sir Jeremy Smith to be a Commissioner of the Navy in the room of Pen; which, though he be an impertinent fellow, yet I am glad of it, it showing that the other side is not so strong as it was. And so, in plain terms, the Duke of York did tell me that they were every day losing ground; and particularly that he would take care to keep out Child: at all which I am glad, though yet I dare not think myself secure, as the King may yet be wrought upon by these people to bring changes in our Office and remove us ere it be long. To White Hall, to a Committee of Tangier, where I see all things going to rack in the business of the Corporation, and consequently in the place, by Middleton's going. Thence walked a little with Creed, who tells me he hears how fine my horses and coach are, and advises me to avoid being noted for it, which I was vexed to hear taken notice of, being what I feared: and Povy told me of my gold-laced sleeves in the Park yesterday, which vexed me also, so as to resolve never to appear in Court with them, but presently to have them taken off, as it is fit I should, and so called at my tailor's for that purpose.

11th. My wife again up by four o'clock, to go to gather May-dew; and so back home by seven, to bed.   In the evening my wife and I all alone, with but the boy, by water up as high as Putney almost, with the tide, and back again, neither staying, going nor coming; but talking, and singing, and reading a foolish copy of verses upon my Lord Mayor's entertaining of all the bachelors, designed in praise to my Lord Mayor.   Some trouble at Court for fear of the Queen's miscarrying; she being, as they all conclude, far gone with child.

12th. To Westminster Hall; and there by chance met Roger Pepys, who came to town the last night: I was glad to see him. After some talk with him and others (and among others Sir Charles Harbord and Sidney Montagu, the latter of whom is to set out tomorrow towards Flanders and Italy) I invited them to dine with me tomorrow.   After dinner my wife and I to the Duke of York's playhouse, and there, in the side balcony, over against the music, did hear, but not see, a new play the first day acted, 'The Roman Virgin,' [1] an old play, and but ordinary, I thought; but the trouble of my eyes with the light of the candles did almost kill me.   Thence to my Lord Sandwich's, and there had a promise from Sidney to come and dine with me tomorrow; and so my wife and I home in our coach, and there find my brother John, as I looked for, come to town from Ellington,[2] where, among other things, he tells me the first news that my sister Jackson is with child, and far gone, which I know not whether it did more trouble or please me, having no great care for my friends to have children, though I love other people's.   So, glad to see him, we to supper, and so to bed.

13th. At noon comes my Lord Hinchingbroke and Sidney and Sir Charles Harbord and Roger Pepys, and dined with me; and had a good dinner, and very merry with us all the afternoon, it being a farewell to Sidney; and so in the evening they away, and

---

[1] A tragedy, altered by Thomas Betterton, from Webster's *Appius and Virginia*.

[2] In Huntingdonshire, the residence of Pepys's brother-in-law, Mr. Jackson.

I to my business at the office, and so to supper, and talk with my brother, and so to bed.

14th. At noon with Mr. Wren to Lambeth, to dinner with the Atchbishop of Canterbury, the first time I was ever there, and I have long longed for it: where a noble house, and well furnished with good pictures and furniture, and noble attendance in good order, and a great deal of company, though an ordinary day; and exceeding great cheer, nowhere better, or so much, that ever I think I saw, for an ordinary table: and the Bishop mighty kind to me particularly, desiring my company another time, when less company there. Most of the company gone, and I going, I heard by a gentleman of a sermon that was to be there; and so I stayed to hear it thinking it serious, till by and by the gentleman told me it was a mockery, by one Cornet Bolton, a very gentleman-like man, that behind a chair did pray and preach like a Presbyter Scot, with all the possible imitation in grimaces and voice. And his text about the hanging up their harps upon the willows: [1] and a serious good sermon too, exclaiming against Bishops, and crying up of my good Lord Eglington,[2] till it made us all burst; but I did wonder to have the Bishop at this time to make himself sport with things of this kind, but I perceive it was shown him as a rarity; and he took care to have the room-door shut, but there were about twenty gentlemen there, and myself, infinitely pleased with the novelty. So over to White Hall, to a little Committee of Tangier; and thence walking in the Gallery I met Sir Thomas Osborne, who, to my great content, did of his own accord fall into discourse with me, with such professions of value and respect, placing the whole virtue of the Office of the Navy upon me, and that for the Comptroller's place no man in England was fit for it but me, when Sir J. Minnes, as he says it is necessary, is removed: but then he knows not what to do for a man in my place. And in discourse, though I have no mind to the other, I did bring in Tom Hater to be the fittest man in the world for it, which he took good notice of. But

---

[1] Psalm cxxxvii, 2.

[2] The person here alluded to is probably Alexander Montgomerie, the sixth Earl of Eglinton, called Greysteel, who was a rank Presbyterian, and a ruling Elder of the General Assembly, when the solemn League and Covenant were drawn up. He fought against Charles at Marston Moor, whilst his son and successor was in the king's army; but he afterwards became a Royalist, and died in 1661, *æt.* 73. The son was a consistent supporter of monarchy, and there seems no reason why he should have been made an object of satire. His death occurred only two months before the unseemly scene at Lambeth.

in the whole I was mightily pleased, reckoning myself fifty per cent securer in my place than I did before think myself to be. Thence to Unthank's, and there find my wife, but not dressed, which vexed me, because of going to the Park, it being a most pleasant day after yesterday's rain, which lays all the dust, and most people going out thither, which vexed me. So home, sullen; but then my wife and I by water with my brother as high as Fulham, talking and singing, and playing the rogue with the Western bargemen, about the women of Woolwich, which mads them.

15th. Up, and at the office all the morning. Dined at home, and Creed with me, and I did discourse about evening some reckonings with him in the afternoon; but I could not, for my eyes, do it, which troubled me, and vexed him that I would not; but yet we were friends, I advancing him money without it. And so to walk all the afternoon together in the garden; and I perceive that he do expect a change in our matters, especially as to religion, and fits himself for it by professing himself for it in his discourse. He gone, I to my business at my office, and so at night home to supper, and to bed.

16th. (Lord's day.) My wife and I at church, our pew filled with Mrs. Backwell and six more that she brought with her, which vexed me at her confidence. I all the afternoon drawing up a foul draft of my petition to the Duke of York, about my eyes, for leave to spend three or four months out of the office, drawing it so as to give occasion to a voyage abroad, which I did, to my pretty good liking; and then with my wife to Hyde Park, where a good deal of company and good weather.

17th. My wife and I and brother John by coach to the King's playhouse, and saw 'The Spanish Curate' revived, which is a pretty good play, but my eyes troubled with seeing it, mightily. Great news now of the French taking St. Domingo,[1] in Spaniola, from the Spaniards, which troubles us, that they should have got it, and have the honour of taking it, when we could not.

18th. Dined in my wife's chamber, she being much troubled with the toothache, and I stayed till a surgeon of hers come, one Leeson, who had formerly drawn her mouth, and he advised her to draw it: so I to the office, and by and by word is come that she

---

[1] St. Domingo, on the southern coast of Hispaniola, the oldest European establishment in America, was founded by Columbus's brother in 1496. A town named Isabella had been built in 1493, on the northern coast, but it was afterwards abandoned.

hath drawn it, which pleased me, it being well done.   So I home to comfort her.

19th. With my coach to St. James's; and there finding the Duke of York gone to muster his men in Hyde Park, I alone with my boy thither, and there saw more, walking out of my coach as other gentlemen did, of a soldier's trade than ever I did in my life: the men being mighty fine, and their Commanders, particularly the Duke of Monmouth; but methought their trade but very easy as to the mustering of their men, and the men but indifferently ready to perform what was commanded in the handling of their arms. Here the news was first talked of Harry Killigrew's being wounded in nine places last night by footmen, in the highway, going from the Park in a hackney coach towards Hammersmith, to his house at Turnham Green: they being supposed to be my Lady Shrewsbury's men, she being by in her coach with six horses, upon an old grudge of his saying openly that he had intrigued with her. Thence by and by to White Hall, and there I waited upon the King and Queen all dinner-time in the Queen's lodgings, she being in her white pinner, and appearing like a woman with child; and she seemed handsomer plain so, than when dressed.   And by and by, dinner done, I out, and to walk in the Gallery, for the Duke of York's coming out; and there meeting Mr. May, he took me down about four o'clock to Mr. Chiffinch's lodgings, and all alone did get me a dish of cold chickens, and good wine; and I dined like a prince, being before very hungry and empty.   By and by the Duke of York comes, and readily took me to his closet, and received my petition, and discoursed about my eyes, and pitied me, and with much kindness did give me his consent to be absent, and approved of my proposition to go into Holland to observe things there, of the Navy; but would first ask the King's leave, which he anon did, and did tell me that the King would be a good master to me (these were his words) about my eyes, and do like of my going into Holland, but do advise that nobody should know of my going thither, and that I should pretend to go into the country somewhere, which I liked well.   In discourse this afternoon the Duke of York did tell me that he was the most amazed at one thing just now, that ever he was in his life, which was that the Duke of Buckingham did just now come into the Queen's bed-chamber, where the King was, with much mixed company, and, among others, Tom Killigrew, the father of Harry, who was last night wounded so as to be in danger of death, and his man is quite dead;

and Buckingham there did say that he had spoke with someone that was by, which person all the world must know must be his mistress, my Lady Shrewsbury, who says that they did not mean to hurt, but beat him, and that he did run first at them with his sword; so that he do hereby clearly discover that he knows who did it, and is of conspiracy with them, being of known conspiracy with her, which the Duke of York did seem to be pleased with, and said it might, perhaps, cost him his life in the House of Lords: and I find was mightily pleased with it, saying it was the most impudent thing, as well as the most foolish, that ever he knew man do in all his life.

20th. Up, and to the office. At noon, the whole Office—Brouncker, J. Minnes, T. Middleton, Samuel Pepys, and Captain Cox—to dine with the Parish, at the Three Tuns, this day being Ascension day, where exceeding good discourse among the merchants. With my eyes mighty weary, and my head full of care how to get my accounts and business settled against my journey, home to supper and to bed. Yesterday, at my coming home, I found that my wife had, on a sudden, put away Matt upon some falling out, and I doubt Matt did call her ill names by my wife's own discourse; but I did not meddle to say anything upon it, but let her go, being not sorry, because now we may get one that speaks French, to go abroad with us.

21st. I waited with the Office upon the Duke of York in the morning. Dined at home, where Lewis Phillips, with a friend of his, dined with me. In the afternoon at the office. In the evening visited by Roger Pepys and Philip Packer; and so home.

23d. (Lord's day.) Called up by Roger Pepys and his son, who to church with me; and then in the afternoon carried them to Westminster, and myself to St. James's, where, not finding the Duke of York, back home, and with my wife spent the evening taking the air about Hackney, with great pleasure.

24th. To White Hall, where I attended the Duke of York, and was by him led to the King, who expressed great sense of my misfortune in my eyes, and concernment for their recovery; and accordingly signified not only his assent to my desire therein, but commanded me to give them rest this summer, according to my late petition to the Duke of York. W. Hewer and I dined alone at the Swan; and thence, having thus waited on the King, spent till four o'clock in St. James's Park, when I met my wife at Unthank's, and so home.

25th. Dined at home; and the rest of the day, morning and afternoon, at the office.

26th. To White Hall, where all the morning. Dined with Mr. Chiffinch, with Alderman Backwell and Spragg. The Court full of the news from Captain Hubbert, of the *Milford*, touching his being affronted in the Straits, shot at, and having eight of his men killed by a French man-of-war, calling him 'English dog,' and commanding him to strike, which he refused, and, as knowing himself much too weak for him, made away from him. The Queen, as being supposed with child, fell ill, so as to call for Madam Nun, Mr. Cheffinch's sister, and one of her women, from dinner from us; this being the last day of her doubtfulness touching her being with child; and they were therein well confirmed by her Majesty's being well again before night. One Sir Edmund Berry Godfrey,[1] a woodmonger and Justice of Peace in Westminster, having two days since arrested Sir Alexander Frazier[2] for about £30 in firing, the bailiffs were apprehended, committed to the porter's lodge, and there, by the King's command, the last night severely whipped; from which the Justice himself very hardly escaped, to such an unusual degree was the King moved therein. But he lies now in the lodge, justifying his act as grounded upon the opinion of several of the Judges, and, among others, my Lord Chief Justice; which makes the King very angry with the Chief Justice, as they say; and the Justice do lie and justify his act, and says he will suffer in the cause for the people, and do refuse to receive almost any nutriment. The effects of it may be bad to the Court.

27th. Presented this day by Mr. Browne with a book of drawing by him, lately printed,[3] which cost me 20s. to him. In the afternoon to the Temple, to meet with Auditor

---

[1] The history of Sir Edmund Berry Godfrey is too well known to require any comment, though his tragical end has never been satisfactorily made out. In the *Gentleman's Magazine* for October 1848 there are some interesting details about the knight's family, and a description and plate of a silver cup, which seems to have been presented to him by the king for his important services during the Plague and Fire of London, and is now in the possession of the corporation of Sudbury.

[2] One of the king's physicians.

[3] A curious and uncommon book, entitled 'A Compendious Drawing-Book, composed by Alexander Browne, limner, collected from the drawings of the most celebrated painters in Europe, engraven by Arnold de Jode.' A second edition with letterpress, and additions, was published in 1675, under the title of *Ars Pictoria*.

Aldworth,[1] about my interest account, but failed of meeting him. To visit my cousin Creed, and found her ill at home, being with child, and looks poorly. Thence to her husband, at Gresham College, upon some occasions of Tangier; and so home, with Sir John Bankes with me, to Mark Lane.

28th. To St. James's, where the King's being with the Duke of York prevented a meeting of the Tangier Commission. But, Lord! what a deal of sorry discourse did I hear between the King and several Lords about him here! but very mean, methought. So with Creed to the Excise Office, and back to White Hall, where, in the Park, Sir G. Carteret did give an account of his discourse lately with the Commissioners of Accounts, who except against many things, but none that I find considerable; among others, that of the Officers of the Navy selling of the King's goods, and particularly my providing him with calico flags, which having been by order, and but once, when necessity and the King's apparent profit justified it, as conformable to my particular duty, it will prove to my advantage that it be enquired into. Nevertheless, having this morning received from them a demand of an account of all moneys within their cognizance received and issued by me, I was willing, upon this hint, to give myself rest by knowing whether their meaning therein might reach only to my Treasurership for Tangier, or the moneys employed on this occasion. I went, therefore, to them this afternoon, to understand what moneys they meant, where they answered me by saying, 'The eleven months' tax, customs, and prize-money,' without mentioning, any more than I demanding, the service they respected therein: and so, without further discourse, we parted upon very good terms of respect, and with few words, but my mind not fully satisfied about the moneys they mean. With my wife and brother spent the evening on the water, carrying our supper with us, as high as Chelsea, making sport with the Western bargees, and my wife and I singing to my great content.

29th. The King's birthday. To White Hall, where all very gay; and particularly the Prince of Tuscany very fine, and is

---

[1] Richard Aldworth, of Stanlake, Berkshire, then one of the Auditors of the Exchequer, represented Reading in the first Parliament after the Restoration, and died in 1680. He was the paternal ancestor of the second and third Lords Braybrooke. In 1762 the auditor's grandson, Richard Neville Aldworth, succeeded to the estates of the Nevilles of Billingbear, in Berkshire, in right of his mother, who was their sole heir, and whose maiden name he assumed.

the first day of his appearing out of mourning since he came. I heard the Bishop of Peterborough [1] preach but dully; but a good anthem of Pelham's. Home to dinner, and then with my wife to Hyde Park, where all the evening: great store of company, and great preparations by the Prince of Tuscany to celebrate the night with fireworks, for the King's birthday. And so home.

30th. (Whitsunday.) By water to White Hall, and thence to Sir W. Coventry, where all the morning by his bed-side, he being indisposed. Our discourse was upon the notes I have lately prepared for Commanders' Instructions; but concluded that nothing will render them effectual without an amendment in the choice of them, that they be seamen, and not gentlemen above the command of the Admiral by the greatness of their relations at Court. Thence to White Hall, and dined with Mr. Chiffinch and his sister: whither by and by came in Mr. Progers and Sir Thomas Allen, and by and by fine Mrs. Wells, who is a great beauty; and there I had my full gaze upon her, to my great content, she being a woman of pretty conversation. Thence to the Duke of York, who, with the Officers of the Navy, made a good entrance on my draft of my new Instructions to Commanders, as well expressing his general views of a reformation among them, as liking of my humble offers towards it. Thence being called by my wife, we to the Park, whence the rain sent us suddenly home.

31st. Up very betimes, and continued all the morning with W. Hewer upon examining and stating my accounts, in order to the fitting myself to go abroad beyond sea, which the ill condition of my eyes and my neglect for a year or two hath kept me behind-hand in, and so as to render it very difficult now, and troublesome to my mind to do it; but I this day made a satisfactory entrance therein. Had another meeting with the Duke of York at White Hall on yesterday's work, and made a good advance: and so, being called by my wife, we to the Park, Mary Batelier and a Dutch gentleman, a friend of hers, being with us. Thence to the World's End, a drinking-house by the Park; and there merry, and so home late.

And thus ends all that I doubt I shall ever be able to do with my own eyes in the keeping of my journal, I being not able to do it any longer, having done now so long as to undo my eyes almost every time that I take a pen in my hand; and, therefore, whatever comes

[1] Joseph Henshaw: *ob.* 1679.

of it, I must forbear: and therefore resolve from this time forward to have it kept by my people in long-hand, and must be contented to set down no more than is fit for them and all the world to know; or, if there be anything, which cannot be much now my amours are past and my eyes hindering me in almost all other pleasures, I must endeavour to keep a margin in my book open, to add, here and there, a note in shorthand with my own hand.

And so I betake myself to that course, which is almost as much as to see myself go into my grave: for which, and all the discomforts that will accompany my being blind, the good God prepare me!

S. P.

May 31, 1669.

END OF THE DIARY

PRINCIPAL EVENTS IN THE LIFE OF SAMUEL PEPYS

JUNE 1669—MAY 1703

1669. Soon after abandoning the *Diary* Pepys made a trip with his wife to France and Holland; but not long after their return Mrs. Pepys died (10th November), and was buried in the church of St. Olave, Hart Street.

1673. In the summer of this year Pepys was nominated secretary to the newly appointed commission of the Admiralty.
On 4th November he was elected to Parliament as member for Castle Rising: the Committee of Privileges declared the election void, but as the House was prorogued before coming to a vote, he retained his seat in the interval. Soon after this he was accused of being 'a papist and popishly inclined.' He denied the charge, which was quickly dropped.

1676. Pepys was elected Master of Trinity House.

1677. He became Master of the Clothworkers' Company, and published his *Portugal History* (see Bibliography, vol. 1, p. viii).

1679. In March Pepys was again elected to Parliament, this time as member for Harwich. In May he and his colleague, Sir Anthony Deane, were accused of supplying naval information to France, and of conspiring to extirpate the Protestant religion. They were committed to the Tower under the Speaker's warrant on the 22nd of that month, and William Hayter succeeded to Pepys's office at the Admiralty. The original deposition of their accuser, one Scott, was not supported, and on 12th February 1680 they were discharged. Pepys remained out of office for four years.

1683. In August he accompanied Lord Dartmouth on his expedition to Tangier to destroy the fortifications, and evacuate the garrison. His journal of this voyage has been edited. (See Bibliography, vol. 1, p. viii.)

1684. In March Pepys returned to England, and three months later was restored in office as Secretary of the Admiralty. In this capacity he instituted the special commission for the recovery of the Navy.
In November he was elected president of the Royal Society.

1685. After attending the coronation of James II as a Baron of the Cinque Ports Pepys was re-elected to Parliament in May as member for Harwich, and later in the year was chosen first Master of Trinity House under its new charter.

1689. He resigned office on 20th February, and was succeeded on 9th March by Phineas Bowles. On 25th June he was committed to the Gate-house on a charge of giving information to the French. His failing health caused him to be allowed to return to his house and the charge was soon dropped. Thereafter he lived at the home of William Hewer at Clapham, in correspondence with his numerous friends, taking an active interest in Christ's Hospital, of which he was treasurer, and working on the last pages of his *Memoirs of the Navy.*

1690. Publication of the *Memoirs* (see Bibliography, vol. 1, p. viii).

1703. Pepys died of the stone at Clapham on 26th May. He was buried next to his wife in St. Olave's, Hart Street, on 5th June.

INDEX

INDEX

Abbot (Abp. George), his hospital at Guildford, I 165; III 261; his tomb at Guildford, III 261

Abelson, Capt. James, II 120

Abergavenny, Mary, Lady, I 488

Abingdon, III 242

Abrahall, Mr., I 467

Abraham, boatswain, I 366

Abury (Avebury), stones at, III 247, 248

Ackworth, Mr., his case, III 265, 270, 316; *alluded to*, I 58, 129, 344, 355; III 204, 374

Ackworth, Mrs., I 344

Adams, Mr., I 9

Adams, Sir Thomas, III 201

Ady, Mr., I 111

Æsop's Fables, by Ogilby, I 126, 132; II 224

Africa, proposal to dig for gold in, I 99

African House in Leadenhall Street, I 486; II 5

Aglaura, II 47; Burt breaks his leg fencing in, I 298

Albemarle, General George Monk, later Duke of, with the Army in Scotland, I 1; ordered to London, I 4; his letter to Parliament, I 7; doubts as to his proceedings, I 10; three citizens meet him, I 10; his concurrence with Parliament, I 13; answer to his letter, I 15; room to be made for his soldiers, I 16; at Whitehall, I 17; in Palace Yard, I 18; his soldiers abuse the Quakers, I 19; secures the Common Council, I 19; pulls down the City gates and chains, I 20; at St. Paul's, I 22; appointed with Montagu as general at sea, I 29; feasted at the twelve City halls, I 30; checks his soldiers, I 32; a dull heavy man, I 33; his life-guard, I 34; created K.G., I 67; made Lieutenant of Ireland, I 92; at the Sessions House, I 101; plot against him, I 120; at Trinity House, I 125; Master of Horse in royal procession, I 158; tastes a bit of the first dish to go to the King's table, I 160; dangerously ill, I 188; in favour of indulgence to the Presbyters, I 292; eager against a company of poor wretches, I 309; member of the Tangier Commission, I 310; proposes that the Life Guards shall pass through its City, I 315; presents a fray, I 385; Parliament confirms royal grants of land to him, I 392; a perfidious man, I 451; his wound at Newhall, I 472; Clarendon Park bought of him, I 491; II 29; his view of retrenchment, II 63; acting Lord Admiral, II 98; walks much in the Park, II 155; his chaplain preaches, II 188; to be lieutenant-general of combined forces, II 201; his portrait, by Lely, II 246; he goes to sea, II 249; his conduct condemned, II 269; disagreement with the Duke of York, II 272, 339; has high words with Sir W. Coventry, II 276; tries to make the best of his defeat, II 278; his interest in the City, II 324; is under a cloud, II 341; ballad in his praise, II 421; a Commissioner of the Treasury, II 465, 467; reported made High Constable, II 486, 487; Parliament favourable to him, III 91; his portrait by Cooper, III 202; and *passim*

427

Albemarle, Lady Monk, afterwards Duchess of, interferes in the appointment of Clerk of the Acts, I 75; book dedicated to her, I 106; a plain homely dowdy, I 143; disposes of the places Edward Montagu hoped to have, I 237; *alluded to*, I 74, 143; II 183, 211, 228, 287, 290, 355, 436, 437, 463, 466; III 88, 110, 202

Albumazar, at the Duke's House, III 176

Alchymist, the, acted at the theatre, I 177; at the King's House, III 396; one of Clun's best parts, II 39

Alcock, Harry, Pepys's cousin, I 267, 272

Alcock, Tom, Pepys's schoolfellow, I 33, 149, 151; III 232

Aldborough, II 262

—— Bay, II 91

Aldersgate, limbs of the traitors on, I 104

—— Street, II 57; III 206; New Prize office, II 390; house set on fire, III 1, 3

Aldgate, I 246, 281, 304; III 75, 366; hackney-coach stand there, II 326

Aldworth, Richard, auditor, III 419

Algerines break the peace, III 342; take £13,000 out of E. India ships, III 379

Algiers, life of Christian slaves at, I 138; the Mole destroyed, I 230; fleet for, I 142, 156; actions at, I 220; Sir J. Lawson's peace with, I 255, 320, 323; plague brought to Amsterdam from, I 443; Diwan of, I 450; commanders going against, I 467; war proclaimed against, II 10; Captain Allen makes peace, II 69; complaints of the Turks of, III 261; peace with, III 367; war with, III 393; *alluded to*, I 121, 200, 202, 256, 455; III 261, 389

Alicante, Lord Sandwich ill at, I 187, 191

Alice, Pepys's cookmaid, II 130; she leaves his service, II 240

Alington, William, Lord, II, 426, 430

All-hallows', Church, Thames Street, the King's Arms set up in, I 42

All's Lost by Lust, at the Red Bull Theatre, I 145

All Souls' College, Oxford, III 241

Allen (Alleyn), Alderman Sir Thomas, Lord Mayor, I 7, 21, 34, 56, 69, 101, 154, 237

Allen, Bab. *See* Knipp, Mrs.

Allen, Capt., father of Rebecca Allen (*q.v.*), I 150, 153, 155, 177; III 179, 381, 382

Allen, Mrs., III 381

Allen, Rebecca, afterwards married to Lieut. Jewkes, I 150, 152, 153, 177, 178; III 381; bridesmaid, I 279; is churched, I 416; intercedes for her husband, II 434

Allen, Dr. Thomas, I 448, 454; II 241

Allen, Capt., afterwards Sir Thomas, makes peace with Algiers, II 69; meets with the Dutch Smyrna fleet, II 85-6; arrives at Portland, II 100; Rear-Admiral, II 131; his complaint against Mr. Wayth, II 243; portrait by Lely, II 264; an elder brother of Trinity House, II 367; condemned to be hanged, flies to Jersey, II 442; instruction for, III 261; *alluded to*, I 196, 406, 442, 464; II 81, 86, 198, 279, 307, 434; III 84, 182, 201, 262, 263, 316, 342, 367, 389, 392, 393, 399, 408

Allestry, bookseller to the Royal Society, III 103

Alsopp, a contractor, II 25, 33; dangerously ill, II 36; death, II 37

Alsopp, Mr., the King's brewer, I 392, 488

Alsopp, minister of St. Clement Danes, I 213

Alstead's Encyclopaedia, I 106

Amsterdam, II 115, 307, 308; plague at, I 443, 447, 461; II 10; strange fires seen there in the air, II 8

Mrs. Pepys, I 325; she leaves, I 326; acts Pyramena in the *Slighted Maid*, I 394; her singing and dancing in the *Rivals*, II 49; at the Duke's Playhouse, III 238, 259, 339

Gosport, I 248

Gotier Mons, I 420

Gothenburg, ship cast ashore at, II 53

Gouge, Thomas, will not read the new service-book, I 282

Grabut Louis, Master of the King's band, II 412; III 72, 107, 211

Gracechurch (or Gracious) Street, I 321; II 159, 195, 521; III 267, 312; corner to the stocks, I 119; poulterer dies there, I 320

Graffam, I 437

Grammont, Marshal de, I 411

Grandison, George, Viscount, III 62

Grant, Mr., or Capt., I 345; III 216; his report on Sir W. Petty's double keeled vessel, I 425

Grant's, Mr., his collection of prints, I 374

Grant's Observations on the weekly bills of mortality, II 141

Grantham, the, I 44

Grateful Servant, at the Duke's House, III, 356

Gravel-pits, the, II 263

Graveley, manorial court of, I 198

Graves, drowsy Mr., I 320

Gravesend, I 38, 71, 149, 259, 279; II 119, 148, 150, 172, 176, 479, 485, 490, 499, 503; III 16, 17, 33, 383; plague at, II 152

Gray, Mr., II 47, 74; his views on trade, II 59

Gray's Inn, I 18, 213, 407; II 54; III 371; the barbers there, I 166; barristers and students rise against the benchers, II 465

—— —— Fields, II 275

—— —— Walks, I 166, 178, 187, 245, 251, 284, 373; III 281; store of gallants there, I 179

Grays, Essex, II 172

Greatorex, Mr., mathematical instrument maker, I 102, 105, 172, 262, 427; his sphere of wire, I 6; Pepys bespeaks a weather glass of him, I 298; brings Pepys a thermometer, I 369; his varnish, I 392; his apprentice, III 347

Green, old Mr., I 273

Green Man, II 75

—— ——, on Stroud Green, III 409

Greene, Capt., an idle drunken fellow, III 140, 156

Greenwich house, II 220; Greenwich Palace, I 494; Park, I 244, 265, 270, 278; trees planted and steps made in the hill, I 244; the music house, I 173; picture of Greenwich, III 339, 347, 351, 361; Greenwich church, I 129; and *passim*

Greeting, Mr., the musician, II 417, 418; III 6, 144, 264

Gregory, Thomas, I 23; III 108, 253

Grenville, Sir John, I 48, 51, 56

Gresham, Sir Thomas, his portrait at the Exchange, II 321

Gresham College, meetings of the Royal Society at, I 482; II 55, 91, 95, 97, 98, 101, 109, 112, 214, 225, 244, 265, 323, 324, 362, 364, 370, 388, 499; III 111, 113, 190, 408, 419. *See* Royal Society

Greville, Sir Fulke, *Life of Sir Philip Sidney*, III 137

Grey, Mr., II 358; III 55

Grey of Warke, William, Lord, III 135

Greyhound, in Fleet Street, I 132

Greyhound, the, ship, I 485, 486

Griffen, Col. Edward, afterwards Lord, II 59

Griffin, Mrs., II 465

Griffin, Will, doorkeeper, I 289, 311, 320, 357, 416; II 88, 462; III 155, 157, 159; his maid, II 255

Griffith, Mr., II 363; III 61

Griffith, Sir John, captain of the fort at Gravesend, II 479

Griffith, Matthew, D.D., preaches at the Temple, I 155

13

Wildes, Deputy-Governor of the Tower, I 312, 470

Wildman, Major, the fifth monarchy man, III 122, 123, 125, 299

Wiles, Mr., the coxcomb, III 185

Wiles, Mrs. Elizabeth, her portion, III 26

Wilford, Dean, preaches at Whitehall Chapel, I 293

Wilgness, Capt., of the *Bear*, I 38

Wilkes's, II 329

Wilkins, Dr. John, Bishop of Chester, II 112, 214, 235; III 113, 291; sermon at the Temple, I 116; examiner at St. Paul's School, I 349, 484; his real character, III 117, 229, 230, 236, 254, 291; appointed Bishop of Chester, III 291; spoken of for Lord Treasurer, III 375

Wilkinson, Capt., of the *Charity*, II 119

Wilkinson, Mr., at the Crown, in King Street, I 9, 17, 34, 82, 168; III 176

Will, Pepys's boy, enters Pepys's service, I 76; steals some money, I 93; Pepys tears his indentures, I 95

Will, who sold ale at the door of Westminster Hall, I 3, 8, 9, 12, 15, 16, 19, 22, 33, 99; II 149

Will's Coffee-house, I 483

Willett, Deb, Mrs. Pepys's new girl, III 72, 76, 79, 81, 82, 85, 129, 135, 155, 170, 193, 204, 244, 245, 273, 298, 302, 306, 307, 308, 314, 372, 385, 410; Pepys discharges her, and advises her never to see him again, III 304

Willett, Mrs., Deb's mother, much beloved at Bristol, III 246

Williams, Col. Henry, formerly Cromwell, I 368, 437

Williams, Dr., in Holborn, I 87, 177; his dog, I 196

Williams, Mr., II 296

Williams, Mrs., Lord Brouncker's mistress, sometimes called 'Lady,' II 157, 159, 161, 162, 168, 184, 187, 192, 204, 205, 208, 214, 232, 236,

242, 243, 277, 287, 303, 351, 360, 387, 404, 420, 465; III 40, 41, 187, 200, 263, 355, 387, 409; her impudence, II 193; her lodgings, II 212

Williamson, Capt., to be captain of the *Harp* frigate, I 34

Williamson, Mr., afterwards Sir Joseph, I 427; II 102, 135, 194, 274, 275, 349; III 4, 186, 301, 332, 373, 375, 408; Latin secretary, I 350; a logical speaker, II 68

Willis, Sir Richard, the governorship of Newark taken from him by Charles I, II 89; betrayed by Morland, I 89

Willis, Sir Thomas, I 350

Willoughby, Lord, II 370

Willson, Tom, Sir W. Batten's clerk, I 416; II 310; III 10, 67

Wilson, Mr., II 484

Wilton, the Court goes there, II 151

Wimbledon, I 499

Winchcombe St. Peter, III 65; collar of brawn from, I 215

Winchelsea, Lord, I 50, 51, 52; ambassador at Constantinople, I 88

Winchelsea, II 349

Winchester, Isabella, Marchioness of, III 405

Windham, Mr., killed in action, II 153

Windsor, Lord, appointed Governor of Jamaica, I 244; returns from Jamaica, I 352; kisses the Duke of York's hands, I 358; adventure in Cuba, I 371

Windsor, I 155; II 143, 152, 154, 228; III 339, 406; knights of, II 228

—— Castle, II 229

Wingate, Edward, III 394

Winsly, the, name changed to *Happy Return*, I 62

Winstanley, William, *History of the Tailors' Company*, III 263

Winter, the Algiers pirate, I 269

Winter, Sir John, I 283; II 425, 453; agreement respecting the Forest of